Reference Guide to United States Military History 1919–1945

REFERENCE GUIDE TO UNITED STATES MILITARY HISTORY 1919–1945

CHARLES REGINALD SHRADER

General Editor

Facts On File®

AN INFOBASE HOLDINGS COMPANY

REFERENCE GUIDE TO UNITED STATES
MILITARY HISTORY 1919–1945

Copyright © 1994 by Sachem Publishing Associates, Inc.

Facts On File, Inc.
460 Park Avenue South
New York NY 10016
USA

Library of Congress Cataloging-in-Publication Data
(Revised for volume 4)
Reference guide to United States military history.

   Includes bibliographical references (v. 1, p. 265–268) and index.
   Contents: v. [1]. 1607–1815—v. [2]. 1815–1865.—v. [3]. 1865–1919.—v. [4]. 1919–1945
   1. United States—History. Military—To 1900.
I. Shrader, Charles R.
E181.R34 1991   973   90-25673
ISBN 0-8160-1836-7 (v. 1)
ISBN 0-8160-1837-5 (v. 2)
ISBN 0-8160-1838-3 (v. 3)
ISBN 0-8160-1839-1 (v. 4)

A British CIP catalogue record for this book is available from the British Library.

Composition and Manufacturing by the Maple-Vail Book Manufacturing Group
Printed in the United States of America

10 9 8 7 6 5 4 3 2 1

This book is printed on acid-free paper.

Contents

Text Chapter Authors

Chapter 1	Charles R. Shrader Lieutenant Colonel (Ret.), U.S. Army	Chapter 5	Edward J. Drea U.S. Army Center for Military History
Chapter 2	Henry G. Gole Colonel (Ret.), U.S. Army	Chapter 6	Kenneth P. Werrell, Ph.D. Radford University
Chapters 3 & 4	Carlo W. D'Este Lieutenant Colonel (Ret.), U.S. Army	Chapter 7	Charles R. Shrader Lieutenant Colonel (Ret.), U.S. Army

List of Contributors

Daniel T. Bailey
University of Wisconsin, Madison

Robert H. Berlin, Ph.D.
Combat Studies Institute
U.S. Army Command and General Staff College

M. Guy Bishop, Ph.D.
Seaver Center for Western History Research
Natural History Museum of Los Angeles County

Leo J. Daughterty III
Ohio State University

Gilbert B. Diaz
Major, U.S. Marines

James Sanders Day
Major, U.S. Army
U.S. Military Academy

Edward J. Drea

George B. Eaton
Captain, U.S. Army
U.S. Military Academy

Ralph Eckert, Ph.D.
Pennsylvania State University at Erie

Uzal W. Ent
Brigadier General (Ret.), PNG

Carlo W. D'Este
Lieutenant Colonel (Ret.), U.S. Army

David Friend

Henry G. Gole
Colonel (Ret.), U.S. Army

Lloyd J. Graybar, Ph.D.
Eastern Kentucky University

Russel A. Hart
Ohio State University

Jonathan M. House
Major, U.S. Army

Richard F. Kehrberg
University of Wisconsin, Madison

Roger D. Launius, Ph.D.
Chief Historian
National Aeronautics and Space Administration

Stephen J. Lofgren
U.S. Army Center of Military History

Peter Model

Rod Paschall
Colonel (Ret.), U.S. Army

Mark Pitcavage
Ohio State University

Jeffrey J. Roberts, Ph.D.
Tennessee Technological University

Charles R. Shrader
Lieutenant Colonel (Ret.), U.S. Army

Lewis Sorley, Ph.D.

Steve R. Waddell
Texas A&M University

Kenneth P. Werrell, Ph.D.
Radford University

Vernon Williams, Ph.D.
Abilene Christian University

John F. Wukovits
Woodhaven, Michigan

Photographic Services
by Jim Enos, Carlisle, Pennsylvania

Introduction

The United States played a substantial role in World War I, but the short duration of its participation scarcely allowed its great war-making potential to be mobilized fully, and the war ended before the full U.S. military weight could be felt. Nevertheless, the United States emerged in 1918 as a recognized major industrial and military power and as a key player on the world stage. In the immediate postwar period, the American government and people strived mightily to dismantle the military power so recently called forth. Preoccupied first with the return to normalcy, the pursuit of business interests, and private pleasure, and then by the effort to recover from the economic disaster of the Great Depression, the American public and its elected representatives declined to maintain more than a corporal's guard. By the early 1930s, the United States was ranked only 17th among the world's military powers. Despite the growing threats to U.S. security posed by a revived Germany and an aggressive Japan, warnings about military threats to the Untied States went unheeded, the more so because the human and material costs of the indecisive first world war had brought a traditional streak of antimilitarism and ardent pacifism to the surface of American life.

The spirit of isolationism and pacifism led to the studied neglect of the U.S. armed forces. Between 1920 and 1939, the navy, hobbled by adherence to international treaties limiting naval armaments, remained the first U.S. line of defense, while the army and fledgling air corps were permitted to languish for lack of men and funds. Military leaders made do and focused on domestic tasks and the preparation of cadres for some future conflict. Only in the late 1930s, when it became clear that the winds of war already blowing in Europe and Asia might sweep over the United States as well, did the United States begin the laborious process of rebuilding the physical strength of its long-neglected military forces. The pace and urgency of that effort increased as the war clouds rolled over Europe and China. Vowing to keep America out of war, Pres. Franklin D. Roosevelt also committed the country to support other democratic nations in their fight against totalitarian domination. America's war industries were revived, first to supply its friends and then to modernize and rebuild its own army, navy, and air corps. When war came in December 1941, the U.S. military forces had made great progress but were still scarcely ready for the global conflict that ensued. Transformed by the unprovoked sneak attack of the Japanese on Pearl Harbor and the obvious need to prevent all of Eurasia from falling to the Nazis, the combative American spirit was reawakened and dedicated to uncompromising defeat of the Axis Powers.

The demonstration of U.S. power called forth by World War II has not been matched before or since. Some 16,000,000 Americans were called to the colors, equipped with the finest and most advanced war equipment, and deployed worldwide. Millions more Americans contributed their mental and physical labors to control and support the efforts of the uniformed forces. American industry poured forth enormous quantities of modern ships, airplanes, tanks, and other weapons, enough to supply many of its allies as well as its own forces. American science, too, was harnessed to the task of finding new and better means of defeating enemies of the United States and overcoming the problems posed by large-scale military operations in a variety of terrain and climate. By 1945, the great U.S. reserves of manpower, industry, and know-how had been thoroughly mobilized, and the United States had outproduced and outfought two major enemies in a series of campaigns that took American soldiers, sailors, marines, and airmen to every part of the globe.

The United States emerged from World War II as the undisputed champion of the Free World. Its military power was approached only by that of the Soviet Union, and then only in consequence of the tremendous number of men the Soviets had placed under arms, in part with U.S. aid. So great was the power of the United States and so depleted were the resources of its allies that there was no turning away in 1945 from the responsibilities of leadership. In consequence, the United States entered an era in which its military forces were to be maintained constantly at a size and level of readiness unprecedented in U.S. history.

In large part, the history of the United States is a history of its military establishment—the story of its military leaders and the forces they have commanded in peace and war. The *Reference Guide to United States Military History* seeks to provide a fresh perspective on this important story. As with each of the other four chronologically organized volumes of the *Guide*, Volume IV comprises a thorough examination of the role of the military and its leaders in American life during a given period. Introduced by a short description of the organization, equipment, and doctrine of U.S. military forces, the narrative portion of the volume includes an extended discussion of the course of events and the development of U.S. military institutions from the end of World War I in 1918 to the end of World War II in 1945. The seven narrative chapters are supplemented by biographical profiles of the military and naval leaders of the period, detailed descriptions of the principal battles and events, and the discussion of special topics. The text of the volume is further enhanced by maps and illustrations depicting the nation's military leaders, military life, battles, and other events. This survey of U.S. history as viewed through the perspective of U.S. military activities thus provides a unique reference work for school and library use and should appeal to a variety of readers interested in this important aspect of the American national experience.

Obviously, every detail of the military history of the United States cannot be addressed even in a five-volume series. The editors of the *Reference Guide to United States Military History* have thus selected for emphasis only those aspects that seem to be most important for understanding the course of U.S. military history and the role of the military in American society. Any selection process is sure to omit personalities and events that many readers may deem significant. The themes and topics stressed in all five volumes represent those that the editors believe to be the most important to the development of U.S. military history and of attitudes toward the military in American society from the colonial period to the present. Special attention thus is

given to such key questions as what should be the role of armed forces in a democratic society and what should be the size, nature, and functions of the American armed forces. Similarly, the themes of citizen (militia) forces versus professional (standing) forces, competiton among the various elements of the U.S. military establishment for resources and prestige, and ways in which American attitudes toward such matters have differed in time of peace and in time of crisis are also emphasized. The unique American solutions devised to coordinate military strategy and the organization of forces to meet perceived threats are investigated in some depth. The adaptation of technology to military ends occupies an especially important place in U.S. military history in view of the country's consistent preference for substituting technology for manpower and thus receives special attention. Another prominent theme is the perpetual and characteristic failure of the United States to prepare adequately for war in time of peace. The attitudes toward soldiers, sailors, and their leaders displayed by American political leaders and ordinary citizens are another important aspect on which the *Guide* focuses. Throughout the five volumes, special care has been taken to highlight the independent nature of the American soldier and sailor and the conditions under which he or she was required to operate. By repeatedly returning to these themes and topics, the editors hope to give focus to the series as well as to explain better the course and importance of military affairs in U.S. history.

The scholars who have contributerd to this as well as to the other volumes of the *Reference Guide to United States Military History* are among the best of the younger generation of scholars working on the problems of U.S. army, naval, and air-power history. Some are serving military officers; others are civilian historians in government service, professors in colleges and universities, or independent scholars from across the nation. Each contributor was chosen for his or her expertise on a particular topic as well as for an ability to explain complex ideas and events clearly and concisely. Chapter authors are identified in the table of contents, and all contributors are recognized in the list of contributors.

The editors have worked diligently to make this volume of the *Reference Guide to United States Military History* as complete, accurate, and readable as possible. It is hoped that they have succeeded and that the users of this and all other volumes of the series will find the work useful, regardless of their individual interests and levels of expertise. Errors of fact and interpretation are inevitable in any work of this magnitude. Readers are therefore encouraged to bring any errors to the attention of the editors for correction in subsequent editions.

Charles R. Shrader, Ph.D.
General Editor
Reference Guide to United States Military History

PART I

The Organization of American Armed Forces and Their History

1

United States Military Organization, Doctrine, and Technology: 1919–1945

Following World War I, the American people and government turned their attention to domestic concerns. Dreams of lasting peace and a fetish for economy in government produced a period of isolationism, pacifism, and meager military appropriations. Thus, when the war clouds again gathered over Europe and the Far East in the late 1930s, the United States was far from ready for another world war. However, U.S. efforts to aid the opponents of fascism between 1939 and 1941 did much to prepare the United States for the struggle that was to follow, and by the time of the Japanese attack on Pearl Harbor on Dec. 7, 1941, the foundation had been laid for a fantastic mobilization of men and matériel. World War II posed enormous challenges of scope, scale, and complexity for U.S. military leaders in that operations were conducted worldwide in every conceivable climate and terrain against enemies who were themselves well armed and trained. The eventual triumph of the United States and its allies in World War II highlighted the efficacy of the planning, doctrinal development, and educational efforts of the penurious interwar years as well as the amazing war-making potential of the United States.

THREATS TO SECURITY

In 1920, few Americans acknowledged any serious threat to their national security. Conditions on the Mexican border remained somewhat turbulent, and there was some concern about challenges to U.S. economic interests in the Pacific and Caribbean, but even the rise of aggressive regimes in Germany and Japan in the early 1930s was not viewed as a direct threat by many Americans. Only in the late 1930s did most Americans acknowledge that the totalitarian states posed a significant danger to the United States. All uncertainty vanished, however, in the flame and smoke of Pearl Harbor. The true nature of the threat posed by Japanese expansion in Asia and the Nazi domination of Europe was then fully revealed.

Strategies

American strategy for most of the period concentrated, as usual, on the defense of the continental United States and its overseas possessions, principally Panama and the Philippines. For some time after World War I, it was assumed that any future conflict would involve the United States in a unilateral defense against a single foe in a fairly restricted area. Only gradually did American strategic planners come to the view that a future conflict might again involve the United States in an all-out coalition effort against more than one major enemy. Accordingly, a series of strategic plans were devised to accommodate such an eventuality, and when war finally came in 1941, the basic strategic decisions had already been made. Unable to devote equal resources to the two principal opponents simultaneously, U.S. planners chose to concentrate first on the defeat of Germany while maintaining a defensive posture

3

A machine-gun crew reacts to the Dec. 7, 1941, Japanese attack at Pearl Harbor, Hawaii, which propelled the United States into an unparalleled global war. (U.S. Navy)

against Japan in the Pacific. Once Germany had been defeated, U.S. military resources could then be directed toward the defeat of Japan. This strategy was followed in principle but was not entirely observed in practice, as demands for greater efforts against Japan soaked off resources and perhaps delayed the defeat of Germany.

Public Attitudes

Many Americans were profoundly disillusioned by the outcome of World War I and consequently developed a very negative view of military affairs. The traditional American antimilitarism was strengthened, and as a consequence, the military services were allowed to decline in size and effectiveness. In the 1920s, Americans were preoccupied with making money and living the good life, and the Great Depression of the early 1930s focused attention on simple economic survival and the restoration of a battered economy. The failure to address pressing issues of military preparedness was compounded in the 1930s by an increasingly widespread and vocal pacifist movement opposed to all military expenditures and adventures. This

The magazine of the destroyer Shaw *explodes after being bombed by Japanese aircraft at Pearl Harbor in 1941.* (U.S. Navy)

attitude changed quickly after the surprise attack on Pearl Harbor, and the equally traditional warlike spirit of Americans when faced by naked aggression was quickly aroused. From December 1941 until September 1945, there was no doubt as to the commitment of the American government and people to the utter military defeat of its enemies, and this was reflected in the enormous effort and resources devoted to pursuing the war against the Axis Powers.

Budget Levels

The prevalent lack of interest in military affairs was, of course, reflected in the funding of the army and navy in the 1920s, and the Great Depression further reduced the resources available to maintain the armed forces at what some considered to be adequate levels. From 1922 through 1934, army expenditures averaged only $417 million per year while those of the navy averaged about $350 million per year. Although air-power advocates failed to secure a separate budget for the Army Air Corps, direct expenditures for army aviation during 1921–34 averaged $22 million annually. Penurious budgets directly affected training, the provision of modern weapons and equipment, and overall readiness. As war approached and the economy began to stabilize in the late 1930s, greater attention was devoted to the renovation and modernization of the armed forces and their increase in size. Appropriations began to rise after 1935, and in 1940, the army spent just over $907 million, the navy nearly $892 million, and the Army Air Corps more than $108 million. Expenditures for all the services jumped dramatically in World War II. Army expenditures peaked at nearly $50.5 billion in 1945, and navy expenditures topped $30 billion in the same year. Air Corps expenditures peaked at more than $13 billion in 1944 and then dropped slightly to just over $11.3 billion in 1945.

LAND FORCES

Following World War I, the land defense of the continental United States and its overseas possessions was the army's first priority task. This mission focused on guarding the Mexican border and providing miniscule garrisons in Alaska, Hawaii, Panama, and the Philippines. The suppression of domestic disorder, particularly labor and racial conflicts, was another traditional mission emphasized in the 1920s and 1930s. The army was also tasked with disaster relief efforts, and in 1933, the army assumed responsibility for administration of the Civilian Conservation Corps. The mission of organizing and executing offensive operations to defeat an enemy far from U.S. borders did not arise until December 1941 and then became the primary focus of army efforts.

Size

The great army created in 1917–18 for the war against the Central Powers was quickly disbanded after the armistice. By Jan. 1, 1920, there were only 130,000 men under arms. The National Defense Act of 1920 set the maximum strength of the regular army at 17,717 officers and 280,000 enlisted men, but Congress immediately began to reduce that authorization. By June 1922, Congress had limited the regular army to 12,000 officers and 125,000 enlisted men plus 7,000 Philippine Scouts. A further reduction in the number of enlisted men to 118,750 occurred in 1927, but after 1933, the size of the army was permitted to increase slowly. By the summer of 1939, the strength of the regular army had risen to about 190,000 officers and men, and on Sept. 8, 1939, Pres. Franklin D. Roosevelt authorized an emergency increase that raised the authorized strength of the regular army to 227,000 enlisted men and expanded the officer corps by calling a number of reserve officers to active duty. After 18 months of rearming and the institution in 1940 of a peacetime draft, the army on Dec. 7, 1941, totaled 120,000 officers and 1,524,000 men.

In 1941, army planners envisioned the eventual mobilization of 10,000,000 men in 213 combat divisions of which 3,600,000 were to be on active service by the end of 1942. By the end of 1942, the army had in fact grown to more than 5,400,000 officers and men in 73 combat divisions. The actual peak strength of the U.S. Army in World War II was reached in 1945 and totaled some 8,300,000 soldiers in 89 combat divisions, plus enough nondivisional combat units to form about 7 more divisions. As has been the case after every war, the U.S. Army quickly demobilized after peace came in August 1945. In 10 months, the size of the army fell to 1,889,690 soldiers, despite the continuing demands for occupation forces, worldwide deployments, and a growing Soviet threat.

Minority Representation

The traditional black regiments of the army (the 24th and 25th infantries and the 9th and 10th cavalries) continued to serve during the interwar years, but with the onset of World War II, black Americans once again had to struggle to serve their country. Eventually a peak of more than 700,000 black soldiers on active duty was reached, of which more than 500,000 were serving overseas. Relegated to segregated, mostly service-type units, black soldiers actively sought combat duty. But only two black infantry divisions, a fighter group, and a number of separate combat arms battalions were formed, despite the large numbers of black men eager for combat service. However, the urgent need for combat replacements during the Battle of the Bulge in December 1944 induced the army for the first time to experiment with the integration of black soldiers into previously all-white combat units.

An all-black unit in training marches at Fort Huachuca, Arizona.
(U.S. Army Military History Institute: Fort Huachuca Collection)

Women also aggressively had to seek active service in World War II. The Women's Army Auxiliary Corps, created on May 14, 1942, was made a regular component of the army as the Women's Army Corps (WAC) on July 1, 1943. Headed by Oveta Culp Hobby, the WAC reached a peak strength of 6,000 officers and about 94,000 enlisted women on Apr. 30, 1945. Women served in a variety of administrative and service units, many of which were deployed to the active theaters of operations. The first contingent of enlisted women were sent overseas to Algiers on Jan. 27, 1943. Just after V-E Day there were 8,000 Wacs in the European theater and 5,600 in the Pacific theater. More than 62,000 women also served in the Army Nurse Corps, which grew from about 7,000 nurses in December 1941 to a peak of 55,950 in August 1945.

Reserve Forces
At the end of World War I, Army Chief of Staff Peyton C. March proposed a permanent regular army of 500,000 men to be organized as a half-strength skeleton field army of five corps that could be expanded in time of war by the addition of conscripts. March's proposal was inconsistent with the mood of Congress and the public, and in the debates preceding passage of the National Defense Act of 1920, the alternative proposal of Lt. Col. John McAuley Palmer emerged as the preferred solution. Palmer advocated a small but full-strength regular army supplemented in time of need by a citizen army. Consequently, the National Defense Act of June 4, 1920, divided the army into three components: the regular army, the National Guard, and the Organized Reserve Corps.

The National Defense Act of 1920 authorized a National Guard strength of 436,000, but the actual strength stabilized at about 180,000. The National Guard was thus the largest of the components from 1922 to 1939. Occasionally called

out to suppress domestic disturbances, most National Guardsmen participated in just 48 drills and 15 days of field training per year. The Organized Reserve Corps was authorized a strength of about 100,000. Although the Enlisted Reserve Corps remained very small, the Officer Reserve Corps prospered with input from both the Reserve Officer Training Corps (R.O.T.C.) and the Civilian Military Training Corps (C.M.T.C.). In 1928, there were 225 senior R.O.T.C. units that produced about 6,000 new reserve officers per year and had an enrollment of 85,000. The C.M.T.C. involved about 30,000 volunteers in four weeks of training each year. After four years, C.M.T.C. participants were eligible for a reserve officer's commission.

In the summer of 1939, the National Guard numbered about 200,000 officers and men comprising the partially trained cadres of 18 combat divisions. As war approached, both the regular army and the National Guard were increased in size. On September 8, President Roosevelt authorized the expansion of the National Guard to 235,000 and expanded the officer corps by assigning reserve officers to active duty. On Aug. 27, 1940, Congress authorized the president to call the National Guard and Organized Reserve Corps into federal service for one year, and less than a month later, on September 16, the Burke-Wadsworth Bill provided for the first peacetime draft. Although soon submerged in the sea of draftees and hastily trained officers ("90-day wonders"), the men and officers of the National Guard and Organized Reserve Corps played a key role in the army in World War II.

High Level Command
The office of the chief of staff of the army emerged from World War I with enhanced authority and sense of purpose. The old question of the relative rank and authority of the chief of staff and the senior commander in the field, seen in the wartime conflict between Chief of Staff March and Gen. John J. Pershing, commander of the American Expeditionary Force (A.E.F.), was at last resolved with the assignment of Pershing as chief of staff in 1921. The National Defense Act of 1920 further clarified the chief of staff's responsibility for the military aspects of mobilization and war preparations and assigned responsibility for procurement to a newly created assistant secretary of war.

Following the recommendations of the Harbord Board in 1921, Pershing formally reorganized the 92-man War Department General Staff on the French pattern with a Personnel Division (G-1), an Intelligence Division (G-2), an Operations and Training Division (G-3), and a Supply Division (G-4), plus a War Plans Division (WPD) for strategic planning and related preparations. The operational responsibilities assumed during the war were stripped away, and the activities of the General Staff were refocused on planning and policy formulation. The General Staff system established in the early 1920s was continued with

The first Women's Army Air Corps unit in North Africa stands in formation. (U.S. Army Military History Institute)

only minor modifications until the pressures of global war forced a major change in overall army organization in March 1942. By that time, the system had become unwieldy and reorganization was clearly needed. Consequently, the War Department was reorganized on March 9, with a revised General Staff and three major army field elements: Army Ground Forces (AGF), Services of Supply (later renamed Army Service Forces [ASF]), and Army Air Forces (AAF). The aim was to simplify and increase the efficiency of staff actions and to provide for more effective control of forces in the field by placing them under separate commands. All of the General Staff sections except for the War Plans and Intelligence divisions were reduced in size and limited to broad planning and policy guidance. The WPD, renamed the Operations Division (OPD), was greatly expanded and became the chief of staff's central command post for controlling army operations worldwide.

Under the 1942 reorganization plan, the AAF was granted practical autonomy in administering training, per-

sonnel, and supplies peculiar to air operations. The new AGF assumed responsibility for the organization and training of ground forces. The missions of determining army supply requirements and distributing supplies as well as the mission of controlling the technical and administrative services of the army (including management of most U.S. installations) became the responsibility of the ASF. As before, responsibility for procurement was charged to the undersecretary of war.

The reorganized General Staff was designed to work smoothly with the new Joint Chiefs of Staff (JCS) organization. Created in February 1942 to provide a means of integrating U.S. and British efforts, the JCS was established formally in July 1942 when the president's personal military chief of staff was added to the army chief of staff, the chief of naval operations, and the commander of the AAF to form a collective body to direct strategic operations against the Axis Powers. The JCS emerged as the highest authority in the U.S. military hierarchy and focused on strategic plans and directions, while the various service headquarters focused on the organization, training, and equipping of forces for active operations.

Administrative Organization

With passage of the National Defense Act of 1920, the old territorial division of the United States into military departments was abandoned and replaced by nine corps areas and three overseas departments (Panama, Hawaii, and the Philippines). The nine corps areas were primarily housekeeping organizations, but until 1932, they also directed training of the regular army and National Guard. In 1932, all tactical units in the United States were organized under four army headquarters. In 1936, selected officers of the General Staff were designated for future duty with General Headquarters (GHQ), a new organization designed to command army forces in the field. GHQ was activated in July 1940, and in October, the four army headquarters actually assumed command of ground units in the United States. New commands were established for Puerto Rico and Alaska, and the corps areas were left with purely administrative functions. On Mar. 17, 1941, the United States was divided into four defense commands that were to become theaters of operations if the United States were invaded. Each defense command fell under the command of one of the four armies. On March 25, GHQ was empowered to supervise and coordinate the planning activities of the four defense commands, and in July, the responsibility of GHQ was extended to the planning and command of all military operations in the continental United States. GHQ was subsequently abolished in the reorganization of March 1942, and the four armies as well as the overseas theaters of operations thereafter reported directly to the OPD of the General Staff.

Stationing

U.S. troops remained overseas long after the Armistice of 1918. Some 5,000 Americans operated under British command in North Russia in opposition to the Bolsheviks from August 1918 to June 1919. Another 10,000 officers and men under Maj. Gen. William S. Graves were sent to Siberia for the same purpose in August 1918 and remained until April 1920. The U.S. 3d Army, assigned to occupy a portion of defeated Germany on Dec. 1, 1918, still numbered 15,000 men at the beginning of 1920. The last 1,000 men of the American Army of Occupation returned home on Jan. 24, 1923. During the interwar years, army troops were also stationed in China and garrisoned U.S. overseas possessions including the Panama Canal Zone, Puerto Rico, the Virgin Islands, Alaska, Hawaii, and islands in the Pacific. The largest contingent was in the Philippine Islands, where 31,000 U.S. Army troops (one-third of whom were Philippine Scouts) were incorporated in the Philippine army of 10 divisions and 130,000 men. In the summer of 1939, about one-fourth of the regular army was stationed in U.S. overseas possessions, and some 140,000 men garrisoned 130 posts, mostly of battalion size, in the United States. On Dec. 7, 1941, the U.S. Army had fewer than 200,000 men deployed overseas, but at the end of April 1945, some 5,400,000 men and women were overseas: 3,000,000 in Europe and 1,200,000 in the Pacific.

Tactical Organization

The higher-level tactical structure of the army remained much the same from 1920 to 1939. Brigades, divisions, corps, and armies continued to be the formations for unit control at higher levels, although they existed primarily on paper. The nine corps areas were purely administrative units; however, in early 1940, tactical corps and army headquarters were reconstituted and GHQ was established to command army units in the field. Unlike the corps area in the United States, the combat corps was primarily a tactical unit. Commanded by a lieutenant general, it consisted of a headquarters and a flexible complement of corps troops (including field artillery, antiaircraft, armor, tank destroyer, engineer, and service units) and controlled two or more combat divisions. Two or more corps were controlled by a field army commanded by a full general. A self-contained organization with both administrative and tactical responsibilities, the field army consisted of a headquarters and a flexible contingent of army troops.

The size and scope of World War II operations in Europe required an additional echelon of command, the army group. The largest field organization under a single commander, an army group controlled 400,000–1,500,000 men. It was designed to facilitate control by the theater commander and was often a ''combined'' organization including contingents from the various Allied nations. Only three U.S. army groups were formed in World War II: the 12th Army Group in northwest Europe under Gen. Omar N. Bradley, the 6th Army Group in southern France under Gen. Jacob L. Devers, and the 15th Army Group in Italy under Gen. Mark W. Clark. In May 1945, Bradley's 12th Army Group consisted of four field armies with 12 corps headquarters and 48 divisions. With more than 1,300,000 men, the 12th Army Group was the largest exclusively American field command in history.

The scope of World War II also required the creation of theaters of operations to control and direct the massive forces deployed against Germany and Japan. The principal World War II theaters were the European, Mediterranean, Africa-Middle East, China-Burma-India, and Pacific (the latter divided into a Southwest Pacific Area and a Pacific Ocean Area). Theaters had both strategic and logistical responsibilities and were commanded by senior generals who reported directly to the JCS.

The organization of the heavy ''square'' (or 4 regiment) infantry division with which the U.S. Army fought World War I was changed only slightly in the 1920s. A smaller,

Army divisions were reorganized to accommodate technological advances, such as this self-propelled 105-millimeter howitzer used by the 14th Field Artillery, 2d Armored Division, during World War II. (U.S. Army Military History Institute)

more flexible division structure was urged by General Pershing in 1920. Low budgets, however, prohibited any major changes in equipment and organization until the mid-1930s. In June 1936, a new "triangular" division structure was proposed to meet the need for greater mobility and to accommodate the recent advances in weapons, transport, communications, and air power. The triangular division was tested in 1937 and 1939, and the 2d Infantry Division was converted to this arrangement in 1939. After the fall of France in May 1940, the new triangular structure was formally adopted to replace the square division. The regular army divisions were immediately reorganized, the National Guard divisions were reorganized after Pearl Harbor, and the new divisions activated after March 1942 were all triangular in format.

With adoption of the new triangular (or three regiment) structure, brigade headquarters were eliminated and the 10,275 officers and men (later increased to 14,981) of the division were organized in three infantry regiments supported by four artillery battalions and a selection of supporting troops. Limited shipping and the need for manpower in the industrial base and in service units resulted in a streamlining of the infantry division in July 1943. The strength of the triangular division was reduced by eight percent to 14,253 officers and men, and certain equipment changes were introduced, such as the substitution of the towed 105-millimeter howitzer for the self-propelled version.

In March 1942, the War Department directed activation of new wartime divisions in six standard types: infantry, motorized, armored, airborne, mountain, and cavalry. There was of course some variance in the strength and organization of the "standard" infantry divisions. For ex-

ample, the 1st Cavalry Division, in reality an infantry division, retained the square division format throughout the war. The 1st Infantry Division in 1945 was a typical triangular infantry division with an authorized strength of 781 officers and 13,472 men in three infantry regiments, three direct-support 105-millimeter howitzer battalions, one general-support 155-millimeter howitzer battalion, a mechanized reconnaissance company, a combat engineer battalion, a signal company, a quartermaster company, an ordnance company, a medical battalion, and a headquarters and military police company. The 1st Infantry Division was provided additional support by the attachment of a tank destroyer company, an antiaircraft artillery automatic weapons battalion, and a 4.2-inch chemical mortar battalion. A tank unit was also attached when required. Up to 1939, the Field Service Regulations prescribed that each infantry division would have an organic company of light tanks. The requirement was dropped in 1939, and organic infantry division tank units were not restored until after World War II.

Each infantry regiment of the triangular infantry division was commanded by a colonel and consisted of three infantry battalions, a headquarters company, a cannon company equipped with 6 short-barrel 105-millimeter howitzers, a service company, and an antitank company equipped with 12 37-millimeter antitank guns. The infantry battalion, commanded by a lieutenant colonel, consisted of three rifle companies and a heavy weapons company. The heavy weapons company was equipped with 6 81-millimeter mortars, 8 .30–caliber heavy machine guns, 7 2.36-inch rocket launchers ("bazookas"), and 3 .50-caliber machine guns. Each rifle company was commanded by a captain and had three rifle platoons and a weapons platoon. The armament of the weapons platoon consisted of 2 .30-caliber light machine guns, 3 60-millimeter mortars, 3 2.36-inch rocket launchers, and 1 .50-caliber machine gun for antiaircraft defense. The rifle platoon, led by a lieutenant, had three rifle squads. Under the triangular organization, the infantry squad was enlarged from 8 to 12 men led by a sergeant and a corporal. Each squad was armed with a total of 10 M-1 rifles, 1 Browning automatic rifle, and 1 1903 Springfield rifle.

Two special infantry divisions were also formed: the 71st Infantry Division (Light, Jungle) and the 89th Infantry Division (Light), but they were soon converted to normal triangular infantry divisions. The specially equipped motorized divisions were also dropped for reasons of economy. One mountain division saw combat in its specialized role. In November 1944, the 10th Mountain Division consisted of 14,101 officers and men in three mountain infantry regiments and had 36 75-millimeter pack howitzers for artillery support. Its motor transport was largely replaced by horses and mules. The airborne division was also accepted as a standard division type. Originally established in October 1942 with 8,505 officers and men in one parachute infantry regiment and two glider infantry regiments with 36 75-millimeter pack howitzers for artillery support, the airborne division was reorganized in December 1944. The revised airborne division had 12,979 officers and men in two parachute infantry regiments and one glider infantry regiment as well as 60 75-millimeter pack howitzers. Five such airborne divisions were formed in World War II.

The other major combat formation of the U.S. Army in World War II, the armored division, underwent several modifications during the war. All of the armored division reorganizations resulted in a decreased number of light tanks, an increased number of medium tanks, an increase in the relative strength of the infantry elements, the elimination of unneeded command echelons, and the reduction of service elements. As originally designed in 1940–42 the U.S. armored division was modeled on the German panzer division, with a high ratio of tanks to infantry. It had about 400 tanks and 14,620 officers and men in 2 tank regiments of 3 battalions each, 1 armored infantry regiment of 3 battalions, and 3 armored field artillery battalions. On Mar. 1, 1942, the two fixed brigade headquarters were replaced by two combat command headquarters designed to control a flexible number of battalions. The ratio of light to medium tanks was reversed, leaving the division with 2 armor regiments (each with 2 medium and 1 light tank battalions), and the artillery was reorganized as 3 separate battalions. The 1942 armored division thus had 14,620 men, 232 medium tanks, and 158 light tanks. On Sept. 15, 1943, the armored division was again reconfigured for greater flexibility and to accommodate the decreasing availability of personnel for combat. A third, smaller combat command was added, and the tank regiment structure was replaced by separate armor battalions. The new, smaller armored division consisted of only 3 medium tank battalions of 4 companies each, 3 battalions of armored infantry, and 3 armored field artillery battalions, for a total of 12 tank companies, 9 armored infantry companies, and 9 armored field artillery batteries. The 1943 armored division thus had 10,937 men, 186 medium tanks, and 77 light tanks. A total of 16 armored divisions were formed in World War II. Most were organized in 1943 under the new, leaner format, but the 2d and 3d armored divisions continued under the heavier 1942 model.

Under the direction of AGF commander Lt. Gen. Lesley J. McNair, a great deal of effort went into streamlining the division structure and conserving critical resources of men and matériel while maximizing combat power. The concept of "pooling" specialized weapons, equipment, and units was a key part of this process as was the "task force" concept of constructing units for specific missions from standard units at hand. Organizations larger than the division were not standardized. Thus, corps, armies, and army groups were essentially task forces without permanently assigned units other than the headquarters, which was itself a nonstandard, tailored organization. Combat, combat support, and service units were attached as required by the needs of the operations contemplated. After 1942, most such nondivisional combat and service units were organized as separate companies or battalions and could be assembled and controlled as necessary by group or separate brigade headquarters.

In December 1941, the army consisted of 36 divisions (29 infantry, 5 armored, and 2 cavalry). The Victory Program of 1941 envisioned an army of 213 divisions including 71 infantry, 61 motorized, 10 airborne, 61 armored, 10 mountain, and no cavalry divisions and controlled by 5 field armies, 23 corps, and 18 armored corps headquarters. In May 1945, the United States actually had 89 divisions (66 "standard" infantry divisions, 1 mountain infantry division, 5 airborne divisions, 16 armored divisions, and 1 cavalry division [organized as infantry] controlled by 12 field army and 24 corps headquarters. In fact, 91 divisions had been formed, the 2d Cavalry Division being twice deactivated. That more divisions were not formed was due primarily to increased demands for manpower in the industrial base and for the air forces. The tactical lessons of war, as well as the inability to produce and transport the necessary equipment overseas, limited the number of specialized divisions, eliminating altogether the 61 planned motorized divisions. Given the support of America's allies and other factors, it turned out that not all of the 213 divisions were required.

Tactical Doctrine

The indecisive slaughter of trench warfare in World War I produced a search for new tactical doctrines that would return mobility and decisiveness to the battlefield. The British, and particularly the Germans, subsequently devised new tactics emphasizing mobility, envelopment, and coordinated use of infantry, tanks, and aircraft to achieve decisive results. This new blitzkrieg approach to land warfare was to be the dominant form in World War II. American ideas on tactics were heavily influenced by the French (U.S. allies in World War I), but most U.S. officers recognized the potential importance of new weapons and the coordination of infantry, tanks, and tactical air power. Immediately after World War I, the tank was considered merely as a supporting weapon for the infantry, but by the late 1930s, the concept of independent tank formations employing firepower, speed, and shock action to penetrate deep into enemy formations was well accepted. U.S. tacticians also recognized the value of mobility represented by the motor vehicle, and by 1941, the U.S. Army was the most thoroughly motorized of any in the world.

World War II tactics were characterized by the close coordination of mobile infantry, mechanized cavalry and tank units, and the use of aircraft for tactical reconnaissance and close air support of ground combat forces. Extensive reconnaissance was employed to fix the enemy's position. Offensive maneuvers, which included the specialized forms of airborne and amphibious assault, were characterized by the massive breakthrough on a narrow front with maximum combat power. Ideally, independent armor forces would make the breakthrough and the attack would be sustained by infantry and artillery. Envelopments and turning movements became the principal forms of offensive maneuver. At the lowest level, the infantry squad relied on the use of cover and concealment and the advance by bounds supported by fire to seize objectives. Defensive doctrine contemplated the organization of battle positions in depth, the use of security forces, and the retention of a mobile reserve. The main battle position comprised a zone of resistance consisting of a number of mutually supporting defensive areas disposed irregularly in width and depth and organized for all-around defense with artillery and antitank fires echeloned in depth. The World War II infantry division theoretically could hold a front of more than 4 miles with a density of 1.75 men per yard of front. Although the tank was considered the best weapon for killing other tanks, the U.S. Army also relied on tank destroyer units with towed or self-propelled antitank guns that were also used on some occasions as field artillery. U.S. tactical doctrine relied particularly on effective communications and recognized the critical importance of logistical support to the success of tactical operations.

NAVAL FORCES

Between 1920 and 1945, the navy, viewed as America's first line of defense, continued to be responsible for protecting seaborne commerce, maintaining sea lines of communication with U.S. overseas possessions, and defending the coasts from enemy attack. In time of war, it was assumed that the U.S. fleet would engage and destroy the enemy's surface forces, seize advanced bases with the use of the Marine Corps, and protect U.S. and allied shipping against submarines and surface raiders. In addition, the navy continued to play an important role in diplomacy by providing protection to U.S. diplomats and other interests abroad and, when necessary, providing a show of force or actual expeditionary forces.

Ships

When the Versailles Peace Conference began, the U.S. Navy was the world's largest, with 29 first-line capital ships in service or under construction and more than 2,100 aircraft. However, like the army, the navy quickly underwent a drastic demobilization, and in the 1920s and 1930s, naval armaments were further reduced in accordance with a series of multilateral treaties concluded with the other principal naval powers. The Washington Naval Treaty of February 1922 placed limits on the number, size, and armament of capital ships. The limits were further modified by the London naval treaties of 1930 and 1936. As a consequence of the naval agreements, no new capital ships, except for aircraft carriers, were constructed between February 1922 and October 1937, when the *North Carolina* was laid down. The first U.S. aircraft carrier, the *Langley*, was launched in 1922, and in 1927, the *Saratoga* and the *Lexington*, both converted battle cruisers, were commissioned. Another carrier, the *Ranger*, was authorized in 1929. By the mid-1930s, the concept of the fast carrier task force had achieved acceptance, and the United States undertook a major carrier building program. The *Enterprise* and the *Yorktown* were laid down in 1933, the *Wasp* in 1934, and the *Hornet* in 1935.

The construction of new naval vessels other than aircraft carriers actually began to accelerate in 1934 when the Vinson-Trammell Act initiated a systematic program of ship replacement to bring the United States up to treaty limits. In 1938, authorized naval tonnage was increased by another 23 percent, and by 1940, the navy had some 2,000 ships and 1,750 aircraft. The Vinson-Walsh Two Ocean Navy Act of July 1940 provided for another 20 percent increase in naval strength, a total of 1,325,000 new tons of combat vessels, 15,000 naval aircraft, and 100,000 tons of auxiliary shipping. Consequently, on the eve of U.S. entry into World War II, the navy had 1,120,000 tons of naval vessels and 430,000 tons building. The navy expanded steadily between 1940 and 1943. On May 13, 1942, the Five Ocean Navy Bill provided an additional 1,900,000 tons, and on May 26, 1943, 1,000,000 tons of landing and district craft were authorized. At the end of World War II, the navy had 1,194 major combatant vessels, 1,256 amphibious transports, and more than 41,000 aircraft.

Personnel

Traditionally, the navy has had less trouble in getting new ships than in manning them, and that situation persisted throughout the 1920s and 1930s. In December 1918, the navy counted 32,309 officers and 494,358 sailors; by 1923, the number had been reduced to 8,410 officers and 85,684 enlisted men. The nadir was reached in 1933 when only 9,947 officers and 81,283 enlisted men were on active duty. With the influx of new ships and the gathering war clouds of the late 1930s, the strength of the navy was substantially increased. The 13,604 officers and 147,939 men serving in 1940 were increased to 19,092 officers and 255,335 men in 1941. Enlisted strength nearly tripled between 1942 and 1943, and by the end of World War II in 1945, the navy had 331,379 officers and 3,049,438 enlisted men on active service.

Minority and Female Representation

Black Americans had long served in the U.S. Navy, but in the 1920s and 1930s, they were largely relegated to service jobs such as being mess attendants. Although real integration of the navy would not come until long after World War II, some black sailors were used in combat roles. The destroyer escort *Mason* and the subchaser *PC1264,* for example, had almost entirely black crews. Ensign Bernard Robinson, the first black navy officer, was commissioned in June 1942.

Women also sought a role in the navy in World War II. A Navy Nurse Corps had been created in 1908, and women had been admitted to the naval reserve in August 1916 with a number of ''yeomanettes'' serving in administrative positions at various shore stations during World War I. The women's naval reserve was formally established in July 1942 under the name WAVES (Women Accepted for Volunteer Emergency Service). The 1942 act established an initial goal of 10,000 enlisted women and 1,000 female officers. Popularly known as Waves, the women of the navy were commanded by Capt. Mildred H. McAfee, who was WAVES director until February 1946. Peak strength of the WAVES was reached shortly before the end of the war with some 8,000 officers and 78,000 enlisted women serving. Approximately 18 percent of all navy personnel assigned to continental shore establishments in World War II were women.

Reserve Forces

A naval reserve was established in World War I and continued during the interwar period, but the real reserve of the navy was provided by the U.S. Coast Guard. Assigned in peacetime to the Treasury Department, the Coast Guard in time of war was transferred to the operational control of the navy. In 1939–40, the Coast Guard assumed a number of important new missions. The Lighthouse Service became part of the Coast Guard, icebreaking duties were added, and the Atlantic Weather Observation Service became the Coast Guard's responsibility. The Coast Guard was also deeply involved in the Neutrality Patrol from September 1939. Port security became a Coast Guard function in June 1940, and the Dangerous Cargo Act subsequently involved the Coast Guard in the safety of loading and transporting explosives by sea. On Nov. 1, 1941, the Coast Guard was transferred to the control of the navy for the duration of the war. Coast Guard strength in 1941 included 1,490 officers and 17,745 enlisted men. By 1945, its strength had increased to 12,683 officers and 158,509 men. At the end of June 1945, 49,283 Coast Guardsmen were serving on navy vessels, 6,851 on army vessels, 25,966 on Coast Guard vessels over 65-foot, and 89,100 at shore stations. Some 572 Coast Guardsmen were killed in action in World War II, and total deaths reached 1,878. The navy relinquished control of the Coast Guard to the Treasury Department on Jan. 1, 1946.

The actual naval reserve was composed primarily of officers. The first Naval Reserve Officer Training Corps (N.R.O.T.C.) units were established at George Washington University in Washington, D.C., and St. John's College in Annapolis, Maryland, in 1924. By 1927, some 5,500 reserve officers had been commissioned. Spurred by Sen. Carl Vinson, the naval reserve program was revived in the late 1930s, and a naval reserve aviation cadet program was instituted.

Higher Level Command

Between the end of World War I and the end of World War II, the three main elements of the navy remained in place. The Navy Department, including the office of the secretary of the navy, the office of the chief of naval operations (CNO), and the various bureaus, provided a headquarters responsible for overall direction, planning, and policy. The Shore Establishment consisted of field activities, such as district and base commands, which supplied and maintained the Operating Forces. The Operating Forces comprised the active fleets, special forces, and other operating forces.

At the highest level, civilian direction of the navy fell to the secretary of the navy, administration and supply were directed by the various bureaus, and planning and operational direction remained the responsibility of the CNO and his staff. The old struggle between line and staff continued until the early 1940s. The office of the CNO, created in 1915, provided a senior officer of the navy responsible for systematic planning, but the incumbents failed to gain control of the various navy bureaus until March 1942, when Adm. Ernest J. King combined the posts of CNO and commander in chief, U.S. Fleet.

The staff elements remained quite small. As late as 1940, Sec. of the Navy Frank Knox operated his office with a staff of only seven officers and seven civilian employees. On July 12, 1921, a new Bureau of Aeronautics under Rear Adm. William A. Moffett was added, reflecting the increased importance of aviation, and an assistant secretary of the navy for air was created in 1926. The Naval Reorganization Act of June 20, 1940, merged the Bureau of Construction and Repair and the Bureau of Steam Engineering to form a new Bureau of Ships and provided for an undersecretary of the navy.

Administrative Organization

The Atlantic Fleet was abolished on Dec. 6, 1922, and was replaced by a Scouting Force and a Control Force under the commander in chief, U.S. Fleet. In the Pacific, navy forces were organized as a Battle Force with the 12 most modern battleships and the carriers *Lexington* and *Saratoga.* In addition, there was a Base Force for training and logistics, the Asiatic Fleet, Naval Forces Europe, the Special Service Squadron, and the Naval Transportation Service. The fleet was again reorganized on Apr. 1, 1931. The Control Force in the Atlantic was abolished, and the Pacific Battle Force was reorganized with subordinate battleship, cruiser, destroyer, mine, and air commands. The Scouting Force in the Atlantic was similarly reorganized, and a separate Submarine Force and Base (Logistic) Force were also provided.

The Scouting Force was sent from the Atlantic to join the Battle Force in the Pacific in early 1932, leaving only the Training Squadron in the Atlantic. The Training Squadron was reinforced in July 1937 and renamed the Training Detachment. From 1939, the U.S. Fleet was almost equally divided between the Atlantic and the Pacific. The Pacific Fleet was based at Pearl Harbor, Hawaii, and the Atlantic Fleet operated from bases on the eastern seaboard. Various smaller contingents covered the Caribbean and other areas. On Feb. 1, 1940, Adm. Husband E. Kimmel in Hawaii was named commander in chief, U.S. Fleet, and Adm. Ernest J. King received command of the reactivated Atlantic Fleet.

After World War I, the naval district system for shore establishments was extended from coastal areas to the entire country and U.S. overseas possessions. In March 1942, Sea Frontier commands were organized for antisubmarine warfare (ASW) and the naval districts became purely administrative commands. In May 1943, the 10th Fleet was established in the Atlantic to coordinate all ASW activities.

Tactical Organization

For much of the period, the tactical organization of naval forces retained its traditional echelons of squadron, flotilla, and fleet, but the basis of World War II navy tactical organization became the task force. Specifically assembled for a particular mission, either functional (escort, attack, support, countermine operations, etc.) or operational (for example, the amphibious invasion of Saipan), task forces were composed of a varying number of types of vessels required by the specific mission. The fast carrier task force was a special type of task force designed to effectively integrate the employment of naval carrier air power and supporting vessels. Similar task forces were organized for amphibious operations. A naval force (task force) normally consisted of numbered groups composed of smaller units, the smallest unit being the individual ship.

Naval Tactics

In most respects, naval tactics changed very little between the two world wars. The tactics of surface and submarine operations were of course modified by the innovations in naval construction, ordnance, and communications introduced between 1920 and 1945, and radar in particular had a significant impact on the range at which and the condi-

An LVT (landing vehicle, tracked), shown here on the Aleutian Islands, could operate on land and sea and was first used during the battle for Guadalcanal; it was nicknamed "alligator." (U.S. Army Military History Institute)

tions under which targets could be engaged. The German "wolf pack" tactic for the employment of submarines provoked considerable reaction in the form of improved ASW techniques devised with the assistance of the new science of operations research and supported by new forms of technology. The major transformation in naval tactics was occasioned by the integration of air power with naval power. Airplanes were of course extremely useful for reconnaissance, coastal patrol, and ASW, but the real tactical revolution was in the emergence of carrier-based air power as the main naval striking weapon, both against shore targets and against other naval vessels. In the 1920s and 1930s, naval air-power enthusiasts worked out tactical doctrine and techniques for the employment of carrier-based aircraft. Their theories were tested and modified under the pressures of World War II, particularly in the Pacific, and it became obvious by 1945 that the fast carrier task force had become the dominant factor in naval tactical operations. The battleship was no longer the centerpiece of the navy's tactical doctrine; henceforth, the doctrine of naval tactics would focus decidedly on how the carriers and their supporting vessels were maneuvered and how carrier-based aircraft were employed to achieve tactical decisions. Another type of naval operation that was prominent in World War II was the amphibious assault. Here, too, the navy, in conjunction with the Marine Corps and the army, developed new tactical doctrine and techniques for amphibious operations on a scale scarcely imagined in 1919.

MARINE CORPS FORCES

The extended deployment of marines as ground combat troops with the army in World War I was viewed as an aberration, and after 1918, the marines again turned their attention to providing ship, base, and embassy guard and to deploying small expeditionary forces to maintain peace and stability while protecting U.S. citizens and interests in Haiti, the Dominican Republic, Nicaragua, and China. Gradually, another major role for the Marine Corps emerged: the conduct of land operations in support of the fleet for the initial seizure and defense of advanced bases. The "advance base concept" quickly developed as a major mission for the Marine Corps and was formally acknowledged in 1927 with the publication by the Joint Army and Navy Board of the document entitled *Joint Action of the Army and Navy,* the first attempt by the two services to delineate responsibilities in joint operations.

Size

Marine Corps resources for the advanced base force mission as well as its other responsibilities were slim in the 1920s and 1930s. In 1919, the strength of the Marine Corps was 2,270 officers and 46,564 men. In 1920, Congress reduced the authorized strength to 27,400 officers and men but appropriated funds for only about 20,000. Just 1,104 officers and 16,061 enlisted marines were on duty in June 1920. The Marine Corps had little trouble recruiting up to near its authorized strength, however, and until the late 1930s, the actual strength of the Marine Corps hovered near 1,200 officers and 18,000 men. The Marine Corps did not begin to expand to meet its projected wartime missions until 1939. By mid-1940, the actual strength of the corps had risen to 1,800 officers and 26,545 enlisted men, but the real expansion began when the president declared a limited national emergency on June 27, 1940. On the eve of war, in December 1941, the Marine Corps numbered 65,881 officers and men, and by June 30, 1942, the corps had swollen to more than 143,000 officers and men. The Marine Corps reached its peak World War II strength in August 1945 with 37,660 officers and 447,440 enlisted marines, half of whom were serving overseas. In all, some 669,000 men and women served as marines in World War II.

Minority and Female Representation

Beginning in 1942, the Marine Corps somewhat reluctantly began to enlist both women and blacks as members of the Marine Corps Reserve. More than 20,000 women served as marines in World War II, principally in administrative positions. A few all-black units with white officers were formed in 1942 and 1943, and two black defense battalions were sent to the Pacific, although neither saw combat. The 63 black depot and ammunition companies (service units) saw greater use. By the end of the war, the Marine Corps included approximately 15,000 black marines.

Reserve Forces

The Marine Corps Reserve Act of Feb. 28, 1925, established two classes of reserves: the Fleet Marine Corps Reserve and the Volunteer Marine Corps Reserve. The authorized Fleet Marine Corps Reserve companies were eventually organized in 17 marine infantry battalions, 1 artillery battalion, and 12 aviation squadrons. In 1935, a 12-week-long platoon leaders course (PLC) for college students was initiated to provide officers for the reserves. The Naval Reserve Act of 1938 reorganized the Marine Corps Reserve into an Organized Marine Corps Reserve consisting of units with active training responsibilities and a Fleet Marine Corps Reserve and a Volunteer Marine Corps Reserve composed of individuals with reduced obligations. In 1939, there were 850 officers and 14,000 enlisted men in the Marine Corps Reserve. All Organized Marine Corps Reserve units were ordered to active duty on Oct. 15, 1940, but added only about 5,000 men to the Fleet Marine Force. When all of the Marine Corps Reserve reported for duty in the summer of 1941, an additional 15,000 marines augmented the active duty force.

Higher Level Command

Before 1917, the Marine Corps lacked a permanent headquarters staff system, but the experience of serving with the army in World War I induced its introduction. A Planning Section at Marine Corps headquarters was created at the end of 1918. As commandant of the Marine Corps 1920–29, Maj. Gen. John A. Lejeune exercised a great deal of influence over the development of his headquarters staff. In November 1924, Lejeune created a War Plans Committee, which became the War Plans Section of the Division of Operations and Training. In the late 1920s, the headquarters staff was reorganized with a new Operations and Training Division as its heart. A separate aviation section was established in 1935 and became the Division of Aviation with its own director in 1936. In 1939, the Division of Operations and Training became the Division of Plans and Policies.

Tactical Organization

Tactically, the marines were organized much the same as the army, while Marine Corps aviation units were similar to their navy counterparts. Until February 1941, the largest permanent Marine Corps unit was the regiment, although for the most part, marines were employed in much smaller increments.

The core element of Marine Corps tactical forces was the Fleet Marine Force, created on Dec. 7, 1933. The Fleet Marine Force was the lineal descendant of the original Advanced Base Force, which was the force designed to fulfill the mission of seizing and defending advanced bases for the fleet. A 1938 navy study resulted in the creation of four marine defense battalions with the mission of providing antiaircraft and antiship defense for U.S. possessions in the Central Pacific. Seven such 1,000-man defense battalions were created before Pearl Harbor. In December 1941, approximately half of the Marine Corps' strength was in the Fleet Marine Force, which included the seven defense battalions, the 1st and 2d marine aircraft wings (created in July 1941), and two marine divisions activated in February 1941: the 1st Marine Division at Camp Lejeune, North Carolina, and the 2d Marine Division (the ''Hollywood Marines'') at Camp Pendleton, California. By August 1945, the Fleet Marine Force in the Pacific included the III Amphibious Corps (1st, 4th, and 6th marine divisions), the V Amphibious Corps (2d, 3d, and 5th marine divisions), and the 1st, 2d, 3d, and 4th marine aircraft wings as well as several separate marine raider and parachute battalions. By V-J Day, 98 percent of all marine officers and 89 percent of all enlisted marines had served in the Pacific, a proportion much higher than the overall armed forces average of only 73 percent that served abroad in World War II.

The Marine Corps had the only U.S. aviation units actually involved in combat between the wars (in the Caribbean), but Marine Corps aviation remained a small organization. In June 1939, only 210 officers and 1,142 enlisted marines were assigned to aviation duties. Under 1940 legislation, the Marine Corps was authorized to add 32 squadrons, but by the end of 1940, there were still only 425 marine pilots and fewer than 3,000 enlisted marines in two small marine aircraft groups. However, marine aviation expanded quickly from 13 squadrons on Dec. 7, 1941, to a peak of 145 squadrons in 1944. By the end of World War II, marine aviation almost constituted a separate corps, with more than 100,000 officers and men, 61,000 of whom were overseas in four marine aircraft wings, four marine carrier air groups, and a variety of ground support and headquarters squadrons.

Tactical Doctrine

In general, Marine Corps tactical doctrine for land warfare followed that of the army from 1920 through 1945. The Marine Officers School at Quantico, Virginia, established in April 1917, used army books and doctrine except for material pertaining to the advanced base concept. However, marines made important conceptual and practical advances of their own in the coordination of naval gunfire, the use of artillery, and air-ground coordination. In one area, they took the lead. To fulfill its responsibilities to the navy under the advanced base concept, the Marine Corps developed the doctrine and procedures for the amphibious assault of a defended coast, one of the characteristic military operations of World War II. In 1933–34, students at the Marine Corps School at Quantico helped write the so-called *Tentative Manual* and an accompanying *Text for the Employment of the Marine Corps Aviation*. The results of their studies and experimentation were incorporated in the *Manual for Naval Operations Overseas* (1938), which established basic doctrine for amphibious warfare.

AIR FORCES

In 1920, the principal mission of the Army Air Service was to support the Army Ground Forces by providing observation, liaison, and air-ground attack services. As the doctrine of air power coalesced in the 1920s and 1930s, the mission of strategic bombardment emerged as the principal tactic of the Air Corps, at least among the airmen themselves. Air superiority (the defeat of enemy air power), close air support of ground forces, reconnaissance, and air transport received relatively little attention, although all would be important Air Corps missions during World War II and after. During the interwar years, the Air Corps was also called upon to perform a number of peaceful missions, perhaps the best known of which was flying the mail for three months in 1934.

Aircraft

The Army Air Corps underwent substantial growth in the 20 years between the world wars, increasing the number of aircraft by two and a half times and adding one-third more tactical units. In 1926, the Air Corps had only 60 pursuit and 169 observation planes. No bombers or attack planes were considered standard, and the total number of planes including trainers was fewer than 1,000. The Air Corps Act of July 2, 1926, authorized modernization and expansion of the army's air arm over five years to a total of 1,800 serviceable planes. The goal was not achieved, due to the lack of appropriations, although important work proceeded on the design of new fighters, bombers, and transport aircraft. In September 1938, President Roosevelt announced the desire to expand the Air Corps to 20,000 first-line aircraft by 1941. However, U.S. aircraft production in 1939 produced only 568 military planes, and the policy of supporting the Allies significantly inhibited the growth of U.S. air forces. In December 1941, the Air Corps had only 12,297 aircraft of all types, but by July 1944, the number of planes had peaked at 79,908. It subsequently fell to 63,715 at the war's end in August 1945.

Personnel

The Army Air Service numbered 195,023 officers and men on Nov. 11, 1918. By 1920, the number had fallen to 9,050. The National Defense Act of 1920 authorized the Air Service a strength of 1,516 officers and 16,000 enlisted men, including a maximum of 2,500 cadets. However, the strength of the Air Corps throughout the 1920s hovered near 10,000 officers and men, well below the authorized level. The totals began to rise slowly but steadily in the 1930s, and by June 1, 1941, the Army Air Corps had expanded to 9,789 officers and 143,563 enlisted men. On the eve of war, in December 1941, the Air Corps numbered

Lt. Charles B. Hall was the first pilot of the all-black 99th Fighter Squadron to shoot down two Japanese planes. (U.S. Signal Corps)

22,524 officers and flying cadets and 274,579 enlisted men. The peak World War II strength of the Army Air Forces was reached in March 1944, when 2,411,294 officers and men were on active duty.

Minority and Female Representation

Black Americans served with distinction in the Army Air Forces (AAF) in World War II. Most served in air service and construction units, but after a long struggle, a pilot training program was established at Tuskegee Institute in Alabama, which produced more than 300 black pilots. Several all-black air combat units were formed, including the famous 99th Fighter Squadron and the 332d Fighter Group, which served in Europe.

Women also played a prominent role in AAF activities in World War II. More than 40,000 women served on active duty. About 30,000 members of the Women's Army Corps (WAC) served in the AAF as Air Wacs. In addition, there were some 6,500 Air Force nurses, of whom 500 were flight nurses. An additional 1,200 women served as Wasps (members of the Women's Army Service Pilots), ferrying aircraft.

Reserve Forces

The first official aviation unit of the National Guard was the 1st Aero Company, Signal Corps, National Guard of New York, which was established in April 1908. No National Guard aviation units served in World War I. The reorganization of the National Guard under the National Defense Act of 1920 provided an initial authorization of 19 aero squadrons, and another 10 were added just before

World War II. All 29 were ordered to active duty in September 1940 with 800 officers, 4,000 enlisted men, and some 400 observation aircraft. The first Air Reserve Officer Training Corps camp was opened at Fort Sill, Oklahoma, in spring 1921. However, before World War II, the Army Air Corps reserve was very limited. As late as 1939, only 2,800 officers and men were enrolled.

To relieve the Army Air Corps of some of its noncombat domestic missions, the Civil Air Patrol (CAP) was created in December 1941 in the Office of Civil Defense. On May 4, 1943, the AAF was given responsibility for directing CAP operations. The AAF was also augmented by a number of civilian employees, many of whom were women. By 1944, the total had grown to more than 350,000. Additional support was provided by the Ground Observer Corps, the Aircraft Warning Corps (25,000 men and women at its peak), and the AAF Women Volunteers, about 25,000 family members who performed various support and morale tasks.

Higher Level Command

The National Defense Act of 1920 made the Air Service a separate combat arm of the army, but in the immediate postwar period, army aviation was controlled by the corps area and departmental commanders. Many airmen, including most prominently Brig. Gen. William (''Billy'') Mitchell, argued aggressively for completely independent air forces, and several major steps were taken in that direction. The Air Corps Act of July 2, 1926, created an assistant secretary of war for air as well as an air section in each major division of the General Staff. The act also created an Army Air Corps to replace the Air Service, and Maj. Gen. Mason Patrick was named the first chief of the Army Air Corps.

On Mar. 1, 1935, General Headquarters Air Forces (GHQAF) was established at Langley Field, Virginia, under the command of Brig. Gen. Frank M. Andrews, to provide centralized tactical direction of a combat air force. GHQAF was charged with controlling all combat aviation to support ground operations or to act as a separate arm as the commander in chief in the field might determine. The GHQAF of the late 1930s was the prototype of the numbered (i.e., 1st, 2nd, etc.) air forces of World War II and reported directly to the War Department General Staff.

The most important step toward an independent air force came with the reorganization of March 1942, when the Army Air Force (AAF) was created to coordinate the Air Force Combat Command (the former GHQAF) and the activities of the office of the chief of the Army Air Corps. Maj. Gen. (later General of the Army) Henry H. Arnold was named to command the AAF, and under his direction in World War II, the AAF became an independent branch of the armed services in all but a legal sense.

Civil Air Patrol members march in formation at a New Jersey base during World War II; their red shoulder tabs distinguished them from regular army personnel. (Civil Air Patrol)

Administrative Organization

The structure of the AAF in World War II included a headquarters in Washington consisting of the commanding general of the AAF, a deputy commanding general, and the Air Staff; 4 continental air forces; 11 combat air forces in the theaters of operation; and 6 AAF commands and other agencies engaged in specialized activities. Among the latter were the Air Matériel Command, responsible for procurement; the Air Service Command, responsible for supply and maintenance of aviation-peculiar material; the Air Training Command, responsible for training of pilots, aircrews, and technical support personnel; and the Air Transport Command, responsible for both domestic and overseas air transport and ferrying operations.

At the end of August 1939, the Army Air Corps was distributed on some 69 regular air bases (in 1944 there would be more than 1,400). Most of the 26,500 officers and men and 2,473 planes of the Army Air Corps were assigned to the three combat wings stationed at March Field in California, Langley Field in Virginia, and Barksdale Field in Louisiana. GHQAF controlled four bomb, three pursuit, and two attack groups. In addition, nine observation and three balloon squadrons were based in the

United States to support the AGF. Approximately one-third of the combat squadrons were overseas. The 18th Wing in Hawaii consisted of three bomb, two reconnaissance, one attack, and two pursuit squadrons. There were one bomb, two reconnaissance, one attack, and two pursuit squadrons in Panama, and one squadron each of bomb, pursuit, and observation aircraft in the Philippines.

On Feb. 26, 1940, the Air Defense Command was established at Mitchell Field, New York, as a planning agency to integrate U.S. air defenses. Four numbered air forces, responsible for domestic administration and training and for the defense of the continental United States, were created in March 1941: the 1st Air Force covered the eastern United States, 2d Air Force the West, 3d Air Force the Southeast, and 4th Air Force the far West. The wartime deployment of the other numbered air forces was as follows: 5th Air Force in the Southwest Pacific (renamed Far East Air Forces when combined with 7th Air Force in 1944); 6th Air Force in the Caribbean; 7th Air Force in the Central Pacific; 8th Air Force in the United Kingdom (responsible for the strategic bombing campaign against Germany); 9th Air Force in the United Kingdom (responsible for tactical air operations); 10th Air Force in the China-

Burma-India theater; 11th Air Force in the Aleutians and northern Pacific; 12th Air Force in North Africa and Italy (responsible for tactical air operations); 13th Air Force in the Southwest Pacific; 14th Air Force in China; 15th Air Force in Italy (responsible for strategic bombing operations); and 20th Air Force in the Pacific (responsible for the strategic bombing campaign against Japan). In April 1945, 52 percent of the AAF's strength was deployed overseas.

Tactical Organization

The tactical organization of air forces in World War II was relatively simple, and the scheme remains much the same today. Combat aircraft are organized in *flights* of two or more planes for tactical purposes. Two or more flights constitute a *squadron*, the smallest air force unit with both tactical and administrative duties. Squadrons include a number of supporting ground personnel as well as pilots and aircrew members. Two to four squadrons, plus the necessary headquarters and support personnel, compose a *group*, which has both tactical and administrative functions. Two or more groups make up a *wing*, which is primarily a tactical organization. Two or more wings constitute an *air division* or *command*, and two or more *air divisions* or *commands* may be controlled by a numbered *air force headquarters*.

Tactical Doctrine

The main operational task of army aviation in World War I was to support the ground forces. By World War II, the advocates of air power had succeeded in promoting the view that strategic bombardment should be the major task

of air forces. Obsessed with strategic bombing, the Army Air Corps seriously neglected the development of tactical air power in the interwar period, but the tactics and techniques of both strategic bombing and close air support were developed in great detail in World War II. World War II fighter tactics emphasized quick reactions, speed, firepower, and maneuverability in the attack of enemy ground targets or in air-to-air combat. World War II bomber tactics involved formations designed to facilitate mutual support against enemy fighter attacks, supporting fighter air cover, and precision high-altitude daylight bombing aided by such technological marvels as the Norden bombsight and radar. Marine and navy aviators as well as AAF personnel also developed effective tactics and methods for the use of aircraft, primarily fighter-bombers, to provide close air support for ground forces.

Overall, the AAF in World War II proved an important factor in achieving tactical and strategic victory. The AAF flew 1,693,565 sorties against Germany, dropping some 1,554,463 tons of bombs, and destroying 29,916 German and Italian planes while losing 18,418. Against Japan, the AAF flew 669,235 sorties, dropped 502,781 tons of bombs, and shot down 10,343 Japanese planes with a loss of 4,530.

TECHNOLOGY

Many of the most dramatic changes between World War I and World War II took place on the technological front. Those innovations ranged from individual weapons to weapons of mass destruction that forever altered the face of warfare.

Two ''bazooka'' teams practice shooting the 2.36-inch rocket launcher during World War II training. (The Armored School)

Infantry Weapons

With two notable exceptions, the U.S. Army fought World War II with exactly the same infantry weapons used during World War I. One exception was the M-1 Garand semiautomatic .30-caliber rifle adopted as the standard infantry weapon in 1936. Veterans still debate the merits of the M-1 as compared to those of the 1903 Springfield (which continued to be used for special purposes such as sniping), but both rifles were certainly among the best military rifles ever made. Another major addition to the infantryman's arsenal in World War II was the 2.36-inch rocket launcher, nicknamed the bazooka. First issued to U.S. troops en route to North Africa in 1942, the bazooka gave the infantryman at least some chance of defeating the many enemy armored vehicles on the World War II battlefield and also proved useful for destroying point targets such as bunkers and pillboxes.

Tanks

The potential of armored vehicles for restoring decision to the battlefield by firepower, speed, and shock action was recognized in World War I, and most major nations developed tanks during the interwar period. The major trends in tank design were toward greater speed, increased cross-country maneuverability, heavier armor, and larger, more effective main gun armament. U.S. tactical doctrine, which emphasized the role of the tank as an infantry support weapon until comparatively late in the 1930s, inhibited the development of suitable medium tanks in the United States. The American inventor J. Walter Christie developed a very effective high-speed tank chassis in the 1920s but was unable to sell it to American ordnance officers. He did find a buyer in the Soviet Union, and the Christie chassis became the basis for the Russian T-34, the workhorse of Soviet armor in World War II. However, the standard U.S. medium tank of World War II, the M-4 Sherman, proved effective, if not ideal, and was used extensively in Europe. Most World War II tanks weighed 18–40 tons and mounted a main gun of 37-75 millimeters. Some later model Shermans had a 90-millimeter high-velocity gun. The extensive use of tanks on the World War II battlefield prompted the development of better antitank weapons as well. The bazooka was considered a marginal tank killer at best, and major attention was devoted to the development of towed or self-propelled antitank guns, including standard models in 3-inch, 37-millimeter, 57-millimeter, and 90-millimeter versions. Perhaps the most famous antitank gun of the war was the German 88-millimeter, which actually had been designed as an antiaircraft weapon.

Artillery Weapons

Improvements in field artillery weapons in the interwar period were marginal, although artillery ammunition, fire direction equipment, and techniques were much improved.

The tank, used since World War I as a support weapon for the infantry, came into its own during World War II; here, an M-4 Sherman tank is used for training infantry troops in Britain. (U.S. Army Military History Institute)

The major change for the army was the replacement of the 75-millimeter gun with the 105-millimeter howitzer as the standard light field artillery piece. The 105-millimeter howitzer in both towed and self-propelled versions could fire 13 different types of shells at a rate of about 20 rounds per minute to a maximum effective range of about 12,000 yards. The 105-millimeter howitzer, backed by its heavier 155-millimeter, and 8-inch relatives, was the field artillery workhorse of World War II. The much smaller 75-millimeter, in a pack version capable of being disassembled and transported by parachute or mule, was standard in specialized units such as the airborne and mountain infantry division. One of the most remarkable technical developments of World War II was the proximity, or variable time, fuze. Essentially a small, self-contained radar set, the proximity fuze was first developed for use with shipboard antiaircraft guns. Tested in August 1942, it was released for general use in December 1944 and made possible controlled airbursts of artillery shells over enemy infantry. New fire direction techniques worked out during the interwar period facilitated the coordinated massing of artillery fires characteristic of World War II operations. New electronic gun directors such as the M-9 significantly improved the speed and accuracy with which antiaircraft fires could be directed and were the forerunners of modern electronic computers.

Naval Vessels

Although the major characteristics of modern naval combatant vessels were established well before 1920, naval architects and naval ordnance specialists continued to provide improvements throughout the interwar period. Perhaps the most obvious advances were in the design of aircraft carriers. The first carriers were built on converted merchant or cruiser hulls. As the carrier task force assumed a prominent place in naval tactical doctrine, great efforts were made to

Landing craft, such as LSTs (landing ship, tank) (left) and others, were invaluable during the amphibious operations that were *characteristic of World War II, especially in the Pacific theater.* (U.S. Army Military History Institute)

design and build large, seaworthy carriers capable of high speed and maneuverability. The trend was toward large fleet carriers, but the demand for convoy protection in the Atlantic in World War II was met by the development of the escort, or "jeep" carrier, a smaller version built on what was essentially a merchantman hull.

The most important naval warfare advances were in the field of antisubmarine warfare (ASW). The British *asdic* (named from the Anti-Submarine Detection Investigation Committee), subsequently known as *sonar* (sound navigation ranging) in its American versions, exploited the piezo-electric effect of quartz crystals, which vibrate at very high frequency, to develop sensitive echo-ranging equipment for the detection of both submarines and surface vessels. Sonobuoys with hydraphones were also employed to detect submarines that could then be killed by the *hedgehog,* a multiple depth charge dispenser that threw a pattern of depth charges ahead of the ship so as to allow it to maintain sonar contact with the enemy submarine. The scientific techniques of operations research were also applied to optimize convoy defenses and ASW procedures.

Amphibious operations were a characteristic feature of World War II, and a variety of efficient new landing craft were developed. The progenitor of the World War II-era LCVP (landing craft, vehicle, personnel) was the "Eureka" boat with a retractable bow ramp developed in the 1930s. Heavier landing craft such as the LCM (landing craft, mechanized), capable of carrying tanks and other large pieces of equipment, were developed during the war. Perhaps the most useful and durable, as well as largest, of the amphibious assault vessels, the LST (landing ship,

tank), was actually an oceangoing ship with clamshell doors in the bow. Amphibious armored assault vehicles such as the LVT (landing vehicle, tracked), adopted in 1941 and nicknamed the "Alligator," were also mass-produced and saw considerable combat action.

Aircraft

Tremendous advances were made in aircraft technology between the wars, and even greater developments took place during World War II itself. Among the key technical improvements in aeronautical engineering were the replacement of wood, wire, and fabric by metal; improved performance, reliability, and safety of both engines and airframes; streamlining; metal variable-pitch propellers; better brakes; directional gyroscopes; more accurate instruments; and air-to-ground radio communication. Perhaps the most important developments before World War II were the changeover to monoplane (single-wing) design and all-metal construction. The first all-metal single-wing bomber was the Boeing YB-9, accepted in 1933 and an ancestor of the best-known American bomber of World War II, the high-speed, long-range, high-altitude B-17.

Few of the aircraft in the U.S. inventory in September 1939 played a major combat role in World War II, but the A-20, P-40, B-17, and B-24 were already on order, and the twin-engined P-38 fighter and the very heavy long-range B-29 bomber were under development. On Oct. 2, 1942, the first flight of a turbojet aircraft in the United States was made at Muroc, California, by the Bell XP-59A. Meanwhile, the Germans introduced jet- and rocket-powered aircraft as well as the use of jet-propelled flying

The P-40 Warhawk, flown by the "Flying Tigers" under Claire Chennault in China in the late 1930s and early 1940s, was the first fighter plane that was mass produced (1940–44) in the United States. (U.S. Army Military History Institute)

bombs (the V-1) and rocket-powered ballistic missiles (the V-2). The United States also developed a number of air- and sea-launched missiles and guided bombs.

A wide variety of munitions were developed for use by aircraft, including rockets, guided bombs, incendiaries, and napalm. The 70-pound, M-47 incendiary bomb used jellied gasoline (napalm), which was also adapted to infantry flamethrowers, giving them greater range, better control, and improved accuracy. The M-69 incendiary bomb was the forerunner of the present-day cluster bomb, encapsulating a number of smaller incendiary bomblets in a single container that burst in the air to disperse its contents.

The Atomic Bomb

Of all the technological innovations of the World War II era, none matched the power and long-term impact of the atomic bomb. The $2 billion Manhattan Project, which oversaw the bomb's development, was established on June 18, 1942, and placed under the direction of Brig. Gen. Leslie R. Groves, who had supervised construction of the Pentagon. Between 1942 and 1945, thousands of American and emigré scientists, technicians, and administrators labored feverishly to fashion the power of the newly discovered atomic reaction into a practical, and enormously destructive, weapon. Their efforts, led by scientists such as Leo Szilard and J. Robert Oppenheimer, produced the first nuclear explosion at Alamagordo, New Mexico, at

5:30 A.M., July 16, 1945. Less than a month later, the first operational atomic bombs were dropped on the Japanese cities of Hiroshima and Nagasaki, causing enormous damage and loss of life and ushering in a new era in military history.

Communications

Strategic and tactical communications were greatly improved by technological innovations introduced before and during World War II. At both the strategic and the tactical levels, radar revolutionized naval air operations. The first operational radar was perfected by Sir Robert Watson-Watt in England in spring 1935 to detect aircraft. Aircraft detection radar played a key role in the Battle of Britain, and the British invention of the multicavity magnetron in 1940 made possible the reduction of radar wavelength from 1.5 meters to 10 centimeters. The much shorter wavelength made for clearer pictures on scope and greater accuracy. The United States, France, Germany, and Japan also developed radar independently during the war, and radar was adapted for use by ships, airplanes, antiaircraft guns, and submarines. It proved particularly valuable for beacon bombing, antiaircraft range finding, and navigation.

Extensive use of vehicle-mounted and man-packed radios made both voice and CW (continuous wave) radio nets for battlefield command and control practical for the first time in World War II. New man-packed radios such

The technology involved in the LCM (landing craft, medium), shown here off-loading supplies at Okinawa, enabled faster unloading of supplies for the troops. (U.S. Army Military History Institute)

as the SCR-54, which weighed 20 pounds and had a range of about five miles, coupled with improved wire communications, gave the commander a greater ability to control his forces on the battlefield. Other advances in electronic and surveillance equipment included improved serial photography, infrared sniperscopes, the metascope, better sound and flash systems, the cathode ray tube, facsimile transmission, and improved teletype and cryptographic equipment.

Mobility

Strategic mobility was greatly enhanced in World War II by the use of long-range aircraft, as well as by larger and faster ships. Tactical mobility was improved even more significantly. The extensive use of motor transport facilitated the movement of men and matériel on and near the battlefield and quickened the pace of operations. The jeep and the 2.5 ton truck were thus among the most significant tools of the war. The protected front-line movement of troops was also enhanced by the introduction of partially armored personnel carriers (M2 and M3 halftracks), the

forerunners of today's fully armored infantry vehicles. Transport aircraft also helped to revolutionize tactical mobility. Parachute and glider insertion of troops onto critical objectives and aerial resupply by airdrop introduced an entirely new dimension to combat operation.

Medical

Advances in the healing arts significantly reduced mortality in World War II and set the pace for even greater advances in medical science after 1945. Effective new drugs, such as sulfa and penicillin, were introduced, x-ray techniques and equipment were improved, and new surgical methods saved thousands of lives during the war and after. The worldwide deployment of U.S. forces also spurred research into the causes, prevention, and treatment of a variety of diseases until then little known or understood. Malaria and other endemic diseases were even eradicated in certain areas as part of the U.S. military public health and preventive medicine efforts. Evacuation techniques were also much improved over World War I standards and even included the first experiments with the evacuation of battlefield casualities by helicopter. The new medicines and techniques had a profound impact on the battlefield in that significantly fewer diseased or wounded soldiers died in World War II than in World War I. Deaths from disease in World War II occurred at a rate of 0.6 per 1,000 compared to a rate of 16.5 per 1,000 in World War I. Deaths from wounds (after reaching medical treatment) fell from 8.1 per 100 wounded in World War I to 4.5 per 100 wounded in World War II.

Even so, the casualty toll for the United States in World War II was not negligible. Out of 16,535,000 men and women who served in World War II, there were 405,449 deaths (291,557 battle deaths and 113,842 nonbattle deaths). Out of the 11,260,000 men and women who served in the army in World War II, 234,874 were killed in action or died of wounds and another 83,400 died of disease, accidents, or other causes. Some 565,861 soldiers were wounded and 114,558 were taken prisoner of war. Some 1,204 soldiers were listed as missing in action and not subsequently accounted for at the end of the war. Navy casualties in World War II included 36,950 killed in action and 37,778 wounded in action. The marines lost 19,733 killed in action or died of wounds and 67,207 wounded in action out of a total of 669,100 officers and men who served. While supplying less than 5 percent of the forces, the marines took almost 10 percent of the casualties.

New technology, such as these landing vehicles on Leyte (Philippines) in 1944, was spurred by the war and enabled the United States to emerge as a formidable global force. (U.S. Army Military History Institute)

CONCLUSION

The armed forces of the United States emerged from World War II as arguably the greatest military machine ever assembled. The U.S. Army, Navy, Marine Corps, and Air Forces had conducted decisively successful operations around the globe in a wide variety of climates and terrain, defeating two well-armed, well-trained, and determined enemies. Important new technology had been added to the American arsenal, including advanced communications and electronic equipment, vehicles, ships, aircraft, artillery, and, of course, the atomic bomb. Given the weak, ill-trained, and ill-equipped forces that were available in 1941, the mobilization, equipping, training, and deployment of more than 16,000,000 men and women around the world were nothing less than spectacular. In August 1945, only the Soviet Union, based principally on the number of men under arms, posed a significant threat to the United States. The post-World War II history of the armed forces of the United States would be the story of American efforts to counter that threat in its many manifestations.

2

The Interwar Period: 1920–1941

It was not unreasonable to believe that the defeat of Germany in 1918 and the exhaustion of the other European powers from their efforts in World War I insured that there would be no major war for a very long time. Both the tradition of avoiding the maintenance of a large standing army and the political climate in the 1920s and 1930s in the United States reinforced the notion that the defense budget should be slashed. The result was that professional military men would receive fewer national resources than they thought necessary to insure even minimal military preparedness.

The possibility of a naval war with Japan had been recognized in the United States since shortly after the Japanese defeated Russia in 1905. Therefore, the navy had to be maintained as a force in being prepared to fight on short notice despite serious efforts by the United States to get universal limitations on the numbers and size of warships.

A small army in peacetime was considered adequate. In the event of war, there would almost certainly be enough warning time, thanks to broad oceans and weak neighbors, to allow for the mobilization of America's enormous industrial and demographic resources. Concrete evidence of the nation's attitudes regarding its military in the period between World War I and World War II can be found and put in perspective by considering some statistics. A few remarks by senior leadership about the armed forces illustrate the distance between public opinion reflected among the lawmakers and those upon whose shoulders responsibility falls in war.

Defense Expenditures and Status

Expenditures of the War Department in 1919 were more than $9 billion and in 1945 were more than $50 billion. From 1922 through 1935, however, expenditures remained less than $500 million per year, sometimes less than $400 million. From 1936 until 1940, expenditures climbed from more than $600 million to about $900 million and reached almost $4 billion in 1941.

The strength of the active army was almost 2,500,000 in 1918 and would exceed 8,000,000 in 1945. For most of the 1920s and until 1935, army strength would average fewer than 140,000. The nadir was 133,243 in 1923. From 1936 until 1940, strength would climb steadily from 168,000 to 270,000. In 1941, almost 1,500,000 men would be in army uniforms.

Funding for the Department of the Navy was roughly parallel to that of the War Department. The 1919 expenditures were more than $2 billion, while those for 1945 reached some $30 billion, but for most of the interwar period, navy expenditures were close to $400 million with a low point of $333 million in 1923. Steady increases can be noted from 1936, and in 1941, navy expenditures were back at $2 billion. Similarly, navy and Marine Corps strengths parallel declining army strength from the end of World War I. They bottom out to some 80,000 for the navy and 17,000 for the marines in the 1920s and 1930s before turning upward in 1936 to peak in 1945 for the navy at 3,000,000 and for the marines at 500,000.

The size and funding of the U.S. Armed Forces were modest, and frugality had its price in quality. In 1932, former army chief of staff Peyton C. March called the army "impotent" and asserted that the United States had of its own volition made itself weaker than the Treaty of Versailles had made a defeated Germany. Army Chief of Staff Douglas MacArthur in 1933 said that the U.S. Army in active strength stood 17th among the armies of the world. He also declared that his tanks were useless for combat with a modern foe. On Jan. 28, 1938, Pres. Franklin D. Roosevelt told Congress, "Our national defense is

World War I general Peyton C. March, shown here being awarded the Distinguished Service Medal by Sec. of War Newton D. Baker in 1920, deplored the downsizing of the U.S. military services during the interwar period. (U.S. Army Military History Institute)

inadequate for purposes of national security and requires increase.'' Almost a year later, the entire General Staff concurred in a War Plans Division study, reporting that the United States did not have a single complete division, while Germany had 90 and Italy 45. Japan had 50 actively employed on the China mainland alone. In 1938, the United States was a third-rate military power. In 1939, outgoing chief of staff Malin Craig lamented that ''time is the only thing that may be irrevocably lost,'' and pointed out that ''sums appropriated this year will not be fully transformed into military power for two years.''

On Sept. 1, 1939, the day that Hitler attacked Poland to begin the shooting war in Europe, George C. Marshall took charge of an army that, at a time when the world was clearly on the brink of general war, had no definitive operations plan for the immediate future; had almost no money, modern weapons, or public support; had a commander in chief whose sentiments clearly lay with the navy; and had army enlisted ranks adequate for little more than garrison duty and a mix of quality and deadwood in the officer corps. In his 1941 annual report, army Chief of Staff Marshall called that service ''ineffective,'' a most damning word in the military lexicon.

The navy would have been pleased to get a larger share of the nation's treasure, but no admiral in 1941 went as far as the army's Marshall in describing the U.S. Navy. Scholars noted that soldiers of the period, presumably out of a scrupulous discipline and loyalty to the principle of civilian-elected authority, became mute once the president or the

Congress decided on the budget or the size of the army. The navy, on the other hand, had friends willing to engage in public relations. They stressed the peacetime utility of the fleet to back up diplomacy and to protect commerce. Despite sound reasons for a large navy, the financial stringencies of the times prevented Congress from bringing the navy even to strengths authorized in the naval agreements. The situation improved after the inauguration of Roosevelt, himself a former assistant navy secretary, as naval appropriations increased each year in the 1930s. No doubt it would have been reassuring to the admirals to have had the ships sooner, but the late start meant that many of the navy's ships incorporated the latest technology when it counted, in war. As a matter of perverse fact, all of America's armed forces would go to war with the most modern arms and equipment precisely because of the late start. A combination of circumstances explains the deliberate choice to maintain the country's armed forces, particularly the army, at very modest levels after World War I and to raise those levels in the late 1930s.

INTERWAR MILESTONES

A number of milestones marked the way as the United States retreated to isolationism after the great adventure in World War I, and then rather late in the game found it necessary to mobilize rapidly for World War II. The depression of the 1930s, combined with America's isolationist mood (dating from the 1920s) plus the absence of a clear and present danger to American security for most of the period between the wars, resulted in neglect of the nation's armed forces. The gradual recognition of the disturbers of world peace in the middle and late 1930s drew a reluctant United States into World War II, a war from which the country would emerge as a superpower. Even the strong and popular President Roosevelt had to move very carefully in the late 1930s when he concluded that war was probably unavoidable, for it was evident from the Gallup polls begun in 1935 that the American people wanted to stay out of it, if that were possible.

Army leadership had to consider the possibility of another world war in the future, but American military tradition looked mainly to the defense of the continental homeland. It was not evident which part of the army's past should shape its future, the long years as a frontier army or the brief European intervention of 1917–18. The former suggested a force structure emphasizing mobility for small wars of maneuver, while the latter suggested weight and power suitable for large wars and the massive application of power. Without a clearly defined enemy on the horizon and in the absence of a perceived threat to national security, neither the purpose nor kind of an army was apparent to the public or to military planners. The army remained ambivalent on this key issue up to and including World War II, when it was shown to be seriously undergunned in battles with German tanks despite having decided upon the massive application of power that has been called "the American way of war."

Military Missions

Following the World War I armistice of Nov. 11, 1918, the American Expeditionary Force returned to the United States for swift demobilization, except for a 15,000-man occupation contingent in Germany that was phased out by January 1923 and an expedition of some 15,000 U.S. troops active in Russia until 1920. By June 30, 1919, an astounding total of 2,608,218 enlisted men and 128,436 officers had been discharged. Once the army troops pulled out of Germany and Russia, the Marine Corps provided most of the small overseas garrisons and conducted the foreign military expeditions required by the United States, particularly in the Caribbean region. The exceptions were the 1,000 army troops in Tientsin, China, from 1912 until 1938 and a force of another 1,000 men sent to Shanghai for five months in 1932. Army garrisons were routinely maintained in Panama, Hawaii, and the Philippine Islands, but overall, few U.S. troops were found on foreign soil.

Domestic Tasks

The generally low regard in which the army was held by the population at large was not enhanced when the regular army was called upon in the summer of 1932 to disperse a gathering of World War I veterans. "Bonus Marchers" seeking payment of a promised bonus for military service in World War I encamped in Washington near the Capitol. Federal marshals failed in an attempt to evict a group of veterans, and blood was spilled. The army was ordered in. Some 600 troops—including Dwight D. Eisenhower and George S. Patton, Jr.—and some tanks, all under the personal leadership of Chief of Staff Douglas MacArthur, settled the situation without firing at the demonstrators. There were few injuries, and they were minor, but the use of military force against civilians who were war veterans damaged the image of the army and probably contributed to the defeat of Pres. Herbert Hoover in his bid for reelection.

More positive for the army's image was the way it managed resources in emergencies arising from natural disasters. In hurricanes and floods, for example, the army responded swiftly and efficiently in providing food, beds, tents, and blankets. The army's Corps of Engineers was visible in its work in harbors and rivers to improve navigation and control floods. The Air Corps flew the mail for several months in 1934 at the direction of President Roosevelt, but there were fatal accidents in this effort. The army had not prepared for the task, and unnecessary risks were taken to advertise aviation. The most significant

nonmilitary function of the army in the 1930s, however, was a consequence of the Great Depression.

Civilian Conservation Corps

In 1933, Roosevelt directed the army to organize and supervise large numbers of jobless men into what became the Civilian Conservation Corps (CCC), whose work would be reforestation and land reclamation. In seven weeks, the army established 1,315 camps manned by 310,000 volunteers. Although the army was explicitly ordered not to make the CCC a military project, the mobilization of the young men was itself a useful experience for the army. The entire operation produced useful long-term results, but the army was not initially pleased with the short-term costs.

About 3,000 officers and many noncommissioned officers, taken from tactical units, were committed to the CCC project in its first year. The resulting shortage of leaders rendered tactical units ineffective, and military training simply stopped, obviously to the great displeasure of the army's leadership. However, as if to prove that every cloud does have a silver lining, a War Department solution to the problem at hand in the middle of 1934 contributed to the partial solution to some larger problems of military readiness. The War Department called some 9,300 reserve officers to active duty so that the regulars could return to their units. The reserve officers thus had the chance to exercise the officer's reason for being: leadership. An unexpected benefit to the regular army was that this windfall of officers was not counted against army strength. Further, many reserves called up for duty with the CCC remained on active duty until the United States entered World War II in 1941. They were available and more ready than they would have been had it been necessary to call them from their normal lines of work. Thus, the army's unhappiness with an interruption in normal operations and training clearly worked to the advantage of national defense. Mobilization of large numbers of men, training of reserve officers, and a disciplined routine for hundreds of thousands of young Americans were among the unintended benefits of a CCC program designed to give productive employment to the jobless. Many veterans of the CCC served as soldiers, sailors, and marines in World War II.

National Defense Act of 1920

The Congress and the American people were not ambivalent as they recoiled from foreign involvement and pinned their hopes for security on international negotiations, war weariness around the world, and disarmament. When the General Staff proposed to Congress a permanent regular army of 500,000, the National Defense Act of June 4, 1920, which governed the organization and guided the regulation of the army until 1950, cut that number to just under 300,000, a level that would not be seen until 1940.

As a matter of fact, army actual strength in most of the interwar period was one-half authorized strength.

The National Defense Act authorized army strength, but actual strength depended on the amount of money appropriated annually by Congress. The Congress, not at all sure that U.S. military involvement in World War I had been a good idea, was disinclined to spend much on the war and navy departments. Appropriations in the interwar period generally amounted to about one-half of what full implementation of the National Defense Act would cost. Half-funding resulted in half-strength. The navy, the first line of defense, was not lavishly funded, but it fared better than the army. There seemed to be an understanding or assumption in the Congress that in the eleventh hour before catastrophe, a country like the United States would be able to fill the ranks of the army, but it would take a long time to build a modern warship.

The act of 1920, among other things, established a single promotion list—except for doctors and chaplains—a step that made the opportunity for advancement more equal in the officer corps. It also added three new branches to the army: the Air Service, the Chemical Warfare Service, and a Finance Department. Aviation and chemical warfare emerged from combat experiences in France; the establishment of a separate Finance Department reflected the army's efforts to adopt and adapt the modern management techniques then being developed in the civilian sector.

The Tank Corps, which briefly enjoyed an independent function, was put in the infantry, suggesting doctrinal confusion as well as fiscal constraints. Some military planners saw the tank as a mobile machine gun, others saw it as a kind of assault gun, and still others worried about keeping tanks fueled and operating if they were used in great numbers. The army wrestled with how to integrate tanks into the force—as part of the infantry or cavalry, or as a separate arm. It could not, in any event, afford to buy many tanks. More experience with real tanks might have prevented errors that had to be corrected in the course of ground combat in World War II.

The army reestablished the Armored Force on the eve of war. Foreign armies had thought through tank warfare more thoroughly than had the U.S. Army, and, perhaps more significant, they tested technical and tactical ideas in the field. Had U.S. armor enthusiasts enjoyed the freedom of their aviation colleagues, U.S. tank units almost certainly would have had greater initial success in combat, but in the long run, a balanced army and a combined arms mentality served the nation well.

Planning and supervision of industrial procurement were assigned to the assistant secretary of war, a civilian manager. The military aspects of mobilization planning and preparation for war were assigned to the chief of staff and the General Staff.

ORGANIZATION AND STAFFING

The War Department General Staff was organized by Gen. John J. Pershing in 1921 along the lines of his wartime "G" staff in France in 1918. Until its reorganization by Chief of Staff Marshall on the eve of U.S. entry into World War II, the staff had five divisions: G-1, personnel; G-2, intelligence; G-3, operations and training; G-4 supply; and the new War Plans Division (WPD). The WPD, because it did the strategic planning and preparation for war and was the nucleus for the wartime General Headquarters, became the focal point for the General Staff in its dealings with outside agencies and departments. It was the WPD that developed the various "color plans" in the event of war with a specific country. Plan Orange, for example, was war with Japan.

For 20 years, ground units had to manage with the weapons and equipment left over from World War I. Further, it was rare for large formations to train together since the units were skeletonized and widely dispersed to a number of posts whose military utility really had ended with the close of the 19th century. In 1932, for example, the 24 infantry regiments in the country were spread among 45 posts, 34 of them housing a battalion or less. This meant that many senior U.S. commanders in World War II experienced prewar troop command at levels no higher than battalion, and most of them were limited to company command. The best opportunities to command fully manned and larger formations were to be found in Hawaii, the Philippines, Panama, and in the school system, where fully manned school troops afforded student-officers the opportunity to experiment in the presence of their peers. That so many senior officers commanded tens and hundreds of thousands of soldiers with distinction in the war after the rather limited experience of commanding mere hundreds in the lean years is a tribute both to the individual officers and to the military school system. A number of professionals resigned to modest careers nevertheless prepared themselves for what in fact happened: a world war requiring American soldiers and sailors to command at the highest levels. Command at the lower levels fell overwhelmingly to citizen soldiers whose desire to serve and to lead had to compensate for minimal training obtained on a part-time basis.

Reserve Components

America's principal military reliance would be on the citizen soldiers of the National Guard and an organized reserve for enlisted soldiers and officers. In the decade after World War I, there were a great number of trained officers and men in the civilian community. Few of them chose to remain in the Enlisted Reserve Corps, but a large number of officers continued training as members of the

Men between the ages of 21 and 36 were required to register for the draft by the Selective Service Act of 1940; at the Douglas Court House in Omaha, Nebraska, the draft registration office was set up alongside a voter registration office. (U.S. Army Military History Institute)

Officer Reserve Corps through extension courses and in short tours of active duty. There were some 100,000 serving in the Officer Reserve Corps between the wars as newly commissioned men, products of the Reserve Officers Training Corps (R.O.T.C.) or the Civilian Military Training Corps (C.M.T.C.), gradually replacing the veterans of 1917–18. In 1928, R.O.T.C. units were found at 325 schools, some 225 of them "senior" units enrolling 85,000 college students, 6,000 of whom were commissioned each year in the Officer Reserve Corps. Regular army officers were detailed as professors of military science in the R.O.T.C. program.

At 180,000 men, the National Guard was the largest component of the U.S. Army. The National Defense Act of 1920 contemplated a National Guard of 436,000, but that number was trimmed by the fiscal constraints affecting all of the armed forces. Each year, members of the Guard drilled in their armories 48 times and spent 15 days training in the field. Although not as prepared for war as the regular army, the Guard relieved the regular force of any requirements regarding domestic disturbances in the states. The Guard was also available to be integrated into the active force as the need arose. In the years between the wars, the War Department spent about 10 percent of its military budget on the Guard, provided regular officers as instructors and advisers, and provided large quantities of materials, mostly of World War I vintage.

When the next war came, there was an orderly mobilization of Guard and reserve units and individuals into the active army. The R.O.T.C. men proved to be a particularly useful element in providing junior leadership at a time of mass conscription in the early 1940s. These programs were cost-effective and were, along with the regulars, the nucleus of what would become an army of more than 8,000,000 men and women.

There was a price to bear for the low pay, often boring duty, and slow promotions. It took, for example, 13 years to go from first lieutenant to captain, and some captains remained in grade for 17 years. Many talented men left the service; others stagnated. When war came, it was necessary to weed out from both the active force and the reserve components those who were incompetent or otherwise unfit for the demands of combat and stress. On the bright side, the gifted officers shot to the top as they never could have done in peacetime.

Recruiting enlisted men for the navy and aviation between the wars was no problem, and the quality of the men was high. The army had a recruiting problem in the 1920s that was fixed in the 1930s. A private earned 70 cents a day in the 1920s when some unskilled civilians made that much in an hour. The Great Depression solved the procurement problem for a time, and conscription was imposed just before the start of World War II. The regular army between the world wars would be little more than a small school for professional soldiers, but most students of the army in this period regard the attention to professional education and the development of officers as a major contribution to success in World War II.

EDUCATION

The U.S. Armed Forces in the war would be overwhelmingly citizen soldiers: men conscripted, or those who volunteered for service after the Japanese attack, or reservists with little training for war. Top and middle leadership, however, consisted of dedicated and competent military professionals who had carefully reflected on war for many years. The best among them made it a point to take advantage of the service schools as much to be with kindred reflective souls as to absorb the curriculum.

It was a small military force, so small that it was possible for an officer to know almost all of his year group and all officers of his branch. Patton, Eisenhower, and Omar N. Bradley knew one another for years before World War II, and Marshall made it a habit to keep track of the army's bright officers in a little black book. Similarly, in the navy, those who became household names in the course of the war in the Pacific had established their professional reputations among one another in the slim interwar years when the navy was tiny.

The Army

Despite the antipathy to internationalism and a marked preference among the American people to tend their own gardens in peace, professional military officers recognized the profound political and technological changes that would make a return to a frontier army mentality impossible. Denied troops and hardware, the best among the officers carefully studied the art of war at all levels. The U.S. Military Academy and the R.O.T.C. provided initial schooling for officers, and 31 branch schools trained officers and men of both the regular army and the citizen soldiers of the reserves. Extension courses augmented those attended by residents. The capstone of the army schools consisted of three: the oldest, at Fort Leavenworth, Kansas, known from 1928 as the Command and General Staff College; the Army War College in Washington, which, according to one wartime leader, provided "the Ph.Ds of the army"; and, after 1924, the Army Industrial College, whose establishment showed the appreciation of industrial mobilization and logistics in modern war and the need to educate officers as modern managers of resources as well as leaders of men.

The Navy

The U.S. Naval Academy trained midshipmen, and the Naval War College in Newport, Rhode Island, educated its students at roughly the level of the courses conducted by the army at Leavenworth and in Washington. The War Colleges exchanged both faculty and students in the 1920s and 1930s. For example, a senior commander or a captain of the navy was normally on the faculty of the Army War College, and Capt. William F. Halsey—"Bull" Halsey of the Pacific battles in World War II—attended the Army War College as a student in 1933–34, the year after he completed the 1932–33 Newport course of instruction. Fleet Adm. Chester W. Nimitz, commander in chief of Pacific Forces in World War II, said of the Newport experience that "nothing that happened during the war was a surprise," since the war with Japan had been fought many times in many ways in the game rooms of the Naval War College in the two decades before the bombing of Pearl Harbor in 1941. Marines selected for schooling at the war college level for the most part attended the school at Newport, but there were usually two senior marines attending the Army War College from 1920 to 1940.

AMERICA'S MOOD

It is ironic that President Woodrow Wilson insisted that the League of Nations was central to peacemaking in 1919, for his country never joined that organization. Senate resistance to U.S. membership caused Wilson to say that the United States had retreated into "sullen and selfish isolation" as he took his case to the American people. In the course of his strenuous advocacy of the League, he suffered a stroke (1919) that incapacitated and eventually (1924) killed him. Because the Covenant of the League of Nations was attached to the Treaty of Versailles presented to the Germans on May 7, 1919, it was not until July 1921 that Congress, by a joint resolution, terminated war with Germany and Austria-Hungary. Separate treaties with those countries were ratified in October 1921. The United States had begun to withdraw from foreign entanglements and to move toward isolationism.

Disarmament and Arms Reduction

Pres. Warren G. Harding responded to a Senate resolution at the end of 1920 by inviting the principal powers, except Russia, to the Washington Armament Conference (Nov. 12, 1921–Feb. 6, 1922) to consider naval disarmament and questions concerning the Pacific and Far East. In addition to scrapping ships already built or in construction, it was agreed to fix the tonnage of capital ships (defined as those displacing 10,000 tons or mounting guns larger than 8 inches) at a ratio of 5 (U.S.): 5 (Britain): 3 (Japan): 1.67 (France): 1.67 (Italy). Those same five powers also agreed to a 10-year naval holiday during which no new capital ships were to be built. The United States was signatory to a number of treaties with the various nations. Among them were agreements restricting the use of submarines in war, outlawing poison gas, and guaranteeing China's independence and territorial rights. The Pacific powers—the United States, Britain, Japan, and France—agreed to respect each

Pres. Warren G. Harding, shown here with his wife, called the Washington Armament Conference that planned naval disarmament among the major powers and provided for open communication regarding the Pacific area. (Library of Congress)

other's rights in the Pacific and to consult in the event of "aggressive action" in the Pacific. The U.S. Senate ratified all of the treaties with a pointed reservation stating that "there is no commitment to armed force, no obligation to join in any defense." The U.S. legislature jealously guarded the power to declare war and scrupulously resisted any commitment that even suggested automatic U.S. involvement in war.

Kellogg-Briand Pact

Further attempts to control arms and even to outlaw war were made, and the results were mixed. Pres. Calvin Coolidge called for a conference on naval disarmament in 1927 in Geneva (June 20–August 4). France and Italy refused to attend, the United States and Britain were unable to agree on cruiser restrictions, and the conference adjourned without accomplishment. Two years later, the United States decided to build 15 cruisers in the 10,000-ton class, but the impulse to find a way to peace was strong, even utopian. Memories of bloody war in the trenches that had cost Europe a generation of young men were still fresh.

From March to August in 1928, a series of French-American conversations resulted in the Kellogg-Briand Pact. This bilateral treaty to outlaw war became a multinational treaty eventually signed by 62 nations. Lacking means to enforce the treaty, it stands as yet another example of the victory of hope over experience.

Naval Conferences

In 1930, at the initiative of Britain's prime minister J. Ramsay MacDonald, another naval conference was at-

tended by the five naval powers—this time, in London between January 21 and April 22. France refused Italy's demands for parity, and neither of those countries signed some important provisions of the treaty. The United States, Britain, and Japan agreed to a plan to limit cruisers, but Britain needed an escape clause that would permit Britain to start construction should France or Italy threaten Britain's traditional policy of maintaining a fleet equal to any two European navies. It was contended that the concerns and responsibilities of a world power, such as Britain or the United States, differed from those of a regional power, such as Italy, and these realities had to be reflected in the treaty. Japan was seen as a regional power, despite the fact that Japan, like Britain, was an island nation—hence, the 10 (U.S. and Britain): 6 (Japan) ratio in capital ships and the 10:7 ratio in other types that the treaty delineated. Japan resented being assigned to second-class status. By the same reasoning, France, as both an Atlantic and a Mediterranean power, could not accept Italy's claim to parity with France, since Italy was a naval power only in the Mediterranean Sea. The U.S. Senate approved the London Treaty, which would expire on Dec. 31, 1936.

The League continued disarmament efforts, and the United States, although not a member, participated in the general disarmament conference in Geneva in 1932, proposing the abolition of all offensive armaments. When the conference failed to adopt the proposal, the United States proposed a 30-percent overall reduction in arms. The disarmament movement wound down from 1933 and was effectively dead by 1936. Germany withdrew from the League in 1933, the same year in which Japan announced its intention to leave in 1935 because the United States and Britain denied Japan equal status as a naval power. In 1936, Japan withdrew from the London Naval Conference of 1935–36, and Germany, Italy, and Japan were showing signs of bellicose intentions: Germany remilitarized the Rhineland in violation of the Treaty of Versailles; Italy waged war in Ethiopia; and Japan was on the march in China.

Anglo-American Cooperation

The naval limitation movement between 1922 and 1936 resulted in a gradual improvement in Anglo-American relations. Animosity was generated by the failure to reach an agreement at the Geneva naval conference in 1927, when Britain was still close to Japan because of the Anglo-Japanese Treaty, which dated back to 1902 but had lapsed after the Washington Armament Conference agreement in 1922. However, shared cultural values, shared interests, and mutual distrust of the Japanese intentions in the Far East brought the Americans and the British together in the late 1930s. The personal ties between the two former "naval persons" of World War I, Winston Churchill and Franklin Roosevelt, bound the English-speaking powers

During Pres. Herbert Hoover's administration, the London Naval Conference (1930) restricted the construction of naval vessels among the major powers. (Library of Congress)

together in an intimate manner that managed to overcome some very real policy differences. The importance of this personal relationship cannot be exaggerated, and the similar interests of the English-speaking democracies in confronting aggression in Europe and in Asia resulted in the special relationship that characterized the Anglo-American alliance in World War II and into the last decade of the 20th century.

FINANCIAL ISSUES

The issue of debts stemming from World War I promoted an anti-American feeling in Europe and isolationism in the United States. From a European perspective, U.S. insistence upon repayment of war loans made to allies and loans made after the armistice to relieve suffering in an economically dislocated Europe seemed petty. Further, pragmatic American bookkeeping seemed to contrast sharply with idealistic and utopian American verbiage. The United States was owed more than $10 billion. The United States joined the war late, suffered relatively light casualties, left Europe as quickly as it had arrived, attained the status of a great world power, uttered sanctimonious pronouncements about international peace, and then insisted upon repayment. Indeed, the remark of President Coolidge regarding the debt—"They hired the money, didn't they?"—hardly sprang from the idealism found in the Wilsonian principles and pronouncements of just a few years earlier when Wilson had been cheered in the streets of Europe as a savior of civilization.

The American Attitude

Americans saw the issue of war debts differently: the New World had pulled the Old World's chestnuts out of the fire only to find corrupt Europeans prepared to renege on their just and legal obligations as they reverted to their old bad habits. Further, as the 1920s became the 1930s, the incorrigible Europeans—and the duplicitous Japanese—continued to play a power game that endangered world order and peace. George Washington's admonitions regarding foreign entanglements were recalled. They seemed particularly applicable to Americans prepared to regard Europeans as ingrates. These general perceptions nudged the United States further toward isolationism.

Nevertheless, realism dictated the course of action taken by the United States and the world community regarding interallied war debts. The economic and financial realities in Europe caused the United States to reduce both debts and interest on debts owed by allies. The debt picture was complicated by the extraordinarily large German indemnities and reparations imposed by the victors in the Treaty of Versailles. Byzantine arrangements found Germany being propped up so that it could make payments to nations that would, in turn, make payments to the United States. A succession of adjustments—the Dawes Plan in 1924 and the Young Plan in 1929—affected German reparations until they were reduced over 90 percent by 1932.

The war debt story is a tale of almost universal acrimony, one of the consequences of what has been called "a bitter peace." Almost immediately after the Treaty of Versailles was signed, some economists were predicting very negative long-term consequences of the 1919 peacemaking. Germany's Adolf Hitler later flagrantly used the reparations and indemnities clauses—and the war guilt clause—of the treaty as examples of what he called "the shame of Versailles" to portray the Germans as martyrs and victims of a "stab in the back." The French, who knew that the future would find Germany stronger than France due to unalterable demographic facts, used the treaty as an excuse to occupy the Ruhr in 1923 along with the Belgians. Americans used the treaty as a reminder of George Washington's advice and as yet another reason to distance the United States from bickering Europeans. Europe, however, was just one of the regional concerns of the United States.

THE INTERWAR NAVY

The U.S. Navy long operated as a military subculture, one that clearly saw its mission as providing American's first

In 1922, the Langley, *originally a collier (coal-carrying ship), was converted to an aircraft carrier; it is shown here at Pearl Harbor in 1938.* (U.S. Navy)

line of defense. The Spanish-American War of 1898 had thrust the country onto the world stage. The defeat of Spain made the United States a force to be reckoned with in the Pacific and Caribbean regions. The United States competed with Germany and Japan, all latecomers to the colonial game at the beginning of the 20th century. Until 1906–07, the U.S. Navy considered Germany the leading candidate for a U.S. wartime enemy in the Pacific and in the Western Hemisphere. Japanese victory in 1905 in a war with Russia was another case of a non-European power defeating a European power, and Germany's defeat in 1918 made Japan the most powerful indigenous player in the Pacific region and a likely U.S. foe sooner or later. The Anglo-Japanese Treaty of 1902 did not lapse until 1922, after which British-American cooperation increasingly aligned those two countries against Japan, whose expansionist tendencies became increasingly apparent as the 1930s wore on.

It was widely believed in the army that the U.S. Navy would have the paramount role in the most likely war, the war with Japan. The army's supporting role in the Pacific was generally accepted by soldiers who were not quite sure if the army of the future was to be designed for frontier defense or for something like the 1918 experience in Europe. In any event, the vast ocean expanses between islands in the Pacific suggested the importance of navies in that part of the world. Certainly, army thinking between wars viewed the navy as the star of any show in the Pacific.

However the army saw the future, the navy had no doubt about its purpose: it would sooner or later fight Japan in the Pacific. An entire generation of officers attending the Naval War College war-gamed Orange, the color plan for war with Japan. Mainstream naval thinking focused on capital ships, battleships, and slugging it out in great and

decisive surface fleet actions like Trafalgar, Tsushima, or the very recent—if less conclusive—Jutland. In fact, the opposing forces were correctly foreseen, and the general strategic scenario was correctly anticipated, but the outcome of battle would be determined far more by a new element of sea power than by the big guns of the battleships. Not even the most prescient planners and enthusiastic aviators could have predicted that battles in the Pacific in World War II would normally be fought by fleets that never saw one another. Nevertheless, the navy deserved high marks for its preparation for the coming war.

Naval Aviation

The potential of land-based and ship-borne aircraft as scouts was recognized early: the airplane would find the enemy fleet, and naval gunfire would fight it. But the rapid evolution of aircraft from the fragile frame of World War I to light metal construction and powerful engines soon after permitted a much heavier payload that led to dive-bombing techniques and airplanes capable of launching torpedoes. In 1922, the collier *Langley* was converted to an aircraft carrier, and naval aviation doctrine—still quite similar at the end of the 20th century—took its first steps. In 1927, the much larger *Lexington* and *Saratoga* joined the aircraft carrier fleet.

The complex techniques of carrier operations were developed and rehearsed almost simultaneously with the working out of equally complex political decisions. Among them were funding, arms limitations, the possible consolidation of the army and navy in a single air service—indeed the establishment of a unified department of defense was seriously considered. The roles and missions of the services were reviewed regarding coastal defense and amphibious

During the interwar years, aircraft carriers were built that allowed the United States mastery of the seas in World War II; here, several aircraft carriers are under way in the Pacific. (U.S. Navy)

assault, and the navy had to decide how much of its limited funding should be dedicated to surface combatants and how much to submarines, logistical support, or naval aviation.

The navy marked the importance of aviation early in the period between the wars by establishing its Bureau of Aeronautics (BuAer) in 1921 and by qualifying senior officers as pilots or aerial observers. Among the latter were William F. Halsey and Ernest J. King, both of whom would become noted leaders in the Pacific in World War II, and William A. Moffett, who, as chief of BuAer, reduced resistance to naval aviation by emphasizing that it augmented rather than challenged the potency of the fleet. Moffett said that naval aviation would go to sea on the back of the fleet. This formulation had the advantage of being both true and of assuaging surface fleet admirals dubious about what some of them took as a challenge to naval tradition. One of the results of the Morrow Board—appointed by President Coolidge to review aviation—was a law of 1926 that provided a five-year plan to build 1,000 planes and to organize a Naval Air Reserve. By the mid-1930s, the fast carrier task force was taking shape and finding acceptance in the navy.

The characteristics of ships, however, were not entirely dictated by operational or engineering considerations. Treaty obligations and fiscal constraints also affected the configuration of aircraft carriers. The navy would have preferred to build carriers of the *Essex* class authorized in 1940, after the restrictions on tonnage had lapsed and when funding had become available. However, adhering to applicable international agreements, the navy earlier built carriers half the size of the *Essex*. In 1929, the *Ranger*

became the first ship the United States built from the keel up as a carrier. Those built earlier used keels designed for other types that were limited by treaty. The National Industrial Recovery Act allowed President Roosevelt to build the *Enterprise* and the *Yorktown* in 1933 and the *Wasp* in 1934, all of which became famous in the course of the Pacific war. It is ironic that an era of American isolationism and pacifism ushered in the fast carrier task force that has allowed the United States mastery of the seas for a half-century. Another anomaly that worked to the long-term advantage of the United States was the failure to fortify U.S. Pacific bases in the period between their acquisition in 1898 and the war with Japan.

Amphibious Operations

After World War I, the focus of naval affairs shifted to the Pacific Ocean where the war's victors confronted one another. British forces were spread around the world as Britain attempted to maintain its empire while honoring its European commitment. Japan, a regional power since 1905, seized the German colonies in the Marshalls, the Carolines, and the Marianas during World War I, thus putting Japan astride the U.S. route to China and the Philippines. U.S. bases on Guam, Midway, Wake, and indeed the Philippines were threatened by forward Japanese airfields and fleet operating bases. These outposts would be taken by the Japanese early in World War II.

The U.S. bases were not fortified. The Five Power Treaty of 1922 prohibited the fortification of bases in the Pacific, but it was generally believed that Japan was secretly fortifying its bases in violation of the treaty. Even when the treaty lapsed in the mid-1930s, Congress was not disposed to invest in the construction of bases for at least two reasons: it was thought that fortifying bases would provoke Japan, and while the United States was mired in the Depression, members of Congress preferred to spend money on projects closer to home.

In the event of war with Japan, an eventuality to which the navy enthusiastically returned in 1919, military insiders recognized that Japan was capable of overwhelming the small U.S. garrisons in the Pacific—including the Philippines—in the early days of any war between those two Pacific powers. In 1920, the chief of naval operations (CNO) told the Marine Corps commandant that Plan Orange would determine navy thinking and planning for the foreseeable future. Accordingly, he advised the commandant that the marines should provide a force of some 6,000–8,000 men on the West Coast, prepared to deploy within 48 hours for a campaign in the Marshall and Caroline islands to secure naval bases for the fleet. Unlike the army, the Marine Corps had "a definite point aim," a mission, early in the interwar period.

The marines were so successful in developing all aspects of amphibious warfare that combat assault on beaches has become synonymous with the Marine Corps. The various pieces of this complex form of war, however, were slow in coming together. The clear mission statement provided by the CNO in 1920 allowed thoughtful marines to develop a sound concept early on, but the perfection of techniques necessary for efficient execution came slowly through trial and error. The theory cost mental effort; implementation would cost actual resources simply not made available to the tiny Marine Corps of the 1920s and 1930s. Persistence and faith kept the concept alive until funding allowed practical development in World War II.

The defeat of the British at Gallipoli in 1915 had convinced many military professionals that the inherent strength of defenders in prepared fortifications armed with modern firepower made amphibious assault a very risky and bloody proposition, perhaps even an exercise in futility. Despite the risks, the prognosis for the course of war in the Pacific demanded at least careful analysis and tentative plans to seize bases in the Pacific to support the fleet.

Commandant John A. Lejeune assigned Major Earl H. Ellis the task of fitting a Marine Corps role into the navy's Plan Orange. By early 1921, Ellis had produced several drafts of "Advanced Base Force Operations in Micronesia," Operations Plan 712. Prescient in outlining what would in fact occur 20 years later, it served as a guide for marine training in the interim. Ship-to-shore movement by waves of assault craft under the cover of massive naval gunfire and tactical air support to penetrate beach defenses characterized the Ellis concept. (Ellis took an extended leave, with Lejeune's cooperation, to the Marshalls and Carolines disguised as an American businessman. In the course of his reconnaissance, he died under mysterious circumstances in the Palau island group in 1923.) But more than a concept was needed.

Personnel, equipment, and many rehearsals were required to coordinate the many elements that constitute an effective amphibious assault. From 1922 to 1926, exercises were conducted annually in Hawaii, the Canal Zone, Cuba, and Puerto Rico, but the cost of this activity caused an interruption in the program of landing exercises from 1926 until 1934. In addition to the amphibious mission, the marines also trained to fight as traditional infantry and to perform security missions aboard ship, both at home and abroad. Marines also performed occupation duties in the Caribbean and in China. The nonamphibious missions were actual here-and-now requirements that sometimes enjoyed higher priority for the 15,000-man corps than preparing for war.

In 1933, the amphibious assault force was named the Fleet Marine Force (FMF), a new name innocuous to pacifists, as "expeditionary" and "assault" were not. The name also put the marines squarely in the fleet, a clever

During the interwar years, the Marine Corps refined the concept of amphibious warfare, which was a major type of attack used against the Japanese in World War II, as at Leyte, Philippines. (U.S. Army Military History Institute)

way to get funds and to encourage the navy operating forces to dedicate assets to training for amphibious warfare. The FMF became a conceptual reality in the Navy Department. The ''Tentative Manual for Landing Operations'' completed in 1934 allowed that clear doctrine to permeate the Marine Corps, and from 1934 until 1941, the FMF conducted fleet landing exercises, producing practical experience matching the soundness of the concept in place since 1921.

The inadequate ships' boats were finally replaced by the innovations of New Orleans boat designer Andrew Higgins, whose solution to the problem of operating in bayou waters was a shallow-draft, broad, flat bow for landing and retracting, and a protected propeller. The later addition of a bow ramp for troop disembarkation produced the basic LCVP (landing craft, vehicle, personnel) of World War II fame. Larger variations would transport tanks, artillery, and other vehicles over the beach. Eventually, a tracked landing vehicle mounting guns was developed, thus providing a kind of amphibian tank for the additional shock and firepower so important early in an assault. Personnel shortages in the small corps were partially addressed in an enlightened Marine Corps reserve system that provided both individual replacements and units up to battalion size.

Despite the progress in the Marine Corps, the General Board (the navy's equivalent to the army's General Staff) assessed the navy's readiness for war in 1939 in a pessimistic report listing many ''critical deficiencies.'' The amphibious warfare mission dominating the outlook of the Marine Corps took a back seat to the navy's concerns for fleet action on the high seas and the defense of fixed naval bases. The proof of the good work done by the marines on slim budgets came later as they seized island stepping stones in the Pacific en route to Japan.

WAR PLANS AND PREPARATIONS

In the period between the world wars, the United States dedicated relatively few resources to its armed forces compared both to other nations and to what America would do after World War II. There were several factors that contributed to public reluctance to provide more than modest maintenance to the armed forces—attitudes favoring isolationism, arms reduction, and outlawing war and the economic impact of the Great Depression were among them. There was also a basic consideration that went to the heart of public attitudes and congressional funding: until the late 1930s, there was no obvious threat to the nation. Broad oceans, weak neighbors, and sheer distance from powerful potential enemies provided the country with a degree of security undreamed of by most of the world's nations. Only by interfering in the business of other people

could the United States become involved in war. Neither the Congress nor the people planned a policy that would put the nation in harm's way.

Only military professionals, and chiefly naval officers, were deeply concerned about Japan's ambitions in the Pacific region, thus illustrating a fundamental difference between the society at large and the military as they think about national security: American society tends to limit its concern for security to the expectation that its military will win its wars. The professional military thinks about security as preparation for war in peacetime and execution in times of war.

With the enemy defeated in 1918 and the rest of Europe exhausted by World War I, the United States faced no serious security challenge. The absence of an immediate threat, allegations that greedy munitions makers and ambitious generals had led the United States into war, the ''never again'' message of war literature, the hope that international agreements and law might regulate international relations and eliminate war, and the Great Depression that focused attention on domestic needs—all of these hopes and considerations added up to a strong inclination to stay out of war, indeed, to avoid becoming involved in the affairs of other nations.

The military, however, continued its mission of planning and preparing for wars. Events would show that the U.S. military planned quite well for the war that came in 1941 and for wars that did not take place. Preparation of the future military leadership was excellent; preparation of forces in being and industrial mobilization, however, would be postponed until the eleventh hour. U.S. admirals and generals were concerned that their forces were not ready for combat during the 1920s and 1930s, but in retrospect, it appears that the essential concepts necessary to put combat forces in action were in place. Those concepts, unequaled productive capacity, and the time to match the two allowed the United States to lead a coalition to victory in World War II.

Plan Orange

Fleet Admiral Nimitz, commander of Pacific forces in World War II, said after World War II that nothing that happened in the Pacific surprised naval leadership. All graduates of the Naval War College had thoroughly war-gamed Plan Orange—war with Japan—and had thought through almost all of the possibilities. No such claim was made by an army officer regarding the war in Europe, but from 1934 until the Army War College closed in 1940 ''for the duration,'' a two-ocean war had been studied and war-gamed. In the Army War College plans and scenarios, the leader of the enemy coalition in Europe, called ''the Nazi Confederation,'' was Germany. Japan was the foe in the Pacific. As the United States confronted enemies on two fronts, it would number among its allies Britain, France, Russia, and China. The plans were worked out in great detail and came very close to describing the way in which the war actually unfolded.

Plans Green and Purple

Plans for the defense of the Western Hemisphere grew out of Plan Green, which concerned U.S. intervention in Mexico. The basic premise in Plan Green was Mexican debt default that might invite intervention by a power from outside of the hemisphere. Beginning in 1938, Plan Purple evolved from Plan Green. It entailed a corps-sized expeditionary force to support Brazil against an insurrection promoted by Germany and Italy, a scenario based upon the large numbers of Italian and German immigrants in South America and upon German-Italian cooperation in the Spanish Civil War. The premise in Plan Purple from 1938 until the time of U.S. involvement in the war was that the United States must initially secure the Western Hemisphere while preparations and mobilization of U.S. resources went on. In some later phase, U.S. power would be projected abroad.

Plans Red and Crimson

The much maligned Plan Red, war with Britain, and Plan Red-Crimson, war with Britain and Canada, were unrealistic considering the close cooperation between Britain and the United States dating from both World War I and particularly from the interwar naval disarmament conferences in which the English-speaking powers aligned themselves against Japan. Enmity toward Japan and cooperation with Britain intensified after the *Panay* incident in late 1937, when the Japanese attacked a U.S. gunboat in China, resulting in the loss of American lives. However, if war planners were to imagine threats from all directions for training purposes, the only threat from the north had to involve Canada. Similarly, the only plausible threat to the U.S. East Coast had to come from the only power capable of threatening that coast, Britain.

In fact, the very detailed intelligence portion of Plan Red (indicating British capabilities and vulnerabilities) would prove useful as U.S. war planners from 1939 through 1941 determined what was needed to keep Britain in the war with Germany so that the United States would not be forced to confront the Axis Powers alone in the event that Britain (and in later planning, Russia) was defeated by those powers. Such data and analysis from Plan Red would result in the Lend-Lease arrangement, the trade of old U.S. destroyers to Britain in exchange for American basing rights in British territories in the Western Hemisphere.

Rainbow Plans

Known collectively as the Rainbow Plans, the various color-coded plans provided options for the top U.S. politico-military leadership on the eve of war for the development of a strategy to win a two-ocean war. The essence of the formal plans adopted came directly out of the work done by students at the Army War College from 1934 until the college closed in 1940 (to be reopened in 1950). From 1934 until 1937, one student committee each year planned exhaustively for war with Germany or Japan. Each year, the students pondered U.S. actions and priorities in the event of a two-ocean war with an enemy coalition. The students also considered that the United States would be in a wartime coalition. Thus, between Sept. 1, 1939, and Dec. 7, 1941, actual American planning with Britain and Canada for war with Germany, Italy, and Japan could build on the work already done at the Army War College. U.S. planning for war in the transition period from 1939 to 1942 was also influenced by the fact that graduates of the Army and Naval War Colleges in the 1920s and 1930s were in key staff and command positions. They were intimately familiar with the formal color plans and the scenarios they addressed at the colleges.

MOBILIZING FOR WAR

Although manning, arming, and equipping U.S. forces were carried out slowly until the late 1930s, the pace of U.S. military preparations picked up as Germany, Italy, and Japan more clearly emerged as disturbers of the peace. The enormous potential of the United States in material and human resources had to be translated into actual military power. Sound planning was needed, but so was political will, a factor that was extremely sensitive to public opinion in a democracy.

Industrial Mobilization

Preparation for war in the mid-20th century entailed more than target practice, marching, and courage. One of the major lessons of World War I was the need for unprecedented masses of matériel to keep a modern army in the field. The rate at which artillery ammunition was used in 1914–18, for example, vastly exceeded the expectations of prewar planners. In World War II, mechanization and motorization would add staggering requirements for fuel, and logistical efforts would be projected far from North America. Total war pitted entire societies against one another, and the side most capable of directing its economy to that end would be the probable victor. The Industrial Mobilization Plan of 1930 put the principles in place, and constant updating assured the nation a plan in 1939 for the war that soon came.

Human Resources

Planning for the required human resources came to fruition in the 1937 Protective Mobilization Plan. It specified the early call-up of the National Guard. The Guard and the regular army would constitute an Initial Protective Force of some 400,000 men. That force and the navy would protect the nation while a further methodical buildup of forces took place. There were planned strengths of 1,000,000, 2,000,000, and 4,000,000 to be met mostly by conscription, but twice the larger number would be necessary for the army before World War II was over, and more than 13,000,000 for all of the armed forces combined. In the summer of 1941, Maj. Albert C. Wedemeyer, War Plans Division, War Department General Staff, wrote the Victory Plan he was directed to prepare. He estimated the number of men needed by the army ground and air forces to be 8,795,658; in May 1945, the actual army strength was about 8,500,000.

In addition to establishing manning levels, there was a plan to train the new soldiers for modern war. It included printing training manuals; developing unit and individual training programs; establishing the location, size, and capacity of training centers; founding schools; and making schedules to handle the flow of millions of men through the system. Despite jokes about making truck drivers of cooks and cooks of truck drivers, the military did an impressive job of testing and sorting out the mass of civilians that it sent to defeat enemies scattered around the globe.

The Strategic Triangle

The concept of a "strategic triangle" described by Alaska-Hawaii-Panama was advanced by the army in connection with the Protective Mobilization Plan, behind which further preparations would be made. The navy took this as evidence of army provincialism and resented the fact that it left out the Philippines. Recalling the navy's obsession with Plan Orange, the future war with Japan, the navy view is understandable. Differences between the army and the navy stemmed largely from simple facts. The navy was a force in being that required augmentation, but essentially it was ready to go to war at all times. The army as late as 1940 knew that it was incapable of mounting even a sustainable corps of some 60,000 men to foreign shores. The army needed time.

Public Opinion

The attack on Pearl Harbor by the Japanese on Dec. 7, 1941, resulted in the declaration of war on Japan by the U.S. Congress, after which Hitler accommodated a rational American military strategy by declaring war on the United States. Considering the strong anti-Japanese feelings in the United States, the anticipation of an all-out war in the Pacific, and the need to gear up for war, it would have been difficult to get a U.S. declaration of war against Germany had Hitler not declared war first. Measures taken

in the United States in 1939 and 1940 had permitted the country to become the "arsenal of democracy" before it entered the war and had provided two years for an industrial mobilization unprecedented in world history. Bellicose behavior by the Axis Powers also made the first peacetime conscription of American men politically possible, though narrowly, in 1940.

The factors that in retrospect seem to have made American involvement in World War II inevitable were not seen that way in the 1930s. Neutrality acts passed by Congress between 1935 and 1937 were the American response to aggression taking place in Asia and Africa and to Hitler's clear intent to revise the Treaty of Versailles. The United States hoped that reason and diplomacy would prevail, as is suggested by the Good Neighbor Policy toward Latin America, the promise of independence to the Philippines, the withdrawal of marines from the Caribbean, and the normalization of relations with the Soviet Union. The American public did not want to send American soldiers and sailors to die on foreign battlefields for obscure causes. It took Japan's surprise attack on Pearl Harbor and the German declaration of war on the United States to arouse a war fever in a people previously disposed to stay out of war.

Weapons and Equipment Developments

The nation's antipathy toward military affairs had some fortuitous results. Because the country was decidedly not in an arms race until late in the 1930s, it was slow to mass-produce new weapons and military gadgets and inclined merely to note new developments, perhaps building a prototype for study. The army would make do with 1918 vintage arms and equipment. Therefore, when the United States finally went to war, its prodigious unused industrial capacity responded to demand to produce masses of technologically advanced military hardware. Perhaps the best rifle in its time was the Garand M-1 semiautomatic rifle that replaced the 1903 Springfield, a bolt-action weapon, on the eve of World War II. Similarly, the mobile 105-millimeter howitzer became the basic divisional artillery piece, replacing the antiquated 75-millimeter gun of World War I fame. Fire direction and forward observer techniques developed at the army's Field Artillery School at Fort Sill improved communication, and the new pieces made U.S. artillery in World War II as effective as any in the world. State-of-the-art tanks and trucks tumbled off assembly lines, thanks to the very late departure of horses and mules from army transportation. The B-17 bomber was produced and continuously improved from the mid-1930s and during the war. There were advantages to the late development of military matériel, but there was a cost in lives as well for the dollars saved in peacetime.

The U.S. Navy's standard torpedo was vastly inferior to those of the Japanese at the beginning of the war in the

Building bridges under battle conditions tested the U.S. Army Corps of Engineers; here, army engineers construct a bridge on Guadalcanal. (U.S. Army Military History Institute)

Pacific. It was alleged that in the cost-conscious peacetime U.S. fleet higher priority was attached to recovering torpedoes than to hitting targets. The Japanese also proved to be more effective at night fighting on land and at sea than the Americans. Initially, U.S. fighter planes were not as good as Japanese, German, or British fighters, but late in the war, the P-51 was probably the best fighter in the skies until a German jet aircraft was developed, but too late to affect the war's outcome. German and Russian tanks were better than U.S. tanks. Radar was known to the U.S. military, but the British developed the technology before the war, while the United States did so during the war. Generally, the U.S. fighting forces had superior weapons and equipment—particularly late in the war—but in certain areas other nations provided their forces with better war materials.

The U.S. logistics and intelligence services performed outstandingly during the war. Getting mountains of warfighting material to troops far from home was accomplished routinely, ports and airfields were built under stressful conditions in all climates, and bridges were constructed under fire. Both the army and navy experts in communications intelligence did well in enabling the United States to break enemy codes, such as the Japanese "purple" code, and to monitor diplomatic and military traffic.

THE EVE OF WAR

President Roosevelt was keenly aware that the United States would either be drawn into war or risk standing alone in a world dominated by militaristic Germany and Japan. He also knew that his country wanted peace. Therefore, he had to be circumspect in making preparations he regarded as prudent without provoking either domestic or foreign enemies. His unprecedented election to a third term by a wide margin in November 1940 showed his success in knowing the mood of the American people.

Hemispheric Defense

At the beginning of 1939, a campaign of limited preparedness was begun. Concerned that European foes might establish air bases in the Western Hemisphere, thus undermining the security provided by the Atlantic and Pacific oceans, the policy of hemispheric defense replaced the more limited defense of the "strategic triangle" and North America. The large numbers of Germans and Italians in South America and their economic influence, particularly in the aviation industry, were a potential threat in the hemisphere. Further, other nations might develop bombers like the American B-17, an aircraft capable of carrying heavy payloads across the Atlantic. Defense of the hemisphere became the sine qua non of each of the five options provided in the Rainbow Plans drafted by the army and navy to supersede the individual Color Plans in 1939. Later, after France fell, 21 nations of the Western Hemisphere signed the Act of Havana on July 30, 1940, which proclaimed collective security to keep Germany out of the hemisphere. The following month, the United States and Canada established a Permanent Joint Board on Defense.

Buildup to War

On Sept. 8, 1939, Roosevelt declared a limited national emergency after the war began in Europe on September 1 with Germany's invasion of Poland. The regular army increased enlisted strength to 227,000 and the National Guard to 235,000, while in April 1940, 70,000 troops took part in the first corps and army training maneuvers ever held in the United States. The latter revealed a number of weaknesses and deficiencies, but fortunately once identified they could be corrected in training in the time remaining before the United States was engaged in a major land war.

In response to Hitler's victories in the west from Norway to France in the spring of 1940 and during the Battle of Britain that followed, the first peacetime conscription in the United States was introduced. The Selective Service Act of Sept. 16, 1940, required men between the ages of 21 and 36 to register and provided for the training of 1,200,000 troops and 800,000 reservists for one year.

Navy efforts matched those of the army as a two-ocean naval program was announced to address the simultaneous threats of Japan in the Pacific and Germany and Italy in the Atlantic, a particularly ominous prospect should Britain be defeated. In the last six months of 1940, there was a doubling of the active army, and by mid-1941, 1,500,000

In anticipation of the need for naval bases in the north, Hitler's army occupied Denmark and Norway in 1940; here, German warships leave a Norwegian fjord base during World War II. (U.S. Navy)

men were serving. An Armored Force was established in July 1940, and a new General Headquarters assumed responsibility for training in the same month. Later, antiaircraft and tank destroyer commands were established. In October 1940, four armies took charge of ground units in the continental United States and trained them under the control of General Headquarters. In the fall of 1941, 27 infantry, 5 armored, and 2 cavalry divisions were being trained in the United States along with 35 air groups and a great number of supporting troops. Even the substantial resources of "the arsenal of democracy" were strained as hard decisions were made regarding the distribution of old and new U.S. equipment to training units, combat units, and allies to prevent their defeat by the Axis Powers.

The Atlantic and Europe

Two days after the invasion of Poland, in one of his "fireside chats," President Roosevelt publicly revealed his attitude when he said: "This nation will remain a neutral nation, but I cannot ask that every American remain neutral in thought as well." The Neutrality Act of 1937 was modified on Nov. 4, 1939, to permit "cash and carry" export of arms and munitions, an action favoring maritime Britain. After the fall of France in June 1940, Germany dominated Europe. On Sept. 2, 1940, the United States obtained naval and air bases from Britain in British Guiana, Antigua, Trinidad, St. Lucia, Jamaica, the Bahamas, Bermuda, and Newfoundland on a 99-year lease in exchange for 50 overage U.S. destroyers desperately needed by Britain. Germany, Italy, and Japan could only regard this as an unfriendly act by the United States.

The Lend-Lease Act, signed by Roosevelt on Mar. 11, 1941, removed all pretense of neutrality. It authorized the president to transfer, lease, sell, or exchange war materials to "any country whose defense the President deems vital to the defense of the United States." Congressional and public opinion hoped for peace, but analysis of public opinion polls and voting records in the Congress during the war in Europe after September 1939 indicates a gradual acceptance of the need for the United States to rearm and to help Britain, and later the Soviet Union. The vote for Lend-Lease, for example, was 60 to 31 in the Senate and 317 to 71 in the House.

The nation's defense policy broadened from one of hemispheric defense to an undeclared participation in the

Pres. Franklin D. Roosevelt, shown with his wife, Eleanor, used the radio as a medium to communicate with and reassure the public during World War II. (Library of Congress)

Diplomat and statesman W. Averell Harriman served as President Roosevelt's envoy for the Lend-Lease program begun in 1941; during the later years of World War II, he was ambassador to Moscow. (Library of Congress)

war. By the time U.S. and British military representatives met for staff conversations concluded in Washington at the end of March 1941, the U.S. military had already decided that Germany was a greater threat than Japan. If it came to war in the Atlantic and Pacific at the same time, the United States would defeat Germany first, a concept explicit in Rainbow 5, the strategy that would guide American and British conduct in the war.

In April 1941, the U.S. Navy was directed by President Roosevelt to patrol the western half of the Atlantic Ocean as the British did the same in the east. In May, Roosevelt proclaimed an unlimited national emergency, the United States assumed responsibility to develop and operate military air routes across the Atlantic via Greenland in the north and Brazil in the south, and the president directed the army and navy to prepare an expeditionary force to be sent to the Azores to block possible German movement into the South Atlantic. In June, Hitler attacked his Soviet ally, and U.S. Army troops landed in Greenland to protect it from German attack while building air bases there to facilitate the ferrying of aircraft from North America to Britain. In July, U.S. troops relieved British troops securing Iceland, and in August, Roosevelt met with British prime minister Winston Churchill in Newfoundland to draft and proclaim the Atlantic Charter, outlining the terms of a

just peace. October saw the U.S. Navy escorting convoys in the North Atlantic, while in November, American merchant ships were armed and permitted in combat zones, producing an undeclared war between the United States and Germany.

Conditions in the Pacific

The incremental steps toward war in the Atlantic were accompanied by a deterioration of U.S. relations with Japan. Japanese aggression in China antagonized U.S. public opinion, long paternalistic regarding China, and Japan was warned by the United States not to take European possessions in Asia and the Pacific made vulnerable in 1940 as Germany rolled over Western Europe. Economic sanctions imposed by the United States in an effort to influence Japanese policy had the opposite effect when Japan decided on war rather than accepting what it regarded as yet another humiliation imposed by non-Asians. Japan failed to see how the United States could take the proprietary stance expressed in the Monroe Doctrine while denying Japan an analogous stance in its part of the world. In July 1941, Japan sent troops into French Indochina. The United States retaliated by curtailing oil shipments to Japan and by freezing its assets in the United States, and it reinforced the U.S. garrison in the Philippines.

Japan's strategic decision to strike for the rich resources of Southeast Asia—rather than cooperating with Germany to defeat the Soviet Union—meant that Japan could not ignore the flank exposed to the Americans in the Philippines. The same logic convinced Japan to launch the strike aimed at destroying the U.S. fleet in Hawaii, despite the known risks resource-poor Japan would take in a contest with a very large and rich United States.

INTERWAR SUMMARY

The preparations by the U.S. services between the world wars demonstrated both strengths and weaknesses in the American approach, but on balance, the services showed good sense. A deficiency that defied correction in the interwar period was addressed by the creation of a Department of Defense at the end of the 1940s. Despite army and navy cooperation in planning together on the Joint Army and Navy Board from shortly after the turn of the century, the existence of an Army-Navy Munitions Board since 1922, and the exchange of student officers and faculty at the war colleges, the two services insisted upon their uniqueness at the expense of complete cooperation in the national interest. The thought of generals commanding navies and admirals commanding armies—as is the case in the unified commands of the U.S. military in the 1990s—was inconceivable in the years before World War II. The best the services could do was to accept the principle of "paramount interest," allowing, for example, that the navy had paramount interest in the Pacific and in Plan Orange. The experience of senior commanders in working with other U.S. services and with foreign military and political leaders during the war made a deep impression on men like Dwight D. Eisenhower. He did his best after the war to eliminate military provincialism by establishing joint schools and joint staffs—with some success. For the most part, each service before the war saw the world narrowly through the lenses of its own interests.

The Army

The army was ambivalent about mobile light forces and powerful heavy forces. The negative consequences of such ambivalence are often lost in the overall success of the effort; total victory and unconditional surrender of enemy forces tend to obscure the bad news. However, the prewar army emphasized the traditional arms, particularly infantry, to the detriment of U.S. armored forces. The latter would enter the war undergunned and thin-skinned compared to foreign armies, most notably the German army. This emphasis on mobility was striking since force development stood in sharp contrast to a doctrine suggesting the use of overwhelming force to annihilate the enemy in decisive battle. The bloody experience of the Germans, British, French, and Russians in World War I stimulated more vigorous research, development, testing, and evaluation of tanks in Europe than that undertaken by the Americans. On the other hand, the U.S. emphasis on the development of a highly professional officer corps resulted in the maintenance of a balanced—if third-rate—army rich in intellectual capital and poor in physical resources. The nucleus of a balanced force exploited sound concepts, a large population, and an untapped industrial capacity to transform the tiny professional army into an army of 8,500,000 well-equipped amateurs that produced victory.

The Navy

The navy of the late 1930s has been criticized for emphasizing a big battleship force that sought a Trafalgar-like victory in the coming war and for relegating aviation, submarine, antisubmarine, and amphibious warfare to supporting roles. In fact, unlike the army, the navy trained many of its most promising middle-grade and senior leaders in aviation and integrated into the fleet both naval aviation and the Fleet Marine Force with its tactical air capability. The navy also turned a perceived disadvantage into an asset that would become the envy of the world's navies to the end of the 20th century. Denied fortified forward bases in the Pacific, the U.S. Navy developed a logistical system of replenishment at sea that allowed its ships to remain at sea for long periods of time, thus producing a force multiplier effect. While foreign navies had to return to port for supplies, the U.S. Navy continued its mission.

Aviation

The Army Air Service, later called the Air Corps, in focusing on the heavy bomber and autonomy as a separate service, presented the army leadership with the problem of reconciling the nurturing of aviation with the maintenance of a balanced force. Army leaders were characterized as unimaginative traditionalists and impediments to progress wedded to the idea of horse cavalry and other old-fashioned notions. Aviators and the general public were mesmerized by flight and the idea that aviation would enable the bomber to leap over armies locked on the ground to go for the destruction of the enemy's "vitals." The army's insistence upon tactical air support of the fighting forces ran counter to the doctrine of strategic bombardment and deep interdiction, a difference that continued long after World War II. In the 1920s and 1930s, the issue was even more fundamental as the army stressed the auxiliary nature of air power while the air arm declared its centrality and fought for the autonomy that was achieved after the war.

The Marines

The way in which the Marine Corps willingly integrated itself into the embrace of the fleet contrasts sharply with the acrimonious struggle of army aviation for independence. Because the primary mission was so clear—amphibious warfare in the Pacific to seize bases from the Japanese for the fleet—the Marine Corps drew the appropriate conclusions and conducted itself accordingly. Because it was totally dependent upon the larger services for support, a balanced combined arms approach to combat and a cooperative attitude were the keys both to success in war and to survival as a Marine Corps in peace.

Conclusion

To interpret the condition of the American military between the wars as a hibernation from which it was jarred by the Japanese attack on Pearl Harbor on Dec. 7, 1941, would be an exaggeration. The nation had other legitimate concerns and inhibitions, but its military leadership was prepared to use the abundant national resources rationally as they became available during the transition to war at the end of the 1930s and in the early 1940s. In fact, the army of 1,643,477 at the end of 1941 marked the first time the nation went to war with a large army already in uniform and with an industrial base already making the changes necessary for war production. The nation's armed forces were prepared to defend the Western Hemisphere against invasion even as the Japanese attacked. Time was required to develop the forces that would be sent thousands of miles across the oceans.

After the attack on Pearl Harbor, a mobilized United States focused on winning the war. The capable leadership, sound service doctrines and plans, unmatched industrial capacity, and enthusiastic public support insured that the United States would be transformed in a remarkably short time from a society with a strong isolationist bent to one of unmatched military and political might that inspired the coining of the word ''superpower.''

3

North Africa, Sicily, and Italy: 1942–1945

The British victory by Gen. Bernard Montgomery's 8th British Army over German field marshal Erwin Rommel's Panzerarmee Afrika—first at Alam Halfa in August 1942 and again two months later at El Alamein—was the turning point for the Allies of the war in the West. After two years of one successful Axis campaign after another, during which all of Europe and a large portion of Russia had fallen, it was also the first visible signal that Adolf Hitler's self-proclaimed thousand-year Reich was not invincible after all.

For the British, the war had been a calamitous series of setbacks ever since Dunkirk. Norway, Greece, Crete, Burma, Hong Kong, Singapore, Dieppe, and Tobruk had all earned a permanent place in the lexicon of British military disasters. Less visible but equally deadly was the Battle of the Atlantic, where the Allies were steadily losing the struggle with German U-boats, which were sinking Allied shipping faster than it could be replaced.

When Hitler unleashed Operation Barbarossa, the surprise attack against the Soviet Union in June 1941, more than 3,000,000 German ground troops, supported by 3,000 tanks and 2,000 aircraft, swarmed over a front extending from the Black Sea to the Arctic, catching the Red Army flatfooted. Two unlikely allies, Britain and the Soviet Union, had made their cause a common one, and both were now on the defensive across Europe and in the Mediterranean. Russian tenacity, the dreadful cold of winter, and Hitler's miscalculation that the war in the East would be quickly won combined to enable the Red Army to continue the fight in 1942.

In the West, the dramatic reversal of British fortune took place near the Egyptian border with Libya. There, in the bloodiest battle of the desert war, a little-known British general led a revitalized 8th Army over Rommel, the celebrated Desert Fox. Thereafter, the names of both El Alamein and Montgomery were immortalized. British prime minister Winston Churchill later proclaimed, "Before Alamein we never had a victory. After Alamein we never had a defeat."

In early 1941, Hitler sent Rommel's expeditionary force to North Africa to bolster the sagging fortunes of his Italian ally. For the next 18 months, the British 8th Army fought a series of losing battles against the Afrika Korps across the vast North African desert. The British were humiliated at Gazala and Tobruk, and by July 1942, the 8th Army was defending Alam Halfa, the final obstacle to the Axis conquest of Egypt. Churchill had already removed Gen. Sir Archibald Wavell as commander in chief, Middle East, in 1941 and in August 1942 did the same to Gen. Sir Claude Auchinleck. It was the arrival of Gen. Sir Harold R. L. G. Alexander and Montgomery that heralded a new era of British success in North Africa.

By late 1942, Rommel had concluded that continued Axis presence in North Africa was a futile gesture, and he urged Hitler to withdraw German forces while there was still time. His blunt assessment was that there was no hope of victory and "the abandonment of the African theater should be accepted as a long-term policy . . . if the Army remained in North Africa it would be destroyed." Rommel's warning was given a chilly reception by Hitler, who declined to acknowledge the growing plight of his forces in North Africa, which were seriously deficient in manpower, weapons, food, and fuel. Despite mounting evidence that the desert war had turned in favor of the

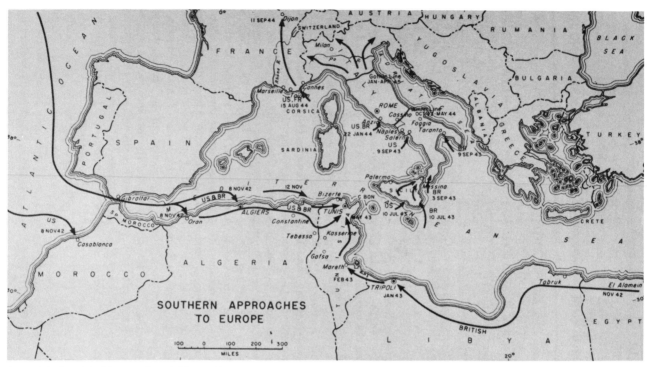

From ROTCM 145-20: American Military History: 1607–1958 (Washington: HQDA, July 1959), Map 39

British, Hitler, who never considered North Africa anything more than a sideshow, spurned Rommel's counsel. The leadership in Germany and in the West believed that the decisive battles of the war would be fought on the soil of Europe, not along the shores of the Mediterranean.

Allied Strategy

From the time of the formal entry of the United States into the war, shortly after Pearl Harbor, the policy of the United States was to defeat Germany by the most direct means, irrespective of political considerations. In December 1941, the United States and Britain had agreed to placing priority upon the defeat of Germany first, rather than of Japan in the Pacific. Gen. George C. Marshall, the architect of American strategy, wanted no part of a U.S. commitment to the Mediterranean. He believed that the decisive campaign of the war would be fought in northwestern Europe. To this end, he relentlessly pursued the development of sufficient forces and equipment in the United Kingdom, from which a cross-channel invasion of France would be mounted at the earliest possible moment.

By the summer of 1942, however, there was no agreement as to what the Allies would do nor where they would do it. An invasion of Europe in 1942 was not even remotely feasible, and Marshall began backing plans for such an operation in 1943. Pres. Franklin D. Roosevelt was more concerned that a suitable role be found for U.S. combat forces as quickly as possible and was unwilling

to tolerate a delay into 1943. Heated Anglo-American negotiations resulted in a compromise: in return for an American commitment to military operations in the Mediterranean, the British agreed to a massive buildup of American forces in Britain for a cross-channel operation in 1943.

Marshall was compelled to accept the commitment of American troops to the Mediterranean, which was to commence with landings in French North Africa. This first joint Allied venture was scheduled for November 1942 and given the code name Operation Torch. Separate invasion forces from the United States and Britain were to rendezvous off North Africa, where three task forces would go ashore simultaneously on the morning of Nov. 8, 1942. The Allied commander for Torch was Dwight D. Eisenhower, then a virtually unknown junior American major general.

NORTH AFRICAN CAMPAIGN

For the first time, Britain and the United States challenged Axis control of the Mediterranean. Inexperienced in amphibious operations and yet to fight their first battle, U.S. forces nevertheless entered into their first campaign of the war with equally green British forces in one of the world's most inhospitable regions. The formidable Allied task was to land and seize nine important objectives along a nearly 1,000-mile coastal front from French Morocco to Algeria.

Once the vital port cities of Algiers, Oran, and Casablanca were secured, the Allies were to thrust quickly into Tunisia to capture Bizerte and Tunis. The Western Task Force, commanded by Maj. Gen. George S. Patton, Jr., seized Casablanca, Safi, and Port Lyautey on the Atlantic side of French Morocco. The two other task forces—a U.S. force of 39,000 men commanded by Maj. Gen. Lloyd R. Fredendall—landed at Oran, and a similar Anglo-American force of 23,000 British and 10,000 U.S. troops seized Algiers. In all, 117,000 troops were committed to Torch, 75 percent of them American.

The situation in French North Africa was complex and beset with intrigue and a confusion of loyalties among the French military, some of whom were loyal to Marshal Henri P. O. Petain's Vichy regime, while others supported the Allies. The reaction of the French to an Allied invasion of their North African colonies was uncertain, and fraught with the possibility that their forces might bitterly resist Operation Torch.

Early Campaigning

Torch was carried out under very unfavorable sea conditions that were nearly disastrous. Inadequate communications, mechanical failures, the absence of engineers (who were left stranded on troop transports), and the wrong priorities for landing equipment were among the problems encountered. A last-minute cease-fire directive by Adm. Jean Darlan, the French commander in chief, generally averted bloodshed except at Oran, where the French fought furiously for two days before surrendering to the U.S. 1st Infantry Division.

To emphasize his determination to hold North Africa, Hitler reacted to the Torch landings by ordering the immediate reinforcement of Tunisia and creating the 5th Panzer Army under Col. Gen. Jurgen von Arnim, who took control of all German forces. The first of some 100,000 additional German and Italian troops began arriving in Tunisia in a steady flow in early November, as the German air force, the Luftwaffe, made Allied movement a costly proposition on land, while at sea, German U-boats sank Allied shipping with distressing regularity.

To the east, the 8th Army continued the pursuit of Rommel's Panzerarmee Afrika as it executed a deliberate retreat toward the Tunisian border. In mid-November, as Allied forces struggled to establish a fully operational front in western Tunisia, the 8th Army reached Tobruk, the scene of its severe defeat six months earlier. The early days of the Tunisian Campaign in November 1942 were a race to determine who could solidly establish themselves in Tunisia first. In mid-November, an Axis force of about 25,000 men resourcefully improvised a bridgehead that delayed the Allied advance and left Bizerte and Tunis under Axis control.

The senior German commander in the Mediterranean was Field Marshal Albert Kesselring, a Luftwaffe veteran whom the Allies came to regard as one of the outstanding German commanders of the war. Kesselring had long urged the establishment of a new front in Tunisia and welcomed its reinforcement. Arnim's mission was not only to defend Tunisia and hold Bizerte and Tunis, which were vital bases for mounting an invasion of southern Europe, but to destroy the Allied expeditionary force.

The original aim of Allied operations in Tunisia was to secure the ports and lines of communication and then to trap and destroy Rommel's army in Tripolitania between the advancing 8th Army and the British 1st Army. The first round of the Battle for Tunisia was an unequal struggle, won by the Axis, whose ground forces were aided immeasurably by the Luftwaffe, which aggressively disrupted and delayed the Allied advance into western Tunisia. It was one of the few times during the war in the West that the Luftwaffe would claim success. By contrast, there were too few Allied air squadrons and a deficit of supporting equipment and services. The closest all-weather air base was at Bone, more than 120 miles from the front lines, while the Luftwaffe operated with virtual impunity from all-weather fields as close as 5 miles to the battlefield. Thus, the first stage of the Battle for Tunisia became in equal measure a contest for domination of the air as well as for control of the ground.

Allied troops and airmen were not lacking in courage, but their inexperience and the unsuccessful results of their first battles left no doubt that there would have to be considerable improvement before they would be an equal match for the veteran German troops in Tunisia. The race for Tunis also became an attempt to beat the winter weather. The Allies lost on both counts, obliging Eisenhower to cancel further Allied offensive operations in Tunisia in 1942.

During the winter of 1942–43, Allied forces in Tunisia were seriously understrength. Their 250-mile-long front along the Western Dorsal Mountains was manned with only single British, French, and American corps. In the south, Fredendall's U.S. II Corps guarded a vast area between the Eastern and Western Dorsals, from Gafsa to a point midway between the Faid and Fondouk passes.

By early February 1943, the German Afrika Korps had retreated westward into the formidable Mareth line. An attack by the 8th Army was inevitable, but Rommel's major concern was that he might be attacked from the rear by Allied forces in Tunisia. Rommel understood that he had no chance whatever to defeat the 8th Army, but by defending the Mareth line with minimum forces an opportunity existed to defeat the inexperienced Allied forces in southwestern Tunisia.

Both Rommel and Kesselring recognized that an opportunity existed to strike a blow that could split the Allies in two by driving a wedge through the Western Dorsals to the Mediterranean as far west as Bone. The attack, to be delivered by all of the panzer strength left in the Afrika Korps and in the 5th Panzer Army, would center around Gafsa and be aimed at destroying the untested and understrength U.S. II Corps. In addition to inexperience, the tanks and guns of the U.S. forces guarding the passes through the Eastern Dorsals were no match for the superior German armament. Tactically, the Allied commanders made the Axis task easier by their faulty dispositions, which left almost no capability for mutual support.

On Feb. 14, 1943, a powerful German tank-infantry force consisting of the 10th and 21st panzer divisions, backed by Luftwaffe dive bombers, surprised U.S. forces at Faid and Sidi Bou Zid. The Americans were quickly overwhelmed, with enormous losses. The German plan was flawed by a clash between Rommel and Arnim that left no one in overall command. Not only was Arnim uncooperative with Rommel, but he made no attempt to exploit his overwhelming success at Sidi Bou Zid, and his inaction proved to be the most telling of the Axis mistakes in Tunisia. Even though Kasserine Pass fell to Rommel, he had not received promised panzer reinforcements from Arnim in time, and U.S. troops had held the pass long enough to delay the advance. Although Axis forces won a major victory at Kasserine, strategically they had gained little of consequence. Unable to turn the Kasserine Offensive into a deep exploitation capable of collapsing the Tunisian front, Rommel called off the offensive on February 22 and began withdrawing toward the Eastern Dorsals.

Sidi Bou Zid and Kasserine were humiliating defeats for American arms, defeats that had serious consequences. The British regarded the battle as clear evidence that American fighting ability was mostly bravado. Not only were U.S. tactics and dispositions unsound, but once attacked by the Germans, some troops had abandoned their positions and equipment and fled to the rear in panic. Equally disturbing was the fact that American armor and artillery were simply no match for the superior German armament. Kasserine convinced the Americans that unless there was an immediate improvement in leadership and training, the long-term effects would be disastrous.

Allied Victory

Unmistakable evidence soon appeared that Kasserine had imbued the senior U.S. leadership with the necessary determination to reclaim their lost honor. Considerable credit for this was due Maj. Gen. Ernest Harmon, a veteran cavalry officer whom Eisenhower sent to the front to help reverse the situation. The aggressive Harmon took temporary control of II Corps and brought stability to the rapidly deteriorating front when it was most needed. The inept Fredendall was dismissed by Eisenhower, and Patton was hastily summoned from Morocco to assume command

Maj. Gen. Ernest Harmon, arriving in Tunisia, was sent by General Eisenhower in 1943 to revitalize and stabilize U.S. troops after two major defeats. (U.S. Army Military History Institute)

of II Corps on Mar. 6, 1943. Patton brought about a dramatic transformation of U.S. forces by convincing his troops that they were capable of defeating the Germans. In Patton, the U.S. Army in Tunisia now had a Rommel-like warrior.

Equally important was the appointment of General Alexander as the commander of all Allied ground forces in Tunisia. Alexander brought to the campaign a stability it had so badly lacked previously. His campaign plan was to unite his ground forces with the 8th Army, which was to breach the Mareth line and drive into southeastern Tunisia. The 18th Army Group, as the combined Allied forces were designated, would then drive Axis forces into northern Tunisia, while the air force and navy prevented the arrival of reinforcements and sealed off any escape by sea.

Although the American commanders in Tunisia had the highest personal regard for Alexander, they bitterly resented the patronizing attitude of the British. The problem facing American commanders was clear-cut: to improve the performance of U.S. troops and in the process to convince their skeptical British ally that the fighting qualities of the American soldier were the equal of any in the world. The leadership that would accomplish that was now on the scene in the persons of Patton, Maj. Gen. Omar N. Bradley, and a growing number of excellent division commanders.

Rommel's final battle was in early March at Medenine, when he launched an ill-conceived spoiling attack that was intended to disrupt the forthcoming 8th Army attack against the Mareth line. Montgomery had established powerful defensive positions between Medenine and Mareth, into which the unsuspecting Afrika Korps plunged. The results were swift and bloody, with more than 50 panzers left burning on the battlefield. Medenine was the nadir of Rommel's illustrious career. He had left Africa the day before the battle, disheartened and ill from two grueling years in the desert. In Berlin several days later, he was severely rebuked by Hitler, who steadfastly spurned his plea that "for the Army Group to remain in Africa was now plain suicide." North Africa, which has been called "the graveyard of generals," had claimed its most famous victim.

In late March at El Guettar, Patton's II Corps won its first victory of the war by defeating a veteran German panzer division. By the standards of World War II, this battle was a minor engagement, but for U.S. forces, it was a significant victory. The lesson for Arnim and the Axis commanders was equally clear: the U.S. Army was no longer to be taken lightly as an adversary. By early April, the 8th Army cracked the Mareth line and joined the Allied forces in Tunisia. Arnim's Army Group Afrika managed to elude entrapment. Nevertheless, although the ultimate fate of the Axis forces in Tunisia was now clear, the campaign was far from over. Arrayed against Arnim was a massive Allied force consisting of the British 1st and 8th armies, a French corps, and the U.S. II corps. Alexander's continued mistrust of American fighting ability was made crystal clear in his plan for the decisive battle of the campaign. II Corps was relegated to the minor role of protecting the Allied left flank, while the British would make the main effort to corner Army Group Afrika in the Cape Bon peninsula.

Bradley, the new American II Corps commander, was dissatisfied with the minor role assigned to U.S. forces and persuaded Alexander to employ II Corps in an independent role of driving to Bizerte in order to block an Axis escape to the west. As II Corps closed the jaws of the trap by capturing Bizerte and cutting off Arnim's only escape route, British and French forces completed the operation by forcing Army Group Afrika onto the plain of Tunis, where it was compelled to surrender.

The fate that befell the Axis army in Tunisia was a bitter pill for Arnim, who belatedly learned that Hitler had ruthlessly and needlessly left his army to wither and die in the Allied trap, his appeals for food, fuel, and ammunition ignored by Berlin. Although starved for resupply, the troops of Army Group Afrika gamely resisted Alexander's relentless onslaught to an honorable end. On May 12, 1943, Arnim surrendered, and the 250,000 survivors of Army Group Afrika became Allied prisoners of war. The Germans could ill afford to lose an entire army group to a hopeless venture, when on the Eastern Front, German troop losses were rising to alarming proportions.

The following day, Alexander cabled Churchill to announce that the Tunisian Campaign was over: "All enemy resistance has ceased. We are masters of the North African shores." For the Allies, the Tunisian venture had been a testing ground. As Bradley later noted, "In Africa we learned to crawl, to walk, then run." Tunisia also became a harsh lesson that U.S. commanders were doggedly determined never to repeat. With the Allies in complete control of North Africa, another turning point in the war had come. Henceforth, the Allies, not Hitler, would dictate the time and place of future engagements.

INVASION OF SICILY

The defeat of Axis forces in North Africa left the German and Italian high commands certain that the Allies would soon employ their massive sea, air, and ground forces elsewhere in the Mediterranean in order to gain a foothold into southern Europe. Among the obvious sites was the island of Sicily.

What the Axis leadership did not suspect was that the Allies were seriously divided over future strategy in the Mediterranean and that some of the most contentious disagreements of the war were to occur in the process of agreeing upon a common strategy. Although Allied planners had for some time been developing a number of possible options for future action after the campaign in Tunisia ended, there had been no firm agreement between Britain and the United States. The British were fully committed to a strategy that not only would exert pressure upon the Axis but would support Russia by drawing German forces away from the Eastern Front, where the Red Army was still on the defensive despite its crushing victory at Stalingrad. In pursuit of this policy, Churchill was determined to remove Mussolini and the Italians from the war once and for all.

Moreover, in early 1943, the British simply were not prepared to support, in more than token form, the American desire for a cross-channel invasion of northeastern Europe that year. Although he accepted the eventual necessity of the cross-channel invasion, and indeed was the first to proclaim that the decisive campaign would have to be fought in Nazi-held Europe, Churchill sought to buy time

Pres. Franklin D. Roosevelt (third from right) *and British prime minister Winston Churchill* (third from left) *met at Casablanca, Morocco, in 1943 to discuss future military strategy; also seated were Americans Gen. Henry Arnold* (left), *Adm. Ernest King* (second from left), *and Gen. George Marshall* (right). (U.S. Army Military History Institute)

for its planning and preparation by nibbling away at what he termed "the soft underbelly" of Germany. As the prime minister saw it, any action to restore the balance in the Far East was clearly out of the question for the foreseeable future. Only in the Mediterranean was there any immediate possibility of continuing the momentum of victory that had begun in North Africa.

The Casablanca Conference

An Anglo-American clash was inevitable when the Allied leadership met at Casablanca in January 1943 to resolve its future strategy. Gen. Sir Alan Brooke, the chief British strategist and head of Britain's chiefs of staff, came to Casablanca fully committed to an invasion of Sicily to follow the Tunisian Campaign. Marshall strongly disagreed with further operations in the Mediterranean and argued forcefully for an invasion of Europe in 1943.

Churchill and Roosevelt remained aloof and left the resolution of their differences to the Combined Chiefs of Staff, who wrangled with one another for nearly 10 days during some of the most arduous negotiations ever to occur between the two allies. Eventually, the two sides reached a compromise. The British agreed to renewed planning for the cross-channel invasion, Operation Overlord. In the meantime, the Allies would exploit their growing strength in the Mediterranean by invading the island of Sicily, which would not only signal the return of the Allies to Europe but eventually enable them to carry their effort into mainland Italy. Command of the invasion forces of what

was code-named Operation Husky was given to the current Allied commander in the Mediterranean, Eisenhower.

Alexander was appointed as the ground commander in chief. Command of Allied naval and air forces also went to British officers: Adm. Sir Andrew Browne Cunningham and Air Chief Marshal Sir Arthur Tedder. The designated invasion commanders were Montgomery, whose British 8th Army would form the ground element of the Eastern Task Force, and Patton, whose U.S. 7th Army would form the Western Task Force.

Planning Operation Husky

From its inception as a strategic compromise at Casablanca, the planning of Operation Husky was plagued by interminable problems of organization and command. Alexander was preoccupied with the Tunisian Campaign and paid scant attention to the preparations for Sicily. The first weeks of planning were extremely critical and urgently required someone to provide guidance at the highest level so that the various planning staffs would understand the direction their effort was expected to take. In theory, the planning of a joint amphibious operation should center on the requirements of the ground forces and their mission. In practice, many factors combined to ensure that this requirement was lost in a morass of confusion, disorganization, and disharmony.

For three months, the Allied commanders failed to agree upon an invasion plan that all would accept. A number of proposals were considered, but none were accepted. In early May 1943, a compromise plan proposed by Montgomery was accepted that called for the 8th Army to land along a 50-mile front in southeast Sicily, from Syracuse to the Pachino Peninsula. At the same time, along the south coast, Patton's 7th Army would make its primary landings at Gela and Scoglitti with the U.S. 1st and 45th infantry divisions, while to the east at Licata, the heavily reinforced 3d Division would land to protect the 7th Army's left flank. The object of the two assault landings on July 10, 1943, was to seize a firm Allied bridgehead in southeastern Sicily and to capture the key ports of Syracuse and Licata and the airfields near Gela, from which Allied aircraft would support the ground forces.

Once ashore, the 8th Army's mission was to drive north to capture the port city of Messina, the gateway to Sicily, in the extreme northeastern corner of the island. Messina was the primary Axis logistical lifeline to the Italian mainland across the Strait of Messina. Other than the capture of the important airfields near the southeastern coastal town of Gela, the U.S. 7th Army's only mission was to protect the 8th Army's left flank. Although Messina was the only strategic target in Sicily, Alexander elected to allow the land battle to develop before committing himself to a course of action by his two armies.

The island of Sicily was garrisoned by an Italian army of more than 300,000 men and a small German contingent that until June 1943 never consisted of more than a division. Until the loss of North Africa, only token attention was paid to the island as a possible Allied target. The new Axis commander, Italian general Alfredo Guzzoni, arrived in May 1943 and found Sicily's ground, naval, and air forces woefully unprepared to resist an invasion.

Guzzoni's dire warnings of the poor state of Sicily's defenses went unheeded in Rome, where Italian dictator Benito Mussolini boasted that any invader would be smashed "at the water's edge." After the debacle in Tunisia, Hitler agreed to send only token reinforcements totaling two divisions. Guzzoni and Kesselring disagreed over how to defend Sicily, and the result was that Axis forces were hopelessly split between eastern and western Sicily.

Before D-Day, the Allied air forces conducted an exceptionally successful air campaign against targets in Sicily, Sardinia, mainland Italy, and elsewhere in the Mediterranean to neutralize the Axis air capability. Both Axis air forces were left a shambles, with the Italians all but extinct as a fighting unit and the Luftwaffe severely crippled.

Combat Operations

The landings were to be preceded by U.S. airborne and British glider landings to seize key targets around Gela and Syracuse as part of a bold night operation, the first of its kind ever attempted. The British glider force encountered dangerously high winds, smoke from the island, and heavy flak both from enemy guns and, unexpectedly, from friendly naval vessels that, contrary to orders, mistakenly

Prior to the invasion of Sicily, Allied air-power attacks severely crippled the German air force, destroying planes like these Stuka dive bombers. (U.S. Army Military History Institute: Jarrette Photo)

fired upon the aerial armada. Of the 147 gliders involved, nearly half crash-landed in the sea, drowning 252 British soldiers. The factors of inexperience, wind, and enemy flak were a fatal combination that turned the first stage of Husky into a disaster. The U.S. airborne landings fared little better, and more than 3,000 paratroopers were scattered over a 1,000-square-mile area of southeastern Sicily.

Unlike the airborne and glider operations, the amphibious invasion was a great success. The 8th Army landings were so successful that Montgomery ordered his two corps commanders to push inland and up the coast toward Catania without delay. The most important of the three American landings took place at Gela, where the 1st Infantry Division landings occurred along the beaches opposite the plain of Gela. For two days, the Americans fought off Axis counterattacks to drive them back into the sea by the Hermann Göring Division and the Italian Livorno Division. The Axis strategy of dividing German forces had backfired; by July 12, the two Allied armies were in control of firm bridgeheads and in Sicily to stay.

Hitler acknowledged that Axis forces had no hope of reversing the Allied invasion. However, despite the generally feeble resistance of the Italians, the Germans had no intention of ceding Sicily without a fight. A German corps headquarters was ordered to the island, as were elements of the elite 1st Parachute Division, which was alerted to drop into the plain of Catania to reinforce a beleaguered German battlegroup operating northwest of Augusta, in an attempt to block the coastal highway to Messina. During the night of July 13–14, Montgomery launched a third night airborne and glider operation to seize a key bridge on the northern edge of the plain of Catania. The target, Primosole Bridge, was not lightly held by the Italians as supposed, but by a regiment of veteran German paratroopers of the 1st Parachute Division that had landed several hours before the British operation commenced.

The airborne landings again failed, and only a handful of British paratroopers landed near Primosole Bridge. Even when reinforced, the British failed to advance north of the bridge and capture Catania and the undefended coastal road to Messina north of the city. The city was virtually undefended from a seaborne assault, and an amphibious brigade-size landing at Catania would have succeeded in trapping the Germans and opening the road to Messina. Such an operation was planned but never carried out. After a savage five-day battle, Montgomery conceded failure and switched his main offensive effort to the northwest, where XXX Corps was ordered to break the German defenses along the newly formed Etna line and sweep around the northern edge of Mount Etna to the coast below Messina. However, by shifting his main effort to the west, Montgomery had split the 8th Army and unwittingly presented the Germans with an opportunity to delay the XXX Corps advance long enough to establish the Etna line.

On July 17, Patton arrived unexpectedly at Alexander's headquarters in North Africa to seek a more important role for his army. With the British in serious trouble in the plain of Catania and unable to crack the Etna line, Alexander agreed to Patton's plan to employ II Corps to thrust to Sicily's northern coast, while the remainder of the 7th Army cleared western Sicily. In reality, this was merely a clever ploy by Patton to maneuver the 7th Army into a position to capture Messina. His army was ideally positioned to outflank the Etna line and encircle the Germans.

Alexander could have struck a killing blow with the 7th Army. The Etna line defenses were incomplete and were weakest precisely where Alexander might have used the U.S. II Corps to break them, and thus tighten a noose from which the only escape was retreat or surrender. Instead, Patton was permitted to carry out independent secondary operations in western Sicily that had no immediate impact on the outcome of the Sicily Campaign. When U.S. forces liberated Palermo on July 21, they were greeted by thousands of flag-waving, cheering Sicilians. While the publicity focused on Palermo and the sweep into western Sicily, neither of which were of any strategic importance, Patton ordered a new offensive along the north coast and across north-central Sicily by two U.S. infantry divisions.

At a meeting of the Allied ground commanders on July 25, Montgomery proposed that the 7th Army rather than his 8th Army capture Messina. Patton now had the full backing of both Alexander and Montgomery to seize Messina and end the Sicily Campaign. By early August, the Germans had skillfully carried out a succession of delaying actions by using the mountain terrain to maximum advantage. Although the German formations in Sicily had performed brilliantly, they now faced entrapment in the northeastern corner of the island. Their choices were limited: evacuate Sicily or surrender. While the XIV Panzer Corps conducted a series of delaying actions that made

Gen. George S. Patton, commander of the 7th Army, maneuvered his troops through western Sicily, enabling them to capture Messina. (U.S. Military Academy)

American progress a painful and costly experience, plans were implemented for a mass evacuation across the Strait of Messina.

German Withdrawal

During the first 11 days of August, the Germans withdrew more than 13,000 troops and considerable equipment. Ferry traffic in the Strait of Messina was efficiently organized and performed flawlessly under the cover of heavy antiaircraft support. The Allied air forces made a halfhearted and largely futile effort to interdict the evacuation. When the Germans began their flight from Sicily, they fully expected catastrophic losses. But instead, the Germans accomplished a stunningly successful strategic withdrawal. By the time it ended on the morning of Aug. 17, 1943, they had extricated nearly 55,000 troops, 9,789 vehicles, 51 tanks, and 163 artillery guns from Sicily. When the U.S. 3d Division entered the smoking ruins of Messina that same morning, it found that the last German had long since departed.

The final days of the Battle for Sicily were a dismal conclusion to a campaign that had been beset from the start by controversy and indecision. For 38 days, the Allies had fought some of the most difficult battles of the war, in terrain every bit as harsh as they would find ahead of them in Italy. Yet their enemy had defied them to the end and accomplished one of the most successful strategic withdrawals in military history. The Germans had saved not only themselves but virtually every weapon and vehicle capable of being ferried to the mainland.

One historian has aptly described Sicily as "an Allied physical victory, and a German moral victory." The reasons were varied and included Alexander's failure to take charge of the battle, his unjustified mistrust of U.S. fighting ability, Montgomery's changes of strategy, the failure of the air forces to make more than a token effort to impede the German evacuation, and the navy's failure to block the Strait of Messina. The Allies needlessly prolonged the reduction of Sicily by fighting a frontal battle of attrition. The result was that a German army corps that never exceeded 60,000 men and that was devoid of air and naval support managed to delay for 38 days two Allied armies whose combined strength exceeded 480,000 troops.

MAINLAND CAMPAIGN

The invasion of Sicily hastened the downfall of Mussolini and his fascist government, both of which were deposed in late July 1943. King Victor Emmanuel III immediately appointed Field Marshal Pietro Badoglio to head the Italian government. Although Badoglio proclaimed that the war would go on as before, within weeks, the new Italian leader began secretly negotiating an armistice with the Allies, which led to Italy's unconditional surrender on Sept. 9, 1943.

The fall of Mussolini led the German leadership to revive quickly earlier contingency plans for a series of military actions to be taken in the event of an Italian collapse. Rommel was hastily recalled from a special mission to Greece and given command of the newly formed Army Group B. As Rommel made preparations to intervene, the Germans began moving fresh troops into Italy under the pretense of reinforcing Kesselring in the event of an Allied invasion.

After months of indecision, the Allies at last acted upon Eisenhower's recommendation that an invasion of Italy follow the fall of Sicily. The Casablanca Conference had failed to formally ratify such a move, even though it was tacitly accepted that the Allied campaign would continue into Italy. Operation Overlord (the invasion of France) was not scheduled until the late spring of 1944, and the massive Allied force in the Mediterranean could not be left in Sicily and North Africa without a new mission.

Eisenhower was authorized to begin planning two operations to be directed against Italy. The U.S. 5th Army had been organized in the spring of 1943 under Lt. Gen. Mark W. Clark to plan and execute operations in Italy, and for months had been preparing for an amphibious invasion

south of Naples, at Salerno. Toward the end of the Sicily Campaign, Montgomery withdrew the British XIII Corps to begin planning Operation Baytown, an invasion of the region of Calabria, in southeastern Italy.

Churchill's Mediterranean strategy envisioned continued Allied operations into Italy and, if possible, an offensive that would carry them into northern Italy, from where Allied aircraft could be employed in a direct support role in Overlord operations. Marshall remained determined that nothing detract from Overlord and resisted any operations after the capture of Rome. What was lacking then or at any time during the Italian campaign was a statement of Allied grand strategy. If the political goals were vague, even less clear were the aims of the forthcoming military operations in Italy. At Casablanca, it was never resolved whether Sicily was to be the stepping stone to a larger objective in Italy or merely an end in itself. The British continued to believe passionately in the necessity for a strong Allied presence in the Mediterranean as a vital ingredient to the defeat of Germany and had long feared that the United States would insist on halting further active military operations in the Mediterranean once Sicily was successfully conquered and Allied control of the region in the air and on the sea was supreme.

At the Quadrant Conference held in Quebec in August 1943, the U.S. and British military chiefs clashed over future operations in Italy and the scope of Operation Avalanche, the Salerno operation. They did agree, however, that Operation Overlord would take precedence and that Eisenhower would have to carry out operations in Italy with considerably reduced forces and a secondary priority on both replacements and logistics.

Operation Baytown

The allied commanders, worried about control of the southern regions of Sicily and the vital shipping lanes of the Strait of Messina, decided that a force was necessary in southern Italy to draw valuable German reserves away from Salerno. The shortage of landing craft was a major problem throughout the war in the Mediterranean and northwestern Europe. There were never enough to meet commitments in both Europe and the Pacific, and it became a constant problem to obtain adequate numbers for amphibious operations in both theaters of operations. The situation was especially acute in the Mediterranean, where, by early 1944, most of the Mediterranean-based shipping would be shifted to the United Kingdom for Overlord. It also meant that Baytown, the drive into southern Italy, must necessarily precede Avalanche; there simply were not enough vessels for simultaneous landings. Once Montgomery gained a foothold in the toe of southern Calabria, the landing craft would be committed to the Salerno landings, which were scheduled for Sept. 9, 1943, a week after Baytown.

British field marshal Bernard Montgomery, standing in a jeep, salutes the citizens of Sousse, Tunisia; he went on to lead Britain's 8th Army through the Sicilian and Italian campaigns of 1943–44. (U.S. Army Military History Institute)

Montgomery believed that Baytown was a wasteful and unnecessary operation where the same lack of coordination and strategic goals that had characterized operations in Sicily now threatened operations in mainland Italy. His attempt to persuade Eisenhower to cancel Baytown and use the threat of landings in Calabria as a means of tying down forces that might otherwise imperil Clark's 5th Army at Salerno was rejected.

The Italian Campaign opened on September 3 when Canadian and British infantry landed on the Italian side of the Strait of Messina only to find that the Germans had withdrawn several days earlier and now occupied positions in the rough mountainous terrain of central Calabria, at the neck of the Italian boot. During the first five days of the new campaign, the 8th Army advanced with relative ease some 100 miles to the point where the Italian boot joins the leg of southern Italy.

Salerno Landings

The governing factor in the decision to invade Salerno was the effective range of Allied tactical aircraft. Naples represented the maximum range of the Sicily-based squadrons. Even at this distance, air cover would only amount to approximately 20 minutes over the battlefront. Hence, the Allied planners recommended that the U.S. 5th Army invade Italy along the Gulf of Salerno, approximately 20 miles south of Naples.

The invasion of Salerno intended to take advantage of the imminent collapse of Italy by gaining the Allies a foothold on the Italian mainland. Once the invasion force gained a bridgehead, Clark's 5th Army would link up with Montgomery's 8th Army driving north from Calabria. Together, the two armies would continue offensive operations toward Rome under the command of Alexander,

whose 15th Army Group would control all Allied ground operations in Italy. Although the Salerno landings were to be carried out by two corps, the shortage of landing craft exerted an enormous influence on the Avalanche invasion plan, reducing the scope of the landings to three divisions (two British and one American), and small U.S. ranger and British commando forces.

Opposing the Allies in Italy was a German army group under the command of Field Marshal Kesselring. His imprint on the Battle for Tunisia had been minimal, but as the fighting shifted to Italy, Kesselring dictated German strategy by skillfully maneuvering his forces against the Allies during what became the longest and bloodiest campaign fought by the Allies in the West during World War II. Many in Berlin believed that the German army should defend Italy in the northern Apennines. Kesselring disagreed and finally convinced Hitler that German strategy should be to defend south of Rome along Italy's narrowest point: from the vicinity of Pescara on the Adriatic through the Liri Valley to the Gulf of Gaeta, north of Naples, the area that later came to be known as the Gustav line.

Such a defense offered the advantage of denying the Allies vital air bases in central and northern Italy and discouraged any attempt to invade the Balkans and threaten the crucial sources of raw materials used to feed the German war machine. Kesselring realized that he could not hold southern Italy indefinitely, but he far preferred defending there than in the Apennines and the Po Valley. Despite Hitler's penchant for interfering in the conduct of battles, Kesselring, unlike most of the other German theater commanders, was permitted to conduct the Italian Campaign according to his own conception and strategy, which was to make the Allies pay dearly for every foot of ground in southern Italy.

This resistance began with the invasion of Salerno, which was bitterly resisted by the 16th Panzer Division. The German 10th Army lost no time in reacting to the Allied landings. German divisions from as far north as Rome and as far south as Calabria were ordered to Salerno to contest the Allied landings. The relentless defense of the Salerno beachhead by the German army was typical of what the Allies encountered in their battles in the Mediterranean. When they could, the Germans fought tenaciously to retain their positions; when that was impossible or militarily impractical, they fought delaying actions until they could establish new defenses elsewhere. In Sicily, they had been outnumbered, outgunned, and outmaneuvered and had been unable to meet the Allied invaders on the beaches. At Salerno, however, despite being outnumbered, the Germans controlled the high ground and the exits from the invasion beaches and demonstrated they had every intention of driving the Allies back into the sea.

The invaders might not have survived without the timely and often valiant support of the Allied fleet. Time and again, destroyers and gunboats braved the intense German fire to maneuver close to the shore so as to deliver counter-battery fire or to suppress a German counterattack.

The 5th Army beachhead was perilous because of a seven-mile gap between the British X Corps and the U.S. VI Corps, which would have to be closed before the Germans were able to exploit it and roll up the flanks of the Allies. By the third day, the situation on the beaches of Salerno had become so dire that Clark was now contemplating the unthinkable: being driven back into the sea. He began making plans to reembark VI Corps and land it in the British sector. There was one slender thread of hope, and Clark seized upon it. If the 5th Army could hold on long enough for the 82d Airborne Division to respond, there was still a chance to retain the beachhead. Across the front came the order to "hold at all costs." As the battle raged, U.S. losses began to mount with disturbing speed. Units were isolated from one another and were being chopped to pieces. Communications were severed, and the battle became a struggle for survival. Clark had already committed his slender reserves and had virtually nothing left with which to stop a determined German counterattack.

At the height of the battle, 3,500 paratroopers of the U.S. 82d Airborne Division were parachuted at night into the beachhead in one of the most successful airborne operations of the war. For the first time, VI Corps could constitute a reserve. A combination of sheer tenacity by the front-line troops, superb gunnery on the part of the Allied navy and the artillerymen ashore, and valiant air support enabled the 5th Army to hold its ground long enough for additional reinforcements to arrive and for the Germans to exhaust their resources in unsuccessful counterattacks.

By September 13, it had become clear to the German commanders that the Allies would hold their beachhead. German equipment losses were mounting, and fatigue was beginning to take its toll when Kesselring ordered a phased withdrawal that would disengage the 10th Army without further serious losses. By September 17, the Germans were on the move to the north, and when Naples fell to the Allies on October 1, the first phase of the Italian Campaign was over.

Despite their inability to drive the invaders of Salerno back into the sea, the Germans nevertheless had managed to stifle the invasion landings and in the process had come close to inflicting a humiliating defeat upon the Allies. More important, Salerno was the proof that Kesselring needed to convince Hitler that his forces could indeed successfully defend central Italy. Had the Allies employed their resources better at Salerno, Kesselring might have drawn a different conclusion and thus altered the entire course of the war in Italy.

Even though the German 10th Army had voluntarily withdrawn from the Salerno bridgehead and offered little resistance on the road to Naples, it still managed to make the 5th Army advance difficult by creating every possible obstacle to Allied movement, including blown bridges and numerous booby traps.

Advance to the Gustav Line

As the 10th Army was withdrawing from Salerno toward the Gustav line, Kesselring was hastening completion of his main defenses, which were to be anchored along the mountains overlooking Cassino at the southern end of the Liri Valley. In order to buy time, the retreating 10th Army delayed the Allied advance along a series of natural defensive barriers. The XIV Panzer Corps had the responsibility for defending the primary Allied route to Rome, while to the east a mountain corps covered the sector running from Cassino to the Adriatic coast.

The Allied high command mistakenly believed that the German defense of Salerno presaged a full-scale retreat to the north and a defense in the Apennines centered on Pisa and Rimini. From Eisenhower down, the belief prevailed that the 15th Army Group would soon capture Rome, probably by the end of October 1943.

However, unless they were to initiate another amphibious landing north of Salerno, the geography of Italy dictated that the Allies must advance on Rome along the Mediterranean (western) side of the great chain of mountains that bisect the center of Italy from the Alps to the Italian boot in Calabria. Although Allied strategy centered on keeping German forces fully committed in Italy, so that its veteran divisions could not be shifted to France to help repel the cross-channel invasion, Churchill was emphatic that Rome must fall by the end of 1943.

To attack the Gustav line, the Allies found they first had to get past a series of hastily fortified defensive belts manned by crack German troops. The mountainous terrain of central Italy was the worst imaginable place to fight a large-scale military campaign, and it became Kesselring's greatest ally. Not only were the mountains formidable obstacles, but the many rivers; the cold winter weather; the wind, mud, and rain; and the limited road network made any advance against a well-prepared defender a nightmare. The mountains had to be negotiated via mule train, by sweating, weary soldiers who had to take over the portage of guns, ammunition, and supplies themselves when the trails became too steep even for mules.

No less difficult were river-crossing operations where the logistics were enormous, the execution demanding, and rapid exploitation essential. In Italy, the Allies were forced to breach such obstacles during the most difficult time of year. Italian rivers run mostly west or east; thus the old adage about "one more river to cross" took on a grim reality throughout the campaign. What had been anticipated as an offensive of short duration to capture Rome turned out to be a methodical and deadly advance. The first German obstacle was based along the Volturno River, 35 miles north of Naples. The Germans succeeded in delaying the 5th Army offensive until mid-October when the British

X Corps and the U.S. VI Corps launched attacks that gained footholds north of the river at heavy cost.

The difficulty facing the Allies in Italy was that the successful crossing of a river or a mountain led them only to yet another series of identical obstacles. After the time-consuming and costly operations to gain a bridgehead north of the Volturno, the Allies then faced the hasty defenses of the Barbara line, which marked the outward boundary of what the Germans called the Bernhard line and the Allies called the Winter line. Anchored on the Garigliano River on their left and a formidable mountain barrier in the center and on the right, the Winter line was the most serious obstacle the Allies had yet encountered in their march on Rome.

Most of the Allied troops were exhausted after months of combat and in poor shape to sustain an offensive under the conditions they faced in Italy. The most seriously affected was the British 8th Army, whose many veteran divisions were simply worn out from endless fighting that for most dated back to El Alamein the previous year. As it struggled to gain a foothold across the Volturno, the U.S. 5th Army was in equally rough shape.

Attempts in November to continue the advance toward the Gustav line lacked sufficient strength to breach the German defenses along the Winter line, and it was not until early December that the Americans were able to regroup and launch a fresh offensive. A series of bloody battles lasting into mid-December did gain considerable ground, but failed to attain the final objective, the Liri Valley and the capture of the town of Cassino. The 5th Army was unable to gain a foothold north of the twin obstacles of the Garigliano and Rapido rivers, and as 1943 drew to a close, the campaign had turned into a stalemate.

Allied strategy shifted toward finding a means of advancing into the Liri Valley. In November, Alexander had come to the conclusion that he could not advance to Rome unless the Allies initiated an amphibious end run and drew away German troops manning the Gustav line. This operation, code-named Shingle, was to be an amphibious landing 80 miles to the north at Anzio by the U.S. VI Corps. Both Shingle and the river crossings were to be carried out by the 5th Army in January 1944.

Battle of the Rapido River

The necessity for thwarting an Allied breakthrough at the Rapido River was not lost on the German commanders. Lt. Gen. Fridolin von Senger had assumed command of the XIV Panzer Corps and had aligned his defenses to prevent the Allies from establishing a bridgehead north of the Rapido. Clark's plan called for the 36th Division to assault and hold a bridgehead across the Rapido for the U.S. 1st Armored Division, which was to move up and debouch into the Liri Valley. The 5th Army commander's optimism for the operation overlooked the simple fact that

the swampy terrain along both sides of the Rapido was wholly unsuitable for the employment of armor.

Diversionary operations to breach the Garigliano River by the British X Corps caught the Germans by surprise and were so successful that Kesselring was obliged to commit his only strategic reserve, two panzer grenadier divisions based near Rome. Clark failed to seize the initiative and exploit the Garigliano success, insisting instead on carrying out the Rapido operation.

For some time, the Germans had been anticipating an Allied end run into their rear and had been preparing contingency plans to react. The problem was that there were simply too few formations to meet Kesselring's requirements. If he committed his only strategic reserve to meet the Allied threat on the Garigliano, there would be no forces readily available to counter an amphibious landing near Rome. Without the slightest hesitation, and counter to the advice of some of his senior staff officers, Kesselring elected to commit his reserves then and there. In his judgment, the threat posed by the British success on the lower Garigliano was so grave that he must react or risk the collapse of the Gustav line.

The U.S. 36th Division assault of the Rapido River the night of Jan. 20, 1944, was one of the bloodiest failures of the war. The 15th Panzer Grenadier Division manned positions astride the west bank of the Rapido that enabled them to pour a devastating volume of fire upon the assault troops who had no cover, no artillery support, and insufficient numbers to force a successful crossing. Two attempts were repulsed by the Germans with heavy American losses.

Planning Operation Shingle

The failure at the Rapido left the 5th Army stalled at the mouth of the Liri Valley, with little prospect for breaking the Gustav line in the foreseeable future. The failure came at the very moment VI Corps was about to launch the Anzio landings, 35 miles southwest of Rome. Alexander believed that the key to this operation lay in the rapid seizure of the Alban Hills, 20 miles northeast of Anzio. If an Allied force seized and held the Alban Hills, it could block all German reinforcement by road and rail and would likely render Kesselring's position so untenable that he would be forced to abandon the Gustav line and retreat to the Apennines.

The key to the success of Shingle was that the operation be launched in conjunction with a major 5th Army offensive that would enable it to link up with the Anzio force within 10 days. This meant that Clark would have to crack the Gustav line and drive 30 miles north to at least the vicinity of Frosinone, a town on Highway 6 approximately halfway between Cassino and Rome. Due to a severe shortage of landing craft, the fate of Shingle was uncertain until late December, when Churchill became involved and pressured the Combined Chiefs of Staff to delay the return of landing craft to the United Kingdom.

Between Alexander and Clark, there were major differences of opinion as to what VI Corps was to accomplish at Anzio. Alexander's intention was to strangle Kesselring and open the road to Rome by seizing and holding the Alban Hills. After Salerno, Clark began to view the problem in terms of avoiding another disaster on the scale of Avalanche. Clark and Maj. Gen. John P. Lucas, the invasion commander, thought that there was unwarranted optimism by Alexander and Churchill. Lucas believed from the outset that Anzio was an ill-conceived operation that would likely end badly.

The ill-fated Rapido crossing destroyed the entire premise of the end run to Anzio and ensured there would be no early linkup between VI Corps and the remainder of the 5th Army. Nor did anyone ever question if the 36,000 troops of the Allied invasion force were of sufficient size to seize and hold both the Alban Hills and a logistical lifeline to the port of Anzio.

Another question that the Allied high command failed to resolve was what would be Kesselring's response to the landings. The Allied high command mistakenly believed that the threat posed by the Shingle force would be sufficient to compel Kesselring to move to the Pisa-Rimini line. However, such a premise was valid only if Lucas could move VI Corps into the Alban Hills and isolate the German 10th Army. Without an adequate force, Lucas could defend the Alban Hills or defend his logistic lifeline to the port of Anzio, but not both.

Anzio Campaign

The Anzio landings were successfully carried out on Jan. 22, 1944, against scant opposition from the few German troops based near Anzio. Although Kesselring had long expected the Allies to launch an amphibious end run somewhere near Rome, the Shingle landings nevertheless caught the Germans flatfooted. Despite the surprise, the Germans had made plans to react on short notice to any Allied amphibious landings, and within hours, divisions from northern Italy, Germany, Yugoslavia, and France were on the move to Anzio. Kesselring's immediate concern was to contain the Allied beachhead, and to do so, he thrust every unit near Rome into the breach to block an Allied advance to the Alban Hills. At all costs, the Allies were not to be permitted to establish themselves along this crucial terrain.

Kesselring need not have worried that Lucas would make a dash to seize and hold the Alban Hills. The American general had long since made up his mind that VI Corps must be securely established ashore and no major offensive action undertaken until the security of the Allied beachhead was assured. Moreover, Clark's instructions to Lucas left him the option of capturing the Alban Hills at his discretion.

Kesselring was confident he could detach formations from the stalemated Cassino front to reinforce Anzio.

By the end of the first day, the Germans had moved 20,000 reinforcements to the vicinity of Anzio, and in the days that followed, the German buildup continued at a relentless pace. By January 24, Col. Gen. Eberhard von Mackensen's 14th Army numbered 40,000 troops. The Germans had thus gained vital time to establish defensive blocking positions and by January 29 had massed nearly 70,000 troops, supported by large numbers of tanks and artillery, in a tight ring across the Anzio beachhead. It was only a matter of time before Mackensen initiated a powerful counterattack to drive the Allies back into the sea. The Allies now found themselves with no place to go. At the end of January, Lucas launched an offensive to capture the Alban Hills that came too late.

This was a decisive moment in the war in Italy. Not only was the stalemate at Cassino unbroken, but within days, Anzio became an extension of the same stalemate. Anzio had turned into a colossal liability for the Allies, who, like Kesselring, were obliged to rush reinforcements from the south to meet the threat of the massive German buildup opposite VI Corps. Instead of facing one stalemate at Cassino, the Allies now found themselves deadlocked on two widely dispersed fronts.

Preliminary attacks took place in early February and made only limited gains for the Germans, who were forced to regroup for their all-out offensive, which commenced in the early morning hours of February 16 as both ground forces and the Luftwaffe responded to Hitler's order of the day to "lance the abscess south of Rome" by driving a wedge into the Allied left flank and destroying the beachhead. Lucas was obliged to commit every available resource to aid the beleaguered units defending the approaches to Anzio on his left flank.

By February 18, the battle had reached the final Allied defensive line outside Anzio, where a last-ditch stand was made. If the Germans had broken through, the entire left flank of the Allied line would have collapsed, and the battle would have been lost. Waves of tanks and infantry hurled themselves upon the British and American defenders in a furious and ultimately futile series of attacks that failed to break the Allied line. The German attackers were cut down by machine-gun fire and the heaviest Allied artillery bombardments of the entire war in the Mediterranean. By February 19, the intensity of the German attacks had waned and the beachhead was saved. The German counteroffensive of February 16–20 marked the turning point of the Anzio Campaign. Lucas, the Allied commander, was relieved of command even though he had been given a mission that he had no practical likelihood of achieving.

From London, Churchill observed the events in Italy with considerable trepidation that failure would have an adverse, if not fatal, impact on the success of Operation

Allied troops man an antiaircraft emplacement at the Anzio, Italy, beachhead; a landing craft is unloaded (right). (U.S. Army Military History Institute)

Overlord. Despite repeated reassurances from Alexander, Churchill's frustration at the inability of the Allied military commanders in Italy to break the stalemate and capture Rome led to his now famous remark about Anzio that "I thought we were landing a tiger cat; instead all we have is a stranded whale."

Cassino Campaign

The failure of two major Allied offensives resulted in a stalemate on the two major battlefields in early 1944. After the Rapido disaster, Mark Clark launched a fresh offensive in early February to capture the town of Cassino, the western anchor of the Gustav line, over which stood the Abbey of Monte Cassino, one of the holiest shrines of Roman Catholicism.

During the bloody First Battle of Cassino, the U.S. 34th Infantry Division could not capture the monastery and its surrounding heights. A second offensive in mid-February resulted in one of the most hotly debated incidents of the war, the destruction of the Abbey of Monte Cassino by more than 200 Allied bombers. The ground forces were unable to take advantage of the bombing until nearly three days later. It was too late, and the Cassino heights remained firmly in German hands until May. The bombing of the abbey became the most visible example of the failure of Allied strategy in Italy in 1944. The Allies had not reaped a single tangible military benefit from it and had instead committed a major blunder that ended the Second Battle of Cassino. The Third Battle of Cassino began in mid-March with a two-pronged assault on Cassino that was preceded by a thunderous artillery barrage from 900 guns and a massive aerial bombardment of the town, which was

pulverized by more than 1,000 tons of bombs. Again the follow-up ground attacks ended in failure.

On both fronts, the stalemate dragged on into the spring of 1944 with neither belligerent posing a serious threat to the other. Across the Anzio front, the Allies turned the battle into a holding action where nothing would happen until the Allies attacked Cassino for the fourth time in the spring of 1944.

Operation Diadem

During the lull, Alexander's staff created a plan, code-named Diadem, to break the Gustav line. This involved a sweeping realignment of forces that would concentrate the British 8th Army opposite Cassino for the main attack by three corps. The 5th Army was to be shifted to the Garigliano sector and would be joined there by Gen. Alphonse Juin's Corps Expéditionnaire Français, while the Polish II Corps took over the former French sector on the 8th Army right flank.

Unlike the piecemeal tactics so unsuccessfully employed by Alexander and Clark, Diadem called for the 8th Army to concentrate its vast array of firepower, supported by the full weight of the Allied air forces, in simultaneous attacks upon key points in the German defenses. Diadem was to be a battle of annihilation, not attrition. Once the Allies were in control of Highway 6, the Gustav line would be effectively cut and German troops from the Anzio and Cassino fronts could not reinforce one another.

Although Diadem and the breakout operation from Anzio were separate plans, the aims of each were closely linked. As the U.S. official history notes, "General Alexander described the coming offensive in terms of a one-two punch, with the Eighth and Fifth Armies throwing the first punch on the southern front and the Fifth Army's VI Corps the second punch—a left hook from the Anzio beachhead."

Allied preparations included the most massive buildup of artillery ever undertaken in the war. There were 124 battalions, consisting of more than 1,500 guns, preparing to fire several million rounds of ammunition in support of Diadem. Despite the vast edge in Allied firepower, the German lines held during the opening days of Diadem. Finally, in the west, a thrust by the Corps Expéditionnaire Français tore a gaping hole in the right flank of the Gustav line. With the loss of this vital anchor, the Gustav line collapsed when the Polish II Corps succeeded in capturing the Abbey of Monte Cassino on May 17. The long-sought breakthrough was at last realized.

With Monte Cassino in Polish hands, his right flank in shreds after Juin's attacks, and British armor threatening to thrust clear to Rome along Highway 6, Kesselring was left with few options and little hope. He was forced to rush two divisions from Anzio, but these proved unable to redeem the situation at Cassino. Their departure in turn severely weakened the 14th Army on the Anzio front.

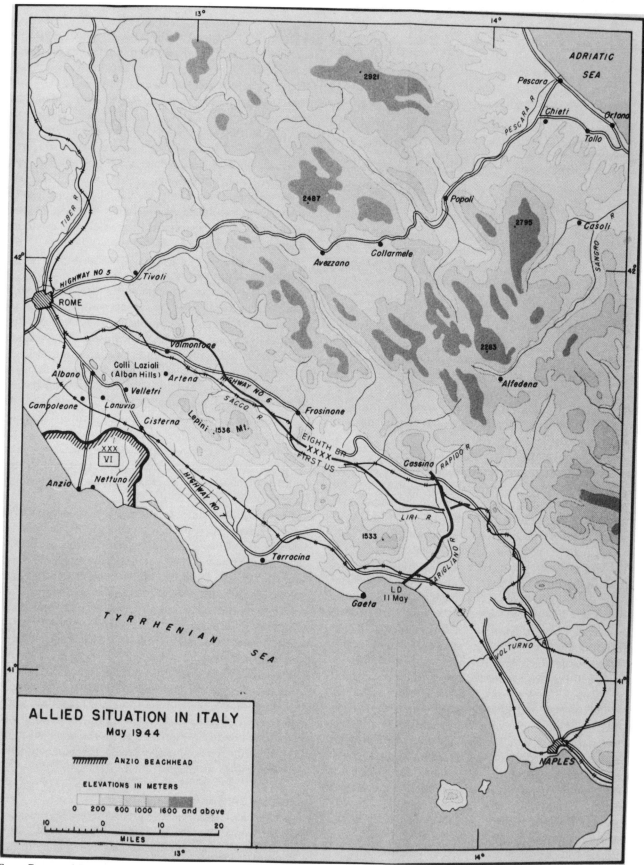

ALLIED SITUATION IN ITALY
May 1944

//////// ANZIO BEACHHEAD

ELEVATIONS IN METERS

0 200 600 1000 1600 and above

10   0   10   20
MILES

From Command Decisions, *ed. by Kent Roberts Greenfield* (U.S. Army Chief of Military History, 1959) Map VI

Allied troops observe the town of Monte Cassino, held by the Germans. (U.S. Army Military History Institute)

On May 23, more than 1,000 Allied guns signaled the opening of the Allied breakout offensive from the Anzio beachhead. The long stalemate at Anzio may have been over, but the first two days brought few rewards as the Germans stubbornly resisted across the entire front. Allied losses were heavy, and progress continued to be painfully slow as Mackensen's stripped-down army fought stubborn rearguard actions across the Anzio front.

The collapse of the Gustav line forced Kesselring to abandon the Cassino front and begin a full-scale retreat on May 22. If the remnants of the 10th Army were to make good their escape, they must pass through the Valmontone bottleneck at the northern end of the Liri Valley before VI Corps could block their retreat to the Pisa-Rimini line. However, at the last moment, Clark decided to switch the main VI Corps axis of advance northwest toward Rome, instead of toward Valmontone. Neither thrust was successful. By denuding his main attack force for the Valmontone thrust, Clark insured the escape of the 10th Army. At the same time, his new main thrust toward the northwest also failed when the 14th Army stubbornly held blocking positions on the roads to Rome and in the Alban Hills.

Although the two fronts had linked up the morning of May 25, thus ending the siege of Anzio, which had lasted over four months, the difficult and bitter final days of the Allied drive on Rome were characterized by the same bloodletting and painfully slow advances that were the hallmark of the entire Italian Campaign. During the first five days, Allied casualties were more than 4,000, exceeding those of the great German counteroffensive of February 16–20.

By the night of June 2–3, 1944, the Germans had reached the limits of their ability to delay the Allied advance. Only scattered units were left behind to harass, delay, and protect the German rear as the remnants of the 10th and 14th armies made good their northward retreat.

To his credit, Kesselring realized that there was nothing to be gained by fighting for Rome or seeing the city destroyed. He declared Rome an open city and left only minimal forces to cover the German escape.

On June 5, the Allies occupied Rome. After five months, victory had come, but at a terrible price. During the desperate months of the Anzio beachhead, the Allies lost 7,000 killed, and 36,000 more were wounded or reported as missing in action. In addition, another 44,000 were hospitalized from various nonbattle injuries and sickness. On the morning of June 6, 1944, the fall of Rome was all but forgotten as Operation Overlord—the long-delayed, long-debated cross-channel invasion of Normandy—commenced in France.

Effects of Operation Anvil

Now that the 5th and 8th armies were able to engage in mobile warfare, the Allies were in a position to end the campaign once and for all, provided Alexander could retain all of his forces in Italy. The problem was that Operation Anvil, the invasion of southern France in support of Overlord, had become a reality that would soon cost Alexander his two best corps. Led by Churchill, the British were openly critical of the Anvil plan, but Eisenhower, the Overlord commander in chief, rejected British arguments that to carry it out would wreck Allied strategy in the Mediterranean. The debate had been simmering for months, and as the date for Overlord grew closer, Churchill stepped up his attempts to convince Roosevelt and Eisenhower to cancel Anvil.

The British case hinged on their Mediterranean strategy and their conviction that too much had already been invested in the Italian Campaign to rob it of the potential to end the war in Italy at the very moment when the Germans were in disarray after the fall of Rome. Churchill pleaded to Roosevelt that there should be no troops or landing craft pulled from Italy. Roosevelt's reply insisted that Anvil proceed as scheduled and was a clear message to the British that the road to Berlin ran through France and western Europe, not Italy and the Balkans.

The effects of Anvil on the campaign in Italy were enormous. The decision meant that Alexander was stripped of a considerable part of his resupply capability and a significant portion of his combat forces, which included Maj. Gen. Lucian K. Truscott's U.S. VI Corps and Juin's Corps Expéditionnaire Français, the only mountain-trained Allied force then in Italy.

The Gothic Line

The principal military beneficiary of the Allied decision to proceed with Anvil was Kesselring, who was able to put into practice his plan to relocate the German army in Italy along the Gothic line in the northern Apennines. Kesselring intended to pursue the same strategy in northern Italy as

A part of Italy's Gothic line, which ran from Pisa across the Apennine Mountains to the Adriatic Sea, was fortified with impenetrable fences, rock-slab piles, and other obstacles. (U.S. Army Military History Institute)

he had for the previous 10 months: fight strong delaying actions to stifle the Allied advance and then defend for as long as possible along a natural, well-fortified defensive line. Although preparations for its eventual manning had been ongoing for some time, the Gothic line was somewhat less formidable than the Gustav line.

The Gothic line was the strongest of a series of defensive barriers designed to slow and then eventually halt the Allies. Located in the mountains north of Florence, the Gothic line ran from Pisa on the Mediterranean, across the Apennines to the Adriatic. German engineers had fashioned every conceivable obstacle, from tank traps to concrete fortifications, all of which took advantage of the rough terrain. Kesselring's aim was to stop the Allied advance until the winter weather set in, thereby continuing the war in Italy into 1945. In short, German strategy was to be a repeat of Cassino and the Gustav line.

The great Allied offensives had cost the Germans more than 38,000 casualties, many of whom would never be replaced as manpower reserves were severely drained by the Allied invasion of France, but Army Group C was far from beaten. During their deliberate withdrawal north of Rome, the Germans extracted an exceedingly heavy price by inflicting 34,000 casualties. At the Arno River, the Allies were forced to halt their advance and regroup. Ahead lay another series of epic battles to sever the Gothic line. Alexander believed he could have thrust through the Gothic line and driven the Germans from Italy during the summer of 1944. Instead, the irretrievable loss of 7 veteran divisions for Anvil left the 15th Army Group with a force of 20 divisions against Kesselring's 22.

Unrelenting late summer and autumn offensives by the Allied armies cracked but failed to break the Gothic line. Allied troops were exhausted, units were understrength, and the manpower crisis that had for so long plagued the British finally caught up with the U.S. 5th Army. To Clark's bitter disappointment, operations had to be halted for the winter. The Allied failure to end the war in the west in 1944 guaranteed the continuation of the campaign in Italy into 1945. By the time Clark, now the commander of the 15th Army Group, launched the final offensive of the Italian Campaign, it was the spring of 1945.

German Defeat in Italy

The 10th Army commander, Gen. Heinrich von Vietinghoff, succeeded Kesselring in early 1945 and, in an effort to avert the destruction of Army Group C, attempted a series of withdrawals, first to the natural defensive barrier of the Po River, and when the Allied armies could no longer be contained, by further delays until they reached the safety of the alpine pass. With no reserve and the loss of several divisions sent to Germany to be consumed in the final defense of the Reich, Vietinghoff had no other options. The choice was stark: either reposition Army Group C or face certain annihilation when the Allied spring offensive got under way.

The Germans were dazed by the intensity of the Allied blows when they finally fell, first on April 9 from the 8th Army and then, five days later, from the 5th Army. Supported by massive artillery bombardments and the Allied air forces, the Germans could not withstand the powerful pressure that squeezed them from two directions without letup. With the Allies now advancing into the Po River valley, and the Germans under attack on the ground and from the air, the river became an impassable barrier to their retreat. Most of the bridges across the wide and swiftly flowing Po were destroyed, and some 100,000 German troops found themselves trapped and forced to surrender. Those who succeeded in retreating across the river were soon run to ground as the Allied spearheads now swept away all before them.

While Hitler refused to countenance surrender, a secret overture was made to the Allies by Gen. Karl Wolff, the head of the Schutzstaffel (SS) in Italy. Wolff's representative secretly met in neutral Switzerland over a period of weeks and worked out tentative terms for an armistice in Italy with American Allen Dulles of the Office of Strategic Services (OSS). The Wolff-Dulles negotiations culminated in the formal signing of unconditional surrender documents at Alexander's headquarters in the royal palace at Caserta on April 29. On May 2, all German forces in Italy were ordered to lay down their arms. In the north, the cease-fire was carried out on May 4.

So ended the Italian Campaign. The cost in human misery was staggering. The numbers of dead and homeless Italians can only be estimated, but for those who fought in Italy there are more precise figures. Allied forces in Italy ranged from a low of 400,000 to a high of approximately 500,000. Overall Allied casualties were 312,000 of which

189,000—about 60 percent—were sustained by the 5th U.S. Army. Overall, 31,886 troops were killed in action. Most were American (19,475 killed of 109,642 total U.S. casualties). Of the British and Commonwealth troops who served under the 5th Army, 6,605 were killed of 47,452 total casualties, while French losses were 5,241 killed of 17,671 total casualties. German losses in Italy have never been accurately calculated, but it is known that their army casualties totaled 434,646. Of these, 48,067 were killed in action and another 214,048 were reported missing. Most of the missing were never accounted for and presumed dead.

Italy was devastated by the war, and its economy was shattered. With the exception of Rome, which received only minor damage, devastation lay wherever there had been fighting. The German scorched-earth policy ensured no less, and the warring parties completed the cycle.

The Italian Campaign had lasted 20 months and covered 1,100 miles, from Cape Pessaro on the southeastern corner of Sicily to the foothills of the Alps. Along the way, the Germans and the Allies fought the bitterest battles of World War II in the west. From the Baytown landings in early September 1943 to the final surrender on May 2, 1945, the Italian Campaign consumed 602 days in some of the most forbidding terrain on earth.

The Germans' presence in the Mediterranean was never more than a sideshow to their operations to the north, and the employment of the German army by Hitler in North Africa was nothing short of criminal. An entire army was needlessly sacrificed to Hitler's stubbornness during a critical stage of the war. Delaying defeat for several months, the Germans fought defensively to protect their southern flank and to keep the maximum number of Allied forces tied up fighting in a secondary theater of war. The Allied grand strategy in Italy, rather than being aimed at winning, seemed to be to drag out the war there for as long as possible, to prevent Army Group C from being dispersed to fight on other fronts. The Allies particularly wanted to keep Army Group C from France, where it was feared these formations might have made the difference between success and failure when Operation Overlord was finally carried out in June 1944.

Alexander had no mandate in Italy other than to capture Rome, and at critical points in the campaign he was denied the men and the logistical assets needed to conclude the campaign. However, for all his personal courage and other soldierly qualities, Alexander was an unimaginative strategist whose tendency to defer to his subordinates made the Allied task all the more difficult. By contrast, Kesselring was highly regarded by his adversaries and was a master of the art of defense who managed to stave off defeat time and again. Although the major partners in the Allied coalition never fully agreed on a mutually acceptable strategy, it remains that the war in the Mediterranean was the longest sustained series of campaigns fought by the western Allies during World War II.

4

Northern Europe: 1944–45

The D-Day landings by the Allies on the beaches of Normandy, France, on June 6, 1944, were the culmination of what had four years previously been thought of as a virtually unattainable goal. When the British withdrew their forces from Dunkirk in May 1940, few entertained illusions as to the fate of Britain.

After Dunkirk, British prime minister Winston Churchill envisioned a second front in the form of a cross-channel invasion of northern France as the key to the eventual defeat of Germany. Although the British vigorously pursued operations in the Mediterranean during 1942 and 1943, Churchill remained committed to an invasion of northwestern Europe. What the British never agreed to was a timetable as ambitious as that advocated by U.S. chief of staff George C. Marshall, who pressed for an invasion as early as 1942. Churchill firmly believed that an amphibious operation across the English Channel could only succeed with a massive force and meticulous planning.

Churchill began to redress British unpreparedness for global war by creating a Combined Operations Staff to begin preparing for a second front. In October 1941, Churchill appointed to head it the dynamic Capt. Lord Louis Mountbatten, who was told: ''You are to prepare for the invasion of Europe, for unless we can go and land and fight Hitler and beat his forces on land, we shall never win this war.'' Marshall's vision of a cross-channel invasion in 1942 was never possible. Various high-level conferences in 1942 led to Operation Torch in North Africa and, in 1943, the invasion of Sicily, followed by the opening of a southern front in Italy in September 1943. Although the United States was the dominant partner of the alliance, in reality it was the British who controlled the timetable for Operation Overlord, as the cross-channel invasion was code-named.

After nearly two years of quarrels, debates, postponements, and growing pressure from Soviet premier Joseph Stalin to open a second front, the Combined Chiefs of Staff at the Quebec Conference in August 1943 finally agreed on a firm timetable for Overlord. The operation would be mounted from the United Kingdom in May 1944.

By early 1943, Combined Operations had identified Normandy and the Pas-de-Calais region of northern France as the two best areas for an invasion. The Pas-de-Calais was the closest point to Britain, provided the most direct route of advance into Germany, and afforded maximum air cover from airfields in southern England. Its drawback was that the Pas-de-Calais was such an obvious invasion site that the Germans had heavily reinforced its defenses and concentrated the bulk of their troops in France in this region. Moreover, there were few adequate ports to accommodate the enormous flow of troops and material required in the post-invasion buildup.

Normandy, with its lengthy sandy beaches and many excellent port facilities, was considered a far better choice. By the spring of 1943 it was recognized that there needed to be a separate headquarters created to plan Overlord. British lieutenant general Frederick Morgan was appointed to create and head a staff of Anglo-American planners designated ''Cossac'' (an acronym for ''chief of staff to the Supreme Allied Commander''), a position the Allies had yet to fill. Morgan was given a scant three months to turn what had heretofore been a series of loosely related proposals and plans into a tangible outline plan ''to defeat the German fighting forces in northwest Europe.''

By July 27, 1943, Cossac presented a solution to the longstanding question of where and how a cross-channel invasion could be launched. The Cossac plan rejected the Pas-de-Calais in favor of Normandy. Although it would stretch Allied air coverage to the maximum range of its aircraft, the Cossac planners reasoned that Normandy met every test for a successful amphibious operation. Because they were severely restricted by an acute shortage of land-

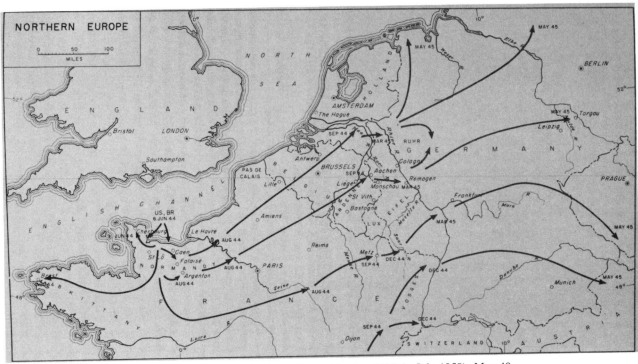

From ROTCM 145–20: American Military History: 1607–1958 (Washington: HQDA, July 1959), Map 40

ing craft, the original Overlord plan called for only a three-divisional invasion along a 30-mile front in the Caen sector, followed by the early capture and development of airfield sites and the capture of the port of Cherbourg. Concurrent with the assault, an airborne force would seize the city of Caen. Once established ashore, armored forces would mount a strong thrust south and southwest to gain airfield sites and to allow sufficient depth for a turning movement to the west to seize Cherbourg within the first two weeks. By then, there would be 18 divisions in action, along with some 33 supporting fighter squadrons. The Supreme Allied Commander would then decide whether to drive east and seize the Seine River ports or to occupy first the ports in Brittany. The Seine would then be breached, and it was expected the Germans would retire to form a strong defense.

One of the most serious problems in mounting Overlord was the designation of its commanders, most of whom would have to come from the Mediterranean theater. The first U.S. appointment was Lt. Gen. Omar Bradley, who was given command of the U.S. ground invasion force, designated as the 1st Army.

Throughout the fall of 1943 there was intense behind-the-scenes maneuvering over the appointment of the Supreme Commander. Both Marshall and Britain's chief of the general staff, Gen. Alan Brooke (later 1st Viscount Alan-brooke), aspired to this command, but neither Pres. Franklin D. Roosevelt nor Churchill could afford to lose his most valuable officer. Churchill openly favored the appointment of Gen. Sir Harold Alexander, a move fiercely re-

sisted by the British chiefs of staff, who considered him ill-suited. In the end, there was unanimous agreement for a compromise candidate, Gen. Dwight D. Eisenhower, who left Italy in December 1943 to fill the position. There was also disagreement over who would command British ground forces. Both Eisenhower and Churchill wanted Alexander but finally agreed to the only possible alternate choice, Gen. Sir Bernard Montgomery. Montgomery was given not only command of the newly formed British 21st Army Group, but, as the senior Allied general, also command of all Allied ground forces until such time as Eisenhower could establish Supreme Headquarters, Allied Expeditionary Force (SHAEF) in France and assume command of the operation.

Air Chief Marshal Sir Arthur Tedder was appointed Eisenhower's deputy, and Air Chief Marshal Sir Trafford Leigh-Mallory commanded the Allied air forces. Adm. Sir Bertram Ramsay, the man who was instrumental in saving the British Expeditionary Force at Dunkirk, became the naval commander in chief. Bradley was ordered to form an army group headquarters to take control of American ground forces when a second field army landed in Normandy during the buildup phase after D-Day. Although Lt. Gen. George Patton remained in Sicily in command of a paper army after the incidents in which he slapped soldiers in August 1943, both Marshall and Eisenhower considered him indispensable. In January 1944, he was summoned to London and given command of the 3d U.S. Army. Patton's appointment was kept a secret. Publicly, it was revealed he was to head the 1st U.S. Army Group. Created by the

Gen. Dwight D. Eisenhower (left), *shown with Gen. George S. Patton, was chosen to be Supreme Allied Commander in Europe in late 1943.* (U.S. Military Academy)

Allied deception planners under the code name of Fortitude, Patton's command was a nonexistent force designed to convince the Germans that the Allies intended to invade the Pas-de-Calais with his army group.

In the months prior to D-Day, the Allies executed the most massive and successful hoax in the history of warfare. Nonexistent units were created and fake emplacements installed in eastern England that included rubber and wooden tanks and vehicles, fictitious radio traffic, and false reports to Berlin by British agents posing as German spies. All combined to convince the Germans that the Allied target was indeed the Pas-de-Calais.

PREPARATIONS FOR OVERLORD

Beginning in 1944, the Allied buildup throughout the United Kingdom continued on an unprecedented scale. Southern England became a virtual armed camp as training for Overlord continued at a frantic pace. Amphibious training exercises took place in Scotland and off the south coast of England. In April, during Exercise Tiger, more than 700 American troops drowned off Slapton Sands when their landing craft were attacked by German motor torpedo boats (''E-boats'') based in Cherbourg. Their deaths were kept a secret, and, in what has been regarded as one of the most controversial acts of the war, their bodies were consigned to an unmarked common grave, there to remain nameless until 1987 when a memorial was dedicated at the site.

Prior to 1944, Adolf Hitler's so-called Fortress Europa was, except for the Pas-de-Calais, nonexistent. In early 1944, Hitler appointed Field Marshal Erwin Rommel the commander of Army Group B, with orders to prepare Germany's defenses in the west against a second front. Rommel was responsible for an area from Holland to Brittany, and he responded to this challenge in the same manner that had earned him the nickname ''Desert Fox'' in North Africa. He tirelessly prodded Berlin for more troops, supplies, and construction equipment. Although he had no particular suspicion that Normandy was to be the Allied target, the sector from Caen to the Cotentin Peninsula received special attention. Mines were emplaced along the beaches along with metal spikes and other obstacles that were set below the low-tide line. Potential airborne landing zones inland were studded with metal spikes topped with antipersonnel mines (called *Rommelspargel*—''Rommel's asparagus'').

Allied and German Strategies

As the senior Allied ground commander, Montgomery was responsible for the invasion plan and for the development of the strategy to be employed during the Battle of Normandy. He was dissatisfied by the original Cossac plan and began orchestrating significant changes. Montgomery recognized that the Cossac bridgehead was far too confined and would impede both the capture of Cherbourg and the establishment of a secure bridgehead that could withstand the certain German counterattacks that Rommel would launch to push the Allied invaders back into the sea. The invasion sector was widened from 30 to 50 miles, and two additional divisions were added to the D-Day assault force.

Montgomery's blueprint was to expand the invasion frontage and to employ two U.S. airborne divisions to seize and hold the critical approaches to Cherbourg in the Cotentin Peninsula. Allied strategy was to concentrate in the initial stages of the operation on quickly gaining control of the main centers of road communication—Caen, Bayeux, and Carentan—followed by deep thrusts by armored formations between and beyond these points to gain and control terrain that would make it difficult for German reserves to get past them and threaten the bridgehead. The assault was to be organized under the control of one British and one U.S. army. The area from Bayeux eastward to the

Orne River was British and from Bayeux westward, American.

With heavy naval and air gunfire support, the infantry would seize the Caen-Bayeux beachhead, thus enabling the armored brigades to land and quickly push inland. The U.S sector was to extend eastward as far as the Cotentin, where the 4th Infantry Division would land on Utah Beach in the Carentan estuary, protected by the 82d and 101st airborne divisions, which were to parachute in and seize key points along the Cotentin around midnight of June 5.

Montgomery knew Rommel well from their previous confrontation in North Africa, and he anticipated the German strategy for defeating the invasion would be to repel the assault at or near the beaches by heavy panzer counterattacks to push the Allies back into the sea. Rommel's only hope of success, in fact, lay in a such a counterthrust before the Allies could gain a firm foothold. Rommel was under no illusions about what would happen if he failed. Normandy was more than 400 miles from the Third Reich, at the end of a tenuous supply line, and, with Hitler giving the Eastern Front priority, Rommel knew that he would have to make do with the meager forces at his disposal. Although the Allies would have difficulty with their initial logistics and troop buildup, once firmly established, there was little hope of stopping them. If the might of their air, sea, and ground forces could be brought to bear upon the German defenders, the end result was inevitable.

Montgomery's basic problem was how to anchor the eastern (left) flank and block any attempt by Rommel to roll him up and defeat the invasion or to interfere with Bradley's assault on Cherbourg. Once Cherboug was captured, the attention of the Allies could be directed toward an offensive to the south and, when the entire Cotentin Peninsula was secured, to a breakout into Brittany by Patton's U.S. 3d Army to secure its many potentially valuable ports.

Caen became the most important place in Normandy to both combatants. If the Allies could seize it quickly and establish themselves on dominant high ground to the southeast, they not only would gain the airfields vital for close tactical air support but would block the most direct German route of reinforcement of the Normandy front. If the Germans could retain control of the city and prevent its encirclement, they could seriously slow the Allied advance and buy enough time for the desired counterattack by the reserves of Gen. Geyr von Schweppenburg's Panzer Group West. In short, no matter what happened in the U.S. sector, the Germans had to hold the Caen front or risk strategic defeat. Caen thus became the focal point of strategy for both Rommel and Montgomery.

Montgomery correctly surmised that Rommel would hold his mobile divisions inland until certain where the main effort was being made and then strike a hard blow to dislodge the invaders. Rommel's problem was not unlike those he faced in Tunisia, where control of the panzer divisions was not entirely his. Hitler's near paranoic distrust of his generals led him to fragment control of assets in the Western Front. In overall command of the German Supreme Command (OB West) was Field Marshal Gerd von Rundstedt, an aristocratic Prussian who was no admirer of Rommel nor his reputation. Although the mobile armored reserves were under the command of Schweppenburg, his Panzer Group West was under the direct operational control of the Oberkommando der Wehrmacht (OKW, the high command of the German armed forces) and therefore could not be released to Rommel without permission from Berlin.

Rommel and Schweppenburg strongly disagreed over the employment of Panzer Group West, with the latter supporting their stationing near Paris so as to respond to an invasion either in the Pas-de-Calais or in Normandy. Rommel wanted this mobile strike force nearer Normandy and under his direct control. He unsuccessfully attempted to convince Hitler and OKW that time was the critical factor in repelling an invasion and that movement would be difficult or even impossible with the Allies in control of the air. Thus, while once again a fragmented German command structure may have protected Hitler against a coup, it ultimately aided the Allied cause. Rommel was left without control of his most important asset: the mobile reserves. On D-Day, this would prove disastrous.

Final Preparation

During April and May 1944, the Allies finalized the most massive and complex military plan ever conceived. On May 15, in the presence of King George VI, Churchill, and Eisenhower, the Allied commanders each explained his role in Overlord, using a terrain model of the invasion site.

Montgomery delivered a brilliant and simple summary of what lay ahead. "We have the initiative," he said; "we must rely on the violence of our assault, our great weight of supporting fire from the sea and the air, simplicity and robust mentality." Quoting Henry V before Agincourt, he reminded his distinguished audience, "He that hath no stomach for this fight, Let him depart."

Various factors had required the changing of the date for D-Day from May to the first full-moon period of June. After months of intensive planning and preparation, D-Day was set for June 5. For nearly three months, northern France had been intensively bombed to sever all German transportation links to Normandy without revealing where the invasion would be launched. The Allied air forces succeeded beyond all expectations and turned the French railways leading to Normandy and the Pas-de-Calais into a vast "railway desert" of smashed rail lines, bridges, depots, and equipment. Meanwhile, Fortitude had succeeded in convincing the German supreme command that Patton was to lead the invasion against the Pas-de-Calais.

Gen. Dwight D. Eisenhower encourages troops before the implementation of Operation Overlord, the invasion of Normandy, France. (Library of Congress)

Hundreds of thousands of Allied troops, ships of every description, and masses of military hardware were crammed on ships and landing craft awaiting the final order to embark. The final days prior to Overlord were an agony of waiting. To preserve secrecy, once the final briefings were given and the target at last revealed as Normandy, the troops were restricted to their encampments. At SHAEF, there was deep concern when the chief meteorologist reported deteriorating weather conditions and high winds. By June 4, when elements of the invasion force had embarked, a full-blown storm rendered any hope of invading on the morning of June 5 impossible and threatened to wreck the entire invasion timetable. While the armada waited, Eisenhower ordered a 24-hour postponement. By late on June 4, the meteorologists offered a glimmer of hope for June 6. While the weather would remain poor, visibility would improve and the winds would decrease just enough to risk launching the invasion.

This was arguably the most important weather prediction in history: a mistaken forecast for D-Day could turn the entire tide of the war in Europe against the Allies. After

consulting with each of the invasion commanders, Eisenhower announced that the invasion of Normandy would take place the morning of June 6. ''O.K., we'll go,'' he said, and the course of the war changed forever.

D-DAY: JUNE 6, 1944

During the night of June 5–6, only hours before the amphibious landings commenced, the skies over Normandy were suddenly filled with the parachutes and gliders of three Allied airborne divisions. The British 6th Airborne was landed north and east of Caen by parachute and glider with the formidable tasks of securing intact the critical bridges over the Orne River and of taking out the German communications centers and strongpoints that menaced the landings of the 3d British Division on Sword Beach. In the west, the 82d and 101st airborne divisions landed in the marshy areas of the Carentan estuary with the mission of protecting the landings on Utah Beach.

The surprise so critical to the success of the Allied plan was achieved. Soon after midnight, the alarm spread throughout the German 7th Army as reports began to come in of the airborne landings. By 3:00 A.M., the Germans had correctly diagnosed that a major invasion was underway, but OB West and Army Group B remained skeptical, believing that this was merely an expected diversionary tactic prior to the main effort against the German 15th Army in the Pas-de-Calais. Rommel himself was absent in Germany, convinced that the bad weather would not permit an Allied invasion prior to his return. The OKW staff was afraid to waken Hitler, who did not learn of the launch of Overlord until midday June 6.

Offshore, hundreds of ships could be discerned through the smoke. The first British assault came at H-Hour of 7:00 A.M., when hundreds of assault craft moved ashore as two British and one Canadian infantry division stormed Sword, Gold, and Juno beaches. Each met with varying degrees of resistance. Near the Orne, a British commando force assaulted critical objectives on the eastern flank, while west of Bayeux, an American ranger force stormed the Pointe du Hoc, the site of a deadly battery of German 155-millimeter guns, which it was later found had been moved inland months before the invasion.

In the U.S. sector, the Utah Beach landings went speedily and with minimal resistance. The landings on Omaha Beach by the veteran 1st Infantry Division and the 29th Division of V Corps were less successful. Unknown to Allied intelligence, the German 352d Division had been moved into the Omaha sector three months earlier. Along the steep bluffs overlooking Omaha, two divisions were now defending the most formidable strip of beach in Normandy. The Allied bombardments had left the defenders virtually unscathed, and the result was nearly a disaster.

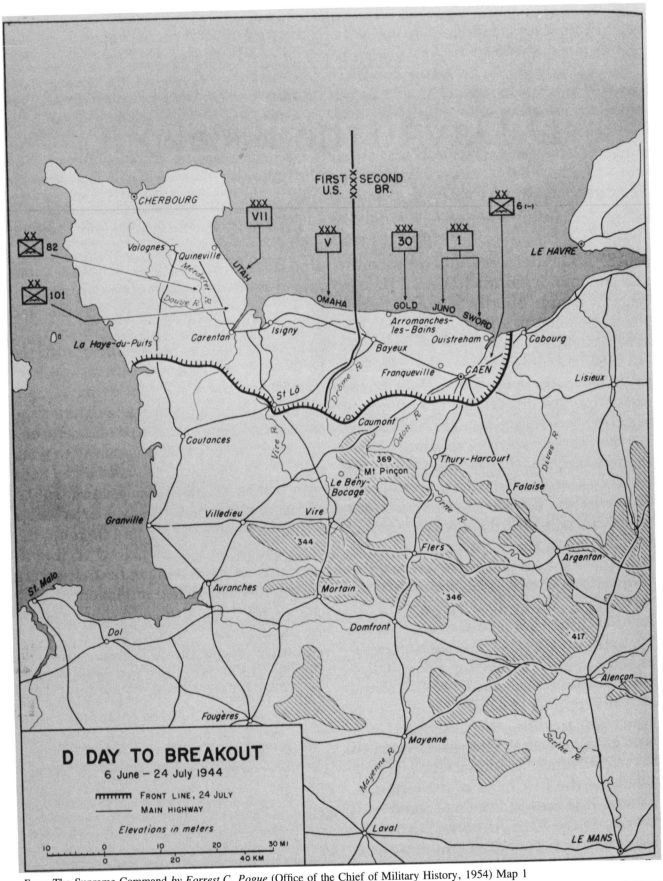

D DAY TO BREAKOUT

6 June – 24 July 1944

⊓⊓⊓⊓⊓⊓ FRONT LINE, 24 JULY

——— MAIN HIGHWAY

Elevations in meters

CHERBOURG

Valognes

Quineville

Mercieret R.

Douve R.

VII

UTAH

82

101

Oo

La Haye-du-Puits

Carentan

Isigny

OMAHA

V

GOLD

30

JUNO

1

SWORD

6 (~)

LE HAVRE

FIRST
U.S.

SECOND
BR.

Arromanches-
les-Bains

Ouistreham

Cabourg

Bayeux

Drôme R.

Franqueville

CAEN

Lisieux

St Lô

Caumont

Odon R.

Vire R.

Coutances

369

Mt Pinçon

Thury-Harcourt

Dives R.

Falaise

Le Bény-
Bocage

Villedieu

Vire

Orne R.

Granville

344

Flers

Argentan

St. Malo

Avranches

Mortain

346

417

Dol

Domfront

Alençon

Fougères

Mayenne

Mayenne R.

Sarthe R.

Laval

LE MANS

10   0   10   20   30 MI

0   20   40 KM

From The Supreme Command *by Forrest C. Pogue* (Office of the Chief of Military History, 1954) Map 1

The jaws of a Coast Guard LST (landing ship, tank) open up in the middle of the English Channel to transfer motorized equipment to the flat deck of a low-riding "rhino" during the early morning hours of D-Day; gun crews on deck watch for Nazi planes. (U.S. Coast Guard)

Although progress could sometimes be measured in yards and casualties were high, the Americans on Omaha Beach eventually succeeded in clawing their way up the steep bluffs overlooking the sea and managed to carve out a tenuous beachhead that somehow withstood furious German counterattacks. The Germans' belief that the main invasion would soon assault their 15th Army in the Pas-de-Calais, the fragmented and muddled German command structure, and the failure of the German high command to react promptly to the airborne landings on the night of June 5–6 proved colossal blunders that benefited the Allies beyond measure. On D-Day, the full extent of this blundering could be seen when Rundstedt ordered the 12th SS Panzer and Panzer Lehr divisions to the front without first obtaining OKW approval. About 7:30 A.M., the OKW notified Rundstedt that permission was denied because Hitler was asleep and no one dared awaken him. Orders for the movement of both divisions were not received until 4:00 P.M., June 6. The 12th SS Panzer Division was within striking distance of the British sector, and the time lost was crucial when the presence of a second German armored division at Caen might have been decisive.

Allied Advances

The mission of the British 3d Division on D-Day was to seize Caen and the crossing points where the Orne River flowed through the southern end of the city so that the armored brigades could move forward and seize the vital Caen-Falaise plain. By mid-afternoon, after a difficult exit from the beaches, where there were terrific bottlenecks and heavy resistance from a formidable strongpoint called "Hillman," elements of the 3d Division had advanced to within three miles of Caen. However, they could not capture the city without the tanks of the supporting armored brigade, most of which were still bogged down on Sword Beach.

The afternoon of June 6 became a race between British and German armor for the control of the vital approaches to Caen. Although the British won a brief but fierce tank battle, the 3d Division was stretched too thinly to have any real hope of capturing Caen that day. By the time they were able to assemble a force of sufficient size, the 21st Panzer had established blocking positions.

Across the British front there was mixed success. The landings had gone well, but the Canadians ran into tough resistance from elements of the 12th SS Panzer Division west of Caen. By evening, the entire division had arrived from Lisieux, and any chance of seizing river crossings over the Orne and Odon rivers was lost. The two U.S. airborne divisions that landed were scattered far and wide across the marshy Carentan estuary, but, as they had in Sicily, the paratroopers fought brilliantly in small groups to protect vital bridges and road junctions until the 4th Division (whose casualties were the lowest of the invasion

Troops of the U.S. 1st Infantry Division, dispatched from an LCVP (landing craft, vehicle, personnel), wade ashore at Omaha Beach, Normandy, on June 6, 1944. (U.S. Coast Guard)

forces—"a piece of cake," Bradley called it) was established safely inland.

The Allied air forces had complete mastery of the skies, where the German air force, the Luftwaffe, was rarely seen, and the warships of the fleet pounded targets ashore at will. In spite of the unexpected setbacks at Omaha, where the toehold remained slender but improving, the invasion had been a stunning success. The greatest amphibious invasion in history on the most important day of the war had been won by the Allies.

THE BATTLE FOR NORMANDY

For the German army, D-Day was a disaster. Of its many mistakes that day, the greatest seems to have been Rommel's absence in Germany. His forceful presence on June 6 could have changed events substantially, in particular the costly delay in moving the two panzer divisions. When he hurriedly returned that night, after an all-day dash by automobile from Germany, all Rommel could do was attempt to stitch together his defenses across the breadth of Normandy. Despite the enormity of the invasion, both Hitler and the OKW continued to be misled by Fortitude into believing that the Normandy landings were merely an Allied feint to draw off German reserves from the Pas-de-Calais.

Hitler had issued "fight to the death" orders and had forbidden retreat or withdrawal. Rommel's assessment was more realistic. His troops were everywhere being pushed back across a broad front. If the British were able to debouch onto the Caen-Falaise plain where their armor could be employed, Normandy would be lost. Rommel's defenses were too thin and his defenders were within range of the deadly offshore naval gunfire that was inflicting steadily worsening casualties. Hitler had approved the dispatch of panzer reinforcements from the Eastern Front, but these would take many days to arrive. Day and night, Allied harassment from the air made the reinforcements' march to Normandy sheer hell.

To make matters worse, there was little Rommel could do about launching a decisive counterattack to throw the British 2d Army back into the sea unless he could establish suitable defenses behind the natural barriers of the Orne and Odon rivers, out of range of Allied naval gunfire. Despite personal pleas by Rommel and Rundstedt, Hitler would not hear of it. Rommel was thus required to improvise in order to cope with Montgomery's tactics. Outgunned, outmanned, and often outflanked; harassed day and night; and short of virtually every logistic necessity of war, the German defenders of Normandy nevertheless fought a remarkable delaying action.

The ensuing battles were not engagements between an invader and a well-prepared defender able to fight a conventional land battle. Instead, the Normandy campaign rapidly turned into a series of small-unit engagements, a classic confrontation at close quarters with no holds barred where, as it is in most wars, the dirty business of winning battles fell to the infantryman. Despite their many problems, the Germans in Normandy were aided by the close, confined terrain that provided an advantage to the defender. Most of the Normandy battlefield was dominated by the bocage— thousands of small fields ringed by earthen banks and dense shrubbery that usually made it impossible to see beyond a single field at a time.

British attempts to capture Caen had bogged down badly since D-Day, as the Germans stiffened their defenses to the point where the British and Canadians were all too frequently able to measure their advance in yards. The lack of progress soon began to trouble not only Montgomery but the Allied high command, where questions were beginning to be asked about why Caen had not fallen.

Controversies

The failure of the British XXX Corps to exploit an open flank at Villers-Bocage in mid-June left the 2d Army stalled outside Caen. In more than 10 days, there had been no strategic and little tactical success on the British front. The aim, said Montgomery, was merely to draw off the German armored reserves from Bradley's front to Caen, where the British would act as a pivot while Bradley launched a breakout in the west. His critics, who included Eisenhower, Tedder, and the senior American commanders, were charged with misunderstanding what he alleged had always been the aim of 2d Army operations in the Caen sector. After the war, the battle for Caen became the subject of rancorous debate. In recent years, a mass of new documentation not only has cast considerable doubt on Montgomery's claims, but has established that the German control of Caen was the most serious problem faced by the Allies in Normandy.

Bradley encountered his own problems fighting in the difficult bocage and marshes of the Cotentin Peninsula. The most important U.S. objective in western Normandy was to capture Cherbourg, which was required to meet the huge logistical needs of the Allied expeditionary force. Hitler was determined to keep Cherbourg out of Allied hands and ordered it held to the death. Although the German fortress commander failed to do so, the German defense of the Cotentin was stubborn, time consuming, and costly for both sides. The American drive on Cherbourg was delayed when the most powerful storm in 40 years struck Normandy with gale-force winds that wreaked havoc on the beaches, sank shipping, and destroyed the Mulberry floating pier at Omaha beach. By the time Cherbourg was finally captured on June 27, the Germans had destroyed its harbor facilities, and it was weeks before the port began to function anywhere near its intended capacity.

Bradley now began operations to the south and southwest toward St.-Lô. On July 3, the 1st Army launched an offensive across the entire front that soon ground to a halt far short of its objective in the dense bocage north of St.-Lô. Not until June 26 were the British able to mount a new offensive against Caen. VIII Corps, backed by the most massive artillery support yet employed in Normandy, launched Operation Epsom, an attempt to outflank the city from the west by a powerful right hook across the Odon River. Epsom became a desperate infantry struggle and

one of the bloodiest battles fought in World War II by either side. With supporting corps-sized Allied attacks by I Corps on the left and XXX Corps on the right, the 60,000 men of VIII Corps found the going deadly. When casualties on both sides became so high that it became dammed up with corpses, the usually placid river was dubbed the "Bloody Odon." Progress was measured in yards along a formidable obstacle called Hill 112, which the Germans defended with great tenacity.

The battle left both sides battered and too exhausted to carry out their respective aims. The VIII Corps' losses during the five-day battle were 4,020, and infantry casualties ran to 50 percent. These grievous losses prompted the British commanders to examine how much more their units could endure. British manpower was at this point in the war stretched to the breaking point. Losses often could not be replaced, and within days, Montgomery was forced to disband a division in order to plug the manpower gaps in his front-line units.

Even worse, the failure of Epsom to make anything more than modest territorial gains left Caen still firmly in German hands. Finally, Montgomery decided to accept an offer from the air commanders to employ their heavy bombers in direct support of the ground forces in an attempt to blast a gap in the German lines that would enable the 2d Army finally to capture Caen. On the night of July 7–8, Allied heavy bombers dropped 6,000 tons of bombs, and in the two days of hard fighting that followed, the northern half of Caen was captured. While Montgomery had unquestionably improved his position, the vital Caen-Falaise plain remained in German hands and Bradley's offensive remained stalled in the mud and bocage of western Normandy. The Normandy Campaign had become a stalemate.

Breaking the Stalemate

During the first week of July 1944, the two army commanders met to put forth separate but compatible plans to break the impasse. British general Miles Dempsey devised Operation Goodwood, a massive British tank attack to break the German grip on Caen by again using heavy bombers to blast a path that three armored divisions could exploit to gain access to the Caen-Falaise plain. Goodwood began the morning of July 18, when the heavy bombers turned the battlefield into a cauldron of smoke, dust, and destruction unprecedented in the history of ground combat. Before the day ended, more than 4,500 Allied tactical and strategic aircraft had been in action against the Germans. As with Epsom three weeks earlier, the air attacks were followed up by the massed artillery fire of three corps, supported by naval gunfire, which together hurled nearly a quarter of a million rounds into the battlefield.

The British expected that the sheer weight of their assault would overwhelm the Germans, and once again they were wrong. The Germans expected a major attack and had prepared their strongest defensive positions in Normandy

Amid the rubble, U.S. soldiers advance toward St.-Lô, France; Notre Dame Cathedral in St.-Lô is in the background. (U.S. Army Military History Institute)

to counter this new threat. On July 18, the massive aerial and artillery bombardments failed to knock out all of the antitank guns and panzers situated in and around several hamlets astride the British route of advance.

The massed tanks and vehicles created a huge traffic jam as far as the eye could see. As the lead tanks dashed into the enormous cloud of dust over the battlefield, they made good progress until late morning, at which time the 88s and Tigers that should have been knocked out by the air attack suddenly and unexpectedly came into action and began destroying British tanks, many of which were caught in the open like sitting ducks.

The spearhead 11th Armored Division advance stalled on the slopes of Bourguebus Ridge, and by the time help arrived, it was too late. The British had lost the initiative and were unable to advance on to the Caen-Falaise plain beyond. British tank losses numbered nearly 200, and infantry losses were uncomfortably high. Despite consider-

able gains, the critical terrain remained in German hands, and the stalemate continued on the eastern flank.

Although the Germans could take considerable comfort from their superb defense, their losses continued to mount in both men and matériel for which there were few replacements. As important, they had lost their inspirational commander. Rommel was badly wounded on July 17 when his staff car was attacked by British fighters. The Desert Fox had fought his final battle; several months later, he killed himself in the aftermath of the abortive putsch against Hitler on July 20. Rommel was replaced by Field Marshal Gunther von Kluge, who lasted barely one month before he, too, came under suspicion for involvement in the plot and committed suicide.

Two days after Operation Goodwood, Bradley opened his own offensive to break out of the bocage by means of a similar operation called Cobra. Bradley planned to use American fighter-bombers to blast open gaps in the front,

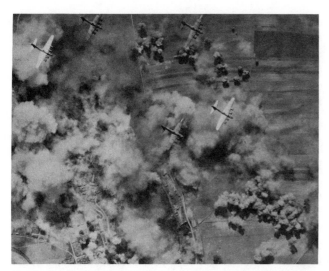

Bombs dropped from B-17s flying over France find their targets.
(U.S. Army Military History Institute: H. U. Milne Collection)

gaps that the massed forces of VII Corps would exploit. Once a gap of about three and a half miles was opened by the bombers, Bradley intended to utilize two infantry divisions to hold open the shoulders of the bulge while three divisions blitzed through toward Avranches and Coutances.

Waiting in the wings was Patton and his 3d Army, which secretly had begun arriving in late June. His presence in Normandy was a closely guarded secret. Incredibly, the Germans were still continuing to believe the Fortitude hoax, and most of the 15th Army remained in the Pas-de-Calais awaiting the main invasion by Patton's fictitious army group. Instead, Patton became Bradley's strategic reserve and his secret weapon to exploit whatever success Cobra brought.

On July 25, there was a virtual repeat of the Goodwood bombardment as fighter-bombers of the U.S. 9th Air Force and 1,500 B-17s of the U.S. 8th Air Force dropped 3,400 tons of bombs. What spelled the difference was a daring gamble by Maj. Gen. ''Lightning Joe'' Collins to deepen his penetration by committing two of his mobile armored columns before the time was ripe for an exploitation. VII Corps suddenly found its progress virtually unimpeded. Bradley recognized that with this sudden turn of fortune, it was time to unleash Patton.

By July 29, four armored divisions began thrusting south of Coutances. The gains were spectacular and threatened complete dismemberment of the German left flank in Normandy as the advancing armor and infantry fought a series of bloody battles with the retreating Germans. After one particularly savage encounter between the 2d Armored Division and an SS panzer force, one American officer described the carnage as ''the most Godless sight I have ever witnessed on any battlefield.''

Within a day, the VII Corps spearhead had driven clear to Avranches, the gateway to Brittany and southern Nor-

mandy. With the combined forces of VII and VIII Corps descending upon Avranches like a torrent, the moment was at hand for an offensive into the Brittany peninsula and a pursuit of the remnants of the shattered German 7th Army.

The Allied Breakout

On Aug. 1, 1944, Patton's 3d Army officially became operational. Bradley moved up to the command of 12th Army Group and was succeeded as 1st Army commander by Lt. Gen. Courtney Hodges. The turning point of the campaign had come, and Patton was determined to take full advantage of the opportunity to employ the great mobility of his army. Although Patton's primary mission was the liberation of Brittany and the seizing of its ports, he quickly concluded that operations in Brittany could be minimized while the remainder of his army turned eastward to drive toward the Seine through the Orleans gap, the unprotected underbelly of Normandy. Bradley agreed, and his historic decision on August 3 changed the course of the campaign: Patton was to leave minimum forces to secure Brittany and was to launch a drive to the east with the preponderance of the 3d Army. Thus, within hours, the original Allied strategy of Overlord was abandoned. What had begun modestly as a breakthrough attempt had turned into a deep exploitation that threatened to encircle the German army in Normandy.

The first week of August was the most decisive period of the Normandy Campaign. As the U.S. 1st and 3d armies advanced east, Hitler ordered a powerful armored counterstroke against the 1st Army at Mortain to cut off all American forces that had advanced beyond Avranches. Bradley and Collins had prepared for just such a counterattack, and the result was a disastrous German defeat. As the 3d Army sped east across southern Normandy and the 1st Army checked the German counterthrust at Mortain, a unique opportunity suddenly developed to trap all remaining German forces in Normandy and end the campaign. The Mortain attack had left the Germans in a trap in the form of a pocket from which the only escape was to retreat eastward before the open neck closed between Argentan in the south and Falaise in the north. If Patton executed a right hook to the north and Montgomery drove south and seized Falaise, the entire German 7th Army would be trapped.

By August 13, the U.S. XV Corps had driven to Argentan and was less than 25 miles from the Canadian 1st Army driving south on the Caen-Falaise plain. Patton intended to continue his drive to the north when Bradley intervened to forbid any further movement. A number of reasons contributed to Bradley's decision, including his belief that it was too dangerous for XV Corps, which was extended across a wide area and vulnerable to German pressure from the direction of Mortain. Bradley also apparently believed that the Canadians would regain the initiative and capture Falaise before Patton could do so. Moreover, Allied aircraft were rampaging across this sector, wreaking severe damage upon the retreating Germans. Bradley did not want Patton's forces caught in the middle of what was certain to be a very determined German attempt to break free of the trap.

However, the Canadian advance on Falaise had run into serious trouble. There were two strategic options open to the Allied ground commanders: what later became known as the short hook, Patton's attempt to close the gap from the south with XV Corps, and a longer envelopment to the east. Bradley elected to pursue the latter, a decision that he later described as choosing a ''solid shoulder at Argentan to the possibility of a broken neck at Falaise.''

With the knowledge from his intelligence officers that the Germans had already begun to break out to the east, Bradley on August 14 ordered two XV Corps divisions to dash eastward to establish blocking positions along the Seine River northwest of Paris. Patton's divisions sliced across southern Normandy with little opposition. LeMans, Orleans, Chartres, and Dreux all fell to the 3d Army, while to the north, Hodges's U.S. 1st Army began a series of drives also aimed at blocking the Seine. When German resistance collapsed east of the Caen-Falaise plain, the Canadian 1st Army and Dempsey's British 2d Army began a similar drive to the Seine.

On August 16, Falaise finally fell to the Canadians after one of the bitterest series of battles fought in Normandy. Montgomery sent the Polish 1st Armored Division, attached to the Canadian 1st Army, and elements of a Canadian corps eastward in an attempt to block the mouth of the Falaise gap. The spearhead Polish armored brigade occupied the commanding high ground of Mount Ormel east of Trun, overlooking the valley below that was filled with the last remnants of the Germans' Army Group B. Although surrounded and cut off for three days, the outnumbered and outgunned Poles wreaked a terrible toll upon their enemy as the Germans launched one furious counterattack after another in an attempt to dislodge them.

On August 19, the U.S. 90th Division joined the hard-pressed Canadians at Chambois, and the gap was finally closed. Those Germans who had escaped were bombed, strafed, and harassed as they attempted to find sanctuary east of the Seine. Except for mopping-up operations, the Battle of Normandy was over.

The legacy of the final battle at Normandy was bitterness sparked by criticism that the Allies had somehow squandered an opportunity of epic proportions by permitting the majority of the surviving German army to escape. Thus, what ought to have been a great moment of triumph marked the beginning of the worst quarrels and greatest controversies of the war in Europe.

The German army absorbed terrible punishment in the final days of the campaign. Some 10,000 perished in the Falaise pocket, and an estimated 50,000 more were taken prisoner. There were thought to be 80,000 Germans

trapped, and although it later proved impossible to make an accurate accounting of how many escaped, the figure is estimated to be about 20,000. Most German units simply disintegrated as troops fled individually and in small groups toward the Seine. Of the 50 German divisions in action in June, only 10 were left as genuine fighting units, and most of these were reduced to small numbers.

The area of the final battles provides the most compelling evidence of the magnitude of the German defeat. In the Falaise gap, the ground was littered with unburied dead, thousands of dead horses (which had become the principal German means of transport), dead cattle, and, everywhere, broken and burning vehicles. Eisenhower described it as unquestionably one of the greatest ''killing grounds'' of any of the war areas. When the Supreme Commander was taken to the battlefield, he encountered scenes ''that could be described only by Dante. It was literally possible to walk for hundreds of yards at a time, stepping on nothing but dead and decaying flesh.''

On the battlefield were found the wreckage of 1,571 tanks, self-propelled guns, artillery pieces, and armored cars; 6,800 vehicles; 669 civilian cars; and 252 other pieces of ordnance. The U.S. official history notes that ''the German remnants east of the Seine, lacking armament, equipment, even demolitions to destroy bridges behind them, could do nothing more than retreat toward Germany.''

General Hans Speidel, Rommel's chief of staff, supported this assessment, noting that there were barely a hundred tanks left out of six panzer divisions. Kluge's successor, Field Marshal Walter Model, reported, ''Five decimated divisions returned to Germany. The remains of 11 infantry divisions allowed us to regroup 4 units, each with a handful of field guns and other minor equipment. All that remained of 11 armored divisions when replenished with personnel and matériel amounted to 11 regiments, each with 5 or 6 tanks and a few artillery batteries.''

Liberation of Paris

In the aftermath of the Normandy Campaign, there still remained the liberation of the greatest prize of all, Paris, the famed City of Light. Militarily, the city was of no value, and, to the contrary, it represented enormous logistical problems for the Allies. An estimated 4,000 tons of supplies per day were required for the civilians of Paris, and these supplies would have to come from those designated to support the Allied armies. Eisenhower would have preferred to bypass Paris entirely. The city's liberation, however, was of immense political importance to the Western world, and on humanitarian grounds alone, it was essential that its 2,000,000 citizens be freed from the yoke of German occupation.

The city of Rome had been spared destruction, but Hitler was determined that Paris be left a vast wasteland. He told

Model, "In all history, the loss of Paris has meant the loss of France," and ordered that the city "must not fall into enemy hands—or if it does, then only as a field of ruins." The German commandant of Paris, Gen. Dietrich von Choltitz, defied the Fuhrer's order and instead surrendered the city.

Maj. Gen. Jacques LeClerc's French 2d Armored Division was given the honor of entering Paris, which was at last freed on August 25 after more than four years of German occupation. Despite attempts to avoid widespread fighting, Paris became a battleground that day when some 1,600 Parisians and resistance fighters died, along with 3,000 Germans. Four days later, there was a colorful parade along the famous Champs Elysees that was as much political as it was ceremonial. To the cheers of throngs of Parisians, an American division paraded through the city in what was a clear gesture by Eisenhower to provide Gen. Charles de Gaulle with a show of force that would establish his authority as the new leader of the provisional government of France.

ALLIED DRIVE ON GERMANY

The collapse of the Normandy front that culminated in a disastrous German defeat left the German army in full retreat as surviving elements fled across the Seine River and began the long march toward the distant borders of Germany. The original Allied intent to pause and regroup at the Seine was scrapped in favor of pursuit operations designed to crush the German army before it had an

Gen. George S. Patton, standing in a jeep, leads the 3d Army across the Seine on a bridge built by army engineers during the drive to the German border. (U.S. Army Military History Institute)

opportunity to fight again in defense of borders of the Reich.

The final days of August and the first week of September saw a flurry of movement as British, Canadian, and American troops swept across France during the most fluid period of World War II in the Western Front. The 21st Army Group slashed its way across the French border into southern Belgium. The Canadian 1st Army was given the task of clearing the Pas-de-Calais and the heavily defended Scheldt estuary around Antwerp. A sign that the heady days of unhindered exploitation were near an end occurred at Le Havre, where the British I Corps fought a brutal two-day battle in the rubble-strewn streets of that port city after Bomber Command and the Royal Navy had poured tons of bombs and shells into the city. During August, the 1st Army reached the Marne River, and Patton's 3d Army continued its sweep to the east into Lorraine as the rout continued.

Broad Front versus Narrow Front

The decision not to pause at the Seine led to one of the greatest controversies of the war, the "broad front" versus "narrow front" question that pitted Eisenhower and Montgomery against one another. Eisenhower's post-Normandy strategy called for a broad advance by the Allied armies into Germany. Montgomery's 21st Army Group would approach Germany through Belgium toward the Ruhr Valley industrial complex, while Bradley's 12th Army Group advanced to the south, covering the British right flank.

The sudden German collapse in mid-August gave rise to a far different proposal from Montgomery, for what he called a single, "full-blooded" thrust toward the Ruhr with the two army groups abreast, a total of some 40 divisions. Pivoting on Paris, the object, said Montgomery, would be "to secure bridgeheads over the Rhine before winter began, and to seize the Ruhr quickly."

Later referring to the plan as a mere "pencil-like" thrust, Eisenhower rejected it out of hand, arguing that there were adequate sources of logistical support to give priority to the 21st Army Group. Instead, he let stand the broad front plan. Bradley's 12th Army Group would continue to push eastward toward the Saar River and the Frankfurt gap. Montgomery would be permitted to thrust northeast toward the Ruhr, but first would have to capture the port of Antwerp, which Eisenhower correctly judged the vital key to supporting the Allied advance. Antwerp was the largest and best-equipped port in Europe, and, with the Normandy ports becoming more and more incapable of handling Allied logistic requirements, as well as being too far from the front lines, Antwerp was the obvious alternative.

The British would advance north of the Ardennes Forest, while the Americans advanced to the south. To protect his right flank, Montgomery asked for and received the attachment of Hodges's 1st Army, over the strenuous objection of Bradley. Because there were inadequate supplies, particularly of gasoline to support both thrusts simultaneously, Eisenhower allocated priority to Montgomery, much to the annoyance of Bradley and Patton, whose mission was reduced to that of a minor offensive into Lorraine.

Red Ball Express
In addition to the problem of supporting the newly liberated Paris, there were mounting logistical problems facing the Allies. Supplies had to be trucked from the beaches of Normandy and the port of Cherbourg hundreds of miles to reach the rear of the rapidly expanding front lines. By the end of August, the average distance from the beaches to the front was more than 400 miles. There was an acute shortage of fuel. The average daily consumption of motor vehicle fuels in the U.S. 1st and 3d armies had risen to 800,000 gallons per day, and gasoline soon came to be referred to as ''the red blood of war.''

To cope with the ever-widening gap between supplies and the front lines, Allied logisticians created the Red Ball Express. An impromptu version of ''through freight,'' the Red Ball Express was an around-the-clock transportation system in which nearly 6,000 cargo vehicles were utilized to carry supplies to forward depots along a series of one-way highways that stretched from Normandy to Lorraine and northern France. Traffic was controlled by military police, and service and rest areas were established along the Red Ball routes. Although there were enormous problems in establishing such an immense transportation system from scratch on short notice, it nevertheless managed to deliver 135,000 tons of supplies between late August and mid-September 1944. Despite its problems and shortcomings, it was a monumental achievement of American ingenuity. In addition to this temporary measure, air resupply was used, pipelines were laid eastward from Cherbourg, and rail lines were repaired and restored to service. The field armies themselves provided considerable transport by driving long distances to railheads and supply points to pick up fuel, rations, and other badly needed supplies required to enable their advance to continue. Famed war correspondent Ernie Pyle described Allied military operations during this period as ''a tactician's hell and a quartermaster's purgatory.''

Landings in Southern France
For months, a debate had raged at the highest levels over a controversial plan for a second invasion of France, to take place on the Mediterranean coast. Originally proposed to coincide with the Normandy landings, Operation Anvil (whose code name was later changed to Dragoon) was intended mainly as a diversion to draw off German attention and reinforcements from the Normandy front. Lt. Gen. Alexander M. Patch's U.S. 7th Army, which consisted of

French and U.S. troops drawn from Gen. Mark Clark's 5th Army on the Italian front, was to land on the French Riviera.

Churchill and Brooke were vehemently opposed to Anvil, while Eisenhower and the U.S. chiefs of staff firmly backed the operation. Although Anvil was eventually postponed until August due to the chronic shortage of landing craft, the quarrel over its necessity continued virtually up to the time of the landings, which took place on Aug. 15, 1944. The question of strategic necessity for Anvil/Dragoon was never resolved. Its many critics maintained that it was never a viable operation of war and that events in Normandy had by August 15 rendered it unnecessary. Fundamentally, Anvil/Dragoon represented the diverse opinions that existed among the Allied leadership over grand strategy. Protagonists on both sides of the question had valid arguments. Churchill and Brooke considered it a foolish waste of valuable manpower that ought to have been kept in Italy. Eisenhower's stated reasons were based on the same rationale he had used since early May 1944: that the Allies required additional ports, particularly Marseilles, and that the second invasion force would serve to protect the right flank of the broad Allied advance toward Germany.

Why was Eisenhower so determined to retain Anvil even though it had to be delayed well past the Normandy landings? In addition to his desire to have Anvil draw off German reserves and protect the southern flank of the Allied armies, Eisenhower was not at all optimistic over the usefulness of the ports in Brittany, which he believed would be destroyed by the Germans before they could be captured. He may have had political reasons as well. In the preceding months, Churchill had been advocating a plan to seize Vienna via Italy and Yugoslavia's Ljubljana gap, and the retention of Anvil served as a guarantee that Overlord would retain its priority against Churchill and Brooke, who still envisioned a widening of the Italian Campaign. Anvil thus became Eisenhower's hole card to insure that Overlord did not lose emphasis to Italy. Moreover, Hitler's insistence in early August on the destruction of the Breton ports and resistance to the bitter end had unwittingly reinforced Eisenhower's belief in the necessity of capturing Marseilles, which had the best port facilities in France; it also hardened his insistence that Anvil/Dragoon take place as scheduled.

Except for heavy fighting around Toulon and Marseilles, the campaign in southern France progressed rapidly as the German 19th Army began retreating up the Rhone River valley toward Alsace. On August 25, Avignon fell to the Allies and three days later, Toulon and Marseilles were surrounded. By September 2, the U.S. 7th Army was nearly to Lyons, while far to the rear, massive numbers of reinforcements (including Gen. Jean de Lattre's French II

Corps) and supplies continued to pour ashore. So far, nearly 200,000 men, 41,000 vehicles, and some 220,000 tons of supplies had been landed.

Allied War Machine Slowed

The acrimonious debates over strategy in the late summer and early autumn of 1944 were in large measure a reflection of the importance of logistics. The insatiable appetite of the increasing numbers of Allied divisions and support troops was a dominant consideration for Allied planners. As Patton found to his dismay, without gasoline, his 3d Army sputtered and then simply ground to a halt in the mud and cold of Lorraine. The war of the logisticians claimed its victim when the 3d Army, which previously had been able to sustain reduced operations through conservation of fuel and by the efforts of Patton's adept scroungers, now found itself literally out of gas.

Despite being given priority over the 3d Army, Hodge's 1st Army was in the same predicament even as its spearheads thrust into Belgium in early September. One corps was immobilized so the other two could continue their advance, and infantrymen were forced to walk because there was no fuel for their trucks to transport them. The situation was little better in Montgomery's 21st Army Group, as the insatiable demands for fuel and supplies simply could not be met, the efforts of such expedients as the Red Ball Express notwithstanding.

On September 3, Brussels was liberated by the British, as was Antwerp the following day in what has been widely regarded as one of the great blunders of the war. Neither Montgomery nor Dempsey had ordered the capture of the vital Scheldt estuary, which remained in German hands, thus preventing the opening of the port of Antwerp. By the time attempts were made to seize the crossings over the Albert Canal, all of its bridges had been blown by the Germans. Some of the most savage battles of the war took place as the Canadians began the task of clearing the Scheldt estuary. The weeks that followed saw a return to the sort of painfully slow, bloody warfare that had been fought in Normandy, as German units heeded Hitler's mandate to fight to the bitter end to prevent the port of Antwerp from becoming an Allied staging area for the final battle for Germany itself.

Operation Market Garden

By Sept. 5, 1944, the 1st Army had driven into eastern Belgium and crossed the Meuse River to capture Namur, on the same day that Hitler reinstated Rundstedt as the commander in chief of all German armies in the west. Five days later, 1st Army spearheads pushed into the duchy of Luxembourg. On September 11, advance elements of Lt. Gen. Jacob Devers's 6th Army Group driving up the Rhone Valley formally linked up with the 3d Army.

As their armies advanced ever closer to Germany, the Allies began finalizing plans for the largest airborne operation of the war. In an attempt to keep alive his single thrust concept, Montgomery devised a daring a plan to open the way to the heartland of the German Ruhr by means of airborne landings to seize the bridges across the Waal River at Nijmegen, the Rhine River at Arnhem, the Maas River at Grave, and the rivers and canals around Eindhoven. The airborne landings were to be followed by a ground thrust to relieve the airborne by Dempsey's 2d Army from the Belgian-Netherlands border area. The airborne operation by the 1st Allied Airborne Army was code-named "Market." "Garden" was the ground operation by which the British XXX Corps was to thrust north along the narrow corridor opened by the airborne. Once in control of the vital bridge along the Lower Rhine at Arnhem, the remainder of the 2d Army was to turn the German flank and rapidly assault the Ruhr. By this surprise assault through the so-called back door to Germany, Montgomery hoped to hasten the collapse of the Third Reich and end the war in 1944.

The British 1st Airborne Division was given the mission of seizing Arnhem and the Rhine bridge, while the U.S. 82d and the 101st airborne divisions were to be dropped near Nijmegen and Grave, respectively. In reserve was the Polish 1st Parachute Brigade, which was to reinforce the British at Arnhem. The mission of the 82d Airborne Division was to seize bridges over the canals to the north of Eindhoven, while the 101st Airborne was to capture the key bridges over the Maas and Waal rivers. Ignoring warnings by the 1st Airborne Division commander that the British landing zones were too far away from the Arnhem bridge (from four to nine miles), the planning for Market Garden went full-steam ahead when the air commanders refused to drop the paratroopers or land the glider troops closer in the mistaken belief that German air artillery defenses ringing Arnhem made the operation too dangerous for their aircraft.

On September 17, in the largest airborne and glider operation ever mounted, the massive aerial armada of more than 1,545 troop carriers and 478 gliders literally blackened the skies over England and Holland throughout the day. Over Arnhem and Nijmegen, parachutes and gliders would be seen with the troops of Market, an operation so mammoth that a second wave of the 1st Airborne Division had to be postponed until the next day. In all, more than 5,000 aircraft would participate in the airborne and glider landings.

Although the landings initially went well, Allied intelligence had failed to heed reports from the Dutch underground that Lt. Gen. Wilhelm Bittrich's II SS Panzer Corps was bivouacked near Arnhem. Units of the spearhead 1st Parachute Brigade were thus obliged to march long distances on foot toward their objective, the Arnhem bridge.

Lt. Col. John Frost's 2d Parachute Battalion was the only unit to reach the bridge. The remainder of the division was soon engaged by veteran German panzer troops and pinned down in and around the city of Arnhem. At this crucial moment, not only did the British radios fail, making the growing dilemma of the British airborne even more acute, but the Germans had captured a copy of the Market Garden plan from one of the gliders that had crashed outside Nijmegen.

The success of the operation hinged on the ability of XXX Corps to relieve rapidly the lightly armed airborne troops at each of the bridges along their route of march. Congestion and German resistance along the single narrow road to Nijmegen and Arnhem, which soon earned the nickname of "Hell's Highway," delayed the British ground advance by crucial hours. Even though XXX Corps linked up with the 101st Airborne at Eindhoven on September 18, the U.S. 82d and the British 1st airborne divisions remained unrelieved and engaged in savage battles for survival. On the afternoon of September 20, two assault companies of the 82d Airborne's 504th Parachute Infantry Regiment stormed across the Waal in rubber rafts directly into heavy German fire and seized the northern end of the Nijmegen railway bridge. Despite the heroics of the airborne, XXX Corps failed to exploit the 504th's hard-fought triumph by thrusting through the disrupted German defenses and seizing the Arnhem bridge.

Worst off were the beleaguered British airborne at Arnhem. Frost's battalion controlled the northern approaches to the Arnhem bridge and very quickly was permanently cut off from the rest of the division, which itself had become heavily engaged with Bittrich's troops in Arnhem. Despite the arrival of the 4th Parachute Brigade the following afternoon, the situation in the Arnhem sector grew steadily worse as the Germans began to tighten a noose around the British, who were forced to abandon Arnhem and establish defensive positions four miles to the west in the small village of Oosterbeek.

Frost and his men fought a savage series of battles on the northern end of the Arnhem bridge against the 9th SS Panzer Division that resulted in heavy losses on both sides. The gallant men of the 2d Parachute Battalion held out at the bridge for four days before being overwhelmed and forced to surrender. An attempt by the Polish airborne to reach the bridge turned to tragedy when the Germans attacked the landing zone and sank a ferry that was to take them across the river.

By September 25, it was clear that the operation had failed, and the decision was made to attempt to save what remained of the British 1st Airborne Division. Under the cover of darkness, 2,400 Polish and British paratroopers and glider pilots managed to cross the Rhine to the safety of the south bank in small rubber boats. Of the 10,000 men who had landed at Arnhem on September 17, 1,400

had been killed and more than 6,000 were prisoners of the Germans. The 1st Airborne had ceased to exist as a fighting unit and was never reconstituted in the aftermath of the battle.

What had begun with high optimism turned into a military disaster. Although the heroic stand of Frost's battalion at the Arnhem bridge is widely considered one of the legendary episodes of World War II, Operation Market Garden was an abject failure. Montgomery's later claim that 90 percent of its objectives had been attained was meaningless. The Allies had failed to establish a bridgehead north of the Rhine, an objective that came to be known as "a bridge too far."

Autumn Stalemate

The failure at Arnhem led to a stalemate during the autumn and early winter of 1944. Although Allied forces had advanced to the borders of the Third Reich, the German army under the leadership of Rundstedt and Model had managed to scrape together sufficient forces to establish a hasty defense of Germany's borders. The advent of bad weather left the Allies frustrated and virtually immobilized in the mud and snow of the Ardennes and the harsh terrain of the outer Ruhr Valley. In October at Aachen, American infantrymen fought ferocious street battles before the city fell. Attempts to crack the Westwall (Siegfried line) and gain access to the heartland met with failure across the entire Allied front, from Schmidt and the Roer River in the north, to the Moselle River in the south, where Patton's 3d Army had also ground to a halt in Lorraine. The fortress city of Metz held out throughout October against the siege warfare that Patton detested. The Lorraine Campaign had turned into yet another series of bloody infantry battles. Advancing through the Rhone Valley from the Riviera, Devers's 6th Army Group had better luck in cracking the Belfort gap in the southern Vosges Mountains and driving as far as the west bank of the Rhine before the offensive stalled. Despite the 6th Army Group's success, the German 19th Army still controlled an extensive bridgehead from Colmar in the north to Mulhouse in the south that was dubbed the Colmar pocket.

The most brutal battle of all was fought in the frigid, dense Huertgen Forest, which lay astride the route to the Roer dams that the Germans threatened to demolish and flood if the Allies attempted to penetrate the Westwall through that sector. In a series of misguided engagements often compared to the worst battles of World War I, the U.S. 1st Army commander, Lt. Gen. Courtney Hodges, flung one division after another into the bloody cauldron of the Huertgen in November 1944. Heavily defended by the Germans, the forest became a deathtrap that consumed men at a shocking rate. Before it was finally captured, 8 American divisions were bloodied in the Huertgen, suffering more than 24,000 combat casualties and 5,000 more to

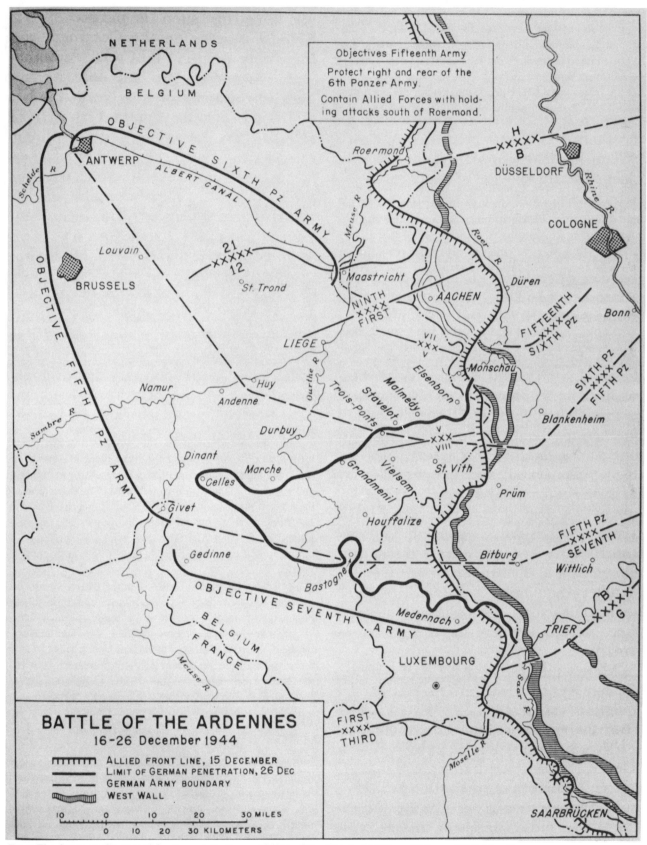

Objectives Fifteenth Army

Protect right and rear of the
6th Panzer Army.

Contain Allied Forces with holding attacks south of Roermond.

NETHERLANDS

BELGIUM

OBJECTIVE SIXTH PZ ARMY

ANTWERP
ALBERT CANAL

Schelde R

Roermond

DÜSSELDORF

H
B
XXXXX

Rhine R

COLOGNE

Meuse R

Roer R

Maastricht

Düren

Louvain

21
XXXXX
12

St. Trond

NINTH
XXXX
FIRST

AACHEN

Bonn

BRUSSELS

OBJECTIVE FIFTH PZ ARMY

LIEGE

VII
XXX
V

FIFTEENTH
XXXXX
SIXTH PZ

Namur

Huy

Ourthe R

Trois-Ponts

Stavelot

Malmédy

Elsenborn

Monschau

SIXTH PZ
XXXXX
FIFTH PZ

Andenne

Durbuy

Blankenheim

Sambre R

Dinant

Marche

Grandmenil

Vielsalm

V
XXX
VIII

St. Vith

Prüm

Celles

Houffalize

Givet

Gedinne

Bastogne

Medernach

OBJECTIVE SEVENTH ARMY

FIFTH PZ
XXXX
SEVENTH

Bitburg

Wittlich

BELGIUM
FRANCE

Meuse R

LUXEMBOURG

B
G
XXXXX

TRIER

Saar R

BATTLE OF THE ARDENNES
16–26 December 1944

FIRST
XXXX
THIRD

Moselle R

IIIIIIII ALLIED FRONT LINE, 15 DECEMBER
━━━━━ LIMIT OF GERMAN PENETRATION, 26 DEC
─ ─ ─ ─ GERMAN ARMY BOUNDARY
IIIIIIII WEST WALL

SAARBRÜCKEN

10   0   10   20   30 MILES
0   10   20   30 KILOMETERS

From The Supreme Command *by Forrest C. Pogue* (Office of the Chief of Military History, 1954) Map 5

trench foot and exhaustion. Overall, during the battles along the Roer River during the autumn of 1944, the U.S. 1st and 9th armies suffered 57,000 combat losses and 70,000 more to the ravages of the elements. When it ended, the Germans remained in control of the vital Roer dams, and the Allies were left with a hollow victory in what was undoubtedly the most ineptly fought series of battles of the war in the West.

Battle of the Bulge

Hitler elected to gamble the fate of Germany on a last-ditch attempt to split Eisenhower's armies by a sudden, lightning blitzkrieg thrust through the Ardennes with the aim of destroying all Allied forces north of a line running from Bastogne to Antwerp. Seeking to repeat the success of 1940, Hitler naively believed his armies could drive clear to Antwerp once they were across the Meuse River and into the Belgian lowlands beyond the Ardennes. With this vital port in German hands, he thought that the Allies would be obliged to sue for peace.

When they first heard of the plan in late October, both Rundstedt and Model opposed Hitler's Ardennes counteroffensive. Model, who had earned the Fuhrer's trust and a reputation on the Eastern Front as ''Hitler's fireman,'' was typically blunt: ''This plan hasn't got a damned leg to stand on.'' Both commanders believed that the seizure of Antwerp was a hopelessly unrealistic goal and attempted to persuade Hitler to scale down its scope from a ''grand slam'' to a ''little slam.'' Their efforts fell upon deaf ears.

Nevertheless, in early December 1944, both Model and his two panzer army commanders, Sepp Dietrich and Hasso von Manteuffel, spoke forcefully at a conference with Hitler, urging that the plan be reconsidered. Hitler again adamantly refused. Under the cover of the most bitter winter weather in years, more than 1,400 tanks, 2,000 guns, and 20 divisions were quietly moved forward into the thick forests of the rugged Schnee Eifel on the eastern fringes of the Ardennes.

Operation Wacht am Rhein (''Watch on the Rhine'') began in heavy fog early on the morning of December 16 when two panzer armies launched the main attack against the most lightly defended sector of the U.S. 1st Army. The thinly held lines of the inexperienced U.S. 106th Division were quickly overrun, and within hours, it was clear that the Germans had unleashed a major counteroffensive. The Ardennes became bedlam as American units became entangled in a series of desperate battles around St. Vith, Elsenborn Ridge, Houffalize, and other small villages and rivers. German panzers and infantry attempted to advance rapidly before the Allies could react to the unexpected attack, while German units dressed in American uniforms operated behind Allied lines to disrupt further an already chaotic situation.

Maj. Gen. James M. Gavin, commander of the 82d Airborne Division, speaks on a field telephone during the Battle of the Bulge in the Ardennes Forest. (U.S. Army Military History Institute)

Although the German advance appeared at first to be unstoppable, weary American fighting men, in some of the most gallant individual and small-unit actions of the war, gained time for reinforcements to arrive by either holding their positions or slowing the German juggernaut by precious hours. These included the paratroopers of Maj. Gen. James M. Gavin's 82d Airborne, who had only months before fought to clear the Nijmegen bridge during Market Garden.

The key to German success lay in the panzer spearheads securing bridgeheads west of the Meuse, and to do so they first had to control the town of Bastogne, through which all major roads in the Ardennes passed. Bastogne was held by the U.S. 101st Airborne Division, which was blocking the advance of the 5th Panzer Army. Although surrounded, the acting commander of the 101st, Gen. Anthony C. McAuliffe, responded to a German surrender ultimatum with the now famous one-word reply: ''Nuts!''

A grim Eisenhower on December 19 summoned his senior commanders to Verdun, where it was decided that Montgomery would take command of all Allied forces north of the German penetration, while Bradley remained in command of all those to the south. With no reserves to call upon and the situation growing more acute by the hour, Patton was ordered to detach immediately elements of his 3d Army in Lorraine and head full speed for Bas-

Refugees and troops of the 101st Airborne Division interact in the town of Bastogne, a major transportation center of the Ardennes. (U.S. Army Military History Institute)

togne. Patton ordered his troops to "drive like hell" to relieve their beleaguered brethren at Bastogne, and they did so with unprecedented swiftness in one of the greatest achievements of military history. On December 22, the 4th Armored Division sliced into the German flank south of Bastogne and Allied aircraft were able to operate for the first time during the battle. Elsewhere, Gen. Ernest N. Harmon's 2d Armored Division established blocking positions near the Meuse and then unleashed a savage counterattack that crushed the 2d Panzer Division and ended any prospect the Germans had of gaining a bridgehead over the Meuse.

Bastogne remained surrounded and was not relieved until the day after Christmas by the 4th Armored Division. Although heavy fighting continued into the new year of 1945, the Battle of the Bulge (so-named for the bulge created by the Germans' deep penetration into Allied lines) was effectively won by Christmas when Manteuffel's and

Dietrich's panzer divisions were choked off from gaining their objectives and began to run seriously short of fuel and ammunition.

The Ardennes counteroffensive was little more than a desperate gamble that had virtually no chance of success, despite achieving surprise. German resources were too few, and the gallantry of American troops fighting in the frozen forests of the Ardennes proved fatal to Hitler's ambition to somehow snatch, if not victory, at least a draw with the Allies and a voice in any terms of Germany's surrender.

By mid-January 1945, not only had the German attacks run their course, but the Allies had gone over to the offensive. As historian Charles B. MacDonald noted, "the cost of this greatest pitched battle ever fought by American arms was on both sides enormous. Out of 600,000 Americans involved—more than three times the number that fought on both sides at Gettysburg—casualties totaled 81,000, of which probably 19,000 were killed, perhaps

15,000 captured.'' German losses, estimated at more than 100,000, were irreplaceable. In late December and early January 1945, there was heavy fighting in the Alsatian sector, centered around Strasbourg as German forces attempted to encircle a substantial portion of the 6th Army Group. Strasbourg held out, and the German attacks were contained, but not before the Germans suffered another 25,000 casualties.

THE INVASION OF GERMANY

It took Allied forces until the end of January to restore the lost ground, and as they contemplated how to conduct the invasion of Germany, the lingering arguments from the previous year resumed. Eisenhower insisted that his armies continue to advance across a broad front to the Rhine in the form of two major thrusts, one in the north under Montgomery, the other in the south by Bradley. Montgomery and the British chiefs of staff continued to support a powerful offensive in the north to breach the Rhine and capture the Ruhr. Moreover, in order to align the Allied front for the final assault on the Third Reich, preliminary attacks were necessary to seize the Roer dams and eliminate the German pockets around Colmar and in the Saar along the Moselle and Saar rivers near Trier. Eisenhower ceded priority of effort to the British and beefed up the U.S. 9th Army, which was attached to Montgomery's 21st Army Group. In what constituted the largest force ever assembled, nearly 4,000,000 U.S., British, and Canadian troops assigned to 3 army groups, 7 field armies, 21 corps, and 73 divisions were poised to launch the final offensive that would finish off Nazi Germany and end the war. By V-E (Victory in Europe) Day in May, these numbers would grow to 4,500,000 men and 91 divisions, while to the east, the Soviet army had more than 2,000,000 troops and 6,000 tanks in action on the Eastern Front.

As Montgomery was preparing for a massive breaching of the Rhine, the German situation grew desperate when a task force of the U.S. 9th Armored Division unexpectedly found a railway bridge over the Rhine at Remagen intact. Taking advantage of this extraordinary good fortune, American troops poured across the river. However, Eisenhower's continued insistence on a broad front approach resulted in a lost opportunity to have established a larger bridgehead east of the Rhine. Instead, the American force of some five divisions was easily contained.

On March 23, Montgomery launched Operation Plunder, his long-awaited offensive that included another large airborne and glider operation by two parachute divisions. The Rhine was breached at numerous points while to the south, the 1st and 3d armies also secured bridgeheads east of the river. By the end of March, the end was near for the German armed forces defending their homeland. As the Soviet army continued its relentless push west toward Berlin, some 300,000 troops of Model's Army Group B were trapped in the rapidly closing Ruhr pocket.

By mid-April, the Ruhr was split in two, and even the loyal Model had had enough. He ordered Army Group B dissolved rather than carry out Hitler's ''scorched earth'' decree. Rundstedt was again dismissed by Hitler, and Kesselring was summoned from Italy in a futile attempt to restore the situation in the Ruhr. Model committed suicide.

In January, the Allied leaders had met at Yalta, and, in what later was often termed a sellout to Stalin, Churchill and an ailing Roosevelt agreed on the division of Germany, which included the establishment of four zones of occupation (French, American, British, and Russian) when the war ended. In return for a Russian commitment to join the war against Japan, the borders of eastern Europe were realigned. Stalin's assurances of free elections in the liberated nations of eastern Europe proved hollow in the aftermath of the war in what Churchill later called an Iron Curtain of Soviet domination.

With the Allies nearly 300 miles away, and the Russians astride the Oder River, a mere 30 miles east of the German capital, the question of Berlin became of paramount importance. Earlier, Eisenhower had expressly stated that Berlin was an Allied objective, but in light of the recent Yalta agreements, he changed his mind and unilaterally announced that the city was no longer of military consequence. The Combined Chiefs of Staff were split on the issue and never overruled the Supreme Commander, thus tacitly validating his controversial directive. Churchill protested that Allied failure to take Berlin would ''raise grave and formidable difficulties in the future,'' but Roosevelt, who was in the last days of his life, endorsed Eisenhower's decision to avoid Berlin and instead halt at the Elbe River. Although the U.S. 9th Army already had established bridgeheads over the Elbe and was fully capable of driving into Berlin before the Russians, the plan was turned down by Eisenhower.

Last Operations

During April 1945, the death knell of the Third Reich sounded as the rampaging Allied armies began mopping up pockets of resistance from the central plains to the Alps, capturing tens of thousands of prisoners and drawing the noose ever tighter. German survivors of the fighting against the Red Army frantically made their way west in order to be able to surrender to the Allies. In mid-April, the Red Army began a three-week siege of Berlin. In what became one of the bloodiest battles fought by the Red Army, German troops responded to Hitler's order to fight to the death by inflicting more than 300,000 casualties. Berlin was reduced to smoking rubble.

By early May, Patton's 3d Army had driven into Austria and Czechoslovakia, but his troops were forbidden to enter the capital of Prague in yet another controversial decision by Eisenhower. When the concentration camps at Belsen, Buchenwald, and Dachau were liberated, the world for the first time learned of the full extent of the gruesome atrocities perpetrated by the Nazis. Shortly before noon on April 25, two separate patrols of the U.S. 69th Division made contact with the Red Army at the Elbe River, and in one of the most epic moments of the war, the Eastern and Western fronts were joined.

With his nation in ruins and his armies destroyed, Hitler committed suicide the night of April 30; his body and that of his mistress, Eva Braun, were burned in a funeral pyre outside his Berlin bunker. To the bitter end, Hitler, who had unleashed the worst conflagration in history, entertained delusions that somehow he would still snatch victory from the jaws of defeat.

On V-E Day, May 8, 1945, the war formally ended when Germany surrendered unconditionally in Reims, France. Europe was devastated, and the cost of World War II in Europe and the Mediterranean had been staggering. Civilian and military deaths have been estimated as high as 50,000,000 dead, more than 14,000,000 of whom were believed to have died in the Soviet Union. Germany lost some 4,600,000 dead, and untold thousands (perhaps several million) of German prisoners of war disappeared into Soviet slave labor camps and were never seen again.

The Occupation

At the Potsdam Conference in July 1945, Churchill, Truman, and Stalin completed the dismemberment of Germany begun at Yalta. East Prussia was split between the Soviet Union and Poland, which also acquired Silesia and Pomerania. The Potsdam agreement also mandated the expulsion of some 14,000,000 Germans living in these regions who were forcibly resettled in the west during the winter of 1945–46. Of these, more than 2,000,000 died of malnutrition, exposure, and brutal mistreatment.

On May 8, 1945, thereafter known as V-E Day, the Germans surrendered unconditionally in Reims, France; here Lt. Gen. Walter Bedell Smith signs the surrender document for the Allies. (U.S. Army Military History Institute)

A realigned Germany was occupied and partitioned among the four Allied Powers, with the erstwhile East Germany placed within the Soviet sector. Berlin became an island in the Soviet sector and came under special four-power occupation, with the right of access guaranteed to the French, British, and Americans.

5

War in the Pacific: 1941–1945

When the Japanese attacked the U.S. forces at Pearl Harbor, Hawaii, on Dec 7, 1941, Japan's war with China had already been raging for more than four years. Sparked by a minor clash outside Beijing (Peking), the fighting between the Japanese and Chinese armies escalated into a full-blown war contested across the landscape of China. Certain Japanese officers expected armed force to resolve the issue quickly in their favor, but the Chinese refused to crumble before Japan's military might and fought on despite fearsome losses. Japanese casualties were also heavy; 40,000 men were lost in the five-month campaign to clear Shanghai and advance up the Yangtze River to Nanking, the Nationalist Chinese capital. Japanese brutality, exemplified by the so-called rape of Nanking in December 1937, only encouraged Chinese resistance, especially among the Communist 8th Route Army led by Mao Zedong. The Nationalist leader, Chiang Kai-shek, eventually shifted his reorganized Chinese government 1,000 miles inland to Chungking, where, safe behind the gorges of the Yangtze River, he held court.

Thus, Japan's plans to subdue China quickly failed, and even before the attack on Pearl Harbor, Japanese casualties in China amounted to 190,000 troops killed and 520,000 wounded. The China fighting drained the army's strength away from Japan's traditional opponent, the Soviet Union. Indeed, Japan was defeated in two major border battles with the Soviets, at Chang-ku Feng on the Korean-Soviet border in 1938 and at Khalkhin Gol on the Outer Mongolian-Manchurian border the following year.

The Imperial Army found itself bogged down in the China morass. By late 1941, 27 of Japan's 51 infantry divisions were fighting in China and another 13 were garrisoning Manchuria. This left Imperial general headquarters in Tokyo with a maximum of 11 infantry divisions and 2 air groups (about 700 planes) available for their opening advance across the Pacific. The Imperial Navy, however, could deploy almost its total surface strength and the bulk of the naval air force (approximately 1,600 aircraft) for Pacific operations.

Japanese Strategy

Japan's initial strategy for a Pacific and Southeast Asian war had limited aims. Imperial headquarters believed that overrunning American, British, and Dutch colonial possessions in East Asia would deprive China of Allied aid and convince Chiang of the futility of further resistance. Similarly, German and Italian military successes would lead to the surrender of Great Britain, which, in turn, would cause the Americans to lose their will to fight. Army leaders viewed Americans as the decadent products of liberalism and individualism, as people who were incapable of fighting a prolonged war of attrition against the morally superior Japanese. There were few "experts" on the United States within the general staff headquarters because Japanese army intelligence had traditionally targeted the Soviet Union, not the United States, as the likeliest opponent.

Japanese army officers naturally thought in terms of offensive operations to open hostilities with Britain and the United States. They gave no consideration to war termination or even to what factors might constitute victory for Japan. Certainly, they never seriously entertained ambitions about defeating the United States, but staff officers remained hazy about operations beyond the seizure of the natural resources of Southeast Asia, which would provide the raw materials needed to feed the Japanese war machine.

Moreover, the continental bias of Japanese army planners appeared in draft operational plans for the so-called Southern Region (Southeast Asia and the Southwest Pacific). They insisted that the army take responsibility for operations in those regions closest to the Asian continent, while

The Japanese aerial attack on the U.S. fleet at Pearl Harbor, Hawaii, destroyed many ships and enabled the Japanese to protect their interests in the Pacific area. (U.S. Navy)

the navy's zone extended far into the Pacific. Consequently, the army assumed initial accountability for the Philippines, North Borneo, Malaya, Sumatra, and Java. The navy's zone extended, among other places, to New Guinea and the Bismarcks, two areas that would ultimately cost the army staggering troop casualties and aircraft losses in the fighting of 1942–44. Such haphazardness underlined Japanese inability to formulate a military strategy and to define the role and scope of operations on extended lines of communications. In short, Japan went to war against the United States on the strength of a five-month plan of operations.

Nonetheless, it was an exceptional operational strategy, one premised on first achieving local air and naval superiority before landing troops. Carrier aircraft crippled the U.S. fleet at Pearl Harbor, thereby protecting Japan's otherwise exposed strategic flank in the western Pacific. Next, seasoned Japanese infantrymen waded ashore at points from Wake Island to Malaya. On December 10, the U.S. Navy base at Guam fell; the same day, Japanese naval infantry occupied Makin and Tarawa in the Gilbert chain; Wake surrendered 12 days later. Within three weeks, the Japanese navy had established a strategic western defensive line against the surviving American fleet. By late January 1942, Japan's reach extended to the great natural anchorage at Rabaul, New Britain, from where the emperor's navy threatened Papua, New Guinea, northwest Australia, and the Solomon Islands.

For the Japanese army, the decisive theater of operations was Southeast Asia. Despite determined air and ground

resistance, landings on Malaya's northeastern coast on Dec. 8, 1941, quickly secured much-needed advanced airfields. Then, the 25th Army, commanded by Lt. Gen. Tomoyuki Yamashita, outmaneuvered a numerically superior, but demoralized, British, Indian, and Australian force. Japanese infantrymen generally avoided direct assaults on fortified areas in favor of flanking attacks. Their initial objectives were always Allied bases and their airfields, from which land-based air power dominated the battlefield. Two days into the campaign, Japanese navy bombers sank Britain's new battleship *Prince of Wales* and its older battle cruiser *Repulse*. With control of the sea and sky, Yamashita's three divisions drove remorselessly toward Singapore. Elsewhere, the Imperial Army landed in the Philippines on December 10 and in North Borneo six days later.

U.S. Strategy

American strategy in Asia rested on the protection of U.S. commercial and colonial interests, although the major U.S. colony, the Philippine Islands, was scheduled to receive its independence in 1946. As early as 1913, the United States saw the distant Philippines as a strategic liability because the islands were vulnerable to Japanese invasion. American prewar strategy rested on the notion of the battle fleet moving across the Pacific, securing its line of communication as it advanced, and relieving the army garrison in the Philippines. The army's role was to hold Manila Bay until the navy arrived; otherwise, the navy had no base from which to operate in Asian waters. The U.S. armed services held radically differing notions of Pacific strategy. The navy thought in terms of offensive fleet operations west of Hawaii, but the army concerned itself with a strategic defensive to hold a triangle stretching from Alaska to Hawaii to Panama.

Such was the Pacific strategy of the United States when World War II erupted in Europe in 1939. Although the United States was not initially a belligerent, it was clear that the United States could ill afford to witness passively the collapse of the British empire. As the U.S. chief of naval operations, Adm. Harold Stark, put it, "If Britain wins decisively against Germany, we could win everywhere; but if she loses, the problems confronting us could be very great; and while we might not lose everywhere, we might possibly not win anywhere." Therefore, in 1940–41, American army and navy planners devised the strategy to defeat Germany, Italy, and Japan, the so-called Axis Powers. The Allies rightly regarded Germany as the most dangerous member of the Axis coalition and the one that had to be defeated first. Italy and Japan, in theory at least, would be handled as opportunities and forces became available.

In the dark days of December 1941, British prime minister Winston Churchill and his chiefs of staff sailed aboard a battleship for the United States. The ensuing meeting with Pres. Franklin D. Roosevelt and the United States chiefs of staff reaffirmed that the "Atlantic and European area was considered to be the decisive theater." Another result of the so-called Arcadia Conference was the decision to create a single unified command for the Pacific region and Asia. Called ABDACOM (for "American, British, Dutch, and Australian Command"), the new command encompassed the region from Burma, Malaya, and the Dutch East Indies to Western New Guinea, Northwest Australia, and (nominally) the Philippines.

In truth, it was a doomed command that Gen. Sir Archibald Wavell led into battle. Little agreement existed about objectives. The British concerned themselves about Malaya and Singapore; the Dutch focused on Java; and the Australians worried about their homeland. U.S. attention centered on the Philippines, where Gen. Douglas MacArthur was leading a stubborn American and Filipino defense against the Japanese invaders.

Allied Defeats

By mid-January 1942, Japanese landings on Borneo provided the catalyst that brought ABDACOM's navy out for battle. Four U.S. destroyers of World War I vintage fought the first American naval battle of the war. This minor night action on January 24 sank 4 Japanese transports, but another attempt to strike at Japanese transports approaching the southern Celebes met enemy air attacks that knocked 2 U.S. cruisers out of the fight.

These losses soon paled, however, beside the news that Singapore's 85,000-man garrison had capitulated on February 15. This disaster rendered the Netherlands East Indies indefensible. Only 10 days later, Wavell closed out his headquarters and turned command of ABDACOM over to the Dutch. On February 24, Allied aircraft sighted large Japanese convoys in the Java Sea. Five Allied cruisers and a dozen destroyers sortied to intercept the approaching Japanese. The resultant Battle of the Java Sea cost the Allies 2 cruisers and 4 destroyers and slowed the Japanese timetable by only one day. Surviving Allied warships trying to escape were hunted down, although the USS *Houston* and the Australian cruiser *Perth* did run into the Japanese invasion fleet. In a confused night battle, both Allied cruisers were sunk. So were 4 Japanese transports, although two of these fell victim not to Allied guns but to errant torpedoes launched from their own destroyers.

Fall of the Philippines

Only in their designs for the Philippines were the Japanese behind schedule. Lt. Gen. Masaharu Homma, commander of the 14th Army, aimed to capture Manila, the Philippine capital and largest city on Luzon. MacArthur declared Manila an open city and withdrew his army, although not all of its supplies, into the rugged Bataan Peninsula. Homma pressed his attack into the mountainous jungled peninsula. Tokyo anticipated an early end to the American

and Filipino resistance, so Imperial headquarters redeployed Homma's veteran 48th Division to the Dutch East Indies. A second-line reserve outfit, the 65th Infantry Brigade, replaced the departing division. Together with the 16th Division, the 65th Brigade would carry the burden of the Bataan fighting.

By the end of January, the Japanese had driven MacArthur's forces about halfway down the peninsula but were themselves on the verge of disintegration. Heavy battle casualties, epidemic malaria, and the ravages of the jungle had whittled away at Homma's forces. A lull settled over the battlefield as the 14th Army suspended offensive operations and asked Tokyo for reinforcements. Throughout February and March, replacements for Homma's depleted units plus additional heavy artillery, warplanes, and battalions of the 4th Infantry Division streamed into Bataan.

There were, however, no replacements for the battered Allies. MacArthur's escape from Bataan in mid-March provided a dramatic moment for the American public. On March 17, after a series of close calls, the general reached Alice Springs, Australia, where he announced, "I came through and I shall return." This fixation on liberating the Philippines dominated MacArthur's strategy throughout the Pacific war.

Meanwhile, on Luzon, General Homma had reconstituted his forces, and on April 3, a tremendous artillery bombardment announced his latest offensive. Although the defenders fought bravely, months without adequate food, medicine, or replacements had left them exhausted. By April 11, the Japanese had conquered Bataan. Landing operations against Corregidor were initiated on May 5, and the island fell the following day. Realizing that further resistance would bring meaningless suffering, and under great pressure from the Japanese, Lt. Gen. Jonathan Wainwright surrendered all forces in the Philippines on May 8. On Luzon, 76,000 Allied soldiers, many weakened from malaria and malnutrition, were herded along in the infamous "Bataan Death March." Perhaps 7,000–10,000 prisoners died (approximately 2,330 of whom were Americans) on the awful trek, during which the Japanese randomly beat, executed, and generally brutalized their captives.

Other Japanese Victories

About 2,000 miles east of Manila, three Japanese divisions were expelling Allied forces from Burma. The main Japanese offensive drove north from Rangoon along the major railroad line and aimed at Mandalay, more than 300 miles distant. Allied resistance collapsed quickly despite the efforts of the newly appointed British commander, Lt. Gen. William J. Slim, and the American Maj. Gen. Joseph "Vinegar Joe" Stilwell, who exercised control of a sort over the Chinese Nationalists' three division equivalents then fighting in Burma. The Anglo-Chinese front in central Burma crumbled in early May when the Japanese took Mandalay and Lashio, about 120 miles to the northwest.

The Philippine army fought side by side with Allied troops against the Japanese invasion of the Philippines. (U.S. Army Military History Institute: H. U. Milne Collection)

Lashio was the point of origin for the Burma Road, and its loss sealed China from overland access to the outside world, besides exposing the British and Chinese left flank. Meanwhile, a smaller Japanese force had flanked Mandalay on the east, threatening to cut that line of retreat. An orderly Allied withdrawal disintegrated into a chaotic flight for the safety of India. From Dec. 25, 1941, through May 12, 1942, at the cost of only 2,431 casualties, Japanese troops overran Burma and inflicted nearly 13,500 casualties on the British and Commonwealth forces.

In April 1942, two Japanese fleets scoured the Indian Ocean, sinking 26 ships, including 2 heavy cruisers and the British aircraft carrier *Hermes*. Elsewhere, Japanese forces had landed on New Guinea. The Japanese sphere of control now stretched in the Pacific Ocean from the Gilberts to New Guinea and into the Dutch East Indies and in the west to the borders of India. Japan's achievements were sensational: 250,000 Allied prisoners of war, 105 enemy ships sunk, and 91 others damaged; the navy alone claimed 460 enemy aircraft shot down in aerial combat and another 1,076 destroyed on the ground. Against this, Japanese losses were about 21,000 killed and wounded; 562 aircraft from both services lost to all causes; 21 ships damaged, but nothing larger than a cruiser sunk. The "victory disease" infected Imperial headquarters.

The series of spectacular victories emboldened the Japanese combined fleet and navy ministry to expand Japan's already acquired wartime gains. Naval planners proposed an invasion of Australia to eliminate the major base and staging area for an Allied counteroffensive. Moreover, severing dominions like Australia from the empire would ensure the collapse of Great Britain. An aggressive strategy would also protect lines of communication between the occupied areas and the Japanese home islands. Army leaders remained unenthusiastic, pointing to shipping and manpower shortages. According to army staff officers, it was better to consolidate existing territorial gains and exploit their resources. They argued that now was the time to construct an impregnable defensive perimeter that could repel the inevitable Allied counteroffensive expected in the latter half of 1943. Nor was the army enthusiastic about the navy's "FS (Midway-Aleutians) Operation," agreeing to cooperate only if the navy guaranteed its success. While Tokyo's leaders pondered future strategy, so did their counterparts in Washington and London.

Allied Responses

Consistent with the "Germany first" strategy, the Anglo-American Combined Chiefs of Staff (CCS) had agreed on Mar. 24, 1942, on a worldwide division of strategic tasks. Under this agreement, the United States took responsibility for the war in the Pacific. Six days later, the U.S. Joint Chiefs of Staff (JCS) placed MacArthur in command of the Southwest Pacific area (SWPA), which included Aus-

Lt. Col. James Doolittle led the bombing of Tokyo that inflicted psychological as well as physical damage on the enemy; Doolittle (right) is shown congratulating two airmen. (U.S. Army Air Corps)

tralia, the Philippines, the Solomons, New Guinea, the Bismarck Archipelago, Borneo, and the Netherlands East Indies excepting Sumatra. MacArthur's arrival in Australia coincided with the appearance of American ground and air reinforcements previously ordered there by Washington. Still, the available Allied forces in Australia were too few in number and too poorly trained and equipped to fight a determined foe.

The navy, commanded by Adm. Chester W. Nimitz, also commander of the Pacific Fleet, assumed responsibility for the remainder of the Pacific in its Pacific Ocean area (POA) theater. POA was further divided into three areas. Nimitz commanded the North and Central Pacific areas directly, while Vice Adm. Robert L. Ghormley took charge of the South Pacific area.

An American settled Japanese strategy. On Apr. 18, 1942, Lt. Col. James Doolittle led 16 B-25 medium bombers against Tokyo and other Japanese cities. The damage the raiders inflicted was insignificant (all 16 aircraft were lost, although not to enemy fire), but the psychological ramifications of the Doolittle raid were enormous. Because the enemy had violated the sacred homeland, opposition dissipated within the navy and army for the FS Operation. Planned operations against New Guinea and the Solomon Islands were accelerated, even though only two carriers were available in the area. The others were refitting for the Midway expedition.

Based on deciphered Japanese navy codes, U.S. naval intelligence had alerted Admiral Nimitz about the likelihood of an attack against Port Moresby, New Guinea, in May. Forewarned of enemy intentions, two U.S. carriers, the *Lexington* and the *Yorktown*, intercepted the approaching Japanese invasion force. On May 7, for the first

time in naval history, a major sea battle occurred between carrier aircraft of opposing fleets that never came within 100 miles of each other. Tactically, the battle was a draw. Japanese pilots sank the *Lexington* and damaged the *Yorktown*, but U.S. airmen sank the carrier *Shoho* and seriously damaged the *Shokaku*. The Japanese realized that, without their carrier air cover, an invasion was impossible and recalled their fleet to Rabaul. Port Moresby was safe for the moment.

Battle of Midway

Attention now shifted to a small atoll in the Central Pacific. Midway is close to the geographical center of the Pacific Ocean, and in early June 1942, it was home to 3,000 U.S. Marines who defended the airfields and other military facilities located there. Aboard his flagship, the superbattleship *Yamato*, Adm. Isoroku Yamamoto, commander in chief, Japanese combined fleet, expected the Midway operation to defeat the U.S. Navy decisively and lead to a negotiated peace. He committed almost the entire Japanese navy to the complex operation, yet he also badly divided his striking power. A diversionary force with two aircraft carriers was hundreds of miles away, steaming north to attack Dutch Harbor, Alaska, on June 5. The 1st Fleet, under Yamamoto, operated well north of the carrier strike force, organized around four carriers and approaching Midway from the southwest. The 2d Fleet, some 200 miles west of the carriers, was expected to mop up the shattered U.S. task force.

Once again, broken Japanese naval codes betrayed their intentions to the Americans and allowed Nimitz to instruct his commanders to position themselves northeast of Midway in position to ambush the enemy but away from the

At the Battle of Midway, the turning point in the war in the Pacific theater, the aircraft carrier Yorktown, *which had been damaged in an earlier sea battle, was hit by enemy fire. (U.S. Navy)*

Repeatedly bombed during the Battle of Midway, the Yorktown *burned and gradually sank.* (U.S. Navy)

flights of Japanese reconnaissance aircraft. By June 5, the Japanese were in the trap, but only the raw courage of American pilots pressing home nearly suicidal torpedo attacks made them pay for their blunder. The *Hornet*'s Torpedo Squadron 8 lost every one of its planes; a torpedo squadron from the *Enterprise* saw 10 of its 14 aircraft destroyed; and 10 of 12 planes from the *Yorktown*'s torpedo squadron went down. None of these desperate attacks damaged a Japanese warship, but they distracted the enemy from the deadly dive bombers hurling themselves against the carriers. Within minutes, 3 Japanese carriers were crippled by bombs. The fourth managed to escape and launch its planes against the *Yorktown*, which went down under repeated bomb and torpedo hits. Vengeance was swift as the surviving Japanese carrier was sunk late that afternoon.

Japanese losses were 4 carriers and 1 heavy cruiser sunk with another heavy cruiser damaged. More important, 285 Japanese planes and their elite pilots perished. The Americans had lost 1 aircraft carrier, 109 carrier aircraft, and 38 land-based planes. The strategic offensive in the Pacific shifted forever to the Americans after the victory at the Battle of Midway. Never again could the Imperial Navy regain the brief glory it enjoyed for six months after Pearl Harbor. Still, the Japanese were far from defeated. They held the local initiative in the South and Southwest Pacific, where events were already in motion to turn those obscure islands into household words.

NEW GUINEA AND THE SOLOMONS

The Imperial Army had little idea of the enormity of the navy's defeat at Midway. The Confidential War Diary entry for June 6, 1942, read: "There seems to have been a decisive surface engagement near Midway. . . . the situation does not permit optimism." Nevertheless, just three days after the Midway debacle, the army started planning to capture Port Moresby by an overland push. MacArthur and his Australian commander of Allied land forces, Gen. Sir Thomas Blamey, received intelligence warning them of Japanese intentions. Both officers thought it impossible that other than "minor forces" could move overland from Buna on New Guinea's north coastline through the uncharted jungle and the rugged Owen Stanley Mountain Range to descend on Port Moresby on the south coast.

In fact, there was little MacArthur could do to block a Japanese landing at Buna. His air force was badly worn, having suffered heavy losses of pilots and machines, and had perhaps 90 operational aircraft available. The theater's two U.S. divisions, the 32d and 41st, needed more training before being thrown into battle, and the Australian brigades had been deployed at Milne Bay, near the southern tip of New Guinea. Once ashore at Buna, Maj. Gen. Tomitaro Horii's 5,000-man South Seas detachment quickly disappeared beneath the jungle foliage as it pressed into the interior. Meanwhile, disquieting intelligence reports reaching the Allies suggested that the Japanese had designs against Milne Bay and that the enemy had constructed an airfield on Guadalcanal in the southern Solomons chain.

In early July, the JCS directed Nimitz and MacArthur to commence operations aimed at seizing the Japanese bastion at Rabaul in order to establish Allied control of the Bismarck Archipelago, to the north of New Guinea. First, the navy and marines would seize bases in the southern Solomons. Next, South Pacific forces would climb the ladder of the Solomons, while Southwest Pacific forces advanced along the northern New Guinea coastline to Lae and Salamaua. Finally, the forces would converge against

Rabaul. General MacArthur's buildup of a staging area at Milne Bay was a part of this strategy, as were Vice Admiral Ghormley's preparations in the Fiji Islands.

Guadalcanal Campaign

However, the invasion of Guadalcanal was a hurriedly thrown together affair in reaction to the known Japanese presence on the island. The 1st Marine Division landed on Guadalcanal unopposed on August 7 and quickly took possession of the Japanese airstrip, which they renamed Henderson Field after a fallen marine aviator. Nearby Tulagi Island witnessed savage ground fighting until marines extinguished the stubborn Japanese garrison. While Japan's 17th Army at Rabaul scrambled to assemble reinforcements to dispatch to the south, the Imperial Navy launched the first of six major surface engagements to challenge American naval supremacy in the South Pacific.

On the night of August 8–9, seven Japanese cruisers and one destroyer managed to slip through Allied picket ships guarding the ''Slot,'' a narrow channel that ran through the Solomons. The resulting night action, known popularly as the Battle of Savo Island, left four Allied cruisers sunk and another damaged. Japanese losses were two cruisers damaged. More important, Japanese boldness and capability convinced Vice Adm. Frank Fletcher to withdraw his warships and transports from the island. The marines were on their own.

On August 18, about 900 men of Japan's Ikki Detachment landed on Guadalcanal's north coast and moved quickly west along the shoreline toward Henderson Field. There had been no time for a reconnaissance, and no one knew how many Americans were even on the island. Col. Kiyonao Ikki insisted that the decadent Americans would flee before his Japanese warriors. Five days later, Ikki launched a night frontal attack across the Tenaru River. Charging into the combined firepower of several thousand marines, his men died in droves, 777 killed or electing suicide. The annihilation of Ikki's force sounded alarm bells in 17th Army headquarters, whose operations against New Guinea had already stretched resources thin.

The indecisive battle of the eastern Solomons played out on August 24–25. The U.S. Navy sank one Japanese light carrier and temporarily blocked ground reinforcements destined for Guadalcanal. During the fighting, however, the *Enterprise* suffered three bomb hits that put the carrier out of commission until October. The same night, Japanese naval infantry landed at Milne Bay, unaware that MacArthur had strengthened its defenses. In confused night fighting in thick jungle, often conducted in torrential downpours, Australian troops first checked the enemy advance and then drove the Japanese bluejackets back during a week of close-in, hand-to-hand fighting. Simultaneously, General Horii's overland trek toward Port Moresby was

coming undone, thwarted by a combination of tenacious Australian infantry and the physical hardships imposed by the mountainous, jungled terrain. Slowly, but steadily, the South Seas Detachment was being pushed back toward Buna.

Throughout September and October, Guadalcanal witnessed a dreadful campaign of attrition as both sides threw reinforcements into the fighting. Japanese air attacks against the island were an almost daily occurrence. At sea, the attempt to interdict each other's transports provoked a series of surface engagements. In the Battle of Cape Esperance on October 11, U.S. warships surprised a Japanese force and sank one enemy cruiser and one destroyer in the first successful night action that the U.S. Navy enjoyed against the Japanese fleet. Just two days later, two Japanese battleships shelled the marines and recently arrived army reinforcements on Guadalcanal. Enemy cruisers repeated the performance the following night. These bombardments were intended to soften up the American defenders for a major Japanese ground offensive. On October 23, the Imperial Army's 2d Division emerged from the rain and jungle and hurled itself against the defenders of Henderson Field. Marines and soldiers stopped the repeated Japanese attacks, killing more than 2,500 of the enemy.

After the Japanese army's latest failure to recapture Guadalcanal, Japan's combined fleet moved south to destroy U.S. naval forces supporting the operation. This time, however, it faced a new opponent, Vice Adm. William F. Halsey, who had relieved Admiral Ghormley as commander in chief, South Pacific, on October 18. In the resulting Battle of the Santa Cruz Islands, the Japanese had 2 carriers damaged and lost 69 planes in exchange for the carrier *Hornet*. Heavy losses of ships and planes, as well as savage ground fighting, left both sides debilitated and the Guadalcanal Campaign stalemated. It now became a race to determine which side could reinforce the island faster.

The Americans committed the 2d Marine Division and two army divisions (the 25th and the American) to the battle, while the Japanese dispatched the 38th Division from Rabaul to Guadalcanal. Three days of sea battles preceded the landing of the 38th Division. This Battle of Guadalcanal saw two Japanese battleships, four destroyers, and six transports sunk in exchange for three American light cruisers and six destroyers. Once ashore on Guadalcanal, the badly depleted 38th Division could not overcome the strengthened U.S. defenses. Although the Japanese contested the island for another month and did not completely withdraw until February 1943, the Guadalcanal Campaign was over.

Approximately 20,800 Japanese soldiers perished on Guadalcanal, most of whom were victims of starvation and disease. The Imperial Navy lost 8 major warships, plus 14

Vice Adm. William F. Halsey relieved Admiral Ghormley as commander in chief of the South Pacific Fleet in October 1942, one month before Halsey's promotion to admiral. (U.S. Navy)

destroyers and numerous transports. It wrote off about 650 land-based and 250 carrier-based naval aircraft. U.S. losses were about 6,300 battle casualties plus 24 warships of all types sunk and about 500 aircraft lost, half to operational causes. As severe as the material losses were, the United States had the industrial base that could simultaneously replace battle losses while producing hundreds of new ships and thousands of new warplanes. Japan, conversely, was hard-pressed to keep pace with its losses, and the enormous discrepancy in the means of production grew ever more pronounced throughout the remaining course of the war.

New Guinea Operations

During the fighting on Guadalcanal, General MacArthur was pressing ahead with his plans to evict the Japanese from Buna, whose airstrip he needed to cover operations against Lae. He launched this ill-starred campaign in early November, hoping to seize Buna rapidly and thereby trap the enemy units retreating from Port Moresby. Instead, his National Guard troops from the 32d Division walked into a jungle nightmare. As at Guadalcanal, the Japanese reaction to MacArthur's thrust was to speed reinforcements to the threatened area, in this case Buna. Siege warfare,

reminiscent of World War I, characterized the unimaginative campaign, in which men fought and died in unspeakable conditions. Disease ravaged the front-line troops, and resupply was exceptionally difficult. When the Americans faltered, Australian troops from two divisions pressed the vicious battle that pitted handfuls of men against one another fighting in bunkers, trenches, or spider holes. After three months, the Japanese had had enough. They had suffered 13,000 casualties, but the Americans and Australians, who carried the brunt of the fighting, had lost 8,500 men (5,698 Australian) in battle and another 27,000 to malaria. Despite the loss of Buna, the Japanese army still held a network of mutually supporting air and naval bases deployed in depth and running in two converging arcs through New Guinea and the Solomons to Rabaul.

The best that can be said about this grim campaign of attrition is that the Allies persevered and triumphed. By later American standards, it was fought on a shoestring, and even this minimum logistics support taxed MacArthur's shipping resources and supply services to the limit. Strong Japanese air and naval units contested the sea lanes off the northern New Guinea coast, threatening to cut Allied lines of communication or to reinforce threatened areas. The Japanese had been ejected from Guadalcanal and Buna, but the cost had been high not only in terms of men and equipment but in terms of time. The front line remained a thousand miles from distant Tokyo and had only inched forward despite six months of terrible fighting in primeval jungles. At that pace, the war could have dragged on for years without decisive result.

During the Buna fighting, Imperial headquarters had created the 8th Area Army on Rabaul. Its commander, Lt. Gen. Hitoshi Imamura, controlled two armies, the 17th on Guadalcanal and the Solomons and the 18th, which oversaw operations on New Guinea. By January 1943, the 18th Army was desperately trying to shuttle troop reinforcement convoys from Rabaul to New Guinea ports such as Lae and Madang in preparation for another offensive. MacArthur's aerial chief, Lt. Gen. George C. Kenney, was an aggressive and innovative airman. Under his leadership, the 5th Air Force pilots forced Japanese resupply convoys to run a gauntlet of aerial bombing and strafing. Kenney's successes prevented sufficient reinforcements from reaching Japanese ground forces fighting near Wau, and by late January, the Australians had taken the offensive.

The 18th Army and the Imperial Navy spent much of February finalizing the transport of the 51st Division from Rabaul to Lae. U.S. Navy code-breakers, however, deciphered enemy naval messages that described the convoy's route, destination, sailing time, and noon positions. With two weeks to prepare for the battle, Kenney devised new, low-level, skip-bombing tactics. From March 2–5, Kenney threw every Allied aircraft he had into a running battle

P-38 "Lightning" fighter planes were used in 1943 to shoot down the bomber carrying Admiral Yamamoto, the architect of the Japanese attack on Pearl Harbor; a P-38 was also the first airplane to land in Japan at the end of war in 1945. (U.S. Army Military History Institute)

with Convoy 81, the Japanese designation for the Lae shipment. Airmen sank eight Japanese transports and four destroyers, killing perhaps 3,000 Japanese infantrymen aboard the vessels. Although 3,900 men of the 51st Division survived the air attacks, only 1,000 oil-soaked soldiers ever reached New Guinea's shores. Henceforth, the Japanese were on the strategic defensive in New Guinea.

The destruction of the 51st Division also critically weakened the southeastern approach to Rabaul and mandated a hurried revision of Japanese joint policy. The Japanese Army-Navy Central Agreement on Southeast Asia Operations of March 25 shifted priority from the Solomons to protect the endangered New Guinea flank. To support this policy, Admiral Yamamoto launched 350 naval aircraft in a four-stage aerial blitz against Allied airdromes and harbors on Guadalcanal and New Guinea. Inexperienced Japanese pilots wildly exaggerated their efforts, claiming 28 ships sunk and 150 Allied aircraft destroyed (actual losses were 4 minor vessels and 12 aircraft). Upon receipt of a congratulatory telegram from the emperor, Yamamoto departed on a morale-raising visit to his front-line pilots.

A deciphered message betrayed his exact time of arrival in the Shortland Islands. Acting on the intelligence, American P-38 pilots intercepted and shot down the bomber carrying the diminutive admiral who had planned the attack against Pearl Harbor. His death coincided with the final massed Japanese air offensive against New Guinea.

CENTRAL PACIFIC STRATEGY

By early 1943, the Australians and Americans had blunted the Japanese advance into the South and Southwest Pacific, had seized the operational initiative from the enemy, and were slowly working their way toward the major Japanese air and naval bastion at Rabaul. The realities of Pacific geography were instrumental in shaping future American strategy. First, the enormous ocean distances in the Pacific made military operations almost completely dependent on water transportation. This fact created an insatiable demand for ships, which were in short supply because of the competing requirements in Europe for shipping to support a cross-channel attack against Germany. Second, the network of Japanese strongholds effectively blocked any Allied advance toward the Philippines. Rabaul defended the Bismarck Sea and New Guinea approach from the southwest. If Allied operations swung northeast of Rabaul, they risked flank attacks from Rabaul to the southwest and the great prewar Japanese naval base at Truk to the northwest. Such a strategy promised bitter fighting for minimal gains in restricted waters that did not allow the U.S. Navy to exploit its growing mobile carrier forces. The alternatives were a drive through the Aleutians, which was not seriously considered, or a Central Pacific advance.

That Adm. Ernest J. King advocated an advance across the Central Pacific is unsurprising because it basically resurrected the prewar Orange Plan that a generation of future naval strategists and commanders had studied in staff and war colleges. King, however, envisioned the Central Pacific drive occurring simultaneously with those in the South and Southwest Pacific. Those ongoing operations, he believed, were essential for the security of Australia and the protection of the Allied lines of communication. A two-pronged attack aimed at the Philippines would whipsaw the Japanese, who would be prevented from concentrating their forces in one area. A Central Pacific drive would also outflank Truk and would be a shorter and more direct route to the Philippines than an approach from the south. Seizing the Philippines would sever Japanese communications to the southern area and would plug the flow of oil and natural resources to the Japanese homeland. The Philippines could also serve as a springboard for Allied landings in China designed to secure a major port that, in turn, would be the entry point for a massive logistics effort to create an infrastructure in China to support aerial operations against Japan.

Obviously, this two-pronged campaign was more than a diversionary effort sublimated to the ''Germany first'' strategy of the Allies. By the end of 1943, for example, 1,878,000 American troops were engaged against Japan, versus 1,810,000 deployed against Germany. About 7,800 aircraft were allocated to the war against Japan, versus 8,800 directed at Germany; and, as might be expected from the geography, the number of U.S. Navy ships operating in the Pacific (713) far exceeded that of the Atlantic and Mediterranean theaters (515).

Indecisiveness among the Allies about the timing for a second front in Europe enabled Admiral King and the JCS to go forward with their Central Pacific drive against Japan, grudgingly approved by the CCS at Cairo in 1943. But even after this highest approval, General MacArthur, the Southwest Pacific commander, adamantly opposed a Central Pacific thrust, in large part because it detracted from his own theater's exploits. It became a question of command, and, although King favored a unified command under a naval officer, the prospects for a unified command were dim, given MacArthur's personality and the persistent rivalry between the army and the navy with which to contend. King finally gave up his dreams of navy control of Pacific operations in favor of preserving his good working relationship with the army chief of staff, Gen. George C. Marshall. Marshall supported MacArthur's position, and King, rather than risk damaging his rapport with Marshall, acquiesced to a divided command.

Recapture of the Aleutians

The Allies were now slowly pushing the Japanese back from the Aleutians to New Guinea. Weather was the enemy in the Aleutians. Perpetual cold and fog, unpredictable storms, and terrain unsuited for construction plagued each adversary's efforts to strengthen its garrisons. Given the scarcity of resources and heavy demands for shipping, equipment, and manpower, the JCS's decision to oust the Japanese from Attu and Kiska made little sense. Nevertheless, the Japanese believed that Kiska would be the first American target and were rushing reinforcements and supplies to the garrison. On Mar. 26, 1943, one such escorted convoy found itself in a long-range, running battle with a U.S. task force. The Battle of the Komandorski Islands cost each side one heavy cruiser damaged and prevented these latest Japanese reinforcements from reaching their destination.

Two months later, on May 11, the U.S. 7th Division invaded Attu Island in the Aleutian chain. After three weeks of costly fighting in an icy wasteland at places like Massacre Valley, U.S. Army troops virtually annihilated the 2,576-man Japanese garrison, taking only 29 prisoners. Under heavy attack in the Southwest Pacific, Tokyo saw no profit in further operations in the Aleutians. As the Allies mounted a major invasion against Kiska, in late July, the Imperial navy skillfully extracted the garrison of more than 5,100 under cover of thick fog. Unaware of the evacuation, about 35,000 American and Canadian troops landed on abandoned Kiska on August 15. It was an appropriate conclusion to an Aleutian strategy that seemed more based on determination to regain U.S. territory than on any military advantage.

SOUTH AND SOUTHWEST PACIFIC OPERATIONS

The Allied counteroffensive in the South and Southwest Pacific was gaining momentum. MacArthur's new timetable for the liberation of the Philippines, code-named Reno, was the basis for his operations from February 1943 through August 1944. The plan envisoned leapfrogging past Japanese strongpoints and employing paratroopers to seize key bases en route to Mindanao in the southern Philippines.

But the so-called Bismarck Barrier—that is, New Britain and its air and naval bases at Rabaul in combination with a series of Japanese airfields along the north coast of New Guinea—blocked his path.

The JCS's directive of Mar. 28, 1943, described Southwest Pacific objectives as a line running across the Dampier Straits from Finschhafen, New Guinea, to western New Britain, the largest island in the Bismarck Archipelago. While MacArthur drove for his goal, the U.S. sailors, marines, and soldiers would clear the Solomons to southern Bougainville Island. This was the basis for Operation Cartwheel, the plan to encircle rather than attack Rabaul. Cartwheel opened on the night of June 29–30 when a battalion-size task force struck at Nassau Bay, New Guinea, while Admiral Halsey's forces invaded New Georgia in the Solomon Islands. Nassau Bay was a minor affair, but it did secure a valuable staging area for MacArthur's next jump, toward Lae. New Georgia, however, proved a much more bitter contest.

Summer–Fall 1943

The objective on New Georgia was the Japanese airfield at Munda, which was defended by about 5,000 soldiers from Japan's 6th and 38th divisions. Fighting in the foul swamps or hilly jungle drained the energy and spirit of the U.S. 43d Infantry Division, which suffered numerous psychiatric casualties. Marines had landed north of the army troops to prevent Japanese reinforcements from reaching the island. The Japanese infantry bypassed the marine roadblock and made its way to the Munda perimeter. By mid-July, the 43d's slow progress convinced U.S. commanders to throw two more army divisions, the 25th and 39th, into the fight. With these reinforcements and extensive use of flame-throwers, the attackers finally broke Munda's defenses, although the surviving Japanese were able to withdraw by sea successfully in early August. The prolonged campaign cost 5,000 American casualties, including 1,000 killed.

As the fighting on New Georgia ground on, an Allied air and amphibious assault isolated Lae in early September. Kenney's pilots had destroyed most of the Japanese air force on the ground at Wewak in surprise raids during mid-August. The cut-off Lae garrison abandoned its positions but had to detour into the rugged mountains to make good its escape. MacArthur and Blamey quickly pushed their advantage by landing farther north on the coast at Finschhafen on September 22. Australian infantrymen met stubborn Japanese resistance. In two months of grueling ground combat, the Australians killed 5,500 Japanese.

When Allied troops captured the jungle-infested island of Bougainville in the Solomon Islands, they were within flying distance of the main Japanese naval base at Rabaul. (U.S. Office of War Information)

While the Australians carried the fighting, Lt. Gen. Walter Krueger was training his growing number of U.S. Army divisions to fight as amphibious task forces. MacArthur appointed Krueger the commander of Alamo Force, an independent operational command, but in reality almost identical to the Southwest Pacific's newly created U.S. 6th Army. MacArthur now had under his control five American divisions, three regimental combat teams (formed by attaching a field artillery battalion to the 503d parachute infantry, 112th cavalry, and 158th infantry regiments), three engineer special brigades, and five Australian divisions. Three more U.S. Army divisions were on the way. There were about 1,000 combat aircraft at his command. His naval force, the U.S. 7th Fleet, had few warships compared to the armadas being assembled for the Central Pacific drive, but it had swelled with transports, cargo vessels, and landing craft. By melding these resources, MacArthur was on the verge of his greatest triumph.

Events continued apace in the northern Solomons. U.S. Army troops bypassed the enemy stronghold on Kolombangara to seize undefended Vella Lavella in mid-August. With Vella Lavella as an advance airbase, New Zealand and American troops took the Treasury Islands in late October and marine raiders wreaked devastation on Choiseul. On November 1, U.S. Marines landed on Bougainville, largest of the Solomon Islands and only 170 miles from Rabaul. From that distance, Allied fighters could escort heavy bombers all the way to the huge Japanese naval base and render it indefensible. Indeed, land-based and carrier air attacks against Rabaul in early November inflicted great damage.

Although 50,000 Japanese garrisoned Bougainville, the absence of roads and the presence of thick jungle vegetation and numerous swamps made overland movement exceedingly difficult. Caught out of position by the 3d Marine Division's landing at Empress Augusta Bay, it took the Japanese four months to move a sizable force along the jungle tracks to the bay. By that time, the Americans, steadily reinforcing by sea, outnumbered the attackers, whom they overwhelmed.

CENTRAL PACIFIC OPERATIONS

As important as the successes in the South and Southwest Pacific were, they paled before the U.S. naval juggernaut appearing in the Central Pacific. The Central Pacific drive commenced in November 1943 with the assault on the Gilbert Islands. Joint planners agreed that the first operation could not fail, so they demanded amphibiously trained, battle-tested "shock troops"—in other words, U.S. Marines—for the attack. The severity of the land battle on the Gilberts' Tarawa eclipsed anything seen to date in the Pacific. In just 72 hours, Japanese guns killed or wounded

The battle for Tarawa in the Gilbert Islands proved to be one of the bloodiest of World War II; here, U.S. marines direct flamethrowers at Japanese bunkers. (U.S. Marine Corps)

more than 3,300 men of the 2d Marine Division. They paid with 4,690 killed, virtually every Japanese member of the naval landing force.

As terrible as Tarawa proved, it might have been worse had the Japanese not diverted proposed reinforcements from the Gilberts to Rabaul to stem the South Pacific advance. Bypassing Tarawa was not possible because its airfield and the other Gilbert Islands were needed as staging and support bases for the planned jump into the Marshall Islands to the north, set for February 1944. Henceforth, the Central Pacific thrust was characterized by amphibious assault forces venturing far beyond the range of land-based air cover, and thereby exposing themselves to Japanese air and surface attack, to seize strongly held atolls too small for maneuver or mass assault. Swiftness was the key to such operations, as U.S. air and naval forces had to establish local superiority and even take on the Japanese combined fleet if it ventured into the contested area.

Mainland Asia Conditions

One objective of the Central Pacific drive was to land on the Chinese coast and establish airfields from which to bomb Japan into submission. As long as this condition held, the China-Burma-India theater received attention. Despite the presence of one of its great World War II commanders, Lieutenant General Slim, the British high command was reluctant to commit itself to any sustained operations against the Japanese in Burma. British strategy aimed at the retaking of Rangoon and Singapore from the sea. But the strategic goal of the U.S. commander in the theater, Major General Stilwell, lay in opening a route to China through northern Burma. The objectives were not only irreconcilable but also geographically divergent. As

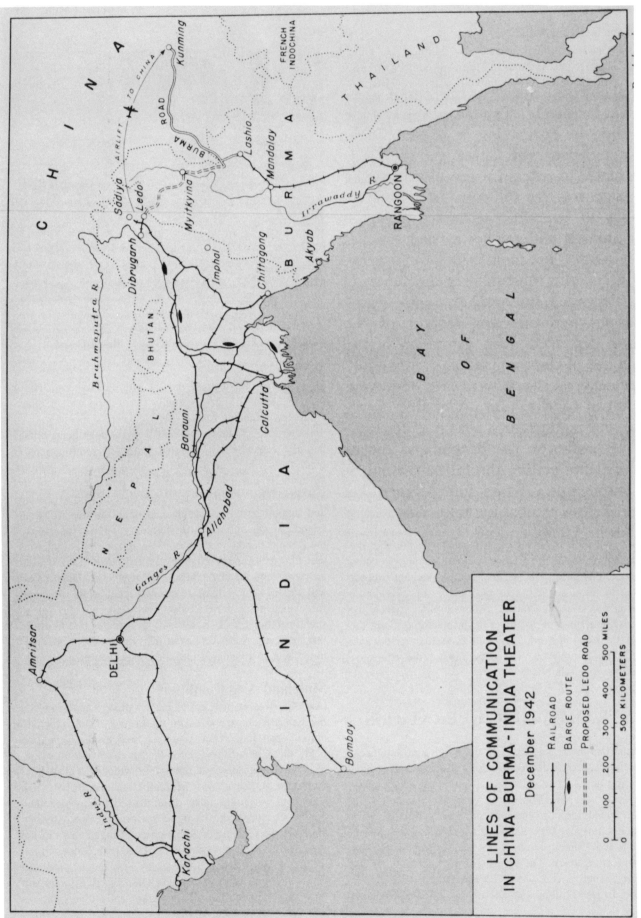

LINES OF COMMUNICATION
IN CHINA-BURMA-INDIA THEATER
December 1942

RAILROAD		
BARGE ROUTE		
PROPOSED LEDO ROAD		

0	100	200	300	400	500 MILES
0			500 KILOMETERS		

From The Sinews of War: Army Logistics 1775–1953 (Office of the Chief of Military History, U.S. Army, 1966) Map 22

U.S. tanks make their way along the Burma-Ledo Road, a major supply route from Ledo, India, across northern Burma, to Kunming, China. (U.S. Army Military History Institute)

long as neither the British nor the Americans tried to execute such operations, the absence of any Allied strategy for Burma could be papered over.

The Cairo Conference of November 1943 endorsed this strategy by sanctioning the plan that the major Allied effort against Japan in Asia would consist of a two-pronged attack on Japan through the Central Pacific and along the New Guinea-Philippines axis. This strategy reduced Slim's efforts to diversionary ones, and even these were failures, such as the ill-considered Arakan offensives of 1943. Brig. Orde Wingate's daring, and some thought foolhardy, Chindit operations deep behind Japanese lines in February and April 1943 were about the only sign of British initiative in Burma. Wingate's newfound fame elevated this brooding mystic to the status of jungle fighter guru and enabled him to form what amounted to his own private army.

Aside from Slim, few were willing to learn from their mistakes. Stilwell's abrasive personality did much to sour relations. He was as uncritical in his admiration of the Chinese fighting man as he was outspoken in his contempt for Chiang Kai-shek. To round it off, Stilwell was a noted Anglophobe who loudly proclaimed British incompetence in Asia to anyone willing to listen. Since his venom contained large doses of truth, Stilwell also had difficulty with the newly appointed commander of Southeast Asia Command, Lord Louis Mountbatten, whom he served as deputy. Mountbatten dismissed Chiang's claim to be a full-fledged ally and with it the strategic concept of Allied positions in China being used to threaten the Japanese flank or home islands. British strategy in 1943 pointed south to Rangoon and Malaya to clear those colonies from the grip of the Japanese. After all, Churchill himself had announced that he had not become prime minister to oversee the dismemberment of the British empire. Still, since Stilwell's ambitions pointed north along the Ledo Road to resupply

China and equip its fighting men to crush the Japanese, friction between the British and the Americans was inevitable. Perhaps it was so acrimonious in 1942–43 because they did little else but argue about objectives. Slim's moment still lay in the future.

Allied Successes: Early 1944

By early 1944, the Allies had accelerated the tempo of their advance along the New Guinea and the Central Pacific axes. In February, Admiral Nimitz moved a mighty task force that leaped more than 1,000 miles from the Gilberts into the eastern and central Marshall Islands and quickly overpowered Japanese defenders on Kwajalein. Because of the feebleness of enemy defenses, Nimitz advanced his timetable by two and a half months to capture Eniwetok Atoll in the western Marshalls. Concurrently, massive carrier air strikes revealed the weakness of the supposedly impregnable Japanese naval base at Truk, to the west, in the central Caroline Islands. Planning commenced for operations to bypass the hollow fortress of Truk.

Meantime, General MacArthur had made substantial but not as spectacular gains. American army and marine forces had landed on southern New Britain in late December 1943. On the north coast of New Guinea, MacArthur then leapfrogged his 126th Infantry Regiment to Saidor to isolate Japanese fighting near Finschhafen and Sio in early January 1944. With the Japanese in retreat, an Australian patrol discovered a trunk containing the Imperial Army's code books. This find enabled U.S. Army code-breakers to read Japanese army messages at a critical juncture in the New Guinea Campaign and allowed MacArthur the luxury of recasting his operations with extensive knowledge of his opponent's condition.

He accelerated his effort by two months when, on Feb. 29, 1944, he dispatched units of the 1st Cavalry Division to Los Negros in the Admiralty Islands, about 360 miles west of Rabaul. Caught off guard, the Japanese garrison fought viciously for five days but was wiped out. Next, MacArthur proposed to the JCS that he make an unprecedented 400-mile leap along the New Guinea coastline to attack the major Japanese base at Hollandia. The operation developed into an enormous undertaking requiring 217 ships to transport 80,000 troops, equipment, and supplies 1,000 miles to make three separate amphibious landings deep behind Japanese lines. Once again, 5th Air Force pilots destroyed Japanese air power on the ground, paving the way for the invasions. On April 22, the 24th and 41st divisions waded ashore at Hollandia, while the 163d Regimental Combat Team took control of Aitape, about 100 miles to the east of Hollandia. The unopposed landings isolated 60,000 Japanese troops in eastern New Guinea and rendered ineffective another 90,000 around Rabaul. It was MacArthur's single greatest victory of the Pacific war

Allied "para-bombs" are dropped on the Japanese airfield at Rabaul; by the spring of 1944, Rabaul was no longer effective as a major Japanese air and naval base. (U.S. Army Military History Institute: H. U. Milne Collection)

and one that he exploited fully in both operational and strategic terms.

Japanese Reactions

On the defensive since August 1942, Japan's Pacific strategy underwent several revisions, notably pulling back to prepared positions or strengthening new ones, but not attempting to recover reconquered territory. Losses on the Pacific fronts were crippling, but Japan was far from defeated. Japanese military planners in September 1943 envisioned the creation of an invincible Inner Defensive Zone that reached from the Kuril and Ogasawara islands in the northern and western Pacific to western New Guinea and then southwest to Sumatra and Burma. Behind this strategic barrier, the Japanese army would marshal its air and sea forces to beat back any future Allied advances. Japanese planners expected to concentrate vast numbers of newly manufactured aircraft in the Pacific to wrest control of the air, and thus of the sea, from the Americans. In fact, Japanese industrial capacity could not produce the 55,000 aircraft the military chieftains demanded, and actual production barely sufficed to keep pace with aircraft losses. For its part, the Imperial Navy would seek the opportune moment for a decisive fleet engagement that would turn the fortunes of war in their favor.

Clearly, the Japanese recognized that they were on the strategic and operational defensive, and their main aim became the protection of the lines of communication between the empire and resource-rich southeast Asia. Aside from a network of supporting bases, the Japanese hurried to adopt antisubmarine warfare techniques that they heretofore had ignored. Naval doctrine presumed that a decisive fleet engagement would decide the course of the war, and not much attention had been given to convoy and antisubmarine tactics. Now U.S. submarines—notably assisted by deciphered Japanese army and navy messages, new wolf-pack tactics, and improved torpedoes—tore at the heart of the Japanese merchant marine. This undersea interdiction campaign threatened the economic isolation of Japan and limited or hindered the redeployment of Japanese ground forces from Asia to the Pacific. It ultimately sank most of the Japanese merchant fleet.

Burma Campaign

Imperial headquarters refused to abandon the idea of driving to India or knocking China out of the war. If either, or better both, plans succeeded, Japan's military might in those theaters could be shifted to its crumbling Pacific front. Since the autumn of 1942, Tokyo had talked about an advance to India, but nothing concrete had materialized because Japan aimed to secure a line in Burma east of the Chin Hills bordering India and the Aykab region on the Bay of Bengal, thereby protecting Rangoon to the south and simultaneously blockading China to the north. Wingate's daring penetrations, however, dramatically affected Lt. Gen. Renya Mutaguchi, commander of the Japanese 15th Army. Mutaguchi believed that if Wingate could live in the jungle, so could the Japanese and their Indian National Army allies. His controversial plan engendered heated debate in high army circles, but on Jan. 7, 1944, Imperial headquarters ordered an advance into India.

Mutaguchi's belief in the Japanese spirit convinced him that willpower could overcome the rugged jungle terrain of northeastern Burma. On the slenderest of logistics lines, he marched his army into the rain forests, across rivers, and over two mountain ranges separating Burma from India. Enduring incredible hardships, the 15th Army's 85,000 Japanese and Indians pushed on and in April 1944 reached the Indian frontier, where they opened a three-month siege of Imphal and Kohima, 80 miles to the north, under appalling conditions.

Here, Slim displayed the resourcefulness of a great commander. He maintained the combat effectiveness of his British and Indian units through extensive aerial resupply. Airlifting supplies enabled his units to fight encircled from "hedgehog" defenses, the so-called administrative-box tactic. To isolate the British formations as they had in 1942 now required that the Japanese own the air above the battleground. It was beyond them. Japanese infantrymen literally beat themselves to death forcing attack after attack against a position without flanks. Slim first smashed the Japanese diversionary attack in the Arakan and next defeated them at Imphal-Kohima. By July, Tokyo had had enough and called a halt to Mutaguchi's quest. Overall, 60,000 Japanese troops perished in the ill-conceived adventure. While this was transpiring, Stilwell was pushing north

Chinese general Chiang Kai-shek fought the Japanese half-heartedly during World War II; he believed that the real threat to China was the Communists. (Library of Congress)

on Myitkyina, and Wingate's columns, minus their leader killed in a plane crash, were fighting behind Japanese lines on missions of their own. Little strategic control of the operations existed. Their cumulative effects and the startling Japanese losses, however, left other points in Burma weakly defended and susceptible to Slim's planned counteroffensive.

China Campaign

Meantime, the Imperial Army had reopened large-scale campaigning in China. In April 1944, Japan's "Ichi-go" operation began. The massive 15-division offensive stretched the length of China and had several related aims. The capture of Chinese airbases in southwest China would prevent their use as B-29 bases for attacks against Japan. Simultaneously, the operation would strengthen the region against British or American counterattacks originating from Burma. Ichi-go would also destroy the Chinese field army and clear a railway route traversing the Chinese mainland. The airfields were captured, but only after heavy fighting. Chiang's refusal to reinforce his besieged commander at

Henyang, in south-central China, soured foreign observers, who took it as proof that Chiang had no desire to fight the Japanese. In a sense, they were right. Chiang judged the Japanese to be an external wound that could be healed, while he considered the Chinese Communists a cancer that had to be eliminated. Thus, Chiang's best Kuomintang troops were withheld from combat against the Japanese and kept in readiness for the showdown with Mao Zedong's Communist armies that Chiang knew awaited.

Stilwell could neither abide nor understand Chiang's reluctance to fight the common opponent, and his denunciations of the Chinese leader grew more outspoken. Yet China's participation in the war far outweighed Stilwell's pungent criticisms, and in October 1944, President Roosevelt recalled his acerbic general. The China-Burma-India theater was then divided into two parts: India-Burma and China. By the time Lt. Gen. Albert C. Wedemeyer arrived in China, Ichi-go had run its course, allowing the Japanese to open an overland route that ran from Saigon, French Indochina, to the port of Pusan, Korea. The overland line of communication helped somewhat to relieve the incessant toll exacted by Allied submarines on Japanese shipping. A secure supply route was critical because the dual offensives in the Central and Southwest Pacific were threatening not only Japan's maritime lifelines but the sacred home islands themselves.

ISLAND FIGHTING

MacArthur had allowed his bewildered opponents in New Guinea no respite. During mid-May 1944, U.S. Army task forces secured a lodgment on the New Guinea coast adjacent to Wake Island and then overwhelmed the tiny island's 600 defenders in two days of close combat. Fighting on New Guinea's mainland during the next month claimed nearly 2,300 American and 4,000 Japanese battle casualties, but it did secure staging areas for MacArthur's future invasions. On May 27, units of the 41st Division stormed ashore at Biak, where Japanese resistance proved much tougher than anticipated. Fighting to the last man from coral caves on the equatorial island, the Japanese threatened not only MacArthur's timetable to return to the Philippines but also the transport fleet that supported Krueger's soldiers fighting on Biak.

Adm. Soemu Toyoda, commander in chief of the Japanese combined fleet, saw the 7th Fleet off Biak as an overexposed and tempting target. Determined to hold Biak, whose airfields the Japanese needed in order to execute Operation "A," a combined air and sea strike against the Americans, Toyoda ordered Operation Kon. It was a combination effort to reinforce Biak and, if possible, to force the American fleet into a decisive engagement. Australian and American warships thwarted the first two Kon efforts, and the third, to be led by the superbattleships *Yamato* and *Musashi,* was canceled when Imperial headquarters received word of an American fleet approaching the Marianas.

Marianas Campaign

Saipan, Tinian, and Guam were the three Mariana island targets of Nimitz's latest offensive. Located about 1,000 miles west of Eniwetok, the islands were only 1,200 miles from Japan's home islands, which placed the homeland within range of the newly available, but mechanically plagued, B-29 very-long-range bombers. When U.S. marines invaded Saipan on June 15, the 1st Mobile Fleet sortied through the Philippines toward the Marianas in Operation A. Vice Adm. Jisaburo Ozawa expected that combined land-based air attacks from Guam, Yap, and Rota and carrier aircraft strikes launched from his fleet would cripple the American invasion armada. Ozawa's massed carrier and land-based air attacks, flown by inexperienced Japanese pilots, were cut to ribbons by veteran American fliers. About 65 percent of the approximately 600 Japanese planes were lost in the so-called Marianas Turkey Shoot. Next, the Americans turned on the enemy carriers. When the Battle of the Philippine Sea ended, 3 Japanese carriers had been sunk and 4 damaged. American losses amounted to 2 carriers, 2 battleships, and 1 cruiser damaged, plus 117 planes lost, most of whose pilots were recovered.

On Saipan, the bloody battle continued for three terrible weeks as more than 26,000 soldiers and 15,000 sailors of the emperor died in battle. There were nearly 15,000 U.S. casualties. For the first time in the Pacific war, U.S. marines and soldiers encountered large numbers of Japanese civilians. About 5,000 civilians were killed or committed suicide during the fighting, creating the specter of a nation determined to die before surrender. Marines invaded Guam on July 21 and secured the island within three weeks. Again, the cost was high; American casualties exceeded 7,000, and Japanese losses were nearly three times as high. Tinian was attacked on July 24 and fell after a week of fighting. Marines suffered nearly 2,000 battle casualties as they eradicated the 15,000-man garrison. Another 3,500 Japanese civilians added to the carnage by committing suicide. The Marianas were in the hands of the Americans, but at a high price in blood and matériel.

Victory in New Guinea

During the Marianas fighting, MacArthur kept unrelenting pressure on the Japanese in western New Guinea. Unable to gain control of Biak's airdromes quickly, he ordered the 158th Regimental Combat Team to seize Noemfoor Island, about 60 miles west of Biak. Based on erroneous intelligence, General Krueger ordered the 503d Parachute Infantry Regiment to reinforce the 158th on the island. As

it developed, reinforcements were unnecessary, but 128 paratroopers were injured in the jump, more than were lost during the fighting. Noemfoor's airfield provided fighter air support against Biak and the impending Sansapor operation set for early August.

A major threat remained to MacArthur's seaborne blitzkrieg along New Guinea's north coast. After the Japanese 18th Army's 60,000 men had been bypassed during the Allied landings at Hollandia and Aitape, the isolated Japanese turned west in an attempt to break the encirclement. Following a two-month trek through the New Guinea jungles on meager rations and under constant Allied air attacks, about 50,000 Japanese troops had assembled east of the Driniumor River. Their plan was to break through the weak U.S. Army covering force along the river and then drive toward Aitape, about 20 miles farther west.

Numerous deciphered Japanese army messages spelled out their order of battle, plan of attack, and even the exact date of the offensive. U.S soldiers along the river warned of an impending attack. Nonetheless, for a variety of reasons, both MacArthur's intelligence officer and the IX Corps' commander discounted such reports. When 20,000 Japanese burst across the Driniumor on the night of July 10–11, 1944, they achieved operational surprise and precipitated a month-long struggle in the New Guinea jungle. In the largest land battle of the campaign, 10,000 Imperial soldiers perished to inflict 3,000 American casualties, 440 of them killed. The defeat left the 18th Army trapped between the Americans in the west and the Australians moving from the east. In mid-December, the Australians began a methodical drive toward Wewak, which finally fell on May 10, 1945. Australian losses were 451 killed, 1,163 wounded, and 3 missing. Another 7,000 Japanese died, while perhaps 13,000 surrendered in eastern New Guinea in September 1945.

With the fighting along the Driniumor on the wane, MacArthur's final assault landing on New Guinea shores took place at Sansapor, a weak point between two known Japanese strongholds on the Vogelkop Peninsula. Rather than fight on the enemy's terms, MacArthur employed his forces' well-tested amphibious capabilities to seize Sansapor. Its two airfields supported the subsequent invasion of Morotai, Halmaheras.

The casualty returns from New Guinea bring the campaign into stark relief. As many as 125,000 Japanese soldiers never returned from New Guinea, while another 50,000 were isolated and left to their own devices until the war ended. It was not a cheap victory. More than 1,300 5th Air Force planes were lost, and 4,000 American airmen were listed as casualties. Another 2,000 Australian aircrew were lost. In the first 20 months of the campaign, the ground forces endured 24,000 battle casualties, about 17,000 (or 70 percent) being Australian. Including the Hollandia landing, Allied losses were 9,500 battle casualties, mostly American, to leap 1,500 miles in just 100 days.

Command Decisions

MacArthur's series of amphibious hooks from April through early August 1944 had neutralized Japanese forces on New Guinea and broken the southwest flank of Japan's so-called invincible defense zone. Nimitz's massive 1,000-mile thrust from the Marshalls to the Marianas in June and July had isolated Truk and pierced the core of Japan's defensive zone. These successes encouraged Washington planners to advance the timetable for the Pacific campaign. This could be accomplished by either advancing target dates for currently scheduled operations or bypassing previously selected objectives. Because deciphered Japanese army messages had made known the enemy buildup along the southern approaches to the Philippines, the Joint Chiefs, especially Admiral King, were predisposed to bypass the Philippines and strike directly at Formosa.

Such a strategic course of action was anathema to MacArthur. He revised his own timetable to accelerate his return to the Philippines. MacArthur personally took his proposals to Hawaii, where, from July 26 to 29, he and Nimitz described for President Roosevelt the future course of the Pacific war. Despite the high drama and MacArthur's eloquent argument that the United States had a moral obligation to liberate the Philippines, Roosevelt made no decision about Formosa versus Luzon. The argument raged back and forth throughout the summer of 1944 as the JCS preferred vacillation to decision. Admiral Halsey, in effect, made the decision for them.

In September 1944, Halsey's fast carriers launched a series of raids on Japanese bases in the Philippines. So weak was the Japanese reaction that Halsey recommended an immediate invasion of the central Philippines. Although strategic intelligence revealed clearly that the Japanese were strengthening, not withdrawing, from the islands, Nimitz was won over. MacArthur had been convinced all along, and on September 15, the JCS ordered the date for the invasion of the Philippine island of Leyte be accelerated to October 20. Ironically, on September 15, MacArthur was incommunicado aboard his flagship *Nashville,* overseeing the 31st Division's assault on Morotai in the Halmaheras. His staff, however, quickly signaled their acquiescence to the advanced date for a landing on Leyte.

The same day, Nimitz sent the 1st Marine Division against Peleliu in the southern Palau Islands, southwest of the Marianas. The Palaus, it is true, served as the major transshipment point for Japanese troops moving into the South and Central Pacific. Yet, the islands' value was diminishing because the seizure of the central Philippines would isolate them from further reinforcements. Japan's 14th Division resisted so ferociously that 5,044 U.S. marines and 279 U.S. soldiers fell in the bloody, month-long struggle for the rugged lump of coral that in retrospect was unnecessary as a support base for the Leyte operation.

The decision to invade Leyte, in the mid-Philippines, had not settled the question of Luzon, the northernmost of the major Philippine islands. Nimitz still favored an invasion of Formosa, north of Luzon and therefore closer to Japan, once Leyte was secured. By this time, however, the extended range of the new B-29 Superfortress made Formosa less attractive as a major airbase complex. Luzon would serve as well. Furthermore, logistics difficulties involved in any assault on Formosa grew more complex with each passing day. On October 3, the JCS announced that Luzon would be taken and Formosa bypassed. Technology had overcome the initial strategic requirement for airbases in China and with it the need for a Chinese port. After Luzon, the Allies could jump directly to Okinawa, which would serve as one of the major staging bases for the invasion of the main islands of Japan.

The loss of Saipan in mid-July had split Japan's strategic inner defensive perimeter and opened the way for an Allied thrust across the Central Pacific toward the Philippines. It thus threatened to cut off Tokyo from its resource-rich Southeast Asian conquests. It was the proximate cause of the downfall of Prime Minister Gen. Hideki Tojo's cabinet. Finally, the breach in the Marianas spurred Imperial general headquarters to develop the "Sho" (Victory) operation on July 21, 1944. There were four Sho variations. Sho 1 was the plan to defend the Philippines; Sho 2, the defense of Formosa; Sho 3, southern and central Japan; and Sho 4, Hokkaido and the Kurile Islands. Wherever the enemy struck in these areas, the full might of Japanese air, ground, and naval forces would be hurled against it. At that time, Tokyo and the Southern Army foresaw Luzon as the site of the decisive ground battle and were hurrying divisions from Manchuria to the Philippines. The U.S. Army's landings on Leyte shifted the scene of Sho to Leyte Gulf in the central Philippines.

PHILIPPINE CAMPAIGN

Leyte became the focal point where MacArthur's Southwest Pacific and Nimitz's Central Pacific forces converged in a mighty assault that capped a two-and-a-half-year advance across the Pacific. For Japan, the Philippines would probably offer the last chance for either a decisive naval or ground engagement against the Allies.

Naval Battle for Leyte

After their assault landings on Leyte, U.S. troops moved swiftly inland against little enemy opposition because the first part of the threefold Sho 1 for defense of the Philippines involved directing the combined fleet against the

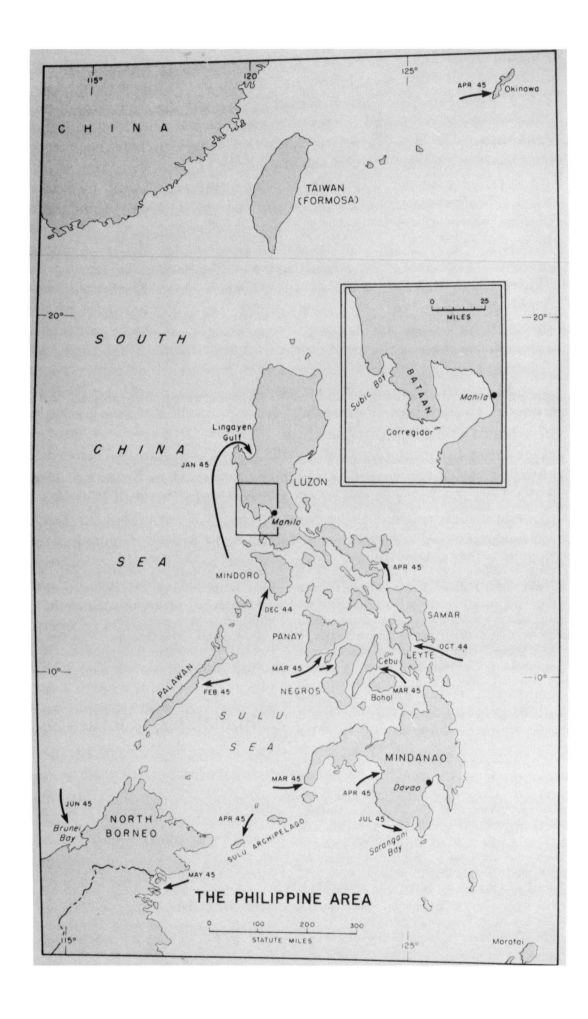

THE PHILIPPINE AREA

American naval forces. Three Japanese fleets were converging on Leyte by October 23. U.S. submarines sighted the 1st Diversion Attack Force (2d Fleet), led by Vice Adm. Takeo Kurita, near Mindoro. The locations of the Japanese 3d Fleet's carrier striking force remained unknown, although naval intelligence believed it was at sea and proceeding to the Philippines.

Kurita's force split into two battle groups: the Central Force, commanded by Kurita, and the Southern Force, skippered by Vice Adm. Shoji Nishimura. U.S. picket submarines spotted the Central Force in the early morning hours of October 24 and located Nishimura's smaller fleet around noon that day. Amply forewarned by these sightings, Vice Adm. Thomas C. Kinkaid positioned his battleships and torpedo-carrying ships to block the entrance to the Surigao Strait, through which the Japanese Southern Force would have to pass. In the early morning of October 25, the waiting Americans ambushed Nishimura's fleet, sinking or seriously damaging virtually every one of his ships. At the same time, covered by darkness, Kurita steered his fleet toward the San Bernardino Strait, which opened into Leyte Gulf.

Off to the northeast, Admiral Ozawa's carrier force was doing its best to lure Halsey's fleet away from the vital strait. Once U.S. pilots spotted the Japanese carriers, Halsey went after the lure and steered north to attack Ozawa. With Halsey gone, Kurita steamed toward Leyte Gulf to confront the U.S. 7th Fleet's slow and vulnerable escort carrier groups, the only U.S. warships in his way. If Kurita could break through the weak American force, which given his superior firepower and speed seemed likely, he could then smash MacArthur's fragile transports anchored off Leyte and isolate Krueger's Alamo Force on the island. Yet, for reasons never satisfactorily explained, after two and a half hours of fighting, Kurita broke off the engagement and withdrew. The Battle of Leyte Gulf was over and the Imperial Navy's bold gamble lost.

Japanese losses amounted to 4 carriers, 3 battleships, 6 heavy and 4 light cruisers, 11 destroyers, and 1 submarine sunk. About 500 planes were lost and some 10,500 sailors and airmen were killed. U.S. losses amounted to 1 light and 2 escort carriers, 2 destroyers, 1 destroyer escort, and more than 200 aircraft. About 2,800 Americans were killed and another 1,000 wounded. The Japanese reacted to the disaster that befell their naval surface units in the October 24–25 battle by intensifying their air and ground efforts to destroy the U.S. invaders.

Land Battle for Leyte
Massed Japanese air attacks struck Kenney's hastily constructed airfields on Leyte, as well as shipping offshore. A new Japanese weapon, the suicide plane, or kamikaze, first appeared in the skies above Leyte. In Manila, the recently appointed commander of army forces in the islands, General Yamashita, wanted to fight the main ground action on Luzon. Operating on shorter lines of communication and with more room to maneuver, Yamashita believed that he could conduct a skillful defense. Imperial headquarters thought otherwise and ordered him to reinforce Leyte immediately. By late October, the 1st Infantry Division, an elite unit from Manchuria, was fighting for control of a series of ridges along Leyte's mountainous central spine. Some of the bloodiest engagements occurred along "Breakneck Ridge" as three American divisions slowly ground down the 1st Division. Altogether, Yamashita threw more than five divisions into the desperate battle. Convoy interdiction efforts by American carrier and land-based aircraft as well as warships inflicted heavy losses en route. Six U.S. Army divisions were needed to crush Japanese resistance. The determination of Imperial headquarters to win on Leyte had destroyed more than five Japanese divisions and cost more than 70,000 lives. Leyte became a graveyard of Japanese hopes. The great Allied victory severed Japan's maritime lifeline to resource-rich Southeast Asia at proportionately low cost: 15,500 army and 2,500 naval battle casualties. The Japanese massive effort had delayed MacArthur's schedule to return to Luzon by just two weeks.

Luzon Campaign
On December 15, toward the end of Leyte's heaviest fighting, the Southwest Pacific commander invaded the island of Mindoro, east of central Luzon, to seize its airdromes to support his Luzon operation. This leap of about 300 miles northwest from Leyte gave Kenney's airmen staging fields within easy striking distance of Manila and other key Luzon targets. Mindoro was lightly defended, but the Allied invasion convoy had to run a fearsome gauntlet of kamikaze attacks that heavily damaged the *Nashville*, two destroyers, and several minor auxiliary ships. Repeated kamikaze attacks on Allied shipping at Mindoro continued into early January and destroyed or damaged several transports, minor warships, and auxiliaries such as oilers, minesweepers, and tenders. On the day after Christmas, six Japanese destroyers and two cruisers lunged at the Allied landing area off Mindoro but found only four Allied transports anchored there. After conducting gunfire and torpedo attacks that left one Liberty ship on fire, the Japanese withdrew rapidly northward. The action was notable as the last time that major surface units of the Japanese fleet interfered with Allied shore operations in the Philippines.

From ROTCM 145–20: American Military History: 1607–1958 (Washington: HQDA, July 1959), Map 43

In 1945, U.S. paratroops of the 503d Parachute Infantry land on the island of Corregidor, where U.S. and Philippine forces had been defeated in 1942. (U.S. Army Military History Institute)

The Mindoro landings set the stage for an attack against Luzon. During the invasion fleet's five-day approach to Luzon, kamikazes pounded the convoy, sinking 3 U.S. ships and damaging another 27. Despite the losses, on Jan. 9, 1945, four Army divisions and one separate regimental combat team stormed ashore in Lingayen Gulf, the northern terminus of Luzon's Central Plain, about 100 miles north of Manila. Yamashita had divided his forces into three large concentrations: Shimbu Group in the rugged northeastern mountains, Kembu Group around the major airbase complex at Clark Field on the route to Manila, and Shobu Group just south of the capital city. The defeat on Leyte, however, had so weakened Yamashita that he could fight little more than a forlorn defensive action. General Krueger's methodical advance southward toward Manila did not suit MacArthur, who prodded the 6th Army commander to move faster.

The main U.S. advance soon gained momentum. By the end of January, Kembu Group was driven from Clark Field and left isolated in the mountains to the east. Meantime, on January 29, the U.S. XI Corps landed on Luzon's west coast, north of the Bataan Peninsula. Two days later, the 11th Airborne Division and units of the 24th Infantry Division went ashore south of Manila to form one arm of the pincer movement closing in on the city. Still, the Japanese soldiers and sailors displayed the stubborn resistance that was their intimidating trademark in the Pacific war. Their fanatical defense of Manila left that great city a smoldering ruin. Japanese troops slaughtered thousands of Filipino civilians and torched much of the city.

Three American divisions had to destroy the enemy in Manila in house-to-house fighting that lasted into early March. During this fighting, XI Corps cleared the Bataan Peninsula, and a combined airborne and amphibious assault

wrested control of Corregidor from the Japanese. Fighting continued against the Shimbu Group east of Manila until June 1945, while in northern Luzon, Yamashita held out until the war ended.

Luzon was the greatest ground campaign fought by the United States in the Pacific war. Between Jan. 9 and Aug. 15, 1945, 10 Army divisions and 3 independent regimental combat teams suffered a total of 44,253 battle and 93,400 nonbattle casualties as they relentlessly destroyed 7 Japanese divisions, 2 independent brigades, and numerous combat support units. As many as 200,000 of the estimated 287,000 Japanese defending Luzon perished.

Last Operations

Despite the prolonged, heavy fighting on Luzon, MacArthur reassigned three divisions from 6th Army to 8th Army, which began operations in late February to liberate the rest of the central and southern Philippines from Japanese occupation. The decision drained much-needed units from the Luzon fight and delayed the liberation of the main island. The U.S. 8th Army's numerous amphibious landings met little opposition on the beaches. The Americans quickly drove inland to dig out Japanese garrisons usually hiding in the rugged, jungled interior. The major amphibious strikes in the 8th Army's swift-moving series were the landings on Palawan (February 28), Zamboanga (March 10), Basilan (March 16), Panay (March 18), Cebu (March 27), Negros (March 29), the Sulu Islands (April 2), Jolo (April 9), Bihol (April 11), and Mindanao (April 17, May 10, June 25, and July 12). American forces suffered slightly more than 9,000 casualties in these operations, while killing 50,000 Japanese. Filipino guerrilla bands assisted the army units, serving as guides and porters and in irregular combat formations.

The guerrilla formations had evolved slowly after the American defeat in 1942. At Southwest Pacific Area headquarters, the Allied Intelligence Bureau reestablished contact with the multiple guerrilla groups and during 1943 and 1944 merged their activities to complement the invasion of Leyte. The stronger and better-organized guerrilla bands operated in the southern islands, where Japanese garrisons were weak, and they proved very helpful to the 8th Army's operations. On Luzon, where the enemy was strong, the guerrillas were constantly harried. Nevertheless, following the January 1945 invasion of Luzon, guerrilla units attacked Japanese rear areas and sabotaged rail lines and highway bridges. The guerrillas also assisted U.S. units, most notably in the raid against Cabanatuan that rescued 500 Allied internees and in the 11th Airborne Division's daring rescue of 2,100 Allied prisoners from the Los Baños prison camp.

FINAL PACIFIC CAMPAIGN

From late 1944, as the Allies advanced in the Philippines, Japan's inner defense perimeter was constantly breached.

Pressures built up on the Japanese government as Allied planes attacked the home islands and as Japanese troops on mainland Asia suffered defeats.

Air and Navy War on Japan

While the Philippine battles were fought out, the U.S. XXI Air Force was sending B-29s from the Marianas to the skies over Japan. The first raid from Saipan occurred on Nov. 24, 1944. It was a microcosm of the problems facing the new bomber. Bad weather, in particular high winds, forced a week-long postponement of the first attack. Two B-29s were lost in the raid, the returning formation straggled widely, and bombing results were disappointing. Despite changes in tactics and adjustments for weather, by March 1945, not a single major target had been destroyed by the much-heralded Superfortress. Moreover, losses were unacceptably high as Japanese fighters pressed home attacks and rammed the big bombers often enough to convince American pilots that it was a standard enemy tactic. In January 1945, Maj. Gen. Curtis E. LeMay took command of the XXI Air Force and devised radical tactics to destroy Japanese targets.

LeMay determined that Japanese industry was too dispersed for conventional high-explosive bombs to inflict much damage. Instead, Japan's cities had to be destroyed. The fatal combination of a high density of wooden buildings and an antiquated air defense system incapable of responding against low-level air attacks would doom one Japanese city after another. LeMay tested his theories with deadly effect on the night of March 9–10. Roaring in at altitudes of several hundred feet, more than 330 B-29s dropped their loads of incendiary bombs onto Tokyo. LeMay had stripped machine guns from his bombers in order to stuff them with more incendiaries. The result was, in a technical sense, very effective. About 16 square miles of Tokyo were burned out and perhaps 100,000 Japanese perished. Thousands more were left homeless, their lives devastated.

Two fire raids against Nagoya and one each against Osaka and Kobe followed within seven days. LeMay expanded his firestorm, torching Japanese cities from Hokkaido in the north to Kyushu in the south. More than 340,000 civilians perished in the bomb-ignited firestorms that engulfed city after city. LeMay's incendiary campaign burned Tokyo, Yokohama, Osaka, Nagoya, and other great cities almost to the ground. Then he switched to fire raids against 60 smaller urban areas, with equally destructive results. Of 69 cities attacked, 42 were more than 50 percent destroyed by fire. From the American viewpoint, the Japanese were reaping the whirlwind that they had sowed at Pearl Harbor.

The U.S. Navy was simultaneously blockading Japan. American submarines had broken the Japanese fleet, sinking almost 5,000,000 tons of the fleet, most of it in 1944 and 1945. Now the navy launched an ambitious campaign to mine Japan's coastal waterways. Code-named Operation Starvation, the aim was to choke off Japan's ports and starve the nation into surrender. Imperial headquarters found itself buffeted by the loss of the Philippines, the increasing devastation of LeMay's air war, and the heavy losses to its merchant fleet.

Japanese Countermoves

These disasters in the Pacific brought Tokyo to the realization that the decisive battle would now take place on Japan's shores. Defensive preparations went forward on Okinawa, a prefecture of Japan, and Iwo Jima, administratively part of Tokyo municipality. As desperate as the Japanese situation was, there were bright spots. Japan had 26 divisions in China at the end of 1944, and during the spring of 1945, several of them were on the move against U.S. airfields there. After capturing fields in west-central China, the Japanese turned their attention to strengthening coastal defenses against a possible Allied invasion. They also called up reserves and conscripts to flesh out new divisions, especially in Manchuria. The elite Manchurian divisions had been or would shortly be transferred to the Pacific front. Because the threat of war with the Soviet Union remained, newly organized formations had to replace these losses. Simultaneous with a mobilization in Japan itself, 700,000 Japanese and Koreans were recalled or pressed into new units of the Kwantung Army. Lacking training, equipment, and leadership, there was little that they could do except sit in defensive positions throughout Manchuria and hope that the Soviets would not invade.

Burma

Disaster struck the Japanese in Burma. Forced on the defensive after the fiasco at Imphal in 1944, Japan's Burma Army by January 1945 had fallen back to southern Burma. Its new mission was to hold that area in order to protect the flank of the vital Malaya-Sumatra-Indochina region. By then, Tokyo had given up on its strategy of cutting off Allied forces in China from those operating in India. Not coincidentally, January 1945 marks the date that the first American truck convoy crossed the eastern borders of Burma en route to Kunming, China.

In March 1945, Slim's XIVth Army crossed the mighty, mile-wide Irrawady River south of the city of Mandalay, isolating Japanese forces there. In a race against the spring monsoon (at which time the Americans would be forced to withdraw their air power), Slim's army struck south for Rangoon, 350 miles distant on the Bay of Bengal. The XIVth Army, pressing forward in a 300-mile-long salient that was usually 1–2 miles wide, liberated the city in early May, just as the first rains came. The Japanese in Burma were a shattered remnant, cut off from resupply and reinforcement. Of the 330,000 Japanese officers and men available at the outset of the Imphal Campaign, at least 200,000 had been killed in action or had died from disease and starvation. Britain's Lord Mountbatten began making plans for the reconquest of Malaya.

Iwo Jima and Okinawa

There was no letup in the Allies' strategic pincer movement closing on Japan. Iwo Jima was prized for its three airfields, which lay only 750 miles from Japan. On February 19, three U.S. Marine divisions assaulted the southeastern side of the small, pear-shaped island. The Japanese defenders were well dug-in and fought back with suicidal fury. From atop Mount Surabachi, Japanese observers called in deadly artillery and mortar fire on the marines below, who were struggling though the volcanic ash. Prying the defenders from an intricate and interconnected bunker system cost the marines more than 25,000 casualties by the time the fighting ended in late March. The Japanese lost almost their entire 21,000-man garrison, but for the first time in the war, the emperor's soldiers had inflicted greater losses on their attackers than they had suffered.

Okinawa was invaded on April 1, 1945. The Americans needed the narrow, 60-mile-long island's port and air bases as major staging areas for the anticipated invasion of Japan. The landing itself was deceptively peaceful, as were the first five days of the operation. Then, the American infantry and marines encountered the outpost defenses of the so-called Shuri line. From that point on, the carnage on and near Okinawa was appalling. Massed kamikaze attacks, suicide boats, defenders fanatically resisting to the last man, mass civilian suicides, and utter destruction were Okinawa's fate.

Most of the ground fighting was centered on the southern third of the island. There were 39,393 U.S. battle casualties

The U.S. Navy lies offshore at Iwo Jima, as seen from the Hamlin *on Feb. 20, 1945.* (U.S. Navy)

in the ground war (plus another 26,211 nonbattle ones) in the two-month struggle. Kamikaze fliers sank 36 Allied ships and damaged another 368 vessels of all types. About 8,000 sailors became casualties, and 763 aircraft (98 British) were lost fending off such attacks. On the Japanese side, there were 65,000 battle casualties as the 32d Army was wiped out. The Japanese army and navy air forces lost 7,830 aircraft, 4,155 in combat. Among these were 2,500 kamikaze planes. Perhaps 100,000 civilians were killed or wounded as they found themselves trapped in the terrible artillery bombardments that marked the siege warfare on Okinawa. One school of Japanese thought maintains that

Soldiers of the U.S. 7th Infantry Division observe the enemy on Okinawa from behind some of the island's monoliths, or large stone sculptures. (U.S. Army Military History Institute)

the high command intentionally sacrificed the people of Okinawa to the invaders' guns to make the point to the Allies that Japan would fight to the bitter end.

Japan's Defeat and Surrender

The specter of Okinawa indeed haunted the JCS and the new American president, Harry S Truman, as they prepared for the invasion of the Japanese home islands. Despite an aerial pounding of the homeland that since March 1945 had killed more than 200,000 Japanese and left more than 1,300,000 homeless, Japan's military leaders were determined to fight until they could achieve an honorable peace. For the Allies, the end of the war against Japan might have been in sight in June 1945, but only after a showdown on the home islands. Since April, the Japanese high command had been preparing for just such an eventuality. Hundreds of thousands of men were rushed to southern Kyushu and deployed in depth along the likely invasion beaches. By August, 900,000 Japanese troops were crowded into fortress Kyushu.

The U.S. Army, in particular Generals Marshall and MacArthur, believed that an invasion of the home islands was necessary to end the war. From strategic intelligence reports, the specific shape of the Japanese reinforcement effort on Kyushu was well known, so Marshall and MacArthur also favored Soviet participation in the war to tie down Japanese troops in Manchuria. The U.S. Navy felt that a combination of air attacks and a sea blockade would compel a Japanese surrender. The JCS opted for a direct invasion, Operation Olympic, slated for Nov. 1, 1945.

In mid-June, the atomic age was inaugurated in a test explosion in a New Mexico desert. The new weapon, the atomic bomb, quickly convinced Sec. of War Henry Stimson that Soviet entry into the war against Japan was no longer needed because the new weapon would win the war. Marshall was uncertain of the potential effect of the bomb, and MacArthur was not informed until shortly before a B-29 dropped an atomic bomb on Hiroshima on August 6. Even after the first atomic attack, Marshall worried that an invasion would be necessary. The Japanese leadership was indecisive, unable to agree on a means to capitulate to the Allies. A second atomic attack, on August 9, was delivered against Nagasaki. At dawn that same day, Soviet forces, as promised in February 1945 by Joseph Stalin at the Yalta Conference, entered the war against Japan. More than 1,700,000 Soviet troops, in 80 divisions, launched a blitzkrieg on three widely separate fronts against Japanese troops in Manchuria. Japan's last hopes for a mediated settlement gone, Emperor Hirohito announced at an Imperial conference that his nation must surrender and "bear the unbearable." The Pacific war ended with the same suddenness that it began when Japan agreed to surrender on August 15.

Japan's surrender was formalized aboard the Missouri *in Tokyo Bay on Sept. 2, 1945; Gen. Douglas MacArthur stands at the left.* (Library of Congress)

On September 2, General MacArthur, the newly appointed Supreme Allied Commander in Japan, accepted the formal surrender of the Japanese on board the battleship *Missouri* at anchor in Tokyo Bay. Elsewhere in Asia, the war ended on a ragged note. In Southeast Asia, British and Indian troops took Japan's surrender. Colonial rule was reinstated temporarily at least in French Indochina, Burma, Malaya, and the Netherlands East Indies. All would soon gain independence—in three cases, by revolting against their colonial rulers. The British had accomplished their immediate aim, to secure the empire east of Suez, but the victory was ephemeral. China's victory also proved temporary. Within a few months of Japan's surrender, civil war again broke out between the Communists and Nationalists. Mao's triumph in 1949 marked the end of an American presence in China until Pres. Richard Nixon's historic visit more than 20 years later. The Soviets withdrew from Manchuria and the northern half of Korea but left behind well-trained, well-equipped, and thoroughly indoctrinated Communist armies.

Thousands of miles to the south, Australian troops found themselves accepting the surrender of Japanese on New Guinea, Rabaul, and the Netherlands East Indies. The Australians had carried the bulk of the early fighting against Japan, and then found themselves consigned to a thankless mop-up role at war's end. As a minor partner in the Allied coalition, perhaps it was inevitable that Australia was overwhelmed by the United States. In the Philippines,

General Yamashita was escorted out of his mountain redoubt to surrender.

The United States fought its Pacific war much in the fashion that the U.S. Navy always thought that it should be fought. It was, however, the unmatched and undamaged industrial reserve of the United States that spewed forth the matériel needed to make the two-front Pacific war a success. The great Allied victory stands as a tribute to a strategy that was broad enough to encompass theaters of enormous diversity, strong enough to withstand the inevitable coalition clashes of personality and objectives, flexible enough to seize and exploit opportunities, and farsighted enough to defeat a tenacious foe in the greatest war the world has ever witnessed.

6

The Air War against Germany and Japan: 1942–1945

World War I is remembered for its duration and indecisiveness, but most of all for its human slaughter. A number of new weapons emerged during the conflict, one of the most important of which was the airplane. Although aircraft were primarily used in support of troops (reconnaissance, observation, and artillery spotting roles) and were probably most noted for the air-to-air exploits of the aces, bombing was also practiced. Bombing was directed against tactical targets, ground troops, or targets close to the front. Little attention was given to strategic operations—that is, bombing of targets in the enemy's homeland—because of the limitations of technology and the more urgent needs of the combatants. During World War I, the Germans initiated bombing of cities on both the continent and in Great Britain, and the Allies responded; however, they never bombed Berlin. The Allies had ambitious plans for bombing, but the war ended before their ideas could be carried out. While little damage was done, the concept of strategic bombing stirred the imaginations of some who saw possibilities for the future. Most military men saw how aircraft would be important in future wars in supporting troops; some envisioned that planes could do more: strategic bombing could win wars and thus avoid the bloodshed and indecisiveness of World War I trench warfare.

Interwar Developments

Aviation rapidly developed following World War I. In less than 20 years, aircraft power dramatically increased as improved engines, new propellers, and higher-octane fuels boosted performance. More noticeable were the changes in airframes, as construction changed to all-metal monoplanes, with retractable landing gear, enclosed crew posi-

tions, and wing flaps. Multiengine aircraft—airliners and bombers—were the first to benefit from this new technology, as clearly demonstrated with the first flight of Boeing's daring four-engine bomber in July 1935, which was redesignated the B-17. It could outfly the finest pursuit plane of the day and was to be the best-performing bomber until the B-29 first flew in September 1942. At the same time, Carl Norden developed a highly accurate bombsight. Essentially, the U.S. strategic bombing program was initially built around the B-17 and the Norden bombsight.

Meanwhile, airmen in a number of countries developed a doctrine of strategic bombing—men such as Hugh Trenchard in Great Britain, Giulio Douhet in Italy, and Brig. Gen. William (''Billy'') Mitchell in the United States. These men shared the ideas that the airplane was essentially an offensive weapon, that nothing could stop it in the air (''the bomber would always get through''), and that the proper targets were cities and civilians.

In the late 1920s, American airmen went beyond this premise and developed a distinctive American strategic bombing concept. They espoused the idea that the strategic bombing offensive should consist of precision attacks on key targets within the ''industrial web,'' targets whose destruction would fatally undermine the enemy's economy. During the 1930s, the airmen studied the U.S. economy and looked at such target systems as finance, utilities, raw materials, oil, food, and electricity. To destroy such targets, the American airmen developed tactics for precision daylight bombing. A serious complication of these tactics was that fighter escort of the bombers was precluded by the long distances involved, leaving daylight operations prey to enemy defenses. The solution the airmen proposed

The four-engined B-17 Flying Fortress, first tested in 1935, could fly at high altitudes and carry a heavy payload. (Army Air Corps)

was to fly fast, heavily armed bombers in tight formation to fend off enemy fighters and to fly high enough to evade enemy antiaircraft artillery. Credit for developing the American strategic bombing theory belongs to a group of army airmen who taught at the Air Corps Tactical School at Maxwell Field, Alabama.

Aerial combat during the 1920s and 1930s provided the airmen with mixed signals as to the validity of their theory. Most of these conflicts were waged with small numbers of obsolete equipment, and the results were therefore of little use. The one exception was the Spanish Civil War (1936–39), to which Germany, Italy, and the Soviet Union sent significant numbers of airmen and modern aircraft. The Germans and Soviets learned the impact of close air support, especially when Soviet airmen single-handedly defeated an Italian armored and motorized column that had advanced without air cover at Guadalajara. Few cities were bombarded, although Guernica was devastated in a notorious terror attack. As far as strategic bombing was concerned, the Spanish Civil War indicated that bombing was less effective and civilian morale much tougher than predicted. Some believed that fast, unescorted bombers could get through, although others held there was a need for escort. One American air attaché wrote that "the peacetime theory of the complete invulnerability of the modern-type bombardment airplane no longer holds," and another noted that "the comparison of an airplane to a flying fortress is possible only in the minds of the theorists."

World War II Begins

World War II exploded in September 1939 following the German invasion of Poland, and aircraft proved very important, but in a tactical role supporting fast-moving German tanks and mechanized infantry in the famous

Blitzkrieg. Poland quickly succumbed to overwhelming German forces, and then the Germans turned westward. Superior German leadership, training, morale, and doctrine (not superior numbers) defeated the British and French armies during the Battle of France in 1940.

The Battle of Britain in the summer of 1940 proved a better test of air power. The British were able to defeat the German air force (Luftwaffe) in this the one truly decisive air battle of the war. The Luftwaffe was defeated, German arms were repulsed, and the myth of the bomber was punctured. Bombers could get through, but they suffered heavy losses and were rendered ineffective by modern fighters directed by a control network based on radar. German aircraft were forced to operate at night to evade the deadly British defenses, as were Royal Air Force (RAF) bombers, which met similar resistance and suffered comparable losses over Germany.

Despite these events, the view of the U.S. Army airmen did not change. They believed that neither European combatant had American equipment or doctrine, and thus the American strategic bombing theory remained intact. Meanwhile, the airmen added another weapon to their arsenal when the Consolidated B-24 first flew in December 1939. The B-17 and B-24 were the two U.S. heavy bombers that waged the strategic air war against Germany. The airmen also ratified their concept with an air plan for the defeat of Germany, called AWPD-1. It summarized the prewar doctrine, identified 154 targets in Europe, and called for 60,000 aircraft.

8TH AIR FORCE OPERATIONS

In February 1942, Maj. Gen. Ira Eaker and a small advance party arrived in Britain to prepare the way for what would become the largest of the U.S. Army Air Forces (AAF) units in World War II: the 8th Air Force. Eaker commanded the bombers organized under VIII Bomber Command, while his longtime friend and colleague Maj. Gen. Carl Spaatz was in overall command of the 8th Air Force. It was Eaker, flying in a B-17 named *Yankee Doodle,* who led a dozen B-17s on the first AAF heavy bomber raid from Britain on Aug. 17, 1942, which attacked a coastal target in France. The initial missions, protected by heavy fighter escort, were short-range attacks against targets mostly in France. The first tough mission was against the industrial city of Lille on October 12, when, for the first time, more than 100 U.S. heavy bombers were launched. Three aspects of this mission provided warning signs for the future. First, the Germans downed four bombers—the most lost in one day up to that time. Second, only half of the bombs dropped could be identified. Third, the bomber crews claimed to have destroyed 56 German aircraft, a large percentage of the total German air strength in the

Lt. Gen. Carl Spaatz (left) *and Gen. Henry Arnold* (right) *visit a 9th Air Force landing strip in France in 1944; Spaatz had become commander of the U.S. Strategic Air Forces at the beginning of the year.* (U.S. Army Military History Institute)

west. These claims were eventually reduced to 21 German aircraft destroyed. Overclaiming was a problem that persisted throughout the war on both sides.

In the fall, the growth of the American bombing campaign was stunted by the demands of the North African Campaign and by the switching of targets to submarines. The former drained off men and machines as the 8th Air Force's most experienced units deployed to North Africa. The latter diverted the bombing effort to difficult and frustrating targets assigned to the 8th Air Force from late October 1942 into the spring of 1943. The worst example of the futility of the submarine objectives was the bombing of submarine pens in France, shelters with roofs measuring 12–19 feet thick, which were impervious to even direct hits by the light American bombs. On Jan. 27, 1943, AAF daylight bombers finally attacked targets in Germany.

Expanded Operations: 1943

As the 8th Air Force grew more ambitious in size and scope, German air-force resistance intensified. Between January and October 1943, the Germans shifted fighter units from other areas to the west to double the number of single-engine fighters and added more airfields, radar, and antiaircraft guns. The Luftwaffe learned that the Allied bombers were most vulnerable on their bomb runs, that the least defended position was the nose, and that the unescorted bombers, flying in tight formations, were easy prey to twin-engine fighters firing heavy cannon and, later, air-to-air rockets. As a consequence, U.S. losses increased, with 16 bombers downed on the Apr. 17, 1943, raid against Bremen, Germany, twice the previous high for one day.

To counter this opposition, in early 1943, the 8th Air Force developed tighter formations, adopted tactics to deceive the enemy, and changed from each bombardier individually aiming to a lead-bombardier system in which the formation dropped its bombs on the signal of one bombardier, permitting the others to man nose guns during the bomb run. The 8th Air Force also used fighter escort as much as possible, introducing the P-47 into action in April 1943. Although limited by its size, the P-47 Thunderbolt proved superior in the escort role to the predominant fighter aircraft in Britain, the Spitfire. The 8th Air Force's fighters had to overcome problems of inadequate numbers, weather, mechanical problems, and inexperience. One innovation that did not work was to arm a B-17 heavily and have it act as a "convoy defender." Flying in combat between May and July 1943, the experiment failed but did produce a nose ("chin") turret fitted to later model bombers, which greatly enhanced the bombers' forward firepower.

Damage from "friendly" forces was another continuing problem. In a three-month period early in 1943, 25 percent of the machine-gun damage to the U.S. bombers was from 8th Air Force guns, and through December 1943, 16 percent of the damage was from American bullets, while another 17 percent was from shell cases. Nevertheless, by the spring of 1943, the U.S. airmen believed that the shakedown period of equipment, organization, and men was complete and that the aerial destruction of Germany's war machine could begin.

Into the spring of 1943, both Spaatz and Eaker believed that a force of 200–300 bombers could operate unescorted. On May 21, 1943, the 8th Air Force was able to send out almost 280 bombers. But missions in late July proved the American leaders wrong. In six missions in seven days, the American airmen were dealt heavy blows, losing 87 bombers, and worse was yet to come.

The AAF flew two of its most famous missions during August 1943, against the Ploesti oil refineries in Rumania and a dual attack against the Regensburg fighter factories and the Schweinfurt ball-bearing plants in Germany. The 8th Air Force planned this dangerous dual mission against these key targets to utilize mutual support and surprise. The surprise was that the Regensburg attackers would fly on to North Africa instead of returning to Britain. Weather wrecked the concept by delaying the Schweinfurt force, and each had to attack alone and was butchered. The Regensburg bombers led by Col. Curtis LeMay lost 24 of

Maj. Gen. Ira C. Eaker (right), *who had played a key part in organizing the 8th Air Force, believed that large numbers of bombers could fly their missions unescorted by fighter planes.* (U.S. Army Military History Institute)

146 B-17s, while the Schweinfurt force lost 36 of 183. The crews expended more than 1,000,000 rounds of .50-caliber ammunition and initially claimed 280 enemy aircraft destroyed, over half of the number they encountered. The Germans admitted losing between 58 and 70 fighters that day.

Despite these high Allied losses, the bombing offensive continued. Weather turned the early September mission against Stuttgart into a disaster when only 46 of the 338 bombers that were launched dropped their bombs, and the Germans destroyed a total of 45 planes. The "time of truth" arrived during the second week of October; the target was again Schweinfurt. During this epic mission, the American airmen encountered 300–500 German aircraft, as well as the usual intense flak from antiaircraft batteries, and lost 60 bombers. Another 4 made it back but were too damaged to fly again. This was a high percentage of the 292 bombers launched and the 228 that actually bombed a target. The bomber crews initially reported the destruction of 288 Luftwaffe fighters, claims later reduced to 99, although German air force records indicate only 40 fighters were lost that day.

The extent of U.S. bomber losses was the most significant factor in the July–October bombing campaign. On 13 missions into Germany in good weather between July 25 and mid-October, 381 American bombers were lost. On 4 raids during October 8–14, the 8th Air Force lost 148 bombers in action, plus 12 others that returned but could not be economically repaired. The severity of the losses is made clear when these numbers are compared with the 8th Air Force's average daily effective strength of 417 heavy bombers during October. The 8th Air Force's heavy bomber loss rate for October 1943 was 9.2 percent, and no unit could sustain such losses for long. Despite brave talk, the AAF bombers had failed to prove that unescorted bombing in daylight could succeed, despite efforts marked by widespread heroism, devotion to duty, and high enemy casualties.

As a result of these losses, the 8th Air Force stopped deep penetration missions into Germany. The U.S. daylight strategic bombing effort had been defeated, but unlike the Germans and the British, who also suffered heavy losses in daylight bombing, the Americans did not turn to night operations. Among the primary factors that saved their concept and permitted the daylight strategic campaign to continue were the growing and overwhelming numbers of aircraft and aircrews the Americans pushed into action. The size of the 8th Air Force grew from a handful of bombers in 1942, to the several hundred in 1943, to more than 1,000 bombers in May 1944.

Technical Innovations

At the same time, two technical innovations became available that changed the strategic air war. The first, and most significant, was the extension of fighter range. In July 1943, drop tanks—external fuel tanks that could be jettisoned at will—were used in combat for the first time and extended escort range by 75 miles. The Americans overcame technical and numerical difficulties with this important piece of equipment and continued to extend the range of the escorts. Modifications were made to the P-47 Thunderbolt that increased its engine power and overall performance. But the most noticeable change, and one that has been overemphasized by writers ever since, was the appearance of the North American P-51 Mustang. It first flew an escort mission in December 1943 and became the premier escort fighter of the war. The P-51 was a delight to fly, a pleasure to observe, and the best performing piston-powered fighter of the war. The Mustang's most important attribute was its range: by the end of the war, it could fly farther than a B-17.

The second technical innovation was the introduction of blind bombing capabilities. Weather proved to be one of the biggest constraints upon the strategic bombing effort, not only while taking off but also while forming up and recovering and especially while bombing. The AAF

P-51 Mustangs could fly farther than any other fighter planes and were used to escort bomber formations during World War II. (Army Air Corps)

adopted some British airborne radar and flew their first nonvisual mission on Sept. 27, 1943. Radar bombing allowed the AAF to operate on days that were otherwise impossible for missions and also gave them an advantage because American pilots were better trained in all-weather operations than were the Germans. Unfortunately, the accuracy of radar bombing was poor. While the AAF's heavy bombers using visual bombing could put about half their bombs within 1,500 feet of the target by the end of the war, radar bombing accuracy was measured, when possible, in miles. Nevertheless, approximately 40 percent of the bombs that the U.S. strategic bombers dropped on Germany were aimed by radar.

The 8th Air Force also employed two antiradar devices during the fall. "Carpet," first used in October 1943, was an electronic device that when activated produced static on radar. A second device was "chaff," aluminum foil strips, similar to Christmas tree tinsel, which the bombers released while in flight and which complicated the enemy radar operator's task. First used by the British in July 1943, chaff was put into service by the 8th Air Force in December. Throughout the war, the Anglo-American Allies enjoyed technological superiority in electronics, and when applied in both carpet and chaff, it cut their bomber losses.

In December 1943, the AAF reorganized its strategic air forces in Europe and formed USSTAF (United States Strategic Air Forces) as the overall headquarters for the British-based U.S. 8th Air Force and the Italian-based U.S. 15th Air Force. Spaatz was appointed command of USSTAF, while the commanders of the two numbered air forces were switched, with Brig. Gen. James Doolittle coming to the 8th and Eaker going to the Mediterranean theater to command Allied air forces there. These organizations and these commanders were the major players in the U.S. strategic air effort against Germany for the remainder of the war.

Operations in 1944

In early January 1944, the 8th Air Force resumed operations deep into Germany. On January 11, it ran into both bad weather and heavy Germany resistance. The unit launched more than 650 bombers but then recalled about two-thirds of them because of weather. This gave the Luftwaffe crews their opportunity, and they downed 60 U.S. bombers. The two opposing forces were not to engage again in earnest until February.

The Allied airmen were waiting for clear weather to hit the Germans, most especially their fighter plane factories. What followed were the most intense series of bombing missions of the war and the heaviest losses. The RAF opened with a raid on the night of February 19 and closed what came to be called "Big Week" on the night of February 25. In all, the RAF flew four missions, the 8th Air Force five, and the 15th Air Force five. The Allied bombers logged more than 6,000 sorties, dropped about 20,000 tons of bombs, and suffered severe losses—243 American and 151 British heavy bombers.

The 8th Air Force followed Big Week with the first daylight attacks on the German capital of Berlin. After two abortive efforts early in the month, on March 6, the 8th Air Force hit Berlin and lost 69 bombers, with 3 more classed as junk upon their return. American claims were also high, the bomber gunners reporting 97 German fighters destroyed and escort pilots reporting 78 (the Germans admitted losing 72). Two days later, the 8th Air Force again hit the German capital and again encountered stiff resistance, losing 36 bombers and 17 fighters, while claiming a total of 141 Luftwaffe aircraft (the Germans put their losses at 57). But on the next mission against Berlin, German resistance was minimal. Although the German air force could fight and inflict heavy losses on the Americans—for example, downing 64 bombers on April 11 and April 29—their aircraft no longer came up in force to meet the Allied missions every time, but became more selective in their defense operations. The 8th Air Force had won daylight air superiority.

Much to their chagrin, U.S. airmen were not able to exploit their air superiority as they would have wished or as had their prewar doctrine indicated. The overriding objectives of the cross-channel invasion scheduled for spring 1944 forced the U.S. air forces to change their role.

For two months prior to the June 6 invasion of Normandy and for two months after it, the AAF was tied down in support of the ground assault. Not until late summer were the airmen able to hit their first-priority target: the German oil refineries and supply centers.

TACTICAL AIR OPERATIONS

American tactical operations were pioneered in the sands of North Africa during the brief campaign there in late 1942 through early 1943. Meanwhile, the 8th Air Force—trained, equipped, and intended as a strategic air force—was engaged in a number of nonstrategic, or tactical, projects even before the invasion support in North Africa. Early in the war, the 8th Air Force detached some aircraft for maritime reconnaissance (antisubmarine) missions. Another operation, code-named Nickeling, that began in October 1943 involved one squadron of B-17s that dropped propaganda leaflets at night. In another night operation, code-named Carpetbagger, a group of B-24s first dropped equipment to anti-German partisans in January 1944. The group could not meet the requirements of the French partisans following the Normandy invasion, so an entire air division was enlisted to make four mass daylight supply deliveries between June 25 and September 9. A further diversion was the bombing effort against German V-weapons. The Germans used both pilotless aircraft (V-1s) and ballistic missiles (V-2s) against the Allies in World War II. Allied airmen bombed both the factories and the launch sites for these weapons, beginning in August 1943. The bombing delayed the firing of the first V-1 against Britain until mid-June 1944 and the first V-2 until early September; otherwise, this tremendous effort yielded meager results. The largest diversion from the strategic bombing effort, however, was support of the ground troops.

Normandy Invasion

The western Allies focused their mighty resources on the major effort of the war, the cross-channel invasion of France, Operation Overlord. The airmen had three tasks: (1) to neutralize the Luftwaffe, (2) to disrupt German communications, and (3) to support directly the ground forces. The AAF accomplished the first task in early 1944 with its costly bombing campaign against German fighter factories, leading to the decisive air-to-air battles won by American escort fighters. To maintain air superiority, the Allied air forces pounded German airfields in Western Europe and also continued their raids deep into Germany to prevent the Luftwaffe from shifting its forces westward. The airmen made good Gen. Dwight D. Eisenhower's boast: "If you see fighting aircraft over you, they will be ours."

The attack on German communications caused considerable controversy. Neither the British nor the American strategic airmen wanted to attack French rail centers on the massive scale envisioned by the Overlord planners. Not only would this effort divert them from strategic bombing, it risked large numbers of French civilians—some estimates of potential casualties were as high as 80,000 to 160,000, 25 percent of whom would be killed. Nevertheless, Eisenhower insisted on his preferred objective and the transportation campaign went forward. By D-Day, June 6, 1944, 51 of the 80 rail centers targeted had been demolished. The airmen also attacked bridges, using all types of aircraft. Fighter bombers proved most successful, requiring about half as many bombs as medium bombers and one-third as many as heavy bombers to destroy each bridge. Rail lines were also cut. While this air effort reduced rail traffic, delaying and battering German forces on the move, military traffic still got through. On the positive side, the airmen inflicted far fewer casualties on French civilians than estimated, approximately 11,000.

During the days immediately before the D-Day invasion, the airmen hit coastal defenses. On June 6, they engaged in massive carpet bombing of the five beachheads and communications checkpoints in Normandy. In all, the 8th Air Force launched almost 2,700 bombers and dropped almost 4,800 tons of bombs at a cost of 3 bombers lost and 7 too damaged to fly again. The 8th Air Force also contributed to the fighter cover that protected the invasion. The Allies put up 171 fighter squadrons and were opposed by a mere 100 planes in the day and 175 at night—only 2 Luftwaffe aircraft got over the beachhead during the day.

Allied air superiority, actually air supremacy, gave the ground forces tremendous advantages. The Allies had reconnaissance capabilities, and the Germans did not. This enabled the Allies to deceive their enemies and that, along with Hitler's interference, tied down German troops expecting the main assault to come at Pas-de-Calais. The Allies owned the air so that Allied troops seldom saw the German air force, much less were attacked by them. The Allied airplanes, along with the ships, also lent great firepower to the ground forces. Finally, the airmen greatly restricted German mobility. The Battle of Normandy was as much a contest of who could reinforce the battlefield quickest as any other factor. Most commentators agree with one high-ranking German who remarked, "It can safely be said that the principal reason [for the invasion's success] was the overwhelming air superiority which allowed the enemy his complete freedom of maneuver and robbed us of ours."

The Allied invasion, however, stalled at the beachhead. Airfields were carved out of the sand and soil to accommodate smaller aircraft, and tactical aircraft were in the thick of the action in the attempt to spring the Allied forces loose. Heavy bombers were also employed. After a British effort with heavy bombers at Caen on July 7, a huge force of British and U.S. aircraft attacked on July 18, including almost 1,100 8th Air Force B-24s. Although the British were able to advance, they were unable to break out. On July 24, the heavy bombers were again used in an attempt by the U.S. 1st Army to break out at St.-Lô in Operation Cobra. Bad weather allowed only 484 of the 1,586 bombers launched to drop their ordnance, with only 15 percent of their payloads falling within the target area. Some bombs fell in friendly territory, killing 27 and wounding 137. The next day, the 8th Air Force returned and more than 1,500 bombers participated, but once again there was short bombing, this time by 35 heavy and 42 medium bombers, which wounded 463 and killed 101 Americans, including Lt. Gen. Leslie McNair. As a result of the casualties and air tactics, this operation continues to create controversy. The controversy should not, however, obscure the fact that U.S. troops were able to break out in early August.

The Germans counterattacked on August 7 toward Mortain, which gave the Allied airmen targets that they attacked with vigor. While the bulk of the German mobile forces escaped, the trap cost the Germans about 70,000 casualties. Heavy bombers were used at the same time to help the British advance at Caen. Again there was short bombing, this time killing 25 and wounding 131.

Advance Across France

The war in western France at this point became a race between the two combatants. The rapid Allied advance, coupled with the voracious appetite for supplies, created acute problems after August 21. Supplies were so tight that air transport was enlisted to try to keep war matériel, and thus the troops, moving. Four groups of bombers were used to transport cargo, especially gasoline, and more than 2,200 sorties were flown in support of this effort.

The heavy bombers continued to be used in tactical operations, along with tactical aircraft. The 8th Air Force's heavy bombers attacked targets around the fortifications of Brest four times between August 11 and September 5. The 8th Air Force was also involved in the ambitious and abortive Operation Market Garden in September 1944. On September 17, about 850 B-17s bombed antiaircraft positions, while other airmen escorted and supported the airborne assault. Later, the 8th Air Force flew 246 aerial resupply sorties, flying its last mission on September 26. It contributed about one-third of the sorties to the operations, a total of more than 4,200 sorties at the cost of 91 aircraft written off.

In early November, the 8th Air Force planned another gigantic air effort around the forts at Metz and Thionville in support of Gen. George Patton's 3d Army; the attempt on November 9, however, was nullified by weather. One week later, the 8th Air Force, along with other American and British air forces, supported the U.S. 1st and 9th

In September 1944, about 850 B-17s like these bombed antiaircraft positions during Operation Market Garden, aimed at capturing strategic bridges in the Netherlands. (U.S. Army Military History Institute: H. U. Milne Collection)

armies near Eschweiler. Although these operations avoided most of the short bombing and casualties, results were limited.

More important was air support in response to the German attack in the Ardennes in December 1944. This assault caught the undermanned Americans by surprise and sparked the last major U.S. battle of the European war, the Battle of the Bulge. The Germans picked a period of bad weather to attack, a tribute to the effectiveness of the Allied air forces. Once the weather broke, however, the aviators were not to be denied. The 8th Air Force mainly hit German communications to disrupt the attackers' logistical operations. The largest mission of the war was flown on December 24, when the British launched 1,200 sorties and the Americans almost 3,600. The 8th Air Force launched 2,031 bombers and 891 fighters on this day (the greatest number of German aircraft aloft on one day during the battle was 849 on December 18). Air power helped to defeat the Germans and to turn the Battle of the Bulge into their last offensive, and a costly one at that.

Allied airmen continued to support the advancing troops during the last months of the war. One operation involving the heavy bombers was the British crossing of the Rhine River near Emmerich and the Anglo-American airborne assault near Wesel. The Allies hit German transportation targets as well as airfields and other military targets in March 1945. The 8th Air Force supported the troops with supplies, as well as flying defensive patrols and attacking German communications and airfields. The last major tactical operation was the effort in France to clear the Germans from the Gironde estuary and thus open the port of Bordeaux to the Allies. The French aircraft began the attack on April 13, followed by further Franco-American attacks on April 15 involving almost 1,300 U.S. bombers, and on April 16 with close to 500 bombers.

The Strategic Campaign

Having failed to create a bottleneck in military vehicle production through their attacks on German ball-bearing plants, the Allied air forces searched for other targets of sabotage. Petroleum facilities and supplies proved to be the correct choice, but it was not until May 1944 that the 8th Air Force began to hit these targets systematically. Then the invasion support intruded. Once the airmen returned to bombing petroleum sites, however, the demise of the German war machine was swift. Germany was short of oil before the war and was forced to curtail flight training early in the war. The bombing of petroleum targets had a dramatic impact, reducing German land, sea, and air operations. One of the great "might have beens" of the war is what if the bombing of oil supplies had taken place earlier.

Once the support of the Normandy invasion was over, the 8th Air Force's routine became essentially one of transporting large tonnages of bombs onto German targets. More than 70 percent of the bombs dropped on Germany by the Allies fell after July 1, 1944. One dramatic campaign, really a series of missions, was Operation Frantic, which consisted of shuttle bombing runs—taking off from an air base in one country, dropping bomb loads in a second country, and landing in a third country for resting, refueling, and rearming—between U.S. air bases in England, Italy, and Russia. The first such mission was flown by the 15th Air Force on June 2, 1944, when General Eaker personally led 130 B-17s to the Soviet Union, returning on June 11. The 8th Air Force launched its first Frantic mission on June 21, but it is best remembered as a great German, not American, air force success. German bombers caught the 8th Air Force's aircraft on the ground and destroyed 47 B-17s at Poltava, Russia. Frantic was primarily a political operation, yet it probably aggravated, not helped, U.S.-Soviet relations.

Another great "might have been" was the German introduction of jet and rocket-powered fighters in the summer of 1944. While these aircraft could fly 100 miles per hour faster than the best Allied fighter, there were too few of them and they arrived too late to make any difference in the war. Allied advantages of numbers and aggressive fighter pilots, coupled with German technical problems and mistakes, prevented these machines from doing much more than scaring the Allies. While jets were spectacular, as

were the V-1 flying bombs and V-2 ballistic missiles, they could not change the course of the war, and they obscured the reality of inferior German technology in more crucial areas: radar, radar countermeasures, proximity fuzes, and flak rockets.

By the fall of 1944, the German armed forces had become spent. The Luftwaffe was able to down numbers of U.S. bombers on occasion but paid a very high price. The toughest German resistance was around their most crucial targets, synthetic oil plants. Some, such as Leuna, were protected by more than 500 antiaircraft guns, as well as by jet and rocket-powered fighters. In 18 attacks against the oil targets at Leuna, the 8th Air Force lost 128 bombers. The campaign to cripple German petroleum sources was successful, but it was expensive.

The air war in 1945 is remembered for two controversial missions, both flown in February. The deadly and much-criticized attack on Dresden was primarily conducted by the British, although a number of U.S. 8th Air Force bombers also bombed the city's marshaling yards. American airmen were more involved in an extensive, nonstandard attack on railroad targets in small German towns on February 22 and 23, an operation code-named Clarion. The Allied air forces—the U.S. 8th and the British 15th—used both bombers and fighters to attack in small formations at low levels, hitting targets that had not been previously attacked. Accuracy was good and results were mixed, but the controversy ensued because one of the objects of the attack was German morale. The Allied strategic bombing campaign officially ended on April 16.

MEDITERRANEAN AIR OPERATIONS

Although the prewar planners had thought that the major thrust of operations would come from Britain, other bases were considered. U.S. air power was soon engaged in another theater following the Anglo-American assault into North Africa in November 1942 (Operation Torch). B-17s organized into the 12th Air Force and B-24s organized into the 9th Air Force hit airfields and ports, hardly strategic targets, but losses were low. Living and working conditions, however, were terrible. Airmen serving in North Africa envied the 8th Air Force's ground facilities as they suffered with rained-out runways, mud, sand, tents, poor food, and disease, as well as all kinds of shortages.

It was not until late February 1943 that the 12th Air Force's bombers hit a target outside of Africa. This was an increasing trend, and by April, the bulk of their bomber missions were against targets in mainland Italy, Sicily, and Sardinia. Perhaps the most famous U.S. operation during this period was Operation Flax, the effort to destroy the

A damaged B-17 remains in the air during Operation Flax, designed to prevent German supply planes from reaching German airfields in North Africa in 1943. (Army Air Corps)

German aerial resupply of its besieged troops in Africa. In April, Allied airmen hit the German airfields and the Luftwaffe in the air. The most famous incident was the "Palm Sunday Massacre" (Apr. 18, 1943), in which Allied fighters downed 86 aircraft. On May 13, the remaining Axis forces in North Africa surrendered.

Tactical air operations began for U.S. forces in the Mediterranean theater. Despite their usefulness in World War I, the American airmen neglected tactical operations because they flew in the face of the move toward air autonomy and because of the difficulties of tactical missions. The doctrine the airmen developed between the world wars emphasized interdiction missions, hitting convoys on the road, troops on the move, railroads, and bridges, but only attacking near the front as a last resort. Strategic bombing was clearly the major focus of the U.S. air forces.

German success with the Blitzkrieg early in the war forced Allied thinking to change. The exploits of fast-moving tanks and motorized infantry, supported by dive bombers, caught the attention of all. The U.S. Army, realizing the power of this German weapon and that American airmen preferred strategic operations, pushed for U.S. aircraft like the German Stukas. The result was not satisfactory—at first. Neither the equipment nor the concept of operations that would break air power into small packets under different army commanders worked well. The British used this scheme and met disaster in the North African desert. The Americans' turn came in short order as dramatically demonstrated at the Kasserine Pass debacle in February 1943. The AAF did change its doctrine and, like the British, centralized its tactical aviation. The Americans also discovered, as did the British, that fighter-bombers were better in the tactical air role than dive bombers. The P-47 served admirably in that function because it was a robust machine that mounted heavy armament (eight .50-caliber machine guns) and could carry heavy bombloads.

Sicilian Campaign

The Allies now shifted their attention to further advances in the Mediterranean. First, Allied air forces pounded the

Italian island of Pantelleria between May 8 and June 11, 1943, forcing the garrison to surrender before Allied troops stepped ashore. Next came Sicily. The thrust of the air attacks in support of the July 10 invasion was against Axis airfields. There were other raids as well, including the first U.S. attack of Rome, on July 19. One bad experience for the airmen took place on the night of July 11–12, when the Allies attempted to reinforce their airborne troops with an aerial resupply. Allied gunners ashore and aboard ships opened fire on the transports and the gliders they were towing, destroying 23 of 144 aircraft, killing 157 troops and airmen, and wounding 162 more. A further miscue occurred in action around the Straits of Messina. Despite Allied air superiority, air attacks on targets in this area failed to hinder seriously the evacuation of 100,000 German troops and 10,000 vehicles from Sicily to the Italian mainland. The Sicilian campaign ended when Gen. George Patton's troops entered Messina on Aug. 17.

Raid On Ploesti

About this same time, the AAF launched one of its most famous and costly missions, the low-level attack on the Ploesti oil refineries in Rumania. Ploesti was a key target for Allied air forces because it produced about 60 percent of Germany's oil. It was the target of the AAF's first bomber attack of the European war, when 12 B-24s hit the Rumanian target on June 11, 1942, with little damage. AAF planners in Washington subsequently came up with the low-level scheme, which offered the benefits of surprise and better bombing accuracy although it conflicted with AAF doctrine. On Aug. 1, 1943, three groups of 8th Air Force B-24 Liberators joined two groups of 9th Air Force B-24s to launch 177 aircraft from airfields near Benghazi, Libya.

B-24 Liberators, shown here bombing Germany, were capable of delivering payloads of five tons from high altitudes; they were used in the raids on the Ploesti oil refineries in Rumania in 1942. (Army Air Corps)

The mission was cursed by bad luck: the loss of the lead aircraft, the abort of the deputy lead, and the mistake of the resulting leader who made a wrong turn. The B-24 Liberators met not only flak and fighters but also barrage balloons and smokestacks. Despite fierce resistance and heavy losses, the crews pressed on and lost 54 bombers and 532 aircrew. Although initial bomb damage estimates concluded that 40 percent of Ploesti's oil capacity was destroyed, the damage was not permanent. Any mission that merits the award of five Medals of Honor and costs one-third of the force without inflicting significant or lasting damage has to be judged a failure. The Ploesti raid was a heroic deed, a daring operation, but an unrealistic, costly operation. This attack came only two and a half weeks before another famous and equally disastrous AAF operation, the August 17 raid on Regensburg and Schweinfurt in Germany.

Mainland Italy

The Allied air forces now turned their attention to attacks on the Italian mainland, primarily railroads and airfields. The war-weary Italians signed an armistice on Sept. 3, 1943, but the Germans quickly reacted, taking over most of Italy and continuing to fight. Early in September, the Allies invaded the mainland and met stiff German resistance, as they did for the remainder of the war in the Italian theater. The air forces supported the slow and frustrating advance northward.

During the same period, on October 1, the AAF's African-based B-17s attempted to bomb the aircraft near Munich, Germany, their first attack on a target in Germany. There were a few more attacks on German and Austrian sites, but the principal targets during the last three months of 1943 continued to be airfields and railroads in Italy. This soon changed following the movement of the African-based B-17s and B-24s to airfields near Foggia, Italy, and the formation in December of both the 15th Air Force and USSTAF. As already noted, Generals Spaatz and Doolittle moved to England, while General Eaker came to the Mediterranean theater. Gen. Nathan Twining took over the newly established 15th Air Force.

While the 8th Air Force hit targets in northwestern Europe, the 15th Air Force attacked targets in eastern and southern Europe. The 15th's heavy bombers were also engaged in supporting the troops more directly, attacking airfields and railroads, especially helping the ground forces in the Anzio assault and the controversial bombing of the Benedictine monastery at Cassino on February 15. The latter cultural site was flattened, but this destruction did not assist the ground forces as the rubble provided effective defensive positions. During the Big Week operation, the 15th Air Force suffered the highest percentage of losses of the three Allied strategic air forces during that campaign—

Gen. Nathan F. Twining, head of the 13th, 15th, and 20th air forces and of the Mediterranean Strategic Forces at various times during World War II, became chairman of the Joint Chiefs of Staff in the late 1950s. (U.S. Army Military History Institute)

three times those of the 8th Air Force. The town of Cassino was bombarded by heavy and medium bombers on March 15, but again with mixed results. The bombing did not break German resistance but did result in short bombing that killed 17 military personnel and 40 civilians. Another notable tactical air operation was the attempt by the Allied air forces to cut off German supplies in Operation Strangle. Beginning on March 19 and ending on May 11, the airmen attacked railroads, bridges, and ports in Italy, employing fighters and bombers. However, without an adequate night bomber capability and diverted by other tasks (such as Anzio and Cassino), this effort failed.

Perhaps the most important series of missions flown by the Mediterranean-based bombers was against the heavily defended Ploesti oil fields. Between June 1942 and August 1944, the AAF heavy bombers flew 20 missions against the Rumanian target and suffered 5.2 percent losses. Although the airmen estimated that the bombing cut the oil exports by more than half, it was the Soviet army that eventually stopped the flow of Rumanian oil to Germany.

The 15th Air Force faced few German fighter planes after the summer of 1944 but did battle German flak up until the very end of the war. Poor weather was the main problem, however, and it was only partially overcome by the use of radar-assisted bombing. Together with the 8th Air Force, Mediterranean-based bombers concentrated their efforts on heavily defended German oil targets. The 15th Air Force also bombed rail targets. The last notable mission of the war for the Italian-based airmen was their one attack on Berlin. Due to differential winds, the 15th Air Force was able to fly more than 800 miles each way to bomb a tank factory in the German capital on Mar. 24, 1945. Of the 169 B-17s and 289 fighters on the mission, 9 bombers and 5 fighters were lost.

In the waning moments of the war, the 15th Air Force hit rail targets. There was one major tactical effort, when in early April the unit launched large numbers of bombers (more than 800 bombers on three days, as well as more than 700 bombers on two others) against German army positions near Bologna. On April 16, General Spaatz announced the end of the strategic air war, yet the 15th Air Force continued to bomb communications targets into early May. The Germans surrendered, effective at 11:00 P.M. on May 8, 1945. The war in Europe was over.

SUMMARY: EUROPEAN AIR WAR

There is considerable controversy over the bombing of Europe by Allied air forces during World War II. Some authorities claim that it was wasteful, others assert that it was counterproductive or futile, and there are those who see it as immoral. Near the end of the war, the federal government set up the United States Strategic Bombing Survey, a blue-ribbon commission to study the impact of the strategic bombing of Germany and Japan. Bombing survey members entered the enemy's homeland along with the troops—in fact, some were killed in the effort—and put together a monumental study, more than 100 volumes on each theater. These volumes are the best source on the results of the bombing, not only because of the high caliber of people who were involved but because they had access to Allied and Axis records, interviewed the enemy, and made their own observations. Much cited, but seldom read, the survey is the key source of information on the strategic bombing.

Certainly, the bombing did not win the war and did not break German morale, but it did, despite uninformed opinions to the contrary, lower it. Beyond a doubt, however, the bombing effort was large and costly. Heavy bombers from the two U.S. air forces flew about 400,000 sorties, dropped approximately 1,000,000 tons of bombs, and lost 6,700 bombers. In personnel, the 8th and 15th air forces suffered 62,000 men killed, missing, or captured (about 60 percent of whom survived captivity). In comparison, the U.S. Army suffered 63,000 casualties (19,000 dead) at Normandy alone.

Air War Achievements

What did the airmen achieve for this tremendous cost in effort and life? First, the strategic bombing played a major role in defeating the Luftwaffe, which gave the Allies a significant advantage in the war. Attacks on German fighter plane factories helped, but most of all, air-to-air combat drove the German air force from the sky. Second, the bombing throttled German petroleum supplies, already in short supply. Third, the heavy bombers smashed German transportation, adversely affecting both the German economy and war machine. Fourth, the bombing campaign destroyed vast amounts of war matériel before it reached the German troops (one estimate holds that 20 percent of German war production during the last 16 months of the war was lost to the bombing). Fifth, the bombers diverted vast resources from the Germans' offensive war effort. About 1,000,000 individuals were involved in direct air defense; another 1,000,000 in rescue, repair, and cleanup operations. The cost in matériel was also immense. Perhaps 30 percent of heavy artillery tubes and ammunition and 55 percent of electronics production went into air defense efforts. In addition, the tactical air effort added a number of other advantages to the Allied cause. These tactical flights gave the Allies reconnaissance that the Germans lacked. Allied aircraft denied their foes mobility and restricted their movement to night or bad-weather conditions. And, of course, the tactical operations delivered considerable firepower, quickly. Finally, operating under Allied air dominance during the later years of the war, the Allied ground forces did not have to ward off German air attacks. Thus, while the cost was high, the air effort gave the Allies numerous advantages that enabled them to win the war sooner and with fewer Allied lives lost than would otherwise have been the case.

PACIFIC AIR OPERATIONS

Operations in the Pacific theater were far different from those in the European theater. Not only were the Japanese a different foe, so were the obstacles, equipment, and tactics. In contrast to the European war, the major problems proved to be weather and logistics rather than enemy opposition. Unlike the strategic air war over Europe, which was fought by two types of American heavy bombers and three types of fighters, the strategic air war against Japan was carried out primarily by only one aircraft type—the Boeing B-29 Superfortress. The American theory of daylight precision bombing did not work in the Pacific and was replaced by a different scheme. Finally, the Pacific air war was much briefer and less costly (to the Americans) than that waged in Europe.

Early Operations

From the very beginning, the Japanese were neither as highly regarded nor as feared as the Germans. Besides stemming from ignorance and racism, this attitude was fostered by the fact that the Japanese economy was only one-tenth the size of the U.S. economy. The attack on Pearl Harbor ignited the war, and it, along with Japan's subsequent startling victories, shocked Americans. Defeats at various island outposts, as well as in the U.S. colony of the Philippines, demoralized the American home front.

In order to strike back and boost American morale, the United States launched a daring attack on the Japanese homeland in April 1942. Sixteen army twin-engine B-25 bombers, fittingly known as "Mitchells," were launched from the carrier *Hornet*. Led by veteran aviator Lieutenant Colonel Doolittle, the bombers were to hit various Japanese targets and then recover on bases in free China. The operation, however, was compromised by a Japanese patrol vessel, and the raid began farther from Japan and earlier than planned. The aircraft bombed in broad daylight at low level, which made a clear propaganda statement to both the Americans and the Japanese. But as the B-25s that survived the Japanese defenses arrived over China in the dark and could not find friendly airfields, all were lost, although most of the crews survived. When Doolittle returned to the United States, he did not know if he would be greeted with a court-martial or a medal—he received the Medal of Honor from the hands of Pres. Franklin D. Roosevelt and became one of America's early heroes in

Very often, airplanes flew above the fleet, especially in the Pacific area, to protect against aerial attack by the enemy. (U.S. Army Military History Institute)

the war. While only a stunt, Doolittle's Tokyo Raid raised American spirits during the dark early days of the war when nothing seemed to go right. Japan's main islands did not see U.S. aircraft again or feel U.S. bombs for another two years.

For the United States, the war in the Pacific centered on navies. The Pacific Ocean was not only vast in size but devoid of friendly bases. Carrier aviation dominated sea warfare, while the strategic thrust was over bases. The Allies had to grab land and then develop it into bases for the next step toward Tokyo and victory. The scarcity of bases, along with the vast Pacific spaces, put a premium on aircraft range. The B-17 and B-24 bombers were only of limited utility in this theater.

Targeting Japan

The aircraft that fought the strategic air war was the Boeing B-29 "Superfortress," the best performing bomber of the war. It was developed in record time; it was requested by the U.S. air forces in January 1940, and a contract was signed in September. The aircraft was so desperately needed that almost 1,700 were on order when the first took to the sky in September 1942. The haste to get the superbomber—officially classed as "very heavy bomber" or "very long range bomber"—into combat created numerous difficulties. It was not the giant bomber's innovations, notably a pressurized cabin and remote controlled guns, that caused the bulk of the problems but its engines. Nevertheless, the B-29 was a much better performing aircraft than its predecessors in terms of firepower, bomb load, speed, altitude, and range. Developed too late for the European conflict, the B-29's long range made it especially useful in the air war against Japan.

B-25 bombers, shown here over Italy, were used in the 1942 Tokyo Raid, a daring foray over Japan by aviator Lt. Col. James Doolittle and 15 other pilots. (Army Air Corps)

If the B-29s were much more potent weapons than the B-17s and B-24s, Japan's air defenses were much weaker and its homeland was more vulnerable to strategic air attack than Germany's. From the start, the Japanese air force was not as strong as the German air force, and by 1944, it had been greatly worn down by attrition. Japanese aircraft were inferior, radar facilities poor, high-altitude interceptors almost nonexistent, and night fighters inadequate. Japan's flak was less concentrated and less lethal than its Axis partner's. Additionally, Japan's civil defense and fire-fighting capabilities were inferior to the Germans. Japan was more susceptible to air attack as its industry was smaller, its economy was dependent on imports, and its cities, with much wood construction, were more vulnerable to fire bombings than were Germany's.

Getting the B-29s within range of the Japanese homeland was a major problem for the U.S. military. Efforts to obtain bases in Siberia failed, as did technical attempts with air-to-air refueling. Therefore, the AAF had to use more conventional means to obtain airfields. The Joint Chiefs of Staff (JCS) established the 20th Air Force in April 1944 to fight this air war, initially with the XX Bomber Command stationed in India and later with the XXI Bomber Command stationed in the Marianas. The command arrangement was unique: the 20th Air Force reported directly to Gen. Henry ("Hap") Arnold, chief of the AAF, and through him to the JCS. As the island-hopping campaign edged toward Tokyo, the AAF deployed B-29s to India. Here, and at forward areas in free China, airfields were established under difficult conditions with minimum equipment, primarily making use of enormous numbers of native laborers, including more than 300,000 Chinese, for example. The bases were almost literally halfway around the world; the distance between factory and airfields, from Kansas to the bases in Bengal, was 11,530 miles, plus another 1,200 miles over the highest mountains in the world to the Chinese bases. U.S. air force commanders recognized the obstacles but had no alternative. If the physical difficulties were not enough, there were severe political problems as well. One reason for employing Chinese bases was to bolster the sagging forces of Chiang Kai-shek, a difficult ally. There were also problems with the "spirited" American commanders in the area—Lt. Gen. Joseph W. Stilwell, Maj. Gen. Claire L. Chennault, and Gen. Douglas MacArthur—as well as complications with the British under the command of Lord Louis Mountbatten.

Even using forward bases in China, the B-29s could only reach targets in southern Japan. Nevertheless, on June 5, 1944, one day before the D-Day invasion in Europe, the XX Bomber Command flew its first mission against Bangkok, Thailand, and attacked a target in Japan on June 14. Weather and logistics (it required four escort sorties to support one bombing sortie), the initial operating problems

In an unsuccessful experiment, aircraft such as the P-47s shown here—disassembled and being towed—were shipped to airfields in India to be used in bombing raids over Japan during World War II. (U.S. Army Military History Institute)

of the B-29, and the extreme range proved too much. Even relieving the unit's command and bringing in the legendary General LeMay could not make this effort work. Bombing from China ceased in January 1945, and the Indian operation was shut down in March. In this testing period, operating under some of the worst conditions that any air force had to deal with throughout the war, the B-29s dropped fewer than 1,000 tons of bombs on targets in Japan, about 10 percent of their total effort. The unit had failed, as it did not effectively bomb Japan.

Attacking from the Pacific

Meanwhile, a second B-29 force was being set up on recently taken Pacific islands. At the same time the Chinese-based bombers began their operations in June, U.S. troops stormed ashore in Saipan. Here, and on Guam and Tinian, a series of five bomber bases was established. While these island bases were somewhat easier to develop and supply than those established in India and China, they also had serious problems. Nevertheless, B-29s based here flew their first mission against Tokyo on Nov. 24, 1944. But the attempt to use the prewar U.S. strategic bombing doctrine failed—not because of enemy resistance, as had been the case over Germany, but because of weather and equipment. Not only was Japan shielded by clouds, but the high-altitude (above 30,000 feet) operations of the B-29 posed problems. The airmen discovered the jet stream, winds at high altitude often exceeding 100 miles per hour that made accurate bombing extremely difficult. In addition, the B-29s had mechanical problems. The heavy weight, high-temperature takeoffs, and high-altitude operations were hard on the engines, which failed at an alarming rate. Mechanical difficulties and weather provided more protection for Japan than did its air defenses. Arnold, never known for his patience, relieved the 20th Air Force commander in early January 1945 and brought in General LeMay.

At first, LeMay, one of the outstanding combat air commanders of all time, could do little better. He shook up the high command, instituted further training, and made some other changes based on the European experience. Some of the problems lessened as the crews built up experience, as supplies and more aircraft streamed into the Marianas, and as Iwo Jima was taken. The capture of Iwo Jima meant that a key Japanese fighter field and radar site were neutralized and that the Americans now had an emergency airfield and fighter field midway to their targets. The first B-29 landed on the volcanic island on March 4, to be followed by 2,400 more through the course of the war. This, along with a well-developed Air Sea Rescue service, which saved half of those who went into the ocean, kept losses low and morale high. Escort fighters were positioned on the airfield as well, flying their first mission on April 7. What few fighter defenses the Japanese had were soon swept from the board.

Still, the basic problems of weather and the B-29 remained. LeMay showed the same imagination and flexibility that had propelled him to the top in the 8th Air Force and made a dramatic change. He took all the ammunition from his bombers, a net weight savings of 3,200 pounds, flew his bombers at night, singularly, at relatively low level (7,000 feet), and employed incendiary bombs. In short, LeMay was jettisoning the U.S. bombing doctrine of day precision bombing for the British doctrine of night area bombing. LeMay's decision was not only a break from AAF doctrine but also a bold and risky move.

On the night of Mar. 9, 1944, LeMay's experiment was tested as 334 B-29s went out against Tokyo and dropped 1,700 tons of bombs, mainly incendiaries. The result was the most destructive air raid of all time (including the atomic bombings of Hiroshima and Nagasaki). One-quarter (16 square miles) of the Japanese capital, Japan's largest city, was destroyed, and more than 80,000 people were killed. The raid showed that Japanese night defenses were almost nonexistent (only 14 B-29s were lost on the raid), and operations at lower altitudes lessened mechanical problems and permitted greater bombloads. LeMay followed

with similar attacks on three other urban areas in the next nine days. These four missions burned out a total of 32 square miles at the cost of only 22 B-29s. In this flurry, the B-29s delivered three times the weight of bombs they had dropped prior to March 9. The campaign was curtailed by a shortage of incendiary bombs, as LeMay's change in tactics relied on a higher percentage of incendiaries and the lower altitudes allowed a greater number to be carried than previously. After a delay, there was a short spurt on April 13 and 15 that destroyed a further 21 square miles of urban areas. A lull followed for about a month as the B-29s were diverted to attack Japanese airfields in connection with the invasion of Okinawa.

The 20th Air Force continued to bomb using visual means when it could, but the focus of its operations was incendiary attacks on Japanese cities. All of these operations were at lower altitudes, which permitted twice the bomb load, increased accuracy from 12 to 37 percent within 1,000 feet of the target, and lessened mechanical problems. By June 15, the airmen had destroyed 106 square miles of the six largest urban areas in Japan and then had turned their attention to smaller cities. Between March 9 and August 14, 70 percent of the B-29 attacks were urban incendiary raids. Japanese resistance was so weak that the Americans dropped leaflets warning civilians in a dozen cities that they would be attacked next, and then went on to attack four of these. The 20th Air Force destroyed 40 percent of the built-up area in 66 cities, about 170 square miles of urban area, before it ran out of targets. The conventional bombing and the two atomic bombs killed about 330,000 Japanese, rendered 30 percent of the urban population homeless, and led to the evacuation of one-quarter of the urban population. Along with the death, destruction, and misery dealt the civilian and military populations, the bombing destroyed the heart of the Japanese economy. By July 1945, overall industrial output was at 40 percent of its 1944 peak, with some areas far lower; for example, oil was at 15 percent and aluminum at 9 percent. The B-29s also helped blockade Japan from the sea. One wing of B-29s engaged in mining Japanese waters, which proved very effective in cutting off Japanese imports.

THE ATOMIC BOMB

The B-29s' destruction of Japanese cities and industry was overshadowed by the two atomic bombs that many have erroneously credited with winning the war. The Allies built the bombs because they feared that the Germans would get the weapon first. Following the revelations by two refugee scientists of German efforts in this field, physicist Albert Einstein wrote President Roosevelt a letter in August 1939, urging him to push work in this area. Thus, the Manhattan Project was born, harnessing the best brains of the Western

Physicist Albert Einstein urged the U.S. development of the atomic bomb because he feared that the Germans were close to developing theirs, but he worked for international control of nuclear energy after World War II. (Library of Congress)

Allies (the Soviet Union was not informed of the project) and tremendous financial resources. Entire cities rose at Oak Ridge, Tennessee; Los Alamos, New Mexico; and Hanford, Washington, to develop and build this untried, super, secret weapon. The defeat of Germany and the death of Roosevelt did not slow the effort. The new president, Harry S Truman, after being informed of the bomb's development, established a committee to advise him on its use. The Interim Committee, which consisted of top U.S. civilian scientists and political leaders, issued its report on June 1, 1945, recommending that the bomb be used as soon as possible, without warning, against a joint civilian-military target (a city). Efforts by some scientists in the project to take a different course (stage a demonstration; make the decision an Allied, not an American, one; and inform the Soviets) were in vain. A nuclear device was tested in mid-July at Alamogordo, New Mexico, and on July 25, the War Department ordered that the first bomb be dropped on the first visual bombing day after August 3. On July 26, Truman issued the Potsdam Declaration, which called for Japan's unconditional surrender and which the Japanese rejected on July 28.

Hiroshima and Nagasaki

On Aug. 6, 1945, the B-29 *Enola Gay,* named after the pilot's mother, dropped the first atomic bomb on Hiro-

Upon the death of President Roosevelt in 1945, Harry S Truman was sworn in as president; he was immediately faced with the decision of whether to use the atomic bomb against Japan. (National Archives)

shima. The bomb devastated the city, destroying 4.7 square miles (60 percent of the built-up area) and killing 70,000–80,000 people. Three days later, a second B-29 dropped an atomic bomb on Nagasaki that razed 1.5 square miles and killed 40,000 people. Thus, two bombs, without the loss of an American life, destroyed 55 percent of two urban areas, an effort that would have required 345 B-29 sorties. The shock of these two bombs and the threat of further attacks convinced the Japanese to surrender on August 14. The peace was signed on Sept. 2, 1945, aboard the U.S. battleship *Missouri* in Tokyo Bay. The long and costly war was finally over.

SUMMARY: PACIFIC AIR WAR

The strategic bombing effort against Japan had about the same physical impact as the bombing of Germany. The Japanese campaign, however, was much smaller in effort and losses, as well as more concentrated in time. The campaign against the Japanese homeland involved about 15 percent of the tons dropped on Germany, 3 percent of the bombers and 1 percent of the fighters lost by AAF and RAF strategic air arms, and 2 percent of the aircrew dead or missing. The greater capabilities of the B-29, the weaker Japanese defenses, and the more vulnerable Japanese economy help to explain this result. The atomic bombs, while more efficient, gruesome, and clearly adding to the shock of the air war, really were nothing more than what Japan had already suffered from hundreds of B-29s delivering thousands of tons of incendiary bombs. While only 9 percent of the 8th and 15th air forces' bombs were incendiaries and 25 percent of the Anglo-American strategic bombing effort was directed against German urban areas, the 20th Air Force dropped 66 percent of its bombs on cities and 61 percent of its bombs were incendiaries.

Just as the strategic bombing of Germany did not win that war, the same can be said of the war against Japan. The Pacific war was won by the defeat of the Japanese army and navy in the field, the sinking of the merchant fleet, the entry of the Soviet Union into the war, and the destruction of both Japanese cities and industry. The B-29 was only one of the victor's weapons.

7

The War of Logistics: 1941–1945

In 1904, Sec. of War Elihu Root warned, "Our trouble never will be in raising soldiers: Our trouble will always be the limit of possibility in transporting, clothing, arming, feeding, and caring for our soldiers, and that requires organization." Secretary Root instinctively recognized that victory in modern warfare is determined by a nation's ability to organize and direct the vast machinery needed to project combat power onto the battlefield. At no time in U.S. history has Root's prophecy been more clearly borne out than in World War II. The challenges faced by American military and political leaders in providing logistical support for U.S. forces around the world in every conceivable climate and terrain were enormous. Those challenges, however, were met and overcome. Effective plans were made, control organizations were set up, industry was mobilized, war matériel was produced and delivered to the theaters of operations, and personnel were found to staff the factories, lines of communication, and service units supporting the combat forces.

The size and complexity of the "war of logistics" between 1941 and 1945 defy easy description, but understanding the American logistical achievement, and indeed the importance of logistics in general, is crucial to understanding World War II. The war of logistics involved four key aspects: planning and organization, production, lines of communication, and the "tooth-to-tail ratio." An examination of each of these demonstrates how the voracious appetite for logistics of a modern, global, coalition war conducted on land, sea, and air with sophisticated weapons affected U.S. military strategy and operations between 1941 and 1945 and thus how World War II was really

won, not solely on the battlefield but in the factory and on the lines of communication as well.

PLANNING AND ORGANIZATION

U.S. industrial power was just beginning to be felt on the battlefield when World War I ended on Nov. 11, 1918, but the American logistical achievement had been nonetheless impressive. In less than 19 months, the United States, with a heavy contribution by the Allies in shipping and ordnance, had moved 7,452,000 tons of supplies and 2,000,000 men to France; organized 42 oversized divisions, 28 of which saw battle; established 22 bases in France plus the lines of communication of the Services of Supply (SOS); and created an entire system of training and embarkation camps at home. This ability to mobilize, produce, and project the machinery of war far from home was perhaps the most striking aspect of U.S. participation in World War I, an ability that would be tested again, even more severely, just 23 years later. The battle of planning and organizing for that test began soon after the end of World War I.

Logistical Organization: 1919–1940

After World War I, the great logistical apparatus that had been formed to support U.S. forces in France and at home was dismantled, and all of the gains made toward efficient centralization of the army's support structure were abandoned. The National Defense Act of June 4, 1920, required

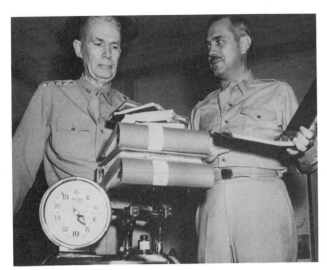

In 1942, Lt. Gen. Brehon Somervell (left) *headed the Army Services of Supply; here, he reviews new procurement regulations.* (U.S. Army Military History Institute)

a return to the traditional pattern of fragmented, diffused authority and responsibility. Effective control of logistical operations reverted to the individual supply departments, and the General Staff surrendered its authority, granted in 1918, as an operating agency directing the activities of the supply bureaus and coordinating the war effort and restricted its activities to planning and simple coordination.

Benedict Crowell, the wartime director of munitions, and others felt that matters of purchasing, production, and contracts were best handled by civilian officials rather than military officers. The National Defense Act of 1920 reflected this view by charging the assistant secretary of war with responsibility for industrial mobilization planning and the supervision of all military procurement. However, the act did not clearly mark out the division of responsibilities between the assistant secretary of war and the General Staff. In 1921, a board headed by Gen. James G. Harbord, the former commander of the American Expeditionary Force's SOS and deputy chief of staff under Gen. John J. Pershing, met to define the relationships that should exist between the General Staff and the assistant secretary of war in procurement and other matters. The Harbord Board recommended that the General Staff G-4 should establish the types and quantities of items needed and determine when and where they were required. The assistant secretary of war would then receive and break down the list of requirements and order the chiefs of the various supply services to procure the necessary items. The supply bureaus would place the contracts, maintain quality control, and receive and store supplies. Finally, the G-4 would direct and supervise the distribution of supplies to the using units. Although the supply departments were to report to the assistant secretary of war on procurement matters and to

the General Staff on other issues, there was no centralized command over the supply bureaus and no close coordination of the whole system below the level of the secretary of war himself. This arrangement, introduced in 1921, remained essentially unchanged until 1942.

Interwar Logistical Planning

War planning between the world wars left much to be desired. Three types of plans were produced. The War Plans Division of the General Staff developed strategic plans that included statements of the forces necessary to achieve the objectives in possible theaters of operations. The General Staff G-3 prepared mobilization plans, and the assistant secretary of war was responsible for industrial mobilization plans. The coordination of these three varieties of plans was particularly poor, and many changes were required after World War II began.

Strategic planning between 1919 and 1940 was impressive when compared to that undertaken before World War II but lacked a proper understanding of probable requirements. In general, the strategic plans were too far from reality to permit any accurate anticipation of the logistical limitations. The Color Plans of the 1920s and 1930s were based on the unrealistic assumption that U.S. forces would act alone to defend the United States and its territories against various combinations of foreign powers. The more likely prospect of another coalition war overseas was ignored until the late 1930s, when the world situation forced the planners to assume that the United States might have to cooperate with allies in operations against an enemy coalition. The most comprehensive of the pre-World War II strategic plans, Rainbow 5, did in fact assume that U.S. forces would be sent to the eastern Atlantic, Africa, and/or Europe to help the British and French in the decisive defeat of Germany and Italy and thus was very close to the eventual reality.

The interwar mobilization plans were also based on faulty assumptions and insufficient information, but their greatest weakness was their near total disregard for logistical factors. Army mobilization planners failed to comprehend the enormous complexity and importance of supply in modern "mechanized" warfare, despite the fact that World War I had proven the absolute dependence of armies on supply. The General Staff mobilization planners were totally preoccupied with manpower issues and ignorantly believed that "supply would have to adjust itself to strategy." In the end, it was strategy that had to adjust to supply.

It was left to the assistant secretary of war to keep alive memories of the tremendous logistical problems of World War I. The assistant secretary of war proceeded with fairly detailed and coordinated planning for industrial mobilization while telling the General Staff strategic and mobilization planners that their pipe dreams could not be supported.

Industrial mobilization planning in the 1920s and 1930s was reasonably well-informed, but it was hampered by a lack of anything except World War I experience to go on, reduced budgets, and pacifist attitudes of the American public. Industrial Mobilization Plans (IMP) were published in 1931, 1933, 1936, and 1939, but none of those plans was ever put into effect. Despite substantial efforts, industrial mobilization planning in the 1920s and 1930s did not achieve tangible success. Nevertheless, the War Department approached World War II with some idea of the raw materials and productive capacity that would be needed and the agencies through which industrial mobilization might be directed.

Until the mid-1930s, strategic plans reflected too few studies of logistical feasibility, and mobilization plans attempted to establish a rate of troop mobilization beyond the capability of U.S. industry to support adequately in the early stages. The gap between strategic "desire" and logistical "reality" was closed somewhat after 1935 when Army Chief of Staff Gen. Malin Craig initiated a serious review of mobilization plans that culminated in a realistic Protective Mobilization Plan (PMP) as the basis for procurement requirements. The PMP attempted to take into account U.S. industrial resources and capabilities and reduced manpower "dreams" accordingly. Despite more realistic planning, the United States remained far from ready for a major global coalition war. The lack of appropriations kept war reserves scanty and equipment obsolete. Logistical support units were practically nonexistent, and there was uncertainty as to what agencies would control mobilization once it became necessary.

Mobilization Agencies

To fulfill his industrial mobilization and procurement responsibilities, the assistant secretary of war organized his office into two branches, the Current Procurement Branch and the Planning Branch, which supervised the supply services in developing their plans and requirements. Each supply department established a procurement planning section in its own headquarters and prepared detailed plans. Both the assistant secretary of war and the General Staff depended on the supply departments for logistical planning information, an arrangement that was not altogether satisfactory. In 1923, Sec. of War John W. Weeks established the Army Industrial College (now the Industrial College of the Armed Forces) on the recommendation of Asst. Sec. Dwight F. Davis. The college was designed to educate officers in industrial mobilization planning and opened in 1924 with nine students. It quickly expanded and gained prestige, and U.S. Navy and Marine Corps students were added in 1925. Planning data and studies prepared by Industrial College students were used in actual planning.

Davis also initiated coordination of industrial mobilization plans with the navy. The Army-Navy Munitions

Board, consisting of the assistant secretary of war and the assistant secretary of the navy, was created in June 1922. The board became the sponsor of the IMP, and it was assumed that in the event of war the board would act as the central control authority for economic and industrial mobilization until an appropriate civilian agency could be set up. In its final (1939) form, the IMP envisaged a war resources administration as the central control agency, reflecting the longstanding belief that "full mobilization" would require a superagency similar to the War Industries Board of World War I. In August 1939, Pres. Franklin D. Roosevelt formed just such a War Resources Board (WRB) under U.S. Steel chairman of the board Edward R. Stettinius, Jr., to conduct an intensive review of the IMP. However, Congress and the public were unreceptive to strong economic controls or central direction of industrial mobilization efforts, and the WRB proved a political liability for Roosevelt. Its recommendations were ignored, and it was allowed to die in November 1939. Instead, Roosevelt asked Bernard Baruch and former navy secretary John Hancock to prepare a modified IMP that would recognize progressive stages rather than a set "mobilization day," would have several agencies reporting to the president rather than one superagency, and would move away from the concentration of emergency powers in the War Department.

The 18-month period of rearmament from June 1940 to Dec. 7, 1941, was crucial to U.S. preparation for World War II, and several important organizational developments took place during that time. In 1940, Sec. of War Henry L. Stimson obtained a change to the National Defense Act of 1920 that returned procurement responsibility to his office with the authority to delegate that responsibility as he saw fit. Stimson subsequently charged the undersecretary of war, Robert P. Patterson, with that responsibility in July 1940, thereby eliminating the assistant secretary from the picture. As war approached, both the president and Congress declined to implement the IMP. The defensive preparations undertaken were not thought to constitute total mobilization, and the army and navy continued to procure supplies and services directly while civilian agencies mobilized and controlled manpower and raw materials. The various military procurement agencies issued contracts independently on the basis of informal bids or under commitments conveyed directly to the War and Navy departments or through the Office of Production Management (OPM).

The Council of National Defense, made up of cabinet members, was revived in the spring of 1940 to help manage the rearmament effort. The actual work was left to an advisory commission consisting of seven prominent representatives of industry, labor, agriculture, transportation, and consumer interests. The Advisory Commission of the Council of National Defense, created on May 29, 1940, was in effect the first mobilization superagency. Its first meeting, held in July 1940, considered such matters as

Henry Stimson, secretary of war during World War II, had served as Pres. Herbert Hoover's secretary of state and had chaired the U.S. delegations to the London Naval (1930) and the Geneva Disarmament (1932) conferences. (Library of Congress)

priorities, scarce materials, the revitalization of industry, the control of contracts, and the building and expansion of defense plants. As requirements grew, the functions of the Advisory Commission were gradually absorbed by various operating agencies, and it was superseded by the OPM in January 1941. That agency was in turn superseded by the Supply Priorities and Allocations Board in August 1941. On Dec. 7, 1941, the Army-Navy Munitions Board remained the only fully functional industrial mobilization management organization.. However, it was soon supplanted by a bewildering array of civilian mobilization agencies, and in February 1942, the board was reorganized. Thereafter, its principal role was to provide liaison with the various civilian mobilization and production agencies. Eventually, the War Production Board (WPB), established in January 1942 and headed by Donald Nelson, became the most important coordinator of industry for national defense programs. The major objective of the WPB was to control plant construction and expansion, provide machine tools, allocate raw materials, and supervise contracting. Introduced in November 1942, the Controlled Materials Plan (CMP) became the heart of the WPB's effective control of the wartime economy.

Military Logistical Reorganization

Perhaps the most important organizational change impacting on U.S. military logistical operations in World War II was the so-called Marshall reorganization of March 1942

and the subsequent development of Army Service Forces. By 1941, it was clear that the organization of the War Department was cumbersome and unsuited to the demands being placed upon it. Some 61 separate offices and agencies had direct access to the army chief of staff, as did 40 major commands and 350 smaller ones. The fragmentation of logistical responsibilities among the War Department General Staff G-4, the Office of the Undersecretary of War, and the chiefs of the six supply services and eight administrative departments was particularly complex and ineffective. To resolve these organizational problems, the War Department was reorganized by presidential executive order on Mar. 9, 1942. All of the General Staff sections except the War Plans and Intelligence divisions were reduced in size and limited to broad planning and policy guidance. The War Plans Division, renamed the Operations Division (OPD), was expanded and became the central War Department command post. The Logistics Group in the OPD provided broad policy guidance and the necessary interface between the forces in the field and the logistical agencies of the government responsible for procurement and distribution.

The Marshall reorganization also divided the army into three major commands: Army Air Forces (AAF), Army Ground Forces (AGF), and the Services of Supply (SOS). The AAF was granted autonomy in administering training, personnel, and supplies peculiar to air operations. The AGF assumed responsibility for the organization, training, and control of ground combat forces. Responsibility for administering the supply and service activities of the War Department was assigned to the SOS, soon renamed Army Service Forces (ASF). The ASF assumed authority over and coordinated the activities of the six technical (supply) services, eight administrative services, nine corps areas (later renamed service commands), six ports of embarkation, and nine general depots. As ASF commander, Lt. Gen. Brehon B. Somervell was responsible for establishing requirements and for distributing supplies, but Undersecretary of War Patterson continued to be responsible for procurement. The creation of the ASF made possible the central direction of army logistical activities in the war and contributed greatly to the final positive outcome. Its establishment marked a major victory in the battle of logistical planning and organization in that it represented the full recognition for the first time of the importance of logistics on the modern battlefield and the advantages of concentrating logistical operations in a single command.

PRODUCTION

The size, complexity, and worldwide distribution of U.S. military forces in World War II were without parallel in the history of warfare. The development and manufacture of the enormous quantities of supplies and services needed

Black American factory workers, many of them women, contributed greatly to the war effort; above, flares are being manufactured. (U.S. Army Military History Institute)

to equip and sustain U.S. forces engaged in a global conflict were one of the most critical battles of the war. The United States and the Allies clearly won the battle by greatly surpassing the Axis Powers in the struggle to produce the quantity and quality of matériel needed by the armed forces while continuing to supply essential civilian needs.

U.S. War Preparations

After the Munich Agreement in 1938, the United States became increasingly aware of its military weakness, but its rearmament program did not begin in earnest until the summer of 1940. In May 1940, 18 months before Pearl Harbor, President Roosevelt appointed William S. Knudsen, an expert on industrial production, to the Advisory Commission of the Council of National Defense. Almost immediately, Knudsen requested guidance from the army and the navy in order to determine the required munitions production capacity of U.S. industry. Knudsen's request resulted in a proposed munitions program that, in its revised form, called for equipping an army of 1,000,000 men by Sept. 30, 1941, 2,000,000 by Dec. 31, 1941, and 4,000,000 at some later, indefinite date. This revised program was approved by the president and passed to Congress on July 10, 1940.

The proposed munitions program represented an attempt to obtain the resources needed to support the existing strategic plans, but even before the United States entered the war, it began to encounter problems meeting the established production goals, principally because of the diversion of much of U.S. arms production to friendly foreign powers. On Apr. 18, 1941, Undersecretary of War Patterson recommended that a new estimate of production requirements be made that would gauge U.S. munitions

production against the capabilities of potential U.S. enemies. Patterson also suggested that the use made of the munitions (that is, the strategic plan) was of less importance than the amount of munitions that could be produced. The War Department General Staff subsequently undertook a new study, which resulted in the Victory Program of 1941, a comprehensive statement of U.S. manpower and production requirements. On Jan. 6, 1942, the Victory Program was redesignated the War Munitions Program and became the basis for U.S. production of war matériel.

Although the raw statistics cannot tell the entire story of how the United States served as the "Arsenal of Democracy" and won the battle of production, a review of army procurement achievements in World War II can suggest the magnitude of the task and the effort required to achieve the desired results. The final statistics are all the more impressive when considered in relation to U.S. status on Dec. 7, 1941. At that time, only 7 of the 34 divisions could be equipped for immediate overseas deployment. The United States had in operation only 12,000,000 tons of ocean shipping with 10,000,000 additional tons under construction. Available supplies and equipment included only 16,000 tons of bombs, 450,000,000 rounds of small-arms ammunition, 2,000 tanks, and fewer than 500 radar sets. There were almost no tractors, airfield planking, Transportation Corps matériel, or chemical warfare equipment available.

Raw Materials

The production of weapons, equipment, and other supplies was of course dependent on obtaining and processing the necessary raw materials. Before World War II, Congress had several times refused to fund stockpiles of critical war materials. Nevertheless, as in so many other areas, the United States was very successful in overcoming the shortfalls. Aluminium production was only 163,500 tons in 1939 but rose to more than 900,000 tons in 1943. Steel ingot production was 53,000,000 tons in 1939 but reached 90,000,000 tons in 1944. Copper production was only 705,000 tons in 1939 but rose to 1,100,000 tons in 1943. The United States produced less than $200,000,000 worth of machine tools in 1939; in 1942, it produced $1.3 billion worth. In 1941, U.S. production of synthetic rubber was only 8,380 long tons; in 1944, it was 797,000 long tons. In October 1939, U.S. shipyards produced 20,000 tons of ocean shipping; at its peak, in December 1943, U.S. production totaled 1,990,000 tons. The daily production of petroleum products rose from an average of 3,900,000 barrels per day in 1941 to 4,860,000 barrels per day in May 1945.

Facilities

The other major factor in production capacity was the number of plants and other facilities available. During

Half-tracks (armored vehicles with tractor treads in place of rear wheels), shown here in Belgium, were one of the many kinds of combat vehicles manufactured during World War II. (U.S. Army Military History Institute)

World War II, the ASF in the United States alone completed 23,200 construction projects worth some $10.7 billion and involving more than 1,000,000 workers. During the war, 17 new supply depots were constructed, as were 61 ordnance facilities and 184 airfields. The ASF eventually managed 149,000,000 square feet of storage area, and 2,000,000 people were employed in handling more than 4,000,000 tons of supplies per month at 125 major storage installations in the United States.

Tanks and Other Vehicles

Between 1919 and 1935, the army's tank production program resulted in just 33 deliveries, and between 1935 and 1940, only 1,000 tanks were produced. In the spring of 1940, the army had no heavy tanks and only 144 medium tanks and 648 light tanks on hand or on order. However, between July 1940 and the end of August 1945, the United States produced 88,410 tanks in 21 different types. In addition to tanks, Ordnance Department deliveries for 1940–45 included 46,706 carriages for self-propelled weapons and 113,967 other combat vehicles. Some 2,382,311 trucks were produced, including 634,569 "jeeps" and 676,433 "deuce and a half" 6 x 6 trucks in 11 different types. Also produced were bicycles, motorcycles, and passenger cars. So great was the U.S. production of automotive vehicles that, at the end of the war, the United States could have loaded and moved all 8,000,000 troops of the U.S. Army on motor vehicles at one time.

Artillery and Infantry Weapons

In World War I, U.S. forces relied on British and French factories for most of their artillery and small arms. However, in World War II, American artillerymen were equipped with 7,803 heavy field artillery pieces, 54,532 light field artillery and antitank guns (including 11,116 workhorse 105-millimeter howitzers), and 27,080 guns and howitzers for self-propelled weapons, all of U.S. manufac-

ture. In addition, 31,104 81-millimeter mortars and 73,706 60-millimeter mortars were produced, as were 156,587 antiaircraft guns. Close-in antitank defense was provided by 476,628 2.36-inch antitank rocket launchers, the famous "bazookas." Infantrymen could choose among the 2,679,819 machine guns, 6,552,290 rifles, and 6,117,827 .30-caliber carbines turned out by U.S. armament factories. Some 188,380 Browning automatic rifles added to infantry firepower. Also available were 2,008,267 .45-caliber submachine guns, 1,877,069 .45-caliber automatic pistols, 889,203 .38-caliber revolvers, and 429,074 12-gauge shotguns.

Ammunition

World War II American ammunition production far surpassed anything dreamed of in World War I. Almost 105,000,000 high-explosive artillery shells were produced, as were 100,000 16-inch naval shells and nearly 82,000,000 mortar rounds. About 13,000,000 2.36-inch HEAT (high-explosive antitank) rockets and more than 10 billion rounds of .50-caliber ammunition of all types were turned out. Small-arms ammunition production included nearly 4.1 billion rounds of .45-caliber (all types) and more than 25 billion rounds of .30-caliber (all types). U.S. factories also produced 4,053,000 1,000-pound general-purpose bombs, 7,309,000 500-pound general-purpose bombs, and 2,455,000 250-pound general-purpose bombs, as well as 8,963,000 fragmentation bomb clusters. In addition, 889,101 AN-CPQ1 proximity fuzes, one of the technological marvels of the war, were produced under Signal Corps supervision. Up to January 1945, $8.5 billion was expended on the manufacture of ammunition alone. In the spring of 1945, ammunition production reached 700,000

The jeep, the versatile, rugged, and chief method of transportation for military personnel during World War II, could even be rigged as an ambulance to carry a wounded soldier. (U.S. Army Military History Institute)

tons per month, or an annual rate of more than 8,000,000 tons.

Communications, Engineer, and Transportation Corps Equipment

Communications were a crucial factor on the World War II battlefield. Between Jan. 1, 1940, and Dec. 31, 1945, the communications equipment produced included 88,040 SCR-300 "walkie talkies," 206,753 SCR-536 "handie talkies," 45,857 SCR-510 radios for armored forces, 1,363,061 EE-8 field telephones, 5,107 SCR-720 air intercept radars, 3,456,452 miles of W-110B communications wire, and 1,050 PG-46-A pigeon lofts. To facilitate battlefield movements, 1,788 M2 Bailey-type panel bridges, 37,613 M2 assault boats, and 702,398 1,000-square-foot sections of steel airplane landing mat were manufactured, as were 7,570 locomotives, 95,290 railway cars (more than 37 types), 1,409 marine tugs (24 types), and 5,839 non-self-propelled marine barges (35 types).

Clothing and Individual Equipment

A good deal of U.S. industrial capacity was given over to the production of clothing and individual equipment. Army Quartermaster Corps procurement alone between July 1, 1940, and Aug. 31, 1945, included 128,315,000 pairs of shoes, boots, and other footwear and 519,122,000 pairs of socks. World War II soldiers donned 259,784,000 pairs of drawers, 212,531,000 undershirts, and 1,024,000 pairs of women's winter panties under 139,069,000 shirts, 229,373,000 pairs of trousers, and 165,531,000 coats and jackets. The soldier's wardrobe was completed by 64,743,000 cotton neckties, 209,685,000 cotton handkerchiefs, 36,585,000 web belts, and 90,811,000 pairs of gloves. The outfit could be topped off with one of the 22,756,000 M1 steel helmets, and the time could be checked by one of the 974,311 wrist watches supplied. To protect against the chemical warfare, which fortunately did not occur, some 23,510,030 military gas masks were produced.

Subsistence

Every army travels on its stomach, and the U.S. Army of World War II was no exception. U.S. farmers, meat packers, and food processors turned out a prodigious amount of subsistence between 1941 and 1945. Among the perishable subsistence items supplied were 461,500 tons of beef, 2,192,000 tons of Irish potatoes, 102,835,000 dozen eggs, 115,500 tons of tomatoes, 178,500 tons of lettuce, 76,000 tons of lemons, and 428,500 tons of butter. Beans are a staple of military cuisine, and in World War II, some 176,500 tons of dry white navy beans were produced for military consumption. Some 2,880,000 tons of white wheat flour, 1,064,500 tons of sugar, and 303,500 tons of rice were produced. Some 51,000 tons of prunes vied with 81,500 tons of canned salmon and 233,500 tons of canned meat and vegetable stew for the title of "least liked" item on the menu. Some 55,500 tons of pickles were available to alter the taste of 136,500 tons of canned luncheon meat. If all else failed, the soldier could survive on 58,000 tons of peanut butter and 120,000 tons of jam, topped off with 171,000 tons of canned fruit cocktail. Lifted to the mouth by 7,173,000 table forks, the whole was washed down with liquids from 6,644,000 5-gallon water cans and 27,842,000 canteens. Afterward, the fastidious soldier could brush with one of the 18,415,000 toothbrushes produced.

Medical Supplies

Heavy fighting on land, sea, and air brought heavy casualties, and worldwide operations, often in hostile climate and terrain, exposed U.S. troops to a wide range of disease and environmentally induced illness. As might be expected, the production of medical supplies between Jan. 1, 1940, and Aug. 31, 1945, was tremendous. Some 237,371,000 2-ounce bottles of insect repellant were supplied to ward off the thousands of exotic insects found in every corner of the world. More than 11,000,000 temperature thermometers were manufactured. Nearly 4 billion quinacrine tablets and more than 747,000,000 quinine sulfate tablets were produced to protect against malaria. More than 2,000,000 20-cc (cubic centimeter) vials of cholera vaccine, nearly 9,000,000 20-cc vials of typhus vaccine, and more than 1,000,000 20-cc vials of plague vaccine were also produced. Some 28,794,919 quarter-pound cans of foot powder were produced. The troops' wounds were dressed with 14,388,577 first-aid packets (brown field dressings); their pain was eased by more than 60,000,000 one-eighth grain tablets of morphine sulfate and more than 16,000,000 quarts of whiskey. Their lost blood was replaced by 3,114,892 500-cc and 3,060,594 250-cc bottles of dried human blood plasma, and more than 146,000,000 envelopes of sulfanilamide powder and 19,875,485 vials of penicillin and streptomycin were applied to prevent or cure infection.

Aircraft

The U.S. approach to winning the war emphasized air power, and aircraft production was one of the true war winners. The U.S. aircraft industry began to expand in 1938 when the Army Air Corps asked manufacturers to prepare to double or even triple their production. They did so with great success. In 1938, there were in operation in the United States only 4 engine factories, 2 propeller factories, and 9 airframe assembly plants employing a total of 32,000 workers. By 1943, there were 22 engine factories, 19 propeller factories, and 67 airframe assembly plants; 500 prime contractors employed some 1,500,000 workers, 40 percent of whom were women. Only 117 aircraft were produced in September 1939; in September 1943, U.S.

The destruction at Pearl Harbor was catastrophic, but new and more modern aircraft and ships replaced those destroyed as the United States geared up its production of war matériel. (U.S. Navy)

factories turned out 7,598. Overall, between January 1940 and December 1945, the AAF accepted from production 231,099 aircraft of all types. Included in this total were 3,899 very heavy bombers (mostly B-29s), 31,000 heavy bombers (including 12,692 of the famous B-17 Fortresses), 16,070 medium bombers, and 18,113 lighter bombers. Fighter production for the AAF Forces amounted to some 68,712 aircraft, including 15,683 P-47 Thunderbolts (or ''Jugs''), 14,686 P-51 Mustangs, and 309 jet fighters (P-59 and P-80). Some 22,885 transport aircraft were produced, including 10,368 C-47 ''Gooney Birds.'' In addition, 1,117 reconnaissance aircraft of various types, 55,712 trainers, and 13,591 liaison-type planes, including 385 helicopters, were manufactured.

Ships

The chief of naval operations, Fleet Adm. Ernest J. King, noted in his final report on navy activities in World War II that ''the capacity of the United States to build warships, auxiliary ships, and merchant ships, while supporting our forces and our allies all over the world, exceeded all former records and surpassed our most sanguine hopes. It proved to be a vital component of that sea power.'' Indeed it was. Between 1940 and 1945, the number of navy combat ships increased by a factor of 8 and the number of logistical vessels by a factor of 28. The losses of combat vessels and merchant shipping were heavy, but were more than compensated for by the enormous U.S. shipbuilding capac-

ity. A total of 72,100 vessels (8,500,000 displacement tons) were built, including 1,200 combat vessels (42.4 percent of the total tonnage), 65,500 landing vessels (36 percent of the total tonnage), and 4,900 merchant ships for the Maritime Commission (51,400,000 tons). Two old battleships were lost at Pearl Harbor; 8 new ones were built. Five carriers and 6 escort carriers were lost during the war; 27 carriers and 110 escort carriers were built. Ten cruisers were lost; 48 new cruisers were commissioned. Fifty-two submarines were lost; 203 were built. In addition, production included 358 destroyers and 504 destroyer escorts.

Research and Development

Underlying the tremendous U.S. production capacity was a large, flexible, and scientifically advanced system of research and development. The scientists and managers involved applied their scientific and engineering knowledge and organizational skills to produce a torrent of new weapons, vehicles, radios and radar, and other equipment, as well as new foods and medicines to support U.S. troops in the field. It was this ability to discover, to innovate, and to move from research to production and distribution quickly that made possible the victory of the United States and its allies over the Axis Powers. To coordinate scientific research and development, the president appointed a National Defense Research Committee on June 15, 1940. A National Inventors' Council was established in July 1940

Leslie Groves (left) *directed (1942–46) the Manhattan Project and oversaw the logistics of constructing an atomic bomb; here, as a major general, he confers in 1944 with David Lilienthal, who later became chairman (1946–48) of the Atomic Energy Commission.* (U.S. Army Military History Institute)

to appraise inventions by civilians for national defense purposes. In June 1941, all scientific research programs came under the Office of Scientific Research and Development. By the end of the war, some 7,500 research projects, exclusive of the atomic bomb project, had been carried out by Army Service Forces alone at an expenditure of $567,000,000.

In terms of expenditure of money and manpower, of scientific and organizational complexity, of overcoming a variety of difficult problems, and of its long-term impact, the $2 billion Manhattan Project to produce the atomic bomb was the greatest research and development project of World War II. The Manhattan Project was established on June 18, 1942, and placed under the direction of Brig. Gen. Leslie R. Groves, who had supervised construction of the Pentagon. Between 1942 and 1945, thousands of scientists, technicians, and administrators labored feverishly to fashion the power of the newly discovered atomic reaction into a practical, and enormously destructive, weapon. Their efforts produced the first nuclear explosion at Alamagordo, New Mexico, on July 16, 1945. Less than a month later, the first two operational atomic bombs were dropped on Hiroshima and Nagasaki, Japan, causing enormous damage and loss of life, bringing the war to an end, and ushering in a new era in military power.

U.S. Support of the Allies

The battle of production for the United States in World War II was complicated by the need to supply its allies as well as its own forces. Allied requirements placed an additional burden on American industry and slowed the pace at which the United States could put its own forces in the field. But U.S. allies, particularly Britain and the Soviet Union, were substantially aided in actively opposing the enemy while U.S. forces mobilized and trained. The Axis Powers were thus denied additional conquests and resources, and by any measure, the diversion of U.S. production to the Allies was well worth the cost.

Many Americans were disillusioned by the outcome of World War I and came to believe that they should never again become involved in "European quarrels." This desire to avoid entanglement was expressed in a series of Neutrality Acts that restricted loans and munitions sales to belligerents. In the summer of 1939, President Roosevelt asked for lifting of the embargo on arms shipments to belligerents, but Congress refused. However, despite the Neutrality Acts, the British and French were allowed to subsidize U.S. plant construction and to place large orders for aircraft and other war matériel, which were delivered through Canada. With the outbreak of war in Europe in September 1939, the United States formally declared its neutrality, and all shipments to the Allies were suspended. The president immediately recalled Congress to repeal the Neutrality Acts, noting that the United States might be able to remain "neutral in deed, but not in thought." After a bitter six-week debate, Congress amended the Neutrality Acts of 1935 and 1937 so as to favor the Allies by providing for a policy of "cash and carry" even for military supplies.

Having won a third term in the 1940 election, President Roosevelt was better able to aid the Allies, the more so because by the late fall of 1940, both isolationists and interventionists had come to believe that the best way to avoid war was by aiding the opponents of fascism. The Roosevelt administration, with the consent of Congress and the general backing of the U.S. public, subsequently undertook a series of steps "short of war" to aid the Allies. Following an appeal by British prime minister Winston Churchill in early December, Roosevelt held a press conference on Dec. 16, 1940, at which he introduced the idea of "lend-lease," using the illustration of lending a garden hose to a neighbor whose house was on fire. In a "fireside chat" on December 29, he spoke of the United States as "the great Arsenal of Democracy" and proposed that U.S. industrial capacity should become the source of matériel that would enable the Allies to defeat the Axis Powers without direct U.S. participation in the war.

Roosevelt's concepts were given concrete form by passage of "An Act to Promote the Defense of the United States," commonly known as the Lend-Lease Act, on Mar. 11, 1941. The Lend-Lease Act provided loans of equipment and supplies to any country whose defense the president deemed vital to U.S. security. Technically, the materials loaned were to be returned or compensated for after the war, but there was actually no assumption that full repayment would take place. To administer the program, an

Representative Lend-Lease Shipments,
1941–1945

Recipient	Tanks	Trucks	Airplanes	Rifles
British Empire	27,755	292,256	26,165	1,425,725
Soviet Union	7,172	432,659	11,450	1
China	100	24,991	1,378	299,712
French Forces	1,406	27,176	1,417	69,129
American Republics	840	9,359	2,089	9,230
Other	50	5,963	522	40,000
Total Lend-Lease	37,323	792,404	43,021	1,843,797
Total Production (Jul 1940–Dec 1945)	88,410	2,382,311	231,099	6,552,290
Percentage Lend-Lease/Total	42.2	33.3	18.6	28.1

SOURCE: "The United States Army in World War II: Statistics-Procurement," Table PR-7; "United States Army in World War II: Statistics—Lend-Lease," Table LL-14.

Office of Lend-Lease was established and placed under the direction of Stettinius, who had remained active in wartime administration since the demise of Roosevelt's War Resources Board in 1939. The Office of Lend-Lease coordinated requirements, pursued appropriations, and oversaw procurement.

The amount and types of war matériel provided to the Allies under Lend-Lease were substantial and varied and represented a high proportion of the total U.S. war production. The annual rate of Lend-Lease disbursements reached $15 billion by 1945, and overall, the program resulted in the expenditure of more than $48 billion between March 1941 and December 1945.

Some 43 countries received Lend-Lease assistance, but approximately 98 percent of the total went to just four major allies: the British Commonwealth, the Soviet Union, China, and France. Britain was the principal recipient of U.S. assistance, receiving more than $31.6 billion in Lend-Lease aid alone. The French also benefited significantly, both before the fall of France in May 1940 and in the later reequipment of Free French forces. The French received more than $3.23 billion in assistance. Nationalist China received $1.6 billion, and despite U.S. hostility to the Communist regime of Joseph Stalin, Lend-Lease was extended to the Russians promptly after the German attack on the Soviet Union in June 1941. Between the end of June 1941 and April 1945, the Soviet Union received $11 billion in Lend-Lease aid.

The prewar activity of U.S. industry in filling British and French orders benefited the United States by increasing employment and spurring the expansion of U.S. factories for the manufacture of aircraft, machine tools, weapons, and ammunition. In all, the United States gained a headstart of some 6–12 months in the conversion and expansion of U.S. industry to meet wartime production requirements. In addition, Lend-Lease prepared U.S. military planners for some of the problems of supporting allies in a coalition and did much to force the adoption of U.S. models of weapons and other equipment, thereby easing somewhat the difficulties of production. On the other hand, by mid-1939, Allied demands had already slowed U.S. rearmament and raised the question of priority in American industry for meeting U.S. needs as against the needs of the Allies. The Army Air Corps especially groaned under the program of aiding the Allies. A plan approved in September 1941 for division of aircraft production through June 1942 provided for more than 68 percent of production (8,985 tactical aircraft) to go to the Allies. Eventually, the General Staff adopted an 80:20 formula as the basis for distributing available equipment. The concept called for 20 percent of production to go to the Allies until the requirements of the Protective Mobilization Plan and one month's maintenance reserve were met. Thereafter, 80 percent would be dedicated to the Allies. Of course, once the United States entered the war, the plan was modified to favor the early preparation of its own forces for combat, but meeting the needs of its allies continued to strain U.S. production capacity to the utmost. For example, 42.2 percent of the total U.S. tank production (37,323 tanks) went to Lend-Lease, roughly enough tanks to equip 139 U.S. armored divisions.

Cost of the War Production Program

The cost of the battle of production far surpassed anything predicted. Between July 1, 1940, and Aug. 31, 1945, the U.S. government spent approximately $336.7 billion. Of that amount, $315.8 billion was dedicated to national defense and related expenditures. War Production Program expenditures totaled $3.6 billion in 1940, $17.8 billion in 1941, $57.4 billion in 1942, $86.2 billion in 1943, $93.4 billion in 1944, and $57.4 billion in 1945. Of the $315.8 billion total, $179.9 billion was charged to the War Department, $83.9 billion to the Navy Department, $21.2 billion to the Maritime Commission and War Shipping Administration, and $30.8 billion to overseas purchases and Treasury Department-procured Lend-Lease. Some $31.4 billion of the $315.8 billion total was dedicated to war construction, $99.9 billion to nonmunitions procurement, and $184.5 billion to munitions procurement. Of the amount dedicated to munitions production, nearly 25 percent ($44.8 billion) went for aircraft production, 23 percent ($41.1 billion) for ships, and just over 10 percent ($20.3 billion) for combat and other motor vehicles; guns and fire control equipment ($9.8 billion), communications and electronics equipment ($10.8 billion), ammunition ($18.1 billion), and other procurement ($38.2 billion) accounted for the remaining 42 percent.

In conjunction with the establishment of the War Munitions Program in January 1942, President Roosevelt stated that "the victory over all enemies will be achieved in the last analysis not only by the bravery, skill, and determination of our men, but by our overwhelming mastery in the munitions of war." He was proved absolutely correct. Even burdened by the need to supply others, U.S. industry and management skills proved more than sufficient to win the battle of production, the key to victory in World War II.

LINES OF COMMUNICATION

Unlike any conflict before or since, World War II was global in scope. In 1942, American armed forces already were conducting operations in six overseas theaters in addition to the United States and its possessions. Each of those distant theaters required its own headquarters, support structure, and line of communication. By the end of the war, material was being sent to more than 127 overseas ports. The effort to construct, operate, and defend the vulnerable lines of communication to U.S. forces around the world was one of the most complex and difficult battles of the war.

The U.S. transportation system for moving personnel and supplies during World War II was complex and efficient; here, Burmese ox carts are being loaded on C-46s for transfer to another area. (U.S. Army Military History Institute)

Total Shipments

In all, the United States moved some 127,000,000 tons of materials from the United States to overseas theaters during World War II: 78,000,000 tons crossed the Atlantic, and 49,000,000 tons crossed the Pacific. Another 8,140,000 tons were moved from overseas theaters to the United States. In addition, a total of 7,300,000 troops and other passengers were transported overseas: 4,600,000 went to Atlantic theaters and 2,700,000 to Pacific theaters. Furthermore, 3,100,000 million passengers, including 568,000 patients, were moved from overseas theaters to the United States.

Air Transport Operations

An important new aspect of the movement of men and supplies overseas in World War II was the existence for the first time of sustained air ferrying and transport operations. Between December 1941 and Jan. 1, 1945, the Air Transport Command (ATC) delivered some 40,000 aircraft to overseas theaters. In 1944, the ATC had 110,000 miles of routes and averaged 12,000,000 miles per month flown in ferrying operations and more than 10,000,000 miles per month in air transport operations. By the end of the war, operations were being flown on 161,000 miles of air routes, 118,900 of which were outside the continental United States. A plane crossed the Atlantic every 13 minutes, and in operations over the ''Hump'' from India to China, 1,250 tons of cargo were delivered by air each day. In all, some 560,000 tons of high-priority passengers and cargo, including 40,000 tons of mail (3.5 billion letters), were transported by air. Most of the 1,200,000 passengers were carried on foreign routes. In addition, from the time air evacuation began in 1942 to the end of the war, a total of 700,000 sick and wounded service members were evacuated by air. However, strategic airlift was still in its infancy, and the real battle of the lines of communication was fought at sea.

The Pacific

Despite the firm U.S. commitment to the early defeat of Germany, the first real overseas deployments of the war were to the Pacific. Although the hard decision was soon made not to reinforce the beleaguered U.S. garrison in the Philippines, the United States began at once to establish the chain of bases and to build up the forces required for the eventual recovery of the Philippines and the defeat of Japan. The navy bore the largest share of the logistical burden in the Pacific, and eventually, 20 percent of the entire strength of the navy was assigned to the Pacific advanced base program. More than 500,000 sailors, including 200,000 Seabees, worked diligently to establish and maintain the U.S. Pacific lifeline. Between March 1942 and October 1945, almost 2,000,000 tons of supplies were shipped to the Pacific in support of the advanced base program; these were in addition to the normal equipment

Seabees, members of the U.S. Navy construction battalions, arrive in the Aleutian Islands to aid in the construction of bases there during World War II. (U.S. Army Military History Institute)

and supplies for the combat forces—land, sea, and air—engaged in active operations. Amphibious operations were terribly complex, and the usual size of combat operations in the Pacific dictated much careful coordination. For example, more than 400 ships were staged for the invasion of Okinawa, and the planned invasion of the Japanese home islands (Operations Olympic and Coronet) would have involved 3,033 combat and noncombatant vessels plus millions of men and hundreds of thousands of tons of supplies. The army and navy were thus forced to work out effective methods of coordinating their logistical operations.

Battle of the Atlantic

The most vulnerable stage on the long road from factory and training camp to battlefront was the ocean crossing, and no battle was more crucial to the outcome of the war of logistics than the battle to control the transatlantic ocean line of communication. In the spring of 1940, Britain remained the only base from which the eventual reconquest of continental Europe could be launched. As a small island nation and center of a great worldwide empire, Britain imported most of its food and raw materials by sea. In World War II, Britain required about 1,000,000 tons per week (roughly 150 shiploads) just to maintain its population and essential industry. Once the decision was made to use England as a base for both the strategic air war against Germany and the eventual invasion of the Continent, the buildup needs added enormously to the monthly shipping requirements. On any given day, approximately 2,500 ships were at sea providing the lifeblood of Britain. Well into 1943 it was not at all certain that the Allies would be able to maintain their transatlantic lifeline against German submarine and surface attack, and for some time, the fate

Hitler considered the German occupation of Norway from 1940 his security in the north; although there was not much combat in this area, it served as a base for German warships and several hundred thousand German soldiers, including ski troops. (Library of Congress)

of Britain and the Allied cause hung in the balance. Churchill later wrote that "the only thing that ever really frightened me during the war was the U-boat peril."

German U-Boat Campaign

In World War I, German submarines came very close to forcing Britain out of the war. Thus in 1939, German admiral Karl Doenitz immediately initiated a U-boat campaign designed to deny Britain the food and raw materials necessary for it to continue the war effort. Doenitz calculated that the Germans needed to sink about 750,000 tons of Allied shipping per month to strangle Britain, but initially the Germans were handicapped by the limited number and range of their U-boats as well as by their restricted access to the Atlantic via the North Sea. As time went on, the Germans developed bigger and better submarines and introduced a number of technological innovations, such as the acoustic torpedo and the snorkel, which made them even more effective. The fall of Norway and France in 1940 also gave the Germans better access to the Atlantic, and Doenitz was thus able to raise the percentage of operational U-boats and their times on station.

Early in World War II, each U-boat was assigned a patrol area and operated independently, generally attacking at night from the surface and then using its superior surface speed to run ahead and prepare another ambush for the following night. However, the Allied convoy system and

other countermeasures soon drove the Germans to adopt new, even more effective tactics. Chief among these was the "wolf pack," a group of submarines operating in a coordinated manner and supported by long-range reconnaissance aircraft and resupply submarines. Wolf pack operations began from Lorient on the French Atlantic coast in mid-1940, and on September 21, a convoy of 41 ships was attacked and 12 vessels sunk using the wolf pack technique.

The U-boat campaign intensified after the fall of France, and Allied losses mounted steadily. In what was called "the happy time," the German wolf packs sank an enormous number of Allied ships. From June through December 1940, 638 ships were lost (three times the number in the previous six months), and in the first six months of 1941, more than 700 ships were lost. Sinkings fell off some in the last half of 1941, but the U-boat campaign hit its stride in early 1942, concurrent with U.S. entry into war. On Jan. 12, 1942, Admiral Doenitz loosed the U-boats on U.S. shipping along the Atlantic seaboard. At first, the United States had no coastal convoy system, and some U.S. cities even refused to observe "blackout," thus making an easy shot for the U-boat commanders on silhouetted Allied ships. Between mid-January and the end of April 1942, U-boats sank 87 ships (515,000 tons) on the U.S. East Coast.

Allied losses of dry cargo ships in the first 10 weeks of 1942 equaled an annual rate of more than 10,000,000 tons, and tanker losses were even more alarming. The toll rose steadily through the spring, and the summer of 1942 brought the worst convoy disaster of the war. In early July 1942, Convoy PQ-17, en route to the North Russian ports of Murmansk and Archangel, met disaster off Norway. Twenty-two out of 33 ships were lost to German submarines, surface vessels, and land-based aircraft. In October and November 1942, the Allies lost almost 1 ship a day in the North Atlantic. Then came the heaviest Allied monthly loss of the entire war: 1,202,000 tons in November 1942.

Allied Countermeasures

British imports declined from a prewar average of more than 50,000,000 tons to 42,000,000 in 1940, 31,000,000 in 1941, and 23,000,000 in 1942. At the beginning of 1943, it appeared that the U-boats might indeed strangle Britain as they intended, but in the first six months of 1943, the tide slowly turned in favor of the Allies as the various technical and tactical U-boat countermeasures took effect. The convoy system developed in World War I to counter the German submarine menace involved very complex planning and coordination, but the British had worked out the techniques very well and immediately instituted a convoy program at the beginning of World War II. The main problem was the lack of suitable escort vessels. A partial answer was found in the small corvette. During the 1939–40 lull in the war, the British were able to build just enough corvettes to see them through, and in late 1940, the British concluded the "destroyers-for-bases" deal with the United States. By April 1941, the United States had provided 50 old four-stack destroyers and 10 "Lake-class" Coast Guard cutters in return for leases on naval bases in the Atlantic and Caribbean. Subsequently, in July 1941, U.S. shipyards began mass production of diesel-engine destroyer escorts, and the escort crisis began to subside.

The assumption by the United States of responsibility for the safety of western Atlantic shipping also helped. On Sept. 5, 1939, the United States established a Neutrality Patrol with limits roughly 200 miles offshore from the Grand Banks south through the Antilles to Trinidad. Under the terms of the Pan-American Declaration in October 1939, the United States declared an area 300–1,000 miles wide adjacent to the coast of North and South America closed to hostile activity by both Axis and Allies. On Apr. 11, 1941, President Roosevelt notified Prime Minister Churchill that the United States would extend its security zone and patrol areas to a line covering all North Atlantic waters west of about 26 degrees, west longitude. On May 21, the American merchant ship *Robin Moor* was sunk by a German submarine in the South Atlantic off the coast of Brazil. On September 4, the destroyer USS *Greer* exchanged fire with a German U-boat and "shoot on sight" orders were issued to U.S. escort vessels. On October 16, the destroyer USS *Kearny* was hit by a German torpedo in

Ships in convoy steam across the Atlantic Ocean; convoying was one tactic used to lessen the possibility of attack by German U-boats. (U.S. Navy)

the middle of a wolf pack attack on a convoy. On October 31, the destroyer USS *Reuben James* was sunk. Consequently, U.S. assistance to the Allies increased, and in December 1941, the United States began escorting convoys bound for the United Kingdom.

From the beginning, the Allies had a slight advantage in scientific devices with antisubmarine warfare applications, and Allied radar and sonar technology remained superior to that of the Germans throughout the war. The destruction of submerged U-boats once they were located was facilitated by the invention of the "hedgehog," a device that dispensed an array of depth charges ahead of the destroyer. Some of the initial efforts to protect convoys from the air bordered on the ludicrous. The infamous "fly and forget" fighter (a British "Hurricane" launched by catapult from a merchant ship or escort) was perhaps the most laughable, although reasonably effective. However, the Allies soon developed more effective search and convoy protection methods and the addition of U.S. aircraft, particularly the long-range B-24 Liberator, soon put the Germans at a distinct disadvantage, which was further increased by the development of the "escort carrier," a small aircraft carrier constructed on a merchant ship hull.

Allied scientific skills were also applied to developing better tactics and techniques for countering the U-boats. Convoy and escort operations were greatly improved by the new techniques of "operational research," which, among other things, indicated the advantage of fewer convoys with a greater number of ships in each and more effective search techniques for the escorts. Perhaps the most significant tactical innovation was the development of the "hunter-killer" groups, unattached escort formations designed to seek out and destroy the U-boat wolf packs.

No longer were the escorts solely reactive; they now actively hunted the U-boats.

The Allies also had a very definite advantage in the field of signals intelligence, which enabled them to monitor U-boat movements and to redirect convoys and escorts accordingly. The British had superior traffic analysis and high-frequency radio-direction-finding equipment to augment their most significant advantage, Ultra. Although the German navy version of the Enigma coding machine was somewhat harder to decipher than the Luftwaffe or Wehrmacht versions and although periodic blackouts in Ultra intelligence were experienced, the Allies were generally able to track U-boat deployments and act in time to avoid the worst concentrations. Fortunately, the Germans had severe problems in making their own radio intelligence information available for operational purposes. By the spring of 1943, the advantage clearly lay with the Allies, and the reduction of the U-boat threat in the Atlantic was at hand.

Defeat of the U-Boats

German U-boat strength reached its peak in January 1943, and in March 1943, it looked as if the wolf packs were gaining the upper hand over the escorts as worldwide sinkings of Allied ships approached 630,000 tons. On Mar. 16, 1943, the U-boats scored a record kill off Newfoundland: 22 ships (more than 146,000 tons) for the loss of only 1 U-boat. But the turning point was reached that same month. The Casablanca Conference in January 1943 had made the defeat of the U-boats a number-one priority, and strategic bombers were diverted against U-boat facilities. Furthermore, in the last six months of 1942, new construction of merchant ships and escorts, primarily from U.S.

shipyards, had more than balanced Allied losses, and 1943 would prove to be the greatest year of the war for Allied shipbuilding, with a net gain of 15,200,000 tons over U.S. losses and a net Allied increase of 16,400,000 tons. By the end of 1943, the U.S. oceangoing merchant fleet alone totaled more than 29,400,000 tons, and by mid-1944, transatlantic cargo shipments threatened to overwhelm British port capacity. The Battle of the Atlantic had been won.

Shipping Losses in World War II

The Battle of the Atlantic was won only at great cost, and, indeed, the overall statistics on Allied shipping losses in World War II are staggering. From Sept. 1, 1939, through Aug. 15, 1945, the Allies lost some 5,150 ships, 2,828 of which were sunk by Axis submarines, mostly German. Overall, some 23,350,000 tons of shipping were lost (about 15,000,000 tons in the Atlantic), but 42,485,000 tons were constructed, a net gain of more than 19,000,000 tons. U.S. shipyards alone averaged 1,000,000 tons per month of new merchant ships after Jan. 1, 1943, for a total of 24,000,000 tons in two years. Due to shipyard production and sea control after 1943, the Allies were able to convert sea communications from a source of weakness to a major asset.

It has been noted that "the Allied victory over the U-boat was a victory of scientific developments, massive merchant shipbuilding programs, and highly skilled use of antisubmarine warfare weapons by the Allied navies," and so it was. But it was also a close victory. The German U-boats in two world wars came very close to achieving their objective of strangling Britain, and in the vast Pacific, the Japanese proved more than a mere nuisance. Only with superior technology and productive capacity, coupled with

Table 2
Allied Shipping Losses and Ship Construction, 1939–1945

Year	Allied Ships Sunk*	New Construction*			Net Gain/Loss
		U.S.	U.K.	Total	
1939#	810	101	231	332	− 478
1940	4,407	439	780	1,219	− 3,188
1941	4,398	1,169	815	1,984	− 2,414
1942	8,245	5,339	1,843	7,182	− 1,063
1943	3,611	12,384	2,201	14,585	+ 10,974
1944	1,422	11,639	1,710	13,349	+ 11,927
1945#	458	3,551	283	3,834	+ 3,376
TOTAL	23,351	34,622	7,863	42,485	+ 19,134

* in thousands of tons

four months only

SOURCE: Fleet Adm. Ernest J. King, *United States Navy at War: Final Official Report to the Secretary of the Navy Concerning the Period March 1, 1945 to October 1, 1945*, p. 29.

ingenuity and courage, were the Allies eventually able to overcome the Axis threat and win the battle of the lines of communication.

TOOTH-TO-TAIL RATIO

Combat power cannot be measured simply in terms of the numbers of weapons and combat troops available. The logistical forces necessary to place the combat troops and their weapons where they are needed and to support them are also an essential part of the equation. World War II demonstrated that modern, complex, mechanized, and technologically sophisticated armies operating worldwide in every climate and terrain, often in conjunction with a coalition of allies, require that a significant portion of the total force, if not the majority of it, must consist of personnel dedicated to providing the required logistical support to the few who actually do the fighting. Historically, U.S. military leaders have resisted the diversion of manpower from combat to support tasks, but in World War II, the overwhelming demand for logistical manpower severely restricted the size of U.S. combat forces. This battle over the "tooth[combat]-to-tail[logistics]" ratio in World War II is perhaps best seen in the Victory Program of 1941.

Victory Program of 1941

The Victory Program presented to President Roosevelt for approval in September 1941 was both the basis for production planning and the blueprint for the organization of combat forces in World War II. The Victory Program estimate of total available manpower turned out to be remarkably accurate, but the types and numbers of combat units actually formed, the proportion of service to combat forces, and other aspects were wide of the mark. An explanation of why the Victory Program was off target can tell much about the impact of logistics and technology on war in the mid-20th century.

The Victory Program, as modified by later staff studies, envisioned an American army of 213 divisions by June 1944. On the day before Pearl Harbor, General Headquarters estimated that the United States would need 200 divisions before opening a major offensive against the Axis. With only 36 divisions available on Dec. 7, 1941, the immediate effort following Pearl Harbor concentrated on mobilizing additional combat divisions. Planning on 10–12 months as necessary to carry a new division from activation to combat readiness, the War Department worked out a plan for activation of three or four divisions per month beginning in March 1942. By mid-1942, the army began to encounter serious difficulties in holding to the schedule for creating new divisions, and neither the total nor the monthly rate was ever met.

The difficulties encountered in meeting the division activation schedule were due to a number of factors, most of which were connected with the war's enormous logistical demands. Some changes in the Victory Program were dictated by tactical lessons, learned early in the war, that demonstrated the lack of need for, or inefficiency of, certain types of units. For example, no motorized divisions were formed because it was soon recognized that they were vulnerable to enemy attack while on the march, were

Table 3
The Victory Program Versus Reality

Category/Type Unit	Victory Program, 1941	Actual, May 31, 1945
Total Men	8,795,658	8,291,336
Ground Forces	6,745,658	5,980,900
Air Forces	2,050,000	2,320,436
Units		
Field Armies	5	12
Corps	23	24
Armored Corps	18	0
Divisions	213	89*
Infantry	71	66
Motorized	61	0
Airborne	10	5
Mountain	10	1
Armored	61	16
Cavalry	0	1**
Air Force Groups	195	243

* 91 divisions were formed. The 2d Cavalry Div. was twice deactivated.
** The 1st Cavalry Div. fought as dismounted infantry throughout the war.

SOURCE: Kreidberg and Henry, *Military Mobilization,* Table 65.

Table 4
U.S. Army in World War II
Percentage of Total Strength by Category

Category	Dec. 31, 1941	Dec. 31, 1942	May 31, 1945
Army Air Forces	16	24	28
Ground Combat Units	53	36	23
Combat Support and Service Units and Other Overhead	31	40	49*
Total	100	100	100

* Includes students and replacements (11% total).

SOURCE: Kreidberg and Henry, Military Mobilization, Tables 68 and 70.

uneconomical in that their trucks were idle much of the time, and demanded too much scarce shipping space. The formation of ground combat units was also constrained by the shortage of equipment. While the demands of the other Allies were a primary cause of such shortages, the extensive requirements for an increasingly mechanized army were also significant. These shortages caused divisions to be activated without enough weapons for adequate and realistic training and ultimately reduced the total number of divisions that could be equipped and supported.

While lessons learned and equipment shortages were important factors, perhaps the most important factor was the competition for available manpower. A series of presidential decisions emphasized industrial production, aid to the Allies, air and naval power, and a high standard of living for U.S. troops in the field. The effect of such decisions was to reduce the manpower available for the formation of ground combat units. As chief supplier of the Allied coalition, the United States had to retain much of its manpower in the industrial economy so that the other Allies could keep their divisions in the field. The manpower requirements of the naval and the army air forces also left fewer men available for combat divisions. The increasing mechanization of war demanded more men to handle and maintain the greater quantities of sophisticated equipment, fuel, and repair parts. Moreover, large numbers of service troops were required to operate the long lines of communication to multiple overseas theaters. More logistical personnel were also required to handle the additional supplies and services needed to maintain a high standard of living in the field. All of these factors meant that the ratio of service troops to combat troops had to be substantially increased.

Combat-Service Troop Ratio

By the end of 1942, the War Department had already learned that it had grossly underestimated the portion of the total force that would have to be dedicated to headquarters and logistical support. The army's ground combat

manpower actually never advanced much beyond the level reached at the end of 1942. On Jan. 1, 1943, the total number of men in ground combat units was 1,917,000, some of whom, of course, had service tasks to perform. About 2,000,000 men were added to the army in 1943, but only 365,000 went into ground combat forces, mostly as replacements. In 1944–45, the number of men allotted to ground combat forces actually declined by 241,000, and by the spring of 1945, only just over 2,000,000 men were in ground combat units. Excluding aviation and antiaircraft artillery troops, U.S. combat forces in 1945 numbered only 300,000 more than in 1918.

Effects of Logistical Troop Requirements

In view of reduced equipment and manpower availability, the program for creation of combat divisions had to be sharply curtailed. Throughout 1942, requirements for nondivisional service units mounted alarmingly, and by the end of the year, it was apparent that something had to be done. The production and mobilization goals for 1942, and even more those for 1943, were clearly beyond the limits of feasibility, especially when realistic estimates of shipping capacity to move troops overseas and other equipment needs were considered. The blueprint for army expansion was thus revised downward in the fall of 1942 to project only 100 divisions by the close of 1943. In January 1943, there was a further postponement of 12 1943 divisions to 1944 due to competing Army Air Forces and service troop requirements. In the spring of 1943, Army Chief of Staff Gen. George C. Marshall slowed the activation of new divisions, and in the summer of 1943, he suspended the creation of new divisions altogether.

Despite the obstacles, the 1942 division program created 37 divisions. Thus, on Jan. 1, 1943, the United States had 73 partially equipped divisions and 167 air groups, of which 17 divisions and 66 air groups had been deployed overseas. Offensive operations against the Axis Powers had begun without the 200 divisions originally considered necessary. After 1942, the main effort turned to the improvement of support and sustaining the efficiency of existing divisions rather than creating new ones. In World War II, the U.S. Army was outstandingly successful in keeping its combat divisions intact. By contrast, in World War I, only 30 of the 42 American Expeditionary Force divisions were integral, effective combat units at the end, having been robbed for service troops and replacements. Thus, with 12,300,000 men mobilized, only 91—not 213—divisions were formed by the United States in World War II. Due to Allied support, the United States probably did not need 213 divisions, but the margin of safety could have been greater. At the time of the German Ardennes offensive in December 1944, the last available U.S. division was hurried to Europe and no more were forming in the United States.

Number of Service Troops

The requirements for men and women to perform supply and service tasks grew tremendously in World War II. Indeed, the supply of trained service personnel never met the constantly increasing demand, and military operations

Privately funded, volunteer organizations, such as the United Services Organization (USO), often entertained troops during rest and recreation and at the battlefront; here, entertainer Jack Benny shares a joke with Allied soldiers. (U.S. Office of War Information)

were often affected by the lack of sufficient numbers of service personnel. Between 1941 and 1945, Army Service Forces (ASF) became the largest single employer in the nation's history. ASF personnel strength peaked in June-July 1943 at 1,577,000 men and women, of whom 554,000 were in uniform and 1,023,000 were civilians. About 1,000,000 ASF troops were sent overseas. By the end of the war, the 8,290,000-person American army included 1,720,000 service troops. Many of the remainder also performed essential supply and service duties. The total proportion of U.S. military forces engaged in logistical tasks also included the many U.S. Navy and Marine Corps personnel assigned to logistical duties.

To a large extent, there was insufficient provision in War Department plans for service troops, and U.S. field commanders tended to neglect the logistical problems of operations. Amphibious operations, in particular, demanded large numbers of support personnel, but invariably, commanders preferred to embark combat units rather than supply and service units with their forces—until the landings were made and it became apparent that the real problem was the lack of necessary troops to unload, store, issue, maintain, and transport critical supplies and equipment. The chronic shortage of trained logistical personnel often required drastic and urgent action to overcome local shortages. Local national personnel and prisoners of war were utilized to some extent, but even so, the theater commanders were constantly demanding more support troops once operations were underway.

U.S. military leaders have always struggled to keep their forces lean and simple. In World War II, they lost the battle of the tooth-to-tail ratio simply because the demands of modern warfare had become such that a high proportion of a nation's manpower was necessarily engaged in supporting the relatively few front-line combat troops. However, the large numbers of personnel diverted to logistical tasks made victory possible by producing, assembling, transporting, and servicing the combat troops and their weapons at the decisive time and place. In that sense, the large numbers of personnel required to take care of the logistical demands of a high-technology, global, coalition war were certainly not wasted.

IMPACT OF LOGISTICS ON STRATEGY

The increasing complexity and importance of military logistical activities since 1898 have resulted in the growing dominance of logistical over strategic or tactical considerations in 20th-century U.S. wars. However, U.S. military leaders have rather consistently tried to ignore this fact at the beginning of each war only to be forced to acknowledge it in the end. In no conflict has this trend been more noticeable than in World War II. From first to last, the strategic and operational decisions in World War II were determined by logistical realities.

Germany-Japan Decision

The basic strategic decision of the war, to defeat Germany first before turning to the defeat of Japan, was confirmed by Allied planners even before the United States entered the war. The decision was clearly dictated by the logistical situation in that the physical proximity of the European theater and the existing lines of communication would permit a more rapid buildup of men and supplies. It was well recognized that manning, training, and equipping the forces necessary to take the offensive in the Pacific would take a much longer time and would require, in addition, the construction of long lines of communication across the vast Pacific Ocean, which would in themselves take enormous quantities of men and matériel to establish and maintain.

An even more fundamental choice, however, underlay the "Germany first" decision, and that was the U.S. choice to dispense with strategy in the first instance and concentrate efforts on outproducing the foe and then worry about how that production could be used to defeat the Axis Powers. If they could be outproduced, they ultimately could be defeated. Even before the first usable strategic plan was formed, U.S. leaders had adopted an approach to warfare that emphasized technology-heavy air and naval power and the weight of matériel that could be brought to bear on the enemy. Continuous supply of U.S. forces with the latest and most sophisticated technology on a lavish scale was a necessary corollary of such an approach and did much to determine subsequent strategic decisions. Indeed, the great strategic conferences of the war produced allocations of available resources to support relatively short-range plans rather than long-range grand strategy.

Impact of Logistics on Strategic Planning

The first step in planning World War II operations, the selection of an objective, was often based on logistical considerations. Enemy factories, roads, railway lines, shipping, and storage depots were subjected to unprecedented aerial attacks, and in the end, the desired effect was achieved, although to a lesser degree of completeness than the advocates of strategic bombing may have hoped. The Japanese were particularly vulnerable in that all raw materials for the Japanese war industry had to be imported by sea, and Japanese forces spread throughout the Pacific and Asia were entirely reliant on sea lines of communication. Indeed, a major factor in the ultimate defeat of Japan was the highly effective antishipping campaign carried out by U.S. and other Allied air and naval forces. Considering only those vessels of at least 1,000 tons, the Japanese

merchant fleet lost more than 1,042 ships (more than 4,200,000 tons) by the end of the war. The U.S. Strategic Bombing Survey conducted after the war concluded that had Allied strategic bombers concentrated on Japanese merchant shipping rather than on strategic bombardment of Japanese cities and factories, the effect would have been greater and the result felt even sooner.

The timing of operations was, in particular, a function of logistics, in that target dates for major operations had to be set far in advance in order to permit the necessary logistical buildup. Forces were armed with intricate mechanized equipment, the production of which had to be scheduled long in advance. When any production or shipping delay occurred, the timing of an operation might be upset. In addition, the scarcity of critical items such as landing craft, which had to be transferred from one operation to the next, meant that a delay in one operation was likely to impact adversely on some other planned operation. Thus, the grand strategy of the war depended on production schedules and shipping possibilities. In short, logistics determined strategy rather than strategy determining logistics, as many operationally oriented commanders would have preferred.

The decision to abandon U.S. forces in the Philippines in 1942 was dictated by logistical reality, and throughout the war, commanders in the Pacific were hampered by the logistical priority afforded the defeat of Germany. In Europe, the priority given to the buildup and invasion of the Continent influenced all other operations. The decision to employ U.S. forces in the invasion of North Africa in 1942 (Operation Torch) was determined in large part by the fact that a sufficient logistical buildup in England for the invasion of the Continent could not occur as soon as hoped. Originally, the Torch planners hoped to use U.S. troops and equipment already in England to shorten the line of communication to North Africa, but insufficient logistical personnel in England to handle the necessary work dictated that a major part of the Torch forces would move directly from the United States. Even then, time and space factors delayed Torch until November 1942, and the size of the force was reduced for logistical reasons. That decision, too, had its follow-on effect. The decision to reduce the number of motor vehicles for Torch produced a bottleneck in the subsequent Allied drive across North Africa in Tunisia and Algeria.

Further operations in the Mediterranean were undertaken, even though it was recognized that they would further delay the invasion of Europe. Fortunately, Operation Husky, the invasion of Sicily in July 1943, was quickly concluded at a lower than expected logistical cost. However, the subsequent Italian Campaign, designed in part to position Allied forces so as to attack German industry and lines of communications, ground on until May 1945, primarily because sufficient men, supplies, and

As barrage balloons fly overhead, vehicles are transferred from a tank landing ship to a "rhino" in the English Channel during the Allied invasion of Normandy in June 1944; the rhino delivered cargo to unload on the beach. (U.S. Coast Guard)

shipping were not available to support overwhelming forces in Italy and invade northwest Europe simultaneously.

Perhaps the greatest logistical and strategic challenge of World War II was Operation Overlord, the invasion of the Continent in June 1944. The buildup for the invasion, Operation Bolero, took longer than initially anticipated and involved a tremendous number of support troops and enormous quantities of supplies. The success of Overlord was in large part due to the ability of Allied logisticians to support the combat forces in establishing a permanent beachhead and in overcoming the difficulties of supporting rapidly moving forces in the race across France to the borders of Germany. It was clear to all that the forward movement of the Allied armies in northwest Europe was regulated by the availability of supplies, the opening of ports, and the establishment of rail and motor transport routes from the beaches and ports to the front-line units. The great debate between the Americans and the British over the "broad front" versus the "narrow thrust" strategy in northwest Europe was basically a debate over how scarce logistical resources were to be apportioned. Indeed, at every turn, logistics dominated the operational decisions.

CONCLUSION

Ultimately, the war of logistics came down to a battle to place the combat troops in position on the battlefield and to provide all of the supplies and services required by a modern army in the field. A thousand such battles took place around the globe in World War II. Although initially unprepared for the contest, the Allies eventually were able to bring to bear against the Axis an overwhelming material advantage. Thus, the Allied victory in World War II can be attributed more to an ability to mobilize and position enormous industrial and military power than to the efficacy of strategic and tactical doctrine or even the superior valor and skill of the Allied soldiers and their leaders. U.S. field commanders in World War II were often uneasy with the fact that combat operations hinged so decidedly on such mundane factors as production schedules; the availability of ocean shipping, landing craft, and ports; and the number of available stevedores and truck companies. In the end, they were forced to admit the obvious: the making of war had become overwhelmingly a matter of logistics.

PART II

Biographies

ALLEN, TERRY DE LA MESA
(1888–1969)

U.S. army officer, Allen was born in Fort Douglas, Utah. He was commissioned in the cavalry in 1912, led an infantry battalion during World War I, and later returned to the cavalry. In 1942, he became a major general and assumed command of the 1st Infantry Division. Allen's handling of the division in North Africa added to his reputation as an aggressive leader, but his superiors worried about the division's lack of discipline. In Sicily, however, the division twice failed to seize its objectives on schedule, and in September 1943, Allen's corps commander, Gen. Omar Bradley, relieved him of command. Allen returned to the United States and took over the 104th Infantry Division. He intensively trained his new unit, especially in night attacks, and took it to Europe in 1944, where it fought well in Holland and Germany. Allen retired in 1946.

Richard F. Kehrberg

ALMOND, EDWARD MALLORY
(1892–1979)

U.S. army officer, Almond was born in Luray, Virginia. He graduated from the Virginia Military Institute in 1915 and received a commission as a regular army infantry lieutenant in 1916. In World War I, he fought in France with the 4th Division. During the interwar years, he graduated from the Command and General Staff School and the Army War College.

As World War II began, he was promoted rapidly, to brigadier general in 1941 and to major general in 1942, when he also assumed command of the 92d Infantry Divi-

Maj. Gen. Terry Allen (left), *with Gen. Omar Bradley in Sicily, was relieved of command of the 1st Infantry in 1943, but returned to lead the 104th Infantry Division in Holland and Germany in 1944.* (U.S. Military Academy)

sion (Colored). Despite the dedication and bravery of the troops of this division, however, the 92d repeatedly failed both in training and in the Italian theater (1944–45). Almond himself, notable for his determined prejudice against minority soldiers, was not held responsible for these failures. Instead, in 1946, Almond was sent to Japan, where he eventually became chief of staff to Gen. Douglas MacArthur in 1949. In the Korean War, he took command of the X Corps in 1950, playing a major role in the Inchon landing. After serving as commandant of the Army War College (1951–53), he retired as a lieutenant general.

Bibliography: Stanton, Shelby L., *America's Tenth Legion: X Corps in Korea, 1950* (Presidio Press, 1989).

Jonathan M. House

ANDREWS, FRANK MAXWELL
(1884–1943)

U.S. army officer and commander, best known for his advocacy of air power, Andrews was born in Nashville, Tennessee. He was commissioned in the cavalry after his 1906 graduation from West Point. Completing flight training in 1918, the young officer missed combat in France during World War I but did become the U.S. Army Air Service Officer during the brief U.S. occupation period in Germany. Rising quickly in the 1920s and 1930s, Andrews, as a major general, became commander of General Headquarters Air Force in the late 1930s, a time when bombing experiments on naval and merchant shipping craft drew some pubic interest and controversy. During this period, the Army Air Corps was being posed as a potential protector of a supposedly vulnerable U.S. coastline. Recommending autonomy for the air force in 1937, the aggressive, assertive Andrews was temporarily quieted by being sent to San Antonio, Texas, and reverted to the rank of colonel. Resurrected by the newly appointed army chief of staff, Gen. George Marshall, in 1939, Andrews was given a high position on the General Staff.

In November 1942, Lieutenant General Andrews was appointed to command U.S. forces in the Middle East and in February 1943 became the overall commander of U.S. forces in the European theater. Just three months later, he was killed in bad weather aboard a B-24 bomber in Iceland. Andrews was a strong and influential advocate of the bomber and a separate air force. He had much to do with the fact that while the U.S. Army had a relatively small ground element on the eve of World War II, its air arm was comparatively formidable.

Bibliography: Craven, Wesley Frank, and James Lea Cate, eds., *The Army Air Forces in World War II*, vol. 1 (Univ. of Chicago Press, 1948).

Col. (Ret.) Rod Paschall

ARNOLD, HENRY HARLEY ("HAP")
(1886–1950)

U.S. army officer and aviation pioneer, Arnold was born in Gladwyne, Pennsylvania. After graduating from West Point in 1907, he was assigned to the infantry and served with the 29th Infantry in the Philippines. In 1911, he applied for service in the Ordnance Department but then accepted an opportunity to enter the new field of aviation with the Signal Corps.

Early Air Experience. Arnold went to Dayton, Ohio, in 1911 to undergo flight training with the Wright brothers and soon earned his wings. He was then assigned to the Air Service at College Park, Maryland, and the next year established a world altitude record of 6,540 feet, for which he received the Mackay Trophy for outstanding accomplishment in aeronautics. Since Arnold was only on temporary assignment with the air arm, he went to the Philippines with the 13th Infantry in 1913 and did not fly again until 1916.

When he came back to the United States, Arnold volunteered for the Air Service and was sent to Rockwell Field, near San Diego, by then the army's premier flying field. He remained there about a year when he was sent to Panama to command the 7th Aero Squadron. At the entrance of the United States into World War I, however, Arnold was recalled to Washington to head the information office of the Signal Corps' Aviation Section. By August 1917, he had been promoted to brevet colonel and placed in charge of all aviation training in the United States. Although he tried to get assignments to France, Arnold never flew in combat during the war.

Air Power Advocacy. In the early postwar period, Brig. Gen. William ("Billy") Mitchell, a flamboyant and galling, yet visionary, officer in the Air Service, began to agitate for greater autonomy in army aeronautics. Arnold was one of several officers who accepted Mitchell's arguments about the primacy of air power to carry destruction to the enemy country's interior and through strategic bombing to break the enemy's will to fight. Mitchell's strident position on this issue resulted in charges of insubordination against him and his being cashiered from the army in 1926, and while Arnold testified on Mitchell's behalf at his court-martial, the younger officer was much more politically astute than Mitchell.

Instead of confronting directly officials who had little interest in aviation, Arnold participated with several other air-minded army officers to win publicity for air power in the late 1920s. He wrote or co-wrote five books on military aviation during the next 20 years, all of which argued that airplanes offered great potential for modern warfare: *Airmen and Aircraft: An Introduction to Aeronautics* (1926); *This Flying Game* (1936), with Ira Eaker; *Winged Warfare* (1941); *Army Flyer* (1942), with Ira Eaker; and *Global*

Mission (1949). These were significant contributions to the development of the doctrine of air power.

In addition, Arnold supported, and in some cases participated in, a number of events designed to demonstrate the potential of military aviation. In 1934, for example, he led a flight of B-10 bombers from Washington, D.C., to Juneau, Alaska, and back. This long-endurance flight earned for Arnold his second Mackay Trophy. While stationed at March Field, in southern California, beginning in 1931, Arnold also built strong relations with the movie industry and supported its efforts to make films built around aviation themes. These activities, and similar ones, were critical to building public support for air power.

During the 1930s, Arnold was also involved in several other important activities that assisted in making the army air arm able to meet the challenges posed in World War II. While at March Field, Arnold began to build close ties with scientists at the California Institute of Technology, setting the stage for greater involvement in aviation issues from the academic community. Arnold also experimented with equipment and tactics associated with the transformation of March Field from a training to an operational base, in the process materially advancing knowledge in these areas.

The Army and the Mail. Of critical importance in both Arnold's career and the development of the Air Corps was its disastrous attempt to fly the mail during the first part of 1934. Following the cancellation of commercial airmail contracts because of questions of malfeasance, beginning in February and lasting through May, the military tried to provide the service. Arnold, by then a colonel, was given command of the Western Zone for this operation. From headquarters at Salt Lake City, Utah, he directed several air routes running through the American West.

The operation was a fiasco of the first magnitude. The army's aircraft were obsolete, its pilots were poorly trained, and the result was 66 crashes and 12 deaths. Some of the accidents were just stupid. Maj. Charles B. ("Barney") Oldfield, who had gotten his wings in 1921 and had more than 100 hours in aircraft with retractable landing gear, on a flight from Salt Lake City to Cheyenne landed his YB-10 wheels up. "I simply forgot I was flying a plane with retractable landing gear," he explained.

The result of such occurrences was a focus on the Air Corps and the development of a program to end its qualitative and quantitative inferiority. Congress began putting money into the Air Corps. In 1934, Congress appropriated $23,300,000 for the use of the army air forces, 8.4 percent of all army appropriations. By 1939, the army air forces received $70,600,000, or 15.7 percent of the army's direct appropriations.

Arnold was pleased with the reaction of the nation's leaders to the airmail disaster, although he was disappointed in the army's showing. He, like most of the rest of his colleagues in the Air Corps, used this funding to procure new aircraft and buttress the air infrastructure. Arnold, who had been promoted to brigadier general in 1935, had a special opportunity to contribute to this work in 1936 when he was called to Washington to become assistant chief of the Air Corps. He held that position until September 1938, when he became chief in his own right, a position he held for almost eight years.

World War II. Arnold was constantly seeking an expansion of the army's air arm, and with the threat of war, he began to find support from several quarters. He was able to secure an appropriation of $2.1 billion for army aviation in 1941. Under his direction, the Air Corps established a global presence during the early 1940s. It built a strategic bombardment force like none ever seen before or since and conducted operations throughout the globe. The overall success of the strategic bombing campaign of World War II has been debated since at least 1945 without resolution, but Arnold and his airmen pointed to it as a primary reason for the Allied victory.

Arnold also assembled the other components of the U.S. air forces. He gave proper attention to fighter forces as escort, air superiority, interdiction, and close air-support forces. He was forward-looking in relationship to the potential of air transportation and supported the creation of aerial logistics systems around the globe. He also stressed the incorporation of the scientific and technical communities into the quest for air power, building a base for postwar advances in the development and maintenance of weapons systems. Without question, although a harsh master who irritated colleagues and subordinates alike, Arnold created a powerful air force of some 2,500,000 personnel, organized into 243 combat groups, with more than 63,000 aircraft, and operating from fields around the world.

The triumph of the United States in World War II was from Arnold's perspective a personal triumph for himself. He had built a major military force and made it run. He retired from the army in March 1946.

Bibliography: Arnold, H. H., *Global Mission* (Harper & Brothers, 1949); Coffey, Thomas M., *Hap: The Story of the U.S. Air Force and the Man Who Built It, General Henry H. "Hap" Arnold* (Viking, 1982); Copp, DeWitt S., *A Few Great Captains: The Men and Events that Shaped the Development of U.S. Air Power* (Doubleday, 1980); Maurer, Maurer, *Aviation in the U.S. Army, 1919–1939* (Office of Air Force History, 1987); Overy, R. J. *The Air War, 1939–1945* (Stein and Day, 1980).

Roger D. Launius

BARBEY, DANIEL EDWARD (1889–1969)

U.S. navy officer credited with the development of U.S. amphibious warfare in World War II and dubbed "Uncle Dan, the amphibious man," Barbey was born in Portland, Oregon. After graduating from Annapolis in 1912, he filled a variety of command and staff billets before being assigned to the War Plans Section, Bureau of Navigation, Navy Department.

Appointed head of the Amphibious Warfare Section in 1941, Barbey conducted training exercises along the North Carolina coast. He viewed this new amphibious force as the "starter" for offensive operations—the amphibious commander would transport troops and equipment to the objective, get the assault force ashore and through the initial battle, and then relinquish control to the ground force commander. This concept required innovative equipment and tactics, and Barbey contributed to both.

Studying the landing craft, vehicle, powered (LCV), derived from the Sino-Japanese War, he developed the DUKW, a dual-purpose boat on wheels that could travel on land, in water, and over reefs. A *Newsweek* reporter described the "Duck" as "a strange mechanical contrivance that looked like the ill-conceived offspring of a motor vehicle and a seagoing barge." In addition, Barbey supervised the development of the LSD (landing ship, dock), the LST (landing ship, tank), and the LCI (landing craft, infantry).

Promoted to rear admiral and transferred to the Southwest Pacific in December 1942, Barbey assumed command of the U.S. Amphibious Force, 7th Fleet in support of Gen. Douglas MacArthur's forces. Studying the amphibious operations on Guadalcanal and Tulagi, he recognized the need for timely logistics and for continuous and sustained air and naval support. Thus, Barbey instituted techniques that reduced the average loading or unloading time for freighters and troopships from five days to five hours. In addition, he managed the flow of logistics in order to prevent stockpiles on the beach and to maximize the support of union-regulated merchant ship crews. To further enhance logistical and fire support, Barbey developed LST hospital ships and LCI(R) rocket-launcher ships. These innovations evolved into principles: (1) on D-Day, use minimum ships for minimum time; (2) unload follow-on echelons when they arrive; (3) build emergency airstrips as soon as possible; (4) employ hospital-rigged LSTs; and (5) maintain unity of command for both assault and service forces.

With an effective amphibious force built on training and discipline, Barbey's process virtually guaranteed success. By 1945, his command included 1,000 ships and 3 independent group commanders. Supporting the "island hopping" drive from New Guinea to the Philippines, Barbey's forces landed more than 1,000,000 men and 1,500,000 tons of cargo in 56 operations. MacArthur deemed him "just about the Number One amphibious commander in the world."

Later, Barbey participated in the surrender of Japanese forces in Korea, helped repatriate more than 2,000,000

Japanese from Korea and China, and took command of the 7th Fleet in November 1945. He retired in 1951.

Bibliography: Barbey, Daniel E., *MacArthur's Amphibious Navy: Seventh Fleet Amphibious Force Operations, 1943–1945* (Naval Inst. Press, 1969); Coletta, Paolo E., "Daniel E. Barbey: Amphibious Warfare Expert," *We Shall Return!*, ed. by William M. Leary (Univ. Press of Kentucky, 1988).

Maj. James Sanders Day

BLANDY, WILLIAM HENRY PURNELL (1890–1945)

U.S. naval officer, Blandy was born in New York City. He graduated from Annapolis in 1913. After service at Veracruz (1914) and at sea during World War I on the USS *Florida,* he took advanced training in ordnance and in gun design. Promoted to captain in 1933 and to rear admiral in 1941, Blandy became chief of the Bureau of Ordnance (1941–43). Although it was slow early in World War II to deal with the problems posed by unreliable torpedoes, the bureau achieved conspicuous success in other areas—for instance, in improving the navy's antiaircraft capabilities. In various capacities, Blandy had been involved in upgrading ships' defenses against aircraft since 1939. Blandy returned to sea in 1944 to command Amphibious Group I in the Central Pacific, a post he retained through 1945. At Iwo Jima and Okinawa, he commanded all prelanding activities, including shore bombardment and underwater demolition.

Commander of the Joint Army-Navy Task Force I in 1946, Blandy directed Operation Crossroads at Bikini Island in the Pacific. He next was appointed commander of the Atlantic's Eighth Fleet (1946–47) and in 1947 became commander of the Atlantic Fleet. He retired in 1950, but returned to active duty in 1953.

Bibliography: Graybar, Lloyd J., "Blandy, William Henry Purnell," *Dictionary of American Biography,* supplement 5 (Scribner's, 1977).

Lloyd J. Graybar

BONG, RICHARD IRA (1920–1945)

U.S. army airman, Bong was born in Superior, Wisconsin. He became the top American fighter ace of World War II, flying a P-38 "Lightning" in the 5th Air Force. He shot down 40 Japanese planes in the Southwest Pacific and was awarded the Medal of Honor. Even while serving as a gunnery instructor in late 1944, he voluntarily continued to fly combat missions, adding to his total. In 1945, after three tours of duty, "Bing" Bong was assigned to the Lockheed plant in California as a test pilot; he died on Aug. 6, 1945, testing the new P-80 "Shooting Star" jet fighter.

Ralph L. Eckert

BRADLEY, OMAR NELSON (1893–1981)

U.S. army officer and chief of staff, Bradley was born in Clark, Missouri. He graduated from high school in 1910 and was ready to enter the University of Missouri when his church school superintendent suggested that he try to enter West Point. An application to his congressman was followed by his appointment to the military academy in 1911. He, Dwight D. Eisenhower, and James Van Fleet were among those of the famous class of 1915 ("the class stars fell on") commissioned second lieutenants of infantry. Bradley considered the four years he spent at West Point among the most rewarding of his life. He believed the academy was the perfect surrogate for the father he had lost at 14. A good athlete, he played both varsity football and baseball.

Bradley requested and was assigned to the 14th Infantry Regiment. Duty with its 3d Battalion at Fort George Wright at the foot of the Rocky Mountains was leisurely. Drill, marksmanship training, and the like occupied mornings; afternoons were free. The 14th was dispatched to the Mexican border in 1916, and Bradley was promoted to first lieutenant. On December 28, he and Mary Quayle were married in Columbia, Missouri. He took his bride to Yuma, Arizona, and the 14th Infantry.

Much to his disappointment, Bradley served out World War I with the 14th in Butte, Montana, guarding copper mines. While there, he was promoted to command Company F. In August 1918, the 14th was assigned to the newly formed 19th Infantry Division, and Bradley was appointed to command the 2d Battalion. In September, he was promoted to major.

After the war, Bradley became assistant professor of military science and tactics in the South Dakota State College R.O.T.C. (Reserve Officers Training Corps) program. In 1920, he was appointed as a math instructor at West Point.

He was a student at Fort Benning, Georgia, in 1924, then was assigned in 1925 to command the 1st Battalion, 27th Infantry Regiment, in Hawaii. Bradley served with the 27th for 20 months, recalling them as the most fulfilling and rewarding of his early career. Then, after a short assignment as liaison officer to the Hawaiian National Guard, he was ordered in 1928 as a student to the Army Command and General Staff College, at Fort Leavenworth, Kansas.

After the staff college, it was back to Fort Benning for four years as an instructor at the Infantry School. He worked under the general direction of Lt. Col. George C. Marshall, assistant commandant in charge of the school's academic department. His immediate boss, in the tactics section, was Joseph ("Vinegar Joe") Stilwell. Bradley recalled Marshall as outwardly austere, cold, aloof, succinct, and prudish, but showing warmth and some sense of fun when off duty. Bradley thought "Vinegar Joe" was an apt nickname for Stilwell, who described himself as "unreasonable, impatient, sour-balled, sullen, mad, hard, profane, vulgar."

Both Marshall and Stilwell advocated war of movement rather than the slow-paced trench style of World War I. Bradley took to this new, dynamic concept, which required simplicity, ingenuity, improvisation, and speed. Marshall was so impressed with Bradley that he made him chief of the weapons section.

Mid-Career Years. In 1933–34, Bradley attended the Army War College at Fort Humphreys (later named Fort McNair) in Washington, D.C. From 1934 to 1938, Bradley served again at West Point, this time in the tactics department. He was promoted to lieutenant colonel in July 1936. In 1938, he was ordered to the G-1 Section (Personnel) of the Army General Staff, Washington, D.C., as an assistant G-1. He again worked for Marshall, now deputy chief of staff of the army.

In February 1941, Bradley was ordered to Fort Benning as post commander and commandant of the Infantry School and was promoted to brigadier general. He pioneered the three-month officer candidate school (OCS) program, which became a model for all future OCS's. During his tenure, new tank and airborne units were formed and trained. Although he had known of George S. Patton in other assignments, at Benning they came into close contact. Patton commanded a Benning-based armored brigade.

World War II. Shortly after the United States entered World War II in December 1941, Bradley was named commander of the new 82d Infantry Division. In June 1942, as a major general, he was given command of the 28th, from the Pennsylvania National Guard. The division—weakened by the army's repeated draining of human resources as replacements and cadres for other commands—was badly in need of leadership. Bradley did the job.

In early February 1943, he was assigned to North Africa, where he served as field aide to General Eisenhower. Later that year, he was given command of the II Corps in North Africa, and he captured Bizerte, Tunisia, in May. This contributed significantly to the fall of Tunisia and the surrender of more than 250,000 Axis troops. Bradley's corps next took part in the Sicilian Campaign.

In September 1943, Bradley was given command of the 1st Army in England. On June 6, 1944, divisions of this army invaded France at Normandy and, with other U.S. and Allied forces, began the liberation of northern Europe. In August, he became commander of the 12th Army Group, consisting of the 1st, 3d, 9th, and 15th armies. His troops drove through France, liberated Paris, defeated a German counteroffensive in the Battle of the Bulge, crossed the Rhine River, and then drove into central Germany to meet Soviet troops attacking from the east.

Postwar Career. Bradley was veterans affairs administrator in 1945–47. In 1948, he was appointed army chief of staff; in 1949, he became first chairman of the Joint Chiefs of Staff, a post he held until retirement in 1953. At the same time, he served as chairman of the Military Committee of NATO (North Atlantic Treaty Organization) until 1950 and then continued on the committee until 1953. In 1950, he was appointed to the five-star rank of General of the Army, becoming the fourth army officer to achieve that rank.

Upon retirement, he accepted a position with the Bulova Watch Company and was elected its chairman in 1958. Bradley resigned as Bulova's chairman in July 1973.

Bradley was a mild-mannered man with a high-pitched voice. To reporters, he was not good "copy." However, his down-to-earth and realistic approach rightly earned him the sobriquet of "a soldier's soldier."

Bibliography: Bradley, Omar N., *A Soldier's Story* (Holt, Rinehart & Winston, 1951); Bradley, Omar N., and Clay Blair, *A General's Life* (Simon & Schuster, 1983).

Brig. Gen. (PNG, Ret.) Uzal W. Ent

BRERETON, LEWIS HYDE (1890–1967)

U.S. army officer and aviation commander, Brereton was born in Pittsburgh, Pennsylvania, and graduated from Annapolis in 1911. Prior to World War I, he transferred to the army where he learned to fly. During the war, he commanded the 12th Aero Squadron in France.

At the time of the Japanese attack on Pearl Harbor (Dec. 7, 1941), which drew the United States into World War II, Brereton was in the Philippines commanding the Far Eastern Air Forces. Suffering terrific losses in defense of the Philippines, just before Christmas he moved what was left of his command to India. There, he received additional resources and began organizing air operations to turn back Japanese incursions and to support the Hump Airlift to China.

In late 1942, Brereton was sent to command the 9th Air Force at Cairo, Egypt, and in February 1943, he assumed command of all U.S. forces in the Middle East, participating in the bombings of the Ploesti oilfields in Rumania. Promoted to lieutenant general in April 1944, he commanded the 9th Air Force during the Normandy invasion in June. Later that year, he commanded the 1st Allied Airborne Army and participated in Operation Market Garden, an assault in the Netherlands to capture the bridges that would provide a direct route into Germany.

Bibliography: Craven, Wesley Frank, and James L. Cate, eds., *The Army Air Forces in World War II,* 7 vols. (Chicago Univ. Press, 1948–1956); Sherry, Michael S., *The Rise of American Air Power: The Creation of Armageddon* (Yale Univ. Press, 1987).

Roger D. Launius

BUCKNER, SIMON BOLIVAR (1886–1945)

U.S. army officer, Buckner was born in Munfordville, Kentucky, the son of Confederate general Simon Bolivar Buckner. He attended Virginia Military Institute for two years before receiving an appointment to West Point with the class of 1908. Commissioned in the infantry, he served in Panama, the Philippines, and Washington D.C., prior to World War I. He spent the war years in the nation's capital and at Kelly Field, Texas. Assigned to the aviation section of the Signal Corps, Buckner commanded and trained the 5th Provisional Regiment as well as the 1st and 3d training brigades.

The interwar years provided Buckner with myriad experiences throughout the army schools system. He returned to West Point in 1919 to teach tactics. As the distinguished graduate of the Command and General Staff School in 1925, he remained as an instructor until 1928. Moving to Washington, D.C., Buckner graduated from the Army War College the following year and then joined the school staff as the executive officer. Leaving that post for another tour at West Point, he served one year as the assistant to the commandant, then served as commandant of cadets from 1933 to 1936.

Departing West Point, Buckner commanded in the 23d, 66th, and 22d infantry regiments. He served one year as chief of staff of the 6th infantry division before transferring to Fort Richardson near Anchorage, Alaska. As commander of the Alaska Defense Force from July 1940 through March 1944, advancing to the rank of lieutenant general in 1943, Buckner directed road and base construction and tested clothing, boots, and sleeping bags. In June 1942, during the Japanese assault on Midway, in the Central Pacific, elements of his command detected a Japanese fleet among the Aleutian Islands off Alaska. Marshalling his forces to defend the Aleutian port of Dutch Harbor, Buckner thwarted the fleet's offensive. Further operations sought to dislodge Japanese forces occupying the Aleutian islands of Attu and Kiska. Subordinated to navy command and obliged to work in an insular environment, Buckner became adept at joint operations.

Selected to form the U.S. 10th Army in the Central Pacific, Buckner assumed command of XXIV Corps and the marine III Amphibious Corps in June 1944. Emphasizing interservice cooperation and coordinated naval and air support, Buckner concentrated on physical fitness, tactical training, logistics, and the care and control of the civilian population. Assaulting Okinawa on Apr. 1, 1945, the 10th Army overcame bad weather and rough terrain to isolate the Japanese forces. On June 18, while visiting a forward observation post, Buckner was killed by a Japanese artillery strike. The defenders capitulated three days later.

Having motivated soldiers through inspired leadership, Buckner was posthumously (1954) promoted to full general. Buckner Bay, a naval anchorage on the southeast coast of Okinawa, and Camp Buckner, the cadet training area at West Point, are named in his honor.

Maj. James Sanders Day

BULL, HAROLD ROE (1893–1976)

U.S. army officer, Bull was born in Springfield, Massachusetts. He graduated from West Point in 1914 and served with the 3d Infantry Division in France during World War I. Between the wars, he graduated from the Infantry School (1927), the Command and General Staff College (1928), the Army War College (1933), and the Naval War College (1934). From 1935 to 1938, he served as assistant secretary of the General Staff. Having risen through the ranks, Bull became a brigadier general in 1941 and a major general in 1942. Following U.S. entry into World War II, Bull became assistant chief of staff for operations and training (G-3) of the War Department General Staff before taking command of the Replacement and School Command, Army Ground Forces (1942–43). He then served as assistant chief of staff for operations and training (G-3), Supreme Headquarters, Allied Expeditionary Forces (SHAEF), from 1944 to 1945. After the war he was chief of staff of the U.S. forces in the European Theater (1945–46) and was commandant of the National War College from 1949 until his retirement in 1952 as a lieutenant general.

Steve R. Waddell

BURKE, ARLEIGH (1901–   )

U.S. naval officer and chief of naval operations, Burke was born near Boulder, Colorado. He graduated from Annapolis in 1923. He drew the battleship *Arizona* as his first assignment and quickly earned a reputation as hardworking and ambitious. As a junior officer, he systematically acquired the in-depth knowledge of naval gunnery that would be so important in his later career. Burke attacked every assignment with enthusiasm and, following his attendance at the Naval War College, became commanding officer of the destroyer *Mugford* in June 1939.

World War II found him stuck on shore duty in Washington as an inspector at the Naval Gun Factory. Although unhappy at being so far from action, his diligence and attention to duty made him invaluable to his superiors and his requests for transfer were routinely denied, but ultimately he obtained a transfer. His eagerness to serve was rewarded by being assigned command of Destroyer Division 43 in February 1943. Earning the nickname ''31-Knot Burke,'' he was known for his innovations in destroyer tactics, which proved highly successful at the battles of Empress Augusta Bay and Cape St. George. He later served as Adm. Marc Mitscher's chief of staff during the Battle of Leyte Gulf in October 1944.

By December 1948, Captain Burke was again in Washington, this time serving as chief of the Organizational Policy and Research Division within the Office of the Chief of Naval Operations. His primary duty was providing advice to the navy on the issue of unification of the armed forces. In this capacity, he provided many position papers to support the naval leadership during its struggles with the air force over primacy in the fledgling Department of Defense. This heated debate was centered on the air force's objections to the building of a super-carrier as an infringement upon the air force's strategic bombing monopoly. Burke's involvement in this so-called Revolt of the Admirals nearly prevented his promotion to rear admiral in 1949.

Selected by Sec. of the Navy Charles S. Thomas to serve as chief of naval operations in 1955, Burke set up the Special Projects Office within the Bureau of Ordnance to investigate methods of firing ballistic missiles from naval platforms as a cheaper, less vulnerable alternative to carrier-based aircraft. The end result was the development of the Polaris missile. Subsequently, during Burke's second tour as chief of naval operations, he saw his life's work rewarded with the 1959 launching of the world's first ballistic missile submarine, the *George Washington*. In 1989, the navy honored Burke by launching the *Arleigh Burke* (DDG-51), the lead ship in the new class of Aegis guided-missile destroyers.

Bibliography: Potter, E. B., *Admiral Arleigh Burke: A Biography* (Random House, 1960).

Maj. Gilbert B. Diaz

BUSH, VANNEVAR (1890–1974)

U.S. electrical engineer, Bush was born in Everett, Massachusetts. After serving on the faculty of the Massachusetts Institute of Technology 1919–39, he was appointed president of the Carnegie Institution of Washington, a scientific research organization. In the early stages of World War II, as the United States mobilized for defense, Pres. Franklin D. Roosevelt appointed Bush chairman of the National Defense Research Committee on June 15, 1940. In late June 1941, Bush was chosen to head the newly created Office of Scientific Research and Development (OSRD). The OSRD was to mobilize science for the nation's defense. As the U.S. scientific coordinator, Bush played a major role in the Manhattan Project, the development of the atomic bomb.

Steve R. Waddell

BUTLER, SMEDLEY DARLINGTON (1881–1940)

U.S. marine officer, Butler was born in West Chester, Pennsylvania. He joined the Marine Corps as a second lieutenant in 1898 and soon saw combat in the Spanish-American War, the Boxer Rebellion, and the Philippine Insurrection. During his later service in Mexico, Central America, and the Caribbean, he won two Medals of Honor.

He returned to the United States from France after World War I to command the marine camp at Quantico, Virginia.

Brig. Gen. Smedley D. Butler, a veteran of the Spanish-American War, the Boxer Rebellion, the Philippine Insurrection, and World War I, was adamant that the United States maintain its neutrality at the beginning of World War II. (U.S. Marine Corps)

While there, he was promoted to brigadier general, and he gained national attention by using marines to reenact the Civil War's Battle of Gettysburg for a crowd of 100,000 including Pres. Warren G. Harding. In January 1924, Butler took a two-year leave of absence from the Marine Corps to serve as the director of public safety for the city of Philadelphia. This strict disciplinarian, who deplored inefficiency, cowardice, laxness, and red tape, declared war on the municipal bureaucracy. He attempted to enforce prohibition, and he fought vice, corruption, and graft in the government. His outspoken demeanor created political enemies, however, and he returned to active duty in February 1926.

Butler commanded a marine expedition to China in response to the Nanking incident of March 1927. By 1930, he was the senior major general in the Marine Corps. His frankness bode ill for him in military life as well as in the civilian sector; he was passed over when considered for selection as the commandant of the Marine Corps. Ever advocating isolationism and an "ironclad" national defense, Butler retired in October 1931 amid considerable controversy. The following year, he campaigned for the U.S. Senate as a Prohibition candidate in his native state of Pennsylvania. Although unsuccessful, he remained active by lecturing and by supporting veterans organizations until his death in 1940.

Bibliography: Archer, Jules, *The Plot to Seize the White House* (Hawthorn Books, 1973); Schmidt, Hans, *Maverick Marine: General Smedley D. Butler and the Contradictions of American Military History* (Univ. Press of Kentucky, 1987); Thomas, Lowell, *Old Gimlet Eye; The Adventures of Smedley D. Butler* (Farrar & Rinehart, 1933).

Maj. James Sanders Day

BYRD, RICHARD EVELYN, JR.
(1888–1957)

U.S. naval officer and explorer and the first man to fly over both the North and South poles, Byrd was born in Winchester, Virginia. He graduated from Annapolis in 1912 and saw his first naval action aboard the USS *Washington* off Veracruz, Mexico. Briefly sidelined into civilian life by sports injuries sustained at the Naval Academy, Byrd got himself recalled in 1917 and earned his pilot's wings at Pensacola. He spent the rest of World War I commanding a naval patrol squadron in Canada. After the war, Byrd invented several navigational tools and busied himself organizing the naval aviation reserve and lobbying for the establishment of the navy's Bureau of Aeronautics.

His polar career began in 1924–25 when he led a small naval aviation detachment accompanying the (Donald B.) MacMillan expedition to Greenland. In 1926, Byrd and pilot Floyd Bennett flew from Greenland over the North Pole to Kings' Bay, Spitzbergen. The following year he and a crew flew the first nonstop transatlantic mail service 4,200 miles from New York to Paris in 39 hours, 56 minutes, ditching the plane off the French coast when their fuel ran out. In 1928, Byrd led a 42–man expedition to establish Little America, the first military base in Antarctica. Byrd's 1929 flight across the South Pole with Danish explorer Bernt Balchen assured his place in aviation history. His polar exploits led to his promotion to rear admiral (retired).

In the years leading up to World War II, Byrd—backed by such powerful patrons as John D. Rockefeller, Jr.; Edsel Ford; Thomas J. Watson; and the National Geographic Society—explored, surveyed, and mapped nearly 600,000 square miles of Antarctica, urging the establishment of military bases. At Byrd's urging, Pres. Franklin D. Roosevelt's administration created the U.S. Antarctic Service, which, long before Pearl Harbor, began training military personnel for frigid-zone warfare.

During World War II, Byrd performed secret wartime missions for the Office of the Chief of Naval Operations; served as an island scout in the planning for Operation Downfall, part of Operation Olympic-Coronet; and was an on-site evaluator of the atomic destruction of Hiroshima and Nagasaki. Details of these missions remain classified.

After the war, he made a fourth expedition to the Antarctic in 1947, leading Operation Highjump, and a fifth in 1955–56 in preparation for U.S. efforts in the International Geophysical Year (IGY), but died before he could participate in the IGY's Operation Deepfreeze. Byrd was the author of four best-selling books: *Skyward* (1928), *Little America* (1930), *Discovery* (1935), and *Alone* (1938).

Peter Model

CARLSON, EVANS FORDYCE (1896–1947)

U.S. marine officer, Carlson was born in Sidney, New York. He served in the army before being commissioned a second lieutenant in the marines in 1922. He served three tours in China, including one in 1937 as an observer with the Communist 8th Route Army whose esprit and success in guerrilla operations against Japanese units impressed him. Carlson resigned his commission in 1939 to write and lecture on the need to take a stand against Japanese expansion in Asia. He reentered the Marine Corps in 1941 and the following year, now a lieutenant colonel, organized the 2d Marine Raider Battalion, elements of which he led on a raid on the Pacific atoll of Makin in August 1942. (The film *Gung Ho!* was based on this operation.) Carlson then led his Raiders on Guadalcanal and finished his World War II service as an observer and in a staff assignment with the 4th Marine Division.

Bibliography: Blankfort, Michael, *The Big Yankee: The Life of Carlson of the Raiders* (Little, Brown, 1947).

Lloyd J. Graybar

CATES, CLIFTON BLEDSOE (1893–1970)

U.S. marine commander, Cates was born in Tiptonville, Tennessee. He returned to the United States after World War I to serve as an aide to Pres. Woodrow Wilson. On Aug. 7, 1942, he landed on Guadalcanal as commander of the 1st Regiment, 1st Marine Division. The following year, he moved to Quantico, Virginia, as commandant of Marine Corps Schools. Returning to the Pacific theater in July 1944, Cates commanded the 4th Marine Division during its assaults on Saipan, Tinian, and Iwo Jima. Appointed commandant of the Marine Corps in January 1948, he resisted personnel reductions and lobbied to retain the marine air arm. Unwilling to retire, Cates served once more as commandant of Marine Corps Schools. He retired as a full general in June 1954.

Maj. James Sanders Day

CHAFFEE, ADNA ROMANZA, JR.
(1884–1941)

U.S. army officer, Chaffee was born in Junction City, Kansas. He graduated from West Point in 1906 and rose rapidly in World War I, which he ended as G-3 of the U.S. III Corps.

From 1927, Chaffee helped organize the army's experimental armored forces. In 1938, he took command of the

7th Cavalry Brigade (Mechanized), which he led brilliantly in maneuvers during 1939 and 1940. Promoted to major general in 1940, Chaffee became commander of the 1st Armored Corps in July 1940, but he died of cancer 13 months later. Chaffee's tireless efforts to create an effective doctrine and force structure were essential to the growth of American armor.

Jonathan M. House

CHENNAULT, CLAIRE LEE (1893–1958)

U.S. army aviator, Chennault was born in Commerce, Texas. At the time of U.S. entry into World War I, he was a factory worker in Akron, Ohio. He applied and was accepted into the officers' training school at Fort Benjamin Harrison, Indiana, in August 1917, entering the infantry reserve.

Early Air Experience. Chennault was enamored with flying from the outset but was refused flight training because of his age and marital status (married with three children). Nonetheless, persistence paid off, and he had completed pilot training by August 1920. There followed several typical assignments as a pilot in the Army Air Service. A high point of his service through 1937 was a three-year stint as commander of the 19th Pursuit Squadron in Hawaii (1923–26), where he became a strong advocate of the use of fighters in air combat.

Another pivotal experience for Chennault came during the early 1930s when he was an instructor at the Air Corps Tactical School. There, he was able to hone his ideas of the use of fighter aircraft and enjoy the stimulation of other air-power theorists. He wrote *The Role of Defensive Pursuit* (1935), which encapsulated his ideas on fighter combat. It was an important but unpopular work, for most of the Air Corps was advocating the primacy of strategic bombardment. When the Air Corps removed him from flying status in April 1937 because of a serious hearing impairment, Chennault retired as a captain.

China Sojourn. In May 1937, Chennault made a major career move, accepting a position as the aviation adviser to the Chinese Nationalist government of Chiang Kai-shek. He was newly arrived and only beginning to settle into his work when the Sino-Japanese War erupted in September 1937 and he was forced to deal with the crisis. He helped organize, equip, train, and direct Chinese air units; in some cases he even led them into battle. He remained in China

Gen. Claire Chennault, shown at bat during recreation in China, organized the ''Flying Tigers'' as a volunteer group of U.S. pilots to aid the Chinese in the Sino-Japanese War; this group became the most effective Allied air unit in the Far East during World War II. (U.S. Army Military History Institute: H. U. Milne Collection)

to fight throughout 1938 and 1939 when the country was on the verge of capitulation and when it seemingly had few friends.

With Chennault's assistance, China created the American Volunteer Group (AVG), better known as the "Flying Tigers." Made up of Americans formed into a separate unit and fighting for the Chinese, this unit was commanded by Chennault. The AVG made a showing comparable to that of the Royal Air Force in the Battle of Britain. The most effective Allied air unit in the Far East, Chennault's Flying Tigers engaged the Japanese from bases in the Chinese interior for several months in 1941 and 1942. It destroyed about 3,000 Japanese aircraft at a cost of 12 AVG airplanes and four AVG pilots lost in combat.

More important, when war news for the Allies was generally bleak, the AVG's "David versus Goliath" act in China was a source of hope and inspiration. Chennault, who had left the Army Air Corps without distinction, now became a hero. His lantern jaw and stoic demeanor became symbols of determined resistance.

China Air Task Force. When the United States entered World War II in December 1941, Chennault was asked to reenter the army air forces with the AVG. In April 1942, he was recalled to active duty and in July took command of the task force. A year later, March 1943, this unit was renamed the 14th Air Force. After the closure of the Burma Road, Chennault organized an aerial logistics pipeline from India to western China, the Hump Airlift, to resupply his forces. This airlift became one of the great resupply feats of the war.

Chennault's command had several stunning victories during the war. With limited resources, which he complained about constantly, in three years of operations, the 14th Air Force claimed about 2,600 enemy airplanes and enormous amounts of supplies destroyed.

Always controversial, Chennault used contacts within the Chinese government, notably with his future brother-in-law Chiang Kai-shek, and among highly placed U.S. leaders to force his wishes on military commanders. He made many enemies in high places; his running fight with Joseph W. Stilwell, U.S. military commander in China, was legendary. Chennault, with the full support of Chiang Kai-shek, demanded the supplies coming into China over the Hump to fight an air campaign against the Japanese. He argued that air power alone could defeat the enemy. Stilwell was convinced that ground efforts would be required and wanted more supplies for that campaign.

Postwar Experience. Eventually these political difficulties forced Chennault to retire a second time—just before Japan's surrender in August 1945. He established Civil Air Transport (CAT) in 1946 and operated it throughout the Far East in the late 1940s. He sold CAT in 1950, and it became a resource for the Central Intelligence Agency's efforts in the region. Chennault remained with CAT until 1955.

Bibliography: Bird, Martha, *Chennault: Giving Wings to the Tiger* (Univ. of Alabama Press, 1987); Chennault, Claire Lee, *Way of a Fighter* (Putnam, 1958); Maurer, Maurer, *Aviation in the U.S. Army, 1919–1939* (Office of Air Force History, 1987); Shaller, Michael, *The U.S. Crusade in China, 1938–1945* (Columbia Univ. Press, 1979).

Roger D. Launius

CHRISTIE, JOHN WALTER (1865–1944)

U.S. inventor and tank designer, Christie was born in River Edge, New Jersey. After first working with marine engines, Christie turned to automobiles and in 1904 founded the Front Drive Motor Company to build and market a front-wheel-drive car he had designed. In 1916, he started to work on military projects, beginning with a four-wheel-drive truck. He soon moved into tank designs, and over the next nine years, his firm built 15 vehicles for the U.S. Army. The two major problems facing tank designs in the 1920s were the short life of tank tracks and low speed. To overcome these obstacles, Christie pioneered the concept of the convertible tank, whereby the tank ran on large rubber tires on the roads and then placed tracks over these same tires for off-road travel. In 1928, he introduced his greatest innovation, an independent suspension system that allowed a tank to travel at high speeds across country and yet remain fairly stable.

The U.S. Army purchased several of Christie's M 1928 tanks, but his designs never found favor there. One factor was Christie's abrasive personality, which made cooperation between the army and the inventor difficult. Another was the expense involved in producing the Christie suspension. Budget-minded ordnance officers preferred cheaper, commercially available systems. Christie's designs found greater acceptance overseas. The Soviet Union used the Christie suspension as the basis of its BT tank series and in the famous T-34. Great Britain also used the suspension in a series of cruiser tanks that served during World War II.

Bibliography: Christie, J. Edward, *Steel Steeds Christie* (Sunflower Univ. Press, 1985); Jones, Ralph E., et al., *The Fighting Tanks Since 1916* (Nat. Serv. Publ., 1933).

Richard F. Kehrberg

CLARK, JOSEPH JAMES ("JOCKO") (1893–1971)

U.S. naval officer, Clark was born in Pryor, Oklahoma. He graduated from Annapolis in 1918 and served on the cruiser *North Carolina* before being wounded in action. Following World War I, Clark spent several years at sea in routine assignments. After a brief tour on the faculty at the Naval Academy, Clark graduated from flight school at Pensacola in 1925 and later attended advanced flight training in San Diego. For the rest of his career, Clark remained with the air arm of the navy.

Commander of the 5th Army, Gen. Mark Clark, shown on the beach at Anzio in 1944, drew criticism for his battle tactics during the capture of Italy, but was admired by his fellow officers. (U.S. Army Military History Institute)

Following more than a decade of aviation assignments, Clark was attached to the carrier *Yorktown* as executive officer. He was promoted to captain in 1942. In 1942–43, Clark brought two carriers into commission, the *Suwannee* and the new *Yorktown*. He commanded the *Suwannee* in Operation Torch. In command of the *Yorktown*, Clark participated in the 1943–44 operations at Marcus Island, Wake Island, the Gilbert Islands, and the Marshall Islands. Promoted to rear admiral in February 1944 and flying his flag in the *Hornet*, Clark commanded task forces in operations at the Caroline and Mariana island groups as well in the battles for the Philippine Sea, Iwo Jima, and Okinawa.

Clark became assistant chief of naval operations (air) in 1946 and later commanded carrier task forces. The last such assignment was on board his flagship *Bonhomme Richard* in operations against North Korea. Clark retired in December 1953 with the rank of admiral.

Vernon L. Williams

CLARK, MARK WAYNE (1896–1984)

Highest-ranking U.S. field commander in the Mediterranean theater of operations during World War II, Clark was born in Watertown, New York. He graduated from West Point in 1917 and was commissioned in the infantry. Within a year, he was a captain commanding the 3d Battalion, 11th Infantry, in the Western Front in France. Two days after taking command, Clark was seriously wounded. Unfit to return to his unit, he spent the remainder of World War I as a staff officer in France. During the interwar years, Clark held a variety of assignments in the peacetime army and graduated from both the Command and General Staff College and the War College.

By 1940, Clark was a lieutenant colonel and had caught the eye of Gen. George C. Marshall. A series of high-level staff appointments followed, and in the summer of 1942, Marshall sent Clark to England as a major general. There, he briefly commanded II Corps, and when Lt. Gen. Dwight D. Eisenhower was named Supreme Allied Commander for Operation Torch, Clark became the deputy commander.

In October 1942, Clark undertook a dangerous secret mission to Algeria that required him to row ashore in high seas from a British submarine. His task was to persuade the Vichy French leaders in French North Africa to either join the Allies or remain neutral when the Torch landings took place on November 8. Despite being nearly captured when the Gestapo raided the beach house in which he had met with the French leaders, Clark's mission was successful, and Allied forces met only limited resistance from Vichy French forces. Clark's reputation soared, and he was decorated with the Distinguished Service Cross for exceptional valor.

He was promoted to lieutenant general in November 1942, and, as Eisenhower's deputy, he successfully negotiated the armistice in French Morocco and Algeria with French admiral Jean Louis Darlan, in what has come to be known as the Darlan Deal. In January 1943, Clark assumed command of the newly formed 5th Army and began preparing its U.S. and French divisions for combat. After the invasion of Sicily in July 1943, it was decided that the Allies would invade Italy. Clark's 5th Army was designated to spearhead the amphibious landings at Salerno.

In his first combat, Clark displayed exceptional bravery as Allied forces fought a furious battle with elements of the German 10th Army in September 1943 that nearly resulted in the loss of the beachhead. During the autumn of 1943, Clark directed the 5th Army as it fought a series of bloody battles in the mountains and along the rivers north of Naples. By December, the Germans had manned the Gustav line, resulting in a stalemate at Cassino. On Jan. 20, 1944, Clark attempted to break the Gustav line in the Liri Valley and push north toward Rome, by establishing a bridgehead across the Rapido River with the 36th (Texas National Guard) Division. The operation resulted in failure and heavy casualties, and the road to Rome remained in German hands.

Clark also directed the ill-fated Anzio landings in January 1944, which resulted in one of the bloodiest stalemates of the war when German forces bitterly resisted this Allied attempt to outflank the Gustav line and capture Rome. In March 1944, Clark's most controversial decision resulted in the bombing and destruction of the Benedictine Abbey of Monte Cassino. In May, his decision to disobey his superior, British general Sir Harold Alexander, by switching the axis of the breakout attack from the Anzio beachhead resulted in the escape of the German 10th Army from Cassino.

On June 5, Clark triumphantly entered Rome, but the celebrations marking the liberation of the Eternal City were soon superseded by a series of bitter battles in northern Italy along the Gothic line. In December, Clark assumed command of the 15th Army Group and directed the final months of the Italian campaign. He was promoted to full general in March 1945 and in early May accepted the surrender of all German forces in Italy. Clark's final assignment in Europe began in July 1945 when he was appointed American high commissioner and commander of U.S. occupation forces in Austria.

Although Clark was a superb organizer and trainer of troops, his performance in Italy was marred by controversy. His relations with Alexander were often adversarial and the result of a mistaken belief that U.S. troops were bearing an unnecessarily high proportion of Allied casualties and that Alexander and the British were attempting to deny what Clark believed was their right to capture Rome. After the war, a congressional investigation cleared Clark of charges that he had negligently squandered American lives at the Rapido.

Bibliography: Blumenson, Martin, "Salerno to Cassino," *The U.S. Army in World War II: Mediterranean Theater of Operations* (Center of Military History, U.S. Army, 1969); —, *Mark Clark* (Congdon & Weed, 1984); Clark, Mark, *Calculated Risk* (Harper & Row, 1951); Fisher, Ernest, "Cassino to the Alps," *The U.S. Army in World War II: Mediterranean Theater of Operations* (Center of Military History, U.S. Army, 1977); Forty, George, *Fifth Army at War* (Ian Allen, 1980); Graham, Dominick, and Shelford Bidwell, *Tug of War: The Battle for Italy, 1943–45* (St. Martin's Press, 1986).

Carlo W. D'Este

CLARKE, BRUCE COOPER (1901–1988)

U.S. army officer, Clarke was born in Adams, New York. He enlisted in the U.S. Army in 1918 and then received an appointment to West Point, from which he graduated in 1925. He participated in the Louisiana Maneuvers in the spring of 1940 and was instrumental in the formation of the Armored Force at Fort Knox, Kentucky. He was deployed to Europe as part of Gen. George Patton's 3d Army, where he emphasized mobility and maneuver. As a brigadier general, Clarke assumed command of Combat Command B, 7th Armored Division, in November 1944 and established a defense at St. Vith, Belgium, where his

forces withstood the brunt of the German counteroffensive. After the war, he was promoted to major general (1951) and commanded a corps in Korea before commanding the Continental Army Command (1958–60), and U.S. Army, Europe (1960–62). Clarke retired in 1962 as a full general.

Bibliography: Clarke, Bruce Cooper, *Guidelines for the Leader and the Commander* (Stackpole Books, 1973); Ellis, William Donohue, *Clarke of St. Vith, the Sergeant's General* (Dillon, Liederbach, 1974).

Maj. James Sanders Day

CLAY, LUCIUS DUBIGNON (1897–1978)

U.S. army officer, Clay was born in Marietta, Georgia. A 1918 West Point graduate, he had a lackluster career with the Army Corps of Engineers until World War II. After revitalizing nearly 500 military air bases and his promotion to brigadier general (March 1942), Clay became deputy chief of staff of matériel, sharply accelerating quality and delivery of front-line supplies. Soon after D-Day (June 6, 1944), he was given command of the Normandy sector, and in April 1945, as civil affairs deputy to Supreme Allied Commander Dwight D. Eisenhower, Clay was promoted to lieutenant general. In 1947, he was promoted to full general and put in charge of the American zone of occupation in Germany. He was the architect of the 1948–49 Berlin Airlift that broke the Soviet blockade of West Berlin. After retiring from the military in 1949, Clay entered private business as chief executive officer of the Continental Can Company.

Bibliography: Clay, Lucius D., *Decision in Germany* (Doubleday, 1950); Smith, Jean Edward, *Lucius D. Clay: An American Life* (Holt, 1990).

Peter Model

COLLINS, JOSEPH LAWTON (1896–1987)

U.S. army officer, Collins was born in New Orleans, Louisiana. He graduated from West Point in 1917, was sent to Germany two years later as an infantry battalion commander, and between the world wars held several important military teaching posts. After serving in the Philippines, Collins in 1940 was assigned to the office of Sec. of War Henry L. Stimson. Promoted to brigadier general and major general in 1942, Collins reorganized and built up defense of the Hawaiian Islands, where he took over the 25th Infantry Division. In the Solomon Islands and Papua New Guinea, he led the 25th Infantry (whose code name of "Lightning" led to his nickname of "Lightning Joe") in the Guadalcanal and New Britain campaigns (1942–43).

Collins was then reassigned to Gen. Dwight D. Eisenhower's European theater, where he was put in charge of D-Day (June 6, 1944) amphibious training. Collins is best known for having led the army's VII Corps from Utah Beach on D-Day through France and the Ardennes, and across the Rhine River to envelop the Ruhr district and then to link up at the Elbe River with the Soviet army. He was promoted to lieutenant general in 1945. After the war, Collins held several staff posts, including chief of information for the War Department and army vice chief of staff (1947–49). Collins, who had been promoted to full general in 1948, succeeded Gen. Omar Bradley as army chief of staff (1949–53). He later served as President Eisenhower's personal representative to South Vietnam (1955–56) before retiring.

Peter Model

CONOLLY, RICHARD LANSING
(1892–1962)
U.S. naval officer, Conolly was born in Waukegan, Illinois. He graduated from Annapolis in 1914. After duty on a destroyer assigned to convoy escort in World War I, Conolly saw many years of service on battleships, cruisers, and destroyers. While on shore, he taught both at the Naval Academy and the Naval War College. As a captain in World War II, he commanded Destroyer Squadron 6, which provided escort for Adm. William Halsey's carriers during the April 1942 Tokyo Raid. Promoted to rear admiral, Conolly spent several months on staff work in Washington before commanding amphibious forces during the 1943 landings on Sicily and then at Salerno, Italy. After Salerno, he was transferred to the Pacific to command an amphibious group, which he led in the Kwajalein, Saipan, Guam, Leyte, and Lingayen Gulf operations. Near war's end, he was involved in planning amphibious operations for the invasion of Japan.

Bibliography: Reynolds, Clark G., *Famous American Admirals* (Van Nostrand-Reinhold, 1978).

Lloyd J. Graybar

CONNER, FOX (1874–1951)
U.S. army officer, Conner was born in Slate Springs, Mississippi. He graduated from West Point in 1898 and was commissioned in the artillery. Attendance at the Leavenworth Schools (1905–06) was followed by appointments to the faculties at West Point and the Army War College. During World War I, he headed the American Expeditionary Force's Operations Staff, reaching the rank of brigadier general.

After the war, Conner held several key positions, including commander of U.S. troops in the Panama Canal Zone, where he became a mentor of Dwight D. Eisenhower. He was also commander of the Hawaiian Department (1928–30) and commander of the I Corps Area (1930–38). He retired as a major general in 1938.

Bibliography: Conner, Virginia, *What Father Forbad* (Dorrance, 1951).

David Friend

In the early 1920s, Brig. Gen. Fox Connor commanded U.S. troops in the Panama Canal Zone, where he encouraged the young Dwight D. Eisenhower to think globally and to strive for a leadership position in the next world war. (U.S. Army Military History Institute)

CORLETT, CHARLES HARRISON
(1889–1971)
U.S. army officer, Corlett was born in Burchard, Nebraska. After graduating from West Point in 1913, he served as a company officer with the 30th Infantry in Alaska, California, New York, and Texas. During World War I, he was detailed to the Signal Corps and went to France in January 1918, rising to lieutenant colonel. Between the wars, he commanded an infantry battalion, was a student and instructor at Fort Leavenworth, graduated from the Army War College, and served from 1934 to 1938 on the War Department General Staff.

Promoted to brigadier general in 1941 and major general in 1942, Corlett commanded the task forces that captured Kiska in the Aleutians and Kwajalein in the Central Pacific. He was sent to Europe to command XIX Corps from March 1944 but was relieved in October due to ill health and lack of progress. Corlett retired in 1946.

Robert H. Berlin

COTA, NORMAN DANIEL (1893–1971)
U.S. army officer, Cota was born in Chelsea, Massachusetts. He graduated from West Point in April 1917, the Infantry School in 1925, the Infantry School Advanced Course in 1928, the Command and General Staff School

in 1931, and the Army War College in 1937. After the outbreak of World War II, he served in a variety of combined operations positions until October 1943, when as a brigadier general he was appointed assistant division commander of the 29th Infantry Division. He performed heroically while leading forward elements of that division ashore during the initial Allied landings in Normandy in June 1944. Promoted to major general, he commanded the division in 1944–45. Cota retired from active duty in 1946, residing for the next 25 years in Philadelphia, where he served for a time as that city's civil defense director.

Bibliography: Miller, Robert A., *Division Commander, A Biography of Major General Norman D. Cota* (Reprint Co., 1989).

David Friend

CRAIG, MALIN (1875–1945)

U.S. army officer, Craig was born in St. Joseph, Missouri, and grew up on various military posts. After graduating from West Point in 1898, he served in Cuba, the Philippines, and China before returning to the United States to attend the army's service and staff schools. During these academic tours, Craig displayed an excellent grasp of strategy and tactics and a marked ability for staff work.

When the United States entered World War I in 1917, Craig, then a major, joined the 41st Division as its chief of staff. Once in France, however, he became the U.S. Army's I Corps chief of staff and served there in the Aine-Marne, St.-Mihiel, and Meuse-Argonne offensives. In recognition for his achievements, he was promoted to brigadier general in June 1918 and made chief of staff of the new U.S. 3d Army in November 1918.

When Craig returned home in 1919, he reverted to his prewar rank of major and became director of the Army War College. Promoted to colonel the next year and brigadier general in 1921, Craig commanded the Cavalry School and Coast Artillery District of Manila before being appointed chief of cavalry and major general in 1924. In 1926, he became the assistant chief of staff for operations and training. Thereafter, Craig commanded a number of corps areas and the Panama Canal Department before becoming commandant of the Army War College in 1935.

In October, Pres. Franklin D. Roosevelt unexpectedly selected Craig to succeed Gen. Douglas MacArthur as chief of staff of the army. Upon entering office as a full general, Craig was very disturbed by the theoretical nature of the General Staff's war plans and ordered a major reevaluation. This study confirmed Craig's suspicion that the current mobilization plan included unrealistically high estimates of the number of men and supplies that would be available in an emergency. Therefore, Craig instituted a new Protective Mobilization Plan (PMP), which provided for a gradual expansion of the army within practical limits.

Craig also moved to improve military training and efficiency. He supervised the reorganization of the Military Intelligence Division and introduced special field exercises for infantry and cavalry units. Moreover, he encouraged experiments with a new three-regiment infantry division in order to increase the army's mobility and flexibility in the field. Craig also pressed for the issue of improved weapons, such as the new semiautomatic M-1 Garand rifle and new tank designs. The army's first purpose-built antitank gun emerged during this time, as did a new emphasis on antiaircraft artillery.

Craig retired in August 1939, but his modernization program had a deep impact on the army in World War II. The PMP formed the basis for wartime mobilization planning, and Craig's reforms in training and equipment laid the foundation for the nation's massive wartime army. Craig himself returned to active duty in 1941 to serve as chairman of the secretary of war's Personnel Board until 1944, when he suffered a stroke. He died the following summer.

Bibliography: Kreidberg, Marvin A., and Merton G. Henry, *History of Military Mobilization in the United States Army* (U.S. Govt. Printing Office, 1955); McFarland, Keith D., *Harry H. Woodring: A Political Biography of FDR's Controversial Secretary of War* (Univ. Press of Kansas, 1975); Watson, Mark S., *United States Army in World War II: The War Department: The Chief of Staff: Prewar Plans and Preparations* (Historical Div., Dept. of the Army, 1950).

Richard F. Kehrberg

CUNNINGHAM, ALFRED AUSTELL (1882–1939)

U.S. marine officer, Cunningham was born in Atlanta, Georgia, and saw action as an enlisted man with the 3d Georgia Volunteer Infantry in the Spanish-American War in Cuba (1898). After a return to civilian life, he enrolled at Marine Officer's School (1909), graduated with the rank of second lieutenant, and began to follow his lifelong interest in aviation. In 1917, as a major, he evaluated the French and British air services, assessed the need for a Marine Corps aviation service, recruited a squadron, and brought it to battle-readiness in time to be a significant force during World War I. During this time, he negotiated an agreement with the army to train marine pilots. After the war, he continued to advance the cause of Marine Corps aviation and brought it from its infancy to its role as an advanced base support for the army. Cunningham served in several administrative and command positions as well as in combat in Nicaragua (1928) before retiring as a lieutenant colonel in 1935.

Leo J. Daugherty III

DARBY, WILLIAM ORLANDO
(1911–1945)

U.S. army officer, Darby was born in Arizona. He graduated from West Point in 1933. Early in World War II, he led a group of U.S. Army volunteer rangers training with British commandos in Scotland. Darby's idea was to form similar small, lethally equipped units for hit-and-run tactics. Instead, his superiors ordered the rangers to operate in battalion strength. Lacking the necessary rank to command a battalion, Darby was rapidly promoted from captain to lieutenant colonel. The rangers' first action was alongside the British and Canadians in the ill-fated Dieppe raid in August 1942. Darby next led the 1st Ranger Battalion in a night landing in Algeria, to knock out local defenses prior to the North African invasion. He later made landings with the rangers in Sicily and on the Italian mainland at Salerno and Anzio. Darby then became assistant commander of the 10th Light (Mountain) Division in northern Italy and was killed in action on Apr. 30, 1945, a few days before the Germans surrendered. He was promoted to brigadier general posthumously, the only army officer so honored.

Peter Model

DAVIS, BENJAMIN OLIVER, JR.
(1912–   )

U.S. army air officer, Davis was born in Washington, D.C., the only son of Brig. Gen. Benjamin O. Davis, Sr., the U.S. Army's first black general. He was appointed to West Point in 1932, becoming only the fourth black to be admitted to the academy and the first black graduate of the 20th century.

Following assignments with the 24th Infantry Regiment and at Tuskegee Institute, he entered the Army Air Corps. In 1943, Lieutenant Colonel Davis was assigned command of the 99th Pursuit Squadron. Later that year, he was assigned command of the 332d Fighter Group. In the postwar integrated air force, Davis held progressively responsible positions, becoming the first black lieutenant general in 1965. He retired from active duty in 1970.

Bibliography: Davis, Benjamin O., *Benjamin O. Davis, Jr., American: An Autobiography* (Smithsonian, 1991).

David Friend

DAVIS, DWIGHT FILLEY (1879–1945)

U.S. military officer and secretary of war, Davis was born in St. Louis, Missouri. A Harvard graduate and prominent businessman, he attended the 1915 Plattsburgh Military Camp that trained civilian volunteers to be reserve officers. He maintained a lifelong interest in citizen soldiers, serving in combat during World War I as a member of the 35th National Guard Division. After the war, Davis became director of the War Finance Corporation. While assistant secretary of war (1923–24), he helped found the Army

As an Army Air Force lieutenant colonel and colonel, Benjamin O. Davis, Jr., commanded pursuit missions over North Africa and Sicily and led the 332d Fighter Group in missions over Italy and Germany. Here, he briefs his all-black pilots before a mission in Italy. (U.S. Air Force)

Industrial College to study the logistical complexities of mobilization. As secretary of war (1925–29), he struggled to support promising experiments, such as the experimental mechanized force, despite severe peacetime economies. Davis later served as governor general of the Philippines (1929–32) and as director-general of the Army Specialist Corps (1942–45).

Bibliography: Bell, William G., *Secretaries of War and Secretaries of the Army* (Washington, D.C., 1982).

Jonathan M. House

DAWLEY, ERNEST JOSEPH (1886–1973)

U.S. army officer, Dawley was born in Antigo, Wisconsin. He graduated from West Point in 1910, was assigned to the field artillery, and participated in the Punitive Expedition into Mexico in 1916. During World War I in France, he was an officer at the Saumur Artillery School and a staff officer with the U.S. 1st Army and at American Expeditionary Force headquarters.

Between the wars, Dawley served in the Tactical Department at West Point (1919–24) and in field artillery assignments at posts in the United States and on staff duty in Washington. During World War II, as a major general, he commanded the 40th Division in 1941 and VI Corps in 1942. Dawley led his corps in the Salerno landing in Italy, but his command at the beachhead was judged to be inadequate and he was relieved in September 1943. He commanded the Tank Destroyer Center at Camp Hood, Texas, and the Reinforcement Command in Europe for the remainder of the war. He retired in 1947.

Robert H. Berlin

DENBY, EDWIN C. (1870–1929)

U.S. secretary of the navy (1919–24), Denby was born in Evansville, Indiana. He graduated from the University of Michigan in 1896 and practiced law in Detroit. After a brief stint in the navy during the Spanish-American War (1898), he served in the U.S House of Representatives (1905–11). He enlisted in the marines as a private in 1917; was assigned to Parris Island, South Carolina, where he instructed recruits on social issues; and was discharged after World War I as a major, the rank with which he entered the Officers' Reserve Corps.

Chosen in 1919 by Pres. Warren G. Harding to serve as secretary of the navy, Denby used his office to build upon an expanding navy but was stymied by the lack of funds and the restrictions agreed upon at the 1921–22 Washington Armaments Conference. The Bureau of Aeronautics grew during his tenure. In 1923, scandal erupted when it was discovered that naval oil reserves at Elk Hills and Teapot Dome had been placed under the Department of the Interior and were being leased to private oil interests in return for favors. Although Denby was not directly involved in the Teapot Dome scandal, he was reprimanded by the Senate and, upon Pres. Calvin Coolidge's refusal to dismiss him, he resigned before an impeachment movement could gain ground.

Leo J. Daugherty III

DE SEVERSKY, ALEXANDER PROCO-FIEFF (1894–1974)

Russian-American aviator and aeronautical engineer, de Seversky was born in Tiflis, Russia, and became a World War I ace for the tsar's air force. He flew more than 50 missions after losing his right leg in combat. After the war, he flew as a test pilot. He came to the United States in 1918 with the Russian Embassy and stayed after the Russian Revolution. Thereafter, he was involved in aeronautical activities as an industrialist and pilot. In 1921, he developed aerial refueling equipment and techniques. Working with Elmer Sperry in 1923, de Seversky invented the first fully automatic synchronous bombsight, the predecessor of all gyroscopically stabilized flight instruments. In 1931, he

incorporated the Seversky Aircraft Corporation, which in 1939 became Republic Aviation.

In 1942, de Seversky published *Victory Through Air Power,* a powerful book on the capability of military aeronautics to defeat an enemy. In it, he advocated the targeting of a nation's entire territory for strategic bombing and of "exterminating" the enemy with air power. It was an eloquent statement that found a ready audience in the crisis-stricken era at the beginning of World War II. De Seversky was thereafter hailed as a prophet of air power and enjoyed that status throughout the remainder of his life.

Bibliography: de Seversky, Alexander P., *Victory Through Air Power* (Simon & Schuster, 1942); Sherry, Michael S., *The Rise of American Air Power: The Creation of Armageddon* (Yale Univ. Press, 1987).

Roger D. Launius

DEVEREUX, JAMES PATRICK SINNOTT (1903–1988)

U.S. marine officer, Devereux was born in Havana, Cuba. He enlisted in the U.S. Marines in July 1923; 18 months later he was commissioned as an officer. He served in East Asia and the United States before he was assigned to Pearl Harbor, Hawaii, in January 1941. During World War II, he commanded 450 marines at the heroic Wake Island defense. He arrived on Wake in October 1941 with orders to defend it against small-scale Japanese raids, but when the enemy hurled a massive invasion force against the island, he could do little but delay the inevitable. Major Devereux succeeded in repulsing a December 11 invasion flotilla, but a more potent invasion force smashed against Wake Island on December 23 and quickly captured the garrison. News of Wake's gallant defense, which included the sinking of two enemy destroyers, electrified the American home front and turned Devereux and his men into instant heroes. Devereux spent the remainder of the war in Japanese prison camps. He retired in 1948 and later became active in politics, serving as a Maryland congressman in the U.S. House of Representatives (1951–59).

Bibliography: Schultz, Duane, *Wake Island* (St. Martin's Press, 1978).

John F. Wukovits

DEVERS, JACOB LOUCKS (1887–1979)

U.S. army officer, Devers was born in York, Pennsylvania, and graduated from West Point in 1909. He spent most of World War I on the staff of the Field Artillery School and became a temporary lieutenant colonel. After a year of occupation duty in Germany, Devers returned to the United States to become an artillery instructor at West Point (1919–24).

Graduating from the Command and General Staff School in 1925, his next assignment was as director of the gunnery department at the Field Artillery School until 1928. Devers pioneered work in developing a new system of fire control for the field artillery that reaped great dividends in World War II. Three years in the office of the chief of field artillery followed, and Devers graduated from the Army War College in 1933.

Devers finally received a permanent promotion to lieutenant colonel in 1934 and to colonel two years later. He received another assignment to West Point in 1936 and directed an extensive building program. Chief of staff of the Panama Canal Department during 1939–40, he was promoted to brigadier general in May 1940. Devers became a major general in October 1940 and took command of the 9th Infantry Division.

Following the death of Maj. Gen. Adna R. Chaffee in August 1941, Devers was named commanding general of the armored force. Although he lacked experience with armored units, it was hoped Devers, an artillery officer, would end the disruptive bickering between infantry and cavalry officers within the armor branch. He proved to be a very capable leader and brought greater harmony among the armored officers. He also directed the organization and training of armored units. His candid advocacy for the employment of the armored division as the centerpiece of the ground combat forces brought him into conflict with Lt. Gen. Lesley J. McNair. Following a War Department reorganization in March 1942, the armored force came directly under McNair, the commanding general of U.S. ground forces. Although the two disagreed vehemently about the role of armor on the battlefield, they remained friends.

Promoted to lieutenant general in September 1942, Devers was ordered to England in May 1943. While Gen. Dwight D. Eisenhower was in North Africa, Devers became the commanding general of the European theater and directed the buildup for the invasion of mainland Europe. He returned these responsibilities to Eisenhower in January 1944 and departed for the Mediterranean to become deputy Allied commander and commanding general of all U.S. forces in that theater. Devers then planned and commanded the invasion of southern France in August 1944. As commanding general of the 6th Army Group, Devers served under Eisenhower for the remainder of the war. It was a strained relationship, however, as Eisenhower looked upon him as a rival.

Devers was promoted to general in March 1945. He returned home in June 1945 and was named head of ground forces, the name of which was changed to Army Field Forces in March 1948. He retained this post until his retirement in September 1949.

Bibliography: Ambrose, Stephen E., *Eisenhower: Soldier, General of the Army, President-Elect, 1890–1952* (Simon & Schuster, 1983); Greenfield, Kent Roberts, et al., *The Organization of Ground Combat Troops* (Department of the Army, 1947); Pogue, Forrest C., *George C. Marshall: Organizer of Victory, 1943–1945* (Viking, 1973).

Daniel T. Bailey

DONOVAN, WILLIAM JOSEPH
(1883–1959)

U.S. attorney and military intelligence administrator, "Wild Bill" Donovan was born in Buffalo, New York. He first came to prominence during World War I when, as a battalion commander in the famed 69th Regiment of the New National Guard (redesignated the 165th), he was wounded three times during the fighting in France and earned the Congressional Medal of Honor, the Distinguished Service Cross, and the Distinguished Service Medal.

Returning to Buffalo, he became a crusading U.S. attorney and soon made national news by raiding his own club for violation of the prohibition statute. During 1924–29, Donovan was an assistant U.S. attorney general, pleading and winning more cases before the Supreme Court than anyone previous. A prominent Catholic layman and a lifelong Republican, Donovan ran unsuccessfully for lieutenant governor, then for governor, of New York, but did much better as the strategist for Herbert Hoover's presidential campaign. Donovan then established the New York law firm that eventually became Donovan, Leisure, Newton & Irvine.

When World War II began in Europe, Donovan was called upon by Pres. Franklin D. Roosevelt to undertake some significant special missions. Sent to England to assess whether the British were in earnest about the war and worth supporting, he reported "definitely yes" on both counts. By June 1941, Donovan had become convinced that the United States was in urgent need of a mechanism for developing strategic intelligence. In a memorandum urging the president to establish such a service, Donovan called the intelligence units of the army and navy inadequate for collecting strategic information and stressed the government's fragmented and uncoordinated means of dealing with the foreign information that became available. He proposed a central intelligence agency.

Coordinator of Information. Thus, in July 1941, even before the United States entered World War II, President Roosevelt established the office of coordinator of information (COI), designed to collect and analyze information bearing on national security, and put Donovan in charge. The COI was supposed to collect and assemble the information it needed from various government departments and agencies, then to collate and analyze them and provide the results to the president and such others as he might direct. A euphemistic reference to "supplementary activities" covered unspecified clandestine activities carried out to facilitate the securing of needed information.

Donovan began by emphasizing the research and analysis function, assembling a group of some 2,000 analysts that included a number of the country's leading scholars, men such as William L. Langer and Edward Mead Earle. British security coordinator William Stephenson, also known as "Intrepid," called it "the most brilliant team of analysts in the history of intelligence." Donovan attracted more talent to staff newly formed intelligence and clandestine warfare elements. Soon he was pouring intelligence reports directly to the president, all the while fighting fierce bureaucratic battles throughout the government with departments and agencies that felt threatened by this new and aggressively energetic organization. Donovan's close personal relationship with the president facilitated his efforts.

Office of Strategic Services. In June 1942, the COI was disestablished, and Donovan, who was eventually made a major general, was put at the head of a successor organization known as the Office of Strategic Services (OSS). He had concluded that such an arrangement would benefit his efforts. Operating now under the Joint Chiefs of Staff, Donovan was in his element.

The OSS was responsible for the full range of intelligence activities: collection, research and analysis, estimates, and special operations—sabotage, guerrilla warfare, espionage, and counterespionage. Many of the people who staffed it were recruited by Donovan personally. "Bill Donovan was a dangerous man to know," said one of them. "If he really liked you, he'd pay you the compliment of having you dropped into Sicily, Sardinia, Corsica, northern Italy, southern France, or someplace else like that."

Donovan himself roamed the world overseeing his enterprise, visiting the head of the Russian secret-police organization NKVD in Moscow, watching Allied landings at Anzio from a PT boat offshore, accompanying U.S. forces on the Normandy invasion, even going behind Japanese lines in a small plane to look at what his people in Burma were doing.

Even as the war continued, Donovan was giving thought to the kind of postwar intelligence agency the United States would need. He tasked aides to draft a statute, telling them it should contemplate an organization that was small, limited to intelligence, and super secret. Then in November 1944, responding to a request from the president, Donovan forwarded his proposal. It involved a central authority under civilian authority, responsible for framing intelligence objectives, collecting and coordinating intelligence for national policy and strategy, coordinating the intelligence activities of existing elements rather than supplanting them, and reporting to the president directly. Donovan also urged that the wealth of talent brought into the wartime government be retained in the new organization rather than dispersed when the war ended, although he returned to

private law practice and was later ambassador to Thailand (1953–54).

Central Intelligence Agency. When a 1947 law established the Central Intelligence Agency (CIA), the new organization was in the image of Donovan's conception. His portrait hangs in its headquarters building, where Donovan is considered the "father of the CIA." Indeed, his legacy is the modern U.S. intelligence community.

Bibliography: Brown, Anthony Cave, *Wild Bill Donovan: The Last Hero* (Times Books, 1982); Dunlop, Richard, *Donovan: America's Master Spy* (Rand McNally, 1982); Troy, Thomas, *Donovan and the CIA* (Central Intelligence Agency, 1981).

Lewis Sorley

DOOLITTLE, JAMES HAROLD
(1896–1993)

U.S. army aviation officer who led the famed 1942 bombing raid of Tokyo, Doolittle was born in Alameda, California. After joining the Aviation Section of the Army Signal Corps in 1917 and spending World War I as a combat and gunnery instructor, he established his excellence as a pilot in 1920s air races and test flights. In 1922, he became the first to cross North America in less than 24 hours. Three years later, he received a doctorate in aeronautical sciences from the Massachusetts Institute of Technology, gaining knowledge he applied in 1929 to help develop the artificial horizon and directional gyros and to complete successfully the first blind, instrument-controlled landing. Doolittle resigned his active commission in 1930 to head Shell Oil's aviation department, where he supported the development of high-octane fuel, used by World War II bombers. Doolittle served on the 1934 Baker Board, which investigated the Army Air Corps' airmail fiasco, and wrote a dissenting report in which he advocated a separate air arm for the U.S. military.

With World War II looming, Doolittle returned to active service in July 1940. On Apr. 18, 1942, he led 16 bombers from the carrier *Hornet* in a raid over Japan that, while inflicting minimal damage to the enemy, succeeded resoundingly in raising an American morale that had been pummeled by repeated Japanese advances. It also shocked the Japanese military into hasty operations that led to the U.S. naval victory at Midway. After being promoted to brigadier general and receiving the Congressional Medal of Honor in spring 1942, Doolittle headed to Europe, where he commanded the 12th Air Force during its operations in North Africa and the 15th Air Force in its bombing offensive against southern Germany.

In January 1944, Doolittle received his largest command—the vast 8th Air Force, situated in London; the same year, he was promoted to lieutenant general. Given the task of destroying German industrial targets in daylight precision bombing runs and eliminating the Luftwaffe, the 8th Air Force involved almost 200,000 men daily. Doolittle quickly switched fighter tactics from an emphasis on protecting bombers to one of actively pursuing the enemy, an unpopular move among bomber crews but one Doolittle regarded as "the most important and far-reaching military decision I made during the war." By spring 1945, his 8th Air Force was fast running out of targets—either in the air or on the ground—to bomb. After Germany's surrender, Doolittle traveled to the Pacific with the 8th Air Force, but that war ended before his bombers could get into action.

Doolittle returned to Shell Oil in 1946. After retiring from both Shell and the military in 1959, he served on a number of boards investigating aviation advances and practices.

Bibliography: Doolittle, James H., *I Could Never Be So Lucky Again* (Bantam Books, 1991); Glines, Carroll V., *The Doolittle Raid* (Orion Books, 1988); —, *Jimmy Doolittle, Master of the Calculated Risk* (Van Nostrand-Reinhold, 1980).

John F. Wukovits

DRUM, HUGH A(LOYSIUS) (1879–1951)

U.S. army officer, Drum was born at Fort Brady, Michigan. He accepted a direct commission in 1898 and remaind on active duty until 1943. His early army years were spent in the Philippines. He served in the U.S. occupation of Veracruz and the Mexican Punitive Expedition and was part of the American Expeditionary Force staff during World War I.

Drum was permanently promoted to brigader general in 1922, major general in 1931, and lieutenant general in 1939. Despite his experience, he received no World War II field command. After briefly heading the Eastern Defense Command, he retired in 1943.

David Friend

EAKER, IRA CLARENCE (1896–1987)

U.S. army officer and air force commander, Eaker was born in Field Creek, Texas. He enlisted in the U.S. Army in 1917 and a short time later was commissioned a second lieutenant in the infantry. He volunteered for the newly formed air corps in 1918 but completed his training too late to participate in World War I.

In 1919, Eaker first met and served under the army's Henry H. Arnold and Carl A. Spaatz, both of whom were to have a great influence on his later career. During the 20 years between the two world wars, Eaker served in the Philippines, traveled extensively throughout Asia, and flew every type of aircraft, often spectacularly, at a time when aviation was in its infancy and flying a very dangerous profession. In 1927, he participated in the Pan American Goodwill Flight to South America and was awarded the Distinguished Flying Cross by Pres. Calvin Coolidge.

In 1929, Eaker was part of a five-man crew that flew a Fokker aircraft nonstop for 11,000 miles, which was not only a record endurance mark but, as the *Washington Post* noted, "the beginning of a new era in commercial and military aviation." For this feat, Eaker earned a second Distinguished Flying Cross. On the eve of World War II, he was one of the most experienced pilots in the Air Corps and was at the forefront of testing and flying new types of aircraft.

By 1941, Eaker was one of only a handful of Americans to have served with the Royal Air Force (RAF) as an observer during the early years of World War II, before the United States entered the war. His training and experience paid off in 1942 when, as a brigadier general, Eaker was given the responsibility for organizing and commanding the first U.S. bomber force in Britain, in partnership with Air Chief Marshal Sir Arthur Harris's Royal Air Force Bomber Command.

The British did not believe daylight precision bombing was feasible, but Eaker insisted that his orders were to make it work. They were soon proven wrong when Eaker not only created and trained the 8th Air Force but pioneered the concept of daylight bombing while the RAF concentrated on night operations. He became the leading American spokesman for the concept of strategic bombing. The resulting combined bomber offensive was known as Pointblank and brought about round-the-clock bombing against Germany as the highest priority commitment of the strategic air forces against the Luftwaffe and German industrial targets.

On Aug. 17, 1942, Eaker personally led the first U.S. B-17 raid on the continent of Europe against the rail yards outside Rouen, France, for which he received a Silver Star. The raid validated not only the U.S. Army Air Corps as an important new force in war against Germany, but also Eaker's belief that properly trained aircrews flying strategic bombers in mass formations with fighter escorts could operate effectively despite the best efforts of the Luftwaffe to stop them.

Eaker was a firm exponent of defeating the Luftwaffe before the Allies attempted the cross-channel invasion of northwest France, and he told the U.S. Army chief of staff, Gen. George C. Marshall, "If you will support the bomber offensive, I guarantee that the Luftwaffe will not prevent the cross-channel invasion." Both generals kept their pledges.

Promoted to lieutenant general in June 1943, Eaker succeeded the RAF's Arthur W. Tedder as commander in chief of the Mediterranean Allied air forces. Based in Caserta, Italy, Eaker now turned his attention to the support of the Italian campaign. Unlike Harris and Spaatz, who never favored the direct support by strategic bombers of major operations on the ground, Eaker backed the attempt to isolate the Anzio battlefield in early 1944. Although he was personally against the bombing that destroyed the Abbey of Monte Cassino in February 1944, Eaker nevertheless loyally supported the Allied ground commanders who insisted it be bombed.

From Italy, Eaker's Allied air forces carried out the strategic bombing of targets in Germany and the Balkans, including the Rumanian oil fields of Ploesti. In March, Eaker initiated Operation Strangle, the saturation bombing of German targets south of the Apennine Mountains, in an effort to compel the Germans to withdraw from central Italy. Although Strangle failed to bring about a German withdrawal, it did cripple the enemy's ability to resupply its armies at Anzio and Cassino.

When he retired in 1947, Eaker was hailed by Gen. Dwight D. Eisenhower, who said of him that his "going will leave a gap that will never be completely filled." Eaker's outstanding pioneering contributions to American aviation were recognized in 1979 when he was awarded a special congressional gold medal. He subsequently worked for aircraft companies and wrote on military subjects.

Bibliography: Arnold, H. H., *Global Mission* (Harper & Brothers, 1949); Copp, DeWitt, *A Few Great Captains* (Doubleday, 1980); Craven, Wesley F., and James Lea Cate, *The Army Air Forces in World War II,* 7 vols. (Univ. of Chicago Press, 1948–51); Freeman, Roger A., *The Mighty Eighth* (Doubleday, 1970); Hastings, Max, *Bomber Command* (Dial Press-James Wade, 1979); Kennett, Lee, *A History of Strategic Bombing* (Scribner's, 1982).

Carlo W. D'Este

EDDY, MANTON SPRAGUE (1892–1962)

U.S. army commander, Eddy was born in Chicago. During World War I, he commanded a machine-gun company and was wounded in action. He returned to action leading the 11th Machine-Gun Battalion in the Meuse-Argonne. After service in Germany, he returned to the United States in 1919. Between the wars, he attended and taught at the Infantry School and served as a member of the Infantry Board. He served in Hawaii and graduated from the two-year course at the Command and General Staff College, continuing as a tactics instructor.

In December 1941, Eddy took command of the 114th Infantry. He became assistant commander of the 9th Infantry Division in March 1942 and took command of the 9th in June. He successfully led the division in the campaigns of North Africa and Sicily during 1943. He took the 9th into Normandy in June 1944. In August, he became commanding general of XII Corps, serving with Gen. George S. Patton's 3d Army in the drive through France, Luxembourg, and Germany. Eddy returned to the

United States shortly before the end of the war due to illness.

After World War II, Eddy was chief of information, commandant of the Command and General Staff College, commander of the European Command, commander of the 7th Army, and commander of U.S. Army, Europe. He retired in 1953.

Robert H. Berlin

EDISON, CHARLES (1890–1969)

U.S. secretary of the navy (1939–40), Edison was born in Llewelyn Park, New Jersey, the son of inventor Thomas Alva Edison. He graduated from the Massachusetts Institute of Technology with a degree in engineering, and after working in the private sector and holding several positions in the New Jersey state government, he served on Pres. Franklin D. Roosevelt's National Recovery Board (1934–36) and was appointed assistant secretary of the navy in 1936. He assumed the secretaryship in 1939 when Sec. of the Navy Claude Swanson died suddenly; Edison was formally appointed later that year. In his position, he supervised the massive buildup in shipping and aviation that took place between 1938 and 1940 and developed the Bureau of Ships, an agency that evolved from the merger of many departments involved in shipbuilding. When he was replaced, inexplicably, in 1940 by newspaper magnate Col. Frank Knox, Edison reentered New Jersey politics and served as the state's governor from 1941 until 1944.

Leo J. Daugherty III

EDSON, MERRITT AUSTEN (1897–1955)

U.S. marine officer, Edson was born in Rutland, Vermont. For World War II service, he organized and trained the 1st Raider Battalion, which attacked the Pacific island of Tulagi in August 1942. On Guadalcanal during the night of September 13–14, Edson's command (including the 1st Parachute Battalion) withstood a ferocious full-scale Japanese assault south of Henderson Field. For his leadership in the vicious fight on "Bloody Ridge" (also known as "Edson's Ridge"), Edson received the Medal of Honor. He led the 5th Marines for the remainder of the Guadalcanal Campaign, then served as chief of staff for the 2d Marine Division during the Tarawa operation. Promoted to brigadier general and appointed assistant commander of the 2d, he participated in the Saipan and Tinian campaigns. In the war's final year, Edson served as chief of staff of Fleet Marine Force, Pacific, stationed in Hawaii.

Ralph L. Eckert

EICHELBERGER, ROBERT LAWRENCE (1886–1961)

U.S. army commander, Eichelberger was born in Urbana, Ohio. He graduated from West Point in 1909 and became a talented staff officer, serving with the General Staff in

Washington during World War I. In the interwar period, he served in Siberia, China, the Philippines, and the United States, usually as a military intelligence officer. In the late 1930s, he transferred to the infantry and later became the superintendent (1940–42) of the U.S. Military Academy.

After the Japanese attack on Pearl Harbor in December 1941, Eichelberger received command first of a division, then of a corps being trained in amphibious warfare. In late summer 1942, Eichelberger was sent to Australia to serve with Gen. Douglas MacArthur, then involved in a flagging counteroffensive against the Japanese in New Guinea, in which U.S. troops performed poorly.

MacArthur gave Eichelberger, now a lieutenant general, his first combat assignment: to take control of and reorganize U.S. forces and to take the port of Buna, ''or not come back alive.'' Eichelberger's task was difficult, given the nature of the terrain and the tenacity of the Japanese defenders, although the completion of an airstrip helped U.S. supply problems. In December, Eichelberger launched a number of offensives aimed at taking Buna, most of which failed with heavy casualties. U.S. forces did not take Buna until Jan. 2, 1943, and not until January 22 did they finish off the Japanese forces in the vicinity, taking more than 8,000 U.S. and Australian casualties in the process.

Eichelberger then served well with commands in Hollandia and Biak, impressing MacArthur, who gave him his next large assignment in September 1944, when Eichelberger was awarded command of the U.S. 8th Army. Eichelberger began operations in the Philippines, supporting Gen. Walter Krueger's 6th Army. The 8th Army landed in Leyte and in south Luzon, taking part in the battle for Manila, but its major role involved the central and southern islands of the archipelago, which MacArthur ordered Eichelberger to capture. Eichelberger, with six divisions, launched in February 1945 a startlingly quick series of amphibious invasions (more than 50 separate operations), which culminated in April-June 1945 with the battle for Mindanao, the largest island in the southern Philippines, where 43,000 Japanese troops were based. At a cost of fewer than 4,000 casualties, Eichelberger's 8th Army inflicted more than 13,000 deaths, gaining control of the island by the end of June, although mop-up operations continued.

After the Japanese surrender in August 1945, Eichelberger's 8th Army took over the military occupation of Japan, and Eichelberger supervised the demobilization of the Japanese army and the occupation of Japan under MacArthur until 1948, when he retired to write his memoirs. He was promoted to full general in 1950.

Bibliography: Eichelberger, Robert L., *Our Jungle Road to Tokyo* (Viking, 1950); James, D. Clayton, *The Years of MacArthur* (Houghton Mifflin, 1975).

Mark Pitcavage

Gen. Dwight D. Eisenhower, future president of the United States, commanded both Operation Torch in North Africa and Operation Overlord, the invasion of France, during World War II. (U.S. Military Academy)

EISENHOWER, DWIGHT DAVID
(''IKE'') (1890–1969)

U.S. five-star general; commander of Supreme Headquarters, Allied Expeditionary Force, in World War II; and 34th president of the United States (1953–61), Eisenhower was born in Denison, Texas, and grew up in Abilene, Kansas. He graduated from West Point in 1915 and was commissioned a second lieutenant of infantry. Much to his regret, Eisenhower missed going to France in World War I and instead was commander of Camp Colt at Gettysburg, Pennsylvania, where he trained men for the Tank Corps. Following World War I, he reverted from the rank of temporary lieutenant colonel to captain. In August 1920, he was promoted to major, a rank he held for 16 years.

Interwar Years. During the interwar period, Eisenhower had both staff and school assignments, including the Infantry Tank School at Camp Meade, Maryland, where he met George S. Patton. After a tour of duty in Panama, where he came under the mentorship of Gen. Fox Conner, Eisenhower attended the Command and General Staff School at Fort Leavenworth, graduating number one in the Class of 1926.

Eisenhower coached the football team at Fort Benning, Georgia, for a year before moving to Washington to work with Gen. John J. Pershing as a member of the Battle Monuments Commission. Between tours with the commission, he attended the Army War College. Service in the assistant secretary of war's office brought Eisenhower into contact with Gen. Douglas MacArthur. Eisenhower served under MacArthur for seven years both in the United States and the Philippines, from the beginning of 1933 until the end of 1939. Eisenhower was military assistant to MacArthur when he was chief of staff and then MacArthur's deputy in the Philippines.

World War II. The beginning of World War II in September 1939 brought Eisenhower the desired opportunity to return to the United States. He went to Fort Lewis, Washington, as a regimental executive and subsequently a battalion commander. Next, he was assigned as chief of staff of the 3d Division at Fort Lewis and then chief of staff of the IX Army Corps. He was promoted to full colonel (temporary) in March 1941. He moved to Fort Sam Houston, Texas, as chief of staff of the U.S. 3d Army and participated in the Louisiana maneuvers in August and September 1941.

Promoted in September 1941 to brigadier general, Eisenhower reported to Washington in December to be deputy chief of the War Plans Division for the Pacific and Far East, working closely with the chief of staff, Gen. George C. Marshall. Promoted to major general, Eisenhower became head of the Operations Division of the War Department, the military's worldwide command post. These assignments clearly qualified Eisenhower to become commander of the European Theater of Operations to prepare in England for the invasion of the Continent.

Although Eisenhower and Marshall favored a prompt invasion of France, their strategy was not supported by the British, who urged instead an Allied invasion of North Africa. Having gained the confidence of British political and military leaders, Eisenhower was selected to command Operation Torch.

His diplomatic skills were tasked in the unsuccessful effort to secure French support for the invasion. However, Anglo-American forces under Eisenhower's command captured the major North African ports, insuring success for the operation. Still, U.S. forces were defeated in their first major battle of World War II at Kasserine Pass in February 1943. Relieving the ineffective corps commander, Eisenhower worked to mold an effective military alliance with the British, and in May, the Axis forces were defeated in Tunisia.

Eisenhower took command in the Mediterranean and oversaw the invasion of Sicily in July and the landings at Salerno, Italy, in September. Throughout these campaigns, Eisenhower was more concerned with furthering cooperation with the British than with operational decisions, which he left to the ground commanders. Eisenhower's selection in December to command Operation Overlord, the invasion of France, confirmed his rise to preeminence among World War II commanders.

Beginning in January 1944, Eisenhower, headquartered in London, undertook, in his words, "the organization of the mightiest fighting force that the two Western Allies could muster." Eisenhower's careful planning and persistence brought the Allied forces to a high state of preparedness for the invasion. He personally interceded to secure strategic air forces to bomb transportation targets and to use U.S. paratroop divisions to drop behind enemy lines prior to the invasion. These decisions were crucial to success.

Ordering the invasion was probably the single most important decision of Eisenhower's military career. A storm in the English Channel delayed the invasion and posed concern for Eisenhower, who made the decision to carry out the successful D-Day invasions of Normandy, June 6, 1944.

Following the invasion, a hard-fought campaign for Normandy ensued until August 25, when the Allied armies reached the Seine River. Eisenhower had to encourage both the U.S. and British army ground commanders, Omar Bradley and Bernard Law Montgomery, both of whom held differing national views on the conduct of the war. Field Marshall Montgomery, who thought Eisenhower was inexperienced and overly cautious, advocated a single narrow thrust attack into northern Germany, while Eisenhower supported a broad front advance into Germany, which his forces pursued.

The advance was temporarily halted by a desperate German counterattack, the Battle of the Bulge, in December 1944. Eisenhower's forces resumed the attack and crossed the Rhine River in March 1945. Germany was defeated, and Eisenhower's mission was accomplished with Germany's surrender on May 7, 1945.

Postwar Career. World War II had made Eisenhower (promoted in December 1944 to the rank of General of the Army) a popular international celebrity. After the war, he served as chief of staff and retired from the army to become president of Columbia University. He returned to active duty in 1950 as the first commander of the North Atlantic Treaty Organization (NATO) military forces.

Sought by both political parties to run for president, Eisenhower accepted the Republican nomination in 1952 and was elected president in November. He served two terms, during which he worked to keep the nation at peace while encouraging economic development and limiting government spending.

Eisenhower forced severe spending cuts on the military services in his desire for a balanced budget. He stressed reliance on nuclear weapons to deter Soviet aggression. His famous farewell address warned the United States about the growing power of the military-industrial complex. In 1961, Eisenhower retired with his wife, Mamie, to their farm in Gettysburg, Pennsylvania. He died in Washington, D.C., on Mar. 28, 1969.

Eisenhower was the outstanding general of World War II. His efforts were critical to the forging of the military alliance that defeated Germany. Soldier and statesman, Eisenhower always placed duty above personal ambition.

Bibliography: Ambrose, Stephen E., *Eisenhower: Soldier, General of the Army, President-Elect 1890–1952.* (Simon & Schuster, 1983); Eisenhower, David, *Eisenhower At War 1943–1945* (Random House, 1986); Eisenhower, Dwight D., *Crusade in Europe* (Doubleday, 1948).

Robert H. Berlin

ELLIS, EARL HANCOCK (1880–1923)

U.S. marine officer, Ellis was born in Inka, Kansas. He enlisted in the Marine Corps in 1900, and by 1901 he was commissioned a second lieutenant. Promoted to first lieutenant in 1903 and captain in 1908, Ellis soon became identified with the concept of the Marine Corps' advanced base force (a base selected to be defended or seized by marines during a naval campaign). Despite several breakdowns exacerbated by excessive drinking, Ellis, as a lieutenant colonel, directed the staff work for the 4th Marine Brigade during World War I. From 1920 until his death, Ellis, assigned to the Operations and Training Section at headquarters, formulated Operations Plan 712-H, an advanced base operations in Micronesia, his strategy for the Marine Corps and navy should a war exist between the United States and Japan. Years later, following the Japanese attack on Pearl Harbor in 1941, his blueprint would become the plan of battle. During a reconnaissance tour of Japanese-mandated islands, Ellis, disguised as a civilian, died mysteriously.

Leo J. Daugherty III

EMBICK, STANLEY DUNBAR (1877–1957)

U.S. army officer, Embick was born in Franklin County, Pennsylvania. He entered the coast artillery after graduating from West Point in 1899. During World War I, he served in the American section of the Supreme War Council and in the U.S. delegation to the Paris Peace Conference. During the interwar period, Embick was promoted to brigadier (1930), major (1936), and lieutenant (1939) general. He rose to be chief of the War Plans Division and deputy chief of staff (1936–38). From these offices, he exerted a

tremendous influence over the formulation of the army's basic strategic policies and war plans, including early combined planning with Great Britain.

He retired in 1941 but was recalled to active duty the same year, as the United States entered World War II. He acted as chairman of the Inter-American Defense Board and also as chairman of the Joint Chiefs of Staff's Joint Strategic Survey Committee, which helped draft the nation's overall strategic plans for the war. He retired for a second time in 1946.

Bibliography: Watson, Mark S., *The Chief of Staff: Prewar Plans and Preparations* (Historical Div., Dept. of the Army, 1950).

Richard F. Kehrberg

ERSKINE, GRAVES BLANCHARD (1897–1973)

U.S. marine officer and administrator, Erskine was born in Columbia, Louisiana. He served in the National Guard on the Mexican border and received a Marine Corps commission in July 1917 following graduation from Louisiana State University. During World War I, he served with the 6th Marines at Soissons, Belleau Wood, and St.-Mihiel, where he was seriously wounded. His assignments between the wars included duty in Haiti, Santo Domingo, Nicaragua, and China.

When World War II began, Erskine was chief of staff, Amphibious Force, Atlantic Fleet, and he subsequently served as chief of staff of marine amphibious forces during the invasions of Kwajalein, Tinian, and Saipan. He assumed command of the 3d Marine Division in October 1944 and led the division on Iwo Jima. In October 1945, he was appointed by Pres. Harry S Truman to head the Retraining and Reemployment Administration. From June 1947, Major General Erskine commanded marines at Camp Pendleton, California, and also served as deputy commander, Fleet Marine Force, Pacific. In June 1950, he led a joint (State and Defense departments) survey of security arrangements in Southeast Asia. Following several other high-level marine commands, Erskine was promoted to four-star rank and retired from active duty in June 1953. From 1953 to 1961, he was director of special intelligence operations in the Defense Department.

Lt. Col. (Ret.) Charles R. Shrader

FLETCHER, FRANK JACK (1885–1973)

U.S. naval officer, Fletcher was born in Marshalltown, Iowa. He graduated from Annapolis in 1906. At the time of Pearl Harbor (December 1941), Fletcher was commanding a cruiser division in the Pacific. Over the next nine months, he commanded carrier-cruiser task forces in raids on the Marshall Islands, in the Battle of the Coral Sea, and in the Battle of Midway. Promoted to vice admiral, Fletcher led U.S. naval forces during the August 1942 landings on Guadalcanal and then in the Battle of the Eastern Solomon Islands. Considered by many to be excessively cautious, Fletcher never again commanded carrier task forces at sea. His peers in the great naval encounters of World War II's first year, William Halsey and Raymond Spruance, gained enduring fame while Fletcher finished the war in comparative oblivion, serving as commander of the Northwestern Sea Frontier (1942–44) and then as commander of the North Pacific area.

Bibliography: Butcher, M. E., "Admiral Frank Jack Fletcher, Pioneer Warrior or Gross Sinner?" *Naval War College Review* (winter 1987).

Lloyd J. Graybar

FOSS, JOSEPH JACOB (1915–   )

U.S. marine aviator, Foss was born in Sioux Falls, South Dakota. He enlisted in the Marine Corps in 1940 and became a pilot in 1941. After duty as a flight instructor and then with a reconnaissance squadron, Foss was named executive officer of VMF-121, which was assigned to Henderson Field on Guadalcanal in August 1942. During two tours there, Foss made 26 kills, tying the record of World War I hero Eddie Rickenbacker and becoming one of the most publicized aces of the time. When VMF-121 left Guadalcanal in January 1943, Foss returned to the United States to receive the Congressional Medal of Honor from Pres. Franklin D. Roosevelt in May and an assignment to public-relations work. In 1944, he returned to the South Pacific to command VMF-115, which flew ground-attack missions from its base on Emirau Island. Foss then served as operations and training officer of the Marine Corps air station at Santa Barbara, California. After the war, he returned to South Dakota to enter business and politics, serving as a Republican governor of South Dakota in the 1950s.

Bibliography: Foss, Joe, with Walter Simmons, *Joe Foss, Flying Marine: The Story of His Flying Circus* (Dutton, 1943).

Lloyd J. Graybar

FREDERICK, ROBERT TRYON (1907–1970)

U.S. army officer, Frederick was born in San Francisco. He graduated from West Point in 1928 as an infantry officer. He organized, trained, and commanded the 1st Special Service Force (nicknamed the Devil's Brigade by the Germans), an elite commando force that fought brilliantly from 1943 to 1945 in the Italian Campaign of World War II. Frederick was wounded in action eight times and ended the war as a major general commanding the 45th Division. One of the most fearless combat commanders of World War II, he earned special praise from British prime minister Winston Churchill, who called him "the greatest

fighting general of all time." After the war, he commanded the 4th Division (1949–50) and the 6th Division (1950–51) before retiring as a major general in 1952.

Carlo W. D'Este

FULLER, BEN HEBARD (1870–1937)

U.S. marine officer, Fuller was born in Big Rapids, Michigan. He graduated from Annapolis in 1889 and later transferred to the Marine Corps, serving in the Philippines and China. A graduate of both the Army and the Navy War Colleges, Fuller commanded the 2d Provisional Marine Brigade in Santo Domingo 1918–19 and received a permanent promotion to brigadier general in 1924.

He spent five years as assistant commandant of the Marine Corps before being named commandant in July 1930 with the rank of major general. Fuller defended the corps against cutbacks and helped make the Fleet Marine Force a reality. In doing so, he solidified the marines' role in amphibious operations and made it their primary mission. Fuller retired in March 1934.

Bibliography: Millett, Allan R., *Semper Fidelis: The History of the United States Marine Corps* (Macmillan, 1980).

Daniel T. Bailey

GEIGER, ROY STANLEY (1885–1947)

U.S. marine officer and aviator, Geiger was born in Middleburg, Florida. He entered the Marine Corps in 1907 as a practicing Florida lawyer and served briefly as an enlisted man before he was commissioned in 1909. By 1915, he was in pilot training and served as a DH-4 squadron commander in France during World War I. Promoted to major in 1920, Geiger flew in Haiti and commanded the 1st Marine Corps Aviation Group from 1921 until 1924. He attended the Army Command and General Staff College in the mid-1920s and the Army War College in 1928–29. Geiger was appointed director of Marine Corps aviation in 1931 and was promoted to lieutenant colonel in 1934. In this position, he was instrumental in developing the close bonds and intimate association between marine ground forces and the marine air arm. On the eve of World War II, Geiger was commanding Marine Air Group 1 of the 1st Marine Brigade.

Geiger took his philosophy of continuous, well-coordinated close air support for ground troops with him when he was placed in command of marine air elements at Guadalcanal in 1942. Managing a tough and costly air campaign on this South Pacific battlefield, Geiger commanded more than 1,000 men whose various tasks included providing support to infantrymen, conducting attacks on Japanese shipping, and maintaining an air defense against enemy bombers. Losing more than 100 planes and pilots, Geiger's airmen claimed more than 400 enemy aircraft and the sinking of 10 Japanese ships.

Geiger exchanged his aviation role for that of an amphibious command in 1943. Taking the helm of the I Amphibious Corps in November, he directed the assault on Guam. This campaign, considered by many a textbook example of interservice cooperation, sustained about half the casualties that Americans had sustained during the Saipan Campaign. However, Geiger's subsequent efforts in the Palaus Islands failed to bring much praise. Criticism was directed at heavy U.S. casualties, the doubtful worth of the operations, and Marine Corps reluctance to ask for help from the U.S. Army.

Criticism was reversed on Okinawa. There, the army's Lt. Gen. Simon B. Buckner was accused of a headfirst, bloody approach against stiff Japanese resistance. Ignoring Geiger's advice to use amphibious landings to outflank difficult Japanese positions, Buckner was killed by Japanese artillery fire in June 1945. Lieutenant General Geiger briefly took over command of the U.S. 10th Army, the only marine officer to claim such a distinction. Much of Geiger's career culminated in the unique close air support doctrine that still exists in the U.S. Marine Corps.

Bibliography: Millett, Allan R., *Semper Fidelis: The History of the United States Marine Corps* (Macmillan, 1980).

Col. (Ret.) Rod Paschall

GEROW, LEONARD TOWNSEND (1888–1972)

U.S. army officer, Gerow was born in Petersburg, Virginia. He was commissioned in the infantry in 1911, served in the Signal Corps during World War I, and returned to the infantry in the 1920s. After a series of school and troop assignments, he joined the War Plans Division (WPD) in 1935. At WPD, Gerow helped lay the basic groundwork for the U.S. Army's strategic plans for the coming war. Promoted to chief of WPD in 1940, Gerow left in 1942 to head the 29th Infantry Division. He took the division to England that fall but moved over to lead the V Corps in July 1943. The V Corps landed on Omaha Beach on D-Day and subsequently fought through northern France and Belgium. In January 1945, Gerow took command of the 15th Army. After the war, he headed the Command and General Staff College and the 2d Army before he retired in 1950.

Richard F. Kehrberg

GHORMLEY, ROBERT LEE (1883–1958)

U.S. naval officer, Ghormley was born in Portland, Oregon. He graduated from Annapolis in 1906 and spent his early years at sea in cruisers and battleships, seeing action in the Nicaraguan campaign in 1912. In 1913, he joined the faculty at the Naval Academy, where he remained until assigned as flag lieutenant to Adm. Albert W. Grant in the Atlantic Fleet during World War I. For the next 15 years,

Ghormley served in a variety of staff positions and held several sea assignments, eventually commanding the *Nevada* in 1935. Ghormley attended the Naval War College in 1937–38 and was promoted to rear admiral in 1938. After a stint as director of the War Plans Office and assistant to the chief of naval operations, he was ordered to England as a special naval envoy.

Promoted to vice admiral in 1941, Ghormley spent most of World War II in the Pacific, where he was responsible for the planning and execution of operations to retake the Solomon Islands beginning in August 1942. Relieved by Adm. William F. Halsey in October, Ghormley spent several months in Washington before taking command of the Hawaiian Sea Frontier and 14th Naval District, based at Pearl Harbor. In November 1944, he was ordered to the European theater, where he eventually commanded all U.S. naval forces in Germany and began the task of demobilizing the German navy. Ghormley retired in 1946.

Vernon L. Williams

GRAVES, WILLIAM SIDNEY (1865–1940)

U.S. army officer, Graves was born in Mount Calm, Texas. He graduated from West Point in 1889, was commissioned in the infantry, and served in a number of Western posts. Although he missed the fighting during the Spanish-American War of 1898, the young officer did participate in the Philippine Insurrection as a company commander with the 20th Infantry. As a captain, he assisted in the aftermath of the 1906 San Francisco earthquake. On the eve of World War I, Graves was posted to the War Department staff and served in positions of great trust and responsibility until March 1918. There, he rose from lieutenant colonel to brigadier general.

Promoted to major general and posted back to California, Graves took command of the 8th Division. In August 1918, he was chosen to lead a deployment of U.S. troops to Siberia. Graves departed for a strife-torn Russia with a letter of instructions personally prepared by Pres. Woodrow Wilson. Wilson's charge to Graves was primarily directed at the provision of assistance to the Czechoslovakian army, then en route from the Eastern Front to the Western Front via the Russian port of Vladivostok. The president's instructions specifically forbade the commander of the American Expeditionary Force to allow U.S. forces to become enmeshed in the ongoing Russian Civil War. Wilson also cautioned Graves that Japanese troops would probably be engaged in territorial expansion and might resist any strong, central Russian authority. However, Graves was permitted to assist the Russians in efforts of self-government and self-defense. In the words of Sec. of War Newton Baker, Graves would be "walking on eggs loaded with dynamite."

In the main, Graves executed his difficult mission with grace and skill, earning the praise of most, but not all, of the various factions in eastern Russia. Generally, Graves

Vice Adm. Robert Ghormley (third from left) *served as commander of naval forces in the Pacific campaigns and of the Hawaiian Sea Frontier at Pearl Harbor before being ordered to the European theater of operations in 1944.* (U.S. Army Military History Institute)

was permitted to interpret his orders and role as he saw fit. His decisions were questioned by the U.S. State Department, the American press, and the American Red Cross, but in the end, his judgments were supported by the war secretary, the army chief of staff, and the president. Many have assumed Graves's role was to assist White Russian military forces in their battle against the Soviets, but in his book *America's Siberian Adventure, 1918–1920*, Graves refutes that notion. On his departure from Vladivostok in 1920, Graves was awarded Czechoslovakian, Japanese, Chinese, U.S., and Italian medals.

Following service in Russia, Graves held a number of high-ranking positions, including a command in Panama. He attained the grade of major general, regular army, in 1925 and retired in 1928. He is buried in Arlington National Cemetery.

Bibliography: Graves, William Sidney, *America's Siberian Adventure, 1918–1920* (Cape and Smith, 1931).

Col. (Ret.) Rod Paschall

GROSS, CHARLES PHILIP (1889–1975)

U.S. army engineer and administrator, Gross was born in New York City. He graduated from West Point in 1914. A member of the Corps of Engineers, he served in France during World War I. Between the wars, he graduated from the Command and General Staff College in 1927 and the Army War College in 1932. He served with the War Department General Staff and helped organize the Civilian Conservation Corps from 1933 to 1936. Other interwar assignments included commanding a provisional battalion surveying Nicaragua for a possible canal and teaching at the Military Academy and the Engineer School. When the United States entered World War II, Gross became chief of transportation of the army service forces. When the Transportation Corps was activated in late 1942, he commanded that organization until the end of the war, when he retired with the rank of major general.

Steve R. Waddell

GROVES, LESLIE RICHARD (1896–1970)

U.S. army officer instrumental in the development of the atom bomb, Groves was born in Albany, New York. He graduated from West Point in 1918 and during World War I served briefly in France, after which he attended the Engineer School from 1918 to 1921.

At the outbreak of World War II, he was serving on the War Department General Staff. Throughout 1942, as deputy chief of the Construction Division, Office of the Chief of Engineers, Groves oversaw the construction of numerous military facilities in the United States, including the Pentagon.

On Sept. 17, 1942, Groves was assigned command of the Manhattan Project, for which he secured priority ratings, materials, land, and tools essential for the development and construction of the atom bomb. The project ultimately employed 120,000 people and consumed more than $2 billion.

Groves remained in command of the Manhattan Project until the formation of the Atomic Energy Commission in 1946. After retiring from active duty in 1948, he worked briefly in the private sector. His autobiographical *Now It Can Be Told: The Story of the Manhattan Project* was published in 1962.

Bibliography: Lawren, William, *The General and the Bomb: A Biography of General Leslie R. Groves, Director of the Manhattan Project* (Dodd, Mead, 1988).

David Friend

Commander of the Pacific Fleet Adm. William F. Halsey's motto, "Hit hard, hit fast, hit often," earned him the nickname "Bull." (Navy Department)

HAISLIP, WADE HAMPTON ("HAM") (1889–1971)

U.S. army officer, Haislip was born in Woodstock, Virginia. He graduated from West Point in 1912 and, as a second lieutenant of infantry, served in South Dakota and Texas and with the expedition to Veracruz, Mexico, in 1914. Major Haislip sailed for France in 1917. In World War I, he served with the Air Service on aerial gunnery and was secretary of the General Staff for V Corps. He participated in the St.-Mihiel and Meuse-Argonne offensives. Between the wars, he was an instructor at West Point; a student at the Infantry School, the Command and General Staff School, and the French war college 1925–27; and a 1932 graduate of the Army War College. Haislip also served in the Office of the Assistant Secretary of War, was an instructor at Fort Leavenworth, and had a tour on the General Staff in Washington.

In 1942, Major General Haislip commanded the 85th Division and organized its training. In February 1943, he became commander of XV Corps, which he trained and led in combat in Europe from July 1944 to the end of World War II. He was vice chief of staff of the army from 1949 to 1951, when he retired as a full general.

Robert H. Berlin

HALSEY, WILLIAM FREDERICK (1882–1959)

U.S. naval commander, Halsey was born in Elizabeth, New Jersey, into a maritime family whose members had sailed American waters since colonial days. Halsey's introduction to the lure of the sea came at the hands of his father, also William, a navy lieutenant and 1873 graduate of the Naval Academy at Annapolis. Although determined to follow in his father's footsteps, his early attempts to secure an academy appointment were hampered by his mediocre academic performance, which delayed his appointment from 1887 until 1900. As a midshipman, he was unexceptional academically but lettered in football his last two years. Following the accelerated graduation of his class in February 1904, he reported to the battleship *Missouri*.

Halsey served aboard several ships as a junior officer and participated in the around-the-world cruise of Pres. Theodore Roosevelt's Great White Fleet. In 1910, the year following both his promotion to lieutenant and his marriage, he was assigned as executive officer of the destroyer *Lamson*. For the next 20 years, he served almost exclusively aboard destroyers, supporting U.S. action against the Mexican port of Veracruz and participating in neutrality patrols off East Coast ports prior to the United States's active involvement in World War I. In February 1918, Halsey was given a temporary promotion to commander and served the remainder of the war escorting convoys to and from Britain.

In 1921, Halsey traded in his beloved destroyers for a permanent promotion to commander and a Washington desk job with the Office of Naval Intelligence. Quickly tiring of his desk, and afraid of being mired in the Washington bureaucracy, he managed to secure an appointment as naval attaché to Germany. He served as attaché for approximately two years before being reassigned to destroyers operating from European ports. By 1925, he was back in the United States serving briefly as executive officer for the battleship *Wyoming* before his promotion to captain and an assignment as commanding officer of the Naval Academy's receiving ship *Reina Mercedes*.

After again serving on destroyers from 1930 to 1932, Halsey left them forever as he successively attended the Naval and Army War Colleges. Offered command of the aircraft carrier *Saratoga,* he was fortunate enough to be forced by naval regulations to attend flight school in Pensacola, Florida. The intent of the regulations was to ensure that officers in command of aviation ships had aviation experience, and the course consisted of nearly the complete pilot training syllabus, less solo flight. As a captain being trained by officers far junior to himself, Halsey refused any special considerations for his rank.

The years immediately prior to World War II provided Halsey with an education in carrier warfare that would serve him in good stead during the war. Reporting to his new command in late 1934, he quickly adapted to maneuvering the large carrier and for the next two years contented himself with skippering the *Saratoga* under the close tactical direction of Vice Adm. Frederick J. Horne, commander, Aircraft, Battle Force. Selected for promotion to rear admiral in 1936, Halsey briefly served as the commandant of the Pensacola Naval Air Station before pinning on his star and assuming command of Carrier Division 2. Completely enamored of his two charges, the new carriers *Enterprise* and *Yorktown,* Halsey soon imprinted his aggressive personality on the ships and their assigned air groups. After briefly serving as commander of Carrier Division 1, he received a temporary promotion to vice admiral and assumed the position of commander, Aircraft, Battle Force, in June 1940.

World War II. As tensions with Japan escalated, Halsey, along with the rest of the battle force, was ordered to a newly designated home port at Pearl Harbor, Hawaii. Nazi successes in Europe and the signing of the Tripartite Pact by the Axis Powers in September 1940 spurred a massive reorganization within the U.S. Navy early the next year. Vice Admiral Halsey, although officially retaining the title of commander, Aircraft, Battle Force, became, in fact, commander, Carriers, Pacific. Acting in this capacity,

he was supervising the ferrying of fighter aircraft to Wake Island by his carriers when the Japanese struck Pearl Harbor.

Stunned by the extent of damage to matériel and morale caused by the devastating Japanese attack, Pres. Franklin D. Roosevelt replaced Adm. Husband E. Kimmel with Adm. Chester W. Nimitz as the new commander in chief, Pacific. Nimitz, knowing that striking back at the enemy would be the best way to rebuild self-confidence and morale in his battered fleet, tasked Halsey with organizing raids on whatever enemy-held islands were within reasonable distance of his carrier forces. Striking at Wake, the Marshall Islands, and the Gilbert Islands, Halsey restored U.S. confidence and earned himself the nickname "Bull" for his aggressive actions. The most famous of these raids occurred on Apr. 18, 1942, when Lt. Col. James H. Doolittle launched his force of B-25 bombers from the decks of Halsey's carriers for a surprise raid on Tokyo.

Although the Tokyo raid was spectacular as a propaganda coup, it proved to be of little military value and worked against Nimitz's interests by causing Halsey's battle group to be too far south to join in the first great carrier action of the war, the Battle of the Coral Sea, in early May. Halsey again missed his chance in June, as a severe case of dermatitis prevented him from seeing action in the pivotal Battle of Midway. Halsey's carrier forces, now guided by Adms. Frank J. Fletcher and Raymond A. Spruance, applied the lessons learned under his command as they sank four Japanese carriers, effectively ending the Japanese advance across the Pacific.

Intercepted Japanese codes detailing intentions to build an airstrip in the Solomon Islands energized U.S. counteraction in the form of Operation Watchtower, the invasion of Guadalcanal. Operating with less than optimal forces due to the "Europe first" strategy of the Western allies, the invasion began on Aug. 7, 1942. The Japanese quickly countered with air strikes from the large Japanese base at Rabaul, New Britain, and with strong naval forces dubbed the "Tokyo Express" by the beleaguered Americans. The land campaign seesawed back and forth as Japanese reinforcements brought in by the nightly runs of the "Express" prevented the U.S. marines and soldiers from gaining the upper hand.

Likewise, the frequent naval surface actions in the passage between Guadalcanal and Florida Island proved frustratingly inconclusive, in spite of the large number of ships lost on each side. By mid-October, the situation was extremely precarious as the land forces were nearing exhaustion and the protecting naval forces were thoroughly demoralized by lack of progress. At this juncture, Nimitz replaced Adm. Robert L. Ghormley with the fresher, more aggressive Halsey as commander, South Pacific Area and South Pacific Force.

Halsey's leadership proved successful as U.S. forces advanced ever closer to Japan. In November 1944, Halsey was ordered to relieve Spruance in command of the newly redesignated 3d Fleet, operating in support of Gen. Douglas MacArthur's invasion of the Philippines. At this point arose the controversy that was to plague Admiral Halsey for the rest of his life. The planned invasion was to be supported by both Halsey's 3d Fleet and Adm. Thomas C. Kinkaid's 7th Fleet, but with no overall commander of naval forces short of Admiral Nimitz in Hawaii. During the confusion engendered by the enemy's three-pronged attack, Halsey believed that Kinkaid could take care of himself and jumped at a chance to obliterate the last known Japanese carrier force. By so doing, the 3d Fleet was diverted north, leaving the 7th Fleet to stand alone against the other two prongs of the Japanese thrust. Adding fuel to the controversy was a message from Nimitz that seemed to cast aspersions on Halsey's conduct. As Halsey realized the seriousness of the situation, and goaded by Nimitz's message, he turned his forces around to rush back to Kinkaid's relief. Fortunately for all, the Japanese forces, battered in their attacks on the 7th Fleet, retreated before Halsey reached the scene.

Unable to stop the U.S. juggernaut, the Japanese began preparing for an invasion of their home islands. By July 1945, aircraft from Halsey's carriers were ranging virtually unopposed against all targets of value throughout the Japanese mainland. Early August saw the dropping of two atomic bombs and the Russian declaration of war against Japan. Defeat was inevitable and on August 14, the Japanese accepted the U.S. surrender terms. The final scene of this great conflict, the signing of the surrender documents, was played out in Tokyo Bay aboard the *Missouri*, one of Halsey's 3d Fleet battleships.

Postwar Career. A victorious but tired Halsey returned to the United States looking forward to retirement. However, Pres. Harry S Truman belatedly promoted Halsey to his fifth star and, in April 1946, Congress passed a resolution keeping all five-star officers on active duty for life. Halsey withdrew from active participation in naval affairs in December 1946 but continued to be an outspoken advocate of naval preparedness. He served in executive positions for several large corporations in the years following his retirement and stayed in close contact with his wartime compatriots. Encouraged to write about his war experiences, he rekindled doubts concerning his actions at Leyte Gulf. Stung by criticism and second-guessing, Halsey continued to be plagued by this controversy until his death.

Bibliography: Hagan, Kenneth J., *This People's Navy: The Making of American Sea Power* (Free Press, 1991); Halsey, William F., and J. Bryan III, *Admiral Halsey's Story* (McGraw-Hill, 1947); Morison, Samuel Eliot, *The Two-Ocean War* (Little, Brown, 1963); Potter, E. B., *Bull Halsey: A Biography* (Naval Inst. Press, 1985).

Maj. Gilbert B. Diaz

HANDY, THOMAS TROY (1892–1982)

U.S. army officer, Handy was born in Spring City, Tennessee. He graduated from Virginia Military Academy, was commissioned in the artillery, and accompanied the 1st Division to France during World War I. Transferring to the 42d Division, the young officer won the Distinguished Service Cross while supporting a brigade commanded by Col. Douglas MacArthur, with whom Handy became friends. During the interwar period, Handy attended both the Army and Navy War Colleges. He became an assistant to Brig. Gen. Dwight D. Eisenhower in the Operations Division of the War Department at the outset of World War II. Taking Eisenhower's post as the chief of the War Plans Division in 1942, Handy kept this position until late 1944 when he became Chief of Staff George C. Marshall's right-hand man as the deputy chief of staff of the army, a position he retained until the end of the war.

Col. (Ret.) Rod Paschall

HARMON, ERNEST NASON (1894–1979)

U.S. army officer, Harmon was born in Lowell, Massachusetts. He graduated from West Point in April 1917, commanded a cavalry troop in combat in World War I, then became a member of the U.S. modern pentathlon team in the 1924 Olympics. As a major general in World War II, he commanded successively the 2d and 1st armored divisions, then the 2d again, then XXII Corps, in North Africa and Europe, leading those units through some of the toughest fighting of the war at Tunis, Bizerte, Cassino, Anzio, and the Bulge. Subsequently, he organized and commanded the celebrated U.S. Constabulary, then served for many years as president of Norwich University.

Bibliography: Harmon, E. N., *Combat Commander: Autobiography of a Soldier* (Prentice-Hall, 1970).

Lewis Sorley

HART, THOMAS CHARLES (1877–1971)

U.S. naval officer, Hart was born in Davidson, Michigan. He graduated from Annapolis in 1897 and served off Santiago in the Spanish-American War (1898) while assigned to the battleship *Massachusetts* as a passed midshipman; he also had duty in the dispatch vessel *Vixen*. Over the next two decades, he taught at the Naval Academy, served in both destroyers and battleships, and had such shore billets as an assignment in the Bureau of Ordnance, as head of the Division of Maintenance and Repair at the torpedo works in Newport, Rhode Island, and as commander of the submarine base at New London, Connecticut. During World War I, Hart commanded a submarine flotilla based at Berehaven in Bantry Bay. Its mission was to conduct anti-U-boat patrols.

During the 1920s, Hart had some of his most rewarding assignments; among them were three years at the Naval War College and then the Army War College and command of the battleship *Mississippi* (1925–27). Between 1927 and 1931, he commanded in succession Submarine Divisions, Pacific Fleet; the Control Force (in effect all submarines in the U.S. Navy); and the torpedo works, which manufactured torpedoes and developed new ones.

A rear admiral since 1929, Hart served as superintendent of the Naval Academy (1931–34) before returning to sea to command a division of heavy cruisers and then all cruisers in the Scouting Force. He next returned to Washington to serve on the General Board, a panel that recommended design changes that should be incorporated in new classes of ships and helped decide what building programs the navy should seek to fund. In 1939, he received command of the Asiatic Fleet.

The title and four-star rank that went with Hart's new command were far more impressive than the fleet itself, as Hart well knew. Much smaller than the Pacific Fleet, the Asiatic Fleet that Hart took over consisted of only 2 cruisers, 13 destroyers, 12 submarines, some auxiliaries and patrol planes, and the Yangtze River Patrol. While the fleet's major installations were located in the Philippines, many of its ships customarily operated out of Shanghai, Tsingtao, and Chefoo, all in China, in these last years of imperialism in East Asia. The Asiatic Fleet commander had many diplomatic responsibilities, and hence ordinarily received four stars in order to place him on an equal footing with the British and Japanese and with the admirals of other navies that he might have to negotiate with over such matters as violations of treaty rights.

In the last half of 1941, even as war with Japan approached, opinion in Washington grew more sanguine about defending the Philippines. Much of the optimism came from the unwarranted assumption that the few squadrons of B-17 bombers then scheduled to operate from bases in the Philippines would give Lt. Gen. Douglas MacArthur, the newly designated commander of U.S. Army Forces in the Far East, the strategic air power to deter the Japanese. Nearly 100 modern fighter planes would also operate from Philippine bases.

Hart briefly shared this optimism, partly because letters from the chief of naval operations, Adm. Harold Stark, spoke of reinforcements for the Far East and partly because Hart actually received 12 new submarines, a tender, and 6 PT boats. Hart believed it likely that Japan would soon initiate war in the Far East, but he now believed the army air forces had sufficient strength to defend the Philippines.

When war began, the Asiatic Fleet was initially spared major attacks while Japanese planes concentrated on bombing air force installations in the Philippines. That done, they bombed naval facilities at Cavite Bay and other locations on Luzon on December 10. Since neither Hart nor the air force had the wherewithal to stop the Japanese air raids, he consequently ordered key staff members and many of his ships to head south (several were already operating from bases in Borneo). He retained in the Philippines little more than the PT boats and submarines. His belief was that the subs would be safe from air attack if they submerged during daylight. Hart, however, was tremendously disappointed in the combat performance of the more than two dozen submarines in the Asiatic Fleet. One of the major problems, it was later ascertained, stemmed from the magnetic exploders used on U.S. torpedoes, the same Mark VI exploder that had been under development while Hart commanded the torpedo station more than a decade before.

With Japanese ground forces nearing Manila, Hart left the Philippines for Java on the submarine *Shark* on December 26. Upon his arrival in early January 1942, Hart's appointment as commander of a unified Allied naval command, ABDAFLOAT (American, British, Dutch, Australian) was announced. He would report to Field Marshall Sir Archibald Wavell, the supreme commander of the hastily formed four-nation ABDA alliance.

In the face of Japanese aerial supremacy, the situation in the East Indies and Malaya was hopeless, and recriminations soon broke out among alliance members over questions of priorities and command. In early February, Hart received a request from Washington that he ask to be relieved from command on the grounds of health. The real reason was to allow a Dutch officer to take command of the rapidly diminishing ABDA naval forces, which consisted of no ships larger than cruisers. Hart complied. During the few weeks under his leadership, ABDA naval forces had had one small success at Balikpapan (January 23–24) and a severe blow when three cruisers were heavily damaged at Makasar Strait (February 4). The strike force had been commanded by a Dutch admiral. Hart's successor fared no better.

Hart left Java in early March. He spent much of his first few weeks back in the United States giving interviews and making public appearances. He was then reappointed to the General Board. In 1944, he was given a more difficult assignment: chairing a board that would take sworn evidence about the Pearl Harbor catastrophe. In early 1945, Hart retired to accept appointment to an unexpired term as a U.S. senator from Connecticut (1945–47).

Bibliography: Hoyt, Edwin P., *The Lonely Ships* (McKay, 1976); Leutze, James, *A Different Kind of Victory: A Biography of Admiral Thomas C. Hart* (Naval Inst. Press, 1981); Morison, Samuel Eliot, *History of United States Naval Operations in World War II; Vol. 3: The Rising Sun in the Pacific* (Little, Brown, 1948); Toland, John, *But Not in Shame: The Six Months after Pearl Harbor* (Random House, 1961); Willmott, H. P., *Empires in the Balance: Japanese and Allied Pacific Strategies to April 1942* (Naval Inst. Press, 1982).

Lloyd J. Graybar

HASBROUCK, ROBERT WILSON
(1896–1985)

U.S. army officer, Hasbrouck was born in New York City. He graduated from West Point in 1917, served in France in World War I, and rose through the ranks to full colonel by the outbreak of World War II. Promoted to brigadier general in 1942, Hasbrouck in 1942–43 headed a combat unit in the 8th Armored Division. In 1943, he was named deputy chief of staff of Gen. Omar Bradley's 12th Army Group in Britain. In November 1944, as a major general, he was given command of the 7th Armored Division. He commanded the 7th Armored at St.-Vith, Belgium, during the December 1944–January 1945 Battle of the Bulge in the Ardennes. Early in 1945, his division participated in the breakout from the Remagen bridgehead and the encirclement of the Ruhr pocket. In August 1945, Hasbrouck became deputy chief of staff for Army Ground Forces. He retired in 1947.

Peter Model

HERRON, CHARLES DOUGLAS
(1877–1977)

U.S. army officer, Herron was born in Crawfordsville, Indiana. He graduated from West Point in 1899 and was the chief of staff of the 78th Division Infantry during World War I. He later served on the War Department General Staff from 1920 to 1923. Promoted to brigadier general in 1934 and major general in 1937, Herron commanded the VI Corps area during January–September 1937 and then the Hawaiian Division.

He took command of the Hawaiian Department in March 1938 and struggled to strengthen its defenses during the next three years. He became a lieutenant general in 1940 and retired in early 1941. Recalled to duty during World War II by his old friend Gen. George C. Marshall, Herron held various posts within the War Department before retiring again in 1946.

Bibliography: Bland, Larry I., ed., *Papers of George Catlett Marshall*, vol. 2 (Johns Hopkins Univ. Press, 1986).

Daniel T. Bailey

HEWITT, HENRY KENT (1887–1972)

U.S. naval officer, Hewitt was born in Hackensack, New Jersey. He graduated from Annapolis in 1907. In World War I, he commanded an escort ship carrying out convoy duty in the North Atlantic. During the interwar years, he ably filled a number of fleet and staff jobs and by 1939 was a rear admiral. In World War II, Hewitt was chosen to command the Western Naval Task Force during the Operation Torch landings in French North Africa (November 1942) and during the Sicily landings (July 1943). In both amphibious operations, he successfully landed troops under the command of Lt. Gen. George S. Patton, Jr.

Hewitt commanded all Allied naval forces for the September 1943 invasion of Salerno, Italy, and for the August 1944 Anvil/Dragoon landings in southern France. At Salerno, his timely naval gunfire support was credited with helping to save the invasion force from disaster.

In 1945, he saw special duty, serving on the committee that investigated the 1941 Japanese attack on Pearl Harbor. He was a consultant at the Naval War College (1946–47) before he retired with the rank of admiral in 1949.

Bibliography: Morison, Samuel Eliot, *History of United States Naval Operations in World War II,* vols. 2 & 9 (Little, Brown, 1947, 1954).

Carlo W. D'Este

HINES, JOHN LEONARD (1868–1968)

U.S. army officer, Hines was born in White Sulphur Springs, West Virginia. He graduated from West Point in 1891, accepting a commission in the infantry. Assigned to the American West, the young lieutenant was swept up in the Spanish-American War, landing on Cuba in the summer of 1898. Participating in the Battle of San Juan Hill, Hines earned the Silver Star for bravery. After the war, he served in the Philippines, fighting during the insurrection there.

Rising to the rank of major, Hines commanded a battalion and was assigned to the Punitive Expedition, serving under Brig. Gen. John J. Pershing as the adjutant for the U.S. effort against Mexico's Pancho Villa. Pershing liked Hines and saw to it that in 1917 the younger officer accompanied the initial deployment of U.S. troops to France during World War I. During the war he commanded the 1st Brigade of the 1st Division. Participating in the Second Battle of the Marne and the Battle of Soissons, Colonel Hines was decorated with the Distinguished Service Cross. By August 1918, he was promoted to major general and took command of the 4th Infantry Division in time to lead the unit during the St.-Mihiel and Meuse-Argonne campaigns. At war's end, he was in command of the U.S. III Corps.

After occupying a number of positions after the war, Hines succeeded Pershing as army chief of staff in 1924. Although very low budgets and thin ranks prevented much innovation within the postwar army, Hines worked to improve professional education and became an aggressive advocate of joint army-navy exercises and maneuvers. He became the army's manager, advocate, and official spokesman during a period when the United States reached a low point in ground forces in comparison to other major powers. Finishing his assignment as chief of staff in 1926, Hines became the commanding general of the Philippine Department, a position he held until his retirement in 1932.

Col. (Ret.) Rod Paschall

HOBBY, OVETA CULP (1905–   )

U.S. army officer and administrator, Hobby was born in Killeen, Texas. After graduating from law school at the

Col. Oveta Culp Hobby, the first director of the Women's Army Corps, visited Allied gun positions in Britain during World War II. (U.S. Army Military History Institute)

University of Texas, she served as parliamentarian of the Texas House of Representatives (1925–31, 1939–41). In 1931, she married former Texas governor William Hobby, then publisher of the Houston *Post*. Over the years, she held increasingly responsible positions with the *Post,* becoming editor in 1938.

In July 1941, she was appointed chief of the Women's Division of the War Department Bureau of Public Relations. In this capacity she was to advise wives and mothers about comfort, food, and recreation of servicemen. Chief of Staff George C. Marshall then asked her to study the feasibility of establishing a women's auxiliary army.

In May 1942, Hobby was sworn in as the first director of the Women's Auxiliary Army Corps (later renamed Women's Army Corps, or WACs). She was initially commissioned a major and later promoted to colonel. Early in her tenure, Hobby studied the wartime activities of British women, inspecting with First Lady Eleanor Roosevelt units of the WRENS (officially W.R.N.S., Women's Royal Naval Service) and the ATS (Auxiliary Territorial Service). By the time Hobby left military service in July 1945, more than 100,000 women had enlisted in the WACs.

After the war, Hobby's public life continued in Texas, where she was active in a number of professional and community organizations. She became politically active in 1952, organizing Texas Democrats for Gen. Dwight D. Eisenhower's Republican presidential campaign. From 1953 to 1955, she served as Eisenhower's secretary of

Health, Education, and Welfare. She resigned to resume her work with the Houston *Post.*

Bibliography: Treadwell, Mattie E., *The Women's Army Corps* (Office of the Chief of Military History, U.S. Army, 1954).

David Friend

HODGES, COURTNEY HICKS (1887–1966)

U.S. army officer, Hodges was born in Perry, Georgia. He entered West Point in 1904 but failed and enlisted in the infantry in 1906. He was commissioned as an infantry lieutenant in 1909. In World War I, Hodges commanded a battalion in combat. In the interwar period, he graduated from the Field Artillery School, the Command and General Staff School, and the War College. He taught tactics at Fort Benning, Georgia, and became commandant of the Infantry School in 1940. During 1942–43, he commanded X Corps and the 3d Army when they were training organizations. In 1944, he went to England as deputy commander of the 1st Army; he took command in August, leading the 1st Army on its drive across France and into Germany. Hodges retired in 1949 as a full general.

Robert H. Berlin

HOLCOMB, THOMAS (1879–1965)

U.S. marine officer, Holcomb was born in New Castle, Delaware. He entered the Marine Corps in 1900, and after World War I, he served in the United States, Cuba, and China. Graduating from both the Navy and Army War Colleges, he served on the staff of the chief of naval operations from 1932 to 1935. After one year at Quantico, Virginia, as commandant of Marine Corps Schools, Holcomb was selected as commandant of the Marine Corps. Due to the expansion of the corps during World War II, he attained the rank of lieutenant general, becoming the first marine to wear three stars. During Holcomb's two tours as commandant, the Marine Corps increased from 16,000 to 350,000 personnel. He continued to oversee the corps' expansion until his retirement in 1943.

Maj. James Sanders Day

HOWARD, SAMUEL LUTZ (1891–1960)

U.S. marine officer, Howard was born in Washington, D.C. During World War II, he drew the unenviable assignment of defending the Manila Bay island of Corregidor in early 1942. His variegated command eventually included his own 4th Marine Regiment, army and navy personnel, Philippine Scouts, and air cadets and various others. Holding Corregidor proved an impossible task because when the Japanese attacked on the night of May 5, virtually all prepared defenses and heavy weapons had been destroyed by intense artillery and aerial bombardment. Corregidor fell the following morning, and Colonel Howard became a prisoner of war. He endured more than three years of

Lt. Gen. Thomas Holcomb, the first marine to attain that rank, served as commandant of the Marine Corps during the years leading up to World War II. (U.S. Army Military History Institute)

imprisonment at camps in Luzon, Japan, and China before being liberated at Mukden in August 1945.

Ralph L. Eckert

HUEBNER, CLARENCE RALPH (1888–1972)

U.S. army officer, Huebner was born in Bushton, Kansas. In 1910, he enlisted in the army and became a sergeant. In 1916, he was commissioned an infantry second lieutenant. He served in several major offensives during World War I with the 1st Division, earning two Distinguished Service Crosses. During the interwar period, Huebner was an instructor at the infantry school for five years and at the Command and General Staff School for more than two years, rising to the rank of colonel in 1941. He was a graduate of all the relevant army schools. He had vast experience teaching and studying tactics.

In World War II, as a major general, he commanded the 1st Infantry Division from August 1943 in North Africa and led it in the Normandy landings at Omaha Beach. He continued to command the division in battles in France and Germany until he assumed command in January 1945 of V Corps, which he led across the Rhine River to the Elbe

River in eastern Germany. After the war, he served as chief of staff of U.S. forces in Europe (1946) and as acting commander of the European command, before retiring in 1950 as a lieutenant general.

Robert H. Berlin

HULL, CORDELL (1871–1955)

U.S. secretary of state, Hull was born in Byrdstown, Tennessee. After opening a law practice, he became a successful politician. His strong standing in the South led to his appointment as Pres. Franklin D. Roosevelt's secretary of state in January 1933.

Under his direction, the State Department increased 400 percent in size. During World War II, Hull tried to keep abreast of foreign affairs, but his administrative talents were overshadowed by the president's iron hand over the administration. Hull resigned in November 1944, after Roosevelt's reelection.

Hull was awarded the Nobel Peace Prize in 1945, and in November of that year, he gave extensive testimony to the joint congressional committee investigating the Japanese attack on Pearl Harbor. In that testimony, he showed that he had predicted a war with Japan in 1941, leading many to speculate that he had forewarning of the attack itself.

Bibliography: Hull, Cordell, *The Memoirs of Cordell Hull* (Macmillan, 1948).

David Friend

INGERSOLL, ROYAL EASON (1883–1976)

U.S. naval officer, Ingersoll was born in Washington, D.C. After graduating from Annapolis in 1905, he served in various sea assignments until he was attached to the U.S. delegation at the Versailles peace conference in 1918–19. During the 1920s, Ingersoll began a long tenure with war plans and staff positions, which led to his assignment as chief of the War Plans Division in 1935. After a brief stint as commander of the Cruiser Squadron, Ingersoll was appointed commander of the Atlantic Fleet and in 1944 assumed command of the Western Sea Frontier while also serving as deputy chief of naval operations and as deputy commander of the U.S. Fleet, where he remained until his retirement in 1946.

Vernon L. Williams

IRWIN, STAFFORD LEROY (1893–1955)

U.S. army officer, Irwin was born in Fort Monroe, Virginia. He graduated from West Point and was commissioned a second lieutenant of cavalry in 1915. He participated in the Punitive Expedition into Mexico in 1916, and after graduation from the School of Fire at Fort Sill, he became a gunnery instructor there. He then transferred to the field artillery and served in Kentucky and

Ohio. He graduated from the appropriate army schools and served in the Philippines.

In World War II, Irwin was artillery commander of the 9th Infantry Division in North Africa and, as a major general, assumed command of the 5th Infantry Division training in England. He led his division into France on July 9, 1944, and commanded it across France and into Germany. In April 1945, he assumed command of XII Corps in Germany. After the war, Irwin served in Europe and Washington and retired in 1952 with the rank of lieutenant general.

Robert H. Berlin

JOHNSON, LOUIS ARTHUR (1891–1966)

Second U.S. secretary of defense, Johnson was born in Roanoke, Virginia. A World War I combat officer and national commander (1932–33) of the American Legion, he was an early champion of veterans' pensions. As assistant secretary of war (1937–40), he drew up the nation's pre-Pearl Harbor defense plans and is credited with presciently proposing (1938) construction of the strategic 1,420-mile Alaska-Canada (Alcan) Highway. After a brief stint in 1942 as Pres. Franklin D. Roosevelt's envoy to India, Johnson ran I. G. Farben's General Dyestuffs Corp. (now GAF Corp.), seized by the United States as a Nazi asset. In 1949, Johnson became Pres. Harry S Truman's secretary of defense, succeeding the beleaguered James V. Forrestal in 1949 and completing Forrestal's controversial unification of the U.S. Armed Forces. Johnson was succeeded at the Defense Department by George C. Marshall in 1950.

Bibliography: Hoopes, Townsend, and Douglas Brinkley, *Driven Patriot* (Knopf, 1992).

Peter Model

KELLOGG, FRANK BILLINGS
(1856–1937)

U.S. secretary of state, Kellogg was born in Potsdam, New York. After developing a prosperous law practice in Minneapolis, he served as president of the American Bar Association (1912–13), as U.S. senator from Minnesota (1917–23), and as ambassador to Britain (1924–25). In 1925–29, he was Pres. Calvin Coolidge's secretary of state. Although marred by the renewal of U.S. intervention in Nicaragua and by ongoing controversies with Mexico that Kellogg had some success in easing through the efforts of a special emissary, Kellogg's term as secretary was featured by the signing of the Kellogg-Briand Pact to outlaw war as "an instrument of national policy." Although many have scoffed at the pact as meaningless, it won Kellogg much praise and the 1929 Nobel Peace Prize. He concluded his career as a judge on the Permanent Court of International Justice (1930–35).

Bibliography: Bryn-Jones, David, *Frank B. Kellogg: A Biography* (Putnam's, 1937).

Lloyd J. Graybar

KENNEY, GEORGE CHURCHILL
(1889–1977)

U.S. army officer, Kenney was born in Nova Scotia, Canada, and grew up in Brookline, Massachusetts. He attended Massachusetts Institute of Technology, enlisted in the Army Air Service, and served as a pilot during World War I, flying 75 missions and shooting down two enemy aircraft. He ended the war as a captain and received the Distinguished Service Cross and the Silver Star.

The air arm of the army during the period between the two world wars was small but filled with young officers, including Kenney, who were fired with a vision of independence based on the possibility of strategic bombing to win future conflicts. Kenney served in a variety of positions, concentrating on aeronautical development and its application to warfare and pursuing the chimera of victory solely through air power.

In August 1942, Kenney assumed command of all Allied air forces in the Southwest Pacific and worked throughout the war as Gen. Douglas MacArthur's air component commander. Kenney found that meeting MacArthur's stiff requirements was not easy. In addition to contending with the initial superior strength of the Japanese, Kenney soon learned that the distances in the Pacific, the demanding climate, the difficulties of logistics, and the dearth of virtually all resources made every campaign an even greater challenge. His abilities as a leader, his willingness to cut through regulations and to innovate with both tactics and equipment, and his unique conceptions on how to organize forces and mass them for victory were critical to success in the Pacific. Kenney's organizational approach of composite units with bombers, fighters, transports, and all support ingredients ensured that smaller units could conduct effective warfare in the expanses of the Pacific.

After the war, in December 1945, Kenney was given an assignment with the Military Staff Committee of the newly formed United Nations. He left this position in 1946 to take command (1946–48) of the newly organized Strategic Air Command. In October 1948, he became commandant of the Air University. While in this position in 1949, he published a significant book, *General Kenney Reports,* which was not only a memoir of his career in World War II but also an explanation of his theories on air superiority. He retired from active service as a full general in 1951.

Bibliography: Kenney, George C., *General Kenney Reports: A Personal History of the Pacific War* (Duell, Sloan and Pearce, 1949); Manchester, William, *American Caesar: Douglas MacArthur, 1880–1964* (Little, Brown, 1978).

Roger D. Launius

KIMMEL, HUSBAND EDWARD
(1882–1968)

U.S. naval officer, Kimmel was born in Henderson, Kentucky. He graduated from Annapolis in 1904. He participated in the Cuba Pacification Campaign in 1906 and sailed with the Great White Fleet in 1907–09, henceforth serving in staff billets through World War I.

During the next 20 years, Kimmel served alternatively at sea and in staff positions, reaching rear admiral in 1937. In February 1941, he was advanced over 46 more-senior officers to the rank of admiral and to the position of commmander in chief, U.S. Fleet and Pacific Fleet, based on board the flagship *Pennsylvania* at Pearl Harbor.

Kimmel was the senior officer present on Dec. 7, 1941, when Japanese aircraft attacked unprepared U.S. positions in Hawaii. He and Gen. Walter C. Short, commanding the Hawaiian Department, were relieved of command and both were blamed for the disaster. Kimmel retired in March 1942 in the rank of rear admiral, pending court-martial. Three investigations followed, with a Presidential Board of Inquiry finding Kimmel and Short derelict and responsible for the calamity. However, a navy court of inquiry in 1944 found no such responsibility nor errors in judgment, and in 1945, a congressional investigation found judgmental errors but no dereliction of duty. In 1955, Kimmel wrote *Admiral Kimmel's Story* in defense of his actions. Recent historical accounts have tended to confirm Kimmel's view of his lack of culpability, but the debate continues to be controversial.

Vernon L. Williams

KING, EDWARD POSTELL, JR.
(1884–1958)

U.S. army officer, King was born in Atlanta, Georgia. After receiving a law degree from the University of Georgia, he joined the National Guard in 1908. As an artillery officer, he served with troop units and was a student and instructor at the Artillery School. He attended and taught at the Command and General Staff School and at the Army War College.

In September 1940, Brigadier General King was ordered to the Philippine Islands, where he had served from 1915 to 1917. He supervised artillery training of the Philippine army and served as Gen. Douglas MacArthur's artillery officer. King's assignment as commander of Luzon Force led to tragedy when he was forced to surrender 78,000 U.S. soldiers at Bataan to the Japanese in April 1942. Major General King, who accepted full responsibility for the surrender, was imprisoned (with cellmate Gen. Jonathan Wainwright) until August 1945. He retired in 1946.

Robert H. Berlin

KING, ERNEST JOSEPH (1878–1956)

U.S. naval officer, King was born in Lorain, Ohio. He graduated from Annapolis in 1901, having seen action in

Adm. Ernest J. King, commander in chief and chief of naval operations of the U.S. Fleet, was responsible for naval strategy in both the European and Pacific theaters of operation during World War II. (U.S. Army Military History Institute)

the Spanish-American War (1898) as a naval cadet. He served aboard the cruiser *San Francisco* on patrols off the coast of Florida defending against Spanish naval activity. He was commissioned an ensign in 1903 and was assigned to battleship duty. He was promoted to lieutenant in June 1906 and ordered to Annapolis to teach ordnance and gunnery. King returned to the fleet in 1909 and served in engineering and staff positions aboard ship until 1912.

In 1912, King returned to Annapolis to serve at the Engineering Experimental Station and assumed editing duties with the *Proceedings* of the U.S. Naval Institute. In the spring of 1914, he arrived in Galveston, Texas, to take command of the destroyer *Terry,* departing the Texas coast for Mexico, where King participated in operations during the crisis off Veracruz in April. Later that same year, he assumed command of the destroyer *Cassin* and concurrently served as aide to Cmdr. William S. Sims, then commander of the Atlantic Fleet Torpedo Flotilla. In December 1915, King was reassigned to the battleship *Arkansas,* flagship of Adm. Henry T. Mayo, then second in command of the Atlantic Fleet. King served as engineering officer and aide to the admiral. The next year, Mayo became commander in chief and King followed the admiral to the *Wyoming* and later the *Pennsylvania,* successive flagships for the Atlantic Fleet. During this period, King accompanied Mayo on several missions to Europe. He remained with Mayo until after World War I.

In the years following the war, King became discontented with the current leadership in the navy, convinced that it was responsible for the lack of progress on the technical front. Emerging from World War I, King served in several assignments on the eastern seaboard, but the 1920s signaled a final break with the surface line. From that point on, his career focused on submarines and aviation.

In 1922, King, dissatisfied with routine duty aboard his supply ship, put in for a destroyer billet. No commands were available, but he was told that senior officers completing submarine school at New London, Connecticut, could get commands. King, then a captain, decided to take the opportunity and transferred to submarines. In January 1923, King took command of a four-submarine division (Submarine Division 11) operating in the Atlantic Fleet. There followed six years of service in submarines, highlighted by two significant salvage operations in which King directed the recovery of two submarines. The wreck of the S-51 (USS *Squalus*, later renamed the *Sailfish*) presented delicate demands on King as he sought to battle rough weather and heightened public interest while raising the vessel with the bodies of 34 crewmen still on board. His success brought favorable attention to King and enhanced his rise within the navy.

King came to the attention of Adm. William Moffett, who actively recruited senior officers for the aviation service and convinced King that the future of the navy rested in the aviation branch. At the age of 48, King earned his wings at Pensacola and over the next few years served in a series of staff and base assignments before assuming command of the carrier *Lexington* in June 1930. In 1933, King was appointed chief of the Navy Bureau of Aeronautics by Pres. Franklin D. Roosevelt. In November 1933, King was promoted to rear admiral and remained in Washington until 1936, when he assumed command of the Aircraft Battle Force. In 1938, he was promoted to vice admiral. Considered for the position of chief of naval operations in 1939, King lost out to Adm. Harold Stark but eventually replaced Stark after the Pearl Harbor disaster in December 1941.

In February 1941, King was promoted to admiral and became commander in chief of the Atlantic Fleet, responsible for directing operations in the undeclared war against German submarine warfare. In late December, he was named commander in chief, U.S. Fleet, and in March, his position was consolidated with chief of naval operations. By March 1942, no other man in naval history had commanded a larger navy or held more naval firepower within his own command.

King became an innovative strategic leader, proving to be a forceful proponent of the navy's position in every Allied planning conference held during the war. His leadership was instrumental in developing an effective strategy against the Japanese empire in the Pacific war and against Hitler's war in the Atlantic sea lanes.

King reached retirement age in 1942 but continued on active service and in 1944 received his fifth star. Although he retired in 1945, he continued to serve in an advisory role on defense affairs well into the 1950s. His memoirs *(Fleet Admiral King: A Naval Record)* were published in 1952.

Bibliography: King, Ernest, and Walter Whitehill, *Fleet Admiral King: A Naval Record* (Norton, 1952); Morison, Samuel Eliot, *History of United States Naval Operations in World War II* (Little, Brown, 1962); Pfannes, Charles, and Victor A. Salamone, *The Great Admirals of World War II; Vol. 1: The Americans* (Zebra Books, 1983).

Vernon L. Williams

KINKAID, THOMAS CASSIN (1888–1972)

U.S. naval officer, Kinkaid was born in Hanover, New Hampshire. His early duty was served primarily on battleships, and after a year at the Naval War College (1929–30), he commanded the heavy cruiser *Indianapolis* before heading to Italy and Yugoslavia as a naval attaché (1938–40). He commanded Destroyer Squadron 8, Atlantic Fleet, for five months in 1941, then as rear admiral headed to Pearl Harbor as commander, Cruiser Division 6.

Kinkaid arrived in Hawaii on December 12, five days after Japan's surprise raid opened hostilities. After participating in the abortive attempt to relieve U.S. forces trapped on Wake Island, Kinkaid's division quickly jumped into the fray with escort operations during the March 1942 carrier strikes against Japanese positions in New Guinea. Kinkaid commanded his cruisers during the major naval battles at the Coral Sea in May and at Midway in June, earning a Distinguished Service Medal. Elevated to commander, Task Force 16, and with his flag on the carrier *Enterprise,* Kinkaid covered U.S. forces landing on Guadalcanal on August 7, then clashed with Japanese naval units in the bitter Solomon encounters. During the Battle of the Eastern Solomons on August 24 and the Battle of Santa Cruz Islands in October, Kinkaid's flagship absorbed numerous hits, and in mid-November, his cruisers helped turn back the enemy's attempt to reinforce its troops on Guadalcanal.

The following January, Kinkaid took command of the North Pacific Fleet, with the objective of halting further enemy drives in Alaska and removing them from positions already seized. In 10 months, his forces secured Amchitka and reoccupied Attu and Kiska, earning for Kinkaid another Distinguished Service Medal and promotion to vice admiral.

Southwest Pacific Operations. On Nov. 26, 1943, Kinkaid received his most challenging assignment when he was named commander of Allied naval forces in the Southwest Pacific and commander of the U.S. 7th Fleet with the primary duties to provide amphibious units for Gen. Douglas MacArthur's drive along the New Guinea coast and to supply beachhead protection. Since bitter feelings existed between MacArthur's headquarters and the navy over how best to employ naval units in the Southwest Pacific, a deft diplomatic touch would be required. The Joint Chiefs of Staff, impressed with Kinkaid's smooth relations with army counterparts in Alaska, hoped he would be able to work successfully with the difficult MacArthur and his even more irascible staff. Kinkaid quickly rewarded their confidence by establishing a workable, although at times difficult, relationship with MacArthur.

Kinkaid wasted little time in letting MacArthur know he would not be pushed around. MacArthur had long maintained a steady barrage of pleas for extra naval forces, but Kinkaid explained he would not likely receive much help because the Japanese combined fleet was operating elsewhere and because ships sent to the Southwest Pacific areas were exposed to enemy land-based bombers. In the December 1943 operations against New Britain, a concerned Kinkaid wrested additional air cover from MacArthur and an agreement that his naval officers would be in charge of the landings until command posts existed on shore. Although Kinkaid impressed MacArthur with his calm demeanor and sound judgment, Kinkaid constantly battled with MacArthur's army staff.

Kinkaid also faced the difficult situation of split command. Although he received his operational orders from MacArthur, Kinkaid's ships and matériel came from Adm. Ernest J. King in Washington, D.C., long a heated critic of MacArthur. Split command haunted Kinkaid at the October 1944 operations at Leyte Gulf, where he controlled the 7th Fleet but had no authority over Adm. William F. Halsey, whose orders came from Adm. Chester W. Nimitz. After his naval forces inflicted heavy blows on approaching Japanese naval units at the Sibuyan Sea and Surigao Strait, Kinkaid, in charge of protecting MacArthur's Leyte beachhead, assumed Halsey guarded the northern approaches at San Bernardino Strait. Halsey, however, in accordance with his orders from Nimitz to pursue the enemy fleet if an opportunity arose, had chased after a decoy enemy fleet and left the strait open. Twenty-one enemy ships slipped through the narrow waters on October 25 to threaten seriously the beachhead. Only the courageous actions of Rear Adm. Clifton A. F. Sprague, commanding the thin-skinned escort carriers off Samar, plus Kinkaid's call that all naval air units immediately dash to the area, succeeded in deflecting the more powerful enemy force from causing havoc at Leyte. The widespread Battle of Leyte Gulf, which involved more naval forces than any previous action, ended as a resounding victory for Kinkaid and a terminal defeat for the Japanese.

Kinkaid and MacArthur squared off the next month over the timing for an invasion of Mindoro, which Kinkaid wanted delayed to give American air power more time to weaken the still-potent Japanese air strength in the Philippines. MacArthur at first demurred, but a determined Kinkaid won a 10–day delay from his superior after lengthy discussions.

Kinkaid continued to support MacArthur's forces until war's end in August 1945. The next month, he accepted the surrender of Japanese troops in Korea, then landed

U.S. Marine occupation forces in China. Relieved of command of the 7th Fleet on Nov. 19, 1945, Kinkaid returned to the United States to command the Eastern Sea Frontier at New York. In June 1946, he took command of the 16th Fleet—redesignated the Atlantic Reserve Fleet the following year—and remained in that position until his retirement in May 1950.

Bibliography: Baldwin, Hanson, *Battles Lost and Won* (Harper & Row, 1966); Garfield, Brian, *The Thousand-Mile War* (Doubleday, 1969); Leary, William M., ed., *We Shall Return!* (Univ. Press of Kentucky, 1988); Morison, Samuel Eliot, *History of United States Naval Operations in World War II; Vol. 12: Leyte* (Little, Brown, 1958); Potter, E. B., and Chester W. Nimitz, *Triumph in the Pacific* (Prentice-Hall, 1963).

John F. Wukovits

KIRK, ALLEN GOODRICH (1888–1963)

U.S. naval officer, Kirk was born in Philadelphia. He graduated from Annapolis in 1909, beginning a long naval career in which he held a variety of command and staff jobs at sea and in Washington. During World War II, Kirk commanded convoy escorts in 1942 and naval Task Force 85 as a rear admiral during the Sicily landings in July 1943. The following year, he was appointed commander of U.S. naval forces for the invasion of Normandy (Operation Overlord) in June 1944 and was promoted to vice admiral. Following the war, Kirk retired as a full admiral and became U.S. ambassador to Belgium (1946–49), the Soviet Union (1949–52), and Nationalist China (1962).

Carlo W. D'Este

KNOX, WILLIAM FRANKLIN (1874–1944)

U.S. secretary of the navy, Knox was born in Boston, Massachusetts. He became the civilian head of the U.S. Navy in 1940 after a long and successful business career in journalism and a less successful political career.

As a member of Pres. Franklin D. Roosevelt's cabinet, Knox led the navy effort in World War II until his death in 1944. He brought to the navy a new managerial style that produced effective team-oriented leadership. Knox became a productive liaison between other civilian leaders and the navy's strategic leaders as he sought to expand the navy's accomplishments in the war. He allowed officers such as Ernest King great latitude in the performance of their duties and never failed to give them the support they needed to succeed.

Vernon L. Williams

KNUDSEN, WILLIAM S. (1879–1948)

U.S. industrialist and war production administrator, Knudsen was born Signius Wilhelm Paul Knudsen in Copenhagen, Denmark, emigrated to the United States in 1899, and eventually became president of the General Motors

Corporation in 1937. He put his production experience to work for the government in 1940 when he joined the National Defense Advisory Committee. Knudsen became director of the newly created Office of Production Management (OPM) in January 1941. Once the United States entered World War II, the OPM was replaced by the War Production Board (WPB), headed by Donald Nelson. Knudsen then became director of production for the War Department. Given the rank of lieutenant general, the first civilian to have such rank, Knudsen traveled around the country solving production problems within the armaments industries.

Steve R. Waddell

KRUEGER, WALTER (1881–1967)

U.S. army officer, Krueger was born in Flatow, Germany, and moved to the United States as a child. He enlisted in the regular army in 1898 and served from 1899 to 1903 in the Philippines, where he rose in rank to second lieutenant. During World War I, he eventually served as chief of staff of the American Expeditionary Force's Tank Corps. After the war, Krueger's reputation as a leader and trainer grew. He spent time teaching at both the Army and Navy War Colleges and commanded the 2d Infantry Division and VIII Corps. In May 1941, he commanded the 3d Army during the Louisiana Maneuvers.

During World War II, Lieutenant General Krueger's appointment to command the 6th Army (1943–45) in the Pacific came as a surprise to many as he was 62 years old. However, he held the confidence of Gen. Douglas MacArthur, and his subsequent performance supported MacArthur's view. Krueger's leadership and planning were severely tested as the 6th Army consistently fought simultaneous engagements in areas hundreds of miles apart in conditions that were almost always primitive and hindered logistics, reinforcements, and communications. General Krueger was often criticized in private by MacArthur and Lt. Gen. Robert L. Eichelberger for being overcautious, but MacArthur later credited that caution for the low casualty rate in the Southwest Pacific theater. Promoted to full general in 1945, Krueger commanded the occupation troops in Japan until his retirement in 1946.

Bibliography: Krueger, Walter, *From Down Under to Nippon: The Story of the 6th Army in World War II* (Combat Forces Press, 1953).

Capt. George B. Eaton

LEAHY, WILLIAM DANIEL (1875–1959)

U.S. naval officer and chief of naval operations, Leahy was born in Hampton, Iowa. He graduated from Annapolis in 1897 and saw action as a midshipman during the Spanish-American War (1898), during the subsequent Philippine Insurrection, and during the Boxer Rebellion in China. He struck up a lifetime friendship with Franklin D. Roosevelt

during the latter's term (1913–20) as undersecretary of the navy. A talent for organization led to Leahy's steady rise in rank: rear admiral (1930), vice admiral (1935), full admiral (1936), and chief of naval operations (1937).

Forced to retire for the first time in 1939, because of age, he was recalled that same year by President Roosevelt, who named Leahy governor of Puerto Rico (1939–40) and then ambassador to Vichy France (1940–42). In 1941, Leahy was sent to prevent French Marshal Henri Pétain from caving in to Nazi demands and to keep the French fleet out of German hands. Recalled to Washington in 1942, Leahy had a dual role for the rest of World War II, serving as Roosevelt's chief of staff and as de facto chairman of the Joint Chiefs of Staff. The plain-spoken Leahy served as a bridge between the White House and the Pentagon's military leaders, while also acting as the president's liaison with British prime minister Winston Churchill. In 1944, Leahy was promoted to five-star rank; the next year he counseled Roosevelt as an adviser at the Yalta Conference. After the war he functioned as Pres. Harry S Truman's point man during the bitter 1946–47 service unification battle. Leahy retired for the second time in 1949 and recounted his career in *I Was There* (1950).

Peter Model

LEE, JOHN CLIFFORD HODGES (1887–1958)

U.S. army engineer and logistician, Lee was born in Junction City, Kansas. He graduated from West Point in 1909 and during World War I served in France, where he graduated from the Army General Staff College at Langres in 1918. During the 1920s and 1930s, Lee worked on a number of Corps of Engineers' river and port projects, in addition to graduating from the Army War College (1932) and the Army Industrial College (1933). Promoted to major general, he took command of the Services of Supply, European theater of operations (later designated the Communications Zone), in July 1942 and oversaw the massive American supply effort in Europe for the remainder of the war. During January–July 1944, Lee also served as the deputy theater commander under Gen. Dwight D. Eisenhower. After the war, Lee commanded all U.S. forces in the Mediterranean theater of operations. He retired from the army as a lieutenant general in 1947.

Steve R. Waddell

LEE, WILLIS AUGUSTUS, JR. (1888–1945)

U.S. naval officer, Lee was born in Natlee, Kentucky. He graduated from Annapolis in 1908. An expert in gunnery, he had five tours in the Division of Fleet Training during the years 1930–42. In 1942, he was promoted to rear admiral and sent to the Pacific. On the night of November 14–15, Lee was in charge of a task force of two battleships and four destroyers with orders to prevent a Japanese force from shelling U.S. positions on Guadalcanal. Although several of his own ships sustained heavy damage, Lee's flagship *Washington* made effective use of radar-directed gunnery to punish the larger Japanese force so heavily that it withdrew. Lee continued to command fast battleship forces in virtually every major operation in the Central Pacific. In June 1945, he was reassigned to Maine waters to develop tactics that might be used against Japanese kamikaze attacks.

Bibliography: Reynolds, Clark G., *Famous American Admirals* (Van Nostrand-Reinhold, 1978).

Lloyd J. Graybar

LEJEUNE, JOHN ARCHER (1867–1942)

U.S. marine officer, Lejeune was born in Pointe Coupée Parish, Louisiana, and graduated from Louisiana State University in 1884. He then entered Annapolis, graduating in 1888 and joining a growing number of marine officers drawn from the ranks of the academy. As was the practice at the time, he spent two years at sea before commissioning. Aboard the *Vandalia,* Lejeune survived disaster at sea when the ship was sunk in a hurricane near Apia, Samoa, in March 1889. When his cadet tenure ended, he applied for the Marine Corps, a request that was disapproved, forcing Lejeune to obtain political help to get his appointment to the corps. The navy did not typically allow Annapolis graduates with high academic records to option for the Marine Corps, wanting those officers to fill billets in the navy. Beginning in the 1880s, most of the new officers in the Marine Corps came from the academy, as the corps began to attract better-educated officers.

Lejeune's early career included service in the occupation of Puerto Rico during the Spanish-American War (1898) and duty in Panama in 1905. In 1909, he became the first marine officer to be accepted to the Army War College, completing the course in 1910. After 1910, he served in several assignments in Cuba, Panama, and Philadelphia, gaining promotion to colonel in February 1914, whereupon he assumed command of the Advanced Base Force along the Gulf Coast.

In April 1914, Lejeune landed with his command at Veracruz, Mexico, relinquishing command to the more-senior Littleton Waller upon his arrival from California. Lejeune served under Waller for the rest of the year, managing aviation and motorized operations in the field before returning to the United States with the brigade. In 1915, Lejeune was appointed assistant commandant under Gen. George Barnett and was promoted to brigadier general the next year. By 1918, Lejeune was in France in command of the only marine brigade in the American Expeditionary Force, eventually taking command of the army's 2d Division, bringing distinction to himself and the Marine Corps in battles at St.-Mihiel and Blanc Mont Ridge and in the

Meuse-Argonne Campaign. He was promoted to major general in July 1918.

In June 1920, Lejeune was appointed corps commandant, and under his leadership, the Marine Corps developed a system of professional education and adopted the doctrine of amphibious warfare, anticipating the demands placed upon the corps in World War II. He retired from the corps in March 1929 and spent eight years as superintendent of Virginia Military Institute before his retirement in 1937.

Bibliography: Bartlett, Merrill, *Lejeune: A Marine's Life, 1869–1942* (Univ. of South Carolina Press, 1991); Millett, Allan R., *Semper Fidelis: The History of the United States Marine Corps,* 2d rev. ed. (Macmillan, 1990).

Vernon L. Williams

LEMAY, CURTIS EMERSON (1906–1990)

U.S. air force officer, nicknamed the "Iron Eagle," LeMay was born in Columbus, Ohio. Failing to receive an appointment to West Point, he attended Ohio State University, where he studied civil engineering (1924–28). Inspired by Charles Lindbergh's transatlantic flight, Lemay joined the army to learn to fly. He was commissioned in the field artillery reserve in June 1928 and attended Army Air Corps flying schools in both California and Texas. LeMay earned a commission in the air reserve in October 1929 and a regular commission in the Army Air Corps in January 1930.

In the next decade, LeMay earned a reputation as a capable pilot, navigator, and bombardier. In 1934, he organized a full-time navigation school in Hawaii that enhanced pilot training for over-water flights. Working with B-17s and B-24s based at Langley Field, Virginia, he flew missions to South America, South Africa, and Europe. Moreover, he instituted the study of maps and aerial photographs by all crew members in an effort to increase bombing accuracy.

In October 1942, Col. LeMay, as commander of the 305th Bomber Group, deployed his unit to England as part of the 8th Air Force. In this capacity, he developed innovative tactics for his B-17s. Close formations, concentrated firepower, and staggered altitudes contributed to increased survivability. Through personal examples, he curtailed evasive action during final bombing runs; this tactic increased accuracy with negligible effect on survivability. On Aug. 17, 1943, LeMay led the first "shuttle mission": after bombing a principal Messerschmitt plant in Regensberg, Germany, his bombers landed in North Africa to refuel before returning to their bases in England. In September, he was made a brigadier general.

Transferred to the China-Burma-India theater in August 1944, LeMay, now a major general, took command of the 20th Bomber Command. This unit of B-29 "Super Fortresses" attacked targets throughout the Far East, including Japan. In six months, LeMay's crews flew 55,000 miles, dropped 4,500 tons of bombs, and downed or destroyed hundreds of Japanese fighters. In January 1945, LeMay moved to Guam, where he assumed command of the 21st Bomber Command. Well within range of the Japanese islands, these B-29s executed low-level, nighttime, incendiary bombing raids on Tokyo. LeMay's innovations included planes stripped of defensive armaments and attacks by solitary aircraft rather than by massed formations. Assuming command of the 20th Air Force in July 1945, LeMay launched the B-29s that dropped the atomic bombs on Hiroshima and Nagasaki in August.

LeMay's leadership principles fostered high morale and service beyond the call of duty. In LeMay's commands, each person understood his job and its importance, commanders established clear goals and monitored progress toward their achievement, and task accomplishment always merited recognition and appreciation.

During the postwar years, General LeMay commanded the Berlin Airlift in 1948, became a full general in 1951, led the Strategic Air Command (SAC) from 1948 to 1957, and served as air force chief of staff from 1957 until his retirement in 1965. He heavily favored the use of nuclear weapons in the Vietnam War. LeMay dabbled in politics as George C. Wallace's vice-presidential running mate on the independent ticket in the 1968 elections.

Bibliography: Coffey, Thomas M., *Iron Eagle: The Turbulent Life of General Curtis LeMay* (Crown, 1986); LeMay, Curtis E., *Mission with LeMay: My Story* (Doubleday, 1965).

Maj. James Sanders Day

LINDBERGH, CHARLES AUGUSTUS
(1902–1974)
U.S. aviator famed for making the first nonstop transatlantic solo flight (1927), Lindbergh was born in Detroit, Michigan. After earning Pres. Franklin Roosevelt's disapprobation because of isolationist speeches, Lindbergh resigned his colonel's commission in the Army Air Force in April 1941. When the United States entered World War II, however, he was eager to help in some capacity, and, as a civilian consultant, he traveled to the Southwest Pacific in 1944 to test various fighter craft. Working mainly with pilots under Gen. George C. Kenney's command, Lindbergh taught them how to increase a fighter's range from 400 to 600 miles through a more efficient fuel mixture, a work praised by both Kenney and Gen. Douglas MacArthur. During his stay in the Pacific, Lindbergh flew 50 combat missions as a civilian and shot down one Japanese aircraft.

Bibliography: Kenney, George C., *General Kenney Reports* (Duell, Sloan and Pearce, 1949); Lindbergh, Charles A., *The Wartime Journals of Charles A. Lindbergh*

(Harcourt Brace Jovanovich, 1970); Mosley, Leonard, *Lindbergh* (Doubleday, 1976).

John F. Wukovits

LOCKWOOD, CHARLES ANDREWS, JR.
(1890–1967)
U.S. naval officer, Lockwood was born in Midland, Virginia. He graduated from Annapolis in 1912. In addition to sea duty in various types of surface craft over the years, Lockwood had many tours in command of submarines (his first was in 1914) and of a submarine division from 1925 to 1928. In early 1942, he was ordered to Fremantle, Australia, to become commander, Submarines Southwest Pacific and was soon promoted to rear admiral. The following year, he was transferred to Pearl Harbor to become commander, Submarines Pacific Fleet (1943–45). Lockwood gave priority to solving the torpedo problems that had plagued U.S. submarines. Finally armed with reliable torpedoes, Lockwood's submarines inflicted heavy losses on Japanese naval and merchant shipping and undertook other duties, including minelaying and lifeguard missions for downed aviators.

Bibliography: Lockwood, Charles A., *Down to the Sea in Subs: My Life in the U.S. Navy* (Norton, 1967).

Lloyd J. Graybar

LUCAS, JOHN PORTER (1890–1949)
U.S. army officer, Lucas was born in Kearneysville, West Virginia. He graduated from West Point in 1911 and was commissioned a second lieutenant of cavalry. He served in the Philippines until 1914 and opposed Mexican rebel leader Pancho Villa in 1916. Lucas joined the Punitive Expedition into Mexico in 1916–17. In May 1918, he went to France, where, after he was wounded in action, he attended the Field Artillery School. He graduated from the Command and General Staff School in 1924 and from the Army War College in 1932. He had numerous field artillery assignments between the wars and served on the General Staff (1932–36).

In 1941, he became commanding general of the 3d Infantry Division at Fort Lewis, Washington, and was promoted to major general. From April 1942 to May 1943, he commanded III Army Corps in Georgia. Lucas was Gen. Dwight D. Eisenhower's representative in the North African and Sicilian campaigns and took command of VI Corps in Italy in September 1943. He led his corps in the Anzio landing in 1944, but when his command failed to advance, he was relieved. After the war, Lucas held commands in the United States and was chief of the Army Advisory Group in China (1946–48). He retired in 1948.

Robert H. Berlin

LUTES, LEROY (1890–1980)

U.S. army supply officer, Lutes was born in Cairo, Illinois. He graduated from the Wentworth Military Academy in 1908. A member of the National Guard, he served during World War I and remained in the regular army as an artillery officer following the war. He graduated from the Advanced Course, Corps of Artillery School (1928); the Command and General Staff School (1930); and the Army War College (1935).

Brigadier General Lutes transferred to the War Department General Staff in 1941. Assigned to the Services of Supply, later designated Army Service Forces (ASF), and promoted to major general, Lutes served as director of operations for the commander of the ASF, Lt. Gen. Brehon B. Somervell. As such, Lutes oversaw the production and distribution of supplies for U.S. army forces throughout World War II. Beginning in 1944, with the creation of the Requirements and Stock Control Division (under Lutes's command), he added procurement planning to his list of responsibilities. The change greatly improved the efficiency of the army supply system. In April 1945, Lutes became ASF chief of staff and later replaced Somervell as ASF head. With the abolition of the ASF in May 1946, Lutes took over the new G-4 War Department General Staff Division, becoming its director of service, supply, and procurement. He retired from the army in 1952 as a lieutenant general.

Steve R. Waddell

MACARTHUR, DOUGLAS (1880–1964)

U.S. general of the army, MacArthur was born on an army base near Little Rock, Arkansas, the son of celebrated general Arthur MacArthur. A noted World War I combat commander, he was superintendent of West Point (1919–22) and then rose to become army chief of staff (1930–35). He retired in 1935 and helped organize the Philippines' military forces before his recall to active duty in 1941. His defense and then recapture of the Philippines was followed in 1945 by his appointment as Supreme Commander of the Allied Occupation of Japan. During the Korean War, his outspoken opposition to President Truman's policies led to MacArthur's relief from command in April 1951.

Early Years. MacArthur graduated from West Point in 1903, first in his class. He then spent a year in the Philippines and, promoted to first lieutenant in 1904, toured the Far East as an aide to his father in 1905. Serving as an aide to Pres. Theodore Roosevelt in 1906–07, he then was assigned to Fort Leavenworth, where he was promoted to the rank of captain in 1911. Assignment to Washington, D.C., culminated in his appointment to the General Staff in 1913. His daring exploits at Veracruz, Mexico, in 1914 were followed in 1915 by his promotion to major.

Gen. Douglas MacArthur, a skilled military leader, used an island-hopping technique to outmaneuver the Japanese and to secure systematically the Pacific area in the Allied drive toward Japan. (U.S. Army)

When the United States entered World War I in 1917, MacArthur, now a colonel, organized and trained the 42d Division, composed of 27 National Guard units, and named it the Rainbow Division. Sent to France as part of the American Expeditionary Force (A.E.F.), the division distinguished itself as did MacArthur, its chief of staff. He was decorated numerous times for bravery under fire. In June 1918, he was promoted to brigadier general and was made commander of his division's infantry. After the war, General MacArthur was appointed superintendent of West Point (1919–22).

Interwar Years. In the 1920s, MacArthur's career was marked by his establishment of the honor code at West Point and by his participation in the controversial court-martial of Brig. Gen. Billy Mitchell. At the Military Academy, MacArthur orchestrated a self-sustaining student ethics system. The cadets administered a code of honor requiring each cadet not only to refrain from lying, cheating, or stealing, but to report those cadets who did. With occasional infractions and failures, the West Point honor system has worked largely as MacArthur designed it. In 1925, assigned as a member of the sensational court-martial of Billy Mitchell, MacArthur dutifully performed his onerous task. An advocate of physical fitness among his troops, MacArthur was chosen to preside over the American Olympic Committee in 1928. In 1930, MacArthur was selected to be the chief of staff of the army in the Herbert Hoover administration.

His tenure as chief of staff (1930–35) came at a time of occasional domestic unrest, and in 1932, MacArthur found the army charged with breaking up of the Bonus Army, a gathering of World War I veterans who assembled in Washington seeking federal bonus payments. Ignoring the choice of leaving this distasteful task to subordinates, the general took a direct hand in the effort to disperse the demonstrators. During this period, he saw the financial support of the army drop to unprecedented lows. The inauguration of Pres. Franklin D. Roosevelt in 1933 coincided with a time of significant military buildups by the Japanese, Italian, and German armed forces. General MacArthur predicted a coming war, and his failed attempts to secure adequate funding for his planned expansion and mechanization of the American army was a great and bitter disappointment for him. In 1935, he headed a military mission to the Philippines and became a military adviser to the fledgling commonwealth. His new duties were centered on creating a commonwealth defense force. His plan called for a Philippine military academy and regular and reserve forces and mobilization facilities in every town. MacArthur retired from the army in 1937.

World War II: The Pacific Theater. After the war he had predicted materialized, MacArthur was recalled to active duty in July 1941 as a major general. Placed in command of all U.S. and Filipino forces in the Philippines, he was soon elevated to lieutenant general and finally to full general. When the Japanese struck the islands after their attack on Pearl Harbor (Dec. 7, 1941), the general's gift of astute leadership seemed to desert him. His bombers were destroyed on the ground. His belief that the Filipinos could be quickly trained and mobilized to hold the island of Luzon worked against the realization of previous planning to make the Bataan Peninsula and Corregidor Island a well-stocked and impregnable fortress awaiting relief. Although the valiant defense of U.S. and Filipino troops did delay the Japanese, better leadership might well have resulted in a more substantial obstacle to Japan's offensive.

Leaving his command in the Philippines at President Roosevelt's order, MacArthur and his family were evacuated to Australia. (His statement, ''I came through and I shall return,'' during this trip became the rallying cry of the war.) There he was given command of U.S. and Australian troops. During the 1942 Papuan Campaign, his forces halted Japan's offensive and then drove the invaders out of southeastern New Guinea. Using a combination of air and amphibious assaults, MacArthur directed his 6th Army in an imaginative offensive that bypassed many Japanese strongpoints while seizing key locations used to support the next move forward. By early 1944, his island-hopping campaign was beyond New Guinea, New Britain, and the Admiralties. Using the Australians to reduce bypassed Japanese garrisons, MacArthur and his Americans moved north of the equator in the last months of the year, striking at Morotai in the Moluccas and then staging a dramatic and well-publicized return to the Philippines.

Invading Leyte in late 1944, MacArthur's 8th and 6th Armies moved on to Luzon. With a deft use of paratroopers and amphibious landings, MacArthur outmaneuvered his opponents and directed several risky but successful rescue operations freeing Allied prisoners. At the same time, Australian forces successfully recovered Borneo and Brunei. MacArthur often pitted his 8th Army commander against his 6th Army commander in a competitive race to go farther and faster. Normally, he would declare a newly assaulted territory secure long before resistance was reduced. However, while other generals might have found difficulty in convincing the press, MacArthur enjoyed near universal acclaim by reporters and basked in the glow of warm and sincere adulation by the American public.

Significance of Philippine Campaign. While many of MacArthur's postwar critics have dwelled on his brazen use of the press for self-glorification, few have considered the alternative or consequences. The Allied grand strategy placed the liberation of Europe as the first priority. That meant largely that MacArthur's air and ground combat needs were subordinated to those of Europe. Further, within the Pacific, the U.S. Navy ensured Adm. Chester Nimitz had first pick of combatants for the effort to drive across the Central Pacific. In Washington, the admirals advocated bypassing the Philippines altogether, securing a lodgment on the Chinese coast, and staging the conquest of Japan from territory nearby the island nation's homeland. This argument was anathema to MacArthur. He believed the people of the Philippines would never forgive the United States if Japanese troops were left to continue their brutal occupation while U.S. forces moved to secure a part of China or free Taiwan. Using his considerable press following, MacArthur appealed to understandable emotions among most Americans when he recommended liberation of the Philippines at the earliest possible moment. At another level, the general's position included the defeat of a large and important Japanese army in the Philippines, a demonstration of American strength and resolve that was not apt to be lost on the leaders in Tokyo.

The swift operations to liberate the Philippines constituted a textbook example of what can be accomplished at the hands of a skilled military leader. MacArthur, with only 17 U.S. divisions, attacked 23 Japanese divisions. He managed one of World War II's few instances where an inferior force rapidly overwhelmed a larger one. Most important, MacArthur's troops attracted Japanese attention in one direction and then moved behind them. It was the greatest single defeat suffered by Japan during the war.

Carefully coordinating the efforts of guerrilla forces with his advancing columns, MacArthur favored the bold move, the maneuver that unhinged his opponents. On Luzon, he largely used the forces of Gen. Walter Krueger. When Luzon was finally secured, Krueger's 6th Army troops completed two years of continuous combat involving 12 major operations, 21 separate amphibious landings, 3 dramatic rescue raids, and a number of parachute and air transport operations. They had advanced more than 3,500 miles and killed more than 260,000 of their enemies, while sustaining 13,423 U.S. deaths.

War's End. Attaining the newly created rank of five-star general at the end of 1944 and as the newly appointed Supreme Allied Commander in early 1945, General of the Army MacArthur accepted Japan's surrender in Tokyo Bay on Aug. 15, 1945. He then began his historic administration of Japan, directing the dramatic social, political, and religious revision of an ancient society.

Analysis. MacArthur's performance during 1943–45 was almost unblemished. During this period, he used specialized forces to the maximum. Rangers, guerrilla organizations, and paratroopers often found themselves badly outnumbered but successful in working behind a confused enemy's lines. Unlike other theater commanders, MacArthur refused to permit the Office of Strategic Services (OSS) to conduct intelligence and partisan operations in his area. He used the press well. In MacArthur's hands, journalists were simply another weapon. Through carefully managed news stories, MacArthur attracted resources that might have gone elsewhere and secured approval of plans that might have been ignored. Finally, a major factor in Japan's decision to surrender, one beyond the use of atomic weapons, was the knowledge of Tokyo's leaders that their forces were unable to halt the oncoming Americans. MacArthur's defeat of a significant part of Japan's armed forces in the Philippines undoubtedly played an important role in convincing Japan's leaders that further resistance was hopeless.

Later Career. As supreme commander in Japan (1945–51), MacArthur formulated a new Japanese constitution and instituted many other reforms. When North Korea invaded South Korea in June 1950, Pres. Harry S Truman recalled MacArthur from Japan to lead the UN forces sent to counter North Korea's aggressors. MacArthur's military strategy was successful in pushing the attackers back beyond the definitive boundary, the 38th parallel, and, eventually, to the Yalu River, the North Korea-China border. At that point, the Chinese entered the war and pushed the UN forces back behind the 38th parallel. MacArthur hoped to expand the war in order to expel the Communists from North Korea, but Truman disagreed, fearing another war. MacArthur disclosed this disagreement to the public through news stories and letters, and, in April 1951, Truman relieved him of his command. In a speech to the U.S. Congress later that month, MacArthur delivered his famous line, taken from an old ballad, "Old soldiers never die, they just fade away."

Bibliography: James, Clayton, *The Years of MacArthur*, 2 vols. (Houghton Mifflin, 1970–75); MacArthur, Douglas, *Reminiscences* (McGraw-Hill, 1964); Manchester, William, *American Caesar* (Little, Brown, 1978); Whan,

Vorin, E., Jr., ed., *A Soldier Speaks: Public Papers and Speeches of General of the Army Douglas MacArthur* (Praeger, 1965); Willoughby, Charles A., ed., *Reports of General MacArthur,* 4 vols. (Dept. of the Army, 1966).

Col. (Ret.) Rod Paschall

MCAULIFFE, ANTHONY CLEMENT (1898–1975)

U.S. army officer, McAuliffe was born in Washington, D.C. He graduated from West Point in November 1918 due to wartime acceleration and was commissioned in the field artillery for service in World War I. In August 1942, during World War II, he took command of the 101st Airborne Division Artillery and, upon the death of Brig. Gen. Don Pratt during the Normandy invasion of June 1944, became the division's deputy commander under Maj. Gen. Maxwell Taylor. In Taylor's absence, McAuliffe commanded the defense of Bastogne, Belgium, during the Battle of the Bulge (December 1944). Responding to a German demand to surrender, he replied, "Nuts!" He assumed command of the 103d Division in January 1945, advanced into Austria, and joined the 5th Army at Brenner Pass. McAuliffe retired in May 1956.

Bibliography: Marshall, S. L. A., *Bastogne: The Story of the First Eight Days* (Infantry Journal Press, 1946); Rapport, Leonard, *Rendezvous with Destiny: A History of the 101st Airborne Division* (101st Airborne Div. Assoc., 1965).

Maj. James Sanders Day

MCCLOY, JOHN JAY (1885–1989)

U.S. assistant secretary of war during World War II, McCloy was born in Philadelphia. As assistant secretary, he held varied responsibilities, including work in the Lend-Lease program, but he is known chiefly for his role in the decision to relocate and intern more than 100,000 Japanese-Americans from the West Coast in the aftermath of the Japanese attack on Pearl Harbor (Dec. 7, 1941).

McCloy considered the Japanese-Americans a potential source for fifth-column activity against coastal industries and military installations. Claiming that time constraints prohibited positive determination of loyalty, McCloy helped convince Sec. of War Henry Stimson, who questioned the constitutionality of the program, to support removal. McCloy defended the deportations as prudent and benign even after the war, opposing those who supported redress for the internees.

Bibliography: Irons, Peter, *Justice Delayed: The Record of the Japanese American Internment Cases* (Wesleyan Univ. Press, 1989).

Jeffrey J. Roberts

MCCOY, FRANK ROSS (1874–1954)

U.S. army officer, McCoy was born in Lewistown, Pennsylvania. He graduated from West Point in 1897, fought in the Spanish-American War (1898), and later led a brigade in World War I. McCoy directed the Red Cross relief efforts following the 1923 earthquake in Japan. He later chaired a commission supervising Nicaraguan elections and was a delegate to the Pan-American Conference in 1928. Promoted to major general in 1929, he represented the United States in 1932 on an international commission investigating Japan's occupation of Manchuria. McCoy retired in October 1938 but was recalled to investigate the Japanese bombing of Pearl Harbor (Dec. 7, 1941) and to chair the Procurement Review Board during World War II.

Bibliography: Bland, Larry I., ed., *The Papers of George Catlett Marshall*, vol. 1 (Johns Hopkins Univ. Press, 1981).

Daniel T. Bailey

MCDOUGAL, DOUGLAS (1876–1964)

U.S. marine officer, McDougal was born in San Francisco, California. He joined the navy as an ensign during the Spanish-American War (1898) and was appointed as a second lieutenant in the Marine Corps in 1900. His early years in the marines were served in the Pacific arena during the Boxer Rebellion; in Veracruz, Mexico, until 1915, and then Haiti and the Dominican Republic; and in Europe during World War I. For a time, McDougal commanded the Garde d'Haiti (1921–29) and reorganized the Guardia Nacional de Nicaragua (1929–31). Commanding general (1935–37) of the Fleet Marine Force and the base at San Diego, California, and then (1937–39) of the base at Parris Island, South Carolina, McDougal was due to command the Department of the Pacific but was forced to retire with the rank of major general because of physical disability in 1940. A noted rifle marksman, McDougal became the first marine commander to lead a rifle team to the International Rifle Matches in 1926.

Leo J. Daugherty III

MCMORRIS, CHARLES HORATIO (1890–1954)

U.S. naval officer, McMorris was born in Wetumpka, Alabama. He was the Pacific Fleet's war plans officer in 1941, but after the debacle at Pearl Harbor in December, the navy sent him to sea as the commander of a cruiser. After playing a successful part in the 1942 fighting off Guadalcanal, McMorris led a task force during the U.S. drive in the Aleutians in 1943. In March, at the Battle of the Komandorski Islands, his task force turned back Japanese reinforcements headed for Attu. These successes, and his reputation as a skilled staff officer, earned McMorris a post on Adm. Chester Nimitz's staff, first in the planning section and then, from June 1943, as chief of staff of the Pacific

Fleet. From this position, which he held for the remainder of the war, Rear Admiral McMorris played a central role in charting the navy's final drive on Japan through the Central Pacific. Following the war, McMorris commanded the 4th Fleet and the 14th Naval District (Hawaii) before his retirement.

Richard F. Kehrberg

MCNAIR, LESLEY JAMES (1883–1944)

U.S. army officer, McNair was born in Verndale, Minnesota. He graduated from West Point in 1904 and received a commission in the artillery. He took part in the 1914 occupation of Veracruz, Mexico, and in the Punitive Expedition of 1916–17. In June 1917, he traveled to France with the 1st Division. Later assigned to the training section of the General Headquarters, American Expeditionary Force (A.E.F.), he became the A.E.F.'s chief artillery trainer and a temporary brigadier general by October 1918.

McNair shipped home in 1919 and returned to his prewar rank of major. He then spent two years at Fort Leavenworth as a student and an instructor before serving on the general staff of the Hawaiian Department (1921–24). His next assignment was to revive the faltering Reserve Officers

Maj. Gen. Lesley McNair was largely responsible for modernizing the U.S. Army in the late 1930s with programs that focused on mobile warfare. (U.S. Army Military History Institute)

Training Corps (R.O.T.C.) program at Purdue University. He succeeded and developed a deep appreciation for the R.O.T.C. in the process. He left Purdue in 1928 and graduated from the Army War College in 1929.

As assistant commandant of the Field Artillery School 1929–33, McNair guided a reform movement that modernized the school's educational program and led to significant improvements in the control of artillery fire. He also pioneered work in the development of antitank guns. A brief but fruitful stint with the Civilian Conservation Corps followed. He was promoted to lieutenant colonel in 1928 and to colonel in 1935.

McNair became commander of the 2d Field Artillery Brigade and a brigadier general in early 1937. When the War Department decided to test the proposed new triangular division, McNair directed the tests as chief of staff of the 2d Infantry Division. He played a key role in determining its final form. In March 1939, he was appointed commandant of the Command and General Staff School. Ordered to rid the school of its trench warfare mentality, he introduced a new program that focused on mobile warfare and stressed speed, simplicity, and flexibility.

The fall of France in June 1940 forced the U.S. Army to begin mobilization. Gen. George C. Marshall named McNair chief of staff of the newly created General Headquarters and charged him with training the ground army. Promoted to major general in September 1940 and to lieutenant general in June 1941, McNair managed the army's training program and directed the huge maneuvers conducted in the summer and fall of 1941.

With a reorganization of the War Department in March 1942, McNair became commanding general of Army Ground Forces. His new responsibilities not only included supervising the training of the ground forces but determining their organization and tactical doctrine as well. Marshall also relied heavily upon his advice in selecting senior field commanders.

With his work at home essentially complete, McNair went to Europe in July 1944 and succeeded Gen. George Patton as commander of the fictitious 1st Army Group in England. Always one to be near the action, McNair was accidentally killed by American bombs while observing the opening attack of the Normandy breakout on July 25, 1944.

Bibliography: Greenfield, Kent Roberts, et al., *The Organization of Ground Combat Troops: U.S. Army in World War II, Army Ground Forces* (Dept. of the Army, 1947); Kahn, E. J., Jr., *McNair: Educator of An Army* (Infantry Journal Press, 1945); MacDonald, Charles B., *The Mighty Endeavor: The American War in Europe* (Morrow, 1986); Palmer, Robert R., et al., *The Procurement and Training of Ground Combat Troops: U.S. Army in World War II, Army Ground Forces* (Dept. of the Army, 1948).

Daniel T. Bailey

MCNARNEY, JOSEPH TAGGART
(1893–1972)

U.S. army officer, McNarney was born in Emporium, Pennsylvania. He graduated from West Point in 1915 and was commissioned in the infantry. He then joined the Air Service and was sent to France during World War I. During the interwar period, McNarney commanded a bomber group and served on the faculty of the Army War College. After Japan attacked Pearl Harbor in December 1941, he served on a board to investigate the debacle.

McNarney's most celebrated feat was his successful redesign of the army staff during the early months of World War II when he was deputy chief of staff to Gen. George C. Marshall. The bitterly contested reorganization resulted in the General Staff being reduced from 800 to only 300 members and the number of officers having direct access to the chief of staff brought down from 60 to 6. With a small staff and a few semiautonomous functional commands, the U.S. Army successfully prosecuted World War II as an efficient organization. In 1944, he became Deputy Supreme Allied Commander under Gen. Dwight D. Eisenhower. After the war, McNarney served as commanding general of U.S. forces in Europe (1945–47). He retired in 1952 as full general.

Col. (Ret.) Rod Paschall

MARSHALL, GEORGE CATLETT
(1880–1959)

U.S. army officer and statesman, Marshall was born in Uniontown, Pennsylvania. He graduated from the Virginia Military Institute in 1901 and received a commission in the army the following year. He served for a year in the Philippines and then saw duty in the West, eventually graduating from Fort Leavenworth's Infantry Cavalry School in 1907. Promoted to first lieutenant, he studied at the Army Staff College there and upon graduation in 1908 remained to teach until 1910. From 1911 to 1913 he saw service in Massachusetts, Arkansas, and Texas and from 1913 to 1916 in the Philippines again, where he impressed his superiors with his knowledge of military tactics.

Promoted to captain in 1916, he served on the staffs of various generals before being part of the American Expeditionary Force (A.E.F.) during 1917–19, as chief of operations on the General Staff of the 1st Army. Marshall went on to serve as chief of staff with the VIII Corps, aiding in planning the St.-Mihiel and Meuse-Argonne offensives (1918). He was promoted to wartime rank of major in 1917 and to lieutenant colonel and colonel in 1918.

In the immediate post-World War I years (1919–24), Marshall, his peacetime rank having reverted to captain and then major and in 1923 to lieutenant colonel, served as aide to Gen. John J. Pershing until 1924. During 1925–27, Marshall served in Teintsin, China. From 1927 to 1932, he acted as assistant commandant of the Infantry School at

Gen. George Marshall, a skilled military tactician, planner, and strategist, became a five-star general in 1944; here, he is shown in the front passenger seat of a jeep (with Lt. Gen. Mark Clark behind him) in Italy. (U.S. Army Military History Institute)

Fort Benning, Georgia, and between 1932 and 1938, he was promoted to colonel (1933) and brigadier general (1936) while serving in various command positions. In 1938, he was detailed to the General Staff as chief of the War Plans Division. He served as chief of staff with the rank of general (1939–45) throughout World War II and emerged as the war's principal strategist. Marshall urged preparedness and worked, before the United States entered the war, to build a force that would be ready to fight. He divided the army into three groups—ground, air, and service; developed an operations service; coordinated army and navy strategies; and cooperated closely with civilian agencies and suppliers.

In opposition to British prime minister Winston Churchill's plan to enter Germany via the Balkan states, Marshall insisted on an entry from the west. His plan, not Churchill's, was accepted. Marshall, along with Adm. Ernest King, were strong advocates of U.S. war plans in the Pacific theater. Marshall and King pushed the Pacific operations forward, often in opposition to the wishes of Churchill. Churchill and Pres. Franklin D. Roosevelt, largely acquiescing to British desires, favored a ''Germany first'' policy. As U.S. chief of staff for army and air forces, Marshall rigidly opposed this tactic. Due primarily to his pressure and determination, the Allies eventually launched Operation Roundup, creating a Second Front in 1943. In 1944, Roosevelt appointed Marshall General of the Army, which entitled him to the rank of five-star general and which was a clear indication of the success of his position. Following the war, Churchill proclaimed Marshall ''the true organizer of victory'' for his work as a planner and strategist.

Almost a prophet of the cold war to come, Marshall, realizing the potential risk for Soviet opportunism in the postwar world, insisted, unsuccessfully, that the Soviet Union's help was not needed in the Pacific theater. Nevertheless, the U.S.S.R. belatedly declared war on Japan, which ultimately led to the Soviet influence in Southeast Asia that Marshall had anticipated.

Following Marshall's retirement from the army (November 1945), Pres. Harry S Truman dispatched him on a mission to China. After Japan had been driven from the region, civil war erupted between Chinese Communists led by Mao Zedong and Nationalists under Chiang Kai-shek. Some 50,000 U.S. Marines and General Marshall were dispatched to the area in hopes of ensuring the peace, but the mission failed. Truman later named Marshall secretary of state (1947–49), and as such, Marshall attended a conference in Moscow with his British, French, and Soviet counterparts. They tried futilely to draw up treaties with Germany and Austria. After seeing firsthand the impending economic collapse of Europe and sensing the Soviet Union's intent to step in and benefit from the resulting turmoil, Marshall returned determined to seek a solution to Europe's problems.

In a commencement address at Harvard University on June 5, 1947, Marshall announced his plan. Officially known as the European Recovery Program, but commonly referred to as the Marshall Plan, it proposed sending more than $13 billion in aid to assist the economic recovery of postwar Europe. The Marshall Plan successfully sparked economic recovery in Western Europe, thus blocking any Soviet penetration from Eastern Europe. Ironically, in 1952, Senators McCarthy and Jenner would damn Marshall and other leading officials for the loss of China and North Korea to the communists.

The American public perceived the Marshall Plan as a generous subvention to war-ravaged Europe. The Soviets, however, viewed the plan in a much different light. They saw it as an attempt to interfere in the internal affairs of other states. Ultimately, the Soviet Union prevented Poland and Czechoslovakia from participating. The Marshall Plan, according to late-20th-century revisionist historians, allowed the United States to remake the European economy in the image of the American economy, thereby providing a more congenial environment for U.S. investment.

Marshall resigned as secretary of state early in 1949 due to health problems. But when North Korean forces invaded South Korea on June 25, 1950, Truman urged Marshall to become secretary of defense. While the defense of South Korea was carried out under the auspices of the United Nations (UN), ultimately 1,800,000 U.S. troops served in Korea. During the one year he agreed to stay in the post, the aging Marshall augmented army strength, secured increased UN aid, and bolstered the North Atlantic Treaty

Organization (NATO), which he had helped to develop in 1948 as a response to imminent cold war.

Marshall retired for the last time in September 1951, after nearly 50 years of military and civilian public service. Strictly nonpartisan, he remained stridently opposed to politics to the point of never voting. For his efforts toward European political and economic reconstruction after World War II, Marshall received the Nobel Peace Prize in 1953.

Bibliography: Bland, Larry I., ed., *The Papers of George Catlett Marshall* (Johns Hopkins Univ. Press, 1981); Mosley, Leonard, *Marshall: Hero For Our Times* (Hearst, 1982); Pogue, Forrest C., *George C. Marshall*, 4 vols. (Viking, 1963–87).

M. Guy Bishop

MERRILL, AARON STANTON ("TIP") (1890–1961)

U.S. naval officer, Merrill was born in Natchez, Mississippi. He graduated from Annapolis in 1912. Promoted to lieutenant junior grade in 1915 and lieutenant commander in 1918, he saw destroyer duty during World War I. After several tours of duty in Europe, the Pacific, and China, Merrill achieved the rank of commander in 1923.

A rear admiral at the beginning of World War II, he commanded Task Force 39 (four light cruisers and eight destroyers) and was involved in the "leapfrogging" drive through the central Solomon Islands. In 1943, Merrill's task force was responsible for confusing the Japanese ships at Empress Augusta Bay in such a way that U.S. Marine amphibious troops were able to land on Bougainville Island. He maneuvered his ships so that enemy ships could neither enter the bay nor get a fix on the U.S. ships. Promoted to vice admiral toward the end of the war, Merrill retired in 1947. He was president of Jefferson Military College (1947–61).

Leo J. Daugherty III

MERRILL, FRANK DOW (1903–1955)

U.S. army officer, Merrill was born in Hopkinton, Massachusetts. He was commissioned in the cavalry after his graduation from West Point in 1929, went to Tokyo in 1938 to study Japanese, and was on a special mission in Burma at the time of the Japanese bombing of Pearl Harbor in December 1941. Assigned to Gen. Joseph W. Stilwell as his operations officer, Merrill participated in the infamous retreat into India in 1942. In October 1943, as a brigadier general, he took command of the 5307th Composite Unit (Provisional), which the press dubbed "Merrill's Marauders." The Marauders participated in the joint Chinese-U.S. offensive into Burma in 1944, including the capture of the Myitkyina airfield, but Merrill's failing health prevented him from playing a major part in the unit's later actions. Merrill left Burma in 1944 as a major general to become

the U.S. 10th Army's chief of staff, and he served there through the Okinawa Campaign. He later served as 6th Army chief of staff and retired in 1948.

Bibliography: Ogburn, Charlton, Jr., *The Marauders* (Harper and Brothers, 1959).

Richard F. Kehrberg

MITCHELL, WILLIAM ("BILLY") (1879–1936)

U.S. army officer and aviator, Mitchell was born in Nice, France. He began his military career as a soldier in the Spanish-American War (1898). He distinguished himself in World War I as a prominent air commander and after the war strongly advocated strategic bombing and a separate air force. Publicizing bombing demonstrations and heralding the airplane's dominance over the battleship, he gained mixed results. Mitchell became a popular hero, but he alienated many of his seniors. Accusing the War and Navy departments of "almost treasonable administration of the national defense," in 1925, Mitchell was convicted by court-martial of insubordination and sentenced to five years' suspension of rank and pay. He resigned in February 1926. Many events of World War II confirmed his theories, however, and Congress posthumously awarded him a special Medal of Honor (1946) for pioneer work and foresight in U.S. military aviation.

Bibliography: Burlingame, Roger, *General Billy Mitchell, Champion of Air Defense* (McGraw-Hill, 1952); Davis, Burke, *The Billy Mitchell Affair* (Random House, 1967); Hurley, Alfred F., *Billy Mitchell: Crusader for Air Power* (Indiana Univ. Press, 1975).

Maj. James Sanders Day

MITSCHER, MARC ANDREW (1887–1947)

U.S. naval officer, Mitscher was born in Hillsboro, Wisconsin. He graduated from Annapolis in 1910 and spent his early years in command of naval air stations, carrier duty, and service in the Bureau of Aeronautics. At the outbreak of World War II, he commanded the *Hornet* during Lt. Gen. James H. Doolittle's raid on Tokyo in April 1942 and in the Battle of Midway in June. During the war, Mitscher held commands in the Pacific, participating in campaigns for the Solomons, the Marshalls, the Marianas, the Philippines, and Okinawa. He was promoted to vice admiral in 1944 and to admiral in March 1946. At his death in 1947, Mitscher commanded the Atlantic Fleet.

Vernon L. Williams

MORROW, DWIGHT WHITNEY (1873–1931)

U.S. attorney, financier, and diplomat, Morrow was born in Huntington, West Virginia. Educated at Amherst College, Morrow became first a corporate lawyer and later a businessman. By the 1920s, he had become involved in Republican politics and was a major supporter of U.S. internationalism.

During World War I, in the years 1914–17, while the United States remained neutral, Morrow was heavily involved in financial transactions supporting the Allied war effort. He helped arrange, through the J. P. Morgan Company, the Anglo-French loan of 1915. At the outset of U.S. involvement in the war (1917), Morrow continued to assist with finances, working on a war savings campaign. In 1918, he helped organize the Allied Maritime Transport Council to ensure the resupply of Allies in Europe, serving in the executive of that council.

During the immediate postwar period, Morrow was involved in reconstruction efforts in Europe, helping to arrange loans for the rebuilding of war-torn nations. At the same time, he continued his political activities and became a close associate of Calvin Coolidge, which led to his chairmanship of the Morrow Board (1925), which studied the use of air power. In 1927, President Coolidge appointed Morrow ambassador to Mexico, where he served until 1929. He remained a force on the diplomatic scene after this posting, participating in the London Naval Treaty negotiations of 1930. At the time of his death, he was serving as U.S. senator from New Jersey (1930–31). Morrow was the father-in-law of aviator Charles A. Lindbergh.

Bibliography: Nicolson, Harold, *Dwight Morrow* (Harcourt, Brace, 1935).

Roger D. Launius

MURPHY, AUDIE LEON (1924–1971)

U.S. soldier who became one of the most decorated heroes of World War II, Murphy was born in Hunt County, Texas. He joined the army in June 1942, being assigned to the 15th Infantry Regiment, 3d Infantry Division. He participated in campaigns in North Africa, Sicily, Italy, southern France, and Germany. In 28 months of combat, Murphy was wounded twice and received 24 decorations for bravery. In addition to the French Croix de Guerre and Legion of Honor, his awards for valor included 2 Bronze Stars, a Distinguished Service Cross, a Silver Star, and the Congressional Medal of Honor (received for action near Holtzwihr, France, on Jan. 26, 1945, when he single-handedly held off a six-tank, 250-man German contingent).

After the war, Murphy became a movie actor, starring in mostly mediocre films. One notable exception was when he played himself in the 1955 film version of his autobiography, *To Hell and Back,* which had been published in 1949. He died in a plane crash near Roanoke, Virginia.

Bibliography: Murphy, Audie, *To Hell and Back* (TAB Books, reprint 1988); Simpson, Harold B., *Audie Murphy, American Soldier* (Hill Junior College Press, 1975).

David Friend

MURPHY, ROBERT DANIEL (1894–1978)

Chief U.S. diplomatic official in French North Africa during World War II, Murphy was born in Milwaukee, Wisconsin. He received a law degree from George Washington University in 1920 and entered the consular service, serving in Switzerland, Germany, Spain, and France. During World War II, he provided intelligence useful in planning the Operation Torch landings in North Africa (1942), while attempting to procure an armistice from Vichy commanders. He continued to meet with Vichy officials after the landings (being briefly held prisoner) and ultimately helped secure the surrender of all Vichy forces in Africa (1942). Thereafter, he continued negotiations with Free French authorities on rearmament, command, and postwar political issues.

Murphy conducted similar armistice negotiations with Italian generals prior to and immediately after the Allied landings at Salerno (1943). He ended the war as Gen. Dwight D. Eisenhower's adviser on German affairs.

After the war, he was U.S. ambassador to Belgium (1949–52) and Japan (1952–53) before joining the State Department.

Bibliography: *Northwest Africa: Seizing the Initiative in the West* (Office of the Chief of Military History, U.S. Army, 1956).

Jeffrey J. Roberts

NELSON, DONALD MARR (1888–1959)

U.S. businessman and war board administrator, Nelson was born in Hannibal, Missouri. He went to work for Sears, Roebuck and Company in 1911 and in 1939 became its executive vice president. When the United States began mobilizing for defense in 1940–41, Nelson put his merchandising experience to work for the government, first with the Council of National Defense and then with the Office of Production Management (OPM) and the Supply, Priorities, and Allocations Board (SPAB). In January 1942, the War Production Board replaced the OPM and SPAB. As chairman of this new organization, Nelson exercised total control over the U.S. economy until a dispute with the army and navy regarding industrial allocations led to his replacement in 1944. He was succeeded by Julius A. Krug.

Steve R. Waddell

NEVILLE, WENDELL CUSHING (1870–1930)

U.S. marine officer, Neville was born in Portsmouth, Virginia. He graduated from Annapolis in 1890, joined the Marine Corps in July 1892, and served in Cuba, China, the Philippines, and Nicaragua. He led the 2d Marine Regiment in the capture of Veracruz in April 1914 and won the Medal of Honor for his bravery. He was a brigadier general during World War I and commanded the 4th Marine Brigade in combat.

As head of the Neville Board following the war, he guided the selection of junior officers and stressed the importance of troop leaders over specialists. Promoted to major general in 1923, Neville was an active force in the development of the Corps' amphibious capabilities. He was named commandant in March 1929.

Bibliography: Millett, Allan R., *Semper Fidelis: The History of the United States Marine Corps* (Macmillan, 1980).

Daniel T. Bailey

NIMITZ, CHESTER WILLIAM (1885–1966)

U.S. naval officer, Nimitz was born in Fredericksburg, Texas. He entered the Naval Academy in 1901, and in response to the need for young officers for the rapidly expanding fleet, the entire Class of 1905 was graduated a semester early.

Early Career. Nimitz spent three years in Far Eastern waters while serving in a battleship and cruiser and then commanding the new gunboat *Panay* and a destroyer. He returned to the United States in 1908 and was given command of a submarine. This was not the duty he preferred, but Nimitz applied himself to his task and became one of the most knowledgeable officers about submarines in the navy and perhaps its foremost authority on diesel engines. After further study of diesel engines in Germany, he was assigned to the Brooklyn navy yard in 1913 to supervise the installation of diesel engines in the new fleet oiler *Maumee*. Rejecting an offer of civilian employment from a firm that manufactured diesels, Nimitz remained with the

Commander in chief of the U.S. Pacific Fleet and Pacific Ocean Area, Adm. Chester Nimitz poses with a group of journalists in front of a map of his area of command during World War II. (U.S. Navy)

Maumee as its executive officer and chief engineer when the ship was ready for sea. While serving on the *Maumee,* he helped prepare the plans for the navy's first effort in underway refueling.

Marked for Success. In 1917, Nimitz was promoted to lieutenant commander and assigned to the staff of Capt. Samuel Robison, commander Submarine Force, Atlantic Fleet. This was a turning point in Nimitz's career, for the change in duty removed Nimitz from his preoccupation with engineering matters and into staff and organizational work and to a normal career progression for line officers. After brief tours as executive officer on a battleship and as commanding officer of the new submarine base at Pearl Harbor, Hawaii, construction of which he supervised, Nimitz studied at the Naval War College and then became aide and assistant chief of staff to Robison, who by this time had moved up to one of the navy's highest positions, commander of the Battle Fleet. Nimitz remained with Robison through 1926, when he was ordered to establish a naval reserve program at the University of California in Berkeley. It was one of Nimitz's most rewarding assignments.

Promoted to captain while at Berkeley, Nimitz then spent several years at San Diego before receiving command of the cruiser *Augusta* in 1934. The following year, he began a three-year stint in Washington as assistant chief of the Bureau of Navigation (BuNav), briefly returned to sea to command a battleship division (*Arizona* was his flagship), and was then appointed chief of BuNav. His promotion to rear admiral had come in 1938. Subsequently renamed the Bureau of Personnel, BuNav oversaw recruitment, training, assignment, and promotion for all naval personnel. As such, it was one of the most important shore assignments in the navy.

World War II. On Dec. 16, 1941, following the disaster at Pearl Harbor, Nimitz accepted the position of commander in chief, Pacific Fleet. After a round of conferences with military leaders, Sec. of the Navy Frank Knox, and Pres. Franklin D. Roosevelt, Nimitz departed for Pearl Harbor, where he took formal command of the battered Pacific Fleet on December 31.

Nimitz's initial strategic responsibilities had already been determined in Washington, where Adm. Ernest J. King had just become commander in chief of the U.S. combined fleet. With authority over all naval forces, King set as priorities for the Pacific maintaining the safety of the Hawaiian Islands (including the outpost at Midway) and the protection of shipping between the United States and Hawaii and between the United States and Australia. King offered the suggestion that the Pacific Fleet should begin to undertake offensive operations as well. Nimitz could not have agreed more, for he believed that continued inactivity in the aftermath of Pearl Harbor and subsequent changes of command could only breed defeatism among the officers and men of the Pacific Fleet.

Although all eight battleships that had been at Pearl Harbor on December 7 had been either sunk or damaged, the means to undertake limited offensive action still existed in the four carriers in the Pacific at the outset of 1942. Nimitz used them to bomb Japanese bases in the Marshall Islands, at Wake Island, and in New Guinea. None of the raids accomplished a great deal, but they gave the Pacific Fleet combat experience and created positive war news.

At the end of March, Nimitz was given the additional title of commander in chief, Pacific Ocean Area. In effect, the Joint Chiefs of Staff (JCS) had divided the entire Pacific into two enormous areas for purposes of command: the Southwest Pacific—Australia, New Guinea, and the Philippine Islands (then almost entirely in Japanese control)—and the Pacific Ocean—everything else except for shipping lanes along the coasts of Central and South America. Within the Pacific Ocean Area, Nimitz would have command of the Pacific Fleet as well as all Allied ground and air forces based in the region. As circumstances required, he would send units of the Pacific Fleet to operate in the Southwest Pacific, which would be under the command of army general Douglas MacArthur. At this time, the Southwest Pacific had little naval power of its own permanently assigned to it.

Save for the Doolittle Raid on Tokyo in April 1942, Japanese actions still determined the course of events in the Pacific. Nimitz had learned to rely upon the information his radio intelligence was able to provide about Japanese intentions. Because of it, he was able to get carrier task forces to the Coral Sea in May and to Midway in June to head off Japanese moves to occupy Port Moresby (in New Guinea) and Midway Island. For the remainder of 1942, the ground and sea struggle for Guadalcanal dominated all else in the Pacific.

Nimitz had long since established his style of command. Much as he would have liked to have been at sea, he recognized from the time of his appointment as Pacific Fleet commander that his responsibilities would be too broad for him to do anything other than command from shore. Inevitably, many of the planning sessions at which he presided developed tensions as officers debated the pros and cons of the operations they were contemplating. Fortunately, the naturally affable Nimitz had an unsurpassed ability to ease tensions with appropriate anecdotes so constructive dialogue could be resumed.

Even though he realized his place was at a desk, he did insist on seeing things for himself. He visited Midway in May 1942 when intelligence first began indicating that the Japanese might be planning to invade the key outpost. In September, he went to Guadalcanal when the operation there appeared to be in jeopardy. The fact that his own South Pacific commander, Vice Adm. Robert Ghormley, never visited Guadalcanal was perhaps one of the reasons he relieved Ghormley and named the aggressive Vice Adm. William Halsey as his replacement. As the war continued, Nimitz visited Tarawa and Okinawa, among other places.

Proposals for the Doolittle Raid and for the assault upon Tulagi and Guadalcanal had been developed by Washington planners, and throughout the war, strategic directives either originated with the JCS or required JCS approval. King, of course, was the navy's representative on the JCS; Nimitz was a loyal subordinate, but he was not one to acquiesce when he believed King was incorrect. The two met about six times a year at King's behest, almost always in San Francisco. For instance, when the Guadalcanal Campaign was at last nearing an end, they met to discuss Nimitz's next operation. King suggested it might be directed against the Admiralty Islands far to the north of Guadalcanal, but Nimitz replied that this would never do. Logistics considerations and the need for land-based air cover would limit an advance to 300 miles at the most, and he convinced King that the Japanese base at Munda Point on New Georgia should be the next step north. He did predict that, with construction on nearly two dozen new aircraft carriers progressing well, more ambitious operations could be planned when the first of these carriers was ready to go to sea in 1943. By 1943, the strategic initiative in the Pacific had passed to Allied forces. With carrier air power becoming available in unprecedented strength, the great drive across the Central Pacific began in the fall of 1943 and gathered momentum thereafter. Individual Japanese bases were isolated, and Nimitz's forces seized the ones that would be of importance to future U.S. operations. Included among these were Tarawa in the Gilberts, Kwajalein in the Marshalls, and Saipan, Tinian, and Guam in the Marianas. The others were bypassed in what proved to be one of history's most sweeping military successes.

With the Marianas in hand by August 1944, subsequent operations were of strategic import. Planners in Pearl Harbor and Washington agreed upon taking Leyte in the Philippines, but King next wanted to seize Formosa, while Gens. George Marshall and MacArthur favored a return to Luzon, where U.S. troops had been defeated in 1941 and 1942. Nimitz and virtually every other senior officer in the Pacific believed that invading Formosa as King proposed would be too ambitious and that an invasion of Luzon followed by assaults upon Iwo Jima and Okinawa promised more at less cost. King, who had refused to allow Nimitz and the combined wishes of almost all Pacific planners to sidetrack him from his determination to invade the Marianas, deferred to Nimitz's reasoning in this instance. As events turned out, the capture of Okinawa in the spring of 1945 was the last of amphibious operations undertaken by Nimitz's forces. In September, on the *Missouri* in Tokyo Bay, Nimitz was one of the signers of the Japanese surrender.

On Nov. 24, 1945, Nimitz relinquished command of the Pacific Fleet and returned to Washington to become chief of naval operations (1945–47). His contribution to American success had already been recognized with promotion to the five-star rank of fleet admiral. He later served as a regent of the University of California.

Bibliography: Hoyt, Edwin P., *How They Won the War in the Pacific: Nimitz and His Admirals* (Weybright and Talley, 1970); Morison, Samuel Eliot, *The Two-Ocean War: A Short History of the United States Navy in the Second World War* (Little, Brown, 1963); Potter, E. B., *Nimitz* (Naval Inst. Press, 1976); Potter, E. B., and Chester Nimitz, *Triumph in the Pacific: The Navy's Struggle Against Japan* (Prentice-Hall, 1963); Reynolds, Clark G., *The Fast Carriers: The Forging of an Air Navy* (McGraw-Hill, 1968).

Lloyd J. Graybar

OLDENDORF, JESSE BARRETT
(1887–1974)

U.S. naval officer, Oldendorf was born in Riverside, California. He graduated from Annapolis in 1909. During World War II, he was promoted to rear admiral (1942) and held various sea commands in the Caribbean and in the Atlantic Fleet. In 1944, Oldendorf was transferred to the Pacific to command a cruiser division during the Marshalls and Marianas campaigns. Assigned next to the 7th Fleet, he commanded a task force consisting of six old battleships (most of which had been at Pearl Harbor), escorted by cruisers and destroyers, that patrolled Surigao Strait should a Japanese naval force try to threaten the U.S. landings on Leyte. When Japanese surface units approached, Oldendorf's destroyers, on Oct. 25, 1944, launched torpedo attacks, and his capital ships then all but annihilated the Japanese force. Oldendorf was promoted to vice admiral and given other commands in the 7th Fleet.

Bibliography: Reynolds, Clark G., *Famous American Admirals* (Van Nostrand-Reinhold, 1978).

Lloyd J. Graybar

PALMER, JOHN MCAULEY (1870–1955)

U.S. army officer, Palmer was born in Carlinville, Illinois. He graduated from West Point in 1892. Assigned to the 15th Infantry, he served in Illinois and Arizona until 1898, when he became professor of military science at the University of Chicago. Palmer saw no active service during the Spanish-American War of 1898 but was sent to Cuba as an administrator in 1899 and subsequently had a brief tour with his regiment in China during the Boxer Rebellion in 1900. He then served for five years as an assistant professor of chemistry at West Point. In 1906, he rejoined the 15th Infantry in the Philippines and later served as governor of the district of Lanao in 1906–07.

Palmer graduated from the Army Staff College at Fort Leavenworth in 1910, and following duty with the "maneuver division," he was assigned to the War Department General Staff. Set to study army organization by Sec. of War Henry L. Stimson, Palmer recommended replacement of the army's traditional geographical organization with one based on tactical units. He also prepared "The Organization of the Land Forces of the United States," a paper in which he advocated abandonment of the idea of an expansible army and reliance instead on a small, ready-to-fight regular army reinforced by a citizen army in time of crisis. His paper was issued as a supplement to the annual report of the secretary of war for 1912, but no other action was taken.

In 1911 and 1912, Palmer attended French and German army maneuvers and then returned to a series of field commands with the 24th Infantry in China, the Philippines, and San Francisco, during which period he was promoted to major. He returned to the General Staff in January 1916 and studied the problems of possible U.S. participation in World War I. He also published *Army of the People*, a book that expressed his views on the benefits of the militia tradition and universal military training. During World War I, Palmer served in staff assignments at general headquarters, American Expeditionary Force, and with the U.S. mission to Italy. In mid-1918, he assumed command of the 58th Infantry and led that regiment during the Meuse-Argonne Offensive. After the armistice, Colonel Palmer returned to the General Staff in Washington and became chief of the War Plans Division in July 1919.

In November 1919, he received special assignment to assist the Senate Military Affairs Committee in drafting the National Defense Act of 1920, which was to remain the principal legislation governing the organization of the army until 1950. Army chief of staff Gen. Peyton C. March proposed a permanent regular army of 500,000 men to be organized as a half-strength skeleton field army of five corps that could be expanded in time of war by the addition of conscripts. Palmer put forward an alternative proposal in which a small but full-strength regular army would be supplemented in time of need by a citizen army. March's proposal was inconsistent with the mood of Congress and the public, and Palmer's plan emerged as the preferred solution and was consequently reflected, although imperfectly, in the law.

Following passage of the National Defense Act of 1920, Palmer commanded the 22d Infantry at Fort Jay, New York, and served for more than two years as aide-de-camp to Gen. of the Army John J. Pershing. He also served on the technical staff of the U.S. delegation to the Washington Arms Limitation Conference of 1920. In September 1923, Brigadier General Palmer assumed command of the 19th Infantry Brigade in the Panama Canal Zone. He retired from active duty in January 1926.

In retirement, Palmer wrote, spoke, and agitated unceasingly for the concept of universal military service. He supported passage of the Selective Service Act, and in late 1941, he was recalled for World War II duty in the office of the chief of staff of the army, where he served until 1946, when he was once again retired. In the postwar period, the concept of universal military training long advocated by Palmer was rejected, but its central element, selective compulsory service (the draft), continued as a fundamental precept of national defense policy until the 1970s.

Bibliography: Holley, I. B., Jr., *General John M. Palmer, Citizen Soldiers, and the Army of a Democracy* (Greenwood Press, 1981); Spiller, Roger J., ed., *Dictionary of American Military Biography,* vol. 2 (Greenwood Press, 1984).

Lt. Col. (Ret.) Charles R. Shrader

PARSONS, WILLIAM STERLING
(1901–1953)

U.S. naval officer, Parsons was born in Chicago. He graduated from Annapolis in 1922. Later trained in ordnance engineering, he remained a line officer but had the expertise to participate in some of World War II's most far-reaching technological innovations: in the early phases of radar studies in the navy, in the field tests of the proximity fuze while on assignment to the Office of Scientific Research and Development in 1942, and, from 1943, as director of the Ordnance Division of the Los Alamos Laboratory. In this capacity, Parsons oversaw the preparation of the gun assembly for the type of atomic bomb used on Hiroshima. He went to Tinian Island in 1945 to head the Overseas Technical Group of the Los Alamos Laboratory and flew on the *Enola Gay* on Aug. 6, 1945, as weaponeer and bomb commander. A captain, Parsons was the most senior naval officer assigned to any of the Manhattan Project's major facilities.

Bibliography: Rhodes, Richard G., *The Making of The Atom Bomb* (Simon & Schuster, 1987).

Lloyd J. Graybar

PATCH, ALEXANDER MCCARRELL
(1889–1945)

U.S. army officer, Patch was born at Fort Huachuca, Arizona. He graduated from West Point in 1913 and commanded the 1st Infantry Division's machine-gun battalion during World War I. During World War II, he organized and trained the Americal Division on New Caledonia in 1942 and led it on Guadalcanal in 1943. Promoted to lieutenant general in 1944, Patch commanded IV Corps in the United States and the 7th Army in Italy and France. After leading the 7th into steady fighting up the Rhone Valley, Patch was able to cross the Rhine in March 1945. His relentless advance into southern Germany was re-

warded by the surrender of German Army Group G on May 5.

Bibliography: Cronin, Francis D., *Under the Southern Cross, The Saga of the Americal Division* (1951).

Brig. Gen. (PNG, Ret.) Uzal W. Ent

PATTON, GEORGE SMITH, JR.
(1885–1945)

U.S. army commander, Patton was born in San Gabriel, California. He attended the Virginia Military Institute for a year before entering West Point in 1904. Difficulty with mathematics delayed his graduation until 1909, when he received a commission in the cavalry. In 1916, when the army launched its Punitive Expedition into Mexico, he engineered an appointment for himself as one of Gen. John J. Pershing's aides.

World War I. When Pershing went to France the following summer as commander of the American Expeditionary Force, Patton went along as well. Once in France, Patton longed to get into combat. In November 1917, he joined the embryonic U.S. Tank Corps and organized the American tank training center at Langres, France. The following August, he led the 304th Tank Brigade into combat during the St.-Mihiel Offensive. The next month, he and his tankers were again in action in the Meuse-Argonne. By the end of the war, Patton had built a reputation as the army's leading tank expert and had been promoted to colonel.

Interwar Years. He returned home in 1919 and served with the Tank Corps at Camp Meade, Maryland, until 1920. That year, he reverted to his prewar rank of captain and Congress transferred control of the army's tanks to the infantry. Rather than become an infantryman, Patton rejoined the cavalry. Over the next two decades, he experienced the regular peacetime cycle of school, staff, and troop duty. Physically, he remained active through polo, fox hunting, and horse jumping. He stayed intellectually active as well, writing for the *Cavalry Journal* and other periodicals and reading military history. Moreover, he maintained his interest in mechanized warfare, although he continued to be a firm believer in the viability of horse cavalry.

North Africa and Sicily. The question of mechanization had taken on an urgent air after the collapse of France in 1940. In July, the War Department created the Armored Force to oversee the development of the army's new armored divisions. Patton assumed command of the new 2d Armored Brigade and, in April 1941, the 2d Armored Division. The army expanded rapidly after the Japanese bombing of Pearl Harbor (December 1941), and in January 1942, Patton took over the I Armored Corps. Soon his colorful image had made him a favorite with the press. He was, nevertheless, a skilled trainer, and he sought to instill qualities of aggressiveness and discipline into his units.

When Gen. George Patton became commander of the 3d Army in 1944, the Germans were misled to believe that he would command an army that would cross the English Channel and attack at Pas-de-Calais. (U.S. Army)

During the spring and early summer, Patton established the Desert Training Center near Indio, California.

On July 30, the War Department ordered Patton east to help plan Operation Torch, the invasion of North Africa, and he led the invasion's Western task force to Morocco in November. His I Armored Corps served principally as an occupation force while other units pushed east into Tunisia. After the disastrous Battle of the Kasserine Pass in March 1943, however, Gen. Dwight D. Eisenhower ordered Patton to take over the battered U.S. II Corps. Patton quickly restored the corps' sagging morale and successfully led it into Tunisia.

His success with the II Corps earned Patton a promotion to lieutenant general and command of the 7th Army for the invasion of Sicily. Gen. Bernard L. Montgomery's British 8th Army was to make the Allies' main effort, a drive on Messina along Sicily's east coast. After landing on July 11, Patton's army was merely to protect Montgomery's left flank. Patton fumed over his secondary role. When the British attack stalled, he received permission to seize Palermo, but then raced Montgomery for Messina. Patton won the race and captured the city on July 22. His zealousness, however, ignited a longstanding feud between himself and Montgomery. Worse, during the campaign, Patton slapped two soldiers suffering from battle fatigue in separate incidents. The uproar over the incidents cost Patton a role in the invasion of Italy and command of U.S. forces in the cross-channel attack on France. Only his reputation as an outstanding commander saved him from relief or dismissal.

3d Army Commander. Patton remained in exile in Sicily until January 1944, when Eisenhower gave him command of the 3d Army. Patton eagerly moved to England and began training his new army. Additionally, he took over "command" of a fictitious army group as part of Operation Fortitude. The Germans considered Patton the Allies' top commander and expected him to lead the upcoming invasion. Fortitude's purpose was to convince the Germans that Patton's "army group" was going to attack the Pas de Calais, a subterfuge that protected the real Normandy landings. Therefore, his role in Fortitude kept him out of France until July 6. On July 27, he unofficially took over Gen. Troy Middleton's VIII Corps until August 1, when the 3d Army became operational.

Patton's army came to life just as the German lines broke around Avranches. The 3d Army poured through the gap and into Brittany and then east toward Le Mans and Orleans. The speed of the 3d Army's advance unbalanced the German defense, and German troops hastily retreated eastward. As Patton's men approached the German frontier, however, they began to outrun their supply lines, and German resistance stiffened. The Patton-Montgomery feud erupted again when Eisenhower chose to send precious Allied supplies north for a British drive on the Rhine at Arnhem in the Netherlands rather than to Patton. After nearly a month of limited activity, the 3d Army attacked again in November, but bad weather and the fortifications around Metz had stalled Patton's advance into the Saar.

As Patton prepared to initiate another offensive, the Germans launched their own attack into the Ardennes in December. Faced with this crisis, Patton wheeled part of his army north to lessen pressure on the southern flank of "the Bulge" and to relieve Bastogne. The 3d Army successfully carried out the difficult maneuver and reached Bastogne on December 26. In February 1945, the Allies began a large-scale offensive aimed at crossing the Rhine north of the 3d Army, in Montgomery's sector. Again assigned a defensive role, Patton nevertheless pushed his men forward through difficult terrain with limited logistical support. After hard fighting, his men captured Trier on March 1 and six days later reached the Rhine at Koblenz. On March 22, Patton put a division across the river—a day ahead of Montgomery. Engineers hurriedly erected bridges over the river, and the 3d Army began expanding its bridgehead toward Frankfurt am Main.

At this point, Patton undertook a controversial operation to rescue nearly 5,000 Allied prisoners of war, including his son-in-law John Waters, held at Hammelburg behind

German lines. A small task force of just over 300 men with 16 tanks fought its way to the camp in late March. The Germans, however, reacted quickly and surrounded the U.S. force. After a sharp fight and a failed breakout attempt, the American raiders surrendered. The press immediately jumped on the story and claimed the task force had been sacrificed solely to rescue Waters.

While Patton complained about the press coverage of the Hammelburg Raid, the 3d Army poured across central Germany toward Kassel. German resistance faltered, although some individual German units still proved dangerous. By mid-April, the 3d Army was in a position to drive into eastern Germany and, Patton hoped, on Berlin. Eisenhower, however, intended to move south against the so-called National Redoubt along the German-Austrian border. Allied intelligence believed that the Germans were massing troops and supplies in the Alps for a last-ditch stand. Concerned, Eisenhower wanted to overrun the region before these plans could be implemented. Patton did not believe the reports but obediently turned the bulk of his army into eastern Bavaria. The 3d Army quickly overran the region but discovered no German troops massing and no National Redoubt. Patton, who did not get to fight for Berlin as he had hoped, received the fourth star of a full general on April 16. In the war's remaining days, the 3d Army pushed into Czechoslovakia and Austria before the German surrender on May 9, 1945.

Post-Combat Career. Patton had expressed an interest in going to the Pacific theater even before the fighting had ended in Europe. Gen. Douglas MacArthur, the army's top commander in the Pacific, however, wanted Gen. Courtney Hodges and his 1st Army rather than the flamboyant Patton. With no immediate prospects for employment in the Pacific, Patton spent June on leave in the United States and then returned to Germany to oversee the 3d Army's occupation of eastern Bavaria. Occupation duty did not appeal to Patton, and his critical comments on de-Nazification quickly landed him in trouble with both the public and his superiors. Faced with mounting public pressure, Eisenhower suggested Patton transfer to the 15th Army, an administrative command charged with collecting and preserving the records of the war and preparing studies on the conflict. Unhappy as military governor, Patton agreed. On October 7, Patton reluctantly relinquished command of the 3d Army. On December 9, the day before he was scheduled to fly home for Christmas, Patton's neck was broken in an automobile accident. He died 12 days ater.

Bibliography: Allen, Robert S., *Lucky Forward: The History of Patton's Third Army* (Vanguard, 1947); Blumenson, Martin, *Patton: The Man Behind the Legend, 1885–1945* (Morrow, 1985); Blumenson, Martin, ed., *The Patton Papers,* 2 vols. (Houghton Mifflin, 1972, 1974); Essame, Hubert, *Patton: A Study in Command* (Scribner's,

1974); Patton, George S., Jr., *War As I Knew It* (Houghton Mifflin, 1947).

Richard F. Kehrberg

PERSHING, JOHN JOSEPH (1860–1948)

U.S. army commander, Pershing was born near Laclede, Missouri. He graduated from West Point in 1886 and served as a cavalry officer in the American Southwest and South Dakota during the Indian Wars of the 1880s. He was appointed as a military instructor at the University of Nebraska (1891–95) and later at West Point (1897–98). Pershing served a tour of duty in the Philippines (1899–1903), was a military observer during the Russo-Japanese War (1904–05), and in 1906 was promoted to brigadier general. As a major general, Pershing commanded Mexican border operations (1916) and in 1917 was appointed commander of the American Expeditionary Force in France in World War I. In October 1917, he was promoted to full general.

Acclaimed as a hero after the war, Pershing received in September 1919 the title of "General of the Armies of the United States," the first to hold the rank. He served as army chief of staff from 1921 until his required retirement for age in 1924. In retirement, he served as chairman of the American Battle Monuments Commission.

M. Guy Bishop

PRATT, WILLIAM VEAZIE (1866–1957)

U.S. naval officer, Pratt was born in Belfast, Maine. He graduated from Annapolis in 1889. Promoted to commander in 1910 and to captain five years later, Pratt was assistant chief of naval operations during World War I (1917–18), returning to sea after the war to command the *New York.* He was promoted to rear admiral in 1921, commanded a division of battleships, and served as president of the Naval War College (1925–27) prior to assuming command of Battleship Divisions, Battle Fleet.

Pratt became chief of naval operations in 1930, a time when the growing severity of the Depression made it apparent that naval budgets would be pared. Pratt believed that the United States should try to build up to the tonnage quotas stipulated in the 1922 Washington and 1930 London naval treaties. He recognized, however, that political realities made achievement of these goals unlikely. He therefore was willing to accept less while trying to bring the navy to peak effectiveness in other ways. He supported and got the modernization of existing battleships, several of which were nearly 20 years old, while calling for the construction of a modest number of new ships. Throughout his tenure, therefore, Pratt was a man in the middle: his fellow officers believed he was too willing to yield to budget cuts at the navy's expense, yet political leaders, both Herbert Hoover and Franklin D. Roosevelt, wanted still greater economies.

Pratt retired in June 1933. He was recalled to duty for six months in 1941 to consult on better methods for protecting North Atlantic convoys. His answer was increased air cover to be provided by planes operating from escort carriers and by navy blimps. Pratt also contributed a well-regarded column for *Newsweek* magazine in which he analyzed the war at sea.

Bibliography: Symonds, Craig L., "William Veazie Pratt," *The Chiefs of Naval Operations,* ed. by Robert William Love, Jr. (Naval Inst. Press, 1980); Wheeler, Gerald E., *Admiral William Veazie Pratt, U.S. Navy: A Sailor's Life* (U.S. Govt. Printing Office, 1974).

Lloyd J. Graybar

PULLER, LEWIS BURWELL (1898–1971)

U.S. marine officer, Puller was born in West Point, Virginia. He enlisted in the Marine Corps in 1918 and was commissioned a 2d lieutenant in 1919. He served in the Haitian Garde (1920–24) and was later part of the expeditionary brigade to establish the Nicaraguan Garde, in which he served as a captain until 1933 with a brief tour in the United States in 1931. In Nicaragua, he earned the first

At retirement in 1953, Lt. Gen. Lewis "Chesty" Puller was the bearer of five Navy Crosses, two of which were awarded during duty in Nicaragua, two during World War II at Guadalcanal and New Britain, and one during the Korean conflict. (U.S. Marine Corps)

two of five Navy Crosses and became noted for leading his men in battle. In 1933, he was assigned to Peking, China, in command of the "Horse Marines" and then, as a major, led a marine detachment on duty aboard a ship in the Asiatic Fleet until 1936. After a U.S. tour (1936–39), he was assigned to Shanghai, China, where he gained fame for driving Japanese troops from the American quarter.

Made commanding officer of the 1st Battalion, 7th Marines, in 1941, he sailed with them to the Pacific in 1942. Now a lieutenant colonel, he distinguished himself at Guadalcanal (third Navy Cross) by standing off a Japanese division with half a battalion, on New Britain (fourth Navy Cross) by leading two stalled battalions under fire to victory, and at Peleliu, one of the bloodiest marine battles during World War II.

In Korea (1950–51), where Puller received his fifth Navy Cross, he became a brigadier general. Known as "Chesty," Puller was the most highly decorated marine of all time. He was promoted to lieutenant general in 1953 and retired in 1955.

Bibliography: Davis, Burke, *Marine! The Life of Lt. Gen. Lewis B. Fuller* (Little, Brown, 1962); Debs, Robert, Jr., *Victory at High Tide* (1968; reprint, Nautical & Aviation Pub., 1979).

Brig. Gen. (PNG, Ret.) Uzal W. Ent

QUESADA, ELWOOD RICHARD (1904–1993)

U.S. army air force officer, Quesada was born in Washington, D.C. He joined the army in 1924 as an enlisted man and in 1927 became an Army Air Corps officer. In 1928, he was among the rescuers of the crew of the German aircraft *Bremen,* which had crashed in Labrador on its maiden east-west transatlantic voyage. Two years later, as relief pilot to Maj. (future air force commanding general) Carl Spaatz, he established a world's endurance record by keeping their plane aloft for six-plus days, thus proving the efficacy of mid-air refueling. After his promotion to brigadier general in 1942, Quesada saw combat in North Africa as an air wing commander and then commanded the 9th Fighter Command in England. He directed air cover for advancing tanks and infantry during the Normandy invasion in 1944.

After World War II, he headed Air Force Tactical Air Command (Air Defense Command after service unification). Involved in testing the hydrogen bomb at Eniwetok in the Pacific, he retired as a lieutenant general in 1951 and joined several defense-related industries. As a long-time advocate of air safety, Quesada was recalled to public life in 1957 by Pres. Dwight D. Eisenhower to help create the Federal Aviation Administration, which he headed until 1961.

Peter Model

RICHARDSON, JAMES OTTO (1878–1974)

U.S. naval officer, Richardson was born in Paris, Texas. He graduated from Annapolis and participated in World War I as executive officer of the battleship Nevada, then gradually rose through the 1920s to become assistant to the chief of naval operations. From 1938 to 1939, Richardson directed the Bureau of Navigation before being elevated to commander in chief of the U.S. Fleet in January 1940. As the nation headed toward war with Japan, Richardson often found himself at odds with Pres. Franklin D. Roosevelt, particularly when the president moved the fleet from California to Pearl Harbor, Hawaii. Richardson was relieved in February 1941 and finished his career serving on various boards, including one investigating armed forces unification. In 1973, he wrote his memoirs, *On the Treadmill to Pearl Harbor*.

Bibliography: Richardson, James O., *On the Treadmill to Pearl Harbor* (U.S. Govt. Printing Office, 1973).

John F. Wukovits

RICHARDSON, ROBERT CHARLWOOD, JR. (1882–1954)

U.S. army officer, Richardson was born in Charleston, South Carolina. He graduated from West Point in 1904 and was a staff officer in France during World War I. He served two years as military attaché in Rome and was commandant of the cadets at the Military Academy from 1929 to 1933. Promoted to brigadier general in 1938, he headed the Cavalry School in 1939–40.

Richardson became a major general and division commander in 1940 and led the VII Corps in training during 1941–43. Promoted to lieutenant general in 1943, he took charge of the Hawaiian Department and later commanded U.S. army forces in the Central Pacific. Talented but difficult, Richardson refused to serve under an Australian officer and lost an important field command in 1942. He retired in 1946.

Bibliography: Pogue, Forrest C., *George C. Marshall: Organizer of Victory, 1943–1945* (Viking, 1973).

Daniel T. Bailey

RIDGWAY, MATTHEW BUNKER (1895–1993)

U.S. army officer, Ridgway was born in Fort Monroe, Virginia. He graduated from West Point in 1917 and rose rapidly through the ranks between the world wars, serving abroad in China, Nicaragua, and Panama and in various U.S. posts, including the War Plans Division of the War Department. As a brigadier general and assistant division commander, Ridgway oversaw the conversion of the 82d Infantry Division into the first U.S. airborne division and then became its commander. In March 1943, he took the 82d into North Africa, and then to Sicily, Salerno, and Anzio.

On D-Day (June 6, 1944), Ridgway jumped with the division into Normandy. In August 1944, he was put in charge of the XVIII Airborne Corps (comprised of the 82d, 101st, and 17th airborne divisions) during the Battle of the Bulge, and also was given the 30th Infantry and 7th Armored divisions. In the front lines all the way from Normandy to the Battle of the Bulge, the disastrous Operation Market Garden, the Remagen Bridge breakout, the Ruhr pocket, the Elbe River crossing (May 2, 1945), and eventual linkup with the Soviet army, the intellectual, much-decorated Ridgway (according to one citation) "displayed an uncanny ability for appearing during crucial moments in the advance, and by his compelling leadership and inspiring presence helped his command to hurdle their obstacles and once more to continue the victorious advance." He was promoted to lieutenant general in 1945 and received numerous decorations for heroism during World War II.

After the German surrender, he was sent to the Philippines to prepare for the invasion of Japan. After the Japanese surrender, Ridgway was posted to the United Nations (UN) Military Staff Committee to help establish the world's first international police force. During the Korean War (1950–53), as commander of the 8th Army, he halted the Chinese counteroffensive, replaced the sacked Gen. Douglas MacArthur as commander of all UN forces in Korea, succeeded Gen. Dwight D. Eisenhower as NATO (North Atlantic Treaty Organization) Supreme Allied Commander, and ended his career as army chief of staff (1953–55). Ridgway recounted his career in *Soldier* (1956).

Bibliography: Ridgway, Matthew B. *Soldier* (Greenwood, 1974).

Peter Model

ROCKEY, KELLER EMRICK (1888–1970)

U.S. marine officer, Rockey was born in Columbia City, Indiana. He was commissioned in the Marine Corps in November 1913 and served in World War I with the 5th Marines at Château-Thierry and Belleau Wood. His assignments between the wars included duty in Haiti and Nicaragua. Following staff assignments early in World War II, Rockey prepared the 5th Marine Division and led it in battle on Iwo Jima. He subsequently commanded the 3d Amphibious Corps and accepted the Japanese surrender in north China. Promoted to lieutenant general in January 1947, Rockey commanded the Fleet Marine Force Atlantic and the Marine Department of the Pacific before his retirement in September 1950.

Lt. Col. (Ret.) Charles R. Shrader

ROCKWELL, FRANCIS WARREN
(1886–1951)

U.S. naval officer, Rockwell was born in Brooklyn, New York. In 1941, he headed the 16th Naval District based at Cavite in the Philippine Islands. After the U.S. Asiatic Fleet left the Philippines in late December, Admiral Rockwell's ragtag collection of minecraft, gunboats, and motor torpedo boats unsuccessfully attempted to stall the invading Japanese. In March 1942, before the final collapse, the navy ordered him to Australia to take charge of U.S. submarines based there. The following January, Rockwell took command of the Amphibious Force, North Pacific, and led it in the campaign to retake the Aleutian islands of Kiska and Attu. Based on this experience, the navy moved Rockwell to the Amphibious Training Command, Atlantic, where he spent the remainder of the war, training units in amphibious warfare.

Richard F. Kehrberg

ROOSEVELT, FRANKLIN DELANO
(1882–1945)

Thirty-second president of the United States (1933–45), Roosevelt was born in Hyde Park, New York. He led the nation through the Great Depression and all but the final months of World War II. Roosevelt pushed hard for the commitment of U.S. aid to Great Britain after France was defeated (1940). His paramount wartime achievement was

Pres. Franklin D. Roosevelt relied heavily on the radio to reassure Americans during the Depression of the 1930s and to inform them during World War II. (U.S. Office of War Information)

his effort to keep the Allies united in purpose. His insistence upon "unconditional surrender" by the Axis powers and his numerous wartime conferences with other Allied leaders were instrumental in shaping the postwar world. At the Yalta Conference in February 1945, the Allies secretly agreed to Soviet demands for regional hegemony, which led to the Cold War era. Shortly after his 1945 inauguration, following reelection for an unprecedented fourth term, and with the United States and its Allies near victory over Germany and Japan, he died.

M. Guy Bishop

ROOSEVELT, JAMES (1907–1991)

U.S. marine officer and presidential aide, Roosevelt was born in New York City, the eldest son of Pres. Franklin D. Roosevelt. Despite a history of heart and ulcer problems, he was a Marine Corps reservist and volunteered for active duty during World War II. In August 1942, he took part in the 2d Raider Battalion's successful raid on Makin Atoll, for which he was awarded the Navy Cross. He assumed command of the 4th Raider Battalion later that year, but illness forced his evacuation to the United States. For the remainder of the war, he served as an intelligence officer on various staffs.

Ralph L. Eckert

ROOSEVELT, THEODORE, JR.
(1887–1944)

U.S. army officer and political figure, Roosevelt was born in Oyster Bay, New York, the son of Pres. Theodore Roosevelt. He graduated from Harvard in 1908 and entered business but left those pursuits to fight in World War I. During the interwar period, he was active in both business and government, including service as assistant secretary of the navy (1921–24), governor of Puerto Rico (1929–32), and governor general of the Philippines (1932–33). In response to World War II, Roosevelt returned to active duty with the 26th Infantry Regiment in April 1941 and fought with the 1st Division in Tunisia and Sicily. As deputy commander of the 4th Division, he was the only general officer in the initial assault at Normandy in June 1944. Roosevelt died of a heart attack on July 12, 1944, while serving as military governor of Cherbourg. With the posthumous award of a Congressional Medal of Honor, Roosevelt won every combat decoration of the U.S. ground forces.

Bibliography: Roosevelt, Eleanor Butler Alexander, *Day Before Yesterday: The Reminiscences of Mrs. Theodore Roosevelt, Jr.* (Doubleday, 1959).

Maj. James Sanders Day

RUSSELL, JOHN HENRY (1872–1947)

U.S. marine officer, Russell was born in Mare Island, California. He graduated from Annapolis in 1892 and joined the Marine Corps two years later. A member of the Naval War College faculty in 1908–10, he later commanded the 3d Marine Regiment and the 1st Provisional Brigade in Haiti. Promoted to brigadier general in 1922, he became the island's chief administrator and directed efforts to improve health conditions and build a unified nation.

Russell departed Haiti with U.S. forces in 1931 and was named assistant commandant of the Marine Corps. At his urging, the name of the marine expeditionary forces was changed to the Fleet Marine Force. Promoted to major general in September 1933, Russell became commandant in early 1934 and continued to enhance the corps' amphibious capabilities. He retired in November 1936.

Bibliography: Millett, Allan R., *Semper Fidelis: The History of the United States Marine Corps* (Macmillan, 1980).

Daniel T. Bailey

SCOTT, NORMAN (1889–1942)

U.S. naval officer, Scott was born in Indianapolis. He graduated from Annapolis in 1911. During World War I, he had duty in the office of the chief of naval operations and as naval aide to Pres. Woodrow Wilson and also served at sea, primarily in destroyers. His first major command was the cruiser *Pensacola* (1939–42). Promoted to rear admiral in 1942, Scott then commanded various World War II cruiser-destroyer task forces, besting the Japanese at Cape Esperance (October 11–12). A month later, Scott, his flag in the cruiser *Atlanta,* escorted three freighters with supplies for Guadalcanal. Scott then joined a larger U.S. task force, commanded by Rear Adm. Daniel T. Callaghan, to oppose a Japanese force that included two battleships. Fighting began just before 2:00 A.M on November 12, Scott and his staff soon dying from enemy gunfire in what became known as the naval Battle of Guadalcanal.

Bibliography: Reynolds, Clark G., *Famous American Admirals* (Van Nostrand-Reinhold, 1978).

Lloyd J. Graybar

SHEPHERD, LEMUEL CORNICK, JR. (1896–1990)

U.S. marine officer, Shepherd was born in Norfolk, Virginia. He graduated from Virginia Military Institute in 1917 and served in France during World War I. As a member of the 5th Marine Regiment, he fought in battles at Aisne-Marne, St.-Mihiel, and Meuse-Argonne, receiving promotion to captain by 1918.

Over the next two decades, Shepherd interspersed routine assignments in the United States with duty in China in 1927–29 and Haiti from 1930 until 1934. By the beginning of World War II, he held the rank of colonel and was a graduate of the Naval War College.

During World War II, Shepherd served in the Pacific theater, eventually being promoted to brigadier general and appointed assistant commander of the 1st Marine Division, seeing action at Cape Gloucester, New Britain, in December 1943. Assuming command of the 1st Provisional Marine Brigade in April 1944, he participated in the invasion at Guam in July 1944. In September 1944, Shepherd was promoted to major general and given command of 6th Marine Division. In April 1945, the 6th Marines participated in the campaign at Okinawa.

During the Korean War, he served under Gen. Douglas MacArthur and participated in the amphibious operations at Inchon. In January 1952, Shepherd rose to the rank of general and was named commandant, serving in that post until his retirement in 1956.

Vernon L. Williams

SHERMAN, FORREST PERCIVAL (1896–1951)

U.S. navy officer, Sherman was born in Merrimack, New Hampshire. He graduated from Annapolis in 1917. During World War II, he commanded the aircraft carrier *Wasp* when it was torpedoed in the Solomon Islands in September 1942. A naval aviator by training, Sherman became chief of staff to the Pacific Fleet's air force commander, Vice Adm. John H. Towers. Promoted to rear admiral in 1943, Sherman was named deputy chief of staff under Pacific Fleet commander Adm. Chester W. Nimitz. Sherman was instrumental in planning the February 1944 air strike on Truk, the ensuing Marianas Campaign, the February 1945 landing on Iwo Jima, and that spring's assault on Okinawa. Vice Admiral Sherman, as postwar deputy chief of naval operations (1945–48) co-authored (with air force general Lauris Norstad and Pres. Harry S Truman's legal adviser, Clark Clifford) the 1947 compromise merger of the three services that avoided the much-feared diminution of the navy's importance. Sherman was subsequently promoted to full admiral and served as chief of naval operations from 1949 until his death.

Bibliography: Clifford, Clark, *Counsel to the President* (Random House, 1992).

Peter Model

SHORT, WALTER CAMPBELL (1880–1949)

U.S. army officer, Short was born in Fillmore, Illinois. He was commissioned a second lieutenant in 1902 and became an expert on the machine gun. His World War I service was largely in training positions in France. After duties as an intelligence officer specializing in the Far East during the early 1920s, Short was given a number of infantry commands, rising to major general by 1940.

In February 1941, he took command of the Hawaiian Department. Eleven months later, when the Japanese made their surprise attack on Pearl Harbor, Oahu, Lieutenant General Short found himself at the center of an enduring controversy over the state of the island's defenses. Consequently, he was reduced in rank to major general, persuaded to retire, and never given a chance to defend himself.

Col. (Ret.) Rod Paschall

SHOUP, DAVID MONROE (1904–1983)

U.S. marine officer, Shoup was born in Battle Ground, Indiana. He was commissioned a 2d lieutenant in the Marine Corps in 1926. He went to China (1934–36) with the 4th Marines at Shanghai and then in Peking. During World War II, having been promoted through the ranks to colonel, he directed the initial waves of U.S. Marines as they battled against withering enemy fire at Betio, Tarawa Atoll (Nov. 20–23, 1943), action for which he won the Congressional Medal of Honor (1945). Despite heavy Japanese opposition and painful shrapnel wounds in his legs, Shoup calmly maintained control from his beach command post and slowly expanded a slim beachhead until reinforcements poured in. After Tarawa, Shoup served as chief of staff for the 2d Marine Division during its tough Marianas Campaign in 1944. He returned to the United States in late 1944, where he served as logistics officer at corps headquarters until 1947. Promoted to brigadier general (1955) and major general (1958), he served in various assignments before becoming Commandant of the Marine Corps (1960–64).

Bibliography: Murphy, Edward F., *Heroes of World War II* (Presidio, 1990); Russ, Martin, *Line of Departure: Tarawa* (Doubleday, 1975); Sherrod, Robert, *Tarawa* (Bantam Books, 1983).

John F. Wukovits

SIMPSON, WILLIAM HOOD (1888–1980)

U.S. army officer, Simpson was born in Wetherford, Texas. He graduated from West Point in 1909, served in the Punitive Expedition of 1916, and distinguished himself during the Meuse-Argonne campaign in World War I. He was a member of the War Department General Staff (1928–32) and, having risen through the ranks, became a major general in 1941. During World War II, he held several training commands (1942–44) and in May 1944 traveled to England to organize the U.S. 9th Army, which became operational in France in September 1944 as part of Gen. Omar Bradley's 12th Army Group. Because of his army's proximity to Field Marshal Bernard Montgomery's 21st Army Group, Simpson found his command shuffled between the two army groups. The 9th Army fought well on the Roer River in December 1944, took part in Montgomery's Rhine River crossing in February 1945, and would have taken Berlin had Simpson not been ordered to let Soviet forces enter the city first. After serving as

president of the War Department Reorganization Board (1945–46), Simpson retired as a lieutenant general.

Mark Pitcavage

SMITH, HOLLAND MCTYEIRE
(1882–1967)

U.S. marine officer, Smith was born in Hatchechubbee, Alabama. After graduating from the University of Alabama Law School in 1903, he sought a commission in the U.S. Army. When no position was made available, he joined the Marine Corps and was commissioned as a second lieutenant in 1905. By 1916, on the eve of World War II, the young officer had served two tours in the Philippines, another aboard a cruiser in the Far East, as well as one period of duty in Nicaragua and one in Santo Domingo.

During World War I, Smith served in France, mostly in staff positions. He was a student at the Army Staff College in Langres and performed staff duties with the Marine Brigade of the 2d Army Division. Later, he was dispatched to become a staff officer with I Corps during the St.-Mihiel and Meuse-Argonne campaigns.

Staff, school, and training assignments continued after Armistice Day and well into World War II. In 1920–21, Smith became a student at the Navy War College. He then filled a staff position on the Army-Navy Planning Committee, a group concerned with war plans. He completed the Marine Corps' field officers' course and was appointed to the staff of the Corps' commandant, becoming the director of operations and training. By 1939, Smith rose to become assistant commandant. Pleasing his superiors in desk jobs, Smith was elevated to brigadier general and was appointed commander of the 1st Marine Brigade at Quantico, Virginia. While in this position, he acquired the nickname "Howlin' Mad," because of his treatment of subordinates. During the first year and a half of World War II, Smith was relegated to Caribbean amphibious training tasks for both marine and army troop units.

Smith's opportunity to fight the Japanese did not come until late 1943 as the commander of the V Amphibious Corps, a major unit of Adm. Chester Nimitz's Central Pacific theater of operations. Smith's initial moves were made against the Makin and Tarawa atolls in the Gilbert Islands. At Tarawa, Smith rightfully argued with his navy superiors for additional amphibious tractors, critical equipment in the bloody landing, one that came within a hair's breadth of failing. In 1944, on the island of Saipan, Smith became embroiled in a bitter and rancorous argument with a subordinate National Guard division commander, a dispute that resulted in the guard officer's relief from command. Most authorities on the Saipan landing side with Smith in the matter; however, when the argument was over, Smith was regarded by many as an unimaginative, argumentative advocate of straight-ahead, bloody pushes into the teeth of Japanese defenses. Later, at Tinian, Smith managed a textbook amphibious operation.

His next defense of his own conduct came with the costly marine invasion of the island of Iwo Jima. By this time, in early 1945, Smith was a lieutenant general in command of the newly formed Fleet Marine Force, Pacific. The assault involved three marine divisions and a stout, well-concealed, and well-dug-in Japanese defense. When U.S. casualties began to mount to unprecedented levels, Smith and other marines continued to argue that their previous recommendations had been ignored by navy officers: Smith charged that the preparatory naval gunfire should have lasted for 10 days instead of the 3 days of firing that preceded the landing.

In July 1945, Smith returned to the United States and was appointed to head the Marine Corps Training and Replacement Command at San Diego, California. Retiring in August 1946 as a full general, he prepared his war memoir, *Coral and Brass* (1948). A book of self-vindication, it is replete with inflammatory criticisms of others. History undoubtedly would have remembered Smith more favorably had he allowed his record to speak for itself.

Indeed, Smith made a solid contribution to the U.S. war effort during World War II by his training duties alone. During 1939 and 1940, Smith took a direct hand in testing and developing Marine Corps amphibious equipment. In his command decisions in the Central Pacific (as opposed to the Southwest Pacific, where there was far more landmass and thus far more opportunity to avoid well-defended Japanese positions), few islands could be bypassed, and thus the Japanese were often well-prepared to resist an American invasion. Additionally, the Central Pacific islands were small enough that there was little doubt about where the favorable landing beach was located and little chance to envelop the defenders. However steeped in controversy, Smith had much to argue in his favor.

Bibliography: Heinl, Robert D., Jr., *Soldiers of the Sea: The United States Marine Corps, 1775–1962* (Naval Inst. Press, 1962); Isley, Jeter A., and Philip A. Crowl, *The U.S. Marines and Amphibious War* (Princeton Univ. Press, 1951); Millett, Allan R., *Semper Fidelis: The History of the United States Marine Corps* (Macmillan, 1980).

Col. (Ret.) Rod Paschall

SMITH, WALTER BEDELL (1895–1961)

U.S. army officer, Smith was born in Indianapolis. He enlisted in the National Guard at age 16. In November 1917, he received an army commission and subsequently served in France with the 4th Division. Between the wars, Smith served in the United States and the Philippine Islands and graduated from both the Command and General Staff School (1935) and the Army War College (1937).

Colonel Smith was appointed secretary of the War Department General Staff in September 1941 and later served as U.S. secretary of the Combined Chiefs of Staff in Washington. In September 1942, he was named chief of staff to Gen. Dwight D. Eisenhower. Known as an able administrator and strict disciplinarian, Smith remained Eisenhower's principal assistant throughout World War II, planning and coordinating the great Allied offensive in Europe. As chief of staff, Supreme Headquarters Allied Expeditionary Force, he signed the surrender of Italy and the unconditional surrender of Germany on Eisenhower's behalf.

In February 1946, Lieutenant General Smith was appointed by Pres. Harry S Truman as the U.S. ambassador to the Soviet Union. He returned to the United States in March 1949 to command the 1st Army in New York. From September 1950 to February 1953, he was director of the Central Intelligence Agency. In July 1951, Smith was promoted to general, and in February 1953, President Eisenhower appointed him undersecretary of state. In 1954, he headed the U.S. delegation at the Geneva Conference on Indochina. General Smith retired from government service in October 1954 and subsequently held several positions in private business.

Bibliography: Eisenhower, Dwight D., *Crusade in Europe* (Doubleday, 1948); Obituary, *New York Times* (Aug. 11, 1961); Smith, Walter Bedell, *My Three Years in Moscow* (Lippincott, 1950); Spiller, Roger J., ed., *Dictionary of American Military Biography,* vol. 3 (Greenwood Press, 1984); *Webster's American Military Biographies* (Merriam, 1978); *Who Was Who in American History—The Military* (Marquis' Who's Who, 1975).

Lt. Col. (Ret.) Charles R. Shrader

SOMERVELL, BREHON BURKE
(1892–1955)

U.S. army officer, Somervell was born in Little Rock, Arkansas. He graduated from West Point in 1914 and was commissioned in the Corps of Engineers. He helped build roads in Mexico for Maj. Gen. John J. Pershing during the Punitive Expedition of 1916 and then served in France during World War I. Somervell was assistant G-4 for the Army of Occupation in Germany 1919–21. He graduated from the Army Engineer School in 1921, the Command and General Staff School in 1923, and the Army War College in 1926. Somervell then served as assistant and district engineer of river and harbor districts in New York City (1923–25), Washington, D.C., and Norfolk, Virginia (1926–30), Memphis, Tennessee (1931–33), and Ocala, Florida (1935–36). From 1936 to 1940, he was Works Progress Administration administrator for New York City.

Recalled to War Department duty with the office of the inspector general in 1940, Somervell was soon appointed chief of the Construction Division, Quartermaster Corps. He oversaw the construction of military facilities needed for the rapidly expanding army. A week before Pearl

Harbor, Brigadier General Somervell was appointed assistant chief of staff, Supply Division. When army chief of staff Gen. George C. Marshall reorganized the War Department in March 1942, creating the Army Ground Forces, the Army Air Forces, and the Army Services of Supply (SOS), Somervell, as a lieutenant general, was selected to head the SOS, later designated the Army Service Forces. Somervell was responsible for providing all logistical support to the U.S. Army during World War II.

Steve R. Waddell

SPAATZ, CARL ANDREW (1891–1974)

U.S. army officer and first chief of staff of the U.S. Air Force, Spaatz was born in Boyertown, Pennsylvania. He graduated from West Point in 1914 and went into the infantry.

Early Air Experience. After serving a tour at Schofield Barracks, Hawaii, Spaatz was sent to San Diego to learn to fly at Rockwell Field. In 1916, he served with Maj. Gen. John J. Pershing's Punitive Expedition against Pancho Villa in Mexico. As a member of the 1st Aero Squadron, Spaatz left San Antonio with eight aircraft on March 13,

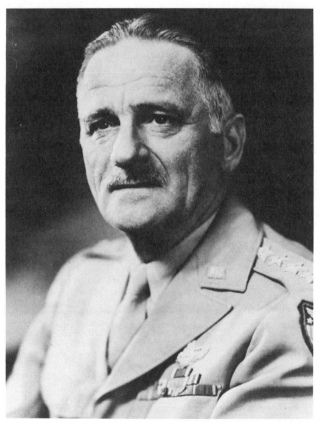

Gen. Carl A. Spaatz, an ardent advocate of air power, directed the bombing of German supply line, oil facility, and transportation targets, which contributed greatly to the success of the Allies in Europe in 1944–45. (U.S. Army Military History Institute)

bound for Columbus, New Mexico. He began flying reconnaissance missions on March 16 and continued until the fall. While the contribution of aviation to this expedition was limited, Spaatz became caught up in the enthusiasm of flying and what it might mean for military operations.

The next year, Spaatz participated in the American Expeditionary Force that went to Europe to fight with the French and British in World War I. Although he was assigned to training duties in the rear echelon, Spaatz took every opportunity to visit the front and on at least one occasion flew on a combat mission with a British Aero unit. He shot down two enemy aircraft during this mission before he ran out of fuel and had to ditch his plane, narrowly avoiding capture while making his way back to Allied lines. These activities earned him both praise and wrath from his superiors; he received a strong reprimand and the Distinguished Service Cross.

Air Power Advocacy. During the 1920s and 1930s, Spaatz was a vocal supporter of the primacy of air power to obliterate the will of the enemy to wage war. A disciple of Brig. Gen. William ''Billy'' Mitchell, whose strident position on this issue resulted in charges of insubordination and cashiering from the army in 1926, Spaatz bluntly and repeatedly told the army that it was wrong in not granting the air arm greater autonomy and increased funding. To prove his point, Spaatz was involved with a cabal of air-minded army officers to win publicity for air power in the latter 1920s. His famous ''Flying Circus'' demonstration team performed aerial stunts for audiences. He was also involved in record-setting flights, notably a January 1929 endurance flight of 151 hours. For his efforts, Spaatz was much disliked by more traditionally minded officers, probably contributing to his long stint, 15 years, with the rank of major.

Spaatz reluctantly attended the army's Command and General Staff College, at Fort Leavenworth, in 1935–36. There, also, he bruised those around him with his air-power advocacy.

World War II. The coming of war in Europe in 1939 brought an opportunity not present previously for airmen such as Spaatz, those the Air Force nostalgically remembered as ''a few great captains,'' to prove their air-power ideas. Spaatz, like his comrades, seized on the opportunity. He went to Great Britain in 1940 to observe the air war. There he was impressed by the ability and flexibility of airplanes to heap destruction on the enemy. It proved, at least to his satisfaction, the air-power theories that had been promulgated during the interwar period.

At the beginning of World War II, Spaatz was a brigadier general. In May 1942, he got an opportunity to carry to fruition his plans for air power by accepting command of the newly created 8th Air Force in England. This bomber force began the systematic destruction of enemy-held territory in Europe in August 1942. Only three months later, having established the form and manner of air operations in Europe, Spaatz became Allied air forces commander under Gen. Dwight D. Eisenhower for Operation Torch, the invasion of North Africa. Spaatz commanded in the Mediterranean theater of operations until early 1944.

He later returned to Great Britain to command the newly established U.S. Strategic Forces in Europe, which would coordinate all air operations for the invasion of the continent. While there, he redirected the bombing of German targets from industrial areas that had been the concentration until that time toward the interdiction of supply lines, logistics bases, and transportation centers. Centering bombing efforts on transportation and oil facilities proved remarkably successful. The lack of supplies and oil products dulled the German counterattack at the Battle of the Bulge (December 1944) and moderated the Germans' use of the new ME-262 jet fighter. In 1945, he was promoted to full general. Spaatz's contention that proper use of air power would have made the D-Day invasion unnecessary, however, was challenged by other officers and remains a major point of debate over the use of strategic air power.

Postwar Experience. Following the war, Spaatz became the first chief of staff (1947) of the newly independent U.S. Air Force, which he had worked so hard to create. After his retirement in 1948, he served in a variety of aeronautics positions, including head of the Civil Air Patrol.

Bibliography: Copp, DeWitt S., *A Few Great Captains: The Men and Events that Shaped the Development of U.S. Air Power* (Doubleday, 1980); Maurer, Maurer, *Aviation in the U.S. Army, 1919–1939* (Office of Air Force History, 1987); Mets, David R., *Master of Air Power: Carl A. Spaatz* (Presidio, 1988); Overy, R. J., *The Air War, 1939–1945* (Stein and Day, 1980).

Roger D. Launius

SPRAGUE, CLIFTON ALBERT FREDERICK (1896–1955)

U.S. naval officer, Sprague was born in Dorchester, Massachusetts. He was in command of the seaplane tender *Tangier* at Pearl Harbor when the Japanese made their attack there on Dec. 7, 1941. After 10 months as chief of staff at the Gulf Sea Frontier based in Miami, Sprague returned in late 1942 to the Pacific, where he commanded the aircraft carrier *Wasp* during its actions in the Wake and Marcus raids, the invasion of Saipan, and the Battle of the Philippine Sea. As commander of Task Unit 77.4.3 (''Taffy 3''), a group of six thin-skinned and lightly-armed escort carriers, he guarded the Leyte beachhead and in a series of bold moves successfully turned back Japanese battleships in the Battle of Samar. He participated in the Iwo Jima and Okinawa assaults before war's end and retired as a vice admiral in 1951.

Bibliography: Morison, Samuel Eliot, *History of United States Naval Operations in World War II; Vol. 12: Leyte* (Little, Brown, 1958); Sprague, C. A. F., and Philip H. Gustafson, ''They Had Us On the Ropes,'' *The United States Navy in World War II,* ed. by S. E. Smith (Morrow, 1966).

John F. Wukovits

SPRUANCE, RAYMOND AMES (1886–1969)

U.S. naval officer, Spruance was born in Baltimore, Maryland. He graduated from Annapolis in 1906 and held a series of posts before being elevated to rear admiral in 1940, earning a reputation for intelligence, logically evaluating situations, and coolness under stress. A commander of Cruiser Division 5, Spruance was at sea with Adm. William F. Halsey's carriers when the Japanese attacked Pearl Harbor in December 1941. Also with Halsey, he participated in the early 1942 raids on Wake Island and the Marshall Islands and in the transporting of Lt. Col. James H. Doolittle's force of bombers close to Japan for its daring Tokyo Raid.

Spruance was given command of Task Force 16 (built around the carriers *Enterprise* and *Hornet*) in place of the ill Halsey when the Japanese approached Midway in June 1942. Rendezvousing at sea with Rear Adm. Frank J. Fletcher's Task Force 17, containing the carrier *Yorktown*, Spruance waited northeast of Midway for the huge enemy armada to approach. He immediately launched all available planes as soon as the Japanese carriers were sighted, in hopes of getting in the initial strike. The planes caught the Japanese in the vulnerable position of switching plane armament and in six minutes turned three carriers into burning wrecks. After his planes sank a fourth enemy carrier, Spruance refrained from a nighttime pursuit of the Japanese, a move that received vigorous criticism from more aggressive officers but one that proved sound, since he thereby avoided steaming straight into a flotilla of potent enemy battleships.

After one year as chief of staff to Adm. Chester W. Nimitz, commander in chief, Pacific Fleet, Spruance took the helm as commander of the 5th Fleet, in August 1943 and guided it during its steady push through the Central Pacific. He opened his drive with the November 1943 assault of the Gilbert Islands, where he helped initiate methods of amphibious assault that were to be employed in future island attacks.

In June 1944, four months after becoming a full admiral, Spruance again faced the Japanese combined fleet when it emerged to counter the American assault in the Marianas. As marines fought on Saipan, Spruance turned his carriers into the Philippine Sea, where on June 19 his planes met and destroyed an astounding 426 Japanese fighters and bombers in what has been called the ''Marianas Turkey

Shoot.'' After submarines sank the carriers *Shokaku* and *Taiho* and planes sank the carrier *Hiyo,* Spruance headed back to protect the vulnerable transports unloading supplies off Saipan. Again, he was criticized by some naval leaders for not chasing the enemy, but Spruance felt it more important to safeguard the Saipan assault force from a sneak attack.

Spruance ended his wartime service by commanding the assaults against Iwo Jima and Okinawa, facing three months of terrifying enemy kamikaze assaults in the latter campaign. He briefly succeeded Nimitz as commander in chief, Pacific Fleet, at war's end, then assumed the post as president of the Naval War College before retiring on July 1, 1948. Four years later, he returned to the Pacific as ambassador to the Philippines.

Bibliography: Buell, Tomas B., *The Quiet Warrior* (Little, Brown, 1974); Forrestel, E. P., *Admiral Raymond A. Spruance, USN: A Study in Command* (Dir. of Naval History, 1966); Potter, E. B., *Bull Halsey* (Naval Inst. Press, 1985); —, *Nimitz* (Naval Inst. Press, 1976).

John F. Wukovits

STANDLEY, WILLIAM HARRISON
(1872–1963)

U.S. naval officer, Standley was born in Ukiah, California. He graduated from Annapolis in 1895. Promoted to captain in 1919 and rear admiral in 1927, he became chief of naval operations in 1933. During his tenure, a modest program of shipbuilding began. He retired at the end of 1936. Recalled to active World War II duty in 1941, Standley held assignments on various boards dealing with production planning, joined the Lend-Lease mission to the Soviet Union in 1941, and then served as ambassador to that nation from February 1942 until his resignation in 1943.

The outspoken Standley disagreed with Pres. Franklin D. Roosevelt's refusal to tie Lend-Lease aid to Soviet cooperation on such matters as furnishing the United States with information on German weapons and tactics. Standley ended his wartime service with an assignment on the Planning Group of the Office of Strategic Services.

Bibliography: Walter, John C., "William Harrison Standley," *The Chiefs of Naval Operations,* ed. by Robert William Love, Jr. (Naval Inst. Press, 1980).

Lloyd J. Graybar

STARK, HAROLD RAYNSFORD
(1880–1972)

U.S. naval officer, Stark was born in Wilkes-Barre, Pennsylvania. He graduated from Annapolis in 1903 and served two years at sea before being commissioned an ensign. In the years before World War I, Stark held sea billets in the Atlantic and Caribbean waters on board the cruiser *Newark,* the *Hartford,* and the gunboat *Newport.* In 1907, Stark

shipped out on the *Minnesota* as the new battleship sailed with the Great White Fleet on its around-the-world cruise in 1907–09.

After the world cruise, Stark spent six years in command of two torpedo boats, then extended his sea service on the destroyers *Lamson* and *Patterson* and the cruiser *Brooklyn*—all concentrated along the Atlantic coastal area.

A brief interlude in the Pacific in 1917 predated his service in World War I as aide to Adm. William S. Sims in London. Following his service with Sims, Stark was attached as chief of staff to Adm. Thomas J. Senn, commander of the Destroyer Squadrons, Battle Fleet.

During the 1920s, Stark served as executive officer on the battleships *North Dakota* and *West Virginia.* He commanded the ammunition ship *Nitro* in 1924–25 and later was appointed aide to Sec. of the Navy Charles F. Adams in 1930–33 and to Sec. of the Navy Claude A. Swanson in 1933. Following his service with the Navy Department, Stark was given the Pacific command of the battleship *West Virginia,* remaining there two years. In 1934, Stark was back in Washington, promoted to rear admiral, and was selected to be chief of the Bureau of Ordnance.

In 1937, he commanded Cruiser Division 3 in the Battle Force and the next year assumed command of all cruiser divisions in the Battle Force. Promoted to the rank of vice admiral, Stark remained with the cruiser command until August 1939, when Pres. Franklin D. Roosevelt named him chief of naval operations (CNO) with the rank of full admiral, passing over 50 more-senior officers. As CNO, Stark oversaw naval preparations for war until the attack on Pearl Harbor destroyed the president's confidence in his leadership. Stark remained as CNO until March 1942, when he was relieved by Adm. Ernest King.

Stark was blamed for the Pearl Harbor disaster by failing to provide Adm. Husband Kimmel with sufficient intelligence on Japanese plans and movements. In 1945, he was reprimanded by a naval court of inquiry, leading to his retirement in 1946. Years later, the findings of the inquiry were moderated, and recent scholarship has taken a more benign approach to Stark's culpability for Pearl Harbor.

Bibliography: Morison, Samuel Eliot, *History of United States Naval Operations in World War II* (Little, Brown, 1962); Reynolds, Clark G., *Famous American Admirals* (Van Nostrand-Reinhold, 1978).

Vernon L. Williams

STILWELL, JOSEPH WARREN
(1883–1946)

U.S. army officer, Stilwell was born in Palatka, Florida, and raised in Yonkers, New York. Controversial, outspoken, and acerbic "Vinegar Joe" Stilwell ranks as one of World War II's great tacticians and brilliant strategists, although a poor politician: his celebrated feud with China's

Gen. Joseph W. Stilwell, well-versed on China and the Chinese language, served as chief of staff to Gen. Chiang Kai-shek (1942–44) and, at the same time, commanded the U.S. troops in China, Burma, and India. (U.S. Army Military History Institute)

Chiang Kai-shek cost him his command of the China-Burma-India (CBI) theater in 1944, when Chiang, supported by Pres. Franklin D. Roosevelt's special envoy, Maj. Gen. Patrick Hurley, demanded Stilwell's recall.

A 1904 graduate of West Point, Stilwell had early developed a lifelong attraction for the Orient. Upon graduation, he requested duty in the Philippines and was posted to the 12th Infantry Regiment on Samar Island fighting the rebel Puljanes. In early 1906, he was reassigned to West Point as a foreign language instructor; he spent the next five years at the academy, also teaching history and tactics and coaching athletics. In January 1911, he got back to the Philippines for three years, then returned to West Point for another three years. In World War I, he was assigned to the 80th Division and then became a staff intelligence officer detached to the French XVII Corps near Verdun, France. He saw battle as an intelligence officer with the U.S. IV Corps in the Meuse-Argonne Campaign and, promoted temporarily to lieutenant colonel, served briefly on occupation duty in Germany until he obtained an assignment to China.

Stilwell spent the years 1920–23 supervising road construction in Shansi (Shanxi) Province, where he befriended the Christian warlord Feng Yu-hsiang. Sent back to the United States for advanced training at the Infantry School at Fort Benning and at the Command and General Staff School, Stilwell then returned to China (1926–29) as battalion commander of the 15th Infantry at Tientsin. His executive officer was George C. Marshall, and they became good friends. Himself promoted to lieutenant colonel in 1928, Stilwell—at the instigation of Marshall, now the Infantry School's assistant commandant—soon found himself back at Fort Benning as head of the school's tactical section. In 1935, now a full colonel, Stilwell returned to China as military attaché in Peking and was able to observe firsthand the Sino-Japanese War. Given command of the 3d Brigade, 2d Division, Stilwell took part in the 3d Army's maneuvers (1940), where he quickly won a reputation for swift and surprising maneuvers that led to his getting command of the newly formed 7th Division at Fort Ord, California, followed by command of the III Corps. As a lieutenant general, Stilwell was next given command of the CBI in January 1942. Also serving as Chiang's chief of staff, he had command over the Chinese. In 1942, Stilwell led the badly mauled Chinese forces out of Burma into India. He spent the next two years rebuilding them on the American model and returned to liberate northern Burma from the Japanese. In 1943, he was made deputy supreme allied commander for CBI, reporting to Adm. Lord Louis Mountbatten. In 1944, he was promoted to full general.

Early on, Stilwell had incurred the enmity of Chiang, who preferred to use air power to crush the Japanese, having little or no faith in his ground troops. Stilwell disdained Chiang's victory through air-power strategy, which he correctly assumed was the work of the Flying Tigers' Maj. Gen. Claire L. Chennault, Chiang's air adviser. Stilwell further despised the Chiang faction personally. In his notebooks, Stilwell described Chiang and his retinue as "a gang of fascists under a one party government similar in many respects to our German enemies . . . sympathy here for the Nazi . . . same type of government, same outlook, same gangsterism."

The lack of supplies and a stream of conflicting orders from Chiang frustrated Stilwell. He no longer tried to hide his contempt for the leader he called "the peanut." With the Grand Alliance at issue, President Roosevelt could not risk alienating the Chinese. Stilwell was reassigned to Okinawa, taking up command of the 10th Army after the battlefield death of Gen. Simon Bolivar Buckner. At war's end, after witnessing the surrender ceremonies in Tokyo Bay, Stilwell returned to the United States to take command of the 6th Army and the Western Defense Command.

Bibliography: Rodzinski, Witold, *The Walled Kingdom* (Free Press, 1984); White, Theodore H., and Jacoby, Annalee, *Thunder Out of China* (Sloane, 1946).

Peter Model

STIMSON, HENRY LEWIS (1867–1950)

U.S. statesman and secretary of war, Stimson was born in New York City. He graduated from Yale University (1888) and Harvard Law School (1890) and served in high government positions from the administration of Theodore Roosevelt through that of Harry S Truman. Pres. William Howard Taft first appointed Stimson secretary of war (1911–13); Pres. Herbert Hoover named him secretary of state (1929–33); and, on the eve of World War II, Pres. Franklin D. Roosevelt reappointed Stimson secretary of war (1940–45).

Stimson served the Hoover administration as chairman of both the U.S. delegation to the London Naval Conference (1930) and the Geneva Disarmament Conference (1932). As secretary of state at the beginning of the Great Depression, Stimson hoped to maintain American power without resorting to military might. In this regard, he formulated and announced the "Stimson Doctrine" (1931), calling for nonrecognition of territories gained through aggression.

Stimson viewed the 1931 Japanese invasion of Manchuria as a lawless act. Under the dictates of the Stimson Doctrine, the United States refused to recognize that any territorial change had taken place by the conquest. But, lacking international support, the doctrine remained ineffective against Japanese expansionism.

It was as F. D. Roosevelt's secretary of war that Stimson had his greatest impact on American life. During the pre-Pearl Harbor days of World War II, he worked to secure congressional approval for conscription, to promote war industries, and to reorganize the War Department. His efforts greatly aided U.S. preparation when war eventually came.

Placing a high value on technological innovation, Stimson encouraged the development of radar and later played a central role in the administration of the Manhattan Project, which developed the atomic bomb. Following Roosevelt's death in April 1945, Stimson was the person who informed President Truman of the existence of the weapon. Stimson continued to serve in Truman's cabinet through September 1945. He was the first American to serve in four presidential cabinets.

A committed internationalist, Stimson favored sharing atomic technology with other nations, including the Soviet Union. He envisioned a stable, U.S.-dominated postwar world order. Stimson was the author of *American Policy in Nicaragua* (1927) and *On Active Service in Peace and War* (with McGeorge Bundy, 1948).

Bibliography: Current, Richard, *Secretary Stimson: A Study in Statecraft* (1954; reprint, Shoe String Press, 1970); Hodgson, Godfrey, *The Colonel: The Life and Wars of Henry Stimson, 1867–1950* (Knopf, 1990).

M. Guy Bishop

STRATEMEYER, GEORGE EDWARD (1890–1969)

U.S. army air commander, Stratemeyer was born in Cincinnati, Ohio. He graduated from West Point in 1915, was commissioned in the infantry, and transferred to the Air Corps in July 1920. He was promoted to the rank of major in 1925 and to that of lieutenant colonel in 1937. During World War II, Stratemeyer served as chief of staff, Army Air Forces (1942–43); commander, Army Air Forces, China-Burma-India theater (1943); air commander, Eastern Air Command (1943–45); and commander, Army Air Forces, China theater (1945–46). In the postwar period, having been promoted to colonel (1944) and brigadier general (1946), he commanded both the Air Defense (1946–48) and the Continental Air commands (1948–49). He was promoted to major general in 1947. While commanding the Far East Air Force (1949–51) in Korea, he advocated air-to-ground liaison teams and the use of jet aircraft as tactical bombers. Poor health forced his retirement in 1952.

Maj. James Sanders Day

SULTAN, DANIEL ISOM (1885–1948)

U.S. army officer, Sultan was born in Oxford, Mississippi. He graduated from West Point in 1907 and early in his career helped design and construct the fortifications at Corregidor, the deeply-tunneled island bastion in Manila Bay that would be overrun by the Japanese in 1942. After brief occupation service in Germany after World War I, Sultan became a junior officer on the General Staff in Washington. Between the world wars, he alternated between high-profile engineering posts and field commands (Nicaragua 1929–31, Hawaiian Islands 1939–41). Promoted to major general before the Japanese attack on Pearl Harbor, Sultan commanded the 38th (National Guard) Division in Mississippi and then VII Corps in the Pacific until joining Gen. Joseph Stilwell in 1943.

Sultan was deputy commander of the China-Burma-India (CBI) theater under the controversial Stilwell when, in September 1944, Stilwell was recalled by Pres. Franklin D. Roosevelt at the insistence of embattled Kuomintang Nationalist Generalissimo Chiang Kai-shek and seconded by Roosevelt's special envoy, Maj. Gen. Patrick W. Hurley, sent to mediate between Stilwell and Chiang. Sultan's primary area of responsibility was ensuring the viability of the supply routes (the Ledo and Burma roads) and the implementation of the Hump Airlift over the Himalayas to Kunming. After Stilwell's recall, the unwieldy CBI theater was split into two commands: Lieutenant General Sultan received Stilwell's turf in Burma and India and the command of two Chinese armies and a British division, and Gen. Albert C. Wedemeyer, more politically in tune with Chiang, was given command in China. After Japan's surrender (September 1945), General Sultan was given an unprecedented fourth Distinguished Service Medal and was named inspector general of the army.

Peter Model

SUMMERALL, CHARLES PELOT
(1867–1955)

U.S. army officer, Summerall was born in Blount's Ferry, Florida. He graduated from West Point in 1892 and served as a major general in France during World War I. Following the war, he reverted to the rank of brigadier general but subsequently climbed the ladder to full general (1929). Having served as commander of the Hawaiian Department and as a judge during the 1925 court-martial of Brig. Gen. William "Billy" Mitchell, Summerall became chief of staff of the army in 1926. After his retirement in 1930, he became president of The Citadel, a military college in South Carolina. While there (1931–53), he made a highly effective effort to increase both the facilities and the student body.

Summerall's performance as chief of staff was not noted for innovation or modernization. Although he saw the army budget rise by 30 percent during his tenure, he resisted the expansion of the air arm and agreed to experiment with mechanization only after considerable pressure. He even opposed the recombination of the field and coast artilleries. Summerall's chief contribution was in integrating artillery and infantry operations, and he was a master at these vitally important techniques during World War I. Chiefly, his postwar record was one of traditional, perhaps even reactionary causes. However, a sound case can be made for his success in strengthening the fundamental branches and institutions of the army during a difficult period of monetary restraint.

Bibliography: Pratt, Fletcher, *Eleven Generals: Studies in American Command* (William Sloan, Associates, 1949).

Col. (Ret.) Rod Paschall

SWANSON, CLAUDE AUGUSTUS
(1862–1939)

U.S. politician and secretary of the navy (1933–39), Swanson was born in Swansonville, Virginia. He attended Randolph-Macon College and the University of Virginia before establishing a law practice in Chatham, Virginia. A Democrat, he served in the U.S. House of Representatives (1893–1906), as governor of Virginia (1906–10), and in the U.S. Senate (1910–33). In 1933, he was appointed secretary of the navy by Pres. Franklin D. Roosevelt and during his tenure oversaw the expansion of the U.S. Navy,

ordering construction of battleships, destroyers, cruisers, aircraft carriers, aircraft, and submarines; an increase in personnel; and an increase in naval reserve forces. If there was a weakness in his department, it involved the revision of war plans, which was usurped by President Roosevelt, and the outfitting of the Marine Corps with the necessary manpower and equipment needed to carry out advanced base force plans during readiness exercises.

Leo J. Daugherty III

SWIFT, INNIS PALMER (1882–1953)

U.S. army officer, Swift was born in Wyoming. He graduated from West Point in 1904 and was commissioned a second lieutenant in the cavalry. He saw combat in the Philippines during the Moro campaign (1910–12) and was aide-de-camp to Brig. Gen. John J. Pershing. He had considerable cavalry experience in Texas and was an instructor at Fort Riley. He participated in the Punitive Expedition (1916) into Mexico. He changed branches to the infantry and sailed in 1918 for France, where he had staff duty with the American Expeditionary Force during World War I. Reverting back to the cavalry, he commanded several units between the wars. By 1939, he had been promoted through the ranks to brigadier general. When the United States entered World War II in 1941, he was promoted to major general. During World War II, he was commanding general of the 1st Cavalry Division (1941–44) and led the division in combat in the Pacific in New Guinea and other island operations and was commander of the task force that recaptured the Admiralty Islands in 1944. He ended the war as commander (1944–45) of the Army I Corps in the Pacific and retired in February 1946.

Robert H. Berlin

SWING, JOSEPH MAY (1894–1984)

U.S. army aviation officer, Swing was born in Jersey City, New Jersey. He graduated from West Point in 1915, was commissioned in the artillery, and participated in the Punitive Expedition (1916) along the Mexican border soon after graduation. During World War I, he served as aide-de-camp to Gen. Peyton C. March. In World War II, as a brigadier general, Swing served in the North African, Italian, and Pacific theaters. He commanded the division artillery of the 82d Airborne Division, the Airborne Command, and, as a major general from 1943, the 11th Airborne Division. With the 11th, he saw extensive combat in the Philippines. On Tokyo's surrender, Swing flew into a still well-armed Japan, leading his lightly equipped paratroopers there to assume occupation duties. Prior to his 1954 retirement in California, he commanded the Artillery Center and the Artillery School at Fort Sill, Oklahoma (1949–50), the Army War College at Fort Leavenworth, Kansas (1950), and the 6th Army at San Francisco (1950–54). He rose to the rank of lieutenant general by

1950. In civilian life, he was commissioner of the U.S. Commission of Immigration and Naturalization (1954–62).

Col. (Ret.) Rod Paschall

TAYLOR, MAXWELL DAVENPORT (1901–1987)

U.S. army officer and administrator, Taylor graduated from West Point fourth in the class of 1922. At the outbreak of World War II, he was serving in the War Plans Division of the War Department. In 1942, as a brigadier general, he took command of the 82d Airborne Division Artillery and in 1944 was promoted to major general and appointed commander of the 101st Airborne Division. He led the division through numerous combat operations in France (including the airborne assault on Normandy on D-Day), the Netherlands, and Germany, receiving several awards for valor.

After the war, Taylor became superintendent (1945–49) of the U.S. Military Academy and, finally, army chief of staff (1955–59). He retired as a full general in 1959 but was recalled by Pres. John F. Kennedy in 1961, subsequently becoming chairman of the Joint Chiefs of Staff (1962–64). After retirement, Taylor served as U.S. ambassador to South Vietnam (1964–65).

Gen. Maxwell D. Taylor led the 101st Airborne Division during the airborne assault on Normandy on D-Day in 1945. (U.S. Army Military History Institute).

Bibliography: Weigley, Russell F., *Eisenhower's Lieutenants* (Indiana Univ. Press, 1981).

Brig. Gen. (PNG, Ret.) Uzal W. Ent

TIBBETS, PAUL WARFIELD (1915–   )

U.S. army officer and the pilot who dropped the first atomic bomb on Hiroshima, Japan, Tibbets was born in Quincy, Illinois. He graduated from Western Military Academy (Illinois) in 1933, attended both the University of Florida and University of Cleveland, and entered the Army Air Corps in February 1937. During the early part of World War II, he flew antisubmarine patrol and later commanded the 340 Bombardment Squadron in England, flying 25 B-17 combat missions.

In September 1944, after a stint as a test pilot for the B-29, Tibbets began work on the Manhattan Project, charged with responsibility for creating the bomb unit and teaching the skills necessary to deliver the atomic device on a target. He moved the 509th Composite Group, of which he was commander, to desolate Wendover Field in the west Utah desert for training. In 1945, this outfit became operationally ready and moved to Tinian Island in the Pacific. From there, flying his B-29, the *Enola Gay,* Tibbets dropped the first nuclear device on Hiroshima (August 6). Three days later, his bombers flew an atomic mission against Nagasaki. After the war, Tibbets remained in the air force and retired as a brigadier general in 1960.

Bibliography: Jones, Vincent C., *Manhattan: The Army and the Atomic Bomb* (Center of Military History, U.S. Army, 1985); Rhodes, Richard C., *The Making of the Atomic Bomb* (Knopf, 1985).

Roger D. Launius

TRUMAN, HARRY S (1884–1972)

Thirty-third president of the United States (1945–53), Truman was born in Lamar, Missouri. Just one month after becoming Pres. Franklin D. Roosevelt's fourth-term vice president, Truman succeeded to the presidency upon Roosevelt's death (Apr. 12, 1945). In World War II, his most dramatic decision was approving the use of the atomic bomb against Japan in August 1945. Earlier in the summer Truman met with other Allied leaders at the Potsdam Conference, which called for the unconditional surrender of Japan and dealt with European problems in the aftermath of Germany's surrender.

Remembered for his congeniality and outspoken bluntness, Truman hoped to maintain Roosevelt's diverse political coalition. His aggressively liberal domestic program (the Fair Deal) helped him retain the presidency in 1948. Truman's foreign policy was internationalist; he saw the United States as a world leader obligated to spread democracy and capitalism. This stance placed Truman's administration in direct conflict with postwar Soviet expansionism. His Truman Doctrine, Marshall Plan, and North Atlantic

Pres. Harry S Truman, who took office in April 1945 following the death of President Roosevelt, had to make the agonizing decision to use the atomic bomb against Japan at Hiroshima and Nagasaki. (Courtesy Harry S Truman Library)

Treaty Organization (NATO) were designed to block Soviet incursions into Western Europe. While these European programs proved highly successful, Truman's Asian policy led to U.S. involvement in the Korean War (1950–53).

Bibliography: McCullough, David, *Truman* (Simon & Schuster, 1992).

M. Guy Bishop

TRUSCOTT, LUCIAN KING, JR.
(1895–1965)

U.S. army officer, Truscott was born in Chatfield, Texas. He enlisted in the army in 1917 and was commissioned a cavalry second lieutenant in the Officer Reserve Corps. He served with the cavalry in Arizona, Hawaii, and Texas before attending cavalry schools at Fort Riley, Kansas, where he also served as an instructor. After commanding a cavalry troop at Fort Myer, Virginia, Truscott graduated from the Command and General Staff School at Fort Leavenworth in 1936 and was an instructor there for four years.

Owing in part to his polo-playing skill, Truscott was selected to serve with the Allied Combined Operations Headquarters in London under Adm. Lord Louis Mountbat-

ten during World War II. Truscott's work with British commandos led to the formation of American ranger units. As a brigadier general in 1942, he participated in the failed Dieppe cross-channel raid. He was Gen. Dwight D. Eisenhower's deputy in North Africa's Tunisian campaign. In March 1943, Truscott took command of the 3d Infantry Division and led the division in successful operations in Sicily.

The 3d Division landed on the Italian mainland at Salerno, Italy, in September 1943 and also made an amphibious landing at Anzio. When the campaign stalled at Anzio, the VI Corps commander was relieved and Truscott replaced him. Truscott led VI Corps in the liberation of Rome and then in the landings in southern France in August 1944. He was promoted to lieutenant general in 1944 and given command of the 5th Army in Italy in 1945.

In October 1945, he replaced Gen. George Patton as commander of the 3d Army and military governor of Bavaria. He retired in 1947. In 1954, Truscott was promoted to general by act of Congress. His memoirs, *Command Missions* (1954), are considered to be the best World War II personal account by a general officer.

Bibliography: Truscott, Lucian K., Jr., *Command Missions,* ed. by Richard H. Kohn (1954; reprint, Ayer Co. Pub., 1979).

Robert H. Berlin

TUCKER, REUBEN HENRY III (1911–70)

U.S. army aviation officer, Tucker was born in Ansonia, Connecticut. He graduated from West Point in 1935 and became one of the first infantry officers to join the newly formed 82d Airborne Division in 1942. Tucker impressed the division commander, Maj. Gen. Matthew B. Ridgway, that he was promoted to colonel in 1943 and quickly advanced to the command of the 504th Parachute Infantry Regiment (1943–45), nicknamed the ''Devils in Baggy Pants'' by the Germans at Anzio. Colonel Tucker ably led the 504th during many of the bitterest battles of the war: Sicily, Salerno, the Volturno River, Venafro, Anzio, Nijmegen, and the Ardennes (Battle of the Bulge).

After the war, he was chief of the Army Field Forces (1951–52) and chaired the Military Assistance Advisory Group in Laos (1962–63). He retired as a major general in 1963.

Carlo W. D'Este

TURNER, RICHMOND KELLY
(1885–1961)

U.S. naval officer, Turner was born in Portland, Oregon. He graduated from Annapolis in 1908. Trained as a surface officer, he gained his pilot's wings in 1927 and spent more than a decade in naval aviation before requesting a return to the surface fleet. After commanding cruiser *Astoria*

(1938–40), he became director of war plans in the Office of Naval Operations until early 1942. For several months thereafter, he remained in Washington as an assistant chief of staff to Adm. Ernest J. King, commander in chief, U.S. combined fleet.

In June, Turner, by this time a rear admiral, was ordered to the Pacific to command the first major U.S. amphibious operation of World War II—the landings on Tulagi and Guadalcanal in the Solomon Islands. Tulagi was quickly secured, but the fighting on Guadalcanal settled down into a battle of attrition in which Turner organized several resupply efforts. On several occasions, Turner accompanied the transports in his flagship *McCawley*.

Turner commanded the landings on New Georgia in June 1943 before being transferred to the Central Pacific to direct the amphibious assault force under Vice Adm. Raymond Spruance's 5th Fleet. In one operation after another, Turner's V Amphibious Force operated successfully—at Makin and Tarawa in November 1943; at Kwajalein, Saipan, Guam, and Tinian in 1944; and finally, in 1945, at Iwo Jima and Okinawa.

Like most American admirals of his generation, Turner knew virtually nothing of amphibious operations at the war's outset, but his thoroughness and his willingness to do the utmost to get the troops to the beachheads and then to supply them once they were ashore made him a masterful leader. During the New Georgia operation, his own flagship was sunk by enemy bombing, but Turner never hesitated to provide the maximum support for the troops going ashore.

Yet, he also had liabilities and has been criticized for not allowing subordinates sufficient leeway to exercise their own judgments, berating them loudly when they failed to comply to the letter with his own lavishly detailed operations orders. In particular, he often forgot that the responsibilities of amphibious command ended at the shoreline. From Guadalcanal on, however, the generals, marine and army both, found Turner trying to tell them what to do, not only where they should go ashore but the strategy and even the tactics they should follow once they and their men were ashore. Recriminations were frequent, but Spruance's chief of staff negotiated a compromise: once the commanding general of an operation had established his command post ashore, Turner would keep his tactical opinions to himself.

The operations Turner headed grew ever larger and more complex. At Guadalcanal, he commanded only a few dozen ships; at Okinawa, he had more than 10 times as many. By this time, his forces included battleships, cruisers, destroyers, and escort carriers, as well as a large and varied array of transports and specialized landing craft. His promotions to vice admiral in 1944 and to admiral in 1945 recognized both his mastery of amphibious warfare and his ever-increasing responsibilities. He retired in 1947 after

serving at the United Nations as the U.S. naval representative on the military staff committee from 1945.

Bibliography: Dyer, George C., *The Amphibians Came to Conquer,* 2 vols. (U.S. Govt. Printing Office, 1972); Potter, E. B., *Admiral Arleigh Burke: A Biography* (Random House, 1990); Spector, Ronald, *Eagle Against the Sun: the American War with Japan* (Free Press, 1984); Wheeler, Richard, *A Special Valor: The U.S. Marines and the Pacific War* (Harper & Row, 1983).

Lloyd J. Graybar

TWINING, NATHAN FARRAGUT
(1897–1982)

U.S. army and air force officer, Twining was born in Monroe, Wisconsin. He graduated from West Point in November 1918. His early service included occupation duty in Germany after World War I and flight training in Texas. By 1926, he was assigned permanently to the air arm of the army. During the years preceding World War II, Twining served with the 18th Pursuit Force in Hawaii (1930–32) and completed courses at the Air Corps Tactical School and the Command and General Staff School. He was promoted to major in 1940.

He commanded the 13th Air Force in the Solomon Islands in the Pacific until relieving Gen. James Doolittle of the 15th Air Force in Britain, in 1944, as well as becoming commander of the Mediterranean Strategic Forces in Italy. During this time, he held the rank of major general (temporary). Twining arrived back in the Pacific in 1945 to command the 20th Air Force and the atomic missions that ended the war. He was appointed chairman of the Joint Chiefs of Staff in 1957 and retired in 1960.

Vernon L. Williams

VANDEGRIFT, ALEXANDER ARCHER
(1887–1973)

U.S. marine officer, Vandegrift was born in Charlottesville, Virginia. He was commissioned a second lieutenant in the Marine Corps in 1909 and within a period of 14 years served in several capacities in the United States and participated in active operations in Nicaragua, Mexico, Haiti, and Panama. While in Nicaragua, Vandegrift served with both Col. Smedley Butler and Col. Joseph Pendleton. In Haiti, he earned a reputation as a determined and skilled leader when he successfully apprehended Caco bandit chief Charlemagne M. Peralte. Additionally, the young Vandegrift aided in the effort to train the Haitian Gendarmerie.

During the 1920s, Vandegrift was often assigned with Butler, serving with the flamboyant officer in Virginia and California. Overseas, Vandegrift and Butler found themselves enforcing extraterritorial rights in China. In 1928, Vandegrift was sent to Washington, D.C., where he became the Marine Corps representative in the Federal

Gen. Alexander Vandegrift, the first active-duty full general in the Marine Corps, was awarded the Congressional Medal of Honor for his leadership during the siege of Guadalcanal. (U.S. Marine Corps)

World War II. Promoted to brigadier general, Vandegrift was appointed to command the 1st Marine Division a few weeks before the Japanese attack on Pearl Harbor (Dec. 7, 1941). Several months later, in June 1942, the division was ordered to the South Pacific to participate in the gathering Allied effort to halt the Japanese. The marines drew the mission of landing in the Solomon Islands, at Guadalcanal. Coming ashore on August 7, Vandegrift suddenly found Adm. Frank J. Fletcher's Task Force 62 withdrawing from the beachhead, still carrying much of the 1st Division's vital supplies. Fearing the vulnerability of being tied to off-loading operations with Japanese naval combatants and aircraft in the region, the U.S. Navy all but left the marines stranded. Thus began a long and perilous fight at Guadalcanal.

The Guadalcanal Campaign amounted to a siege. This early in the war, U.S. air superiority could not be assured. Additionally, the massive firepower and ample supplies that characterized later U.S. operations were missing. Vandegrift and his marines clung to an airfield (Henderson Field) while successive waves of Japanese ground and air elements tried to force the Americans back into the sea. Plagued with supply problems, Vandegrift and his men maintained a somewhat static defense of Henderson Field. The airfield was critical to the marine defense. Not only did it provide the platform to launch U.S. air power against Japanese ground troops, it also provided the quick response to incoming Japanese bombers and naval ships. Gradually, the Americans began gaining the upper hand, and in November the 1st Marine Division began receiving the support it badly needed. Breaking out of their defense perimeter, Marine Corps units began the offensive, bringing the battle to the Japanese. In the end, in December 1942, the victorious but weary 1st Marine Division was relieved by the 2d Marine Division and the army's 25th Division. The 1st Marine Division was so battered and depleted, it was sent for rest and rehabilitation to Melbourne, Australia. For his courage and valor during the Guadalcanal Campaign, Vandegrift was awarded the Congressional Medal of Honor.

In 1943, the Allied offensive in the Pacific began in earnest. Now, the marines could put into practice the amphibious operations that Vandegrift had helped design. Vandegrift, promoted to lieutenant general, was given command of the 1st Marine Amphibious Corps, which in November was engaged in operations at Bougainville. He returned to Washington in 1944 to assume the duties of Marine Corps commandant, a position he held until his retirement in 1947. In March 1945, Vandegrift became the first active-duty full general in the Marine Corps.

Perhaps Vandegrift's most difficult battle was during the Truman administration in the last months of and immediately after World War II. Two events provoked difficult

Coordinating Service, an organ of the Hoover administration dedicated to abolishing duplication in matériel procurement among the armed services. He remained in this position for five years, learning much about the inner workings of the nation's capital and making a number of friendships that would stand him in good stead in later years.

By 1933, Vandegrift was returned to a marine base, at Quantico, Virginia, where he served in staff and school capacities. There, at the Marine Corps School, he helped write new amphibious doctrine. Additionally, he had the opportunity to field-test his theories in exercises. From 1935 until 1937, Vandegrift, now a colonel, once more served in China, this time with the U.S. embassy in Peking.

From 1937 until 1941, he was assigned to various marine staff positions in Washington. Serving the commandant, Maj. General Thomas Holcomb, he became deeply involved in budget, procurement, and supply issues and rose to become Holcomb's assistant. During this period, the corps began to expand as the Franklin D. Roosevelt administration prepared for war, and Vandegrift had an opportunity to influence the direction of the Marine Corps' growth.

times for the commandant: the atomic bomb and the effort to unify the U.S. armed forces. The new weapon and its effects were tested at the Bikini lagoon in 1946. A weapon of such force cast doubt on the ability of the Marine Corps to stage amphibious operations, at least of the type that were normal to World War II. The primary problem was that such operations relied on prolonged concentration of large numbers of ships just off the beachhead. That sort of vulnerable target would be tempting to a nuclear-armed opponent. Vandegrift's reaction was to listen to his advisers and appoint a board to study the problem. Headed by Maj. Gen. Lemuel C. Shepherd, Jr., Maj. Gen. Field Harris, and Brig. Gen. O. P. Smith, the Special Board conducted a thorough review of the entire problem. It recommended an extensive change in Marine Corps amphibious doctrine, stressing the need for a wide dispersion of support shipping on the approach to a beachhead. Also, the board pressed for the use of helicopters to ferry marines from ships to positions behind enemy defenses as opposed to the traditional assault across the beach. Vandegrift approved the findings of the board and once again played a major role in the revision of corps doctrine.

Marine leaders believed the very existence of the corps was threatened by the effort to unify the armed forces in the waning days of World War II. Vandegrift and his advisers were wary of the new president, Harry S Truman. Truman headed a congressional investigation of the armed forces during the war and had become convinced there was far too much duplication, waste, and inefficiency in the branches and much room for streamlining and savings. Truman, however, well knew such a reorganization during the war would be counterproductive. Thus, there was considerable anticipation of dramatic change in the last days of the war. Army and army air force officers favored the president's idea of a single military department, single secretary, and single military commander. Both the navy and the marines bitterly fought against these ideas. Although Truman noted that he favored the continuation of the Marine Corps, marine leaders doubted the president's sincerity. When the initial unification proposals made progress in the Senate Military Affairs Committee, Vandegrift and his aides managed to bring matters before the friendly Senate Naval Affairs Committee. The battle raged all through late 1945 and 1946.

On May 6, 1946, Vandegrift gave a moving presentation to the Senate Naval Affairs Committee. Stating the unique capabilities of the corps, the commandant pleaded for the continuation of the marines and cited the advantages of having some interservice rivalry. Ultimately, compromise was reached. Resistance to unification in the Congress grew to such levels that the administration had to conclude that the independence of the Air Force was threatened unless the marines received legislative protection. In the end, the

Marine Corps was directed by law to develop amphibious warfare doctrine and equipment and given the status of a separate service within the Navy Department. Vandegrift served as commandant until the end of 1947 and retired in 1949.

Bibliography: Asprey, Robert B., and Alexander Archer Vandegrift, *Once a Marine: The Memoirs of General A. A. Vandegrift, USMC* (Norton, 1964); Foster, John T., *Guadalcanal General: The Story of A. A. Vandegrift, U.S.M.C.* (Morrow, 1966); Griffith, Samuel B., *The Battle for Guadalcanal* (Lippincott, 1963); Isley, Jeter A., and Philip A. Crowl, *The U.S. Marines and Amphibious War* (Princeton Univ. Press, 1951).

Col. (Ret.) Rod Paschall

VINSON, CARL (1883–1981)

U.S. congressman, Vinson was born in Milledgeville, Georgia. A graduate of Georgia Military College and Mercer University Law School (1902), he became active in Georgia state government before his election to the U.S. House of Representatives in 1914. During his long tenure (1914–65) in the House, he served as chairman of the Naval Affairs Committee (1932–47) and of the Armed Services Committee (1950–64). His strong commitment to military preparedness helped secure passage of bills for the expansion of the navy in 1940. With these programs in place, the navy was able to recover from the losses of Pearl Harbor. An early and outspoken opponent of Pres. Harry S Truman's armed services unification, Vinson—who feared for the navy's diminution under unification—almost succeeded in scuttling the controversial legislation. Nicknamed the "Swamp Fox" for his cunning, Vinson often worked in legislative tandem with the equally formidable Sen. Richard Russell of Georgia.

Peter Model

VOGEL, CLAYTON BARNEY (1882–1964)

U.S. marine officer, Vogel was born in Philadelphia, Pennsylvania. After studying at Rutgers University, he was commissioned a second lieutenant in the Marine Corps in 1904. His early assignments included service in China (1906–09) and Haiti (1916–18) and in the Judge Advocate Corps (1926–29). He advanced through the ranks to brigadier general in 1939. During service in Haiti from 1930 to 1934, he was given the rank of major general in the Garde d'Haiti, which he shaped into a viable military force. As commander of the 2d Marine Brigade from 1939, he played a major part in the preparedness movement and succeeded, under difficult conditions, to shape his troops into combat readiness. Promoted to major general in 1941, he administered and provided logistical support for the 2d Joint Training Force (later the Amphibious Corps, Pacific). In 1943, Vogel commanded the Fleet Marine Force at San Diego.

He served at Parris Island, South Carolina, from 1944 until his retirement in 1946.

Leo J. Daugherty III

VOLCKMANN, RUSSELL WILLIAM
(1911–1982)

U.S. army officer, Volckmann was born in Iowa City, Iowa. He graduated from West Point in 1934 and was serving in the Philippines when war broke out in 1941. During the early fighting, he commanded the 11th Infantry, Philippine Scouts. When the Japanese prevailed, he escaped to northern Luzon, where he organized and commanded a guerrilla force eventually numbering 20,000 men. His heroic service earned him the Distinguished Service Cross and many other decorations. When the war ended, Volckmann for a time commanded the 2d Division, Philippine Army. He retired in 1957 as a brigadier general and also wrote a book about his experiences in the Philippines, pointedly titling it *We Remained*.

Bibliography: Volckmann, Russell W., *We Remained: Three Years Behind the Enemy Lines in the Philippines* (Norton, 1954).

Lewis Sorley

WADSWORTH, JAMES WOLCOTT
(1877–1952)

U.S. politician, Wadsworth was born in Geneseo, New York, and was educated at Yale University. After managing a ranch in Texas and serving in the New York State legislature, he became a U.S. Senator (1915–27). As chairman of the Committee on Military Affairs, he developed the compromise bill that became the National Defense Act of 1920, creating the regular army/National Guard/army reserve structure that survives to the present. From 1933 to 1951, Wadsworth served in the U.S. House of Representatives. In 1940, he and Edward R. Burke cosponsored the Selective Training and Service Act. Wadsworth's longtime advocacy of universal military training for citizen soldiers led to his appointment as chairman of the National Security Training Commission in 1951.

Bibliography: Holley, I. B., Jr., *General John M. Palmer, Citizen Soldiers, and the Army of a Democracy* (Greenwood Press, 1982).

Jonathan House

WAINWRIGHT, JONATHAN MAYHEW
(1883–1953)

U.S. Army officer, Wainwright was born in Walla Walla, Washington. He graduated from West Point in 1906. He saw action in the Philippines against Moro rebels in 1908 and fought in France during World War I.

Promoted to temporary major general in 1940, he returned to the Philippines and commanded U.S. and Filipino

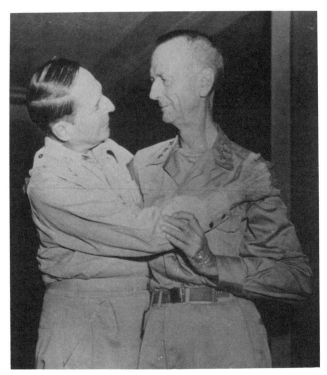

An emaciated Lt. Gen. Jonathan Wainwright (right), after spending more than three years in Japanese captivity, is greeted by Gen. Douglas MacArthur. (U.S. Signal Corps)

forces in northern Luzon when the Japanese invaded in December 1941, at the start of U.S. involvement in World War II. Unable to repel the landings at Lingayen Gulf, Wainwright conducted a difficult fighting retreat southward. He delayed the enemy long enough for his and other troops to withdraw onto the Bataan Peninsula in early January 1942. Defending the western half of Bataan and leading the I Corps, Wainwright bolstered the morale of the "battling bastards of Bataan" by constantly moving among his men in the field. For his bravery and leadership on the peninsula, he was awarded the Distinguished Service Cross.

Wainwright assumed command of all troops on Luzon when Gen. Douglas MacArthur left the Philippines in March 1942. Shortly thereafter, he was promoted to lieutenant general, became commander of all forces in the Philippines, and moved his headquarters to Corregidor Island. Bataan surrendered on April 9, but Wainwright continued to hold out on the island fortress. Lack of supplies, incessant bombardment, and successful Japanese landings finally compelled him to surrender on May 6.

Wainwright spent more than three years as a prisoner of war. His captivity proved particularly trying for several reasons: he watched his men being starved and abused; he personally endured beatings and humiliation; he anguished over how his countrymen viewed his conduct in surrendering his forces. He had no way of knowing that Americans regarded him as a hero fighting against hopeless odds or that he and his men in the Philippines provided a symbol of hope at a particularly dark time in the war.

In August 1945, after imprisonment in camps in the Philippines, Formosa, and China, Wainwright was liberated at Mukden. On September 2, he stood with MacArthur on the USS *Missouri* to receive the formal surrender of the Japanese. He then flew to the Philippines where he witnessed the Japanese surrender of the islands. Returning to the United States, Wainwright was accorded a hero's welcome, promoted to general, and awarded the Congressional Medal of Honor. He retired from the army in August 1947.

Bibliography: Beck, John Jacob, *MacArthur and Wainwright: The Sacrifice of the Philippines* (Univ. of New Mexico Press, 1974); Morton, Louis, *The Fall of the Philippines* (Dept. of the Army, 1953); Wainwright, Jonathan M., *General Wainwright's Story,* ed. by Robert Considine (Doubleday, 1946).

Ralph L. Eckert

WALKER, WALTON HARRIS (1889–1950)

U.S. army officer, Walker was born in Belton, Texas. He graduated from West Point in 1912 and was commissioned a second lieutenant in the infantry. After a series of assignments in the United States, he participated in the Veracruz Expedition of 1914. In World War I, he commanded a machine-gun company and fought extensively in the campaigns of St.-Mihiel and the Meuse-Argonne. In the 1920s, Walker attended the Field Artillery School and the Infantry School. He graduated from the Command and General Staff School in 1926. He was a tactics instructor at the Infantry School, West Point, and the Coast Artillery School.

In the early 1930s, Walker was a major with the 15th Infantry in Tientsin, China. He attended the Army War College in 1935 and joined the War Plans Division of the General Staff in 1937. Prior to U.S. entry into World War II, he commanded an armored brigade, the 36th Infantry Division, and the IV Armored Corps. He established the Desert Training Center in California to train armored units. Walker led XX Corps from its arrival in England in February 1944 to its landing in France in July 1944 as part of Gen. George Patton's 3d Army, through the movement across France, the capture of Metz, and into Germany.

Following the war, General Walker commanded the 8th Service Command and the 5th Army in the United States. He took command of the 8th Army in Japan in September 1948. When the North Korean army invaded South Korea in June 1950, Walker led the defense of the Pusan perimeter. Following the Inchon landings, Walker led his forces

north across the 38th parallel. His forces fell back after Chinese troops entered the conflict. On Dec. 23, 1950, Walker died in an automobile accident in South Korea.

Robert H. Berlin

WEDEMEYER, ALBERT COADY
(1896–1989)

U.S. army officer, Wedemeyer was born in Omaha, Nebraska. He graduated from West Point in 1919. Wedemeyer did much to heal the rifts between the United States and Generalissimo Chiang Kai-shek's Kuomintang (Nationalists). A Mandarin Chinese scholar, Wedemeyer not only spoke the language but was a diplomat. After graduating in 1921 from the Fort Benning Infantry School, he served in a series of infantry and staff posts in the Philippines and with the 15th Infantry in Tientsin, China. In 1936, following graduation from the Command and General Staff school at Fort Leavenworth, Captain Wedemeyer spent two years in Adolf Hitler's Germany at the *Kriegsakademie*—the Prussian war college—returning to Fort Benning, after which he joined the General Staff in Washington. After promotion to major in May 1941, he joined the War Plans Office under Maj. Gen. Dwight D. Eisenhower, where he served as principal author of stratagems implemented after the Pearl Harbor attack in December.

In 1942, Wedemeyer became director of plans in the newly created Operations Division and at the same time served on the Joint (Anglo-American) Strategic Committee. He attended all the major joint Atlantic strategy conferences between British prime minister Winston Churchill and U.S. president Franklin D. Roosevelt, either as an aide to or representative of Gen. George C. Marshall. Promoted to major general in September 1942, Wedemeyer was sent to Burma as Adm. Lord Louis Mountbatten's deputy chief of staff. In September 1944, after the China-Burma-India theater was split in two—with Burma and India given to Gen. Daniel I. Sultan—Wedemeyer replaced the controversial Gen. Joseph W. Stilwell as commander of the China theater and chief of staff to Generalissimo Chiang Kai-shek.

Wedemeyer remained in China until May 1946, skillfully extricating the United States from the coming struggle between Chiang's Kuomintang (Nationalists) and Mao Zedong's Communists, when he was promoted to commander of the U.S. 2d Army. While in that post, Marshall, then secretary of state, sent Wedemeyer back to China to report on the civil war. His blunt report forecast defeat of the Nationalists but was suppressed by the State Department. In 1947, Wedemeyer became director of the army's G-3 (Operations and Training). His last assignment before retiring in 1951 was as commanding general of the 6th Army at the Presidio. In retirement, Wedemeyer published a strategic newsletter (*Wedemeyer Reports!*) and became politically active as a conservative Republican and as a consultant.

Peter Model

WEEKS, JOHN WINGATE (1860–1926)

U.S. politician and secretary of war, Weeks was born in Lancaster, New Hampshire. He graduated from Annapolis in 1881, and, although discharged as part of a reduction in force in 1883, he continued service in the Massachusetts Naval Militia, from which he retired as a rear admiral.

A successful financier in Boston, Weeks served in the U.S. House of Representatives (1905–13) and in the U.S. Senate (1913–19). His campaigning for Warren Harding in the 1920 presidential election led to his appointment as secretary of war (1921–25). He presided over the demobilization of the army after World War I and became involved in the air defense controversy begun by Col. William Mitchell in 1925. Weeks founded the Army Industrial College (later the Industrial College of the Armed Forces) in 1925.

Jonathan M. House

WILBUR, CURTIS DWIGHT (1867–1954)

U.S. secretary of the navy (1924–29), Wilbur was born in Boonesboro, Iowa. He graduated from Annapolis in 1888. He resigned his commission, however, and from 1890 practiced law in California. After his 1924 appointment as secretary of the navy by Pres. Calvin Coolidge, one of Wilbur's first actions was to appoint two boards to define the present status of and to recommend future general policy for the navy and for naval aviation. As a result of the boards' findings, Wilbur authorized the first aircraft carriers, which were converted from the former battleships *Lexington* and *Saratoga,* and instituted programs to meet the navy's call for a substantial increase in personnel. He also directed that the Marine Corps be expanded and strongly advised that the marines become the nation's primary amphibious assault force. Wilbur realized that the airplane and the fleet would become integral elements of the navy's task force.

Leo J. Daugherty III

WILLIAMS, DION (1869–1952)

U.S. marine officer who founded and developed the use of amphibious reconnaissance in the Marine Corps and who laid the foundation for the marine special operations and expeditionary units. Born in Williamsburg, Ohio, Williams graduated from the U.S. Naval Academy in 1891. He was commissioned a second lieutenant in the Marine Corps in 1893 and took part in the Spanish-American War operations in the Philippines in 1898. From 1902, he saw duty in Panama and Puerto Rico. Promoted to major in 1905, he taught at the Naval War College, where he emphasized the

importance of amphibious reconnaissance and urged the organization of advance base forces. From 1906, he served in various staff positions and foreign assignments. He was promoted to brigadier general in 1924, having commanded the 4th Brigade of Marines at Quantico since 1922. Assigned to Nicaragua in 1929, he commanded the 2d Marine Brigade and onshore U.S. naval forces there. He then returned to marine headquarters, where he served until retirement in 1934.

Leo J. Daugherty III

WOOD, JOHN SHIRLEY (1888–1966)

U.S. army officer, Wood was born in Monticello, Arkansas. He graduated from West Point in 1912 and then coached football there, eventually becoming assistant commandant of the academy. During World War I, he commanded artillery units in France. During World War II, he built the 4th Armored Division, which he commanded (1942–45) as a major general, into the foremost element of Gen. George Patton's 3d Army. Wood, known as "Tiger Jack," led the division in the St.-Lô breakthrough and the dash across France. "Unquestionably, in a rapid moving advance, [Wood] is the greatest division commander I have ever seen," Patton later wrote. Subsequently, Wood, agonized over heavy losses among his troops, was relieved from command and relegated to training duties for the rest of the war, retiring in 1946. From 1947 until 1954, he served as chief of the International Refugee Organization in Austria, as well as chief of the United Nations' Korean Reconstruction Administration.

Bibliography: Baldwin, Hanson W., *Tiger Jack* (Old Army Press, 1979).

Lewis Sorley

WOODRING, HARRY HINES (1890–1967)

U.S. secretary of war, Woodring was born in Elk City, Kansas. He won the Democratic nomination for Kansas governor in 1930 and was elected by a margin of only 300 votes. Only the fourth Democrat to serve as Kansas governor, Woodring was defeated by Republican Alfred M. Landon in 1932. Woodring was an avid promoter of Franklin D. Roosevelt in the 1932 presidential campaign and became Roosevelt's secretary of war in 1936, upon the death of Sec. George Dern. His overwhelming support for Roosevelt turned sour, however, when he disagreed with the president's plan to send planes to Britain. An isolationist, Woodring considered this "stripping America's defenses." The president asked him to resign in June 1940. Returning to Kansas, he spearheaded a campaign to block Roosevelt's reelection to a fourth term. Woodring lost the Kansas gubernatorial race of 1946 and met defeat in the Democratic primary 10 years later.

Bibliography: McFarland, Keith D., *Harry H. Woodring: A Political Biography of FDR's Controversial Secretary of War* (Univ. Press of Kansas, 1975).

Maj. James Sanders Day

YARNELL, HARRY ERVIN (1875–1959)

U.S. naval officer, Yarnell was born in Independence, Indiana. He graduated from Annapolis in 1897. During the years 1898–1907, he participated in naval operations in the Spanish-American War, the Philippine Insurrection, the Boxer Rebellion in China, and the Great White Fleet. He held various staff assignments through World War I.

In the 1920s, Yarnell began his service in the air arm of the navy, successfully completing flight school while a captain. His rise to major command culminated in his appointment as commander in chief of the Asiatic Fleet in the rank of admiral in 1936. Yarnell retired in 1939 but returned to service during World War II, ending all active service in 1944.

Vernon L. Williams

PART III

Battles and Events

AACHEN, BATTLE OF (October 21, 1944)

U.S. offensive on one of Germany's oldest cities, which thus became the first German city to fall to Allied troops during World War II. When troops of the U.S. 1st Army crossed the German border on Sept. 11, 1944, Hitler ordered Aachen defended to the last man and rushed reinforcements to the city's defense. U.S. forces encircled Aachen, and, after intense aerial and artillery attack, the 1st Division and the 3d Armored Division began to clear the city. Bitter resistance continued until October 21, when the garrison finally capitulated. Despite widespread damage, the Carolingian cathedral of Emperor Charlemagne miraculously escaped serious harm.

Russell A. Hart

ABC-1 STAFF AGREEMENT
(March 27, 1941)

Farsighted collaboration between the United States and Great Britain on the eve of U.S. entry into World War II. By late 1940, the Axis Powers' successes compelled U.S. and British military planners to conduct secret meetings with the objective of establishing probable national roles during a future emergency. The conversations (hence "ABC," for American-British conversations) were held from January 29 to March 27, 1941. The outcome was an agreement that "if the United States should be compelled to resort to war" with Germany and its allies, the "Atlantic and European area" would be the "decisive theater" and Germany's defeat the top priority. Should Japan enter such a war, the Allies would maintain the strategic defensive in the Pacific until after Germany's defeat. Coming seven months before the Japanese attack on Pearl Harbor, while the United States was still neutral, the conversations were a fundamental statement of what would constitute the cornerstone of Allied strategy during World War II—the "Germany first" decision.

Stephen J. Lofgren

ALEUTIAN ISLANDS CAMPAIGN
(March-August, 1943)

World War II campaign in which U.S. forces retook Japanese-occupied islands in the southwestern extreme of Alaska. In June 1942, planes from a Japanese naval task force twice bombed the U.S. base at Dutch Harbor, Alaska, and seized the Aleutian islands of Kiska and Attu as part of a ruse to divert U.S. attention away from the Japanese offensive in the Central Pacific. The U.S. joint chiefs of staff speculated that the invasions might be part of a Japanese move on the Soviet Union, but they also conceded that the region's weather was too severe to make it an area of major importance. Therefore, U.S. forces would be used elsewhere in the Pacific. Rear Adm. Thomas C. Kinkaid, commander of the North Pacific area, however, proposed

U.S. troops inspect a captured Japanese barge during the campaign to regain the Aleutian Islands, an important link in the Lend-Lease supply line running to the Soviet Union. (U.S. Army Military History Institute)

to use locally available forces to recapture Attu. The joint chiefs agreed and scheduled Operation Landgrab for May 1943.

On Mar. 26, 1943, a Japanese task force carrying reinforcements for Attu encountered a U.S. fleet under Rear Adm. Charles H. McMorris. Although outnumbered, McMorris chose to fight and closed on the Japanese. For four hours, the two fleets engaged in one of the few daylight gunnery duels of the war. McMorris's largest ship, the heavy cruiser *Salt Lake City,* was hit four times, and he decided that he had to break off. As the Americans turned south, the Japanese pursued, but then suddenly broke off themselves and turned west for Japan. The Battle of the Komandorskiye (Commander) Islands thwarted Japan's last attempt to reinforce its garrisons in the Aleutians and set the stage for the U.S. invasion.

After weeks of preliminary air bombardment, U.S. troops from the 7th Infantry Division went ashore on Attu on May 11. Although the Americans heavily outnumbered the Japanese, the offensive immediately bogged down due to thick fog, cold temperatures, muddy terrain, and stiff Japanese resistance. Impatient with the lack of progress, Kinkaid relieved the 7th's commander, Maj. Gen. Albert E. Brown, on May 16. Brown's relief came just as his infantrymen broke the Japanese hold on Attu's high ground and pushed them onto the island's extreme northeast tip. On May 29, the Japanese commander, Col. Yamasake Yasuyo, led his remaining 800 men in a furious night attack but failed to break through the encircling Americans. Japanese resistance collapsed after the attack. The fighting on Attu cost the Japanese 2,379 men and the Americans

549 dead and 1,148 wounded. In terms of the number of men involved, it was one of the costliest assaults in the Pacific.

With Attu secured, the joint chiefs decided to move against Kiska. Air attacks began in July, and on August 15, a strong naval task force carrying nearly 35,000 troops arrived off the island. As the troops landed, however, they discovered that the Japanese had evacuated the island. With Kiska and Attu regained, the joint chiefs considered moving next on the Kuril Islands, but then deferred the issue indefinitely. Although the Aleutians were never an area of great strategic importance, the U.S. offensive there removed a potential threat to Alaska and the Lend-Lease supply line running to the Soviet Union. Perhaps its most important result was removing the psychological burden of having enemy troops occupying U.S. territory.

Bibliography: Conn, Stetson, et al., *United States Army in World War II; The Western Hemisphere: Guarding the United States and Its Outposts* (Office of the Chief of Military History, U.S. Army, 1964); Garfield, Brian, *The Ten Thousand Mile War* (Doubleday, 1969); Morison, Samuel Eliot, *History of United States Naval Operations in World War II; Vol. 7: Aleutians, Gilberts and Marshalls, June 1942–April 1944* (Little, Brown, 1957).

Richard F. Kehrberg

AMERICAN-BRITISH-DUTCH-AUSTRALIAN COMMAND (ABDACOM)

Politico-military union established by the Allied Powers in late December 1941, at the request of U.S. Army chief of staff George Marshall, as a response to the Japanese offensives in the Pacific. ABDACOM's commander, Sir Archibald Wavell, was to coordinate the Allied forces in Burma, Malaya, the Dutch East Indies, western New Guinea, northwestern Australia, and ostensibly the Philippines.

Wavell arrived at Batavia in Java, Dutch East Indies, in mid-January 1942 to begin the task, which proved insurmountable. The different areas under Wavell's command were separated geographically and politically; regions could not reinforce one another nor coordinate their defenses. Nor did they want to; the Dutch were concerned only with the defense of their islands, the British with Singapore, and the Americans and Australians with the approaches to Australia. Wavell was further hampered by mediocre subordinates and a paucity of resources.

Wavell's greatest priority was the defense of Singapore, where he sent the bulk of his disposable forces, but Britain's Gen. A. E. Percival nonetheless surrendered the fortress and more than 100,000 men to the energetic Japanese on February 15. Thereafter, Wavell lost faith in ABDACOM's viability.

After taking Malaya, the Japanese turned their attention to the Dutch East Indies, seizing Sumatra by airborne assault and other islands by amphibious invasion. ABDA-

COM had few remaining troops or aircraft and had to rely on naval forces to defend the islands. On February 24, Japanese naval forces were spotted moving into the Java Sea, and the ABDACOM fleet, under Dutch admiral K. W. F. M. Doorman, steamed forth to meet them, in a last-ditch attempt to protect Java. Doorman's forces were devastated by Japanese forces superior both in number and in skill, especially in night fighting. Most of the surviving warships were sunk trying to escape to the Indian Ocean.

Doorman's defeat gave the Japanese de facto control of Java, which they invaded on March 1, but the Allies had given up even earlier, Wavell recommending that ABDACOM be turned over to the Dutch. In fact, there was nothing else left of ABDACOM other than the doomed Dutch possessions. ABDACOM had never exerted control over the Philippines, and the British positions in Malaya and Burma had been overrun. ABDACOM was a nominal central command that existed more in theory than in fact. Because of the geopolitical realities, it could not assert effective control over its assigned areas; because of Japanese superiority, it could not provide effective defense.

Bibliography: Lewin, Ronald, *The Chief: Field Marshal Lord Wavell* (Farrar, Straus & Giroux, 1980); Spector, Ronald, *Eagle Against the Sun: The American War With Japan* (Macmillan, 1985).

Mark Pitcavage

ANVIL, OPERATION
(August-September 1944)

Planning-stage codename given to Allied combined amphibious and airborne assault against the French Mediterranean coast during World War II; name changed to "Operation Dragoon" when disclosure to Germans was suspected. Anvil, launched on Aug. 15, 1944, was the culmination of one of the lengthiest and most divisive Allied command controversies of the war. Gen. Dwight D. Eisenhower, the Supreme Allied Commander, envisaged a diversionary operation to support the main Allied landings in Normandy. However, the British prime minister, Winston Churchill, favored using the resources in Italy to secure a breakthrough from which the Allies could advance into Austria and the Balkans.

Although Eisenhower's view prevailed, lack of landing craft prevented the execution of Anvil before mid-August, by which time German forces had been considerably weakened by transfers to Normandy and the Allies had already broken out from their bridgehead. Thus, as a diversionary operation, Anvil was redundant by the time it was launched.

The 3d, 36th, and 45th U.S. divisions spearheaded the assault between St. Tropez and Cannes, supported by airborne landings inland. On the first day, 86,000 Allied troops were put ashore at a cost of 520 casualties. The following day, the French 1st Infantry and 3d Algerian divisions landed. On August 17, the massively outnumbered Germans began a general withdrawal from southern and southwestern France. The immobile garrisons of Toulon and Marseilles held out until August 28, the garrison at Bordeaux until the end of hostilities. American forces pursued the retreating Germans up the Rhone Valley, but skillful German delaying actions allowed many combat units retreating from southwestern France to reach safety. Allied forces entered Lyons on September 2, and Dijon fell one week later. On that same day, Allied troops advancing from Normandy linked up west of Dijon with troops advancing from the south. On September 13, the U.S. 6th Army, under Lt. Gen. Jacob L. Devers, took direction of the U.S. 7th and the French 1st armies. As the advance approached the foothills of the Vosges, German resistance stiffened and the speed of the Allied advance and overextended supply lines began to take their toll.

Although the operation netted 100,000 prisoners, very few of these were first-rate combat troops. Moreover, rather than facilitating the encirclement of German forces, the Anvil landings may have precipitated the withdrawal from southern France of German forces that might not otherwise have escaped.

Bibliography: Wilt, Alan F., *The Atlantic Wall: Hitler's Defences in the West, 1941–44* (Iowa Univ. Press, 1975).

Russell A. Hart

ANZIO, BATTLE OF (January-May 1944)

World War II battle at the beachhead at Anzio, a historic Italian seaside resort 35 miles south of Rome. During the four-month-long, seesawing battle, the defending German forces nearly drove the invading Allies back into the Tyr-

rhenian Sea. For 125 days starting on January 22, more than 250,000 Allied and German troops fought for control of the cold, damp lowlands and plains of the Pontine marshes.

Hurriedly planned by Sir Gen. Harold Alexander of Britain and Gen. Mark Clark of the United States to pave the way for troops landed at Salerno in September 1943, Operation Shingle was timidly executed by U.S. VI Corps commander Maj. Gen. John Porter Lucas. The plan was to put pressure on Panzer Gen. Heinrich von Vietinghoff's 10th Army, manning the fortified Gustav line 80 miles south of Anzio. Had Lucas not delayed a week to shore up his beachhead, and had he instead broken out of the perimeter to seize the Alban Hills rising above the Anzio plain 20 miles from the sea, the Allies could have interdicted Field Marshal Albert Kesselring's road and rail supply links from Rome and shortened the Italian campaign by months.

The landing at Anzio and nearby Nettuno began as a lightly opposed U.S. Ranger-led amphibious landing by two Anglo-American divisions. The cost of putting 36,000 men on the beach was low: 13 killed, 97 wounded, and 44 missing. Shingle had been actively promoted by Britain's Prime Minister Winston Churchill, but once Anzio turned into a charnel house, his political enemies invoked images of the 1915 Gallipoli debacle and its 55,000 dead, planned by Churchill, then First Lord of the Admiralty. Ultimately, Anzio cost the Allies 4,400 dead, 18,000 wounded, 7,000 taken prisoner, and 37,000 lost to exhaustion, frostbite, shell shock, and desertion.

At the peak of battle, 110,000 reinforced Allied troops faced the entire German 145th Army, under the command

Operation Shingle, an amphibious landing at Anzio, Italy, to divert the Germans from the defense of the Gustav line, was carried out by Allied troops in early 1944. (U.S. Army Military History Institute)

of Gen. Eberhard von Mackensen. The combat conditions came close to emulating the meat-grinding trench warfare of World War I; there was little in the small semicircular beachhead to distinguish the front line from rear areas. Recuperating wounded even asked to be sent back to the front lines, which were deemed safer. Daytime movement by the Allies became suicidal: one U.S. unit lost 761 out of 767 men.

Ordered by Adolf Hitler to "lance the abscess south of Rome," Kesselring almost succeeded in decimating VI Corps, turning 88-millimeter antiaircraft guns into horizontal field artillery. Horrendous casualties resulted from rolling huge railcar-mounted guns out of specially reinforced caves in the Alban Hills. Nicknamed "Anzio Annie" and "Anzio Express," they were capable of hurling 280-millimeter shells 30 miles onto the beachhead and sometimes at supply ships anchored offshore. The relentless pounding and sniping cost the Allies five times as many men as would be lost on D-Day (June 6, 1944) at Normandy.

Four weeks into the battle, 5th Army commander Clark removed Lucas and replaced him with Maj. Gen. Lucian K. Truscott, Jr. Truscott finally staged a successful breakout on May 23, soon after Cassino fell along with the Gustav line.

Bibliography: Calvocoressi, Peter, et al., *Total War: Causes and Courses of the Second World War* (Pantheon, 1989); D'Este, Carlo, *Fatal Decision: Anzio and the Battle for Rome* (HarperCollins, 1991).

Peter Model

ARCADIA CONFERENCE
(December 22, 1941–January 14, 1942)

Codename for the summit talks held in Washington, D.C., between British prime minister Winston Churchill and U.S. president Franklin D. Roosevelt, in the aftermath of the Japanese attack on Pearl Harbor. The most significant outcome of the conference was the Anglo-American determination that Germany's defeat would be top priority. This sentiment was expressed in the Joint Declaration, in which 26 nations pledged not to negotiate a separate peace until Germany was defeated. Another result was the creation of the Anglo-American Combined Chiefs of Staff, which, as the Allies' supreme military body, would plan global strategy and direct the war effort.

Stephen J. Lofgren

ARGENTIA CONFERENCE
(August 9–13, 1941)

World War II summit talks between U.S. president Franklin D. Roosevelt and British prime minister Winston Churchill aboard two warships in Placentia Bay, Newfoundland, near the Argentia naval base. This second major wartime conference resulted in the Atlantic Charter, a statement of war aims and principles.

As drafted by Churchill and elaborated by Roosevelt, the charter was signed on Aug. 12, 1941. In it, the two denied any interest in territorial gains, asserted the right of self-determination, and called for free trade and access to resources.

While the two political leaders reached such general agreement, their combined chiefs of staff achieved much less in military terms. As in most of the early wartime conferences, the British chiefs of staff in effect set the agenda. They naturally emphasized security of the United Kingdom and anticipated the strangulation of Germany by a combination of blockade, strategic bombing, and subversive operations. American participants found this approach vague and unconvincing. In military terms, therefore, the conference accomplished little except to establish greater cooperation in convoy escorts in the North Atlantic.

Bibliography: Churchill, Winston S., *The Grand Alliance* (Houghton Mifflin, 1950).

Jonathan M. House

ARMS LIMITATIONS CONFERENCES AND TREATIES (1919–1936)

Disarmament deliberations among the major world powers during the years between the two world wars. One of the strongest effects of World War I was a global interest in disarmament. The naval arms race between Germany and Great Britain was viewed as one of the prime causes of the war. Armaments production had incited popular opinion and had depleted the treasuries of every prewar European government. The United States had also become involved in naval armaments building before World War I. However, U.S. popular opinion was decidedly in favor of reduced armaments in the interwar period. In addition to concerns over costs, many diplomats and politicians believed that if large arms caches existed and if nations engaged in arms races the weapons would eventually be used.

Versailles Treaty and Arms Control. Interest in arms limitations began before the end of World War I. Delegates at the Paris Peace Conference began to explore ways to reduce tension and increase security through arms limitations agreements, but in 1919 the immediate interest was in reducing or eliminating Germany's capacity to wage war. Germany's army was reduced to 100,000 while its air force was eliminated as was most of its surface navy and all of its submarine force.

While the Versailles Treaty forced disarmament on Germany and, for the time, guaranteed French security, it was considered by most of the delegates to the Paris Peace Conference as only a first step in global arms reduction. Commitments to continue to discuss arms limitations on a global scale were written into both the Versailles Treaty and the Charter of the League of Nations. The interest in arms limitations was not new. The Hague Peace Conference of 1899 had been proposed in the interest of reducing armaments expenditures, but was generally unsuccessful. The Hague Peace Conference of 1907 quickly degenerated into international bickering as each nation refused to reduce armaments until all others had done so. The United States participated in each of these conferences but remained relatively disinterested in taking a leading role. However, after the experience of World War I, the United States began to take a greater interest in ground arms control and a leading role in the reduction of naval weapons. The interwar period became a constant search for the correct balance of national and global security and reductions in armaments.

Washington Naval Conference. The United States had become a naval power of the first order during World War I. It wanted to preserve that position in the postwar world and sought to control naval spending by limiting the size of navies through international agreements. At the same time, many Americans blamed secret treaties for the outbreak of the war. The only treaty remaining from before the war was the Anglo-Japanese Alliance, which the United States considered a potential threat to its Pacific and Asian interests. The Washington Naval Conference of 1921–22 sought to remedy both of these concerns by superseding the Anglo-Japanese Alliance with a multilateral agreement and by setting enforceable limits on the size of national navies.

The result of the Washington Conference was the Naval Limitation Treaty, which regulated the navies of the United States, Great Britain, Japan, France, and Italy. The United States, while concerned about growing Japanese naval power and about its own security in the Pacific, offered naval parity to Great Britain in order to gain the dissolution of the Anglo-Japanese Alliance. The United States and Great Britain were allowed 525,000 tons of capital ships. Japan was allowed 330,000 tons, while France and Italy were each allowed 175,000 tons. The same ratio of shipping was applied to aircraft carriers. No one ship was allowed to be more than 35,000 tons, and guns larger than 16 inches were banned. In addition, a moratorium was placed on the construction of new capital ships except under carefully defined circumstances. The agreement was hailed at the time as a breakthrough in arms limitations attitudes, as the United States had voluntarily ended the possibility of an arms race with Great Britain while simultaneously accepting a certain amount of risk in its relations with Japan and its security in the Pacific.

The failure of the Washington Naval Limitation Treaty was in not regulating the number of ships less than 10,000 tons and in not covering submarines. Politically, France and Italy were unhappy that they were given smaller ratios than Japan. France was displeased that its fleet and power were considered equal to Italy's. The failures of the

agreement led to a naval arms race in submarines, cruisers, and destroyers.

Geneva Naval Conference. By the mid-1920s, the arms race in smaller naval vessels became acute. Many nations began to face difficult choices between building more technologically advanced ships or funding other parts of their economies. U.S. president Calvin Coolidge proposed a naval conference in Geneva in 1927, but the conference was a complete failure. The United States did not send its best statesmen, while Italy and France sent only observers. The conference devolved into a series of unresolved differences between naval experts over various aspects of cruiser construction.

Kellogg-Briand Pact. The next attempt turned away from agreements on weapons and addressed the legality of war itself. Many believed that if war were outlawed, then weapons would be unneeded and could be negotiated away. Aristide Briand, France's foreign minister, suggested in 1927 a bilateral agreement between France and the United States outlawing war. The United States resisted for several reasons, but U.S. Sec. of State Frank B. Kellogg eventually suggested that the proposed agreement be open to all nations. This was quickly agreed on; however, the Kellogg-Briand Pact (or Pact of Paris), ratified in 1929, was bereft of all meaning when the United States, and then most other nations, asserted a continuing right to self-defense. While an agreement was signed, there remained no global reduction in armaments.

London Naval Conference. The United States again proposed a naval arms conference in 1930, but the London Conference of 1930 was only a partial success. France and Italy again refused to accept any agreement. The United States, Great Britain, and Japan agreed to limits on submarines, cruisers, and destroyers at a ratio of 10:10:6.9, respectively, but included an escalator clause that allowed all tonnages to increase if Italy, France, or other nations built ships. This option was used after the 1935 Anglo-German Naval Agreement.

World Disarmament Conference. The issue of ground weapons had been on the agenda in Washington but was never addressed during the 1922 conference. By the late 1920s, European nations were again concerned about ground disarmament. The consistent point of conflict was a French demand for security against German attack before France would agree to any disarmament. Germany maintained that its disarmament under the Versailles Treaty had been intended as a first step toward global disarmament and accused France of being militaristic. By the 1930s, German rearmament was a poorly concealed secret. In 1932, after several years of staff and committee work, the World Disarmament Conference convened in Geneva. The primary conflict remained German demands for equality countered by French demands for security. The crisis point came when the British suggested a plan that would require the United States to guarantee security in Europe by agreeing to impose economic sanctions against any nation branded an aggressor by the League of Nations. The French almost agreed but balked over the guarantee of security. They wanted the United States and Great Britain to promise armed security. The United States was back to the point when the Versailles Treaty was rejected because membership in the League was considered an infringement of U.S. freedom of action. The United States, after 10 years, still rejected such a restrictive agreement. After more than a year of proposals and deadlock, the conference was abruptly ended in October 1933 when German chancellor Adolf Hitler withdrew from both the conference and the League over the unwillingness to grant Germany equality in ground and air weapons. This was the closest the world came to disarmament between the wars, but it faltered over questions of security.

London Naval Conference. The final attempt at global disarmament before World War II was the London Naval Conference of 1936. Naval limitations again had been muddled after the Japanese renounced in 1934 the agreements of the Washington Naval Conference and Great Britain concluded a bilateral naval agreement with Germany in 1935. The London Naval Conference, the last chance for disarmament, was another failure. As both the United States and Great Britain attempted to control the size of navies while maintaining their security, both the Japanese and Germans demanded naval parity. The conference broke down over the issue of ratios and ship sizes. Great Britain, France, and the United States concluded a pact in March 1936, limiting the size of battleships to 35,000 tons and the ships' arms to 14–inch guns and continuing the building holiday on heavy cruisers and battleships. No other pacts were in effect, and other nations built ships without restriction to size, guns, or numbers. After 1936, the United States returned to a traditional aloofness from European security concerns.

Bibliography: Adler, Selig, *The Uncertain Giant, 1921–1941* (Macmillan, 1965); Offner, Arnold A., *The Origins of the Second World War* (Praeger, 1975); Sontag, Raymond, *A Broken World, 1919–1939* (Harper & Row, 1971); Taylor, A. J. P., *The Origins of the Second World War* (Atheneum, 1962); Wolfers, Arnold, *Britain and France Between Two Wars* (New York, 1940).

Capt. George B. Eaton

ATLANTIC, BATTLE OF THE (1941–1945)

Name given to the four-year period of maritime military activities in the Atlantic theater during World War II. War in Europe assumed grim proportions in early November 1940. Since the supply of food, raw materials, and finished products lies at the heart of a nation's ability to wage war, the restriction of such materials can prove disastrous. German submarines (U-boats) successfully blockaded Brit-

ish ports in 1940–41. By spring 1941, more than 2,000,000 gross tons of supplies bound for England had been lost or captured by the U-boats. On April 11, Pres. Franklin D. Roosevelt informed England's Prime Minister Winston Churchill that the U.S.-protected security zone around Great Britain would be expanded.

Possibly in retaliation, on May 27, 1941, the *Robin Moor,* a U.S. merchant ship, was sunk by a U-boat off the coast of Brazil. Three days later, the British warship *Hood* was sunk in the North Atlantic by the German battleship *Bismarck.* Clearly, German intents were not about to be thwarted by an increased American presence.

Over the next four years, the U.S. Navy provided escorts for the British merchant fleet. Additionally, long-range U.S. aircraft based in North America, Iceland, and Britain progressively worked to reduce the number of German U-boats operating in the Atlantic. Both the boats and their bases in the North Atlantic were targeted.

The Battle of the Atlantic, a term coined by Churchill, passed through distinct phases. From the outbreak of war in 1939 until the fall of France in June 1940, the U-boat fleet had been confined by geographical constraints and Adolf Hitler's concern over U.S. involvement. After Germany gained control of French ports, these constraints were largely removed. Thereafter, the U-boats began to operate undeterred throughout the Atlantic. After December 1941, when U.S. attention was diverted to the Pacific theater, German submarines carried their warfare to the Atlantic coast of the United States and into the Gulf of Mexico, sinking hundreds of thousands of tons of shipping.

By summer 1942, the Battle of the Atlantic appeared to favor the Allies. Measures were successfully taken to route convoys away from known or suspected U-boat patrol zones. Allied intelligence was focused on learning where the German submarines were lurking. Rerouting shipping proved the most effective way to avoid losses. Improved intelligence and the superiority of Allied radar, combined with the Allied ability to replace lost ships, allowed the safe passage of Atlantic convoys.

M. Guy Bishop

BATAAN DEATH MARCH (April 1942)

Brutal 60–mile march by more than 75,000 American and Filipino troops to Japanese prison camps in April 1942. When the Philippine peninsula of Bataan surrendered, its starving defenders were in wretched shape, malnourished and racked by such diseases as malaria, dysentery, diarrhea, and beriberi. Their weakened condition plus Japanese underestimation of their numbers contributed to the staggering mortality on the march, but it was the sadistic cruelty of the guards that made it a deadly nightmare. Contemptuous of anyone who surrendered, the Japanese were clearly indifferent to the suffering of their captives. Prisoners were forced to march under the blazing hot sun, robbed of their personal belongings, and beaten, clubbed, shot, and bayoneted at the whim of their guards. Those who fell out for any reason were killed by execution squads trailing the column. Survivors of the grueling six-day march from Mariveles to the rail center at San Fernando were crammed into poorly ventilated metal boxcars where they baked in the suffocating heat on the four-hour ride to Camp O'Donnell. Years of imprisonment at various camps in the Philippines, Formosa, Japan, and China awaited those who survived the death march. Although death totals on the march are impossible to determine, the best estimates are 5,000–10,000 Filipinos and 600–700 Americans; many thousands more perished in the prison camps.

Bibliography: Falk, Stanley L., *Bataan: The March of Death* (Norton, 1962); Knox, Donald, *Death March: The Survivors of Bataan* (Harcourt Brace Jovanovich, 1981).

Ralph L. Eckert

BATAAN, DEFENSE OF
(December 1941–April 1942)

During World War II, the U.S. and Filipino attempt to defend the Philippines on a rugged 15–20-mile wide and almost 30–mile long peninsula jutting out from southwestern Luzon island. Successful Japanese landings at Lingayen Gulf on Dec. 22, 1941, destroyed Gen. Douglas MacArthur's plans to defeat the invaders on the beaches. On December 24, he ordered all his forces in northern and southern Luzon to withdraw to Bataan and Corregidor Island, where he believed they could hold out until help arrived. MacArthur's men had to conduct a long, difficult fighting retreat just to reach Bataan, but by Jan. 6, 1942, more than 80,000 had escaped to the jungles and mountains of the peninsula.

Shortages became evident immediately. For a variety of reasons, most of the supplies necessary for withstanding an extended siege had been captured or abandoned on the retreat. Lack of food forced the entire command onto half rations in the first week. Worse than malnutrition were the diseases that spread rapidly among the defenders.

Fierce Japanese attacks began on January 9 and, despite determined resistance, pushed MacArthur's men back 10 miles during the next two weeks. At the same time, the Japanese also launched several amphibious assaults along the west coast and engaged in numerous infiltration operations. Although they created confusion and necessitated hard fighting to eliminate them, these threats in the rear had little impact because by January 26, a new line stretching from Orion to Bagac had stabilized.

A two-month stalemate then developed as both armies were exhausted. With the Japanese 14th Army mauled in battle and ravaged by the same tropical maladies sapping their opponents, reinforcements would be needed to take Bataan. Although morale among the "battling bastards of Bataan" ran relatively high, their effectiveness deteriorated

daily. Rations were again halved (to 1,000 calories a day); most men were sick and thousands hospitalized; all supplies ran low, especially medicines for tropical diseases. When MacArthur acceded to Pres. Franklin D. Roosevelt's orders to leave the Philippines on March 11, it became clear to all that help would not be sent—they were expendable.

Heavily reinforced with fresh troops, the Japanese resumed their offensive on April 3. They breached the line three days later and pushed down the peninsula as the starved Americans and Filipinos collapsed before the onslaught. On April 9, Maj. Gen. Edward King unconditionally surrendered all troops on Bataan. Only Corregidor remained, but its days were numbered.

Bibliography: Beck, John Jacob, *MacArthur and Wainwright: The Sacrifice of the Philippines* (Univ. of New Mexico Press, 1974); Conroy, Robert, *The Battle of Bataan: America's Greatest Defeat* (Macmillan, 1969); Morton, Louis, *The Fall of the Philippines* (Department of the Army, 1953); Wainwright, Jonathan M., *General Wainwright's Story*, ed. by Robert Considine (Doubleday, 1946).

Ralph L. Eckert

BISMARCK SEA, BATTLE OF THE
(March 3, 1943)

World War II battle in the Pacific Ocean off New Guinea. Following their defeats at Guadalcanal and at Buna Mission in Papua, New Guinea, the Japanese attempted to strengthen their hold on the central Solomon Islands and at key locations in New Guinea. A Japanese army division sailing in eight transports escorted by as many destroyers headed for Lae on the New Guinea coast. Lt. Gen. George Kenney, commanding Allied air forces in the Southwest Pacific, had recently devised low-level tactics to use against enemy shipping. Employing commerce-destroyers, B-25 bombers modified to hold eight forward-firing machine guns, and a variety of other planes and ordnance, U.S. and Australian aviators hit the convoy hard and often, sinking all transports and half the destroyers. American PT boats completed the onslaught. The ability of Allied air power to control the waters off New Guinea had finally been demonstrated.

Bibliography: Watson, Richard L., Jr., "The Battle of the Bismarck Sea," *The Army Air Forces in World War II; Vol. 4: The Pacific: Guadalcanal to Saipan, August 1942 to July 1944,* ed. by Wesley Frank Craven and James Lea Cate (Univ. of Chicago Press, 1950).

Lloyd J. Graybar

BOMBER AIRCRAFT

Airplanes equipped to carry and drop bombs; developed and advocated by the U.S. military following World War I. Beginning in 1935, the United States began an earnest rearmament campaign to combat what was perceived—

The B-29, the most advanced bomber of World War II, with a payload capacity of 20,000 pounds, dropped the atomic bombs on Hiroshima and Nagasaki. (U.S. Army Military History Institute: Army Air Corps)

peak inventory at any one time was 1,931 in March 1944. Production of the aircraft ended in April 1945.

The B-29 "Super Fortress" was the most advanced bomber of World War II. Development began in 1940, and Boeing, the principal contractor, made the first deliveries of 7 aircraft in July 1943. By the end of August 1945, deliveries had reached a total of 3,763. A four-engine bomber that could carry a maximum payload of 20,000 pounds, the B-29 went on to drop the atomic bombs on Hiroshima and Nagasaki in August 1945 and remained in the U.S. Air Force inventory through the Korean War.

Bibliography: Holley, I. B., Jr., *Buying Aircraft: Matériel Procurement for the Army Air Forces* (Office of the Chief of Military History, 1964); Maurer, Maurer, *Aviation in the U.S. Army, 1919–1939* (Office of Air Force History, 1987); Overy, R. J., *The Air War, 1939–1945* (Stein and Day, 1980); Sherry, Michael S., *The Rise of American Air Power: The Creation of Armageddon* (Yale Univ. Press, 1987).

Roger D. Launius

rightly, as it turned out—as totalitarian aggression. Much of this effort was directed toward the acquisition of new aircraft. By 1939, the army air forces were receiving $70,600,000, or 15.7 percent of the army's direct appropriations, and most of that went to aircraft acquisitions.

The army air forces used this funding especially effectively in developing several bombers that saw extended service in World War II. Replacing antiquated aircraft, some of which were still biplanes of World War I vintage, the first bomber developed was the B-17 "Flying Fortress," a system that became legendary, and while airmen thought it left something to be desired as a fortress, they found that it could fly with all types of damage from enemy fire. The B-17s were first flight-tested in July 1935 at Wright Field, Ohio, and by the end of 1940, the service had accepted 66 of them and large numbers were on order. The B-17, a four-engine aircraft with a bomb payload of 8,800 pounds, carried the brunt of the strategic bombing campaign in the European theater during World War II. The army air forces acquired 12,692 aircraft of that type over the course of the war.

The B-17 was not the only heavy bomber procured during the 1930s buildup; the B-24 "Liberator" program was started in 1939, and by the end of the war, the army air forces had accepted more than 18,000 planes, most of which were used in the Mediterranean and Pacific theaters. In addition, the B-26 "Marauder," a medium bomber, was developed, beginning in 1939 and entering active production the next year from the Glenn L. Martin Company. A twin-engine aircraft, the B-26 could carry about 4,000 pounds of bombs by the end of the war. In all, the army air forces accepted delivery of 5,157 B-26s, but its

BONUS MARCH (July 9–28, 1932)

Demonstration in Washington, D.C., by World War I veterans seeking congressional appropriation for promised funds. In 1924, the Adjusted Compensation Act had mandated land, money, and other benefits to the veterans—to be granted in 1945. The onset of the Great Depression made many anxious to receive their monies sooner, a wish not granted by the federal government. What resulted was an ostensibly grassroots movement in the summer of 1932, a parade of veterans and their families to Washington, in mass protest of what they perceived as their government's uncaring attitude. The first contingent (1,500 from the West Coast) of the so-called Bonus Army arrived on July 9, and their ranks ultimately swelled to 15,000.

Under the leadership of Walter W. Waters, the protesters spent two months at Anacostia Flats in a makeshift campsite, from which they were ordered to leave in late July. While most of the protesters left, close to 2,000 refused. District police attempts to remove them resulted in four deaths, two policemen and two veterans. On July 28, U.S. Army troops, led by Chief of Staff Douglas MacArthur, attacked the remaining veterans, forcing their removal from public property.

Bibliography: Daniels, Roger, *The Bonus Army: An Episode of the Great Depression* (Greenwood Press, 1971).

David Friend

BREST, BATTLE OF
(August 21-September 19, 1944)

World War II campaign focused on a major Breton port and fortified naval base in northwest France. After the Allied breakout from Normandy in July 1944, U.S. forces fanned out into Brittany. The weak German forces retreated into the fortified ports. Allied logistical shortages mandated the rapid capture of Brest. By mid-August, the U.S. 3d Army had assembled 3 divisions, supported by 18 corps artillery battalions, to assault Brest. German defenders totaled 30,000 troops, commanded by General Ramcke. Operations began on August 21, and Brest capitulated on September 18. American casualties totaled 9,831. This high cost dissuaded the Allies from assaulting other defended ports.

Russell A. Hart

BULGE, BATTLE OF THE
(December 16, 1944–January 28, 1945)

Largest land battle fought on the Western Front during World War II. Also known as the Battle of the Ardennes, it was Germany's last major counteroffensive of the war. In early December 1944, Gen. Dwight D. Eisenhower, Supreme Allied Commander, was planning major offensives in the northern and southern sectors of the Western Front. To ensure sufficient power for these offensives, he left his central sector, an 80-mile line on the France-Belgium border in the Forest of Ardennes, lightly defended by Maj. Gen. Troy Middleton's VIII Corps. This "quiet" area was used by both sides to allow new commands to get experience and to train replacements. The forbidding Ardennes terrain and apparently light German force in the area gave Eisenhower reason to hold there with fewer troops. Further, the Allies saw no tactical or strategic objectives in the area.

Allied troops were hampered by snow in the Ardennes forest during the Battle of the Bulge, Germany's last counteroffensive of World War II. (U.S. Office of War Information, National Archives)

The VIII Corps included the 4th, 28th, and 106th infantry divisions; the 9th Armored Division (less Combat Command B); and the two-squadron 14th Cavalry Group. Neither the 106th Infantry nor the 9th Armored had experienced combat, and the 4th and 28th infantries were absorbing thousands of replacements after suffering horrendous casualties in the Huertgen Forest. The 4th Infantry and part of the 9th Armored occupied the southern part of the corps front, then came the 28th Infantry on a 25-mile front, and next the 106th Infantry on a front of close to 16 miles. The 14th Cavalry screened a 9,000-yard sector between the northern flank of the VIII Corps and the southern flank of the V Corps (Maj. Gen. Leonard T. Gerow).

Into this lightly defended area, Germany's Adolf Hitler launched his massive counteroffensive designed to seize Antwerp, Belgium, then isolate and destroy the British army. He felt that the success of this offensive would cause a military and political split between Britain and the United States.

Hitler designated Army Group B, commanded by Field Marshal Walther Model, to make the attack. This group included the 5th, 6th, and 7th Panzer armies, under Gens. Hasso-Eccard von Manteufel, Josef "Sepp" Dietrich, and Erich Brandenberger, respectively. The group numbered 250,000 men, 970 tanks and assault guns, and 1,900 artillery pieces.

Allied intelligence, almost without exception, failed to detect the German buildup. As a result, the offensive came as a complete surprise. German artillery forces opened their offensive at 5:30 A.M., December 16. Disruption of communication led U.S. commanders to believe these to be local attacks.

In the north, the V Corps' 99th Division repulsed the 12th, 277th, and 326th Volksgrenadier divisions (VGDs). The 14th Cavalry, however, was forced to give ground, and elements of Germany's 3d Parachute Division and 18th VGD made some headway against the 106th Division. In the 28th Division sector, the northern regiment (112th) held against elements of the 116th Panzer Division and the 560th VGD. The 110th Infantry Regiment in the center—hit hard by enemy fire—was decimated. Small enclaves of the regiment were individually surrounded and destroyed. The 109th Infantry in the south, although hard-pressed by the 352d VGD and the 5th Parachute Division, held. Elements of the 9th armored and 4th infantry divisions, south of the 28th, also held fast against the 276th and 282d VGDs.

December 19 was a pivotal date in the battle. Eisenhower ordered the 7th and 10th armored divisions in to support the VIII Corps. The 101st Airborne Division was sent to Bastogne, arriving there on December 19. To defend the town, the 101st was joined by Combat Command R, 9th Armored Division; Combat Command B, 10th Armored

Division; the 755th Armored Field Artillery Battalion; the 705th Tank Destroyer Battalion; and remnants of the 28th Infantry Division. Due to the absence of the 101st's commanding general (Maj. Gen. Maxwell D. Taylor), Brig. Gen. Anthony C. McAuliffe, assistant division commander, was named commander of this combined force.

By December 19, both the 28th and 106th infantry divisions had been destroyed, but the German timetable had been irretrievably shattered by the men of these two divisions. Of the 106th, the Germans surrounded and forced the surrender of the 422d and 423d regiments. The division's 424th Regiment extricated itself and moved back to a position west of the Our River. On the same day, Combat Command B, 9th Armored Division, and the 7th Armored Division (Brig. Gen. Robert W. Hasbrouck) came in on the 424th's north flank. The 112th Infantry, from the 28th Division, moved in on its south flank. This diverse force, under the command of Gen. Hasbrouck, defended St.-Vith until December 21, then withdrew into a "fortified goose egg," which it defended for two more days. They then withdrew through elements of the 82d airborne and 3d armored divisions.

Also on December 19, Britain's Field Marshal Bernard L. Montgomery, commanding the 21st Army Group, on his own initiative, deployed his XXX Corps (43d, 51st, and 53d infantry divisions and the Guards Armoured Division) in position between Namur and Brussels. This would block further German advance, if it reached this far. Meantime, the spearhead of the 1st SS Panzer Division, led by Lt. Col. Jochen Peiper, was slowed, then halted by U.S. troops.

From December 19 until relieved on December 26, the 101st, plus supporting armor, artillery, and other miscellaneous units, successfully defended the Bastogne area against determined attacks by the 26th VGD and elements of the 15th Panzer Grenadier Division. When called on to surrender, McAuliffe replied with the word, "Nuts!" The stands at St.-Vith and Bastogne ruined any hope by the Germans that their counteroffensive would succeed. On December 22, the U.S. III Corps (Maj. Gen. John Milliken), consisting of the 26th and 80th infantry and the 4th Armored divisions, from Gen. George S. Patton's 3d Army, began to attack north to relieve Bastogne.

From December 18 on, German rear areas were in chaos. The road network was not adequate to support the German offensive. Roads were jammed with traffic, denying the front of sorely needed reinforcements, ammunition, and supplies. Also at this time, a thaw had set in, slowing tank movements. By December 22, the 6th Panzer Army wallowed in rain and mud, the 5th Panzer Army was slowed by fog and snow, and supply lines were beset by continuous snow. Clearing weather allowed Allied air power to attack the Germans all across the "bulge" area (essentially the center of the Allied line), causing heavy losses and further snarling traffic and resupply efforts. The campaign raged on until January 28, when the Germans were finally pushed back to their original positions.

For the Allies, the Ardennes Campaign was a classic example of a tactical defeat but a strategic victory. The sacrifices of the 28th and 106th infantry divisions and the stands made at St.-Vith, Bastogne, and on the German flanks, combined with snarled traffic in the German rear (subsequently compounded by Allied air attacks), all bought valuable time. This permitted the Allies to realign strategically and to re-allocate troops first to contain, then to reduce relentlessly, the German salient. The cost was severe to both sides. The Germans lost some 100,000 men (almost a third of those engaged), more than 700 tanks, and some 1,600 aircraft. The Allied (mostly American) losses were 80,000 men, 300 tanks, and 300 aircraft. U.S. losses could be replaced, but those of the Germans could not. Hitler's gamble was an irreparable disaster. Although it delayed Eisenhower's campaign by five weeks, it devoured already lean German reserves of personnel, fuel, ammunition, tanks, and guns. Within four months of the end of the campaign, Germany surrendered.

Bibliography: Cole, Hugh M., *The United States Army in World War II. The European Theater of Operations. The Ardennes: Battle of the Bulge* (U.S. Govt. Printing Office, 1965); Dupuy, Ernest, *St. Vith, Lion in the Way* (Infantry Journal Press, 1949); Eisenhower, John S. D., *The Bitter Woods* (Putnam's, 1969); Elstob, Peter, *Hitler's Last Offensive: The Full Story of the Battle of the Ardennes* (Macmillan, 1971); Toland, John, *Battle: The Story of the Bulge* (New American Library, 1959).

Brig. Gen. (PNG, Ret.) Uzal W. Ent

BURMA AND LEDO ROADS

Massive U.S. military project to reopen a land supply route to China during World War II. Construction was begun in 1942 by 28,000 U.S. Army engineers, who with only light equipment had to repair the 600-mile Burma Road from Lashio, Burma, to Kunming, China, and build a new 500-mile road from Ledo, India, to Lashio. The route wound through incredibly difficult terrain, sometimes still contested by the Japanese. The roads took two years to complete (opening in January 1945), cost $150,000,000, and delivered only 34,000 tons of supplies, but it was one of the greatest engineering feats of the war.

Mark Pitcavage

CARGO AIRCRAFT C-46 AND C-47

The two principal cargo aircraft of World War II. The C-47 ("Skytrain") was a variant of the Douglas-built DC-3 first flown in 1935. It entered service with the army air forces in 1941 and more than 10,000, built in 25 different models, made their way into the inventory. An enormously successful design, it could haul three tons of cargo or

An aerial view shows part of the Burma-Ledo Road as it winds it way through the mountains; it was the main supply route to China during World War II. (U.S. Army Military History Institute)

handle 27 paratroopers. At the Skytrain's peak, the military had more than 1,300 C-47s in service during World War II. Not available in large numbers until 1943, the Curtiss-Wright C-46 ("Commando") was a disappointment. The hydraulic and fuel systems had problems, the fuselage leaked in the rain, and corrosion problems were extensive. Even so, because of a larger carrying capacity, more than 700 C-46s were placed in service in World War II. They were phased out of the inventory in the early 1950s.

Bibliography: Burkard, Dick J., *Military Airlift Command Historical Handbook, 1941–1984* (Office of Military Airlift Command History, 1984); Glines, C. V., and W. F. Moseley, *The Legendary DC-3* (Van Nostrand-Reinhold, 1979).

Roger D. Launius

CARIBBEAN, U.S. INTERVENTION IN
(1918–1940)

Intervention during the 1918–40 period centered around the West Indian countries of Haiti and the Dominican Republic, the Central American nations of Nicaragua and Panama, the Panama Canal Zone, and the West Indian island of Trinidad. Even while the United States was involved militarily in France during the last years of World War I, the U.S. Marines were active in Haiti and the Dominican Republic, as well as in Cuba. Besides attempting to restore political and economic order in these countries, the United States, primarily concerned about possible German subversion in Haiti and Cuba, wished to protect its assets in these countries, especially its sugar holdings and production facilities in Cuba.

The 7th Marine regiment was dispatched to Cuba in August 1917 when it was discovered that German agents had been sent there to disrupt sugar production and stir up political unrest. The marines, having effectively kept the sugar industry going and political unrest at a minimum, remained in Cuba until August 1919.

In 1916, rebels had overthrown the government in the Dominican Republic, and at the request of the legitimate government, U.S. warships were ordered to the island country. The rebel government retreated to the city of Santiago, and U.S. Marines began a counterinsurgency campaign, which lasted for three months before the rebel capital was taken. A U.S. military government was then formed, its primary mission being to oversee the reconstruction of government and the restoration of basic services to the population. In 1922, a provisional government was installed, and the gradual transfer of power to it began. A constitutional government was inaugurated in 1924.

In Haiti, attempts to establish peace and to create a native constabulary, or *Garde,* were not as successful; in 1918, the entire northern half of Haiti was in revolt and the U.S. Marines stationed there began conducting massive counterguerrilla sweeps throughout the country. The concept of close air support was used for the first time here when a way was devised for pilots to drop small fragmentary bombs. By May 1920, the marines had conquered the guerrillas, and the United States was able to install a military government, led by Brig. Gen. John H. Russell, that introduced stability to the nation. In August 1934, the U.S. occupation of Haiti ended.

Marines were called to Nicaragua in 1926 to establish a neutral zone along the eastern coast in an attempt to quell revolutionary fervor and in 1927 to guard the property and lives of U.S. citizens. Despite an American presence and a peace plan formulated by Henry L. Stimson, Pres. Calvin Coolidge's personal representative, the fighting continued, and the marines were forced to intervene. Several antibandit campaigns were waged against the rebels, and eventually, an effective native constabulary (Guardia Nacional de Nicaragua), trained and led by marine officers, was developed. (Lessons in the employment of extensive patrolling, jungle fighting, and close air support proved to be invaluable experiences for the marines in World War II. These lessons were recorded by the Marine Corps schools in a 1940 document entitled *Small Wars Manual.*) In 1933, the United States withdrew its forces from Nicaragua.

When a military coup occurred in Cuba in 1933, U.S. Navy warships and marines, in a show of force, were dispatched to Guantanamo Bay. They remained in Cuban waters through January 1934, but no landing was necessary.

As war approached in Europe in the late 1930s, naval officers stationed in the Caribbean stressed the strategic importance of the area in any future European war. Of concern were threats to the security of the Panama Canal and to the oil-producing and oil-processing centers of

Aruba, Curacao, and Trinidad. In 1940, the United States sent a marine advisory team to Trinidad to train local police and militia in basic military skills.

Leo J. Daugherty III

CARTWHEEL, OPERATION (1941–1945)

Code name for overall Allied plan in the Pacific theater during World War II. It was comprised of 13 separate but overlapping westward operations along the New Guinea coast, then north toward the Solomon Islands. Cartwheel's objective was to neutralize the built-up Japanese base at Rabaul, on the eastern tip of crescent-shaped New Britain, the largest island in the Bismarck Archipelago. The strategic plan called for Adm. William F. Halsey's seizure of Woodlark and Kiriwina islands, then the U.S. Army's assault on the New Guinean coastal towns of Salamaua, Lae, and Finschhafen, with Halsey then taking the Shortland Islands prior to moving on Bougainville. The final phase entailed landings at Cape Gloucester by Gen. Douglas MacArthur on the west coast and at Bougainville by Halsey, converging their drives on Rabaul, seized in January 1942 by the Japanese and turned into a heavily fortified fleet and air base. Rabaul had given Japan virtual dominance of the naval and air approaches to New Guinea and the Solomons.

A direct assault seemed out of the question: the Japanese were too well entrenched. The decision thus was made to neutralize the Rabaul complex by carrier- and land-based bombers, which flew nearly 30,000 sorties, but did not directly assault the 91,000 troops of the heavily fortified Japanese garrison.

With Bougainville's capture in November 1943, Rabaul no longer proved threatening and was effectively bypassed. The garrison finally surrendered to the victorious Allies on September 6, 1945—three weeks after Japan had surrendered. Had MacArthur opted to go by land, naval historian Samuel Eliot Morison would later write, "Tarawa, Iwo Jima and Okinawa would have faded to pale pink in comparison with the blood that would have flowed if the Allies had attempted an assault on fortressed Rabaul."

Bibliography: Morison, Samuel Eliot, *The Two Ocean War* (Little, Brown, 1963); Spector, Ronald, *Eagle Against the Sun: The American War with Japan* (Free Press, 1985).

Peter Model

CASABLANCA CONFERENCE
(January 1943)

World War II summit talks attended by U.S. president Franklin D. Roosevelt, British prime minister Winston Churchill, and the Anglo-American Combined Chiefs of Staff (CCS); held at Casablanca, Morocco, in January 1943, to decide joint Allied strategy for the remainder of the war against Germany, Italy, and Japan. Code-named "Operation Symbol," the conference was in reality a series

of meetings of the Anglo-American military leadership, led by Gen. George C. Marshall of the United States and Gen. Sir Alan Brooke of Britain. While Churchill and Roosevelt remained in the background, the CCS, after many days of heated debate, hammered out a series of agreements specifying that priority would go to the defeat of Germany, to Lend-Lease supplies for Russia, and to the Battle of the Atlantic against the U-boats.

Although planning and a military buildup of forces and equipment in Britain for a cross-channel invasion of northern France would continue to be the overall top priority, it was accepted that the Allies could not carry out such an operation before the spring of 1944. Meanwhile, Mediterranean operations were to proceed with an invasion of Sicily in the early summer of 1943. The Allies also announced a policy of "unconditional surrender" for the Axis nations that later led to criticism that it unnecessarily prolonged the war.

Carlo W. D'Este

CASSINO, BATTLE FOR
(February-May 1944)

World War II battle for the town of Cassino, a key German observation post on the Gustav line. Located in central Italy near the Rapido River, the town was the site of a famous 6th-century Benedictine abbey. The abbey's bombing and destruction was one of the most controversial and questionable actions of the entire war. Perched atop 1,715-foot Monte Cassino, the abbey had housed one of Europe's most prized libraries of illuminated manuscripts and religious icons.

After Gen. Mark Clark's U.S. 5th Army crossed the Volturno and Sangro rivers in October 1943, his German counterpart, Field Marshal Albert Kesselring, ordered the removal of the abbey's treasures to Rome, along with most of its monks. Also unknown to the Allies at the time was Kesselring's pledge to the Vatican that, despite its elevated position as an observation post, the Germans would not fortify the abbey and expected the other side to refrain from aerial bombardment.

The tragic misunderstanding began in early February, after U.S. and French units crossed the Garigliano and Rapido rivers north of Monte Cassino and New Zealanders and Punjab troops under the command of Gen. Sir Bernard Freyberg advanced on the town. Pinned down by heavy artillery fire from above, they called for close air support. Aerial reconnaissance personally conducted by Gen. Ira C. Eaker reported seeing a German garrison in the abbey. On Feb. 15, 1944, Eaker dispatched a fleet of B-17s that dropped hundreds of tons of high explosives, pulverizing the ancient abbey. Freyberg's demand for air support recklessly exposed his troops to Allied air bombardment, causing heavy losses. After the bombing, the Allies renewed their assault but still failed to penetrate the town. Ironically, the rubble provided Germans with excellent protection.

In early May, a Polish unit attached to the British 8th Army advanced on the mountain but was repulsed with heavy casualties. It was only after Kesselring was denied reinforcements that the Germans began to pull back. On May 17, a second Polish assault was launched, and Monte Cassino fell the next day.

Bibliography: Calvocoressi, Peter, et al., *Total War: Causes and Courses of the Second World War* (Pantheon, 1989).

Peter Model

CHERBOURG, FALL OF (June 27, 1944)
The Allied taking of a chief Normandy port, located at the northern tip of the Cotentin Peninsula in northwestern France, during World War II. After U.S. troops established a bridgehead on the eastern flank of the Cotentin Peninsula on D-Day (June 6, 1944), U.S. forces broke out across the peninsula on June 16, thereby isolating Germany's Cherbourg garrison under Gen. Wilhelm Schlieben. The assault on Cherbourg proper began on June 22, supported by massive aerial, naval, and artillery bombardments. Schlieben capitulated on June 26, the harbor garrison surrendered June 29, and resistance continued on the western Joburg Peninsula until June 30. The entire harbor was wrecked and was not cleared until late September.

Russell A. Hart

CIVILIAN CONSERVATION CORPS (CCC)
New Deal unemployment relief agency largely administered by the U.S. Army. A combined effort of four governmental departments—labor, agriculture, war, and the interior—the Civilian Conservation Corps was authorized to enroll 250,000 unemployed young men between the ages of 18 and 25 for work in reforestation, soil conservation, flood control, road construction, and other reclamation projects. The War Department opposed participation in relief activities, but when it became clear almost immediately that only the army had the resources to build and operate the camps necessary to house the large number of enrollees, its role expanded dramatically. Army personnel controlled virtually all camp activity except actual supervision of the work itself. Remarkably, in less than three months, more than 250,000 young men were enrolled and at work in more than 1,300 camps—the most rapid and orderly mobilization in U.S. history.

Although the CCC remained a civilian relief organization until its demise in 1942, its success in preserving the nation's natural as well as human resources was primarily due to the efficiency of the army. Despite the disruption of normal military activities, the CCC experience also proved beneficial to military preparedness. In the years prior to

World War II, more than 2,500,000 young men were exposed to military life and partially trained for the armed forces; moreover, thousands of regular officers and reservists gained invaluable command experience in the camps.

Bibliography: Harper, Charles P., *The Administration of the Civilian Conservation Corps* (Clarksburg, 1939); Salmond, John A., *The Civilian Conservation Corps, 1933–1942: A New Deal Case Study* (Duke Univ. Press, 1967).

Ralph L. Eckert

COBRA, OPERATION (July 25, 1944)
Code name for the World War II Allied breakout from Normandy, France, initiated west of St.-Lô by Lt. Gen. Omar Bradley's U.S. 1st Army against Lieutenant General von Choltitz's much weakened LXXXIV Corps. The fall of St.-Lô on July 19, 1944, allowed U.S. forces to exit the difficult terrain and prepare for a major breakout attempt. Massive aerial bombardments opened the offensive, but part of the bombardment fell short, killing hundreds of U.S. troops, including Gen. Lesley J. McNair, the inspector of U.S. ground forces.

The bombardment stunned German resistance, and by July 27, Maj. Gen. Lawton J. Collins's VII Corps had penetrated the German line and threatened to encircle Choltitz's forces against the western Cotentin coast. Gen. Paul Hausser, commanding the German 7th Army, withdrew his threatened flank southwest after determined counterattacks by Lt. Gen. Eugen Meindl's II Parachute Corps failed to restore the situation. This withdrawal allowed Lt. Gen. George S. Patton's 3d Army to seize first Avranches and then a bridgehead across the Selune River at Pontabault on July 30. Patton ferried seven divisions and 100,000 men into the bridgehead in three days and then proceeded to fan out west into Brittany, south to the Loire, and east into the heart of France.

Russell A. Hart

COLMAR POCKET
(January 20–February 9, 1945)
Allied offensive against a German salient in World War II. On Jan. 20, 1945, the French 1st Army (General Jean de Lattre), reinforced by the U.S. 3d Infantry Division, attacked the eight-division German 19th Army (some 50,000 men), which occupied a salient, or pocket, centered on Colmar in northeastern France. Severe shortages of French troops led to the eventual attachment to the offensive of the entire U.S. XXI Corps (3d, 28th, and 75th infantry divisions), commanded by Maj. Gen. Frank Milburn.

The 28th Division reached Colmar on February 2, and the 75th Division neared Neuf-Brisach in the pocket's rear. The U.S. 12th Armored Division was added to the attack. The pocket was split on February 5 when U.S. troops met the Moroccan 4th Division near Rouffach. The French finished off the pocket on February 9. The Allies had lost approximately 18,000 men; German losses were estimated between 22,000 and 36,000.

Bibliography: Eisenhower, David, *Eisenhower: At War 1943–1945* (Random House, 1986); Weigley, Russell F., *Eisenhower's Lieutenants* (Indiana Univ. Press, 1981).

Brig. Gen. (PNG, Ret.) Uzal W. Ent

COMBINED CHIEFS OF STAFF/JOINT CHIEFS OF STAFF

World War II collaboration committee established by the United States and Great Britain during the Arcadia Conference (Dec. 22, 1941–Jan. 14, 1942). Largely because of U.S. Army Chief of Staff Gen. George C. Marshall's adamant proponency, British and American representatives agreed to form a single Anglo-American high command to plan global strategy, set priorities, and allocate war production—in short, to direct the overall war effort. The result was the Combined Chiefs of Staff (CCS), comprised of the American and British service chiefs, which reported directly to the president and prime minister. The committee met in continuous session in Washington, D.C., with representatives generally sitting for the British service chiefs.

The U.S. component of the CCS became known as the Joint Chiefs of Staff (JCS). Its members were Marshall; Gen. Henry H. Arnold, commanding general, army air forces; Adm. Ernest J. King, chief of naval operations and commander in chief of the U.S. combined fleet; and Adm. William D. Leahy, who functioned as de facto chairman and military chief of staff to Pres. Franklin D. Roosevelt. Leahy also provided the navy with a second member, to balance the army's Marshall and Arnold.

Because national and service rivalries persisted, both organizations were the setting for great, sometimes acrimonious, debates. Nevertheless, both contributed significantly to the Allied victory. The CCS brought unprecedented cooperation and communication between wartime allies. The JCS broke the American tradition of complete service autonomy and provided a mechanism for establishing the "U.S. position" in dealing with the Allies.

Stephen J. Lofgren

CORAL SEA, BATTLE OF THE
(May 4–8, 1942)

World War II battle that marked the first time major surface naval forces engaged without actually sighting each other, illustrating the key role intelligence could play in combat. By sending a potent naval armada of three carriers and numerous support ships into the Coral Sea, which lies off Australia's northeast coast, Japan hoped to establish a presence in the Solomon Islands and seize the New Guinea town of Port Moresby, which would place Japan within striking distance of Australia. Aided by superb intelligence work, Adm. Chester W. Nimitz, commander in chief of

the Pacific Fleet, was able to place his two available carriers, the *Lexington* and the *Yorktown* under Rear Adm. Frank J. Fletcher, in position to intercept the enemy.

Opening forays commenced on May 7, 1942, when Japanese carrier planes sank the destroyer *Sims* and badly damaged the tanker *Neosho*. On the same day, U.S. carrier planes sank the light carrier *Soho*, the first major warship lost by Japan in the war. Its loss stunned the Japanese commander, Vice Adm. Shigeyoshi Inouye, who halted the invasion force headed for Port Moresby until the U.S. naval threat was removed. The next day, U.S. torpedo planes and bombers damaged the carriers *Shokaku* and *Zuikaku*, while Japanese pilots so pummeled the *Lexington* that it later had to be sunk by an American destroyer. Although Japan emerged with the tactical victory due to *Lexington*'s loss, the U.S. Navy gained an important strategic victory by turning back Japan's invasion of Port Moresby and by so harming the *Shokaku* and *Zuikaku* that they had to be held out of the coming Midway action.

Bibliography: Costello, John, *The Pacific War* (Quill Books, 1982); Morison, Samuel Eliot, *Coral Sea, Midway and Submarine Actions* (Little, Brown, 1960); Spector, Ronald, *Eagle Against the Sun* (Free Press, 1985).

John F. Wukovits

CORREGIDOR, FALL OF (May 6, 1942)

The Japanese capture of a fortified Pacific island that, along with Bataan, was key to U.S. defense of the Philippines during World War II. Because Corregidor commanded the entrance to Manila Bay and served as headquarters for U.S. forces, when Bataan fell on Apr. 8, 1942, a Japanese assault on Corregidor was inevitable. Corregidor held 13,000 troops, but only 3,000 effectives. Its gun batteries were vulnerable to attacks from the air and from Japanese artillery on Bataan, which bombarded Corregidor until May 8, when 2,000 Japanese landed. U.S. forces initially imposed severe casualties, causing considerable worry to the Japanese, but then surrendered, disorganized and short of water. The Philippines thus belonged to the Japanese.

Mark Pitcavage

DESTROYERS, PREWAR SINKING OF U.S.

Naval actions in September-October 1941 that brought the United States closer to war as neutrality became imperiled by German U-boat operations in the Atlantic. On Sept. 4, 1941, a German submarine mounted a torpedo attack on the USS *Greer*, under the command of Lt. Cmdr. L. H. Frost. All torpedoes missed, and Frost ordered a depth-charge run against the assailant, but the U-boat escaped without damage. Pres. Franklin D. Roosevelt ordered convoy escorts to open fire on any vessel that threatened U.S. shipping or any vessel under American protection.

One month later, on October 17, a German U-boat attacked the USS *Kearney,* under the command of Lt. Cmdr. A. L. Davis, while on escort duty south of Greenland. Eleven sailors of the *Kearney's* company were killed in the engagement, but the ship remained afloat and made port. Two weeks later, another convoy escort, the USS *Reuben James,* commanded by Lt. Cmdr. H. L. Edwards, was torpedoed and sunk by a German submarine. The *Reuben James* lost more than 100 of its crew and was the first U.S. naval vessel sunk by the German navy. These attacks prompted the U.S. Congress to repeal the neutrality acts and begin a more aggressive support of the Allies.

Vernon L. Williams

DESTROYERS FOR BASES

U.S.-British agreement made during World War II, before the United States entered the conflict. On July 24, 1940, U.S. president Franklin D. Roosevelt and British prime minister Winston S. Churchill "agreed in principle" for the United States to give Great Britain 50 old destroyers in exchange for the right to establish air and naval bases on British islands in the Caribbean. This agreement—sealed in writing in September—allowed Roosevelt to skirt the terms of the 1935 Neutrality Act and set the stage for the $50 billion Lend-Lease program that would be implemented the following year. The agreement also marked an auspicious beginning of an extraordinary transatlantic partnership between Roosevelt and Churchill.

Roosevelt knew that sooner or later, the United States would have to enter the war against the Axis, in which case, ships using the Panama Canal from either end would be vulnerable to enemy attack. The United States would therefore require a strengthened military presence in the Caribbean. With Bermuda, the Bahamas, British Guiana, and many outposts in the Antilles, Leeward, and Windward islands under British sovereignty, the Caribbean was in many respects British turf. Could some sort of arrangement be made by which the United States could set up military bases on British soil in exchange for the obsolete destroyers? There would be no sale, merely a barter deal, although Congress would have to be consulted.

Churchill, rallying the British after the fall of France and the miraculous Dunkirk evacuation, needed surface vessels with which to combat the growing German U-boat peril. He knew the U.S. Navy planned to modernize its destroyer fleet and would dispose of its older ships. But even under the amended Neutrality Act of 1935, especially in the face of a growing isolationist mood among U.S. voters, Churchill knew that Roosevelt could not sell these weapons of war to the British.

Churchill coveted the destroyers for their speed, even though they had been built in 1917 and were lightly armed with 4 102-millimeter guns, 12 torpedo tubes, and primitive depth-charge launchers. Roosevelt sought and secured 99-year leases for military bases in the Caribbean. As a bonus, Britain also ceded sovereign rights to bases in Newfoundland and Bermuda.

The first three destroyers were transferred to the British in Halifax, Nova Scotia, and other ships soon followed. All had been laden with provisions that were in great shortage abroad. Once in British hands, all were retrofitted with sonar and new depth-charge equipment and rearmored. In a thoughtful gesture to his benefactors, Churchill ordered the ships be given names common to both countries—such as the HMS *Broadway.* Of the 50 destroyers, 9 were turned over to the Soviet navy in May 1944.

Peter Model

DOOLITTLE TOKYO RAID (April 18, 1942)

Surprise U.S. air assault on Tokyo four months after the Japanese bombing of Pearl Harbor. In response to U.S. president Franklin D. Roosevelt's desire for a morale-boosting raid to answer Pearl Harbor, a plan was devised for aircraft carriers to transport 16 B-25 Mitchell bombers within 600 miles of Japan, from where they would take off and surprise the enemy capital before flying on to friendly bases in Nationalist China. Led by Lt. Col. James H. Doolittle (army air force), the 16 crews rendezvoused at sea with Adm. William F. Halsey, who led Task Force 16, comprising the carriers *Hornet* and *Enterprise.*

On Apr. 18, 1942, Japanese picket ships spotted Halsey's force 100 miles short of its launching point. Halsey and Doolittle decided to launch the 16 bombers immediately (even though it meant some might not have sufficient fuel to reach China) in hopes of surprising the Japanese. The decision worked, and few enemy fighters became airborne before Doolittle's planes dropped their bombloads on steel plants, aircraft factories, and power plants and rushed toward China. One crew landed in Vladivostok and was interned by the Russians, while the others crash-landed short of the Chinese coast or on Chinese land. Eight members fell into the hands of the Japanese, who executed 3, but the remainder of the 80 safely returned with the assistance of Chinese guerrillas.

Japanese morale was shaken by this unsuspected assault deep into its territory. Japanese navy officials were so humiliated that they sped up operations in the South Seas and approved the daring Midway operation. These moves extended Japanese strength and enabled U.S. naval power, with the help of its code-breaking capacity, to check decisively later Japanese offensives.

Bibliography: Costello, John, *The Pacific War* (Quill Books, 1982); Glines, Carroll, *The Doolittle Raid* (Orion Books, 1988); Potter, E. B., *Bull Halsey* (Naval Inst. Press, 1985).

John F. Wukovits

DRAGOON, OPERATION (see ANVIL, OPERATION)

DRESDEN, DESTRUCTION OF
(February 13–14, 1945)
World War II Allied bombing of the German city of Dresden. The capital of the ancient state of Saxony, Dresden had great charm and elegance. During the last year of World War II, it fell victim to Allied bombing efforts designed to "break" the German will to fight. The Royal Air Force bombed Dresden with napalm on the night of Feb. 13, 1945. The next day, the U.S. Air Force also hit the city.

This devastating campaign very nearly leveled Dresden, and casualties, most of which were civilian, have been estimated between 60,000 and 500,000 people. The massive destruction in Dresden prompted Allied pangs of conscience, but the war ended within three months of Dresden's destruction, and serious rethinking of this type of bombing awaited other military contingencies.

Bibliography: Irving, David, *The Destruction of Dresden* (William Kimber, 1963); Kennett, Lee, *A History of Strategic Bombing* (Scribner's, 1982).

Roger D. Launius

ENIWETOK, BATTLE FOR (February 1944)
Battle in World War II for the Pacific Ocean atoll of Eniwetok, located on the extreme western end of the Marshall Islands, 325 miles northwest of Kwajalein and 1,000 miles from Saipan. Eniwetok was of key strategic importance as a staging area for the eventual assault on Okinawa. Launched 11 days after Kwajalein had been secured, the amphibious assaults of Feb. 17–18, 1944, on the northern and southern rims of the atoll by U.S. forces of the marines' 22d Regiment and the army's 106th Infantry Regiment turned out to be the penultimate attack on the Japanese outer defense perimeter. Rear Adm. Richard L. Connolly later said "it gave [the Japanese] no time to fortify their inner defense line that ran through the Marianas."

At first thought to be lightly defended, Eniwetok, like Kwajalein, turned out to be artfully fortified by underground tunnels, pillboxes, blockhouses, and other defenses. It was also manned by the fanatic 3,500–man Japanese 1st Amphibious Brigade, most of whom were annihilated by the orchestrated assault of sea bombardment, artillery, and flamethrowing tanks. The Americans lost 348 killed and missing (many blown apart by a new kind of mine detonated by just 35 pounds of pressure) and took the atoll by February 23. In 1947 Eniwetok was used to test atom bombs and, in 1952, the hydrogen bomb.

Peter Model

FALAISE GAP (August 1944)
Strategic point in northwest France in World War II. After the American breakout from Normandy and the failure of the German Mortain counterattack, the remants of two German armies, totaling 100,000 men, were caught in a 20-mile-deep salient, the neck of which hinged on Falaise in the north and Argentan in the south. Allied efforts to nip off the neck of the pocket and trap the Germans proved protracted. Stubborn German resistance denied Falaise to the Canadians for three days. The British and Americans had managed only partially to close the pocket by August 20 when the German breakout across the Dives River began. Although the retreating Germans lost most of their heavy equiptment, an estimated 50,000 Germans managed to escape.

Russell A. Hart

FIGHTER AIRCRAFT
Airplanes designed for the in-flight protection of bomber aircraft and the destruction of enemy aircraft, five models of which were utilized by U.S. air forces during World War II. During the 1930s, the United States fell behind other nations in the development of fighter aircraft. This was explained in part by the Army Air Corps' concentration on developing long-range bombers. At the opening of World War II, the United States relied essentially on two fighter aircraft. Both the Bell P-39 "Aircobra" and the Curtiss P-40 "Warhawk," designed in the mid-1930s, were single-engine fighters. Each weighed about 4,000 pounds and had from four to six machine guns, depending on the model. Between 1940 and 1944, when production ceased, a total of 9,558 P-39s and 13,738 P-40s were accepted for service in the army air forces. Only the P-40, which was employed with good sucess by U.S. aviator Claire L. Chennault's "Flying Tigers" in China during 1940–42, received notoriety during the war.

The army air forces developed three additional fighters that were used in the war. The Lockheed P-38 "Lightning," with its unique forked tail, was designed in 1937 for high-altitude interception. It was a superior aircraft in terms of performance and firepower, comparing favorably with the British "Spitfire" and the German ME-109. By Pearl Harbor (December 1941), the service had an inventory of only 69 P-38s. In all, 9,536 P-38s were accepted for use in the air forces during the war, and they flew in all theaters.

The Republic P-47 "Thunderbolt" was one of the most significant fighters of the war. By January 1944, approximately 40 percent of U.S. fighter groups serving overseas were equipped with it. Designed in 1940, the P-47 mounted six to eight .50-caliber machine guns and six 5-inch rockets. An excellent escort plane for bombers, it was also a superior ground-attack aircraft. By May 1945, 5,595 P-

47s were in active service with the army air forces in all theaters.

The last U.S. fighter that saw heavy service in World War II was the North American P-51 "Mustang," the so-called Cadillac of the skies. Prior to the war, many bomber enthusiasts had believed that their armadas would be invincible to attack from enemy fighters, a theory that was quickly dispelled during the strategic bombing campaign in Europe. Accordingly, fighters were employed as escorts for the bombers, but none had sufficient range to stay with the bomb groups over Germany. The P-51 was the direct result. It was designed initially for the British in 1940, with the army air forces taking little interest until 1942. Americans were first equipped with P-51s in November 1943. They proved so successful in merging performance, range, and armament that by the end of the war, 5,541 P-51s were in the army air forces' inventory. Along with the P-38 and the P-47, the P-51 carried the brunt of the fighter missions for the army air forces in all but the opening days of the war.

Bibliography: Holley, I. B., Jr., *Buying Aircraft: Matériel Procurement for the Army Air Forces* (Office of the Chief of Military History, U.S. Army, 1964); Maurer, Maurer, *Aviation in the U.S. Army, 1919–1939* (Office of Air Force History, 1987); Overy, R. J., *The Air War, 1939–1945* (Stein and Day, 1980).

Roger D. Launius

GARAND RIFLE (M-1)

A .30-caliber, gas-operated, air-cooled semiautomatic rifle designed by John C. Garand prior to World War II. It was the basic individual weapon in both World War II and the Korean War.

The rifle used a top-loaded eight-round clip. When fired, gas was forced down through a port drilled in the bottom of the barrel into a gas cylinder. This gas thrust an operating rod to the rear, driving the bolt rearward, ejecting the spent shell. A spring-loaded device then pushed the next live round up into position. As the bolt rode forward after ejecting the spent shell, it picked up this round and chambered it for firing. The Garand rifle has been regarded by many users as the best shoulder-fired weapon ever invented. More than 5,500,000 of them were produced.

Bibliography: *Field Manual 23–5, U.S. Rifle, Caliber .30, M-1* (U.S. War Department, 1943); Hatcher, Julian S., *Hatcher's Notebook* (Stackpole Co., 1966); Smith, W. H. B., and Joseph E. Smith, *The Book of Rifles* (Stackpole Books, 1972).

Brig. Gen. (PNG, Ret.) Uzal W. Ent

GUADALCANAL CAMPAIGN
(August 1942–February 1943)

World War II campaign in the western Pacific between U.S. and Japanese forces. The campaign proved to be significantly favorable to U.S. posture and morale in the Pacific theater.

Early Operations. Throughout the spring and summer of 1942, Japanese forces moved down the coast of New Guinea and to Tulagi and Guadalcanal at the southeastern corner of the Solomon Islands. Although Japanese activities on Tulagi had originally attracted the attention of U.S. naval leaders, it was the much larger island of Guadalcanal, some 20 miles away, that assumed paramount importance, for on it the Japanese were constructing an airfield. If marines could seize it and make it operational, the projected U.S. invasion of the Solomons—Operation Watchtower—could succeed. Without the airfield, Guadalcanal could not be secured and Tulagi, even if taken, would be lost as well. Watchtower originated in Washington where Adm. Ernest J. King pushed it through the Joint Chiefs of Staff (JCS), gaining only the reluctant approval of army chief of staff George Marshall.

On Aug. 7, 1942, marines under the overall command of Maj. Gen. Archer Vandegrift landed on Tulagi and Florida islands and two small neighboring islets as well as on Guadalcanal, where there were fewer than 1,000 Japanese combat personnel. The Japanese withdrew to await reinforcements. Heading inland from their beachhead about three miles from Lunga Point on the island's eastern shore, marine units easily reached the still incomplete airfield the second day. With Tulagi and adjacent islands quickly secured, on land, Watchtower seemed to be going well.

However, a sea disaster struck shortly after midnight on August 9 when a support force that included one Australian and four U.S. cruisers was almost wiped out in the Battle of Savo Island. The immediate consequences of this encounter with Japanese night gunnery and the "Long Lance" torpedo cost the Allies a total of four cruisers, one Australian and three American. In the absence of air cover (the carrier task force assigned to the operation had already turned away from the Solomons) and with only a handful of warships still available, the amphibious commander, Rear Adm. R. Kelly Turner, ordered freighters and transports to retire southward with large amounts of supplies intended for the marines still on board.

Turner's decision left the 11,000 marines on Guadalcanal (another 7,000 had landed on Tulagi) with rations for a month but with ammunition sufficient for only four days of sustained combat. Badly needed construction equipment and other supplies, including radar and five-inch guns, had not been unloaded either. Securing Guadalcanal in the face of enemy resistance would be difficult, for the island was more than 80 miles long and 25 miles wide; swarming with insects, poisonous spiders, and scorpions; and rife with malaria-carrying mosquitoes and natural obstacles such as mountains, rivers, swamps, jungle, and sawgrass. It was about halfway between Japan's principal South Pacific base, Rabaul, and the nearest American base at Espiritu

Santo in the New Hebrides, some 600 miles south of Guadalcanal. Efate and New Caledonia, where Vice Adm. Robert Ghormley (commander of the navy's South Pacific area) had his headquarters, were even more distant.

Vandegrift set as his priorities moving available supplies off the beachhead; making the airfield, now named Henderson Field, operational; and establishing a defense perimeter around it. For more than three months, circumstances placed U.S. forces on the tactical defense. Fortunately for Vandergrift's marines, most of whom were from his own 1st Division, the Japanese underestimated U.S. strength on Guadalcanal and committed only 6,000 men to their initial attempt to retake the island on August 21. Marines were waiting for them at the Tenaru River, less than two miles from Henderson Field, and decimated the charging Japanese with a combination of small-arms fire, mortars, artillery, tanks, and, where necessary, bayonets and machetes. By this time, Vandergrift had received 31 planes—dive bombers and fighters—as well as two additional shipments of supplies. Other planes—marine, navy, and army—began arriving to operate in what was known as the Cactus Air Force. All flew under the direction of marine brigadier general Roy Geiger. In the Battle of the Eastern Solomons (August 24), U.S. carriers returned to the area long enough to disrupt a Japanese resupply effort and sink one small enemy carrier.

A pattern of events was therefore established by the end of August. The Japanese were prepared to commit substantial resources to regain uncontested possession of Guadalcanal. However, U.S. forces on Guadalcanal, unlike their compatriots in the Philippines who had surrendered only three months before, were able to receive additional supplies. The operations needed to get the supplies to Guadalcanal were sometimes costly, and the amount brought in at any one time was often meager. Naval and air battles developed as each side attempted to cover its own resupply efforts and to disrupt those of its adversary.

September–October 1942. In covering the transportation of the 7th Marines to Guadalcanal, the *Wasp* was torpedoed and sunk (September 15) by a Japanese submarine, and the battleship *North Carolina* was damaged by still another, yet convoys could not venture north without substantial protection. A month later, a task force of U.S. cruisers and destroyers that had come north to help deliver a convoy carrying the 164th Infantry of the army's Americal Division surprised a Japanese surface force at the Battle of Cape Esperance (October 11–12) and sank one enemy cruiser.

The Japanese, however, were also able to augment their troop strength on Guadalcanal. Regaining control of Henderson Field was their objective, but they were stopped by marines at Edson's Ridge (September 12–14), while their biggest push was halted in battles along the Matanikau River (October 23–26) and on the opposite side of Henderson Field near Edson's Ridge (October 24–26). There, an understrength battalion of marines reinforced by an army contingent held off several times as many Japanese troops. Vandergrift was by no means satisfied with conducting a perimeter defense, but while his forces were able to begin advancing in November, the Japanese proved tenacious in defense, and the final American drive was postponed until early 1943. Throughout the struggle, Vandergrift's men conducted aggressive patrols, including a month-long foray by the 2d Marine Raider Battalion, and also had the invaluable aid of Melanesian scouts native to Guadalcanal. The defenders of Henderson Field also had to contend with Japanese air raids and naval bombardment.

At the same time as Japan's major land effort, the Japanese navy sent large forces to Guadalcanal. American task forces built around the carriers *Hornet* and *Enterprise* moved north to intercept the more powerful Japanese force. Although the *Hornet* was sunk by air attack in the resulting Battle of the Santa Cruz Islands (October 26), severe damage to two of their own carriers led the Japanese to retire to Truk.

Although South Pacific commander Ghormley never ceased to send supplies and reinforcements to Guadalcanal, his superiors came to perceive his attitude as defeatist. He was relieved by Vice Adm. William Halsey on October 16. Whether Halsey had more tactical and strategic acumen than Ghormley might never be known, but he clearly had the ability to inspire that Ghormley lacked. The securing of Guadalcanal had become a significant objective in Washington. Furthermore, Pres. Franklin D. Roosevelt made it clear to the JCS that holding Guadalcanal had the highest priority.

Securing Guadalcanal. Although the Japanese had amassed some 30,000 personnel on Guadalcanal by the end of October, there now arrived a procession of marines, Seabees, army contingents (both air and ground), as well as supplies and heavy artillery. A total of 37 Allied squadrons operated from Guadalcanal at one time or another: 16 of them marine, 10 navy, 9 army, and 2 from the Royal New Zealand Air Force. Japan's last major effort to destroy Henderson Field by naval bombardment was thwarted in mid-November. In two separate night surface encounters—together known as the Naval Battle of Guadalcanal (November 12–15)—U.S. task forces cost the enemy one battleship and damaged another so badly that planes from Guadalcanal were able to catch and sink the crippled vessel when daylight returned. Even though several Japanese destroyers sank three U.S. cruisers at Tassafaronga (November 30), Japanese combined fleet leaders had already decided to give up major operations in the southern Solomons.

In December, the 1st Marine Division began the process of evacuation from Guadalcanal. It would be a year before the depleted and disease-ridden division returned to combat. The army's Lt. Gen. Alexander Patch, who now took over command of operations on Guadalcanal, had at his disposal forces that included 200 planes and two army divisions as well as the 2d Marine Division, enough ground personnel to warrant establishment of a corps headquarters. To liquidate remaining Japanese forces, Patch ordered a drive to Cape Esperance on the northern edge of the island. When his forces reached their objective on Feb. 9, 1943, they discovered that some 12,000 Japanese had already been evacuated. More than twice as many had died of wounds, illness, or starvation. American deaths on land numbered 1,200 marines and about 400 army personnel. Many more men of both nationalities had died in the air and at sea, among them Adms. Daniel Callaghan and Norman Scott. So many ships had been sunk during the contest for Guadalcanal that the waters between Tulagi and Guadalcanal became known as Ironbottom Sound.

Analysis. A battle of attrition, Guadalcanal demonstrated that the Japanese could be beaten, not only on the seas and in the air but on the ground as well. Perhaps more important, the campaign proved that U.S. resources were superior. Less than a year after Pearl Harbor, the Japanese combined fleet had had to call off major naval operations in the Guadalcanal area. Although each contestant lost two dozen warships, it was the United States that was in the process of establishing command of the seas. Moreover, the Japanese had lost large numbers of experienced pilots; their naval aviation had started upon a period of decline that would never be reversed.

Bibliography: Coggins, Jack, *The Campaign for Guadalcanal* (Doubleday, 1972); Frank, Richard B., *Guadalcanal: The Definitive Account of the Landmark Battle* (Random House, 1990); Hough, Frank O., et al., *Victory and Occupation: History of U.S. Marine Corps Operations in World War II; Vol. 1: Pearl Harbor to Guadalcanal* (U.S. Govt. Printing Office, 1968); Morison, Samuel Eliot, *History of United States Naval Operations in World War II; Vol. 5: The Struggle for Guadalcanal, August 1942–February 1943* (Little, Brown, 1943).

Lloyd J. Graybar

GUAM, RECAPTURE OF (July 21, 1944)

The retaking of a western Pacific island by U.S. forces during World War II. A U.S. possession since its acquisition from Spain in 1898, the weakly held island outpost of Guam fell quickly to Japanese forces in December 1941. In July 1944, substantial U.S. naval and ground forces descended on the Marianas, landing first on Saipan, the closest to Japan of the major islands in the group, and then on Guam and Tinian. On July 21, troops from the 3d

Marine Division, the 1st Provisional Marine Brigade, and the army's 77th Division, under the overall command of marine major general Roy Geiger, came ashore on Guam on two separate beachheads. After a week of fighting, the beachheads were consolidated, and Geiger ordered his forces to advance to the north where the Japanese were continuing to resist. The island was declared secure on August 10. With several airfields and an excellent harbor, Guam became the Pacific Fleet's advance headquarters.

Bibliography: Wheeler, Richard, *A Special Valor: The U.S. Marines and The Pacific War* (New Amer. Library, 1983).

Lloyd J. Graybar

HAMBURG RAIDS (July 24–August 4, 1943)

Allied air assaults on Germany's second largest city during World War II. As a result, it was an early and frequent target for the Allied strategic bombing campaign. Prior to the summer 1943 raids, Hamburg had already been bombed more than 130 times. A new wave of attacks was begun on the night of July 24 by 740 Royal Air Force (RAF) bombers. In successive night attacks, Britain's heavy bombers created a firestorm when thousands of individual fires merged into one consuming blaze. The wind drew people into the inferno, and the fire consumed oxygen so that many in shelters suffocated or were baked alive. When the last attack was completed, the Allied campaign had destroyed about 6,000 acres in Hamburg, more than half the city, and killed somewhere between 60,000 and 100,000 people.

Bibliography: Kennett, Lee, *A History of Strategic Bombing* (Scribner's, 1982); Middlebrook, Martin, *The Battle of Hamburg: Allied Bomber Forces Against a German City in 1943* (Scribner's, 1981); Sherry, Michael S., *The Rise of American Air Power: The Creation of Armageddon* (Yale Univ. Press, 1987).

Roger D. Launius

HARBORD BOARD (1921)

Advisory group formed when army chief of staff Gen. John J. Pershing appointed his deputy, Maj. Gen. James G. Harbord, to head a board in 1921 to recommend a further organization for the War Department General Staff. The board recommended the adoption of the "G" system successfully used by the American Expeditionary Force in France during World War I. As a result, the General Staff was divided into five divisions: G-1 (Personnel), G-2 (Intelligence), G-3 (Operations and Training), G-4 (Logistics), and WPD (War Plans Division). An assistant chief of staff headed each division. This basic organization, in one form or another, has remained in effect to the present time.

Steve R. Waddell

HIROSHIMA AND NAGASAKI, ATOMIC BOMBINGS OF (August 6–9, 1945)

The nuclear devastation of two metropolitan sites in Japan by the United States during World War II. Resulting in immense human suffering, these bombings were followed by the unconditional surrender of the Japanese empire.

Atomic Bomb Development. When Vice Pres. Harry S Truman succeeded to the U.S. presidency in April 1945, he learned about the most important weapons research program of the era: the Manhattan Project to develop an atomic bomb. A massive effort employing thousands of scientists and technicians at scores of sites and costing more than $2.5 billion, the Manhattan Project was successful. On July 16, 1945, a nuclear device of devastating power was detonated at the Trinity Site near the desert research center of Los Alamos, New Mexico.

At the same time that these efforts were underway, the army air forces were developing the capability to deliver an atomic weapon on a target. Col. Paul W. Tibbets was given command of the 509th Composite Group in September 1944. Tibbets began training his force at Wendover Field, in the western Utah desert. Although his aircrews had already received flight training and were capable of meeting the normal standards for accuracy, Tibbets's program demanded that each B-29 aircrew consistently hit within 200 feet from the center of a bullseye at an altitude of 30,000 feet. Moreover, bombing was to be done visually, with no radar allowed. Another unique aspect of the crew training program involved practice to deliver a single bomb, immediately followed by executing a tight turn of 158 degrees, but crews were unaware at the time that the reason was to retreat as far away as possible from the target to avoid the expected shock waves from the atomic explosion.

With training completed, on May 29, even before the first successful test of the nuclear weapon, Tibbets relocated his wing to Tinian in the Marianas island chain in the Pacific. There it awaited orders to drop the bomb.

Command Decision. When Truman learned that an atomic device had been successfully detonated, he faced the decision of whether or not to use it. Apparently, he never seriously considered not using every means at his disposal to defeat the enemy—by that time only Japan was continuing its hostilities—and that included atomic weapons. Some advisers urged him not to employ it in combat, suggesting instead that Japan be treated to a demonstration of the bomb's capability, but this was rejected with statements of concern about what might happen if the weapon experienced a malfunction during the test. The

bomb, Truman and his supporters stated repeatedly, had been made to be used, and they rationalized it as a means of saving American lives through an earlier ending of the war.

At the Postdam Conference in late July, Truman gave Japan an ultimatum: unless immediate unconditional surrender was tendered, the United States would use its terrible new weapon without specifying what the weapon was. Japanese officials, thinking that there was little more terrible than the firebombing already taking place, vowed to fight on. Truman then authorized the army air forces to drop the new bomb anytime after August 3.

The Operation. Military officials chose the targets for the atomic devices carefully. There were four major Japanese cities still relatively untouched by strategic bombing. They first settled upon Kyoto, but this was rejected because the city was a religious and cultural center. They decided on the manufacturing city of Hiroshima, about seven miles square and 350,000 in population. At 9:15 A.M. local time on Aug. 6, 1945, Tibbets, flying his B-29, the *Enola Gay*, dropped the first atomic bomb on the city. The result was massive devastation. There was first a blinding flash, then a great rushing wind of fire, and a mushroom cloud rose about the city. Within a second, four square miles of the city were vaporized, and nearly 80,000 people died.

Unconditional surrender did not follow immediately, and three days later, another B-29 from the 509th, *Bock's Car,* dropped a second atomic bomb on Nagasaki. Again, thousands died, and the city center was destroyed. Neither the men that ordered the mission nor the aircrew that flew it could have known that the inner council of the Japanese government was considering surrender, formally doing so on August 14.

Aftermath. The act of dropping the atomic bomb on Japanese cities has caused controversy since it occurred. Some people charged that the bombing made explicit a longstanding Western racism against Asians. Others argued that the use of the weapon was more to frighten the emergent Soviet Union in the opening stages of the Cold War. Regardless of the necessity and motivations of the use of these weapons, the military executed its mission with efficiency and precision and in so doing created a new reality in international relations through the possible use of such a weapon of mass destruction.

Bibliography: Alperovitz, Gar, *Atomic Diplomacy: Hiroshima and Potsdam* (Simon & Schuster, 1965); Jones, Vincent C., *Manhattan: The Army and the Atomic Bomb* (Center of Military History, U.S. Army, 1985); Rhodes, Richard C., *The Making of the Atomic Bomb* (Knopf, 1985); Sherry, Michael S., *The Rise of American Air Power: The Creation of Armageddon* (Yale Univ. Press, 1987); Sherwin, Martin J., *A World Destroyed: The Atomic Bomb and the Grand Alliance* (Knopf, 1977).

Roger D. Launius

HUERTGEN FOREST, BATTLE OF THE

World War II scene of bloody infantry combat within a German forest lying southeast of Aachen; it breached the Siegfried Line defenses barring the path to the heart of Germany. Between September 1944 and January 1945, 120,000 American troops of the U.S. 1st Army (Lt. Gen. Courtney H. Hodges) suffered 33,000 casualties in occupying the bulk of the forest. The stubborn German defense was attributable to a combination of excellent defensive terrain, strong fortifications, and unimaginative American frontal attacks. Indeed, the forest's strategically important Rur (Roer) River dams only fell in February 1945 after the Germans released floodwaters that delayed a crossing of the Roer for two weeks.

Bibliography: MacDonald, Charles B., *The Battle of the Huertgen Forest*, ed. by Hanson W. Baldwin (Lippincott, 1963).

Russell A. Hart

HUMP AIRLIFT (1942–1945)

The most spectacular air transport operation of World War II. After the Japanese cut water and land access to China, Pres. Franklin D. Roosevelt decided to resupply Allied forces in the Chinese interior by air. The airlift, begun on Feb. 1, 1942, became known as the "Hump" because its route crossed the dangerous Himalayan mountain ranges. During the course of its operation, the Air Transport Command's (ATC) C-46, C-54, and C-87 aircraft and crews moved thousands of tons of supplies from eastern India to Allied forces in the Yunnan Province of China. Contending with 16,000-foot mountain peaks, violent turbulence, harsh monsoon seasons, severe cold and icing, and enemy attacks, the ATC maintained a slender logistical pipeline to China, delivering nearly 650,000 tons of supplies and proving that air supply was a viable means of supporting armies in the field.

Bibliography: *Anything, Anywhere, Anytime: An Illustrated History of the Military Airlift Command, 1941–1991* (Office of Military Airlift Command History, 1991); Koening, W. J., *Over the Hump: Airlift to China* (Ballantine Books, 1972).

Roger D. Launius

INDIANAPOLIS INCIDENT
(July 29, 1945)

Sinking of a U.S. cruiser by a Japanese submarine at the end of World War II, for which a rescue mission was tragically belated. In July 1945, after delivering essential ingredients of the atom bomb to the island of Tinian in the Marianas, Capt. Butler McVay headed his unescorted heavy cruiser USS *Indianapolis* toward the Philippines. Traveling in what was deemed a safe rear area, McVay opted not to zigzag his ship at night. Late on July 29,

Japanese submarine I-58 sighted the *Indianapolis* and fired six torpedoes that sank the cruiser in less than 15 minutes. Due to communications problems, the ship was not reported missing or overdue, and for four horrendous days, its surviving crew suffered from exposure and repeated shark attacks before a search plane called in assistance. More than 800 of the total crew of 1,196 safely abandoned the ship, but fewer than 320 remained alive four days later. A court-martial, convened partly to satisfy public opinion, found McVay guilty of failure to zigzag, a verdict that is still heatedly debated.

Bibliography: Costello, John, *The Pacific War* (Quill Books, 1982); Kurzman, Dan, *Fatal Voyage* (Macmillan, 1990); Morison, Samuel Eliot, *Victory in the Pacific* (Little, Brown, 1960).

John F. Wukovits

ITALIAN CAMPAIGN (NORTHERN)
(1944–1945)

Conclusive Allied campaign waged in the late months of World War II in Europe. When the great Allied offensives at Cassino and Anzio in May 1944 finally broke a six-month stalemate in central Italy, Field Marshal Albert Kesselring's German Army Group C began retreating toward northern Italy. Electing not to fight for Rome, Kesselring in early June declared the Italian capital an open city. Although there was German resistance outside the city, it was merely a delaying action to buy time for Group C to get free of the Rome bottleneck and move north as fast as possible.

The Allied ground commander in chief, Gen. Sir Harold Alexander, ordered Lt. Gen. Mark Clark's U.S. 5th Army and Lt. Gen. Sir Oliver Leese's 8th British Army to pursue and engage the German armies before they could reach the sanctuary of the northern Apennine Mountains. Kesselring's rear guards prevented this by successfully covering the withdrawal of the major elements of Group C, inflicting 34,000 Allied casualties in the process.

German strategy was to establish new defensive positions along a series of fortifications known first as the Gothic Line and later as the Winter Line. Situated north of Florence in the heart of the Apennines, the Gothic Line was the strongest of a series of defensive barriers designed to slow and then eventually halt the Allies. Running from Pisa on the Mediterranean Sea, across the Apennines, to Pesaro on the Adriatic Sea, this barrier consisted of numerous obstacles that included tank traps and concrete fortifications.

In late August, British and Canadian forces attacked the Adriatic end of the Gothic Line, and on September 10, Clark's 5th Army opened a major offensive to break through the German defenses and enter the Po Valley. If the offensive succeeded, the Allied commanders believed they could end the war in Italy in 1944. However, after more than six weeks of heavy fighting under exceptionally difficult conditions and extensive casualties on both sides (nearly 16,000 in the 5th Army alone), the exhausted Allies were unable to crack the Gothic Line. The result was the second winter stalemate of the Italian Campaign.

The Allies were unable to resume operations until the spring of 1945, when a massive offensive finally crushed German resistance in northern Italy. More than 100,000 German troops were trapped in the Po Valley and forced to surrender. On May 2, 1945, the campaign ended with the surrender of Kesselring's Group C.

Bibliography: Clark, Mark, *Calculated Risk* (Harper & Row, 1951); Fisher, Ernest, *Cassino to the Alps, (The U.S. Army in World War II: Mediterranean Theater of Operations)* (Center of Military History, U.S. Army, 1977); Graham, Dominick, and Shelford Bidwell, *Tug of War: The Battle for Italy, 1943–45* (St. Martin's Press, 1986); Orgill, Douglas, *The Gothic Line* (Zebra Books, 1986).

Carlo W. D'Este

IWO JIMA, BATTLE OF
(February–March 1945)

Scene of harsh World War II fighting between U.S. and Japanese forces on a tiny island 750 miles south of Tokyo. During the war in the Pacific, the Americans advanced across two fronts: Gen. Douglas MacArthur slogged across New Guinea toward the Philippines, while Adm. Chester Nimitz's amphibious forces leapfrogged from island to island. In February 1944, Nimitz's forces reached the Marianas, a chain of volcanic islands in the Central Pacific.

By the beginning of 1945, the situation for the Japanese had deteriorated badly across the Pacific. Imperial forces formulated a defense plan, code-named Ten-Go (Ten-Ichi-Go), aimed at holding what were considered the most vulnerable points on Japan's remaining defensive perime-

A U.S. tank-landing ship unloads at Red Beach One on the island of Iwo Jima in 1945; three days of bombardment by sea and air secured the beachhead. (U.S. Navy)

ter. U.S. strategists decided that an island on this perimeter must be seized as an emergency landing field for American B-29s. Iwo Jima in the Volcano Islands seemed to be the best choice for such a base.

On Feb. 19, 1945, Gen. Harry Schmidt's V Amphibious Corps (4th and 5th Marine divisions, with the 3d Marine Division in reserve) landed on Iwo Jima. Heavily gunned and garrisoned, and honeycombed with tunnels, the island's defenders subjected the marines to their worst landing experience of the entire war. Three days of battleship bombardment had failed to destroy Japanese positions dug into the island's bedrock. Landing vehicles lost traction on the volcanic rock and, after being ditched on the beaches, were destroyed by salvos from close artillery.

After bitter fighting, U.S. forces captured Mount Suribachi on February 23 and raised the American flag over Iwo Jima on March 16. Correspondent Robert Sherrod, who covered the island landings in the Pacific, labeled Iwo Jima the one with "the greatest possible violence." U.S. casualties numbered 6,821 killed, with about 20,000 wounded, while 21,000 Japanese defenders died almost to a man. Iwo Jima provided a warning of what lay in store as U.S. forces advanced closer and closer to Japan.

Bibliography: Ross, Bill D., *Iwo Jima: Legacy of Valor* (Random House, 1986).

M. Guy Bishop

JAPANESE-AMERICANS, RELOCATION OF

Controversial internment of Japanese-Americans by U.S. military authorities during World War II. On Feb. 19, 1942, in the face of false rumors following the Japanese attack on Pearl Harbor that Japanese-Americans were involved in sabotage, Pres. Franklin D. Roosevelt signed Executive Order No. 9066. The order authorized the War Department to designate certain areas as military zones and gave it the right to exclude anyone from them. In reality, the order was aimed at one group—the 127,000 Japanese-Americans—most of whom lived along the West Coast and were U.S. citizens by birth. Evacuations of Japanese-Americans began the following month. By September, more than 100,000 had been transferred by the War Relocation Agency to 10 permanent camps at isolated inland sites. Although a grievous injustice had been inflicted on a loyal group of Americans, the action was three times upheld by the U.S. Supreme Court in cases such as *Hirabayashi* vs. *United States* (1943) and *Korematsu* vs. *United States* (1944). The camps remained open until the end of 1945. A federal district court overturned *Korematsu* vs. *United States* in 1983, and the federal government offered a public apology to Japanese-Americans, while also stipulating that payments would be made as reparations for suffering.

Bibliography: Bosworth, Allan R., *America's Concentration Camps* (Norton, 1967); Girdner, Audrie, and Anne

Japanese-Americans, required to relocate at isolated inland camps during World War II, gather at a camp reception center. (War Relocation Authority, National Archives)

Loftis, *The Great Betrayal* (Macmillan, 1969); Tateishi, John, *And Justice For All* (Random House, 1984).

John F. Wukovits

JAVA SEA, BATTLE OF
(February 27–March 1, 1942)

World War II South Pacific naval battle in which Allied combatants were decisively bested by the Japanese navy. On Feb. 24, 1942, Allied planes spotted a Japanese convoy heading toward the island of Java, causing the Americans, British, Dutch, and Australians to send a fleet of five cruisers and a dozen destroyers, under Dutch Adm. K. W. F. M. Doorman, to stop the invasion. The Allies intercepted a Japanese force of about equal size on February 27.

After an inconclusive initial engagement, Doorman ordered a night attack, in which the Japanese demonstrated their superiority, sinking two Allied cruisers and four destroyers with minimal losses to themselves. Most of the remaining Allied ships were sunk trying to escape; the Allies had delayed the invasion of Java by only one day.

Mark Pitcavage

JEDBURGHS (1944–1945)

In World War II, code name given to special British and U.S. teams secretly sent behind French enemy lines after D-Day (June 6, 1944) to assist the French Resistance in disrupting German military and political operations. The paramilitary Jedburgh teams usually numbered three operatives: an American from the Office of Special Services

(OSS, forerunner of Central Intelligence Agency), an Englishman (or woman) from Britain's Special Operative Executive (SOE), and a French officer or enlisted person, also from military intelligence. The Jedburghs were recruited and trained by the OSS and SOE and at all times wore uniforms to ensure that when captured they would not be executed as spies but as combatants, a distinction the Germans sometimes ignored. In 1944–45, more than 90 Jedburgh teams were sent into France, and others were later sent into Belgium, Holland, and Norway. In these cases, the third team member would be a native.

Peter Model

JEEP

Popular name for the ubiquitous World War II versatile utility vehicle. Its name may have derived from the pronunciation of its "GP" (general purpose) classification. The jeep, conceived as a reconnaissance vehicle, was adaptable as a headquarters transport communications vehicle, litter bearer, towing vehicle, and quite often weapons carrier. It was used by more Americans than any other tool of war. Built to travel 60 miles per hour on the open road and to traverse rough terrain, the canvas-topped 11-foot-long, 4-foot-high vehicle weighed about 2,500 pounds (depending on how it was equipped) but offered little protection against the weather or the enemy. It had four-wheel drive and a four-cylinder engine. Originally built in 1940 by the American Bantam Car Company, it was adopted by the army in the summer of 1941 and was mass-produced during the war as the M38 utility vehicle by the Ford Motor Company and Willys-Overland Motors (subsequently absorbed into

A jeep, the usual mode of transportation for the Allied forces in World War II, is driven through a French village in June 1944; seated in the back (left to right) *are Lt. Gen. Courtney Hodges, Gen. George C. Marshall, and Gen. Dwight D. Eisenhower.* (Dwight D. Eisenhower Library)

American Motors). Nearly 635,000 jeeps were built during the World War II. The wartime jeep spawned an entire civilian line, now made by Chrysler.

Peter Model

JEEP CARRIERS

U.S. naval vessels designed for use in World War II as antisubmarine escort carriers. In 1940, Pres. Franklin D. Roosevelt ordered the U.S. Navy to convert merchant vessels into small aircraft carriers to combat the alarming German submarine threat in the Atlantic. Carrying up to 24 aircraft, these escort carriers guarded Europe-bound convoys and launched search planes that would aggressively hunt submarines before they stalked the convoy. Subsequent escort carriers, built from scratch, provided valuable cover for Pacific amphibious landings and ferried extra aircraft to fast carriers. Escort carriers achieved their moment of glory in the 1944 Battle of Samar, when a vastly outgunned flotilla of jeep carriers under Vice Adm. Clifton A. Sprague turned back a potent Japanese force intent on disrupting the Allied beachhead on Leyte.

Bibliography: Y'Blood, William T., *Hunter-Killer* (Naval Inst. Press, 1983); —, *The Little Giants* (Naval Inst. Press, 1987).

John F. Wukovits

KAMIKAZES

Japanese volunteer suicide pilots of Special Attack Corps who flew airplanes loaded with explosives into U.S. warships in 1944–45 during World War II. The kamikazes were named for the Japanese word meaning "divine wind," from the typhoon in 1281 that destroyed Mongol ruler Kublai Khan's invasion fleet. Kamikazes were first organized by Vice Adm. Onishi Takejiro as a last desperate move by a matériel-starved Japan to counter the enormous U.S. military machine in its powerful drive across the Pacific. The initial kamikaze attack occurred on Oct. 24, 1944, in Leyte Gulf and succeeded in sinking the escort carrier *St. Lo.* More than 1,500 kamikaze missions seriously threatened U.S. naval forces at Okinawa, where more than 30 ships were sunk. The kamikaze became one of the most feared weapons of the Pacific clash.

Bibliography: Millot, Bernard, *Divine Thunder* (McCall, 1971); Naito, Hatsuho, *Thunder Gods* (Kodansha, 1989); Toland, John, *The Rising Sun* (Random House, 1970).

John F. Wukovits

KASSERINE PASS, BATTLE OF (February 14–22, 1943)

The first major U.S. engagement against Germany during World War II; widely viewed as a humiliating defeat for U.S. forces. In early 1943, Allied forces in Tunisia had adopted a defensive posture and were thinly disposed across

U.S. troops of the 1st Infantry Division march through Kasserine Pass, Tunisia, in 1942; they were called upon to defend the pass against German attack in early 1943. (U.S. Army Military History Institute)

a wide front along the mountains of the Western and Eastern Dorsals. The U.S. II Corps was defending the important pass at Kasserine (or Al-Qasrayn), which was the gateway to the interior and one of the key elements of the Allied defensive positions.

On February 14, Gen. Jürgen von Arnim's 5th Panzer Army attacked and crushed U.S. forces defending Faid and Sidi Bou Zid, the anchor of the Allied defense east of Kasserine. This was the first part of a two-pronged German offensive designed to split the Allies in two and threaten their lines of communication from Algeria. Five days later, Field Marshal Erwin Rommel's Afrika Korps attacked Allied troops guarding Kasserine Pass. U.S. troops were able to delay the German advance sufficiently to enable a hastily assembled Anglo-American task force to contain the 10th Panzer Division at Thala, while a similar force stopped the advance of the 21st Panzer Division at Sbiba. By February 22, Rommel realized he had lost the initiative and ordered the Afrika Korps to withdraw.

Bibliography: Blumenson, Martin, *Kasserine Pass* (Houghton Mifflin, 1967); Howe, George F., *Northwest Africa: Seizing the Initiative in the West (The U.S. Army in World War II: Mediterranean Theater of Operations),* (Office of the Chief of Military History, U.S. Army, 1957).

Carlo W. D'Este

KELLOGG-BRIAND PACT (August 27, 1928)

Multipartite antiwar treaty that, although designed to prevent a second world war, was ultimately ineffectual. The aftermath of World War I brought an attempt to outlaw war, and French foreign minister Aristide Briand openly suggested a treaty between France and the United States renouncing war as a means of settling disputes. U.S. secretary of state Frank B. Kellogg was furious. He felt that Briand should have used diplomatic channels rather than a public forum. Kellogg feared acceptance of the plan would drag the United States into an unwanted alliance with France in the event of future wars. He came back with his own proposal for a multilateral nonaggression pact involving not only the United States and France but also Great Britain, Japan, Italy, Belgium, Poland, and Czechoslovakia. Such an agreement was signed on Aug. 27, 1928, by 15 nations, but Kellogg and Briand knew the treaty lacked force. Yet, public apprehension following World War I demanded an antiwar treaty. While the Kellogg-Briand Pact was hailed publicly, diplomats failed to take the agreement seriously. Only 14 years later, all of the signatories had become belligerents in World War II.

M. Guy Bishop

KWAJALEIN, BATTLE FOR
(January 31–February 4, 1944)
World War II engagement in the Marshall Islands on Kwajalein, the world's largest coral atoll, comprised of a string of 18 islands and dozens of islets, wrapped around an irregular-shaped lagoon 66 miles long and 20 miles wide, considered the most complex of all amphibious Pacific assaults. Strategists had anticipated as bloody a battle as Tarawa three months earlier. However, the sequential amphibious attack on the Japanese administrative, air, and communications island center by the U.S. 4th Marine and 7th Army divisions—the first at the joined islands of Roi and Namur on the north, the second at Kwajalein Island at the south end—went surprisingly well. The atoll had been subjected to relentless aerial bombardment by carrier-based planes. But savage resistance was

offered on Kwajalein Island by the deeply entrenched and fortified Japanese. To subdue this garrison took five days of close combat; all but 35 Japanese died, many by suicide. All told, the enemy lost 7,870 out of 8,675 stationed there, while the Americans posted 372 dead or missing out of 41,000 men committed. Kwajalein was later used for U.S. missile testing.

Peter Model

LANDING CRAFT
Naval vessels designed to deliver equipment and personnel on or close to shore for disembarkment. During World War II, Allied progress in the Pacific theater greatly hinged on the American ability to assault, from the sea, heavily fortified enemy island bases. That amphibious operations succeeded was in large part due to the landing craft designed for these offensives. Landing craft required shallow drafts so they could quickly bring in men and supplies directly to the beachhead and then speedily depart to transport additional cargo. Two basic types appeared. Tractored vehicles, called amphibians, could churn through water to the beach, then continue on land. Other landing craft bore right onto the beach, deposited their cargoes of men or supplies over their forward ramps, and then backed off the beach to bring in more cargo. A slipstream from a protected propeller washed away sand beneath each craft, thus releasing the grounded craft from its sandy grasp and permitting it to ease away.

The smallest landing craft, the LVT (landing vehicle, tracked), first appeared at Guadalcanal and was used through the remainder of the war. Known as "alligators" or "amptracs" and developed in 1933 by Donald Roebling

Some landing craft, such as the LCIs (landing craft, infantry) shown here preparing for the invasion of Sicily, were able to travel long distances; others were dispatched from larger ships near the shore. (U.S. Army Military History Institute)

for use in rescue operations in the Florida Everglades, the tractored LVT could climb over menacing coral reefs to deposit 15–20 men. Sporting one machine gun for protection, an LVT could operate on land or in water. Although hard to manage, even in calm waters, and although the absence of ramps forced the men to climb out over the sides and thereby often expose themselves to enemy fire, more than 18,000 LVTs were built during the war. A second type, the LVT(A), was a turreted gun-vehicle that operated mainly as close-in fire support for landings.

New Orleans boat builder Andrew J. Higgins contributed two other types of landing craft. The LCVP (landing craft, vehicle, personnel), a diesel-powered machine, carried a larger cargo of men or supplies than the LVT and, with its protected propeller, could back off the beach to get more equipment. A forward ramp permitted faster unloading of its cargo. Higgins's other product, the LCM (landing craft, medium), transported heavier items, as well as troops, directly to the beach. Tanks, bulldozers, and heavy trucks were typical cargoes of this craft.

The largest of the four main kinds of landing craft was the LST (landing ship, tank). Designed by John C. Niedermair of the Navy Bureau of Ships, the oceangoing LST carried practically everything in its hold and could transport matériel long distances from supply bases directly to the needed area. As many as 150 troops could fit on board for an amphibious operation. Although displacing 4,000 tons, its shallow bottom also permitted it to discharge troops or smaller vehicles on the beach. In addition to ferrying men and supplies, the LST served many other functions throughout the war, including that of hospital ship and repair vessel for smaller craft. Due to a slow pace of 10 knots, which made the ship vulnerable to enemy airplanes, the LST was often referred to by navy personnel as "large slow targets."

Bibliography: Gregg, Charles T., *Tarawa* (Stein and Day, 1984); Millett, Allan R., *Semper Fidelis* (Macmillan, 1980).

John F. Wukovits

LEAGUE OF NATIONS (1919–1946)

International organization created by the Treaty of Versailles at the conclusion of World War I. After the end of hostilities with Germany (November 1918), leaders of both sides met at Versailles, France, to draw up terms for peace. The Treaty of Versailles, and particularly the League of Nations covenant, mandated that all signees agree to "respect and preserve" the territory of member nations against aggression. Pres. Woodrow Wilson insisted upon this clause, believing the League of Nations to be a moral pledge for enduring peace. Wilson refused to compromise on this issue.

When he returned home with the treaty, the Senate, as strongly isolationist as Wilson was an internationalist,

refused to ratify it. Republican senator Henry Cabot Lodge of Massachusetts, a Senate moderate, sought a compromise, but other irreconcilable Republicans, including California's Hiram Johnson, Idaho's William E. Borah, and Wisconsin's Robert La Follette, advocated complete rejection of the treaty. In October 1919, as the ratification fight dragged on in the Senate, Wilson suffered a debilitating stroke. With Wilson incapacitated and strong opposition from Republican "irreconcilables," U.S. ratification of the Treaty of Versailles was doomed. Finally, in 1921, newly elected Republican president Warren G. Harding stated that the League of Nations "is not for us."

During its years of existence, the League of Nations did resolve some minor skirmishes, but it was ineffective for China when Japan seized Manchuria in 1931 and for Ethiopia when Italy invaded that country in 1936. The league was unable to stop Germany's militarization of the Rhineland in 1936 and did little about events leading to World War II. Member countries left (Germany, 1933; Japan, 1933; Italy, 1937), and the U.S.S.R. was expelled in 1939 when it invaded Finland. The League of Nations was formally dissolved in 1946, the year the United Nations was formed.

M. Guy Bishop

LEND-LEASE ACT

U.S. legislation passed in March 1941 that permitted Pres. Franklin D. Roosevelt to provide goods and services to nations whose defense during World War II he considered to be vital to U.S. defense. The recipient nation was to pay for this material when the war was over.

At first, only Great Britain received help through lend-lease. However, after an Allied meeting in Newfoundland in August 1941, the act was extended to Russia in September. As a result of lend-lease, the Soviets alone received 2,000 locomotives, 11,000 railway cars of various types, 540,000 tons of rails, almost 3,000,000 tons of gasoline, 7,000 tanks, 15,000 aircraft, 350,000 tons of explosives, 51,000 jeeps, 375,000 trucks, and 15,000,000 million pairs of boots. Without American boots and trucks, the Russian advance to Berlin would have stalled in western Russia in 1944.

During the war, among other great amounts of supplies and equipment, Britain received 5,000 tanks, 7,000 aircraft, and 114,000 tons of rubber, all representative examples of the decisive logistical support that the United States provided to the Allies during World War II. Without this support, both Russia and Britain would probably have been defeated.

Bibliography: Eisenhower, David, *Eisenhower: At War 1943–1945* (New Vintage Books, 1987); Keegan, John, *The Second World War* (Penguin Books, 1990).

Brig. Gen. (PNG, Ret.) Uzal W. Ent

LEYTE GULF, BATTLE OF
(October 23–26, 1944)

Series of sea and air engagements fought between Japanese and mostly U.S. forces during World War II in an eastern Philippine gulf. Collectively, these engagements were decisive. As a result, the Japanese combined fleet was crippled, the U.S. invasion of the Philippines could continue unhampered by the Japanese navy, and the Allies gained control of the Pacific. The battle was precipitated by the American amphibious assault on the Philippine island of Leyte on Oct. 20, 1944. The Japanese countered with their Sho-Go ("Victory Operation") plan.

The mission of phase one (Sho-1) of the plan was to "annihilate the enemy invading the central Philippines." To accomplish this mission, Adm. Soemu Toyoda, commanding the combined fleet, divided his forces into a number of task fleets: (1) Task Force Main Body (Vice Adm. Jisaburo Ozawa), with 4 aircraft carriers, 2 hybrid battleship-carriers, 3 cruisers, and 8 destroyers; the carriers had 108 aircraft, about half their normal capacity. (2) First Striking Force (Vice Adm. Takeo Kurita), with 5 battleships, 12 cruisers, and 15 destroyers. (3) Second Striking Force (Vice Adm. Kiyohide Shima), with 3 cruisers and 9 destroyers. (4) Third Task Group (Vice Adm. Shoji Nishimura), with 2 battleships, 1 cruiser, and 4 destroyers. (5) Transport Unit (Vice Adm. Naomasa Sakonji), with 2 cruisers, 1 destroyer, and 5 troop carriers.

Admiral Ozawa's force, sailing from Japan far to the north, was a decoy to draw the U.S. 3d Fleet (Adm. William F. Halsey) away from the Leyte area so that the First Striking Force and the Third Task Group coming from Brunei, Northern Borneo, and Shima's Second Striking Force from the Pescadores could converge on Leyte and destroy the U.S. 7th Fleet (Vice Adm. Thomas C. Kincaid), which was supporting the American invasion. Meantime, the Transport Unit would land reinforcements on the west side of Leyte. In general support of the plan were Japanese army and navy aircraft and 19 submarines. The submarine force (Vice Adm. Shidyoshi Miwa) proved of no value to the Japanese in the forthcoming battle.

Palawan Passage. On October 23, as Kurita's First Striking Force sailed up the Palawan Passage, west of that island, it was attacked by U.S. submarines. Two cruisers were sunk and another so severely damaged that it was escorted back to port by two destroyers. This submarine attack prematurely alerted the Americans that the Japanese intended a naval assault at Leyte.

Battle of the Sibuyan Sea. The next day, Kurita was attacked by U.S. aircraft in the Sibuyan Sea. One battleship was sunk. Two other battleships and a destroyer were damaged. As a result of his cumulative losses and the concentrated American attacks, Kurita temporarily reversed course. The Japanese also launched furious air attacks on

October 24, sinking the light carrier *Princeton* but losing most of their attacking planes in the process.

Battle of Surigao Strait. Meanwhile, Nishimura's Third Task Group, sailing between the islands of Mindanao and Negros, was attacked by U.S. aircraft. A battleship and a destroyer were damaged. Nishimura sailed on into the 7th Fleet's battle line, commanded by Rear Adm. Jesse B. Oldendorf. This line consisted of 38 PT (motor torpedo) boats (as an early warning and attack screen between the islands of Bohol and Camiguin) and a picket of 28 destroyers. This was backed by the main battle line of cruisers and, finally, six battleships. The PT boats attacked as Nishimura sailed through Surigao Strait but failed to score any hits. Next, five U.S. destroyers fired torpedoes at the Japanese formation, sinking one battleship. More destroyers took up the attack as the first five retired. In the ensuing battle, two Japanese destroyers were sunk and another destroyer and a battleship were damaged. Toward the end of the destroyer attack, U.S. cruisers and battleships joined the assault, sinking the damaged battleship. Nishimura finally lost every vessel except one destroyer, which returned safely to its base on October 27.

Admiral Shima's group followed Nishimura and also came under PT and destroyer attack. One light cruiser was lost and another was damaged when it accidentally collided with one of Nishimura's cruisers that had earlier been damaged and was afire. In the ensuing retreat, Shima lost another destroyer, sunk by bombs on October 26.

Battle Off Samar. Admiral Kurita was to have made a joint attack with Nishimura on U.S. naval units off Leyte. When he reversed course, although for little more than an hour, he destroyed all hope of joining Nishimura in a coordinated attack. Kurita turned again toward the Americans, entering the sea off Samar Island at daybreak on October 25. To his amazement, no U.S. ships nor planes were in sight. Incredibly, Halsey, in his haste to chase Ozawa, had left the strait completely open and had failed to notify Admiral Kinkaid. No radar or observation planes detected Kurita's approach.

When the approaching Japanese fleet was finally discovered, Kinkaid launched every available plane from six carriers, which were in Kurita's path of advance. When Kurita opened fire with the 18-inch guns from his superbattleship *Yamato,* the U.S. carriers (armed with light guns) and some of their screening vessels fled, taking evasive action and making smoke. For the next four hours, a furious battle took place, engaging U.S. destroyers (protecting the carriers) and U.S. aircraft against Kurita's ships. The Americans lost an escort carrier, a destroyer, and a destroyer escort. The Japanese lost three cruisers and a destroyer and had two cruisers and a destroyer damaged.

Kurita regrouped his battered fleet, now reduced to 15 of his original 32 ships, and at 12:36 P.M. on October 25 abandoned his penetration of the Leyte Gulf. Unknown to him at the time, Japanese naval aircraft had attacked the U.S. escort carriers, sinking 1 and damaging 3 others.

Battle Off Cape Engaño. Ozama left Hashirashima anchorage near Kure, Japan, on October 20. On October 24, one of his search planes located part of the U.S. fleet, and he launched an unsuccessful carrier plane attack. He then detached the two hybrid battleship-carriers, with screening vessels, to steam south and "attack and destroy enemy remnants."

When Admiral Halsey learned of Ozama's approach, he ordered three carrier groups north with all possible speed to intercept what appeared to be a strong enemy carrier force. By taking this strong, decisive action, Halsey was carrying out what Kincaid had assumed in his operation plan—that "any major enemy force approaching from the north would be intercepted by the Third Fleet." Halsey left the Samar approach open because he believed that Kurita's fleet had been so heavily damaged that it no longer posed a threat.

Halsey attacked Ozawa's ships with wave after wave of carrier planes from 8:15 A.M. to 5:00 P.M. Ozawa lost all four carriers. One cruiser was seriously damaged and sank on the way to Okinawa. Two destroyers were also sunk. Ozawa escaped with the two hybrid battleship carriers, two cruisers, and six destroyers.

Thus ended what might be termed a "banzai" charge by the Japanese navy. In the battles and subsequent retirement, the Japanese lost 4 carriers, 3 battleships, 10 cruisers, and 10 destroyers. U.S. losses were 1 light and 2 escort carriers, 2 destroyers, and 1 destroyer escort. Most of what remained of the Japanese navy had been destroyed. American losses were replaceable, while Japanese losses were not.

Bibliography: Cannon, M. Hamlin, *The United States Army in World War II. The War in the Pacific. Leyte: The Return to the Philippines* (Office of the Chief of Military History, U.S. Army, 1954); Dull, Paul S., *A Battle History of The Imperial Japanese Navy (1941–1945)* (Naval Inst. Press, 1978); MacArthur, Douglas, *Reports of General MacArthur;* Vol. 2, Part 2: *Japanese Operations in the Southwest Pacific Area* (U.S. Govt. Printing Office, 1966); Morison, Samuel Eliot, *History of the United States Naval Operations in World War II;* Vol. 12: *Leyte, June 1944–January 1945* (Little, Brown, 1966).

Brig. Gen. (PNG, Ret.) Uzal W. Ent

LORRAINE CAMPAIGN
(September 1–December 16, 1944)

World War II offensive action in which Lt. Gen. George Patton's 3d Army cleared the German Army Group G from the Lorraine region of northeastern France. In addition to difficult terrain and unusually heavy rainfall, the U.S. advance was hindered by the fact that the Allied advance

through the Low Countries had logistical priority over Patton's parallel advance farther south. Just as Patton finally achieved some success, the German Ardennes Offensive began on Dec. 16, 1944, forcing the 3d Army to pivot to the left and counterattack.

Jonathan M. House

MAKIN, BATTLE FOR
(November 20–23, 1943)

U.S. invasion of an island in the Gilberts (an equatorial Pacific atoll group) by the United States during World War II. Makin, closer to the Japanese-held Marshall Islands than Tarawa (the largest of the Gilberts), was not heavily defended, having fewer than 800 Japanese soldiers, of whom only 400 were combat troops. The invasion forces numbered 6,500, accompanied by a sizeable naval task force. Although numerically superior, the green U.S. troops, burdened by equipment failures, took heavy casualties, capturing the island after four days of fighting. The delay caused the loss of an escort carrier to an enemy submarine on the last day of the battle. Along with the other Gilbert islands concurrently invaded (especially Tarawa), Makin showed the urgency for better amphibious equipment and training.

Mark Pitcavage

MANHATTAN PROJECT

Unofficial code name for the U.S. development of the atomic bomb. It was administered by a section of the U.S. Army code-named the Manhattan District. Pressure for the project began in 1939 when German scientists accomplished nuclear fission. Believing that Germany might soon have the capability to develop an atomic bomb, Albert Einstein and other physicists convinced Pres. Franklin D. Roosevelt to launch a small research program to work on atomic fission. The secret Manhattan Project began in June 1941 under Leslie Groves, a major general from 1944. Research teams from a number of U.S. universities participated. By June 1942, the researchers reported that building an atomic bomb was feasible. A testing site at Los Alamos, New Mexico, was established in 1943 under the direction of Dr. J. Robert Oppenheimer. Over the next two years, workers labored feverishly to perfect the weapon. The first test explosion occurred on July 16, 1945, at Alamogordo, New Mexico. Pres. Harry S Truman ordered the first atomic bomb be dropped on Hiroshima, Japan, just three weeks later.

M. Guy Bishop

MARKET GARDEN, OPERATION
(September 1944)

Code name for an ambitious Allied combined operation to capture river crossings in the Netherlands, especially the Rhine, during World War II. "Market" referred to the airborne part of the operation; "Garden" to the ground advance. On Sept. 17, 1944, the 1st Allied Airborne Army (General Brereton) dropped the 82d and 101st U.S. divisions to capture the bridges at Eindhoven and Nijmegen in the Netherlands. Meanwhile, the 1st British Airborne Division (Major General Urquhart) and the Polish Parachute Brigade (Major General Sosnbowski) dropped at Arnhem, on the Lower Rhine, to capture the bridge there. The Arnhem drop proved to be "a bridge too far," due to the slow ground advance of the XXX British Corps. On September 25–26, 2,000 Arnhem survivors escaped to the southern bank of the Lower Rhine. Of 11,850 Allied casualties, 5,000 were captured.

Russell A. Hart

MARSHALL REORGANIZATION
(March 1942)

Reorganization of the U.S. War Department during World War II by Gen. George C. Marshall. Marshall took such actions with the approval of Pres. Franklin D. Roosevelt, who, on Dec. 18, 1941, had been authorized by the First War Powers Act to reorganize the federal government as needed. Effective Mar. 9, 1942, Marshall decentralized operating responsibilities by creating three new field commands and centralized executive control to direct better the overall war effort. The three new field commands—the army ground forces commanded by Lt. Gen. Lesley McNair, the army air forces commanded by Lt. Gen. Henry Arnold, and the army service forces commanded by Lt.

Dr. Robert J. Oppenheimer established and directed the testing site for the Manhattan Project's atomic bomb at Los Alamos, New Mexico, in 1943. (Courtesy of the Institute for Advanced Study)

The 82d and 101st airborne divisions were dropped from gliders in the Netherlands to capture bridges at Eindhoven and Nijmegen as part of Operation Market Garden in 1944. (U.S. Army Military History Institute)

Gen. Brehon Somervell—were to handle the day-to-day operations of the army, including administrative matters, thereby eliminating most of the paperwork that the General Staff had had to deal with previously. The reorganization enabled Marshall to reduce greatly the size of the War Department, as many of the officers assigned to the General Staff were transferred to the new field commands and other positions such as the offices of the chiefs of the combat arms were eliminated. Marshall ran the slimmed-down General Staff from the Operations Division (formerly the War Plans Division) and was able to devote his time and energies to strategic planning and to coordinating the efforts of the three field commands.

Steve R. Waddell

MERRILL'S MARAUDERS

Nickname given to the 5307th Composite Unit (Provisional), a guerrilla force of volunteer U.S. soldiers trained for missions in Burma during World War II. In August 1943, the U.S. Joint Chiefs of Staff decided to support a large-scale British raid into Japanese-held Burma with U.S. air power and an all-volunteer long-range penetration group, and thus created the 5307th Composite Unit. Modeled after the British "Chindits," the 5307th was to operate behind Japanese lines disrupting supply routes and destroying communications facilities while relying on airdrops and pack animals for their own supplies. In November, the unit began training in India under the command of Brig. Gen. Frank D. Merrill. Given the unit's uninspiring official designation, the press immediately dubbed it "Merrill's Marauders."

Gen. Joseph W. Stilwell, U.S. commander in the theater, decided to use the unit in his offensive into northern Burma instead of enjoining the British, and in February 1944, the Marauders joined him in Burma. Since October, Stilwell had been trying to use his Chinese divisions to envelop the Japanese 18th Division, but the slow-moving Chinese never quite closed the trap. Now he resolved to use the Marauders as his flanking force and sent them on a wide turning movement toward Walawbun. The ensuing campaign cost the Japanese heavily, although they did manage to escape. Stilwell was encouraged by the operation and sent the Marauders on another, longer movement to cut the Japanese line of retreat at Kamaing. The Americans again moved through dense jungle and set up their block, but Japanese counterattacks pushed them back to Nhpum Ga in the surrounding hills. In the face of heavy Japanese attacks, the Marauders held for 13 days until the encircling Japanese gave up and retreated to the south.

Reduced to less than half their original strength, the Marauders looked forward to a rest after Nhpum Ga. Stilwell, however, wanted to move quickly on the important airfield at Myitkyina. He reinforced the Marauders' depleted combat teams with local Kachin guides and 4,000 Chinese soldiers and then sent them across the formidable Kuman Mountains toward Myitkyina. After three weeks of hard marching over torturous terrain, the force emerged from the jungle and captured the airfield against light resistance. The Japanese immediately rushed troops to the area, and attempts to capture the town failed. As the monsoons set in, the battle turned into a prolonged siege. Stilwell committed whatever troops he could find to the battle, including engineers working on the Ledo Road and Marauders from the hospitals. The Marauders, however, were at the end of their endurance, and by June, most had to be evacuated, although a portion of the 1st Battalion remained in the area until the town fell on August 3.

The capture of Myitkyina was the Marauders' last action. By gaining the town, the joint Chinese-U.S. force cleared the way for the Ledo Road and captured a new airfield, which substantially shortened the air supply route to China. In August, the army disbanded the 5307th Composite Unit (Provisional) and the surviving Marauders joined the 475th Infantry Regiment, which continued fighting in Burma until the war's end.

Bibliography: Hunter, Charles N., *Galahad* (Naylor, 1963); Ogburn, Charlton, *The Marauders* (Harper & Row, 1959).

Richard F. Kehrberg

MIDWAY, BATTLE OF (June 3–6, 1942)

Decisive World War II sea and air battle in which the apparent superiority of Japanese naval power was dominated by U.S. fighter planes and the U.S. Pacific Fleet, which made a far more formidable showing than anticipated. The Midway Islands, 1,134 miles west of Hawaii, were a target of Japanese expansion in the Central Pacific during the first year of U.S. involvement in World War II. In the months following their attack on Pearl Harbor (Dec. 7, 1941), the Japanese steadily attempted to expand their sphere of control in the Pacific in the Philippines, the East Indies, Malaysia, and Singapore.

Japan's carrier fleet was second to none at the beginning of the war. At the outset of 1942, it outnumbered that of the United States by a 10 to 3 ratio. Moreover, the Japanese carriers and their air groups were of the first quality.

At Pearl Harbor in May 1942, the U.S. Navy's Lt. Cmdr. Joseph Rochefort, chief of intelligence for the 14th Naval District, was convinced that the heavy volume of Japanese radio transmissions indicated a forthcoming advance. He concluded that the next target of Japan's aggression would be Midway.

Some of Rochefort's superiors remained skeptical. Prior to Pearl Harbor, they argued, the Japanese had maintained strict radio silence: Why would they now send out signals concerning another major move? In order to test Rochefort's theory, U.S. forces on Midway sent a bogus message reporting a water plant breakdown. Two days later, a new

Japanese transmission reported their target to be short of fresh water. Rochefort's speculation had proven correct.

While Midway was Japan's primary target, it was only a means to an end. Such an attack, Japanese military strategists hoped, would bait a trap luring the U.S. Pacific Fleet into a major battle hoped to bring about its annihilation, While weakened by the attack on Pearl Harbor, the American fleet was still a menace to Japanese operations in the Pacific. The battle plan for Midway, as conceived by Adm. Isoroku Yamamoto, commander in chief of the Imperial Navy, called for an even greater armada than that used against Pearl Harbor: 8 carriers, 11 battleships, 20 cruisers, 60 destroyers, 15 submarines, 30 auxiliary vessels, and 16 transports. Yamamoto hoped to destroy the U.S. carriers that had escaped Pearl Harbor.

Yamamoto had the cream of Japan's navy and naval air forces at his disposal. As May waned, he confidently sent the fleet to sea. The odds seemed overwhelmingly in Japan's favor. The United States had only 3 carriers to oppose Yamamoto's 8, 14 destroyers to his 60, and no battleships to his 11. Only in submarines did the Americans enjoy a slight superiority of 19 to 15.

But there was much that the Japanese did not know. Their strike at Pearl Harbor had not been the unmitigated disaster that most observers believed it to be. The attackers had overlooked the U.S. Navy repair facilities at Pearl Harbor and a vital oil tank farm that had escaped undamaged. Also, not a single U.S. carrier had been struck. Had these installations and supplies been destroyed, the U.S. Pacific Fleet under Adm. Chester Nimitz would have been forced to retire to the West Coast.

Yamamoto's confidence was misplaced further in that faulty Japanese intelligence had led him astray. It incorrectly had reported that the U.S. carriers *Yorktown* and *Lexington* had been sunk in the recent Battle of the Coral Sea (May 7–8). Two other American carriers, the *Hornet* and the *Enterprise*, were reported to be far from Midway. As far as Yamamoto knew, there would be no U.S. carriers to challenge his own at Midway.

When Rochefort's false message drew a Japanese reaction, thus confirming his assumptions, U.S. preparations began in earnest for a battle at Midway. Bunkers arose in the atoll's sands, miles of wire were strung along the island's beaches, antiaircraft batteries were rushed in from Hawaii, and Midway's obsolete aircraft were quickly reinforced by the best the U.S. Navy could spare. Also, the *Hornet* and the *Enterprise* under Rear Adm. Raymond Spruance moved quickly to join Task Force 17, which included the *Yorktown*, near Midway.

On June 2, the forces rendezvoused 325 miles northeast of Midway. At dawn on June 4, a U.S. patrol bomber out of Midway spotted the Japanese carriers and reported enemy planes headed toward the island. Within a half hour, every U.S. plane on Midway was in the air. While the bombers headed toward the Japanese carriers, fighters engaged incoming enemy planes. Japan's first strike force returned to its carriers with Midway's defenses still viable.

By the time the Japanese became aware of the approaching U.S. carriers, the die was cast. Adm. Chuichi Nagumo, commanding the Japanese naval air forces, was forced to alter his tactic, resulting in a fateful delay. This lost time worked to the Americans' advantage. Just after 10:00 A.M., Japanese lookouts aboard the carrier *Akagi* warned, "Enemy dive bombers!" As swiftly as the U.S. strike had appeared, it was over. A huge crater now split the flight deck of the *Akagi*. Fire soon swept over the crippled carrier. The devastation was similar aboard the carriers *Soryu* and *Kaga*.

A second Japanese attack was launched from the carrier *Hiryu*. Dive bombers assaulted the *Yorktown,* inflicting fatal blows to the American carrier. With oil gushing from its ruptured fuel tanks and seawater flooding in, at 3:00 P.M., Capt. Elliott Buckmaster gave the order to abandon ship. American planes spent three hours hunting for the remaining Japanese carrier. Moments before the *Yorktown* was destroyed, the *Hiryu* was spotted. About 3:30 P.M., 34 U.S. planes, all that could be mustered, sped toward the *Hiryu*. As the U.S. pilots attacked, four bombs slammed home. The forward third of *Hiryu*'s flight deck was destroyed. The crew fought unsuccessfully to save the ship, but just before midnight, the order to abandon the *Hiryu* was given.

Yamamoto's grand design to destroy the U.S. Pacific Fleet had failed. Early on June 5, he recalled his forces to the west. "The price," he reportedly said, "is too high." His ill-fated venture cost Japan 4 carriers, 1 cruiser, 322 planes, and the lives of 3,500 Japanese fighting men. The Americans had lost 1 carrier, 1 destroyer, 150 planes, and 307 lives. Japan's foreign minister Mamoru Shigemitsu said upon learning of Midway, "the Americans have avenged Pearl Harbor."

Bibliography: Barker, A. J., *Midway* (Prentice-Hall, 1983); Collier, Basil, *The War in the Far East, 1941–1945* (Morrow, 1969); Prango, Gordon W., *Miracle at Midway,* ed. by Donald M. Goldstein and K. V. Dillon (McGraw, 1982).

M. Guy Bishop

MORROW BOARD (1925)

Post–World War I advisory group appointed by Pres. Calvin Coolidge on Sept. 12, 1925, to study the use of aircraft in national defense. The board, headed by Dwight W. Morrow, a New York banker, held hearings and found that there was little agreement about how many usable aircraft the Army Air Service had, or whether the United States had fewer or more than Japan. While the Morrow Board rejected the most extreme claims of air power advocates, the board's report, issued on November 30, recommended appointing two additional airmen as brigadier generals, one to head procurement and the other to command the flying schools. Morrow also recommended increased appropriations for the training of airmen and the development of modern airplanes. Finally, the board recommended changing the name of the Army Air Service to the Air Corps. In response, Congress passed the Air Corps Bill of 1926 to formalize many of these recommendations.

Bibliography: Maurer, Maurer, *Aviation in the U.S. Army* (Office of Air Force History, 1987).

Roger D. Launius

MORTAIN, BATTLE OF
(August 6–12, 1944)

World War II engagement in a town in Normandy, France, begun by an armored German counterattack force that intended to reach Avranches, reestablish its defensive line, and cut off U.S. forces that had broken out of the Normandy beachhead. Striking after midnight on Aug. 6, 1944, the Germans encountered staunch defenders, notably the U.S. 30th Infantry Division. Tactically, the Germans made limited gains, but they were unable to take key positions—such as Hill 317, from which encircled American troops directed devastating artillery fire on German concentrations—or avoid Allied close-air support. Operationally, the attack was a German disaster. The effort to break through U.S. lines, while depleting German armor, served to hold the Germans in place while U.S. forces encircled them from the south, thereby contributing to the subsequent slaughter around Falaise-Argentan.

Stephen J. Lofgren

MULBERRY

Artificial harbor constructed of concrete and steel, used by Allied forces on the Normandy beaches following the June 1944 invasion landings of World War II. Two mulberry units were used: one on American beaches, one on the British beaches. Their purpose was to provide shelter for shipping and the discharge of cargo.

Between June 20 and Sept. 1, 1944, an average of 6,765 tons of supplies per day were unloaded at these harbors. Mulberries gave the Allied planners for the invasion of Europe the freedom to choose logistical landing areas away from heavily defended ports, thus bypassing the strong defenses of the German Atlantic Wall.

Bibliography: Hartcup, Guy, *Code Name Mulberry: The Planning, Building and Operation of the Normandy Harbours* (David & Charles, 1977).

David Friend

NAPLES, CAPTURE OF (October 1, 1943)

Uncontested Allied taking of the largest port in southern Italy during World War II. Naples was a key target for capture by the Allied armies when they invaded Salerno, only 30 miles to the south, on Sept. 9, 1943. After a furious 10–day battle at Salerno, the Germans began a fighting withdrawal to the north, destroying all bridges and mining the roads. The Allies expected to fight a difficult battle for Naples, which they intended to use as a staging area and logistics base for future operations. Instead, the Germans abandoned the city, and when the Allies entered it on October 1, Lt. Gen. Mark Clark described Naples as "a city of ghosts."

Carlo W. D'Este

NATIONAL DEFENSE ACT OF 1920

Post-World War I act that codified the three-component U.S. Army—regular, National Guard, and organized reserve (later army reserve)—and set the course for military organization during the interwar years. In 1918, Army Chief of Staff Peyton March sought to make permanent the perceived lessons of World War I—that the United States needed a large peacetime army and that such a force could not rely on citizen soldiers. March proposed that Congress establish a permanent body of 500,000 regulars with federal reservists, ignoring the National Guard.

Congress delayed consideration of this radical plan until 1919. In October, James W. Wadsworth, chairman of the Senate Military Affairs Committee and an advocate of reserve components commanded by reserve officers, asked for expert testimony from the General Staff's chief of war plans, Lt. Col. John M. Palmer. Palmer openly criticized the March Plan because it clashed with American traditions about citizen soldiers. Wadsworth demanded Palmer's services to draft a new bill.

During the next eight months, Palmer and Lt. Col. John W. Gulick, under Wadsworth's direction, produced a new defense plan. Palmer rapidly recognized that advocates of the National Guard wanted to retain dual state and federal missions. Wadsworth and Palmer also wanted universal military training in peacetime as the source of trained manpower for both National Guard and organized reserve units. However, public opinion was generally opposed to any peacetime conscription, and thus another compromise was necessary.

Ultimately, the House of Representatives would only agree to amend the 1916 act, rather than to create an entirely new law. Palmer was able to insert a provision that left detailed implementation of the new plan to a combined board of regular and reserve component officers, a board on which he served.

The final version of the 1920 act, as elaborated by the officer board, divided the country into nine corps area commands, each having a combination of regular, National Guard, and organized reserve divisions. Given the austere interwar defense budgets and the absence of universal military training, this structure rapidly turned into a skeleton. Still, Palmer's plan preserved the World War I structure, providing a framework for the mobilization of 1940–41.

Bibliography: Holley, I. B., *General John M. Palmer, Citizen Soldiers, and the Army of a Democracy* (Greenwood Press, 1982); House, J. M., ''John McAuley Palmer and the Reserve Components,'' *Parameters: Journal of the U.S. Army War College* (Sept. 1982); Weigley, R. F., *History of the United States Army* (1967; reprint, Indiana University Press, 1984).

Jonathan M. House

NAVAL AIRCRAFT

Airplanes designed to provide aeronautical support in sea battles. By the end of World War II, four main roles had evolved for U.S. naval aircraft: reconnaissance, air interception, bombing, and close support for amphibious operations.

Reconnaissance craft required speed, endurance, and the ability to operate at high altitudes. The PBY Catalina, a flying boat with a range of 3,100 miles, was used for long-range maritime scouting. Boasting superb armament—typically four .30-inch or .50-inch machine guns plus up to 2,000 pounds of bombs—the Catalina often served a dual purpose as a scout or an offensive weapon. The PB4Y Liberator, protected by eight .50-inch machine guns, flew from land bases against shipping and submarines, mainly in the Atlantic, while the smaller Vought OS2U Kingfisher scouted shorter ranges.

Fighters had to be adaptable for fleet defense, offensive sorties, and bomber escort and thus demanded speed, maneuverability, firepower, and range. At the same time, the fighters needed a compact design so they could be stored on aircraft carriers. The F2A Brewster Buffalo carried four .50-inch machine guns and increased armor protection for the pilot, but that extra weight reduced its maneuverability and made it a tempting target for the more agile Japanese Zero. The Grumman F4F Wildcat possessed a sturdy frame along with six .50-inch machine guns, but it also was outclassed by the Zero. American designers produced two answers for the Zero. The Chance Vought F4U Corsair, first used in mid-1942 and flying with the distinctive gull-winged design, boasted increased speed combined with either six .50-inch machine guns or four 20-millimeter cannon. It more than matched the Zero and ended the war with an 11:1 kill ratio. Along with the Corsair, the Grumman F6F Hellcat dominated the Pacific. More maneuverable and sturdier than the Corsair, the Hellcat accounted for close to 75 percent of the U.S. Navy's air-to-air kills. Its six .50-inch machine guns (some versions contained four .50-inch guns and two 20-millimeter cannon) inflicted ghastly punishment on the Japanese during fighting in 1944 in the Marianas.

Like the fighters, navy dive bombers fared poorly when first pitted against the enemy. The Douglas TBD Devasta-tor's slow speed of 206 miles per hour and lack of protection—only two .30-inch guns along with its one 1,000-pound torpedo—turned it into an easy target for enemy fighters or antiaircraft fire. The navy pulled the Devastator from operational use after most of the ones used at Midway were shot down. The Grumman TBF Avenger carried five machine guns and could thus more effectively shoot its way through enemy defenses to drop either its 22-inch torpedo or 2,000 pounds of bombs. The powerful Curtiss SB2C Helldiver, with four .50-inch guns in the wings and two .30-inch guns firing from the rear cockpit, also replaced the Devastator and became more important in the later stages of the war. The main carrier-based bomber, however, was the Douglas SBD Dauntless, a sturdy plane that could absorb an incredible amount of damage. Its speed of 245 miles per hour and range of 1,100 miles, combined with four machine guns and 2,000 pounds of bombs, resulted in the sinking of more Japanese shipping than could be effected by any other dive bomber, while suffering fewer casualties per mission.

Bibliography: Swanborough, Gordon, and Peter M. Bowers, *United States Navy Aircraft Since 1911* (Naval Inst. Press, 1990).

John F. Wukovits

NEUTRALITY ACTS (1935–1941)

Series of laws designed to keep the United States out of war. An August 1935 act banned arms shipments to belligerents (also applied to civil wars in January 1937) and forbade Americans from traveling on belligerent ships except at their own risk. A February 1936 law extended this ban and also prohibited loans to warring parties. Congress in May 1937 made travel on belligerent vessels unlawful and authorized the enumeration of nonmunition items that belligerents could purchase but only on a cash-and-carry basis. Responding to war in Europe, Congress repealed the arms embargo in November 1939, permitting cash-and-carry sales. In November 1941, restrictions against arming U.S. merchant vessels and their entry into combat zones were repealed.

Ralph L. Eckert

NEW GUINEA CAMPAIGN (1942–1944)

World War II Allied drive along New Guinea's northern coast led by Gen. Douglas MacArthur as part of a two-pronged offensive to clear the Japanese from the Solomon Islands and New Guinea. After crack Japanese troops advanced through extremely difficult terrain to within 30 miles of Port Moresby, a strategic Allied supply center only 300 miles north of Australia, U.S. and Australian forces, aided by incessant air attacks from Gen. George C. Kenney's fighters and bombers, pushed back the enemy to the three small villages of Buna, Gona, and Sanananda along New Guinea's north coast.

In early October 1942, Kenney's transports airlifted elements of the 32d Infantry Division to small airstrips near Buna. November assaults through swamps toward heavily bunkered Japanese soldiers resulted in severe casualties for Americans who had to charge into machine-gun fire. Without heavy artillery and flamethrowers to knock out the Japanese positions, the U.S. attack quickly stalled. An angry MacArthur dispatched Gen. Robert L. Eichelberger to relieve the 32d's commander, Gen. Edwin F. Harding, and admonished him to "take Buna—or don't come back alive."

Eichelberger arrived near Buna on December 1 and found the American units in disarray. After halting offensive drives for two days to straighten out lines and reestablish communications, Eichelberger ordered a two-pronged December 5 attack against coastal positions and against Buna itself. Enemy fire pinned down his forces, but the next day, SSgt. Herman Bottcher and 18 men punched a hole in the Japanese defenses by seizing a strip of beach and holding out against repeated enemy counterattacks from both sides. Buna finally fell on December 14, although another three weeks of fighting remained before the Buna area was declared secured on Jan. 2, 1943.

Simultaneously, the Australian 7th Division under Maj. Gen. George A. Vasey had charged Japanese positions at Gona, 20 miles to the north. Like the Americans at Buna, the Australians also ran into stiff opposition and futilely tried to knock out fortified machine-gun nests. Finally, shells with delayed-action fuses succeeded in shredding enemy bunkers, and Gona fell on December 8.

U.S. and Australian troops combined to eliminate the final enemy holdouts at nearby Sanananda. Sensing the end quickly approaching, Imperial general headquarters ordered all troops near Sananando to fall back by land or sea to stronger Japanese defenses further northwest at Lae and Salamaua. Sanananda fell January 22, ending the bloody Allied drive to recapture Papua that cost almost 3,000 dead and 5,500 wounded.

MacArthur next turned to driving the Japanese out of their string of positions in northern and western New Guinea. Lae and Salamaua near the Huon Peninsula were first. MacArthur wanted Lae because of its airfield and anchorage and because controlling it would give him command of strategic valleys opening the way northwest to the important Japanese base at Madang. The Japanese attempted to reinforce Lae and Salamaua with 6,000 men in early March 1943, but 200 Allied bombers practically wiped out the entire convoy as it steamed across the Bismarck Sea. Japanese troops in New Guinea were now cut off from major reinforcement and would have to rely on their remaining supplies and whatever could be brought in by night destroyer runs.

In order to confuse the Japanese into thinking that Salamaua, not Lae, was his main objective and thus switch troops away from Lae, MacArthur landed troops at Nassau Bay to Salamaua's south. At Japanese headquarters in Rabaul, Gen. Hitoshi Imamura fell for the ploy and ordered men to Salamaua. Meanwhile, after Allied engineers constructed a secret fighter base to the west of Lae, which helped Kenney gain control of the air, on September 4, MacArthur sent in Australian troops to Lae's east and American units to its west. Realizing they had been outmaneuvered, the Japanese high command ordered both posts abandoned. Allied units captured Salamaua on September 9, four days before Lae fell, although many Japanese defenders evaded capture and headed for other bases on the Huon Peninsula. Australian troops quickly followed and seized Finschhafen at the peninsula's eastern end to prevent enemy reinforcements from arriving, while other Australian units dashed up the Ramu and Markham valleys to split the peninsula from the rest of Japanese-controlled New Guinea.

Advances in 1944. On Jan. 2, 1944, two battalions from the 32d Division landed near Saidor, a port town at the western end of the Huon Peninsula 70 miles east of Madang. MacArthur needed its airfield, plus he hoped this move would trap the fleeing enemy soldiers. Although Saidor fell with little opposition, numerous Japanese troops managed to evade the Americans and reach Madang.

MacArthur next targeted the Admiralty Islands, lying at the northern entrance to the Bismarck Sea, 300 miles northeast of Madang. Control of these strategic islands would seriously impede Japanese attempts to reinforce New Guinea and would give the Allies possession of one of the Pacific's finest protected anchorages. On Feb. 29, 1944, 1,000 men of the U.S. 5th Cavalry Regiment landed at Los Negros in the Admiralties. Within three days, they had seized the Momote airfield and by the end of March had eliminated most opposition in the Admiralties. Japanese units on New Guinea now had to withdraw hurriedly from the Madang region and embark on an arduous trek through difficult terrain 200 miles west to Wewak to avoid encirclement. The Admiralties Campaign was declared officially over on May 18, with American casualties of 1,400 dead and wounded to Japanese losses of 3,820 dead and 75 captured.

More than 1,000 miles of New Guinea's northern and western coastline still remained in Japanese hands. Before MacArthur pushed on toward his long-cherished goal of returning to the Philippines, his men would have to neutralize the numerous Japanese bases sprinkled along this coast and seize airfields that could be used be U.S. bombers to support his Philippine drive. Fortunately, Allied intelligence kept MacArthur superbly informed of enemy dispositions, enabling the Allied commander to bypass stronger concentrations and hit at vulnerable Japanese posts.

The port town of Hollandia, one of the enemy's main supply centers, lying 450 miles west of Madang, became

MacArthur's next objective. Three Japanese airfields joined fortified enemy positions in surrounding hillsides to transform Hollandia into a formidable objective, but MacArthur cannily tricked Gen. Hatazo Adachi into believing his assault would come 200 miles farther east near Wewak. Kenney's bombers targeted Wewak and nearby areas as though preparing it for an invasion, and when the invasion convoy left the Admiralties for the assault, the ships followed a circuitous route to make the enemy believe they indeed were attacking Wewak. One portion of the convoy, however, headed 125 miles east of Hollandia to grab Aitape's two airfields and to block an expected counterattack from Wewak. Aitape's 1,000 men, mostly service personnel, were quickly overrun.

The April 22 U.S. assault at Hollandia so surprised the 11,000 Japanese defenders that they were forced to abandon their positions and move inland. General Adachi hurriedly organized 20,000 men for the arduous trek toward Aitape, and after a month of marching, Adachi launched his counterattack on July 10. Twenty-five days of bitter fighting thoroughly debilitated Adachi's force, causing him in early August to lead his battered men back to Wewak.

Six hundred miles of coastline remained to be secured. A May 17 assault captured the town of Toem, 125 miles west of Hollandia, but 175 miles beyond lay Biak, a hilly, jungle-clad island containing vital airfields. Intelligence from higher headquarters indicated that more than 7,000 enemy defenders waited on the island, but MacArthur believed his own intelligence, which stated that fewer than 3,000 Japanese held Biak. The assault on May 27 encountered minor opposition on the beaches, but when the Americans moved inland toward the airfields, deadly fire poured down on the Americans from 11,000 defenders from fortified positions in the numerous caves that honeycombed Biak's surrounding hillsides. Although the airfields were secured within a week, mortar and artillery fire from the hillsides plagued the Americans until Biak was cleared in late August. More than 4,700 Japanese were killed and another 220 captured at Biak against U.S. casualties of 2,550.

The final Japanese bases in New Guinea fell by late September. In July, the island of Noemfoor, lying 60 miles west of Biak, was taken, after which 7,300 men seized airfields near the villages of Sansapor and Mar on the Vogelkop Peninsula forming New Guinea's far western reaches. Troops occupied the island of Morotai, resting between the Vogelkop Peninsula and the southern Philippine island of Mindanao, in an unopposed landing on September 15. This completed a remarkable drive by MacArthur, who skillfully employed intelligence and amphibious tactics to target weaker Japanese positions while advancing Allied positions 1,400 miles closer to the Philippines. MacArthur now stood ready for his Philippine assault.

Bibliography: Eichelberger, Robert L., *Our Jungle Road to Tokyo* (Viking, 1950); James, Clayton D., *The Years of MacArthur; Vol. 2: 1941–1945* (Houghton Mifflin, 1975); MacArthur, Douglas, *Reminiscences* (McGraw-Hill, 1964); Milner, Samuel, *Victory in Papua* (Center of Military History, U.S. Army, 1989); Smith, Robert R., *The Approach to the Philippines* (Center of Military History, U.S. Army, 1953); Spector, Ronald H., *Eagle Against the Sun* (Free Press, 1985).

John F. Wukovits

NORDWIND, OPERATION
(January 1–25, 1945)

World War II code name (from the German for "north wind") of the Germans' New Year's (1945) attack on Lt. Gen. Alexander Patch's U.S. 7th Army (6th Army Group) in the Ardennes region·of France. The German XIII SS Panzer Corps struck the U.S. 44th Infantry Division (U.S. VI Corps), and the 256th and 361st Volks Grenadier divisions drove deep on the left flank of the U.S. corps. By January 4, the German XC Corps had penetrated 16 miles into the 7th Army front. The Germans succeeded in forcing the withdrawal of the U.S. VI and XV Corps to positions on and near the Moder River. However, a German six-division drive on January 24 was blunted by the next day, and the enemy began to withdraw soon after.

Bibliography: Weigley, Russell F., *Eisenhower's Lieutenants* (Indiana Univ. Press, 1981).

Brig. Gen. (PNG, Ret.) Uzal W. Ent

NORTH RUSSIAN AND SIBERIAN INTERVENTIONS (1918–1919)

Multinational interventions in revolutionary Russia—in north Russia near Archangel, and at Vladivostok in Siberia—during World War I. Britain, France, Japan, and the United States each intervened for different reasons. National motives often conflicted; interventionist rationales tended to be more emotional than logical; and the means employed often bore little relation to the ends desired. Handicapping contemporary analysis were the diversity of opinions about Russia within individual countries, the overall lack of accurate knowledge in the West about events in revolutionary Russia, and the rollercoaster changes in the military fortunes of anti-German forces during 1918. U.S. Army Chief of Staff Gen. Peyton March best described the situation: "It is extremely difficult to see the light of day in a heaven so completely obscured as this is."

Dismay that the Bolsheviks had overthrown the Russian provisional government turned to overt hostility in March 1918 when the Treaty of Brest-Litovsk removed Russia from World War I. The Western powers viewed the treaty, which greatly benefited Germany, as outright betrayal. Suspicion grew that the Bolsheviks were either pro-German or paid German pawns.

Pressure for American participation in some form of intervention began in December 1917. Pres. Woodrow Wilson resisted. He did not want to lose America's independence as an associated (rather than allied) power, and he believed that the United States did not "share the same goals" as the Allies. Recognizing that U.S. participation in any venture would constitute sanction, and wary of hidden Allied national agendas, Wilson did not want to commit U.S. troops to what would be, in effect, Allied political intrigue. By mid-July 1918, however, three considerations led Wilson to sanction American participation in two interventions.

First, Wilson's antipathy toward the Bolsheviks increased; consequently, so did his desire to succor anti-Bolshevik forces. As his outlook changed, Wilson considered a joint Japanese-American intervention in Siberia. Second, the specific timing of the U.S. agreement to intervene resulted from the second consideration—the "Czech Legion." The Legion was a group of 60,000 former Austro-Hungarian prisoners of war who, while traveling across Russia to Vladivostok for repatriation, seized control of the strategically important Trans-Siberian Railroad following clashes with Bolsheviks. The Legion's predicament, Wilson quickly grasped, provided an acceptable reason for intervention. He also realized that the militarily effective Legion might serve as a shield behind which anti-Bolshevik resistance could form. Simultaneously confronted with Japanese plans for unilateral intervention in Siberia, Wilson agreed to a joint Japanese-American expedition in Siberia on July 6, 1918.

The third consideration stemmed from successive German offensives in the west (using troops redeployed from Russia) during the spring and summer of 1918 that made the British and French frantic to re-create the Eastern Front via North Russia. The Allies further worried that war matériel stockpiled in North Russia would fall into German or Bolshevik hands. Wilson also opposed intervention in North Russia, but, in order to maintain U.S. influence with the Allies, he acquiesced on July 17 after France and Britain indicated their firm intention to intervene (and after Wilson's decision for a Siberian intervention had undercut much of his argument).

U.S. intervention was publicized in an August 3 press release, in which Wilson announced to the public that the United States was intervening only to "guard military stores" that had accumulated and to safeguard the Czech Legion. Wilson informed the Russian people that the United States planned "no intervention in [Russian] internal affairs," but only wished to help them "regain control of their own affairs, their own territory, and their own destiny." Wilson virtually ignored North Russia.

Behind the interventions, therefore, was a transient British and French desire to reestablish the Eastern Front. Anti-Bolshevism provided a second motive, and one that became the sustaining force behind Western intervention as the military situation improved in the west. The Japanese were interested not in anti-Bolshevism nor the Eastern Front, but in establishing a noncommunist Far Eastern Republic that would serve as a buffer between their interests in Manchuria and the Soviet Union. Wilson's desire to maintain his diplomatic leverage with the Allies and his profound dislike of the Bolsheviks made him decide that, despite his own misgivings, the interventions were necessary to further U.S. international political objectives. Thus, although the secretary of war opposed intervention, and March called it "a serious military mistake," Wilson committed the United States to two simultaneous, but completely separate and uncoordinated, expeditions.

North Russia. Allied intervention in North Russia began in April 1918, when British troops first landed. For the American contingent, Gen. John J. Pershing selected from his ranks the 339th Infantry Regiment and supporting units from the 85th Division (1st Battalion, 310th Engineer Regiment; 337th Ambulance Company; 337th Field Hospital; and 310th Sanitary Train) to join the Allies. The majority of the 5,000 men under the command of Col. George E. Stewart disembarked on September 4 at Archangel. There they joined British, French, Canadian, and "White Russian" troops (of dubious quality) in defending a 450-mile strongpoint perimeter.

The British exercised overall command in North Russia. U.S. troops also were generally under British command and control tactically, to the extent of British-led multinational platoons, which rankled most Americans. Colonel Stewart never recognized the larger issues involved in intervention and proved ineffective as a component commander in a demanding coalition environment.

The U.S. soldiers suffered their first casualties within two weeks of disembarkation as the British commander attempted unsuccessfully to expel the Bolsheviks from the Archangel region. During the winter of 1918–19, American troops were involved in substantial combat, losing 136 dead and 266 wounded (including 7 killed and 23 wounded on November 11, the Armistice Day on the Western Front). Living in primitive conditions and unsure why they were in Russia, many troops had morale problems during the long Russian winter. There were also the inevitable nonbattle deaths, notably from disease.

The end of the war with Germany meant the end of all the reasons for intervening in Russia that had been couched in wartime rationales. Public desire grew to bring troops home (especially in Michigan and Wisconsin, homes of the 339th) and cease involvement in foreign entanglements. The intervention was an obvious failure, and Wilson sanctioned its end in February 1919. U.S. field troops were withdrawn during June 3–27, 1919, and the last personnel departed in August. They had suffered 244 deaths and 305 men wounded. A British withdrawal followed later that year.

Siberia. In Vladivostok, Maj. Gen. William S. Graves and 9,000 U.S. troops (the 27th and 31st infantry regiments and 5,000 men from the 85th Division) joined Allied troops, primarily 70,000 Japanese. Graves's orders specified noninterference in internal Russian affairs. Unlike the other intervening powers, he zealously maintained his neutrality, refusing Allied, Japanese, and U.S. State Department efforts to change his mind. As part of an Allied scheme to keep the Trans-Siberian Railroad operating (and funneling supplies to anti-Bolshevik forces), however, Wilson ordered Graves in early 1919 to help guard the railroad and to protect rifle shipments to anti-Bolshevik forces. Graves became responsible for 316 miles of railroad including a section just east of Lake Baikal, approximately 1,700 miles from Vladivostok. This frustrated Graves's efforts to remain uninvolved in the civil war and, inevitably, brought the Americans into conflict with the Bolsheviks and with Japanese-supported Cossack factions. Bolsheviks and disaffected Russian partisans attacked U.S. troops and outposts at night, while befriending them by day.

By the fall of 1919, anti-Bolshevik resistance was foundering. The French and British had withdrawn their small forces from Siberia, and there was growing American-Japanese friction. The U.S. troops began departing Siberia on Jan. 17, 1920, finishing on April 1, while the Japanese remained. That the battle casualties of U.S. troops in Siberia totaled fewer than 100 was testimony to Graves's success and steadfastness.

Summary. The complex reasons surrounding the decisions to intervene largely explain the ignominious results. The interventions were political acts intended to pursue political objectives, yet those objectives (as well as the method by which they were to be achieved through use of military force) remained largely intangible and inadequately defined. The nebulousness of the political objectives meant that U.S. military commanders in the field received little useful guidance from civilian superiors. Unsurprisingly, both interventions were ill-conceived. Given the small size of the intervening forces, it was probably impossible to gain any significant objectives militarily, and hopes that Russian anti-Bolshevism would coalesce quickly proved unfounded. The president and pro-interventionists in the State and War departments did not understand Russian events—a lack of understanding perhaps best exemplified by Wilson's shortsighted belief that the "Russian people" would view his actions exactly as he did and would not be antagonized by a foreign intervention.

Once the bankruptcy of intervention became apparent, the most difficult problem the United States encountered was extricating its troops. In North Russia and Siberia, the presence of British and Japanese forces made the withdrawal of U.S. troops—without major casualties—feasible. Wilson sent enough forces to fuel Soviet propaganda for decades, but not enough to overthrow the Bolsheviks.

Bibliography: Bradley, John, *Allied Intervention in Russia* (Basic Books, 1968); Kennan, George F., *The Decision to Intervene* (Princeton Univ. Press, 1958); Unterberger, Betty Miller, *America's Siberian Expedition, 1918–1920: A Study of National Policy* (Duke Univ. Press, 1956; reprint Greenwood Press, 1969).

Stephen J. Lofgren

OFFICE OF STRATEGIC SERVICES

U.S. intelligence agency established during World War II. Set up by executive order on June 13, 1942, and disbanded on Oct. 1, 1945, the Office of Strategic Services (OSS) gathered essential intelligence and conducted covert activities in support of U.S. war efforts during World War II. It was led by Maj. Gen. William J. Donovan. OSS efforts ranged from the assessment of information by the Research and Analysis Division to the concoction of unorthodox weapons and plots by the Research and Development Division. Another wing of OSS, the Morale Operations Division, staffed by advertising copywriters, journalists, and Hollywood screenwriters, developed propaganda designed to deceive and confuse the enemy.

At the heart of OSS operations were the Secret Intelligence (SI) and Special Operations (SO) divisions. SI's duty was to collect foreign intelligence while SO conducted guerrilla operations and sabotage. SO operatives played a vital role in support of partisan resistance activities in Italy, Hungary, Rumania, and Bulgaria. A freewheeling operation with a predilection for graduates of Ivy League universities, the OSS was the forerunner of the Central Intelligence Agency (CIA) and gave a whole generation of intellectuals and academics a taste of power and an orientation toward government service.

Assessing the type of individual drawn to OSS service, particularly the so-called cowboys of the SI and SO divisions, Dr. Henry Murray, chief psychologist of the OSS, labeled recruits as being attracted by "the idea of being a mysterious man with secret knowledge." Potential OSS recruits for overseas assignments were put through a rigorous screening of mental and physical agility tests. Those who failed were sent back to their former pursuits without knowing why they had been tested.

Upon passing this initial screening, fledgling agents learned how to send Morse code, repair radio transmitters, kill quickly and silently, parachute into enemy terrain, and survive behind enemy lines. One of the most experienced practitioners of such covert activities was Allan Dulles, who went on to become head of the CIA. Dulles, who looked more like a college professor than a spy, spent

World War II in Bern, Switzerland, gathering information about Nazi activities for the OSS.

OSS operatives such as Dulles served throughout Europe and the Far East gathering intelligence, sabotaging enemy war efforts, and encouraging partisan resistance movements. Relying upon teamwork and cooperation, OSS agents provided the know-how for a successful behind-the-lines war effort.

Bibliography: Corvo, Max, *The O.S.S. in Italy, 1942–1945: A Personal Memoir* (reprint; Greenwood Press, 1989); Troy, Thomas F., ed., *Wartime Washington: The Secret OSS Journal of James Grafton Rogers* (reprint; Greenwood Press, 1986).

M. Guy Bishop

OKINAWA, BATTLE FOR
(April 1–July 2, 1945)

World War II battle for Okinawa, largest of Japan's Ryukyu Islands and only 360 miles southwest of Kyushu Island. The Allied armada poised offshore in the South China Sea as part of Operation Iceberg was the largest ever assembled for a single operation, larger even than for D-Day, the massive Allied invasion staged a year earlier in Europe. The 1,200 ships crammed with soldiers of the newly formed U.S. 10th Army were supported by 40 aircraft carriers, 18 battleships, and nearly 200 destroyers. The 10th Army, composed of the marines' Amphibious Corps and the army's XXIV Corps, totaled about 180,000 combat troops and 110,000 support troops.

Capturing Okinawa was an essential prelude to invading the Japanese homelands, and the Japanese knew it as they threw more than 120,000 troops against the U.S. invaders. It would take the Allies 82 days of hand-to-hand combat to conquer Okinawa. Offshore, pilots of the Imperial Navy's Divine Wind (Kamikaze) Special Attack Unit hurled their explosives-laden planes against the armada, but only three percent actually succeeded—the rest either crashed into the sea short of the target or were shot down by antiaircraft fire.

About 6,000 Japanese aircraft were downed in combat against the loss of 763 U.S. planes. During the battle, 263 Allied ships were sunk or damaged; about 4,900 Americans were killed or missing at sea, and more than 5,000 sailors were wounded. On land, some 30,000 U.S. soldiers were wounded and 7,613 died, including 10th Army commander Lt. Gen. Simon Bolivar Buckner, Jr. The casualty toll for the Japanese was much higher: 107,500 soldiers were killed or missing (an average of 1,300 a day), 20,000 were killed in caves sealed up by flamethrower-equipped bulldozers, and approximately 100,000 civilians were killed. Buckner's opponent, Gen. Mituru Ushijima of the 32d Army, committed suicide on June 23.

Bibliography: Ienaga, Sasburo, *The Pacific War* (Pantheon, 1978); Naito, Hatsuho, *Thunder Gods: The Kami-*

kaze Pilots Tell Their Story (Kodansha, 1989); Okumiya, Masatake, and Jiro, Horikoshi, *Zero!* (Dutton, 1956).

Peter Model

OLYMPIC-CORONET, OPERATION

Unrealized two-pronged plan of attack against Japan at the close of World War II. Operation Downfall—the overall Allied plan for invading Japan—consisted of two phases: Operation Olympic, the assault on Kyushu, the southernmost of Japan's home islands, scheduled for autumn 1945; and Operation Coronet, the assault on the main island of Honshu, scheduled for spring 1946 (a security breach in August 1945 caused nervous planners to rename the operation Majestic). Tapped to head the Kyushu phase was Gen. Walter Krueger of the 6th Army. Against Kyushu, U.S. planners envisioned hurling a total of 11 army and 3 marine divisions, bringing in ground troops stationed as far away as Hawaii. Only the southern half of Kyushu, from Tsuno on the east to Sendai on the west, would be occupied so as to give the Allies a staging area for the following year's assault on Honshu, while Honshu (Coronet) would be assigned to Lt. Gen. Robert Eichelberger of the 8th Army. Three divisions each would land on the southern flank of the island, while units of the 10th Army would make a diversionary move off Shikoku. The 10th Army's XXIV Corps would land in the Pusan area of southern Korea.

Figuring on about the same high (35 percent) casualty rate as the Allies sustained taking Okinawa, the invasion strategists warned of as many as 268,000 battlefield American dead, missing, and wounded. The invaders would be facing a ferocious enemy—at least 14 Japanese divisions and 5 brigades (2,300,000 men), plus a civilian army of 4,000,000 men and women. The destruction of Hiroshima and Nagasaki by atomic bombs in early August 1945 and the subsequent surrender of Japan made all these plans moot.

Peter Model

OPERATION . . . (*see* second part of name)

OVERLORD, OPERATION

Code name for the Allied plan for the 1944 invasion of northern France in World War II. It was launched on June 5–6, 1944, by the greatest amphibious operation in the history of warfare, when 155,000 Allied troops stormed the French beaches of Normandy from Caen in the east to the Carentan Peninsula in the west. The long-awaited cross-channel invasion, Operation Overlord, was the result of planning, logistics, and execution on a scale never before attempted.

The invasion of Normandy began late on the night of June 5 and in the early morning hours of June 6, when massive airborne landings took place near Caen and in the western sector in the Carentan Peninsula. The British 6th

U.S. marines from the landing craft in the background gradually make their way up the beach during Operation Overlord, the invasion of northern France via Normandy in 1944. (U.S. Navy)

Airborne Division assaulted both sides of the Orne River and the Orne Canal sector north of the city of Caen by parachute and glider landings. Their mission was to secure intact the vital Pegasus Bridge, the only bridge over both the river and the canal between Caen and the sea, and to take out German communications centers and strongpoints that menaced the nearby landings on Sword Beach by the British 3d Division.

At dawn, elite commandos of Britain's 1st Commando Brigade landed on the extreme left flank of the British sector. Their mission was to knock out the German artillery batteries and garrison at Ouistreham and to link up with the 6th Airborne Division so as to protect the left flank of the beachhead until the British I Corps was established ashore. Between 3:00 A.M. and 5:00 A.M., June 6, more than 1,000 British aircraft dropped more than 5,000 tons of bombs on the German coastal defenses in the British landing sector. As soon as this preliminary bombing had ceased, the guns of the Allied fleet opened fire across the Normandy front.

At the same time, the U.S. 82d and 101st airborne divisions were parachuted into the Carentan estuary to secure the terrain and support the landings on Utah Beach by the U.S. VII Corps. In the darkness, the paratroopers landed over a wide area and were unable to link up with their units. Nevertheless, operating in small groups, they were able to disrupt severely German attempts to interfere with the Utah landings on June 6.

The Allied ground forces were under the temporary command of Gen. Sir Bernard Montgomery, and on D-Day, they landed in three separate sectors. In the east, commencing at 7:00 A.M, Lt. Gen. Miles Dempsey's British 2d Army landed three divisions and three armored brigades of the British I Corps on Sword, Juno, and Gold beaches in the Caen sector. Their mission was to seize

Caen and anchor the Allied left flank by preventing the Germans from reinforcing from the west. Within two and a half hours, 30,000 men, 300 guns, and 700 armored vehicles came ashore. Although the Canadian 3d Division took more than two hours to crush German resistance in the Juno sector and open exits before they could begin moving inland, the British landings went exceptionally well overall.

In the U.S. sector, Omaha and Utah beaches had been subjected to the same bombardment by air and naval forces. The VII Corps assault of Utah Beach began at 6:30 A.M. and was spearheaded by the 4th Infantry Division, which achieved total surprise and the least opposition and fewest casualties of any Allied assault unit. The division quickly moved inland and seized its D-Day objectives. The landings on Omaha Beach by the veteran 1st Infantry Division and a regiment of the 29th Infantry Division of Maj. Gen. Leonard T. Gerow's V Corps ran into heavy resistance from the German 325th Division, which had managed to escape the attention of Allied intelligence when it moved into the Omaha sector three months earlier. From the steep bluffs overlooking Omaha Beach, the Germans poured artillery, mortar, and automatic weapons fire, inflicting heavy casualties on the confused and badly exposed troops.

Heavy seas swamped many of the landing craft, resulting in most of the armor failing to get ashore, along with the demolition engineers whose task it was to clear obstacles from the beach. For the first six hours, the invaders held only a few yards of beach, which remained under intense enemy fire. It soon became evident to the U.S. commanders that it would be suicidal to remain where they were, and they rallied their men to attack or die. One commander strode up and down the beach under fire exhorting his troops, while another led an attack against German machine-gun positions, declaring that "two kinds of people are staying on this beach, the dead and those about to die. Now let's get the hell out of here." Eventually, American leadership and exceptional acts of gallantry by men of all ranks saved the day. Nevertheless, throughout June 6, the situation on Omaha remained so perilous that the U.S. 1st Army commander, Lt. Gen. Omar N. Bradley, seriously considered evacuating the beachhead and switching the follow-up units to the British sector or to Utah Beach.

Although the Germans resisted, often savagely, across the entire invasion front, their reaction to the surprise of the landings was too little and far too late to prevent the Allied invaders from establishing a firm beachhead in Normandy. Although Caen was not captured and the British later became stalled before the city, they had managed to fend off what were mostly weak and badly coordinated German counterattacks. On that momentous day, more than 130,000 Allied ground troops and 23,000 airborne were landed in Normandy. In spite of the unexpected setbacks at Omaha, where the toehold around the beaches was still slender but gradually improving, the invasion was a stunning success.

The numbers bear out the enormity of Operation Overlord: 195,700 naval personnel in 6,939 vessels (1,213 combat ships, 4,126 landing craft, 736 ancillary ships, and 864 merchant ships) participated in the D-Day landings. On June 5–6, the Allied air forces flew 14,000 sorties in support of the landings. In all, the Allies lost 12,000 officers and men killed and 2,000 aircraft in the period April 1–June 5 in support of pre-D-Day operations over France. Total Allied losses on D-Day have never been established precisely but appear to have exceeded 10,000, with U.S. losses of 6,603 the highest, which included 1,465 killed and 1,928 missing in action.

Success and Its Price. U.S. casualties on D-Day in the Omaha sector alone numbered more than 2,000 killed, wounded, or missing. British and Canadian losses were approximately 3,000.

It was the German commander responsible for the defense of Normandy, Field Marshal Erwin Rommel, who in April 1944 had defined the importance of this day when he predicted, "The first 24 hours of the invasion will be decisive . . . the fate of Germany depends on the outcome . . . for the Allies, as well as Germany, it will be the longest day." Rommel was correct: June 6, 1944, was the most decisive day of World War II. It marked the beginning of the end of Adolf Hitler's Third Reich, and after nearly four years of German occupation, it marked the first step in the liberation of France.

Bibliography: D'Este, Carlo, *Decision in Normandy* (Dutton, 1983); Harrison, Gordon A., *Cross-Channel Attack (United States Army in World War II: European Theater of Operations)* (Office of the Chief of Military History, U.S. Army, 1950); Hastings, Max, *Overlord: D-Day and the Battle for Normandy, 1944* (Simon & Schuster, 1984); Keegan, John, *Six Armies in Normandy* (Viking, 1982); Ryan, Cornelius, *The Longest Day* (Popular Library, 1977).

Carlo W. D'Este

PANAY INCIDENT (December 12, 1937)

Pre-World War II naval skirmish, in which the USS *Panay* (PR 5), under the command of Lt. Cmdr. James J. Hughes, was attacked by Japanese aircraft while cruising on China's Yangtze River 27 miles upstream from Nanking. Despite a large U.S. flag painted on each of the two awnings built on the deck fore and aft and a third flag flying from the standard on the stern, the Japanese airmen made repeated attacks on the *Panay,* sinking the U.S. ship. Casualties included 2 killed and 43 wounded. Anxious to avoid war with the United States, the Japanese government accepted responsibility and paid indemnities to the U.S. government and to the families of the crew.

Vernon L. Williams

Gen. Charles de Gaulle, head of the Free French, parades through Paris shortly after its liberation from the Germans in August 1944. (French Embassy Press and Information Division)

PARIS, LIBERATION OF (August 1944)

Allied liberation of the French capital from German occupation during World War II. After the Allied breakout from Normandy, four principals wrestled for control of Paris: German commander Gen. Dietrich von Choltitz had orders to destroy Paris, while Gen. Dwight D. Eisenhower, the Supreme Allied Commander, was determined to bypass Paris. The French Communist resistance hoped to seize the city to improve its political position. Finally, Gen. Charles de Gaulle, head of the Free French, sought to reach Paris first.

On Aug. 19, 1944, the resistance rose in Paris. Choltitz, unwilling to destroy the city, signed a temporary truce with the resistance. The deteriorating situation in Paris, and Gaullist pressure, induced Eisenhower, on August 23, to order the occupation of Paris. Two days later, Gen. Jacques Leclerc entered Paris. De Gaulle triumphantly paraded through Paris, on August 26, amid German sniper fire.

Russell A. Hart

PEARL HARBOR, ATTACK ON
(December 7, 1941)

Devastating surprise Japanese attack on the U.S. air and naval installations on the Hawaiian island of Oahu starting at 7:55 A.M. (Hawaiian time) on Sunday, Dec. 7, 1941— "a date which will live in infamy" in Pres. Franklin Roosevelt's immortal words to an outraged Congress. The attack on Pearl Harbor finally ended U.S. neutrality and brought the nation irrevocably into World War II.

The long-planned air strike was deemed necessary by Japan's Imperial High Command in order to neutralize the United States and thus render the Pacific basin open to unimpeded Japanese conquest for the Greater East Asia Coprosperity Sphere. The attack effectively crippled the

The Phoenix *burns after the Japanese air attack on the U.S. fleet at Pearl Harbor on Dec. 7, 1941.* (U.S. Navy)

U.S. Pacific Fleet anchored off Ford Island in Pearl Harbor. Sunk or damaged were 8 American battleships, 3 light cruisers, 3 destroyers, and 3 smaller vessels, while 177 airplanes (75 percent of the amphibious and ground aircraft parked at Ford Island Naval Air Station, Hickam Field, and Wheeler Field) were destroyed. There were 2,403 American military personnel (mostly sailors) killed or missing, 49 civilians dead, and more than 1,100 military and civilian personnel wounded.

The Japanese, using specially designed armor-piercing bombs and torpedoes built for shallow waters, deployed a total of 350 aircraft: 78 Zero fighters, 129 Val torpedo (dive-) bombers, and 143 Kate horizontal bombers. The Japanese encountered no aerial opposition and lost only 27 planes and 5 midget submarines that were to have penetrated the undersea harbor defenses. The principal U.S. target ships were lined up on "Battleship Row," which flanked Ford Island; to guard against sabotage, the airplanes were parked wingtip-to-wingtip.

Three U.S. carriers that had been targeted—the *Lexington,* the *Enterprise,* and the *Saratoga*—were not in port and thus escaped unharmed. The *Saratoga* was sailing in California waters, while the other two carriers were delivering fighter planes to Wake and Midway islands. Ironically, the carriers had been dispatched by Pacific Fleet Commander Adm. Husband E. Kimmel, who, along with army commandant Lt. Gen. Walter C. Short, would be relieved for having failed to anticipate the attack.

The aerial assault was launched in two waves—75 minutes apart—from a total of 6 Japanese carriers located 230 miles north of Oahu. The carriers were accompanied by 2 battleships, 3 cruisers, 9 destroyers, 30 submarines, and 8 oilers. The attack fleet had steamed secretly from the Kurile Islands in northern Japan the month before while Japanese diplomats in Washington were talking rapprochement with Sec. of State Cordell Hull.

The "sneak attack"—as it was quickly dubbed—was conceived by Japanese Combined Fleet commander in chief Adm. Isoroku Yamamoto (who would be shot down and killed by a U.S. air ambush over the Solomons in April 1943) and executed by naval air commander Mitsuo Fuchida and fleet vice admiral Chuichi Nagumo. Yamamoto was said to have been inspired by a prophetic (1925) British book about a war between the United States and Japan that began with the destruction of the American fleet and by a real-life event—the November 1940 attack by carrier-based British bombers on the Italian fleet anchored at Taranto on the Mediterranean Sea.

Japanese planning failed to anticipate the American resolve (spurred by the slogan "Remember Pearl Harbor") to rebuild the fleet, rearm, and strike back. All but the battleships *Arizona, California, Utah,* and *Oklahoma* were salvaged and eventually returned to active duty in the Pacific. Inexplicably, the attackers did not bomb the huge fuel depots, whose destruction would have forced the remainder of the U.S. fleet to move its operations to San Diego, California, delaying the counteroffensive by months.

The humiliating disaster at Pearl Harbor led to no fewer than eight Congressional investigations and Naval Board of Inquiry hearings that would run longer than the war itself. Military careers would be ruined and questions raised that have never been fully answered.

Bibliography: Prange, Gordon W., *At Dawn We Slept: The Untold Story of Pearl Harbor* (McGraw-Hill, 1983); Toland, John, *Infamy: Pearl Harbor and Its Aftermath*

(Doubleday, 1982); Wallin, Homer N., *Why, How, Fleet Salvage and Final Appraisal* (U.S. Govt. Printing Office, 1988).

Peter Model

PELELIU, BATTLE FOR

Assault, beginning Sept. 15, 1944, against the main Japanese base in the Palau Islands by the U.S. 1st Marine Division and 81st Army Division to secure a base of operations for Gen. Douglas MacArthur's advance into the Philippines during World War II. Marines and army units had to rely on flamethrowers and hand grenades to wrest 10,500 determined enemy defenders from hundreds of limestone caves cut into soaring cliffs, turning what was hoped to be a two-day assault into a grinding, bloody two-month campaign that cost almost 2,000 American lives. When Japanese resistance finally ended in late November, only 300 enemy troops remained alive. Tragically, by then, MacArthur had already established his forces in the Philippines after speeding up his invasion timetable, making the campaign on Peleliu unnecessary.

Bibliography: Costello, John, *The Pacific War* (Quill Books, 1982); Spector, Ronald H., *Eagle Against the Sun* (Free Press, 1985); Wheeler, Richard, *A Special Valor* (New Amer. Library, 1983).

John F. Wukovits

PERSIAN GULF COMMAND

Independent command established in December 1943 to facilitate delivery of Lend-Lease supplies to the Soviet Union via Iran during World War II. Under the command of Maj. Gen. Donald H. Connolly, the Persian Gulf Command (PGC) reached a peak strength of nearly 30,000 men in 1944. PGC responsibilities covered several construction, maintenance, supply, and transportation operations. At times, the PGC provided logistical support to the Mediterranean and Asian theaters. The PGC was also responsible for providing civilian goods and services to Iran. During the PGC's gradual contraction in 1945, its facilities were turned over to the Iranis. Such policies encouraged postwar U.S.-Irani military cooperation.

Bibliography: Motter, T. H. Vail, *The Persian Corridor and Aid to Russia* (Office of the Chief of Military History, U.S. Army, 1952).

Jeffrey J. Roberts

PHILIPPINES CAMPAIGN
(October 1944–September 1945)

Major U.S. offensive against the Japanese in the Pacific theater during World War II. By July 1944, U.S. forces in the Pacific had advanced into the Marianas and western New Guinea. The question then facing U.S. leaders was where to strike next: Formosa or the Philippines. The chief of naval operations, Adm. Ernest J. King, and many in

Washington favored a move on Formosa. The commanders in the Pacific, however, supported an invasion of the main Philippine island, Luzon. U.S. carrier strikes on the southern Philippines in September created the impression that the Japanese were only lightly holding the region. This belief, coupled with a shortage of troops for the Formosa operation, caused the Joint Chiefs of Staff to decide in favor of Luzon. First, however, the Philippine islands of Leyte and Mindoro would be seized to gain air bases for the Luzon attack.

Initial Phases. On October 20, an invasion fleet of 738 U.S. ships carrying more than 160,000 troops appeared off Leyte's east coast. At 10:00 A.M, four army divisions stormed ashore and established a beachhead against scattered resistance. The Japanese navy quickly moved to unleash a counterstroke. Two task forces diverted and fought the U.S. fleet's carriers and battleships, while a third Japanese force appeared off the lightly defended invasion beaches on October 25. The Japanese commander, however, misread his opportunity and thought that he faced the main force of the U.S. fleet. After a sharp fight with U.S. escort carriers and destroyers, he withdrew. Not even the introduction of the new kamikaze suicide units could save the Japanese attack. The Battle of Leyte Gulf cost the Japanese heavily: 3 battleships, 4 carriers, 9 cruisers, 11 destroyers, and more than 500 aircraft lost. Moreover, it left the Japanese troops in the Philippines unsupported and marked the last major fleet action of the war.

With the beaches now secured, the U.S. Army continued to push across Leyte. Despite the defeat in Leyte Gulf, the Japanese were determined to fight a decisive battle on the island and pumped reinforcements into the land battle. U.S. troops quickly spread across the southern part of the island, but Japanese resistance stiffened in the mountains east of the west coast port of Ormoc. By November, troop and supply movements had become difficult due to heavy monsoon rains, and intense fighting developed in the mountains. The U.S. 6th Army commander, Gen. Walter Krueger, proposed bypassing the mountains with an amphibious assault on Ormoc. Delayed for two weeks until sufficient shipping could be found, the 77th Infantry Division landed south of Ormoc on December 7. The division moved rapidly inland and within three days captured the port. The capture of Ormoc sealed the fate of the Japanese still fighting in the mountains. Cut off from supplies and reinforcements, they held out for several more weeks before their final defense collapsed. As the remnants of the Japanese army fought on Leyte, two American regiments landed on Mindoro on December 14 and quickly secured the island.

Battle for Luzon. As engineers built air bases on the recaptured islands, Gen. Douglas MacArthur readied his 6th and 8th U.S. armies for the invasion of Luzon. The Japanese commander on Luzon, Gen. Yamashita Tomo-

U.S. soldiers oversee Japanese prisoners of war during the Philippines Campaign in 1945. (U.S. Army Military History Institute: E. M. Walker Collection)

yuki, also prepared his forces for the invasion. The fighting on Leyte had drained his command of many of its best troops and most of his air power, so Yamashita decided to fight a delaying action in Luzon's rugged mountains. On Jan. 9, 1945, MacArthur's forces came ashore in the Lingayen Gulf. While the troops moved ashore relatively easily, kamikazes harried the invasion fleet, sinking or damaging 25 ships. Nevertheless, the 6th Army quickly pushed down the central plain and toward Manila.

As Krueger's men moved on Manila, other U.S. units began landing on the island. On January 31, the 11th Airborne Division landed southwest of Manila and moved north on the city. While Yamashita had no intention of fighting for Manila, his naval counterpart, Adm. Iwabachi Sanji, did. As units of the U.S 1st Cavalry Division entered the city on February 3, heavy fighting developed. Over the next month, 1,000 Americans, 16,000 Japanese, and more than 100,000 Filipino civilians died as U.S. troops fought a bitter house-to-house battle to clear the city.

As American forces approached Manila, the U.S. XI Corps landed near the village of San Antonio on Luzon's west coast on January 29. After a difficult fight at Zigzag Pass, the corps moved south and liberated the Bataan Peninsula. On February 16, a combined airdrop and amphibious assault landed on the island of Corregidor at the mouth of Manila Bay. Within 10 days, Japanese resistance on the island collapsed, and the Americans turned to clearing the smaller islands at the mouth of the bay.

While fighting still raged in Manila and the bulk of Yamashita's troops still held forth in Luzon's northern mountains, MacArthur ordered Gen. Robert L. Eichelberger's 8th Army to clear the southern Philippines. Beginning with Palawan on February 28, the 8th Army and the U.S. 7th Fleet undertook 14 major and 24 minor amphibious operations over the next 44 days to liberate Panay, Cebu, Negros, Bohol, and Mindanao. Eichelberger's troops worked closely with local Filipino guerrillas and captured the region's important towns, airfields, and roads before the war's end.

After securing southern Luzon, Krueger's 6th Army moved against Yamashita's main force in the north. Rugged terrain and large expanses of thick jungle made fighting difficult. Still, U.S. forces slowly battered their way north along Route 9 and the Villa Verde Trail, while Filipino guerrillas wrecked Yamashita's supply lines. In the face of heavy pressure, the Japanese steadily lost ground, although at the end of the war, they continued to hold the Asin River valley in north central Luzon.

The hard-fought campaign in the Philippines had been costly—nearly 18,000 Americans and more than 450,000

Japanese dead—but it was also an important part of the Allied victory over Japan. The campaign's land and sea battles severely reduced Japan's military power, and possession of Luzon gave the Allies the fine harbor at Manila and air bases to increase their stranglehold over Japan's vital supply line to the East Indies and from which to stage attacks on Japan itself.

Bibliography: Cannon, M. Hamlin, *U.S. Army in World War II: The War in the Pacific: Leyte: The Return to the Philippines* (Office of the Chief of Military History, U.S. Army, 1954); Cortesi, Lawrence, *The Battle for Manila* (Kensington, 1984); Morison, Samuel Eliot, *History of United States Naval Operations in World War II,* vols. 12 & 13 (Little, Brown, 1958); Smith, Robert R., *U.S. Army in World War II: The War in the Pacific: Triumph in the Philippines* (Office of the Chief of Military History, U.S. Army, 1963).

Richard F. Kehrberg

PHILIPPINE SEA, BATTLE OF THE
(June 19–20, 1944)

Pivotal naval engagement during World War II. By April 1944, U.S. naval strength in the Pacific was overwhelming. The battered Japanese fleet was limited in operations by severe shortages of fuel oil and the aggressive actions of U.S. air and submarine forces. Japanese commanders sought to conserve their strength for a climactic battle that would rout the Americans and win the war. When U.S. forces began preparations for the invasion of Saipan in June 1944, the Japanese decided to force the issue by making an all-out attack on the invading forces. Saipan was considered one of the Japanese home islands, and to allow it to fall uncontested would bring about an unbearable loss of face for the Japanese.

The U.S. 5th Fleet, commanded by Adm. Raymond A. Spruance, assigned the invasion of Saipan to Vice Adm. Marc A. Mitscher's powerful Task Force 58, comprised of 15 carriers, numerous other ships of all classes, and almost 900 aircraft. The opposing Japanese naval forces under Vice Adm. Jisaburo Ozawa were inferior in almost every respect, but hoped to use a combination of greater aircraft range, submarine attacks, and land-based fighter support to destroy the Americans. Ozawa relied heavily on the hope that Japanese aircraft based on the islands of Guam, Rota, and Yap would greatly weaken Mitscher's carrier strength prior to the engagement of the two fleets. Thus, when Mitscher's force was spotted by Japanese air patrols on June 10, Admiral Ozawa set his plan in motion.

Things went wrong for the Japanese from the beginning. Mitscher knew the importance of neutralizing Japanese land-based aircraft in the vicinity of Saipan and began offensive air strikes throughout the Marianas on June 11. By June 13, the U.S. battleships were close enough to begin

their bombardment of the landing beaches, and Mitscher's planes had already destroyed approximately 500 Japanese aircraft. Ozawa's forces began moving toward Saipan on June 15 and were immediately spotted by U.S. submarines, which alerted Spruance and Mitscher. Ozawa's own submarines were a dismal failure, destroying no U.S. ships and losing 17 of their number to U.S. destroyer escorts. The aggressive Mitscher was barely restrained by Spruance from launching an immediate attack on Ozawa.

Spruance recognized that a major naval battle was developing but knew that his primary mission was the protection of the landing forces at Saipan. By June 16, the imminence of Ozawa's attack had become clearer, and Spruance gave his final instructions to Mitscher, who remained in tactical command of the operation. The instructions directed that enemy carriers were to be the first target and that complete destruction of the enemy fleet was the ultimate goal. The details were left to Mitscher's discretion, save that the Saipan landings were to remain protected.

On June 18, Ozawa's scout planes began providing him with sufficient details of the disposition of Mitscher's forces to allow him to finalize his plans and prepare to launch his first strikes. He moved his van, including the light carriers *Chitose, Chiyoda,* and *Zuiho,* ahead of his main body and approximately 300 miles from the U.S. forces. This arrangement kept the main body beyond the range of Mitscher's carrier aircraft and gave Ozawa the initiative to start the battle when he felt it most advantageous to the Japanese forces. The Americans, less sure of Ozawa's exact location, still felt that he might try to evade their forces and attack the landings at Saipan. As a consequence, while Ozawa warmed up his aircraft prior to his first launch, Mitscher's forces continued their strikes on known Japanese airfields in the vicinity.

The first phase of the battle, popularly referred to as the "Great Marianas Turkey Shoot," opened on June 19 with a U.S. strike against the Japanese airfield at Orote, Guam. This action had barely begun when U.S. radar picked up a large group of enemy aircraft approaching from the west. Mitscher immediately turned his carriers into the wind and launched every available fighter. The attacking Japanese, the first of four strikes launched by Ozawa that day, were decimated by the more heavily armed and better trained American pilots. Of the 69 Japanese aircraft in this first wave, none reached Mitscher's carriers and only 1 managed to damage a U.S. ship. Only 24 of these planes made it back to their carriers.

Ozawa's second strike fared even worse, achieving no hits and losing 98 of the 130 planes involved. A smaller third wave, consisting of 47 aircraft, failed to find the U.S. ships and returned to their carriers after losing 7 planes. In the fourth and final Japanese strike of the day, Ozawa lost 73 of the 82 aircraft launched without damaging a single

U.S. ship. In this greatest carrier battle of all time, the Japanese lost 346 aircraft and 2 carriers, victims of submarine attacks, against U.S. losses of just 30 planes.

Second Day. After recovering his aircraft, Mitscher ordered the bulk of his forces westward in pursuit of Ozawa. The Japanese proved somewhat elusive as U.S. scout planes were not able to pinpoint their location until late in the afternoon of June 20. Not wishing to miss a chance to destroy the Japanese carriers, Mitscher launched his aircraft knowing that they would return after dark. Mitscher's 10 carriers launched more than 200 planes against an enemy whose remaining strength was unknown and who was located at the extreme range of the U.S. aircraft. Catching Ozawa unprepared for an attack, the American forces sank the carrier *Hiyo,* damaged several other ships, and shot down 65 of Ozawa's remaining 100 aircraft. The attackers lost 20 aircraft to enemy action, but lost four times that number during the difficult night carrier landings that followed. Only Mitscher's courageous decision to order his ships to turn on their lights prevented American losses from being far greater.

Mitscher gave up his pursuit the next day as a thoroughly defeated Japanese fleet steamed toward Okinawa. In the two days of battle, the Japanese lost 3 large carriers and more than 480 aircraft against negligible U.S. losses. This was the third time during the war that Japanese carrier aviation had been decimated, and this time there would be no recovery.

Bibliography: Hagan, Kenneth J., *This People's Navy: The Making of American Sea Power* (Free Press, 1991); Jablonski, Edward, *Airwar* (Doubleday, 1971); Morison, Samuel Eliot, *The Two-Ocean War: A Short History of the United States Navy in the Second World War* (Little, Brown, 1963); Reynolds, Clark G., *The Carrier War* (Time-Life Books, 1982).

Maj. Gilbert B. Diaz

PLOESTI RAID (August 1, 1943)

World War II air assault by U.S. forces on oil refineries at Ploesti, Rumania, reportedly the source of almost one-third of Germany's oil requirements. On Aug. 1, 1943, 165 B-24 bombers of the U.S. 9th Air Force delivered a low-level attack on these refineries. The raid, led by Brig. Gen. Uzal W. Ent's 9th Bomber Command, originated in North Africa and employed five air groups: 98th (Col. John Kane), 376th (Col. Keith K. Compton), 44th (Col. Leon Johnson), 93d (Lt. Col. Addison Baker), and 389th (Col. Jack Wood).

Unknown to the raiders, German intelligence detected the formation, shortly after takeoff, heading for Rumania. Both the mission navigator and deputy were lost while still over the Mediterranean. Ent and Compton, in the leading group, mistook ground features in one area for those marking the point where the bombers were to turn toward Ploesti. The mistake carried part of the force toward Bucharest. The lead group soon corrected its mistake. However, the error resulted in improvised bombing runs and groups hitting targets other than those assigned.

Fifty-three aircraft were lost, 23 reached other Allied bases, and 88 returned home, but only 33 were fit to fly. Of some 1,620 men who reached Ploesti, 310 were killed, 54 wounded, 79 interned in neutral Turkey, and 136 captured. The refineries temporarily lost 40 percent of their throughput and 42 percent of their cracking capacity.

Bibliography: Dugan, James, and Carroll Stewart, *Ploesti* (Ballantine Books, 1973); Wolff, Leon, *Low Level Mission* (Berkley Publ., 1958).

Brig. Gen. (PNG, Ret.) Uzal W. Ent

POTSDAM CONFERENCE
(July 17–August 2, 1945)

Last of the World War II summit talks attended by the United States, Great Britain, and the Soviet Union (the "Big Three"); held in Potsdam, Germany, just outside captured Berlin. It was the first such conference for Pres. Harry S Truman, and British prime minister Winston Churchill was replaced in mid-conference by Clement Attlee after Churchill's election defeat. Talks at Potsdam began on July 17, 1945, and centered on postwar Germany and ending the war with Japan.

On European issues, agreements were difficult as relations among the Big Three were rapidly deteriorating. Poland was granted administration over German territory east of the Oder-Neisse Line. Consensus was reached that Germany must be demilitarized, disarmed, and de-Nazified, but the Big Three could not agree on a common set of rules to govern the four occupation zones. Eventually, the Soviets were granted reparations rights in their zone and 25 percent of reparations from the western zones. It was these economic partitions that led to political partition and full Soviet control over East Germany.

The Allies were more productive in respect to Japan. The Soviets reaffirmed their commitment to declare war on Japan. On July 26, the conference issued the Potsdam Proclamation, demanding unconditional Japanese surrender but allowing the emperor to remain. During the course of the conference, Truman issued the orders to drop the first atomic bomb on Japan. Failure to come to agreement over Germany, failure to gain a guarantee of land access to Berlin, and rising Western concern over Soviet intentions in Eastern Europe mark Potsdam as the bridge from wartime alliance to the Cold War.

Bibliography: Feir, Herbert, *Between War and Peace: The Potsdam Conference* (Princeton Univ. Press, 1961).

Capt. George B. Eaton

QUADRANT CONFERENCE
(August 13–24, 1943)
World War II meeting of British and American military leaders in the Canadian city of Quebec; attended by U.S. president Franklin D. Roosevelt and British prime minister Winston Churchill. During the conference, held as operations in Sicily neared completion, strategists reaffirmed the priority of Operation Overlord. Churchill and Roosevelt agreed to an invasion of mainland Italy, which would tie down German troops and secure air bases, with which to expand the Combined Bomber Offensive. They also agreed to seize Sardinia and Corsica, in order to facilitate an invasion of southern France. The Americans rejected other British proposals, however, that would have delayed Overlord.

Further agreements were reached on Pacific operations, most notably the establishment of the Southeast Asia Command (SEAC). The British and Americans also signed secret agreements on cooperative nuclear research.

Bibliography: Matloff, Maurice, *Strategic Planning for Coalition Warfare, 1943–1944* (Office of the Chief of Military History, U.S. Army, 1958).

Jeffrey J. Roberts

RED BALL EXPRESS
(August 25–November 17, 1944)
Emergency measure implemented during World War II by the Communications Zone, which was responsible for the delivery of supplies to the U.S. forces in the European theater. To keep the rapidly advancing American troops supplied, the Red Ball Express commenced operation on Aug. 25, 1944, and over the next 12 weeks, thousands of trucks operated 24 hours a day along specially designated Red Ball highways, hauling cargo from the Normandy beaches to supply dumps near the front. Cargo tonnage transported peaked on August 29 when nearly 6,000 trucks moved more than 12,000 tons of cargo. Approximately 412,000 tons of gasoline, ammunition, food, and other supplies were moved forward by the Red Ball Express.

Steve R. Waddell

REMAGEN BRIDGE, TAKING OF
(March 7, 1945)
The seizing of a tactically important German bridge by U.S. forces during World War II. In February 1945, the Allies were poised to force their way across the Rhine River, a feat matched by no invading army since 1805. In an effort to forestall the Allied advance, the Germans blew up the most threatened Rhine bridges.

On Mar. 7, 1945, the U.S. 9th Armored Division advanced on Remagen, 60 miles northwest of Mainz, where the Germans had rigged the bridge for destruction. However, two attempts to blow up the bridge failed, and U.S.

troops captured the bridge intact. Within a day, 8,000 troops had crossed and established a bridgehead. Chancellor Adolf Hitler was infuriated and ordered the bridge destroyed from the air and by frogmen, but all attacks failed.

Russell A. Hart

ROER RIVER DAMS, BATTLE FOR THE (February 5–10, 1945)
World War II conflict in which German forces delayed the advance of U.S. troops into Germany by opening a strategically situated dam.

As the U.S. Army approached Germany and the Rhine River in the fall of 1944, the dams on the Roer (or Rur) River posed a serious threat. German control of these dams meant that they could flood the terrain in front of the Americans at will. The Americans belatedly recognized the importance of the dams and made several unsuccessful attempts to take them. In February 1945, in order to protect the U.S. 9th Army and to assist the Canadian offensive farther north, the U.S. 78th Infantry Division received orders to seize the dams. After four days of hard fighting, the division captured the main dam on February 10. It was only a partial victory, however, for the Germans had destroyed the control machinery and discharge valves. The result was a steady stream of water that flooded the front of the U.S. 9th Army and kept it immobile for more than two weeks.

Richard F. Kehrberg

SAIPAN, BATTLE FOR
(June 15–July 9, 1944)
U.S. naval offensive in the Pacific during World War II; part of Operation Forager, designed to seize the strategic Mariana Islands (Saipan, Tinian, and Guam) from Japan to provide bases for the B-29 bombers. Since this would be the first assault against Japan's inner line of defense, the largest U.S. naval force yet assembled gathered for the June 15, 1944, invasion, commanded by Adm. Raymond A. Spruance. More than 31,000 toughened Japanese defenders under Gen. Yoshitsugu Saito and Adm. Chuichi Nagumo bitterly fought in hills, swamps, and coral-limestone caves. Finally overcoming suicidal banzai attacks, U.S. marine and army units secured the island on July 9, but not before helplessly watching 8,000 Japanese civilians commit suicide—most leaping to their deaths from lofty cliffs protruding over the sea—rather than surrender.

Bibliography: Costello, John, *The Pacific War* (Quill Books, 1982); Spector, Ronald H., *Eagle Against the Sun* (Free Press, 1985); Wheeler, Richard, *A Special Valor* (New Amer. Library, 1983).

John F. Wukovits

U.S. troops land on Red Beach near Salerno, Italy, on Sept. 9, 1943; a wrecked P-38 airplane is at the right. (U.S. Navy)

SALERNO, LANDING AT
(September 9, 1943)

Fiercely contested Allied landing at a southwestern Italian seaport during World War II. Selected for its proximity to Naples and its accessability to Allied air cover, Salerno was the focal point of the Allied beachhead during the invasion of the Italian mainland (Operation Avalanche). The American VI Corps landed to the south of the city, while the British X Corps, supported by three U.S. Ranger battalions, landed to the north. A German panzer division stationed nearby curtailed initial progress, and other units arrived to launch repeated counterattacks throughout the first week of the battle, inflicting heavy U.S. losses. Timely reinforcements, extensive naval and air support, and the Allied advance from Taranto and Messina helped suppress resistance, secure the lodgment, and allow for exploitation northward.

Bibliography: Blumenson, Martin, *Salerno to Cassino* (Office of the Chief of Military History, U.S. Army, 1967).

Jeffrey J. Roberts

SCHWEINFURT RAIDS
(August–October 1943)

Part of an Allied strategic bombing campaign during World War II; executed because planners believed a massive blow to German wartime production could be dealt by destroying ball-bearing factories at Schweinfurt, deep inside Germany. On Aug. 17, 1943, 376 U.S. B-17s bombed targets at Schweinfurt and Regensburg. About 60 bombers (16 percent of the force) were lost in that combat. The Allies did not challenge German air power so seriously again until October 14, when 291 B-17s bombed Schweinfurt again. While the mission was moderately successful, the Allied losses were massive: 60 B-17s were shot down (20 percent of the force). For the rest of the year, the U.S. 8th Air Force reeled from this setback.

Bibliography: Kennett, Lee, *A History of Strategic Bombing* (Scribner's, 1982); Sherry, Michael S., *The Rise of American Air Power: The Creation of Armageddon* (Yale Univ. Press, 1987).

Roger D. Launius

SELECTIVE TRAINING AND SERVICE ACT (BURKE-WADSWORTH BILL)
(September 16, 1940)

Act of Congress, passed just 15 months prior to U.S. entry into World War II, that established the first peacetime program of compulsory military service in the United States. This act required all males aged 21–35 to register for possible military training of up to 12 months. It created the Selective Service System, which eventually assumed additional responsibilities beyond the registration, classification, and delivery of draftees. A civilian agency administered primarily by local boards, this system drew its first draft numbers on Oct. 29, 1940. The terms of the original act would be changed frequently—particularly expanding

Basic trainees of the 29th Infantry Division, drafted under the Selective Training and Service Act, train for chemical warfare. (U.S. Army Military History Institute)

and contracting the age limits—but between October 1940 and January 1943, almost 36,000,000 men were enrolled.

Ralph L. Eckert

SEXTANT CONFERENCE
(November 23–26, 1943)

World War II summit talks held outside Cairo, Egypt. The key participants were U.S. president Franklin D. Roosevelt, British prime minister Winston Churchill, and Chinese Nationalist leader Chiang Kai-shek. The conference had originally been intended as an Anglo-American planning conference on Operation Overlord, future military operations in Europe, and forging a united front before meeting with Soviet leader Joseph Stalin at the Tehran Conference, but Pacific matters soon took precedence. While little was decided on European operations, the Pacific theater was raised in importance second only to Europe, and the China, North Pacific, and Southeast Asian theaters were reduced to secondary importance. The Western allies agreed on a dual thrust against Japan in the Pacific.

Capt. George B. Eaton

SHAEF

Acronym for Supreme Headquarters, Allied Expeditionary Force, the unified Allied command that carried out strategic planning and direction of the invasion of France and subsequent campaigns in northwest Europe to defeat Nazi Germany during World War II. The supreme commander of SHAEF was Gen. Dwight D. Eisenhower, who received his orders directly from the Combined Chiefs of Staff. He assumed formal command on Feb. 13, 1944. The deputy supreme commander was Air Chief Marshal Sir Arthur Tedder, and the chief of staff was Lt. Gen. Walter B. Smith. Reflecting SHAEF's unified and combined nature, the naval and air component commanders were British, while their deputies were American. The four deputy chiefs of staff were British. Significantly, SHAEF controlled only tactical air forces, not the strategic bomber forces.

Stephen J. Lofgren

SICILIAN CAMPAIGN (OPERATION HUSKY) (July-August 1943)

Major Allied offensive during World War II. The Allied high command decided to launch Operation Husky, the invasion of Sicily, at the Casablanca Conference in January 1943. The Allies had limited intentions. Seizure of Sicily, they concluded, would secure Mediterranean communications, siphon off German forces from the continent, and weaken Italy's ability and will to continue the war. The U.S. high command deemed more expansive operations in the Mediterranean prejudicial to the buildup for a cross-channel invasion. Only at the Trident Conference in May would the Allies agree to further Mediterranean operations.

Field Marshal Sir Harold Alexander was designated operational commander and would oversee the activities of the invasion force, comprising Gen. George Patton's 7th Army and the British 8th Army under Gen. Bernard Montgomery. The British would land on the southeastern side of the island. Patton's force, comprising elements of the 2d Armored Division and the 1st, 3d, and 45th infantry divisions, would land farther west, to protect the British left.

The Axis troops in Sicily were composed of 12 divisions in theory, but 6 were Italian coastal formations of negligible worth, and 4 others were standard Italian infantry divisions of but slightly better quality. Even the 2 German divisions on the island (the Hermann Goering "Panzer-Parachute" Division and the 15th Panzergrenadier) were under-equipped. While comprising a force of more than 300,000 men, the Axis units were scattered widely across the island, attempting to defend nearly 500 miles of accessible land-ing beaches.

In the morning of July 10, 1943, the Allies began to land elements of eight divisions (four American, three British, and one Canadian), supported by several ranger and commando battalions, in a force comprising more than 180,000 men. Few casualties were sustained in the landings amidst scattered, sporadic, ineffective Italian resistance. (In some areas, in fact, Italian "defenders" were soon helping unload Allied landing craft.) In many cases, how-ever, the accompanying airdrops went badly awry. In-stances of troops being dropped into the sea or shot down by "friendly" forces occurred, and on the whole, the rough winds and inexperienced pilots combined to scatter the forces from their target areas. Small airborne detachments would nonetheless succeed in delaying and harassing en-emy movements toward the beachheads.

Montgomery quickly secured the ports of Syracuse and Augusta, while Patton's forces took Gela and Licata. Fol-lowing the invasion, Axis forces launched a series of uncoordinated attacks against the American perimeter around Gela. Two attacks by the "Livorno" Division, and others by elements of the Hermann Goering Panzer Division, were thwarted by the tough resistance of the 1st Infantry Division and detachments of rangers and para-troopers. A more concerted attack on the following day made more headway but was ultimately turned back with help from naval gunfire and the 1st Division's artillery. By July 15, the Allies had a secure lodgment throughout the southeast corner of the island.

Following the consolidation of the landing areas, Mont-gomery began to advance northward through eastern Sicily across the Catanian plain toward Messina. Patton sent his forces north and westward. The 3d Division, advancing at a rate of more than 20 miles per day, captured Palermo on July 22, and elements of the 1st and 45th divisions reached the north coast the following day.

The Axis resistance, however, soon stiffened. Two Ger-man divisions (1st Parachute and 29th Panzergrenadier) arrived to support those already in Sicily. As the front narrowed, the rugged countryside allowed the Axis defend-ers to exact a heavy toll from the attackers. Typical of the battles was that at the village of Triona, where elements of

the 1st Division struggled for six days in an effort to dislodge the German garrison.

While the Germans reinforced, the Italians began with-drawing their troops following the ouster of Italian dictator Benito Mussolini on July 26. By early August, the German command similarly began withdrawing troops from the island. They succeeded in extracting the vast majority of their troops and equipment. Patton, abetted by a series of amphibious "endruns" around the Axis flanks, reached Messina on the morning of August 17. British forces arrived shortly thereafter.

Campaign Results. The fall of Messina ended Operation Husky. The Sicilian campaign had secured Allied supply lines through the Mediterranean and had provided air bases and ports for use in further operations. It also proved a valuable training ground in a variety of aspects. It led directly to the dismissal of Mussolini, and while he would escape to form a puppet regime in northern Italy, the successor Italian government would negotiate an armistice with the Allies, entering their camp as a "co-belligerent."

From the German perspective, however, the battle had been a successful delaying action. Most of the Germans on the island had gotten away. The Axis had succeeded in evacuating more than 100,000 men and a considerable quantity of matériel across the straits. Sicily produced no vast gaggle of Axis prisoners comparable to that in Tunisia. (Alexander would report more than 100,000 prisoners, but most of these were reservist Italian troops taken early on in the campaign.) German losses totaled 12,000, while Allied losses in the campaign were 5,532 killed, 2,869 missing, and 14,410 wounded, out of some 450,000 men involved in the operation.

Bibliography: Garland, Albert N., *Sicily and the Sur-render of Italy* (Office of the Chief of Military History, U.S. Army, 1965).

Jeffrey Roberts

SQUALUS, SINKING AND RECOVERY OF THE (May 1939)

U.S. submarine training accident, in which the USS *Squa-lus* (S-51), under the command of Lt. O. F. Naquin, sank in waters off Portsmouth, New Hampshire, while undergoing tests in May 1939. The submarine sank in depths making ordinary rescue impossible. Using a diving bell, rescuers saved 59 crewmen, but 26 of the crew perished in the accident. The *Squalus* was successfully raised in salvage operations commanded by Rear Adm. Ernest King. After a refit, the *Squalus,* under the new name *Sailfish,* served successfully in World War II, most notably in its sinking of the Japanese carrier *Chuyo* in a 14-hour engagement.

Vernon L. Williams

STRATEGIC BOMBING SURVEY

U.S. investigative project charged with assessing the success of the strategic bombing campaigns of World War II. Franklin D'Olier, president of the Prudential Insurance Company, was appointed head of the survey, while it was actively directed by Henry C. Alexander, a partner in the financial firm of J. P. Morgan. Soon after its creation in November 1944, the survey sent 300 civilians to Europe, where they, aided by almost 1,000 military personnel, compiled basic information from inspections of bombed sites, captured German records, and interviews. Following the conclusion of the war with Japan, the survey team also conducted similar investigations in the Pacific. The survey issued 208 reports on European strategic bombing and another 108 volumes about the Pacific. The survey found that while the destruction visited on the enemy had been formidable, it had not been decisive in breaking the enemy spirit as had been predicted in prewar air-power arguments.

Bibliography: MacIsaac, David, *Strategic Bombing in World War II: The Story of the United States Strategic Bombing Survey* (Garland, 1976).

Roger D. Launius

TARAWA, BATTLE FOR
(November 20–23, 1943)

U.S. Marine assault on Betio, an isle in Tarawa Atoll and part of the Gilbert Islands, a chain resting along the equator in the Pacific Ocean, 2,500 miles southwest of Hawaii; proportionately, the bloodiest battle of World War II. U.S. forces were commanded by navy admiral Raymond A. Spruance and marine general Holland Smith. The 2d Marine Division, following an intense preinvasion naval bombardment, approached shore in maneuverable amtracs. After crossing a forbidding coral reef, the marines planned to seize Betio's airfield against what was assumed to be light opposition. Rear Adm. Keiji Shibasaki, a commander of Betio's 4,500 defenders, transformed Betio into an armed bastion, replete with sand-covered bunkers and interlocking pillboxes able to withstand the potent American bombardment.

Thus, the initial U.S. assault forces approaching early on November 20 were met by concentrated Japanese fire that shredded their ranks. When shallow waters exposed the coral reef, reinforcements had to wade in to the beach, and by day's end, marines barely clung to a narrow beachhead. Of 5,000 marines participating, 1,500 were casualties before nightfall. Reinforcements started pouring onto Betio the next day after the tide covered the reef, but three days of brutal combat, which included digging out the Japanese from their underground bastions and withstanding a desperate nighttime banzai charge, lay ahead. Betio was declared secured on November 23, with fewer than 20 of its garrison surviving.

When marine casualty figures for the brutal four-day battle reached the American public—more than 1,000 dead and 2,000 wounded—a furor arose as to Betio's value, but the battle for Tarawa taught vital lessons for future amphibious assaults, particularly pertaining to preinvasion bombardment and battle communications.

Bibliography: Costello, John, *The Pacific War* (Quill Books, 1982); Sherrod, Robert, *Tarawa* (Bantam Books, 1983); Wheeler, Richard, *A Special Valor* (New Amer. Library, 1983).

John F. Wukovits

TEHERAN CONFERENCE
(November 28–December 1, 1943)

World War II summit talks held in Teheran, Iran, in which the triad of Soviet premier Joseph Stalin, British prime minister Winston Churchill, and U.S. president Franklin D. Roosevelt met in person for the first time. Stalin voiced strong support for Operation Overlord and for operations in Southern France (Operation Anvil) and secured a commitment to both from the Western Allies. The advance in Italy would continue, as per Churchill's wishes, ostensibly to facilitate Anvil.

Churchill and Roosevelt effectively, although not formally, acceded to Stalin's annexation of eastern Poland. The Allies also agreed to withdraw their forces from Persia and restore Iranian sovereignity there after the war. Some discussion of the status of postwar Germany, the establishment of a united-nations organization, and Russian entry in the Pacific war transpired, but no concrete policy formation occurred.

Bibliography: Matloff, Maurice, *Strategic Planning for Coalition Warfare, 1943–1944* (Office of the Chief of Military History, U.S. Army, 1958).

Jeffery J. Roberts

TINIAN, BATTLE FOR
(July 20–August 1, 1944)

World War II offensive by U.S. forces to take a Japanese-controlled island in the Marianas. Tinian was targeted in 1944 because its airfields would provide an advanced base from which the new B-29 bombers could reach Japan. Aided by an effective diversion, the 4th Marine Division completely surprised the Japanese by landing on two narrow northern beaches on July 20. The 2d Marine Division joined the 4th the next day, and together they secured the island by August 1. U.S. casualties, in what has been described as the most nearly perfect amphibious operation of the Pacific war, numbered 328 killed and 1,571 wounded. Both atomic bombs dropped on Japan in August 1945 were delivered by Tinian-based B-29s.

Bibliography: Hoffman, Carl W., *The Seizure of Tinian* (U.S. Marine Corps, 1951).

Ralph L. Eckert

TORCH, OPERATION (November 1942)

Code name for the Allied invasion of North Africa during World War II. Allied high command sanctioned the operation in July 1942. Although American strategic doctrine called for direct confrontation with the main enemy forces as soon as possible, logistical constraints inhibited an invasion of mainland Europe from across the English Channel. The British further persuaded their allies that the European continent was too strong to be attacked, especially as the U.S. troops needed training and experience before dealing with veteran German forces. Pres. Franklin D. Roosevelt, perhaps more aware of the existing limitations than his generals, supported Prime Minister Winston Churchill's alternate plan for action.

Roosevelt thought it vital to take some action to reinforce his "Europe first" policy while the buildup in England continued. Torch seemed the best option available. The overall goal of the operation, entrusted to the newly appointed Allied commander in chief, Gen. Dwight D. Eisenhower, was to seize Morocco, Algeria, and Tunisia. In time, the invasion forces, in conjunction with Gen. Bernard Montgomery's 8th Army, would trap the Axis troops in North Africa and secure the entire continent as a base for operations northward.

The invasion force was predominantly American, owing both to sheer availability of forces and to Allied recognition of the Vichy French government's continued hostility to Britain. French North Africa was unoccupied by German forces, but the forces there were pledged to resist any invasion. Allied planners nonetheless believed those forces remained fundamentally anti-German.

The Americans attempted to contact anti-Vichy elements within the French army prior to the landings. Eisenhower dispatched his deputy, Gen. Mark Clark, via submarine to Algeria, and later brought French general Henri Giraud to Gibraltar for discussions. Clark and U.S. diplomat Robert Murphy contacted some sympathetic officers, who in certain instances would surrender their commands upon the Allied arrival. Concern for security, however, prevented extensive cooperation, and the Allies came ashore on Nov. 8, 1942, with no guarantees of French compliance.

Three task forces led the assault. The Western Task Force, comprising the 2d Armored Division and the 3d and 9th infantry divisions, and under command of Gen. George Patton, was transported directly from the United States to the vicinity of Casablanca, Morocco. This force included more than 100 ships transporting 60,000 soldiers. The Center Task Force and the Eastern Task Force both left from Britain, for the Algerian cities of Oran and Algiers, respectively. The former, under the command of U.S. general Lloyd Fredendall, comprised about half of the 1st Armored Division and the bulk of the 1st Infantry Division. The largely British Eastern Task Force also included elements of the U.S. 34th Infantry Division.

All three task forces arrived off their respective beaches without serious incident, in part owing to confusion within German intelligence. Although elements of the convoys were spotted by U-boats and aircraft, the Germans remained unsure of their destination. Believing the convoys bound for Malta or the Western Desert, the Germans made no concerted effort to stop them in the Atlantic.

French resistance proved strong in certain areas. The Western Task Force met some of the fiercest resistance. By November 10, however, Patton's forces had seized several airfields and positioned themselves on both sides of Casablanca. They were poised for an attack when word of an armistice came. Total casualties numbered approximately 150 killed and 400 wounded.

The Center Task Force suffered but few setbacks in its effort to encircle and capture Oran. On the third day after the landing, French authorities in Oran surrendered. Total U.S. casualties in the center sector numbered approximately 600.

British forces landing west of Algiers met French troops who had been ordered not to resist, and the U.S. forces met only light resistance. An Allied group that assaulted the city directly, however, was surrounded and briefly held prisoner by French units. The Allied command opened negotiations with Adm. Joseph Darlan, the second-ranking official in the Vichy regime, who was in Algiers when the invasion began. Darlan was persuaded to sign an armistice for Algiers, which he expanded later that evening (November 8) to include the whole of French North Africa.

German dictator Adolf Hitler reacted quickly to the invasion. He ordered troops into unoccupied France and began sending sizeable forces to the Tunisian cities of Tunis and Bizerte. The ill-equipped and often confused French troops in the area could offer little resistance. Following Darlan's action, the Eastern Task Force had begun to push westward toward Tunisia. Lead elements came in contact with the Germans as early as November 20. The difficult terrain, lack of roads, and poor weather, however, limited the Allied advance. Following a series of setbacks, Eisenhower called off immediate attempts to take Tunisia on December 24.

Torch was the first of what would be several successful amphibious operations conducted by Allied forces. The victory further demonstrated the feasibility of joint Anglo-American operations. Torch provided employment and experience for U.S. troops and served as something of a second front for 1942. It also brought many French soldiers into the ranks of the Allied forces. The operation was on the whole a dramatic success. If there was a downside, it was that the relatively easy victory caused overconfidence in the American ranks, which later proved costly at Kasserine Pass and elsewhere during the North African campaign that followed.

Bibliography: Howe, George F., *Northwest Africa: Seizing the Initiative in the West* (U.S. Govt. Printing Office, 1957).

Jeffrey J. Roberts

TRIDENT CONFERENCE
(May 12–25, 1943)

World War II summit talks held in Washington, D.C., between U.S. president Franklin D. Roosevelt and British prime minister Winston Churchill. At this conference, the British high command accepted U.S. proposals for a cross-channel offensive, with a target date of May 1, 1944. With top priority given to Operation Overlord, the Americans proved amenable to British plans for more Mediterranean operations, provided they would facilitate the cross-channel attack. Gen. Dwight D. Eisenhower was directed to plan "operations in exploitation of Husky as [were] best calculated to eliminate Italy from the war and to contain the maximum number of German units."

Both partners agreed to increase the combined bomber offensive and to continue supply operations to China. Also, the British accepted American proposals for a Central Pacific Offensive.

Bibliography: Matloff, Maurice, *Strategic Planning for Coalition Warfare, 1943–1944* (Office of the Chief of Military History, U.S. Army, 1958).

Jeffrey J. Roberts

TRUK, RAIDS ON (1944)

Two World War II aerial attacks by U.S. forces on Truk Island in the Carolines where the Japanese had built a major naval base—"the Gibraltar of the Pacific." It stood as an obstacle to the Central Pacific strategy of the United States. On Feb. 4, 1944, U.S. aerial reconnaissance spotted a major part of Japanese admiral Mineichi Koga's combined fleet at anchor, but by the time U.S. admiral Raymond A. Spruance's carriers got within flying distance, most of Koga's ships had slipped away. At dawn on February 17, Adm. Marc A. Mitscher's carrier-based navy bombers and torpedo planes began a two-day attack on Truk. They pounced on 50 merchant ships at anchor, sinking more than half; took out 265 aircraft; sank a cruiser and two destroyers; and inflicted enormous damage on ground facilities. U.S. navy ships sank another cruiser and two more destroyers. The Americans lost 25 planes. On April 29–30, in phase two of Operation Hailstorm, the U.S. Navy returned, this time completing the job of destroying the atoll's fuel and ammunition storage depots, sinking or damaging two light cruisers, four destroyers, and two submarines, marking the first time in history that a major enemy base was shut down without help of land-based airplanes or an amphibious landing. The second raid cost the navy 30 planes, but 25 pilots were rescued. Left

to wither, like Rabaul, Truk's garrison surrendered on Sept. 12, 1945.

Bibliography: Calvocoressi, Peter, et al., *Total War: Causes and Courses of the Second World War* (Pantheon, 1989); Gilbert, Martin, *The Second World War,* rev. ed. (Holt, 1992); Morison, Samuel Eliot, *The Two Ocean War* (Little, Brown, 1963).

Peter Model

TULAGI, BATTLE FOR (August 7–10, 1942)

Raid during World War II by more than 6,000 U.S. marines that marked the opening phase of Operation Watchtower—the landing at Guadalcanal in the Solomon Islands—and was the first U.S. ground offensive in the Pacific. U.S. forces landed on Aug. 7, 1942, and had taken the island by August 10. Compared to other targeted islands, Tulagi was an insignificant speck of land 20 miles north of Guadalcanal, but the ferocity of its defenders stunned the Americans. "I have never heard or read of this kind of fighting," Maj. Gen. Alexander A. Vandegrift wrote the marine commandant in Washington. "These people refuse to surrender. The wounded will wait till men come up to examine them and blow themselves and the other fellow to death with a hand grenade." The Japanese had seized Tulagi three months earlier as part of their plans to invade Port Moresby, New Guinea, to build a seaplane base to protect newly conquered Rabaul, and to deny the Allies a place from which to scout the eastern approaches to the Coral Sea.

Peter Model

TUNISIAN CAMPAIGN
(November 1942–May 1943)

World War II offensive—following the Operation Torch landings in November 1942—by an Allied expeditionary force (U.S., British, and French troops), the mission of which was to move into Tunisia to block German reinforcement of North Africa and later to link up with the British 8th Army moving west from Libya in pursuit of Field Marshal Erwin Rommel's Afrika Korps. The attempt failed, and Allied troops spent the winter of 1942–43 in defensive positions in the mountains of central and southern Tunisia. After the German counteroffensive at Sidi Bou Zid and Kasserine Pass in February 1943, Allied troops went on the offensive in the spring. The campaign ended in mid-May when an estimated 250,000 Axis troops surrendered on the plain of Tunis.

Bibliography: Howe, George F., *Northwest Africa: Seizing the Initiative in the West (The U.S. Army in World War II: Mediterranean Theater of Operations)* (Office of the Chief of Military History, U.S. Army, 1957).

Carlo W. D'Este

TUSKEGEE AIRMEN

Name given black fighter pilots trained at the Tuskegee Army Air Field in Alabama and formed primarily into the 99th Fighter Squadron during World War II. Sent to North Africa to fill an urgent need for pilots, the "Lonely Eagles," as they called themselves, first entered combat on June 2, 1943, over the island of Pantelleria in the Mediterranean and later participated in action over Italy—where they downed 12 German aircraft in two days at Anzio—Rumania, France, and the Balkans. In 1945, the squadron escorted bombers deep into Germany and proudly boasted that no bomber under their protection was lost to German aircraft. By the end of the war, the 99th, now a part of the 332d Group, had tallied 108 enemy planes and earned three distinguished unit citations.

Bibliography: Nalty, Bernard C., *Strength for the Fight* (Free Press, 1986); Osur, Alan M., *Blacks in the Army Air Forces During World War II* (Office of Air Force History, 1977).

John F. Wukovits

ULTRA/MAGIC

Code names for Allied cryptographic efforts during World War II. All of the war era belligerents used cipher systems for tactical messages and strategic and diplomatic communications. Cipher machines greatly advanced the cryptographic capabilities of both the Allied and the Axis powers.

Ultra. Ultra was the Allied cover name for the largely British effort of intercepting and translating messages sent by the German military on Engima coding machines. During the German invasion of France in May 1940, the commander of the British Expeditionary Force, Lord Gort, had Ultra materials available. Because of a German cipher change, however, there were no Ultra intercepts during the first 10 days of the Battle for France. Gort did use Ultra intelligence in his plans for the British and French withdrawal at Dunkirk.

During the Battle of Britain, Ultra intercepts of Luftwaffe, or German air force, messages enabled British air marshal Sir Hugh C. T. Dowding to understand the strategy, strength, and readiness of the German air arm. Ultra could give advance warning of impending air raids, but it was not always foolproof and the location of the intended target was not always readily evident. The Coventry Raid of Nov. 14, 1941, has been mistakenly given as an example of sacrificing a city in order to keep secret the Ultra capability. Ultra did give the British Fighter Command warning of an attack but could not pinpoint the target city.

German naval ciphers were more difficult to break than their Wehrmacht (army) and Luftwaffe counterparts. Ultra did provide information about the destination of the German battleship *Bismarck,* but it was not until May 8, 1941, when the British captured a U-boat's cipher books and Enigma machine, that a major breakthrough came against the U-boats. Once the British could read the German submarine code, they could reroute their convoys and send aircraft or destroyers to a U-boat rendezvous point. In early 1942, the Germans made a major change in their naval ciphers, and it was not until December 1942 that the Ultra could again read German naval signals with regularity. The loss of this capability is directly reflected in the loss of Allied shipping that year. However, by 1943, the Allies' chances of losing the Battle of the Atlantic were largely over, due, in part, to Ultra.

During the Allied reclamation of German-occupied territory, Ultra provided invaluable information on enemy capabilities. Gen. Bernard Montgomery received detailed information about Field Marshal Erwin Rommel's supply problems in the North African desert in the fall of 1942, and Gen. Dwight D. Eisenhower obtained vital information for Operation Torch. Ultra played an important intelligence role in the invasions of Sicily, Salerno, Anzio, Normandy, and southern France. It forewarned the British and Americans of the German counterattack at Mortain in July 1944. The Germans observed strict radio silence prior to the Ardennes Offensive in December 1944, insuring that the Allies received little warning of that German attack. Despite their intelligence success at the Battle of the Bulge, the Germans' major intelligence failure during the war was their belief that the Enigma system was totally secure.

Magic. Magic was the American code-breaking and radio interception efforts against the Japanese. The Japanese diplomatic code, known as "Purple," was broken in late September 1940. The Japanese naval code, however, proved to be a difficult target, with only 1 in 10 messages being deciphered. The Japanese naval code was lost prior to the attack on Pearl Harbor on Dec. 7, 1941.

Magic provided the U.S. Navy with information about the intended Japanese invasion of Port Moresby in May 1942, information that preceded the Battle of the Coral Sea. Even though the Japanese navy changed ciphers on June 1, Magic intercepted useful messages concerning Japanese plans for the invasion of Midway Island that month.

Magic provided detailed information on the movements of Japanese admiral Isoroku Yamamoto, virtually assuring that officer's death when his plane was shot down in the northern Solomon Islands on Apr. 18, 1943. It also dramatically increased the effectiveness of U.S. submarines in the Pacific when the Japanese merchant shipping code was broken.

Additionally, Magic gave the Americans troop strengths (but not dispositions) on Tarawa. As a result of Magic information, Adm. Chester Nimitz elected to invade Kwajalein Island in 1944. Magic intercepts proved that the Japanese were moving troops from that island to outer islands in the Marshall group.

The U.S. Navy routinely sent radio intercept teams on board command vessels. The most spectacular performance of these teams came during the engagement known as the

"Marianas Turkey Shoot" in June 1944. The Japanese naval air force used a master pilot to lead inexperienced air crews, with the master pilot directing all airborne craft. An American intelligence officer intercepted the master controller's every command, resulting in the loss of more than 300 Japanese aircraft and 3 Japanese carriers versus some 30 American aircraft lost.

While the Japanese changed their ciphers regularly, they, like the Germans, believed their code system was secure. Allied successes in codes and code-breaking ultimately proved to be a significant factor in an eventual Allied victory.

Bibliography: Cave-Brown, Anthony, *Bodyguard of Lies* (Harper, 1975); Lewin, Ronald, *Ultra Goes to War: The First Account of World War II's Greatest Secret Based on Official Documents* (McGraw-Hill, 1978); —, *The American Magic: Codes, Ciphers and the Defeat of Japan* (Farrar, Straus & Giroux, 1982).

David Friend

VOLTURNO RIVER, BATTLE OF THE (October 1943)

World War II conflict in which Allied forces endured severe fighting to cross a German line of defense in south-central Italy. After the capture of Naples in early October 1943, the Allies began advancing north with the object of capturing Rome. To gain time for German engineers to complete formidable new defensive positions near Cassino, called the Gustav Line, Field Marshal Albert Kesselring ordered the German 10th Army to fight a series of delaying actions. One of these was along the natural defensive barrier of the fast-flowing, flood-swollen Volturno River. During the first three weeks of October, U.S. and British troops of Gen. Mark Clark's 5th Army fought a series of costly battles before Allied assaults on the river crossings finally gained bridgeheads north of the river.

Bibliography: Blumenson, Martin, *Salerno to Cassino (The U.S. Army in World War II: Mediterranean Theater of Operations)* (Office of the Chief of Military History, U.S. Army, 1969).

Carlo W. D'Este

WAKE ISLAND, FALL AND RECAPTURE OF (December 23, 1941 and September 4, 1945)

The Japanese capture and ultimate relinquishing of a tiny Pacific atoll, 2,400 miles west of Hawaii, during World War II. Japan seized Wake early in the war to place it in position to threaten Midway and eliminate U.S. interference with Japanese interests in the Marshall Islands. On Dec. 11, 1941, a defense contingent of less than 500, led by marine major James Devereux and navy commander Winfield S. Cunningham, repulsed Japan's initial invasion attempt. A stronger Japanese armada attacked on December

23 and quickly overran the outnumbered garrison. Although Wake had fallen, its spirited defense raised American home-front morale.

The island returned to U.S. control on Sept. 4, 1945, two days after Japan surrendered on board the *Missouri,* when marine brigadier general Lawson Sanderson accepted a peaceful surrender from the Japanese commander, Rear Adm. Shigematsu Sakaibara.

Bibliography: Devereux, James P. S., *The Story of Wake Island* (Lippincott, 1947); Schultz, Duane, *Wake Island* (St. Martin's Press, 1978); Toland, John, *But Not in Shame* (Random House, 1961).

John F. Wukovits

WAR AGENCIES

Temporary civilian bureaus of administration and service established to meet the unique demands of war. While most histories of World War II focus on the fighting in the European and Pacific theaters, another theater of war existed in the United States. The aim of the war at home was to ensure that labor, industry, and transportation meshed in order to deliver to the fighting units the material means required to defeat the enemies of the United States. The war at home was managed by the armed services and a host of war agencies. Many of these agencies were founded during the state of emergency declared in the year before the Japanese attack on Pearl Harbor in December 1941. The early agencies focused on building ships and transporting matériel to Great Britain, but as the war progressed, the agencies controlled and programmed almost every aspect of domestic life and business.

Many of the war agencies were created through executive order. In some cases, there were overlapping spheres of responsibility and no one had control. Some agencies, such as the War Production Board (WPB), were granted, in theory, nearly all-powerful authority over the means of production within the United States, while other, smaller agencies, such as the War Food Administration (WFA), were given powers that often put them in conflict with the WPB. In addition, each of the armed services had its own logistics organization, which it jealously guarded. The various war agencies were forced to cooperate and compromise with a wide range of military and civilian organizations. When cooperation and committees did not work, many of the agencies had direct access to the president, and the final method of establishing priorities was through presidential order. The agencies fell into four broad categories: labor, industry, transport, and all others.

Labor. During the period prior to the declaration of war, industry began to gear up to provide material to future U.S. allies in both Asia and Europe. At the same time, the armed forces began to build up in anticipation of the coming war. Both increases required the same resource—manpower. The demand increased when war broke out. By

1942, the army was planning on increasing to 7,200,000 soldiers and officers while industry required more workers to increase production while losing men to the services.

The War Manpower Commission (WMC) was established in April 1942 to balance and meet competing demands. Headed by Paul McNutt and under the direction of the WPB, the WMC waged a continuing battle to restrict the size of the armed forces while increasing the labor pool available to industry. One innovation was the development of manpower urgency ratings. This helped to prioritize the labor demands in relation to how urgently certain products were needed for the war effort. Another innovation was the Plant Site Board. The WMC would survey the amount of available manpower in different areas. Based on the results, areas were targeted for war contracts if surplus labor was available. In some cases, the WMC forced the services and other government agencies to cancel contracts in areas with a shortage of labor.

While charged with insuring full mobilization and effective utilization of American manpower, the WMC was not given the authority to enforce its policies. Despite this shortcoming, the WMC had great impact on U.S. society and culture. It oversaw the vast increase of female, minority, and foreign workers in the workplace and was indirectly responsible for many postwar societal changes.

Industry. The most powerful and all-encompassing agency of the war period was the WPB, headed by Donald Nelson. Established in January 1942 as the successor to the Office of Production Management, the WPB was charged with the general direction of industrial mobilization. It had the power to establish policy, procedures, planning, and methods for all government agencies engaged in war production and procurement. The WPB had two major obstacles to achieving its task. One was big industry, which did not want to abandon all consumer production. The other was the military, which wanted to control its own procurement. Nelson handled big industry relatively easily by controlling the amount of raw materials allotted for civilian products. Eventually, through the Controlled Materials Plan, Army Supplies Plan, Production Requirements Plan, and other systems of prioritizing requirements and allotting resources, the WPB was able to force big industry, especially the automobile industry, to convert to military production.

While civilian industry eventually came under the control of the WPB, the WPB's relations with the military were difficult. Nelson was reluctant, in the beginning, to strip the military of its contracting and procurement powers. For example, he preferred to leave the Army Services of Supply (later the Army Service Forces) in control of its own procurement. At first, this was a sound decision, as Nelson had a difficult time controlling the civilian side of industrial mobilization and did not need to try to take on the military at the same time. However, as the WPB expanded its control of industry through prioritization and control of resources, the military became a great problem. At one point, when the WPB established a certain level of priorities with the highest priority being "A," the army and navy simply established priorities "AA" and "AAA."

Only through force of personality and control of an expanding system of joint production agencies was Nelson able to gain the cooperation of the armed services and move toward the goal of arming the forces. This cooperation again began to crumble when labor shortages became critical. The WPB considered soldiers in training and awaiting overseas shipment as wasted labor pools and tried to force the reduction of the size of the army. While not successful, the WPB eventually forced the army to loan soldiers to industry and mining operations. The WPB was the supreme authority in running the arsenal of democracy, as it had control of plants, resources, and labor. Despite this power, Nelson resigned in August 1944 in protest to continuing disagreements with Gen. Brehon Somervell, head of the Army Service Forces.

Transport. While the WPB may have controlled the manufacture of war matériel, the War Shipping Administration (WSA), established in February 1942, controlled the movement of products overseas. The WSA was conceived as the transport agency of the Maritime Commission, and both were headed by Rear Adm. Emory Land, who became the wartime shipping czar. His charter was the allocation, operation, purchase, and use of all noncombat shipping, less any ships in the military transport fleets. The primary problem for the WSA was, again, the armed services. Neither the navy nor the army would agree to give up its own transport ships in order to pool shipping more efficiently. In addition, the armed services refused to relinquish control of their port facilities and loading areas and forced the WSA to take over civilian areas or build its own port facilities. Not until the enemy was able to sink a significant amount of Allied shipping was the WSA able to gain some control over the armed forces, and then only because Land also controlled ship construction. However, despite this leverage, the WSA was never able to gain the military's full cooperation in planning, prioritizing, and controlling Allied shipping. Land's assistant, Lewis Douglas, concentrated his efforts on efficiency. The WSA was able to raise the used portion of a ship's rated capacity to more than 95 percent, but the military never followed the lead and often squandered available space.

In addition to these problems, there was also the continuous problem of insufficient off-loading facilities, whether in North Africa or the Southwest Pacific. Goods and matériel frequently could not be taken off ships and placed ashore. A final problem was the physical control of ships once they left WSA ports. Gen. Douglas MacArthur was notorious for appropriating Liberty ships to meet his own plans. Despite a greater control over construction and planning of shipping, the power remained too often theoretical, and the WSA was forced to accept inefficient use of Allied ships.

Other Agencies. Other smaller agencies were also important. One was the Office of War Information (OWI), which was responsible for propaganda. Under the control of Elmer Davis, the OWI disseminated war information and explained U.S. policy and actions at home and abroad. The OWI suffered internal divisions as some of the intellectuals working for the agency resigned in protest against a failure to explain war aims properly. Even the Bureau of Motion Pictures worked for the OWI, as evidenced by Walt Disney Studios' Donald Duck, who urged the public to "Pay your taxes and beat the Axis."

Another agency was the Office of Civil Defense (OCD), organized in May 1941. Initially headed by New York City mayor Fiorello LaGuardia, the OCD was the primary government agency for channeling energies of the home population. It planned air-raid defense, ensured that areas were blacked out, formed the Civil Air Patrol, and established day-care centers. Another agency was the Office of Price Administration (OPA), charged primarily with keeping a check on inflation and administering the rationing system.

Bibliography: Fairchild, Byron, and Jonathan Grossman, *The War Department: The Army and Industrial Manpower,* The U.S. Army in World War II Series (U.S. Govt. Printing Office, 1959); Leighton, Richard M., and Robert W. Coakley, *The War Department: Global Logistics and Strategy,* The U.S. Army in World War II Series (U.S. Govt. Printing Office, 1954; reprint, 1968); Nelson, Donald M., *Arsenal of Democracy: The Story of American War Production* (Harcourt, Brace, 1946); Risch, Erna, *The Technical Services: The Quartermaster Corps: Organization, Supply and Services,* vol. 1, The U.S. Army in World War II Series (U.S. Govt. Printing Office, 1953; reprint, 1987); Risch, Erna, and Chester L. Kieffer, *The Technical Services: The Quartermaster Corps: Organization, Supply and Services,* vol. 2, The U.S. Army in World War II Series (U.S. Govt. Printing Office, 1955; reprint, 1988).

Maj. George B. Eaton

WOMEN IN THE ARMED FORCES

Although they never comprised more than two percent of the country's uniformed services, women were a highly visible and integral element of the U.S. war effort during World War II. The United States had had a positive experience utilizing women in World War I, the navy having enlisted female nurses. After the armistice, however, the "Navy Yeoman (F)" was discontinued and women no longer were in uniform.

During the 1930s, several studies commissioned by the military recommended serious consideration of using women in a future conflict, but no action was taken on the issue until World War II neared. Initial public reaction to the creation of women's service units was surprisingly supportive, the most vocal opposition coming from leaders of the Catholic Church, which saw the military experience as unfit for women. Despite some technical differences among the service branches, ultimately all-women units were created to put females in noncombat assignments, releasing men for combat duty. Congress authorized a women's army corps in March 1942; within a year all the services followed suit.

WAC. The Women's Army Corps was created in May 1942 (its official name was the Women's Army Auxiliary Corps [WAAC] until 1943). As with the other women's units, the War Department selected as WAC director a socially prestigious individual. Ultimately reaching the rank of colonel, Texas publisher and public official Oveta Culp Hobby directed the WAC, in which 99,000 women enlisted during the course of the war. The WAC became part of the regular army after the war.

WAVES. The Women Accepted for Volunteer Emergency Service was the U.S. Navy's all-female unit. Legislation passed on July 30, 1942, allowed women to enter the U.S. Naval Reserve. Impetus for a women's naval corps had come from within the navy itself. Adms. Ernest J. King and Arthur Radford, among other ranking officers, supported the creation of a women's corps. In 1944, the unit was renamed the Women Reserves, and by the end of the war it numbered 90,000. Throughout the war, the unit was directed by Lt. Cmdr. Mildred McAfee, who had been president of Wellesley College. At the end of the war, the Women Reserves were integrated into the regular navy.

SPAR. The women's unit of the U.S. Coast Guard was established in November 1942 under the name SPAR ("Semper Paratus—Always Ready"). Dorothy Stratton, former dean of women at Purdue University and a serving Wave, was appointed its director. At its peak strength in November 1944, the SPAR numbered 10,000 enlisted women and 1,000 officers. The unit was disbanded in November 1946.

Women Marines. The last of the U.S. women's service units to be established was that of the Marine Corps. Corps commandant Thomas Holcomb was one of the high-ranking U.S. officers who needed convincing that women could function in the corps. He soon dropped his objections, and in February 1943, the Women Marines were created. Like Stratton of the SPAR, Ruth Chenery Streeter was a serving Wave when she was appointed to head the Women Marines. An alumnus of Bryn Mawr College known for her philanthropic work, Streeter oversaw a unit that eventually enlisted 23,000 women before it was disbanded at war's end.

Obstacles to Service. While quotas for the other services were low, realistic, and easily achieved, the army experi-

At Yalta in Russia's Crimea, British prime minister Winston Churchill (left), *U.S. president Franklin D. Roosevelt* (center), *and Soviet premier Joseph Stalin* (right) *met in February 1945 to discuss the final campaigns for winning World War II and establishing the postwar order.* (U.S. Army Military History Institute)

enced difficulty achieving its enlistment quotas for women. Wacs were popular with stateside and overseas army commanders, and the continuous demand made it difficult to keep the ranks filled.

Forces both internal and external prevented many women from enlisting. Some families, uncomfortable with the radical shift of tradition, pressured their young women to stay away from military service. Additionally, some women feared military life, and most women had little or no understanding of the jobs they would be expected to perform. And those most familiar with the military, namely wives and mothers, were barred from service.

Officially, the army and navy welcomed women into their ranks. However, a 1943 national smear campaign portraying all women in uniform as sexually promiscuous put a serious dent into recruiting efforts, especially with the army. The Federal Bureau of Investigation traced the

rumors and insinuations to U.S. servicemen eager to keep women from their ranks.

None of the services were willing overtly to recruit black women. In 1944, Pres. Franklin D. Roosevelt ordered that this policy be reversed, but the numbers reveal little compliance: Black Wacs numbered about 4,000; the WAVES and SPAR accepted fewer than 100 blacks each, the marines none.

Common to all services was an unwillingness, based upon national policy and legal restraint, to place women in a direct combat situation. Exposure to enemy bombs was inevitable in some overseas jobs, and some nurses did become prisoners of war. The image of a uniformed woman in combat was, however, overwhelmingly unpalatable to the American public, and despite some attempts to put women into semicombat situations (the army utilized some for staffing antiaircraft posts in the United States), Congress refused to allow full integration of women into units with a combat mission, an exclusion that still exists.

If women were officially deemed necessary to pursue the war effort, a different attitude became prevalent as the conflict neared its conclusion. In early 1945, the government announced that after the war, large numbers of civilians would be sent overseas to assume clerical duties in the occupied areas. While these women would wear WAC uniforms, they would escape military discipline, would be better paid than Wacs, and would have officers' privileges. Once out of uniform, women veterans met a similar fate. The Veterans of Foreign Wars banned them from membership.

Bibliography: Campbell, D'Ann, *Women at War with America: Private Lives in a Patriotic Era* (Harvard Univ. Press, 1984); Treadwell, Mattie E., *The Women's Army Corps* (Office of the Chief of Military History, U.S. Army, 1954).

David Friend

YALTA CONFERENCE
(February 4–11, 1945)

World War II summit talks held in Russia's Crimea, attended by Soviet premier Joseph Stalin, British prime minister Winston Churchill, and U.S. president Franklin D. Roosevelt. The summit's discussion turned from how to win the war to the establishment of the postwar order.

Roosevelt apparently decided to deal directly with Stalin, while Churchill held considerably less power within the alliance. The resulting agreements recognized the physical control the Soviet Army was already holding in the areas it had freed from German control. The Big Three agreed on the Communist domination of the Polish government, although some members of Poland's London-based democratic government were to become ministers.

The Allies also pledged cooperation in applying the principle of self-determination in the freed nations of Eastern Europe in the extremely vague Declaration of Liberated Europe. They agreed to zones of occupation in Germany to include the French and agreed to a commission on the establishment of the German-Poland border after signing away much of Poland's eastern provinces to the Soviets. These agreements almost guaranteed the Soviets a controlling role in the future of Eastern Europe. The vagueness of the agreements and the inability of the Big Three to come to agreements on the future of Poland and Germany were to lead almost immediately to conflict between the Soviets and the West. The key military result, and possibly the reason Roosevelt accepted the other vague agreements, was that the Soviets would declare war on Japan within three months after the defeat of Germany and assist in the final defeat of Japan.

Bibliography: Clemens, Diane Shaver, *Yalta* (Oxford Univ. Press, 1970).

Capt. George B. Eaton

Bibliography

Chapter 1. United States Military Organization, Doctrine, and Technology: 1919–1945

Armed Forces Information School, *The Army Almanac* (U.S. Govt. Printing Office, 1950); Brodie, Bernard, and Fawn M. Brodie, *From Crossbow to H-Bomb* (Indiana Univ. Press, 1973); Brophy, Arnold, *The Air Force: A Panorama of the Nation's Youngest Service* (Gilbert Press, 1956); Coletta, Paolo Enrico, *The American Naval Heritage in Brief* (Univ. Press of America, 1978); Department of the Army, *American Military History, 1607–1958* (July 1959); —, *Army Heritage*, pamphlet 355–27 (Aug. 1963); —, *The Army* (1978); Department of the Navy, *The United States Navy* (Naval History Division, 1969); Dupuy, Ernest R., *The Compact History of the United States Army* (Hawthorn Books, 1961); Glines, Carroll V., Jr., *The Compact History of the United States Air Force* (Hawthorn Books, 1973); Goldich, Robert L., "Historical Continuity in the U.S. Military Reserve System," *Armed Forces and Society* (Fall 1980); Hinter, Edna J., "Combat Casualties Who Remain at Home," *Military Review* (Jan. 1980); House, Jonathan M., *Toward Combined Arms Warfare: A Survey of 20th Century Tactics, Doctrine, and Organization* (Combat Studies Institute, U.S. Army Command and General Staff College, Aug. 1984); Howarth, Stephen, *To Shining Sea: A History of the United States Navy, 1775–1991* (Random House, 1991); Kreidberg, Marvin A., and Merton G. Henry, *History of Military Mobilization in the United States Army, 1775–1945* (Office of the Chief of Military History, U.S. Army, June 1955); Mason, Herbert Malloy, Jr., *The United States Air Force: A Turbulent History* (Mason/Charter, 1976); Matloff, Maurice, ed., *American Military History* (Office of the Chief of Military History, U.S. Army, 1969); Maurer, Maurer, *Aviation in the U.S. Army, 1919–1939* (Office of Air Force History, U.S. Air Force, 1987); Millett, Allan R., *Semper Fidelis: The History of the United States Marine Corps* (Macmillan, 1980); Millis, Walter, *Arms and Men: A Study of American Military History* (Mentor Books, 1956); Ney, Virgil, *The Evolution of Military Unit Control, 500 BC–1965 AD* (CORG memorandum 217, 1965); —, *Evolution of the U.S. Army Division, 1939–1968* (CORG memorandum 365, Technical Operations, Inc., Jan. 1969); Parker, William D., *A Concise History of the United States Marine Corps, 1775–1969* (Historical Div., U.S. Marine Corps Hdqrs., 1970); Rector, Frank, ed., *The Air Force Blue Book 1961;* Vol. 2: *Air Force Facts* (Bobbs-Merrill for Military Publ. Inst., 1960); U.S. Army Air Forces, *AAF: The Official World War II Guide to the Army Air Forces, A Directory, Almanac and Chronicle of Achievement* (Bonanza Books, 1988); Weigley, Russell F., *The American Way of War: A History of United States Military Strategy and Policy* (Macmillan, 1973); —, *History of the United States Army* (Macmillan, 1967).

Chapter 2. The Interwar Period: 1920–1941

Ball, Harry P., *Of Responsible Command, A History of the U.S. Army War College* (Alumni Assoc. of the U.S. Army War College, 1983); Coletta, Paolo E., *The American Naval Heritage* (Univ. Press of America, 1987); Dupuy, Ernest R., and Trevor N. Dupuy, *The Encyclopedia of Military History* (Harper & Row, 1977); Fairchild, Byron, and Jonathan Grossman, *The Army and Industrial Manpower* (Chief of Military History, U.S. Army, 1959); Gallup, George H., *The Gallup Poll,*

Public Opinion 1935–1971 (Random House, 1972); Hagan, Kenneth J., and William R. Roberts, *Against All Enemies: Interpretations of American Military History from Colonial Times to the Present* (Greenwood Press, 1986); Hattendorf, John B., et al., *Sailors and Scholars* (Naval War College Press, 1984); Hewes, James E., Jr., *From Root to McNamara: Army Organization and Administration, 1900–1963* (Center of Military History, U.S. Army, 1975); Huntington, Samuel P., *The Soldier and the State* (Vintage, 1957); James, D. Clayton, *The Years of MacArthur, 1880–1941* (Houghton Mifflin, 1970); Killigrew, John W., *The Impact of the Great Depression on the Army* (Garland, 1979); Kirkpatrick, Charles E., *An Unknown Future and a Doubtful Present: Writing the Victory Plan of 1941* (Center of Military History, U.S. Army, 1990); Kreidberg, Marvin A., and Merton G. Henry, *History of Military Mobilization in the United States Army, 1775–1945* (Dept. of the Army, 1955); Langer, William L., and S. Evert Gleason, *The Challenge to Isolation, 1937–1940* (Harper, 1952); —, *The Undeclared War, 1940–1941* (Harper, 1953); Leighton, Richard M., and Robert W. Coakley, *Global Logistics and Strategy* (Chief of Military History, U.S. Army, 1955); Leutz, James R., *Bargaining for Supremacy: Anglo-American Naval Cooperation, 1937–1941* (Univ. of North Carolina Press, 1978); Matloff, Maurice, *American Military History* (Chief of Military History, U.S. Army, 1969); McFarland, Keith D., *Harry H. Woodring: A Political Biography of FDR's Controversial Secretary of War* (Univ. of Kansas Press, 1975); Millett, Allan R., *Semper Fidelis: The History of the United States Marine Corps* (Macmillan, 1980); Millett, Allan R., and Williamson Murray, eds., *Military Effectiveness;* Vol 2: *The Interwar Period* (Allen & Unwin, 1988); Millis, Walter, with Harvey C. Mansfield and Harold Stein, *Arms and the State* (Twentieth Century Fund, 1958); Paret, Peter, ed., *Makers of Modern Strategy* (Princeton Univ. Press, 1986); Pogue, Forrest C., *George C. Marshall: Education of a General, 1880–1939* (Viking, 1963); —, *George C. Marshall: Ordeal and Hope, 1939–1942* (Viking, 1966); Smith, R. Elberton, *The Army and Economic Mobilization* (Chief of Military History, U.S. Army, 1959); Watson, Mark S., *Chief of Staff: Prewar Plans and Preparations* (Historical Div., U.S. Army, 1950); Weigley, Russell F., *History of the United States Army* (Macmillan, 1967); Vlahos, Michael, *The Blue Sword: The Naval War College and the American Mission, 1919–1941* (Naval War College Press, 1980).

Chapter 3. North Africa, Sicily, and Italy: 1942–1945

Ambrose, Stephen E., *The Supreme Commander: The War Years of General Dwight D. Eisenhower* (Doubleday, 1970); Bennett, Ralph, *Ultra and the Mediterranean Strategy* (Morrow, 1989); Blair, Clay, *Ridgway's Paratroopers* (Dial Press, 1985); Blumenson, Martin, *Bloody River* (Allen & Unwin, 1970); —, *Mark Clark* (Congdon & Weed, 1984); —, *Rommel's Last Victory* (Houghton Mifflin, 1967); —, *Salerno to Cassino* (Office of the Chief of Military History, 1969); Bradley, Omar N., *A Soldier's Story* (Holt, 1951); Clark, Mark, *Calculated Risk* (Harper & Row, 1951); D'Este, Carlo, *Bitter Victory: The Battle for Sicily, 1943* (Dutton, 1988); —, *Fatal Decision: Anzio and the Battle for Rome* (HarperCollins, 1991); Eisenhower, Dwight D., *Crusade in Europe* (Doubleday, 1948); Eisenhower, John S. D., *Allies: From Pearl Harbor to D-Day* (Doubleday, 1982); Ellis, John, *Cassino: The Hollow Victory* (McGraw-Hill, 1984); Fisher, Ernest F., Jr., *Cassino to the Alps* (Center of Military History, 1984); Garland, Albert N., and Howard McGaw Smyth, *Sicily and the Surrender of Italy* (Office of the Chief of Military History, U.S. Army, 1965); Graham, Dominick, and Shelford Bidwell, *Tug of War: The Battle for Italy, 1943–45* (St. Martin's Press, 1986); Hamilton, Nigel, *Montgomery: Master of the Battlefield, 1942–1944* (McGraw-Hill, 1984); Hapgood, David, and David Richardson, *Monte Cassino* (Congdon & Weed, 1984); Hickey, Des, and Gus Smith, *Operation Avalanche: The Salerno Landings, 1943* (Heinemann, 1983); Howe, George F., *Northwest Africa: Seizing the Initiative in the West* (Office of the Chief of Military History, U.S. Army, 1957); Jackson, W. G. F., *The North African Campaign, 1940–43* (Batsford, 1975); Kesselring, Albert, *Kesselring: A Soldier's Record* (Morrow, 1954); Liddell Hart, B. H., ed., *The Rommel Papers* (Harcourt, Brace, 1953); Macksey, Kenneth, *Crucible of Power: The Fight for Tunisia, 1942–1943* (Hutchinson, 1969); Morison, Samuel Eliot, *Sicily-Salerno-Anzio* (Little, Brown, 1954); Nicholson, Nigel, *Alex: The Life of Field Marshal Earl Alexander of Tunis* (Weidenfeld & Nicholson, 1973); Orgill, Douglas, *The Gothic Line* (Zebra Books, 1986); Sheppard, G. A., *The Italian Campaign, 1943–1945* (Praeger, 1968); Trevelyan, Raleigh, *Rome '44: The Battle for the Eternal City* (Hodder & Stoughton, 1981); Truscott, Lucian K., *Command Missions* (Dutton, 1954); Vaughan-Thomas, Wynford, *Anzio* (Holt, Rinehart & Winston, 1961).

Chapter 4. Northern Europe: 1944–1945

Ambrose, Stephen E., *The Supreme Commander: The War Years of General Dwight D. Eisenhower* (Doubleday, 1970); Blumenson, Martin, *Breakout and Pursuit (United States Army in World War II: European Theater of Operations)* (Office of the Chief of Military History, U.S. Army, 1961); Bradley, Omar N., *A Soldier's Story* (Holt, 1951); Butcher, Harry C., *My Three Years With Eisenhower* (Simon & Schuster, 1946); Cole, Hugh M., *The Ardennes: Battle of the Bulge (United States Army in World War II: The European Theater of Operations)* (Office of the Chief of Military History, U.S. Army, 1965); —, *The Lorraine Campaign (United States Army in World War II: European Theater of Operations)* (Office of the Chief of Military History, U.S. Army, 1950); Collins, Larry, and Dominque Lapierre, *Is Paris Burning?* (Simon & Schuster, 1965); Craven, Wesley Frank, and James Lea Cate, eds., *The Army Air Forces in World War II;* Vol. 3: *Europe: Argument to V-E Day, January 1944 to May 1945* (Univ. of Chicago Press, 1951); D'Este, Carlo, *Decision in Normandy* (Dutton, 1983); Eisenhower, Dwight D., *Crusade in Europe* (Doubleday, 1948); Eisenhower, John S. D., *The Bitter Woods* (Putnam's, 1979); Gavin, James M., *On To Berlin* (Viking, 1978); Farago, Ladislas, *Patton: Ordeal and Triumph* (Dell, 1970); Hamilton, Nigel, *Monty: Master of the Battlefield, 1942–1944* (McGraw-Hill, 1984); —, *Monty: The Field-Marshal, 1944–1976* (McGraw-Hill, 1986); Harrison, Gordon A., *Cross-Channel Attack (United States Army in World War II: European Theater of Operations)* (Office of the Chief of Military History, U.S. Army, 1950); Hastings, Max, *Overlord: D-Day and the Battle for Normandy, 1944* (Simon & Schuster, 1984); Irving, David, *Hitler's War, 1942–1945* (Avon, 1990); —, *The Trail of the Fox* (Dutton, 1977); Keegan, John, *The Second World War* (Viking, 1989); —, *Six Armies in Normandy* (Viking, 1982); MacDonald, Charles B., *The Last Offensive (United States Army in World War II: European Theater of Operations)* (Office of the Chief of Military History, U.S. Army, 1973); —, *The Mighty Endeavor* (Oxford Univ. Press, 1969); —, *A Time for Trumpets: The Untold Story of the Battle of the Bulge* (Morrow, 1985); Montgomery, Bernard L., *The Memoirs of Field-Marshal the Viscount Montgomery of Alamein* (World, 1958); Pogue, Forrest C., *The Supreme Command (United States Army in World War II: The European Theater of Operations)* (Office of the Chief of Military History, U.S. Army, 1954); Powell, Geoffrey, *The Devil's Birthday: The Bridges to Arnhem, 1944* (Watts, 1984); Ryan, Cornelius, *A Bridge Too Far* (Simon & Schuster, 1974); —, *The Last Battle* (Simon & Schuster, 1966); —, *The Longest Day* (Simon & Schuster, 1959); Toland, John, *The Last 100 Days* (Random House, 1966); Weigley, Russell F., *Eisenhower's Lieutenants* (Univ. of Indiana Press, 1981); Wilmot, Chester, *The Struggle for Europe* (Harper & Row, 1952).

Chapter 5. War in the Pacific: 1941–1945

Allen, Louis, *Burma: The Longest War 1941–45* (St. Martin's Press, 1984); Blair, Clay, *Silent Victory: The U.S. Submarine War against Japan* (Harper & Row, 1975); Craven, Wesley Frank, and James Lea Cate, eds., *The Army Air Forces in World War II*, vols. 4 & 5 (Univ. of Chicago Press, 1950, 1953); Drea, Edward J., *MacArthur's ULTRA: Codebreaking and the War against Japan, 1942–1945* (Univ. Press of Kansas, 1992); Dull, Paul S., *A Battle History of the Imperial Japanese Navy (1941–1945)* (Naval Inst. Press, 1978); Falk, Stanley L., *Decision at Leyte* (Norton, 1966); Frank, Richard B., *Guadalcanal: The Definitive Account of the Landmark Battle* (Random House, 1990); Hayes, Grace P., *The Joint Chiefs of Staff in World War II: The War against Japan* (Naval Inst. Press, 1983); Horner, D. M., *Crisis of Command* (Australian National Univ. Press, 1978); James, D. Clayton, *The Years of MacArthur;* Vol. 2: 1941–45 (Houghton Mifflin, 1975); Miller, John, Jr., *United States Army in World War II: The War in the Pacific: Cartwheel: The Reduction of Rabaul* (U.S. Govt. Printing Office, 1959); Milner, Samuel, *United States Army in World War II: The War in the Pacific: Victory in Papua* (U.S. Govt. Printing Office, 1957); Morison, Samuel Eliot, *History of United States Naval Operations in World War II*, 15 vols. (Little, Brown, 1947–1962); Morton, Louis, *United States Army in World War II: The War in the Pacific: The Fall of the Philippines* (U.S. Govt. Printing Office, 1953); Prange, Gordon W., *At Dawn We Slept: The Untold Story of Pearl Harbor* (McGraw-Hill, 1981); Smith, Robert Ross, *United States Army in World War II: The War in the Pacific: The Approach to the Philippines* (U.S. Govt. Printing Office, 1953); —, *United States Army in World War II: The War in the Pacific: Triumph in the Philippines* (U.S. Govt. Printing Office, 1963); Spector, Ronald, *Eagle against the Sun* (Free Press, 1985); U.S. Marine Corps, *History of U.S. Marine Corps Operations in World War II*, 5 vols. (Historical Branch G-3, U.S. Marine Corps, 1958–1968).

Chapter 6. The Air War aganist Germany and Japan: 1942–1945

Ardery, Philip, *Bomber Pilot: A Memoir of World War II* (Univ. Press of Kentucky, 1978); Army Air Forces, Headquarters, *Condensed Analysis of the Ninth Air Force in the European Theater of Operations* (Office of Air Force History, 1984); Caidin, Martin, *Black Thursday* (Ballantine, 1960); Coffey, Thomas, *Decision Over Schweinfurt: The U.S. 8th Air Force Battle for Daylight Bombing* (David McKay, 1977); —, *Hap: The Story of the U.S. Air Force and the Man Who Built It, Gen.*

Henry H. "Hap" Arnold (Viking, 1982); —, *Iron Eagle: The Turbulent Life of Gen. Curtis LeMay* (Crown, 1986); Craven, Wesley, and James Cate, eds., *The Army Air Forces in World War II,* 7 vols. (Univ. of Chicago Press, 1948–58); Dugan, James, and Carroll Stewart, *Ploesti: The Great Ground-Air Battle of 1 Aug. 1943* (Bantam, 1962); Fletcher, Eugene, *Fletcher's Gang; A B-17 Crew in Europe, 1944–45* (Univ. of Washington Press, 1988); Freeman, Roger, *Mighty Eighth War Diary* (Jane's, 1981); —, *Mighty Eighth War Manual* (Jane's, 1984); —, *The Mighty Eighth: Units, Men and Machines (A History of the US 8th Army Air Force)* (Macdonald, 1970); Goodson, James, *Tumult in the Clouds* (St. Martin's Press, 1983); Hallion, Richard, *Strike from the Sky: The History of Battlefield Air Attack 1911–1945* (Smithsonian Inst. Press, 1989); Hansell, Haywood, Jr., *Strategic Air War Against Japan* (Air Univ. Press, 1980); Infield, Glenn, *Big Week* (Pinnacle, 1974); Jablonski, Edward, *Double Strike: The Epic Air Raids on Regensburg-Schweinfurt Aug. 17, 1943* (Doubleday, 1974); Johnson, Robert, *Thunderbolt* (Ballantine Books, 1958); Kennett, Lee, *A History of Strategic Bombing* (Scribner's, 1982); MacIsac, David, *Strategic Bombing in World War Two: The Story of the United States Strategic Bombing Survey* (Garland, 1976); Middlebrook, Martin, *The Schweinfurt-Regensburg Mission* (Scribner's, 1983); Muirhead, John, *Those Who Fall* (Random House, 1986); Overy, R. J., *The Air War 1939–1945* (Stein and Day, 1980); Parton, James, *"Air Force Spoken Here": Gen. Ira Eaker and the Command of the Air* (Adler & Adler, 1986); Rust, Kenn, *Eighth Air Force Story: in World War II* (Historical Aviation Album, 1978); —, *Fifteenth Air Force Story: in World War II* (Historical Aviation Album, 1976); —, *The 9th Air Force in World War II* (Aero, 1970); Schaffer, Ronald, *Wings of Judgment: American Bombing in World War II* (Oxford Univ. Press, 1985); Sherry, Michael, *The Rise of American Air Power: The Creation of Armageddon* (Yale Univ. Press, 1987); Smith, Dale, *Screaming Eagle: Memoirs of a B-17 Group Commander* (Algonquin Books, 1990); Stiles, Bert, *Serenade to the Big Bird* (Ballantine Books, 1957); Stokesbury, James, *A Short History of Air Power* (Morrow, 1986); Thomas, Lowell, and Edward Jablonski, *Doolittle: A Biography* (Doubleday, 1976); Turner, Richard, *Big Friend, Little Friend: Memoirs of a World War II Fighter Pilot* (Doubleday, 1969); Twentieth Air Force, "Summary of Twentieth Air Force Operations, 5 June 1944–14 Aug. 1945" (1945); United States Strategic Bombing Survey, *Overall Report (European War)* (n.p., 1945); United States Strategic Bombing Survey, "Statistical Appendix to Over-All Report (European War)," 1947; United States Strategic Bombing Survey, "The Strategic Air Operation of Very Heavy Bombardment in the War Against Japan," 1946; —, *Summary Report (Pacific War)* (U.S. Govt. Printing Office, 1946); Werrell, Kenneth, *Eighth Air Force Bibliography: An Extended Essay and Listing of Published and Unpublished Materials* (Aerospace Historian, 1981); —, "The Strategic Bombing of Germany in World War II: Costs and Accomplishments," *The Journal of American History,* vol. 73 (Dec. 1986); —, *"Who Fears?": The 301st in War and Peace* (Taylor, 1991); Wolff, Leon, *Low Level Mission* (Berkley Publ., 1957).

Chapter 7. The War of Logistics: 1941–1945

Armed Forces Information School, *The Army Almanac* (U.S. Govt. Printing Office, 1950); Arnold, Henry H., *Report of the Commanding General of the Army Air Forces to the Secretary of War* (U.S. Govt. Printing Office, 1944); —, *Second Report of the Commanding General of the Army Air Forces to the Secretary of War* (U.S. Govt. Printing Office, 1945); —, *Third Report of the Commanding General of the Army Air Forces to the Secretary of War* (Schneiderith and Sons, 1945); Campbell, Levin Hicks, Jr., *The Industry-Ordnance Team* (McGraw-Hill, 1946); Coakley, Robert W., and Richard M. Leighton, *Global Logistics and Strategy, 1943–1945 (United States Army in World War II: The War Department)* (Office of the Chief of Military History, U.S. Army, 1968); Coletta, Paolo E., *The American Naval Heritage in Brief* (Univ. Press of America, 1978); Daniel, Hawthorne, *For Want of a Nail: The Influence of Logistics on War* (McGraw-Hill, 1948); Deutsch, Harold C., "The Historical Impact of Revealing the ULTRA Secret," *Parameters, Journal of the US Army War College* (No. 3, 1977); Glines, Carroll V., Jr., *The Compact History of the United States Air Force,* rev. ed., (Hawthorn Books, 1973); Hewes, James E., Jr., *From Root to McNamara: Army Organization and Administration, 1900–1963* (Center of Military History, U.S. Army, 1975); Howarth, Stephen, *To Shining Sea: A History of the United States Navy, 1775–1991* (Random House, 1991); Huston, James Alvin, *The Sinews of War: Army Logistics, 1775–1953* (Office of the Chief of Military History, U.S. Army, 1966); King, Ernest J., *United States Navy at War: Final Official Report to the Secretary of the Navy Concerning the period March 1, 1945 to October 1, 1945* (U.S. News, 1945); Kreidberg, Marvin A., and Merton G. Henry, *History of Military Mobilization in the United States Army, 1775–1945* (Office of the Chief of Military History, U.S. Army, 1955); Leighton, Richard M., and Robert W. Coakley, *Global Logistics and Strategy, 1940–1943 (United States Army in World War II: The War Department)* (Office of the Chief of Military History, U.S. Army, 1955); Mason, Herbert Malloy, Jr., *The United States Air Force: A Turbulent History* (Mason/Charter, 1976); Matloff, Maurice, ed., *American Military History* (Office of the Chief of Military History, U.S. Army, 1969); Millett, John

D., *The Organization and Role of Army Service Forces (United States Army in World War II: The Army Service Forces)* (Office of the Chief of Military History, U.S. Army, 1954); Rector, Frank, ed., *The Air Force Blue Book 1961;* Vol. 2: Air Force Facts (Bobbs-Merrill for Military Publ. Inst., 1960); Ruppenthal, Roland G., "Logistics and the Broad-Front Strategy," *Command Decisions,* ed. by Kent Roberts Greenfield (Office of the Chief of Military History, U.S. Army, 1960); —, *Logistical Support of the Armies,* vols. 1 & 2 (Office of the Chief of Military History, U.S. Army, 1953); Schmidt, Carl T., "The Division Slice in Two World Wars," *Military Review* (Oct. 1951); Stokesbury, James L., *A Short History of World War II* (Morrow, 1980); Sykes, H. F., Jr., "Logistics and World War II Army Strategy," *Military Review* (Feb. 1956); U.S. Army Air Forces, *AAF: The Official World War II Guide to the Army Air Forces, A Directory, Almanac and Chronicle of Achievement* (Bonanza Books, 1988); U.S. Bureau of the Budget, *The United States at War: Development and Administration of the War Program of the Federal Government* (U.S. Govt. Printing Office, 1946); U.S. Navy Bureau of Yards and Docks, *Building the Navy's Bases in World War II: History of the Bureau of Yards and Docks and the Civil Engineer Corps, 1940–1946,* 2 vols. (U.S. Govt. Printing Office, 1947); U.S. War Department General Staff, Director of the Service, Supply and Procurement Div., *Logistics in World War II: Final Report of the Army Service Forces* (U.S. Govt. Printing Office, 1948); Watson, Mark S., *Chief of Staff: Prewar Plans and Preparations (U.S. Army in World War II: The War Department)* (Hist. Div., Dept. of the Army, 1950); Weigley, Russell F., *The American Way of War: A History of United States Military Strategy and Policy* (Macmillan, 1973); —, *History of the United States Army* (Macmillan, 1967).

Index

Boldface numbers indicate main essays;
italic numbers indicate illustrations

Lee, John Clifford Hodges (1887–1958) **182**

Lee Jr., Willis Augustus (1888–1945) **182–183**

Leigh-Mallory, Trafford 62

Lejeune, John Archer (1867–1942) 14, 34, **183**

LeMay, Curtis Emerson (1906–1990) 103, 109, 119–120, **183–184**

Lend-Lease 39, 131–133, *132*, **248**

Lexington (ship) 11–12, 32, 86, 180, 218, 236, 253, 263

Leyte (Philippines) 99, 101, 264

Leyte Gulf, Battle of (October 23–26, 1944) *23*, **249–250**, 264

Libya 43, 115

Lilienthal, David *131*

Lindbergh, Charles Augustus (1902–1974) 183, **184**, 192

Little America (Richard Byrd Jr.) 152

Loans *See* Lend-Lease; War debts

Lockwood Jr., Charles Andrews (1890–1967) **184**

Locomotives 129

Lodge, Henry Cabot 248

Logistics 123–142, 147 *See also* Burma Road; Hump Airlift; Red Ball Express; Transportation

London naval treaties (1930/1936) 11, 30, 227–228

"Lonely Eagles" 275

Lorraine Campaign (September 1–December 16, 1944) 76, **250**

Los Alamos (New Mexico) 121, 250

Los Baños (Philippines) 102

LSD (landing ship, dock) 147

LST (landing ship, tank) 20, *20*, *67*, *142*, 147, 248

LST hospital ships 147

Lucas, John Porter (1890–1949) 55–56, **184**, 225–226

Luftwaffe (German Air forces) 45, 108–117, 163, 275

Lutes, Leroy (1890–1980) **185**

Luxembourg 75

Luzon Campaign 101–102, 264–265

LVT (landing vehicle, tracked) *13*, *20*, 247–248

M

M-1 Garand rifle *See* Garand rifle

M-4 Sherman (tank) 19, *19*

M38 utility vehicle *See* Jeep

MacArthur, Arthur 185

MacArthur, Douglas (1880–1964) *185*, **185–187**, *216*
air war complications imposed by 119
Army funding criticized by 24
Bonus Marchers dispersed by 26, 230
Central Pacific strategy opposed by 91, 186
Japan invasion favored by 105
Japan surrender accepted by 105, *105*, 217
Lindbergh praised by 184
in New Guinea campaign 87–89, 92–93, 95, 97–99, 180–181, 186, 194, 234, 244, 255–257
officers serving under 145, 147, 165–166, 173, 178–179, 182, 198, 202
Philippines defended by 84, 174, 186, 216, 229
Philippines reconquered by 99, 101–102, 173, 186, 194, 264–265
Ridgway replacement of 200
ships appropriated by 277
Southwest Pacific command given to 85

MacDonald, Charles B. 79

MacDonald, J. Ramsay 30

Machine guns 128

Mackensen, Eberhard von 55, 58, 226

MacMillan, Donald B. 152

Magic (radio intelligence) **275**

Makin, Battle for (November 20–23, 1943) **250**

Malaya 83–84, 95, 103, 105

Manhattan Project 21, 120, 131, 211, 242, **250**

Manila (Philippines) 102

Manteuffel, Hasso-Eccard von 78–79, 231

Mao Zedong 82, 97, 105, 190, 217

March, Peyton C.
Army funding criticized by 24
Army reorganization proposals 6, *25*, 195, 254
Russian interventions 257–258
Swing and 210

March Plan 254

Mareth line 45–47

Mariana Islands 33, 98, 103, 119–120, 268 *See also* Guam; Rota; Saipan; Tinian

Marianas Turkey Shoot 98, 266, 276

Marine Corps, U.S. 13–15
command 14
interwar period 26, 33–35, *34*, 41, 233
military education 15, 29
minorities and women in 14, 278
postwar period 215
reserve forces 14
size 14
tactics 14–15, 215

Marine Corps Reserve Act (Feb. 28, 1925) 14

Marine Officers School (Quantico, Virginia) 15

Market Garden, Operation (September 1944) 75–76, **251–252**

Marshall, George Catlett (1880–1959) **189–191**, *190*, *245*
and Andrews 145
Army Chief of Staff appointment 25, 190
and Bradley 148–149
General Staff reorganized by 27, 250–251
and Stillwell 208
women in service and 176
in World War II
activation of divisions slowed by 139

conferences attended by *48*, 234, 236
European campaign 44, 48, 51, 61, 163, 190
officers serving under 155, 166, 173, 175, 189, 217
on Pacific Front 91, 105, 190, 194, 224, 239

Marshall Islands 33, 93, 95, 247 *See also* Kwajalein

Marshall Plan 190

Marshall Reorganization (March 1942) 126, 205, **250–251**

Mason (ship) 12

Massachusetts (ship) 173

Maumee (ship) 193

Mayo, Henry T. 179

McAfee, Mildred H. 12, 278

McAuliffe, Anthony Clement (1898–1975) 78, **187**, 232

McCarthy, Joseph 190

McCawley (ship) 213

McCloy, John Jay (1885–1989) **187**

McCoy, Frank Ross (1874–1954) **188**

McDougal, Douglas (1876–1964) **188**

McMorris, Charles Horatio (1890–1954) **188**, 223

McNair, Lesley James (1883–1944) 10, 113, 161, *188*, **188–189**, 235, 251

McNarney, Joseph Taggart (1893–1972) **189**

McNutt, Paul 277

McVay, Butler 243

ME-109 (aircraft) 238

Medenine, Battle of (March 1943) 47

Medicine 22–23, 129

Mediterranean region *See specific countries (e.g., Italy)*

Meindl, Eugen 235

Merrill, Aaron Stanton ("Tip") (1890–1961) **191**

Merrill, Frank Dow (1903–1955) *191*, 252

Merrill's Marauders 191, **252**

Mexico 5, 36

Mid-air refueling 199

Middleton, Troy 197, 231

Midget submarines 263